Human Resource Management

STRATEGIC ANALYSIS TEXT AND CASES

Raj Kumar
Senior Professor and Director
Maharaja Agrasen Institute of Management & Technology
Kurukshetra University, Kurukshetra, Haryana (India)

I.K. International Publishing House Pvt. Ltd.

NEW DELHI • BANGALORE

Published by

I.K. International Publishing House Pvt. Ltd.
S-25, Green Park Extension
Uphaar Cinema Market
New Delhi – 110 016 (India)
E-mail: info@ikinternational.com
Website: www.ikbooks.com

ISBN 978-93-80578-82-8

10 9 8 7 6 5 4 3 2

Reprint 2012

Published by Krishan Makhijani for I.K. International Publishing House Pvt. Ltd., S-25, Green Park Extension, Uphaar Cinema Market, New Delhi – 110 016 and Printed by Rekha Printers Pvt. Ltd., Okhla Industrial Area, Phase II, New Delhi – 110 020.

Human Resource Management

STRATEGIC ANALYSIS TEXT AND CASES

PREFACE

Success in today's competitive business environment is increasingly a result of effective human resource management. Organizations around the world; be these business, educational or government are remodelling themselves as they respond to the challenges presented by the global economy. The functioning of these organizations depends upon how people work or behave in the organizations because human nature is impulsive and unpredictable. People in organizations need to lead in directions because human resources of an organization constitute its entire workforce.

Structure and technology can be easily duplicated but the factor that sets apart an organization is its people. The quality of the organization's employees, their enthusiasm and satisfaction with their jobs, and their sense of fair treatment all has a significant impact on the firm's productivity, level of customer service, reputation and survival. Human resource management is an art of developing people and their potentialities for their personnel and the growth of the organization.

This book covers all the aspects of Human Resource Management. Following a reader-friendly approach, it provides comprehensive coverage of basic concepts and principles of human resource management relevant to students and highlights its formats and modalities in current use. The book combines the operational as well as the strategic aspects of HRM. The text provides logical and analytical application of concepts. The strategic analysis involves integrative approach of HRM with strategic management. Case studies have been given at the end of each chapter to make the subject more practical and analytical.

The study of the subject is simple, need based and sequential. All relevant dimensions of human resource management, from a learner's perspective, find lucid coverage here. This book provides invaluable text for the students of MBA, M.Com., and other postgraduate students who are specializing in HRM. The book is also designed to meet the requirements of teaching, training and development programmes. Besides, the text provides a valuable guidance to HR professionals and executives of corporate world.

The author invites suggestions from the students, teachers and researchers for further improvements in the book.

Raj Kumar
E-mail: dr_r_kumar@yahoo.com

CONTENTS

CHAPTER

1

Human Resource Management: Operational and Strategic

CHAPTER'S OUTLINE

- Introduction
- Meaning of HRM
- Nature of HRM
- Objectives of HRM
- Importance of HRM
- Line and Staff Aspects of HRM
- Functions of HRM
- Duties and Responsibilities of HR Manager
- Process of HRM
- HR and Technology
- Strategic Role of HRM
- Strategic Planning and HR Management
- HR's Role as a Strategic Partner
- Recent Trends or Emerging Issues in HRM
- New HR Strategies to deal with the Challenges/Trends in HRM
- The Changing Role of HR Management

INTRODUCTION

The basic job of management is the effective utilization of human resources for the achievement of organizational objectives, such as, profitable operations and growth through the satisfaction of certain needs of the customers and society. *It is through the combined efforts of human resources or personnel that technological, financial, physical and all other resources are utilized.*

More specifically, human resource management involves determining the organization's need of human resources, recruiting and selecting the best available employees, developing, counselling and rewarding them, acting as a liaison with unions and government organizations and handling other matters related to the well-being of employees. Each of these functions is necessary to some degree, irrespective of nature and size of the organization. That is why, in most of the organizations, a separate department known as Personnel/Human Resource Department is created for the effective performance of these functions. HR policies are formulated to support company's strategies.

MEANING OF HUMAN RESOURCE MANAGEMENT

In order to explain the meaning of HRM, first it is essential to know the meaning of human resources.

What are Human Resources?

The term 'human resources' may be defined as the total knowledge, skills, creative abilities, talents, and aptitudes of an organization's workforce, as well as the values, attitudes, approaches and beliefs of the individuals involved in the affairs of the organization. It is the sum total or aggregate of inherent abilities, acquired knowledge and skills represented by the talent and aptitude of the persons employed in an organization.

Several terms have been used by various management thinkers to represent human resources. These include *'personnel', 'people at work', 'manpower', 'staff'*, and *'employees'*. Whatever may be the term used, the human resources of an organization include all individuals engaged in various organizational activities at different levels. According to **Leon C. Megginson,** "*From the national point of view, human resource may be defined the knowledge, skills, creative abilities, talents and aptitudes obtained in the population; whereas from the viewpoint of the individual enterprise, they represent the total of the inherent abilities, acquired knowledge and skills as exemplified in the talents and aptitudes of its employees*".

After having discussed the meaning of HR, we can define the HRM. HRM is concerned with people in management. The term HRM is also used to refer as Personnel Management; hence HRM or Personnel Management is defined as *the philosophy, policies, procedures and practices relating to the management of people with in the organization.*

The success of the management lies in attaining organizational objectives which in turn depends upon the quality of human resources in the organization. HRM thus is the qualitative improvement of human beings who are considered the most valuable asset of an organization.

Definitions

According to **Edwin B. Flippo**, *"Personnel Management is the planning, organizing, directing, and controlling of the procurement, development, compensation, integration and maintenance and separation of human resources to the end that individual and societal objectives are accomplished."*

This definition reveals that personnel or human resource (HR) management is that aspect of management which deals with the planning, organizing, directing and controlling the personnel functions of the enterprise. This definition is a comprehensive one and covers both the management functions and the operative functions. The purpose of all these functions is to assist in the achievement of basic organizational, individual and societal goals.

According to the **Institute of Personnel Management (U.K.),** *"Personnel Management or HRM is an integral but distinctive part of management concerned with people at work and their relationship within the enterprise. It seeks to bring together into an effective organization the men and women who staff the enterprise enabling each to make his/her best contribution to its success, both as a member of a working group and as individual. It seeks to provide relationships within the enterprise that are conducive both to effective work and human satisfaction."*

According to **Dale Yoder,** *"The management of human resources is viewed as a system in which participants seek to attain both individual and group goals."*

In the words of **Michael J. Jucious,** *"Human resource management may be defined as that field of management which has to do with planning, organizing and controlling the functions of procuring, developing, maintaining and utilizing a labour force, such that the (a) objectives for which the company is established are attained economically and effectively; (b) objectives of all levels of personnel are served to the highest possible degree and (c) objectives of society are duly considered and served."*

According to **National Institute of Personnel Management of India,** *"Personnel management (or human resource management) is that part of management which is concerned with the people at work and with their relationship within the organization. It seeks to bring men and women who make up an enterprise, enabling each to make his own best contribution to its success both as an individual and as a member of a working group."*

Features of Human Resource Management

Based on the analysis of definitions of human resource management, the following features of HRM can be identified.

1. **Human resource management is concerned with the employees both as individuals and as a group in attaining goals:** It is also concerned with behaviour, emotional and social aspects of personnel. It is the process of bringing people and organizations together so that the goals of each are met.
2. **Human resource management covers all levels and categories:** It applies to workers, supervisors, officers, managers and other types of personnel. It covers both organized and unorganized employees. It applies to the employees in all types of organizations in the world.
3. **Human resource management is a continuous and never ending process:** According to **George Resource Terry,** *"it cannot be turned on and off like water from a faucet; it*

cannot be practiced only one hour each day or one day each week. Personnel management requires a constant alertness and awareness of human relations and their importance in everyday operations."

4. **Human resource management is the responsibility of all line managers and a function of staff managers in an organization:** Human resource managers do not manufacture or sell goods but they do contribute to the success and growth of organizations by advising the operating departments on personnel matters.
5. **Human resource management is the central sub-function of an organization and it permeates all types of functional management:** viz., production management, marketing management and financial management. Each and every management is involved with human resource function. It is the responsibility of all line managers and a function of staff managers in an organization.
6. **Managing of human resources is a challenging job due to the dynamic nature of people:** Human resource management aims at securing unreserved communication-operation from all employees in order to attain predetermined goals.
7. **HRM is development oriented:** Individual employee's goals consist of job satisfaction, job-security, high salary, attractive fringe benefits, challenging work, pride, status, recognition, opportunity for development, etc. Human resource management is concerned with developing the potential of employees, so that they derive maximum satisfaction from their work and give their best to the organization.

NATURE OF HUMAN RESOURCE MANAGEMENT

The nature of the personnel management or human resource management has been highlighted in the following features:

1. **Inherent Part of Management:** Personnel or human resource management is inherent in the process of management. This function is performed by all the managers throughout the organization rather than by the personnel department only. If a manager is to get the best of his people, he must undertake the basic responsibility of selecting people who will work under him. He must also take interest in training and motivating the employees and of appraising their performance for improving their quality.
2. **Pervasive Function of Management:** Personnel management or human resource management is a pervasive function of management. It is performed by all the managers at various levels in the organization. In other words, every manager from managing director to the foreman is required to perform the personnel function on a continuous basis. It is not a responsibility that a manager can leave completely to someone else. However, he may secure advice and help in managing people from experts who have special competence in personnel management and industrial relations.
3. **Basic to all Functional Areas:** Personnel management permeates the functional areas of management such as production management, financial management, and marketing management. That is, every manager from top to bottom, working in any department has to perform the personnel functions. Though the personnel department is created under the

supervision of a person designated as 'Personnel Manager', it should not be assumed that the other managers are relieved of their responsibilities.

4. **People Centred:** Human resource management or personnel management is people centred and is relevant in all types of organizations. It is concerned with all the categories of personnel from top to the bottom of the organization. The broad classification of personnel in an industrial enterprise may be as follows:
   (i) Blue collar workers (i.e., those working on machines and engaged in loading; unloading, etc.) and white collar workers (i.e., clerical employees).
   (ii) Managerial and non-managerial personnel.
   (iii) Professionals (such as chartered accountant, company secretary, lawyer, etc.) and non-professional personnel.
5. **Personnel Activities or Functions:** Personnel management involves all functions concerned with the management of people at work. It includes manpower planning, employment, placement, training, appraisal and compensation of employees. For the performance of these activities efficiently, a separate department known as Personnel Department is created in most of organizations.
6. **Continuous Process:** Personnel management or human resource management is not a 'one shot' function. It must be performed continuously if the organizational objectives are to be achieved smoothly.
7. **Based on Human Relations:** Personnel management or human resource management is concerned with the motivation of human resources in the organization. The human beings cannot be dealt with like physical factors of production. Every person has different needs, perceptions and expectations. The managers should give due attention to those factors. Human relations skills are also required in training, performance appraisal, transfer and promotion of subordinates. If the personnel function is performed properly, the human relations in the organization will be cordial.

OBJECTIVES OF HUMAN RESOURCE MANAGEMENT

The primary objective of HRM is to ensure the availability of a competent and willing workforce to an organization. Beyond this, there are other objectives, too. Specifically, HRM objectives are fourfold—societal, organizational, functional and personal. Figure 1.1 shows these objectives.

1. **Societal Objectives:** The failure of an organization to use their resources for the society's benefit in ethical ways may lead to restrictions. For example, the society may limit HR decisions through laws that enforce reservation in hiring and laws that address discrimination, safety or other such areas of societal concern.
2. **Organizational Objectives:** HRM is not an end in itself. It is only a means to assist the organization with its primary objectives. Simply stated, the department exists to serve the rest of the organization.
3. **Functional Objectives:** Resources are wasted when HRM is either more or less sophisticated to suit the organization's demands. The department's level of service must be tailored to fit the organization it serves.

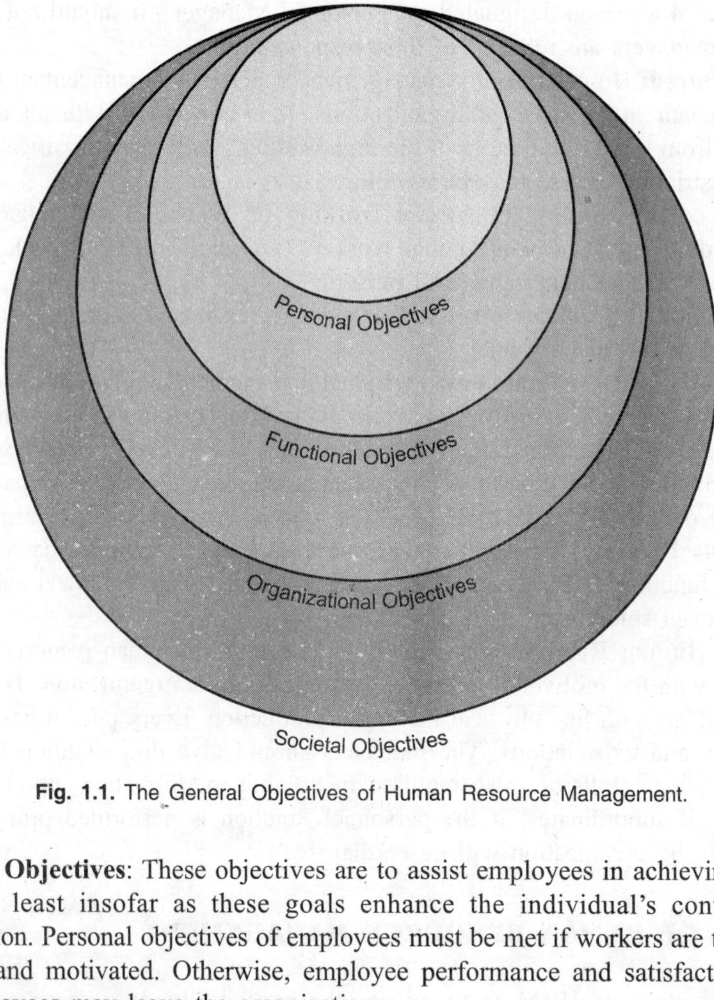

Fig. 1.1. The General Objectives of Human Resource Management.

4. **Personal Objectives**: These objectives are to assist employees in achieving their personal goals, at least insofar as these goals enhance the individual's contribution to the organization. Personal objectives of employees must be met if workers are to be maintained, retained and motivated. Otherwise, employee performance and satisfaction may decline and employees may leave the organization.

Specific Objectives

The specific objectives of personnel management or human resource management may be outlined as follows:

(i) To ensure effective utilization of human resources. All other organizational resources will be efficiently utilized by the human resources.

(ii) To establish and maintain an adequate organizational structure of relationships among all the members of an organization by dividing organization's tasks into functions, positions, and jobs, and by defining clearly the responsibility, accountability, authority for each job and its relation with other jobs in the organization.

(iii) To generate maximum development of human resources within the organization by offering opportunities for advancement to employees through training and education.

(iv) To ensure respect for human beings by providing various services and welfare facilities to the personnel.

(v) To ensure reconciliation of individual/group goals with those of the organization in such a manner that the personnel feel a sense of commitment and loyalty towards it.
(vi) To identify and satisfy the needs of individuals by offering various monetary and non-monetary rewards.
(vii) To achieve and maintain high morale among employees in the organization by securing better human relations.

IMPORTANCE OF HUMAN RESOURCE MANAGEMENT

According to **Rensis Likert** "*All the activities of any enterprise are initiated and determined by persons who make up that institution. Plants, offices, computers, automated equipment and all else that make a modern firm are unproductive except for human effort and direction of all the tasks of management. Managing the human component is the central and most important task because all else depends on how well it is done.*"

The effectiveness with which human resources are coordinated and utilized determines the success in achieving organizational objectives. Human resource management is important to the organization in a number of ways, such as:

1. Importance for the Organization

Human resource management is important for the organization due to the following:
(i) Good human resource practices help in attracting and retaining the best people in the organization.
(ii) In order to make use of latest technology, the appointment of right type of persons is essential. The right people can be fitted into new jobs properly only if the management performs its HR function satisfactorily.
(iii) Globalization has increased the size of the organizations that employ thousands of employees in various countries. The performance of the company depends upon the qualities of the people employed. This has further increased the importance of HRM.
(iv) Human resource planning alerts the organization to the types of people it will need in the short, medium and long run.
(v) Human resource development is essential for meeting the challenges of future. The importance of HRM has increased because of the shortage of really good managerial talent in the country.

2. Importance for the Employees

The human aspect of organizations has become very important over the years. HRM stresses on the motivation of employees by providing them various financial and non-financial incentives. Right organizational climate is also stressed upon so that the employees can contribute their maximum to the achievement of the organizational objectives. Effective management of human resources promotes team work and team spirit among employees. It offers excellent growth opportunities to people who have the potential to rise. It also encourages people to work with diligence and commitment.

3. Importance for the Society

Society as a whole is the main beneficiary of good human resource practices. Good HR efforts lead to productivity gains (ratio of output to input) to the society, since it enables the managers to reduce costs, save scarce resources, enhance profits and offer better pay, benefits and working conditions to employees.

The importance of HR is very intelligently explained by **Herbert E. Meyer** in the following words: "*The name of the game in business today is HR. You can't hope to show a good financial or operating report unless your human relations are in order and it is immaterial, what kind of company you are running. A chief executive is nothing without his people. You got to have the right ones in the right jobs for them and you got to be sure that employees at every level are being paid fairly and being given opportunities for promotion. You can't fool them and any chief executive who tries is going to hurt himself and his company.*"

LINE AND STAFF ASPECTS OF HRM

An organization requires of structural relationships among different departments, people and other resources to achieve the desired objectives. The formal relationship among the people in the organization is the most important factor for its success and that is why, it is very often said that the process of organization involves combining and coordinating the efforts of the persons working in the organization in the efficient manner to produce the desired results. In order to combine and coordinate the efforts of people working at different levels in the organization, proper relationships among them in terms of authority and responsibility should be set up. For this, any of the following types of organization structure may be set up:

(i) Line organization
(ii) Line and staff organization
(iii) Functional organization

From this set, we shall discuss line and staff organization. Here formal relations are divided into line and these relationships are discussed in greater detail below:

Line and Staff Relationships: The relationship with which the managers in an organization deal with one another are broadly classified into two categories, viz., line and staff. Line and staff are often used in ways that are loose and unclear. Attempts have been made in some organizations to dispense with them. Thus, operating managers/departments are frequently substituted for line and auxiliary and service departments are used for staff. Line and staff are characterized by relationship but not by departments. The important category of relationships is line relationship.

1. **Line Relationship:** The relationship existing between two managers due to delegation of authority and responsibility and giving or receiving instructions or orders is called line relationship. Thus, line relationship generally exists between superior and subordinate. Line refers to those positions of an organization which have responsibility, authority and are accountable for accomplishment of primary objectives. Managers identified as line are not subject to command by staff position. In case of disagreement between line and staff, line manager has the right to make final operating decisions.

Line authority represents uninterrupted series of authority and responsibility delegating down the management hierarchy. In other words, Board of Directors delegates authority to the managing director who in turn delegates a part of his authority to the general manager. The general manager in turn delegates part of his authority to different departmental heads and through them to the supervisors. However, the line managers are completely responsible and accountable for the results achieved by the employees of the respective departments and sections. This does mean that though the authority is delegated, responsibility for action taken by a subordinate still rests with the superior.

The second kind of relationship is staff relationship.

2. **Staff Relations:** The staff concept is probably as old as organization itself. It is virtually impossible to busy line managers to perform all their functions and concentrate on all the activities including management of the people in their respective departments. This gives rise to securing advice and help from specialists. This creates staff relationships. The relationship between two managers is said to be a staff relation, when it is created due to giving and taking advice, guidance, information, help or assistance, counselling, etc., in the process of attaining organizational goals.

   Thus, staff managers analyze problems, collect information and develop alternative suggestions and help the line managers to make right decisions quickly. Staff control is monitoring and reporting, which brings the results of information to the attention of the line managers for action by the line. Thus, they reduce the workload of the line managers and allow them to concentrate on their operative issues.

Having discussed two categories of relationships it would be appropriate to apply the line and staff relationship to the organization design.

Structuring Line and Staff Relationships in an Organization

An organization can also be structured on the basis of line and staff. As discussed earlier, line and staff are viewed as relationships but not by departments. Some functional managers have line relations with other managers whilst some other managers have staff relations with other managers in the organization as shown in Figure 1.2. But those functional managers having staff relations may have line relations in relation to the subordinates. Thus, organization structure is designed on the basis of line and staff relationship within the departmental structure. It is often regarded that the personnel manager has staff relations with other managers in an organization. Now we discuss the line and staff relationship and personnel management in an organization.

Line and Staff Relationships and HRM

Regarding the relationship between HRM and line and staff, three main aspects have been highlighted.

1. Human Resource Management is a Line Responsibility

It is widely felt that "*Human resource management is a line manager's responsibility but a staff function.*" As discussed earlier the responsibility of line managers is to attain effective goals of

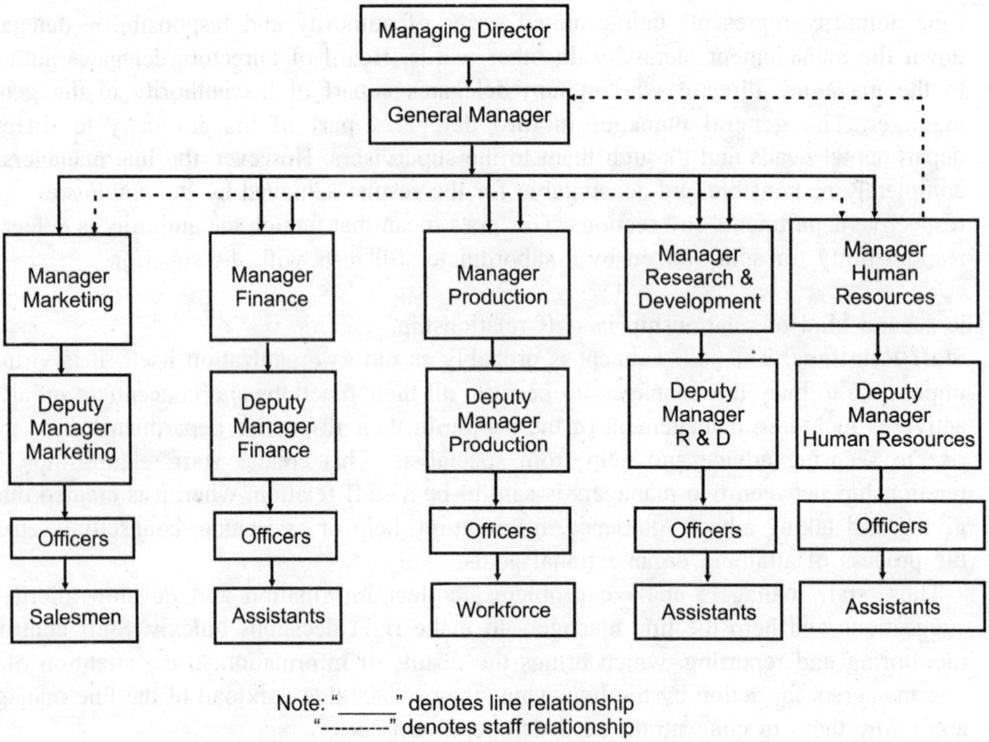

Fig. 1.2. Line and Staff Relationships in an Organization.

their respective departments by the proper management of materials, machine, money and men. Thus, management of four Ms which includes management of personnel in their respective departments is the responsibility of line management. Since management is getting things done through and by the people, responsibility of management of these people rests with line managers. Attaining overall organizational goals is the responsibility of the general manager through proper management of personnel and with the help of the different heads of the departments. In turn, management of personnel in different departments is the responsibility of heads concerned. In the same way, first level superiors are also responsible for managing the men of their respective sections in achieving their goals. Thus, personnel management is a responsibility of all the line managers. It is in this sense that every manager is a personnel manager.

2. *Line Needs Assistance in Managing Men*

In most of the organizations, Boards of Directors delegate operative/technical responsibilities to managing directors and through them to the general managers. Different functional managers are delegated with the technical responsibility by the general manager. Since all these line managers have to concentrate on discharging technical or operative responsibility they may not find time to discharge their responsibilities managing human resources. For example, the production manager has to concentrate on production activities and thus he may not find time to perform the various functions of personnel management relating to the employees of his own department. In such a situation the line managers require help or advice relating to personnel management of their respective departments.

3. Human Resource Management is a Staff Function

Since the top management believes that organizational ability depends on sound management of human resources, it provides specialized assistance to line managers, through personnel managers. Thus, personnel managers are created for the purpose of providing assistance, advice, information, etc., to line managers in order to relieve them from the burden of management of personnel and to allow them to concentrate on their technical operations. Personnel managers perform the various functions of personnel management, viz., employment, training, development, wage and salary administration, motivation, grievance redressal, workers participation in management, collective bargaining, etc. Thus, personnel managers perform certain staff functions relating to management of personnel like advising, assisting, guiding, suggesting, counselling and providing information to the line managers. So personnel management is a staff function.

However, responsibility for the management of personnel still rests with line managers. Thus, personnel human resource management is a line management responsibility but a staff function.

Table 1.1: Line Organization vs. Line Staff Organization

Line Organization	Line and Staff Organization
1. Line refers to those positions which have the responsibility of achieving the primary objectives of the organization.	1. Staff refers to those positions which have responsibility for providing advice and service to the line in attainment of organizational objectives.
2. There are no experts to assist and advise the line officials.	2. There are experts known as staff to assist and advise the line officials.
3. There is strict discipline.	3. There is loose discipline.
4. There is no friction between line and staff.	4. There is always a risk of friction between line and staff people over their respective roles.
5. It is not based upon planned specification.	5. It is based upon planned specialization.
6. Certain line executives become key men as they occupy those positions on which the survival of the organization depends.	6. This is not possible in case of line and staff organization as staff officials always share credit with line officials.

FUNCTIONS OF HUMAN RESOURCE MANAGEMENT

There are three categories of functions which the personnel manager is expected to perform. These are: (1) managerial, (2) operative, and (3) advisory.

1. Managerial Functions

The Human Resource Manager is a member of the management. So he must perform the basic managerial functions of planning, organizing, directing and controlling in relation to his department. These functions are briefly discussed below:

1. **Planning:** To get things done through his subordinates, a manager plans ahead. Planning is necessary to give the organization its goals and directions to establish best procedures to reach the goals. Effective managers recognize that a substantial part of their time should

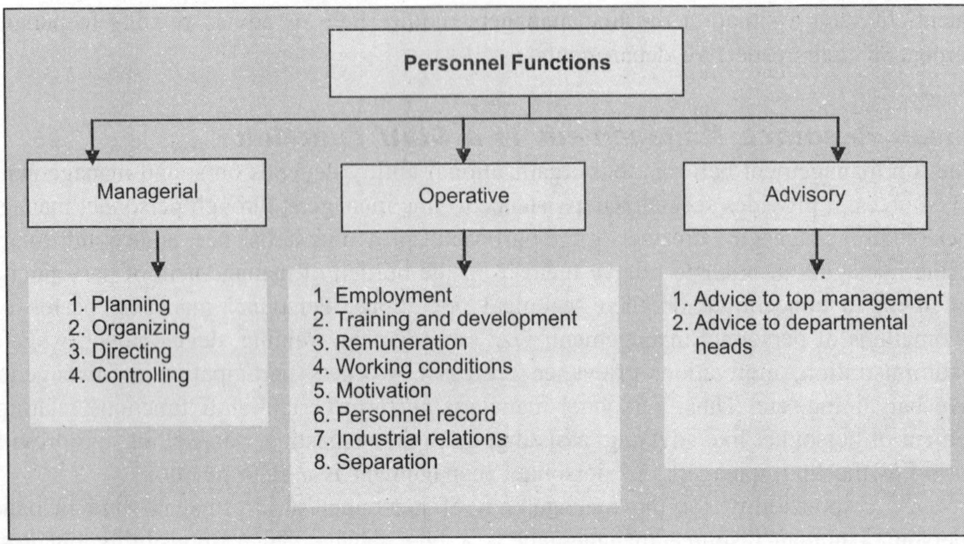

Fig. 1.3. Functions of Human Resource Management.

be devoted to planning. For a personnel manager, planning means the determination in advance of personnel programmes that will contribute to the goals established for the enterprise, i.e. anticipating vacancies, planning job requirements, job descriptions and determination of the sources of recruitment. The process of personnel planning involves three essential steps. Firstly, a supply and demand forecast for each job category is made. This step requires knowledge of both labour market conditions and the strategic posture and goals of the organization. Secondly, net shortage and excess of personnel by job category are projected for a specific time horizon. Finally, plans are developed to eliminate the forecast shortages and excess of particular categories of human resources.

2. **Organizing.** Once the personnel manager has established objectives and developed plans and programmes to reach them, he must design and develop organization structure to carry out the various operations. The organization structure basically includes the following:
   - Grouping of personnel activity logically into functions or positions;
   - Assignment of different groups of activities to different individuals;
   - Delegation of authority according to the tasks assigned and responsibilities involved; and
   - Coordination of activities of different individuals.
3. **Direction**. The plans are to be put into effect by the people. But how smoothly the plans are implemented depends on the motivation of people. The direction function of the personnel manager involves encouraging people to it willingly and effectively for the goals of the enterprise. In other words, the direction function is meant to guide and motivate the people to accomplish the personnel programmes. The personnel manager can motivate the employees in an organization through career planning, salary administration, ensuring employee morale, developing cordial relationships and provision of safety requirements and welfare of the employees.

The motivational function poses a great challenge for any manager. The human resource manager must have the ability to identify the needs of employees and the means and methods to satisfy those needs. Motivation is a continuous process as new needs and expectations emerge among employees when old ones are satisfied.

4. **Controlling:** Controlling is concerned with the regulation of activities in accordance with the plans, which in turn have been formulated on the basis of objectives of the organization. Thus, controlling completes the cycle and leads back to planning. It is the observation and comparison of results with the standards and correction of deviations that may occur. Controlling helps the personnel manager to evaluate and control the performance of the personnel department in terms of various operative functions. It involves performance appraisal, critical examination of personnel records and statistics and personnel audit.

2. Operative Functions

The operative functions are those tasks or duties which are specifically entrusted to the human resource department under the general supervision of human resource manager. These are concerned with employment, development, compensation, integration and maintenance of human resource of the organization.

The human resource department performs the following operative functions:

(i) **Employment:** The first operative function of the human resource department is the employment of proper kind and number of persons necessary to achieve the objectives of the organization. This involves recruitment, selection, placement, etc. of the human resource. Before these processes are performed, it is better to determine the manpower requirements both in terms of number and quality of the human resource. Recruitment and selection cover the sources of supply of labour and the devices designed to select the right type of people for various jobs. Induction and placement of personnel for their better performance also come under the employment or procurement function.

(ii) **Development:** Training and development of human resource is a follow-up of the employment function. It is a duty of management to train each employee properly to develop technical skills for the job for which he has been employed and also to develop him for the higher jobs in the organization. Proper development of human resources is necessary to increase their skills in doing their jobs and in satisfying their growth need. For this purpose, the human resource department will devise appropriate training programmes. There are several on-the-job and off-the-job methods available for training purposes. A good training programme should include a mixture of both types of methods. It is important to point out that human resource department arranges for training not only of new employees but also of old employees to update their knowledge in the use of latest techniques.

(iii) **Compensation:** This function is concerned with the determination of adequate and equitable remuneration of the employees in the organization for their contribution to the organizational goals. The human resource can be compensated both in terms of monetary as well as non-monetary rewards. Factors which must be borne in mind while fixing the remuneration of human resource are their basic needs, requirements of jobs, legal provisions regarding minimum wages capacity of the organization to pay, wage level afforded by competitors, etc. For fixing the wage levels, the human resource department can make use of certain techniques like job evaluation and performance appraisal.

(iv) **Maintenance:** Merely appointment and training of people is not sufficient; they must be provided with good working conditions so that they may like their work and workplace and maintain their efficiency. Working conditions certainly influence the motivation and morale of the employees. These include measures taken for health, safety, and comfort of the workforce. The personnel department also provides for various welfare services which relate to the physical and social well-being of the employees. These may include provision of cafeteria, rest rooms, counselling, group insurance, education for children of employees, recreational facilities, etc.

(v) **Motivation:** Employees work in the organization for the satisfaction of their needs. In many of the cases, it is found that they do not contribute towards the organizational goals as much as they can. This happens because employees are not adequately motivated. The personnel manager helps the various departmental managers to design a system of financial and non-financial rewards to motivate the employees.

(vi) **Personnel Records:** Personnel department maintains the records of the employees working in the enterprise. It keeps full records of their training, achievements, transfer, promotion, etc. It also keeps many other records relating to the behaviour of personnel like absenteeism and labour turnover, and the personnel programmes and policies of the organization.

(vii) **Industrial Relations:** These days, the responsibility of maintaining good industrial relations is mainly discharged by the personnel managers. The personnel managers can help in collective bargaining, joint consultation and settlement of disputes, if they arise. This is because personnel manager is in possession of full information relating to personnel and has the working knowledge of various labour enactments. The personnel manager can do a great deal in maintaining industrial peace in the organization as he is deeply associated with various committees on discipline, labour welfare, safety, grievance, etc. He helps in laying down the grievance procedure to redress the grievances of the employees. He also gives authentic information to the trade union leaders and conveys their views on various labour problems to the top management.

(viii) **Separation:** Since the first function of personnel manager is to procure the employees, it is logical that the last should be the separation and return of that person to society. Most people do not die on the job. The organization is responsible for meeting certain requirements of due process in separation, as well as assuring that the returned person is in as good shape as possible. The personnel manager has to ensure the release of retirement benefits to the retiring personnel in time.

3. Advisory Functions

Personnel/human resource manager has specialized education and training in managing human relations. He is an expert in his area and so can give advice on matters relating to human resources of the organization. He offers his advice to:

(i) **Top Management:** The personnel manager advises the top management in formulation and evaluation of personnel programmes, policies and procedures. He also gives advice for achieving and maintaining good human relations and high employee morale.

(ii) **Departmental Heads.** The personnel manager offers advice to the heads of various departments on matters such as manpower planning, job analysis and design, recruitment and selection, placement, training, performance appraisal, etc.

DUTIES AND RESPONSIBILITIES OF HR MANAGER

There are many different roles and responsibilities that can be performed by the HRM department depending on the size of the organization, the demographic profile of the employees, the industry where the business belongs, values and corporate culture prevalent within, and the priorities of top management, and in the case of a small business, the priorities of its owner. The HRM department or the HRM professional in small organizations may take full responsibility for all human resource activities. Whereas in others, it may share the roles and responsibilities of other departments such as the finance or administration. Still, in some organizations, the HRM acts as an advisor of top management, while in others the HRM makes all the human resource related decisions in support of top management's critical business decisions.

In the last 10 years or more, it is noticeable that more and more organizations are looking into HRM as their strategic partners in quality management, corporate planning, business operations, and most of all, in business profitability. HRM now takes the forefront in lending support to business operations and expansions in ways that enhances the image and value of the organization both for its shareholders and customers.

The main duties and responsibilities of HR manager are as under:

1. Employment and Recruiting

Interviewing, recruiting, testing and temporary labour coordination.

2. Training and Development

Orientation, performance management, skills training and productivity enhancement.

3. Compensation

Wage and salary administration, job description, executive compensation, incentive pay and job evaluation.

4. Benefits

Insurance, vacation leave administration, retirement plans, profit sharing and stick plans.

5. Employee Services

Employee assistance programme, relocation services and outplacement services.

6. Employee and Community Relations

Attitude surveys, labour relations, publications, labour law compliance and discipline.

7. Personnel Records

Information system records.

8. Health and Safety

Safety inspection, drug testing and health, wellness.

9. Strategic Planning

International human resources, forecasting, planning and mergers and acquisitions.

PROCESS OF HUMAN RESOURCE MANAGEMENT

HRM is a process consisting of four functions as shown in Figure 1.4.

The HRM process is a four-step process.

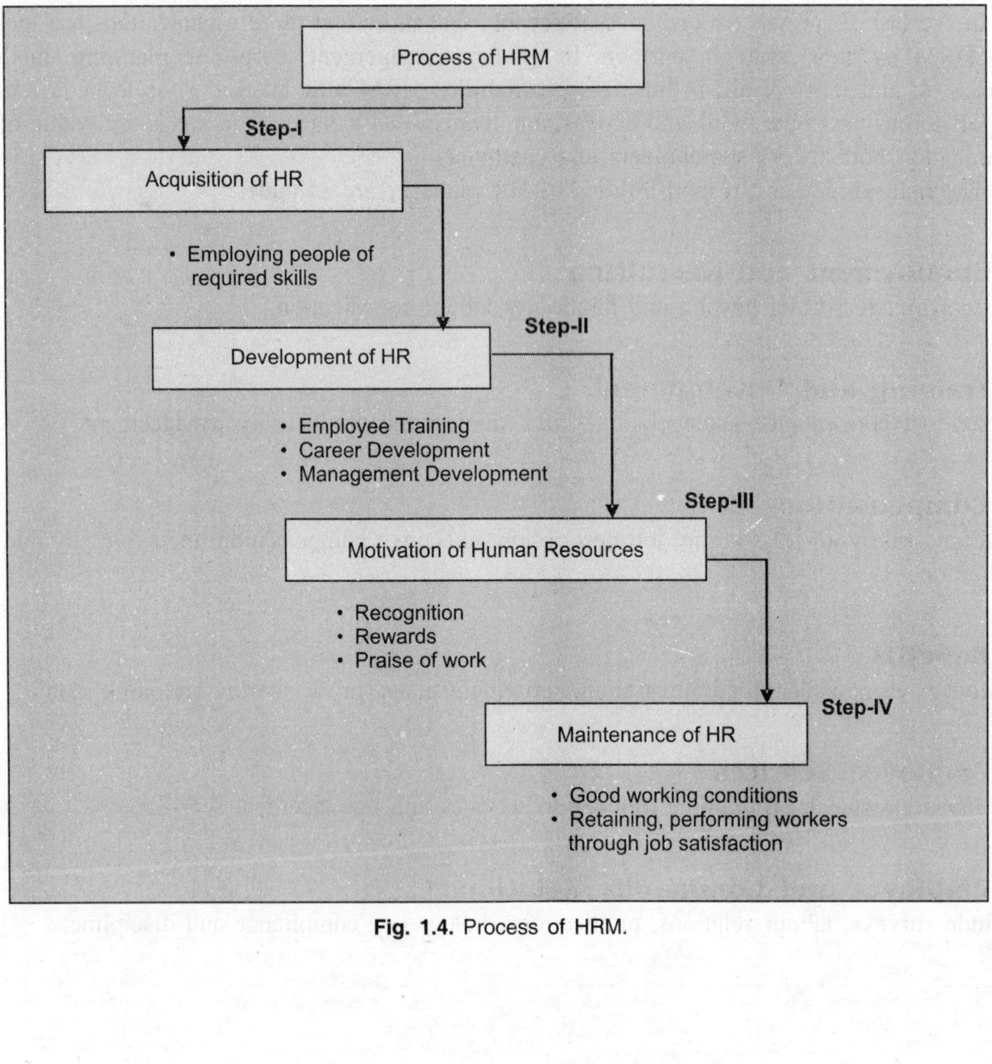

Fig. 1.4. Process of HRM.

1. Acquisition Function of HR

The first step in the process of HR is acquisition of HR. Acquisition process is concerned with securing and employing the people possessing required kind and level of skills necessary to achieve the organizational objectives. The acquisition function begins with planning. It also covers other functions such as job analysis, human resource planning, recruitment, selection, placement, induction and internal mobility.

2. Development Function of HR

The second step in the HR process is development of HR. Development function is the process of improving, moulding and changing the skills, knowledge, creative ability, aptitude and values of the employees. The development function can be viewed along three dimensions:

(a) **Employee Training:** Training is the process of imparting to the employees the technical and operating skills and knowledge. It also includes changing of attitudes among workers.

(b) **Management Development:** Management development is primarily concerned with the knowledge acquisition and the enhancement of an executive's conceptual abilities. It is the process of designing and conducting suitable executive development programmes so as to develop the managerial and human relations skills of employees.

(c) **Career Development:** Career development is a continual effort to match long-term individual and organizational needs. When human resources have been developed effectively, one can expect to have competent employees with up-to-date skills and knowledge.

3. Motivation Function

The motivation function begins with the recognition that individuals are unique and that motivation techniques must reflect the needs of each individual. It is an area of management that deals with integrating people into work situation in a way that motivates them to work together productively, cooperatively and with economic, psychological and social satisfaction.

4. Maintenance Function

The maintenance function is concerned with providing those working conditions that employees believe are necessary in order to maintain their commitment to the organization. The objective of the maintenance function is to retain people who are performing at high levels. This requires that the organization provide safe and healthy working conditions and satisfactory labour relations. If these activities are performed effectively, we can expect to have competent employees who are committed to the organization and are satisfied with their jobs.

HR AND TECHNOLOGY

J.K. Galbraith defines technology as a systematic application of organized knowledge to practical tasks. During the last 100 years, technology has developed beyond anybody's comprehension. Science and technology enabled man to overcome distances; control birth rate; save lives; generate, preserve and distribute energy; discover new materials to substitute existing ones; introduce machines to do the work for humans; substitute mental work with computers; unravel the mysteries of the seas and the space; and provide himself with a lot of leisure and comfort in the process.

How Does Technology Affect the HR Function?

1. **With the advent of technology, jobs tend to become more intellectual or upgraded:** A job which was earlier handled by an illiterate or unskilled worker now requires the services of an educated and skilled worker.
2. **Introduction of new technology dislocates workers unless they become well-equipped to work on new machines:** This makes it obligatory on the part of HRM to train workers and to rehabilitate those who are displaced or cannot be trained.
3. **For those employees who pick up and acquaint themselves with new technology, the job will be challenging and rewarding:** Working class, in general, stands to gain through increased productivity, reduced prices and increased real wages—all by-products of technological advancement.
4. **Along with upgrading jobs, technology has its impact on human relations:** Technology lays down the requirements for much of the human interaction in organizations. The arrangement of a production setup determines who will be near to whom. The work flow determines who needs to talk to whom. And since interaction and activity affect sentiments, technology indirectly determines what individuals in large groups will feel and think about one another and about their work situation.
5. **Job-holders will become highly professional and knowledgeable:** An organization which has adopted the latest technology is flushed with scientists, MBAs, engineers, college graduates and highly-skilled workers. L&T, for example, has 20,000 employees, 70 per cent of whom are engineers and a good part is of the remaining MBAs. Though such an organization can boast of a progressive and modern outlook but due to this the problems faced are serious, to say the least motivating such employees, for instance, is a difficult job. Such mundane incentives as attractive remuneration, job security and just treatment hardly inspire the enlightened employees to work more or harder. They are, instead, motivated by opportunities which offer challenges, achievement and growth. Further, retaining such employees for long is a difficult job. Being cosmopolitan in their outlook, these employees are known for organizational rootlessness and job hopping. The company has to make several allowances to discourage rootlessness. Regular attendance and punctuality have to be relaxed; dual promotion ladders have to be established so that distinguished technical people can rise in their ranks; profit sharing to be provided to give creative persons a financial stake in the ideas they create; participation in professional get-togethers needs to be sponsored; writing of professional articles must be encouraged; foreign jaunts need to be allowed; and 'moonlighting' has to be tolerated. Another problem relates to, what **Galbraith** calls, 'technostructure' which is a composition of scientists and technicians in an organization. The technostructure tries to control the organization by influencing the management's decision-making. While there may be nothing wrong in making decisions prompted by the technostructure, the problem lies in the social effect that is involved. People constituting the technostructure are experts, no doubt, but they are more action-oriented and are yet to learn social problems arising out of business

decisions. The management is, therefore, in a tight position trying to balance the ruffled feelings of technocrats and the social consequences of business decisions.

6. **Growth of HRIS is possible with technology:** More specifically, the main use of technology in HRM is an organization's human resource information system (HRIS). HRIS is a computerized information package that provides the management with increased capacity to record, store, manipulate and communicate information widely, with access to many users. Some organizations store their data in a mainframe linked to personal computers; others use a decentralized network system with smaller computers at workstations in various functional areas.
7. **The Internet has revolutionized one's ability to access technology:** Many firms use company-specific 'intranets', to establish home pages that allow employees to read current job postings and even apply for the positions on-line. Equipped with only a PC and a modem, managers can take advantage of on-line services designed especially for HR departments. With constant advances in technology and work processes, firms are under intense competitive pressure to implement more efficient means of operations. However, the financial considerations of whether to adopt a new technology must be balanced with the number of HR strategic issues.

Thus, to conclude it can be said that HR professionals need a knowledge-base about the current technological possibilities and a general vision about the role that technology might play in their firms. With this knowledge, they will be able to add value to strategic decisions that involve technology.

STRATEGIC ROLE OF HUMAN RESOURCE MANAGEMENT

It has been realized today that the employees are central to achieving competitive advantage. This has led to the emergence of the field known as strategic human resource management.

What is Strategic HRM?

According to **L. Gratton**, "*SHRM has been defined as the process of linking the HRM with strategic goals and objectives so as to improve business performance and develop organizational cultures that foster innovation and flexibility.*"

In the words of **P. Wright and G. McMahan**, "*SHRM is defined as the pattern of planned human resource deployments and activities intended to enable an organization to achieve its goals.*"

After having discussed the meaning of SHRM, we are in a position to highlight the strategic HR and its role. It is as under:

- Strategic HR involves accepting the HR function as a strategic partner in the formulation of the company's strategies.
- Strategic HR involves HR function as a strategic partner in the implementation of the company's strategies through HR activities such as recruiting, selection, training and rewarding the personnel.

- The aim of the SHRM is to build a committed workforce that helps the organization to achieve its goals—the goals to achieve superior levels of customer service and high profitability.
- Another strategic role of HRM is to use various mechanisms to build healthy two-way communications.
- Still another important strategic role of HRM is to screen out potential managers who can be involved and assigned more and higher responsibilities in the organization.
- The strategic role of HRM is also to provide highly competitive salaries and pay for performance incentives and to guarantee to the greatest extent possible fair treatment and employment security for all employees.
- The strategic role of HRM is also to institute various promotions from within activities so as to enable the employees to grow and giving them every opportunity to fully utilize their skills at work.

STRATEGIC PLANNING AND HR MANAGEMENT

The term strategic planning is usually reserved for the company's corporate level and organization wide strategic planning process. Specifically strategic planning outlines the type of business the firm will be doing given the firm's external opportunities and threats and its internal strengths and weaknesses.

The manager's strategic plan will ideally seek to balance the two sets of forces: on the one hand, there are firm's external opportunities and threats and on the other there are firm's internal strengths and weaknesses.

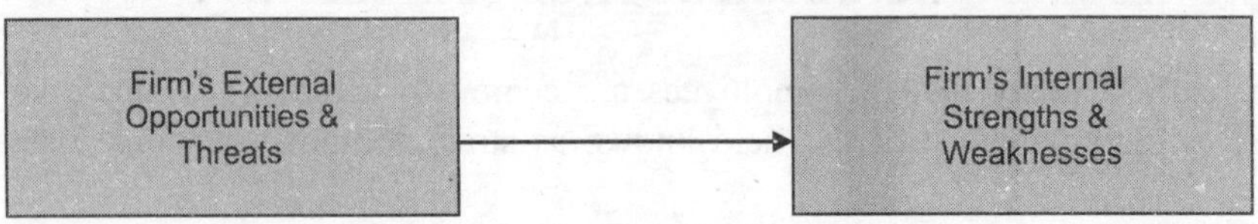

Fig. 1.5. Strategic Plan of an Organization.

> **Illustration**
>
> In 1995, IBM bought Lotus, a software firm, in part to acquire the Lotus Notes networking programs. Sensing the opportunities and threats presented by the Internet's growing popularity and by IBM's relative lack of expertise in networking software, IBM Chairman Louis Gerstner apparently decided to diversify by buying Lotus to position IBM to compete more effectively with other means of linking or networking companies and individuals.

Nature of Business Strategies or Strategic Planning

Normally companies typically formulate three types of strategies under strategic planning:

1. **Corporate Strategies:** Corporate strategies identify the mix of businesses the firm will engage in. For example, many companies such as Pepsi Co. consists of several businesses such as Pepsi, Frito-lay, and Pizza Hut. These companies, therefore, need a corporate-

level strategy. A company's corporate-level strategy identifies the portfolio of businesses that, in total, will comprise the organization and the ways in which these businesses will relate to each other.

2. **The Business-Level/Competitive Strategies** : These strategies identify how each of the firm's businesses will compete. For example, at the next level down each of these businesses such as Pizza Hut is then guided by a business-level/competitive strategy. A competitive strategy identifies how to build and strengthen the long-term competitive position in the marketplace. It identifies for instance, how Pizza Hut will compete with Dominos or how Wal-Mart will compete with K-Mart.
3. **Functional Strategies:** Each business has several functional strategies which identify how the units manufacturing, sales, HRM and other functions will contribute to the business strategy. Functional strategies identify the basic course of action that each of the business departments will pursue in order to help the business attain its competitive goals.

Managers thus engage in three types of strategic decision-making for the firms and each represents different levels of strategic decision-making in an organization. This is shown in Figure 1.6.

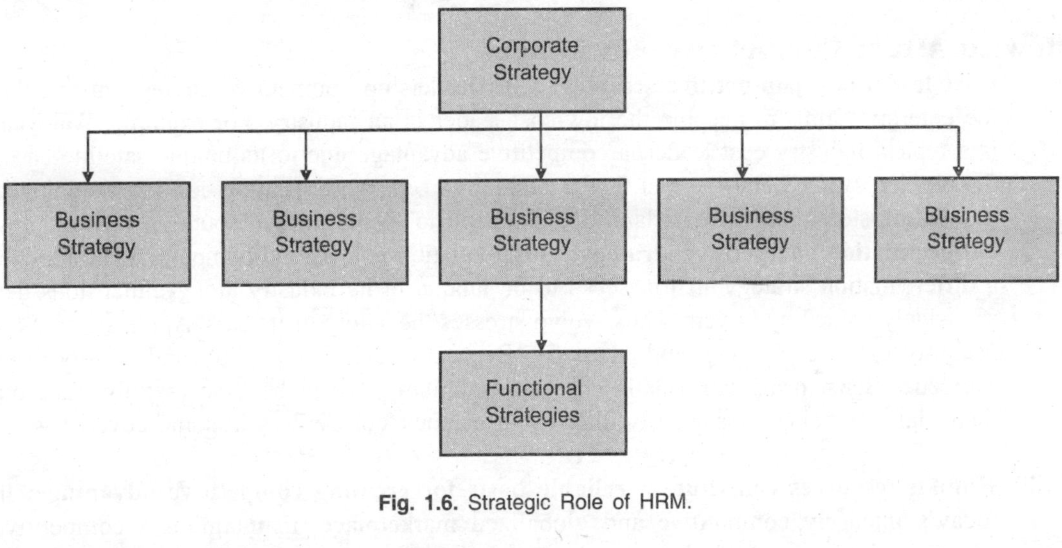

Fig. 1.6. Strategic Role of HRM.

Attributes of Strategic Decision-Making

The three levels of strategic decision-making have the following attributes:

(i) Supportive and interrelated decision-making: Strategic decision-making at three levels and mutually supportive.

Illustration: Let's consider IBM's Lotus acquisition. At the corporate organization-wide level, the acquisition represents an attempt to reposition the giant corporation to compete more effectively in the coming age of networking computers. However, having decided to acquire Lotus, Gerstner then had to make a business-level strategic decision regarding how to organize IBM's new networking business and in particular how to compete with other firms making similar products. In this case John Manzi, the head of Lotus, proposed to Gerstner the merger of Lotus with IBM's other software divisions with Manzi in charge; Gerstner rejected this suggestion, deciding to keep Lotus and its Lotus Notes software separate, and to let Manzi leave the firm.

Corporate and business-level strategic decisions like these in turn help determine what IBM's functional strategies should be. For example, IBM's push into networking has production strategy implications, since it may require phasing out several hardware manufacturing facilities and consolidating the firm's network programme design facilities in fewer locations. Similarly, IBM's marketing and sales efforts may have to be increasingly organized around a networking sales effort. The HR function will also have to accomplish its share. There will be facilities to be closed, new ones to be staffed and new network programme designers to be recruited and hired, for instance.

(ii) Building competitive advantage: A firm tries to achieve a competitive advantage for each business it is in. A competitive advantage can be defined as any factors that allow an organization to differentiate its product or service from those of its competitors to increase market share. Similarly, strategic planning expert **Michael Porter** says that "*Competitive strategy aims to establish a profitable and sustainable position against the forces that determine industry competition.*"

How to Attain Competitive Advantage?

1. **Cost leadership competitive strategy:** Cost leadership competitive strategy means that the enterprise aims to become the low-cost leader in an industry. For example, Wal-Mart is a typical industry cost leader, a competitive advantage due to its unique satellite-based distribution system, and the fact that it generally keeps store location costs to a minimum by placing stores on low-cost land outside small to medium-sized southern towns.
2. **Differentiation competitive strategy:** Differentiation is a second competitive strategy. In a differentiation strategy, a firm seeks to be unique in its industry along dimensions that are widely valued by buyers. Thus, Volvo stresses the safety of its cars, Apple stresses the usability of its computers, and Mercedes Benz emphasizes reliability and quality. Like Mercedes Benz, firms can usually charge a premium price if they successfully stake out their claim to being substantially different from their competitors in some coveted way.

(iii) Human resources constitute a reliable basis for creating competitive advantage: In today's intensely competitive and globalized marketplace, maintaining a competitive advantage by becoming a low-cost leader or a differentiator puts a heavy premium on having a highly committed and competent workforce. Low-cost, high-quality cars like those of Toyota and Saturn aren't just a result of sophisticated automated machines. Instead they're a result of intensely committed employees, all working hard and with self-discipline to produce the best cars that they can at the lowest possible cost.

Many experts have emphasized the strategic role that committed workers play in helping their firms achieve competitive advantage. For example, strategic planning experts **C.K. Prahalad** and **Gary Hamel** say that competitive advantage lies not just in differentiating a product or service or in becoming the low-cost leader but also in being able to tap the company's special skills or core competencies and rapidly respond to customers' needs and competitors' moves. In other words, competitive advantage lies in management's ability to consolidate corporate-wide technologies and production skills into competencies that empower individual businesses to adapt quickly to changing opportunities.

CONCLUSION

In a growing number of organizations human resources are now viewed as a source of competitive advantage. There is greater recognition that distinctive competencies are obtained through highly developed employee skills, distinctive organizational cultures, management processes, and systems. This is in contrast to the traditional emphasis on transferable resources such as equipment.

HR'S ROLE AS A STRATEGIC PARTNER

There is a long history of HR. There are three views in this context.

1. Some still tend to view that HR is strictly operational and that HR activities are not strategic. This view is given by **Peter Boxall** and it is the first view.
2. Another sophisticated view of HR is that its role is simply to fit the company's strategy. In this view HR's strategic role is to adapt individual HR practices (recruiting, rewarding, and so on) to fit specific corporate and competitive strategies. By this view, top management crafts a corporate strategy—such as to buy Lotus—and then HR is told to create the HR programmes required to successfully implement that corporate strategy.
3. A third view of HR management is that it is an equal partner in the strategic planning process. By this view HR management's role is not just to tailor its activities to the demands of business strategy, nor, certainly, just to carry out operational day-to-day tasks like ensuring that employees are paid. Instead, by this third view, the need to forge a company's workforce into a competitive advantage means that human resource management must be an equal partner in both the formulation and the implementation of the company's organization-wide and competitive strategies.

Hence, HR's role as strategic partner is discussed below in two strategic areas (Figure 1.7).

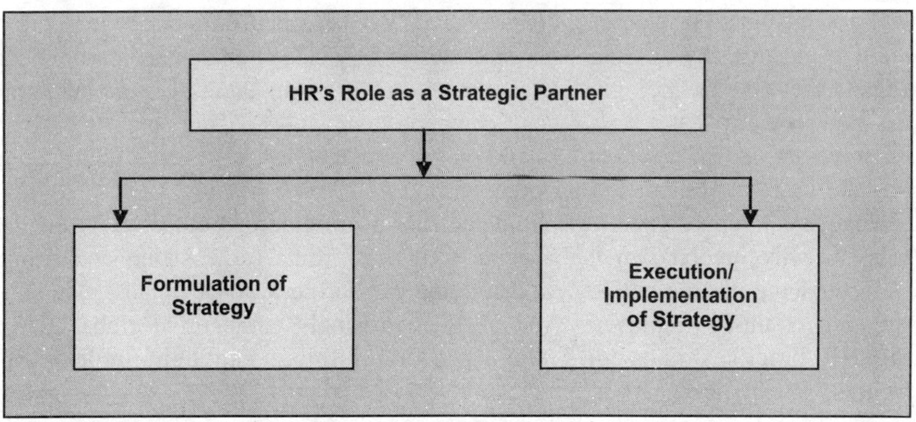

Fig. 1.7. HR's Role as a Strategic Partner.

1. HR's Role in Formulating Strategy

Formulating a company's overall strategic plan requires identifying, analyzing, and balancing two sets of forces: the company's external opportunities and threats on one hand, and its internal strengths and weaknesses on the other. Here comes the strategic HR management.

(i) **HR management can play a role in what strategic planners call environmental scanning**, in other words, identifying and analyzing external opportunities and threats that may be crucial to the company's success. For example, in 1995 both United Airlines and American Airlines considered and then rejected the opportunity to acquire US Air, a smaller and relatively weak airline. While both American and United had several reasons for rejecting the bid, HR considerations loomed large. Specifically, both American and United had doubts about their abilities to successfully negotiate new labour agreements with US Air's employees, and both felt the problems of assimilating them might be too great.

(ii) **Similarly, HR management is in a unique position to supply competitive intelligence that may be useful in the strategic planning process.** Details regarding advanced incentive plans being used by competitors, opinion survey data from employees that elicit information about customer complaints and information about pending legislation like labour laws or mandatory health insurance are some examples.

(iii) **HR also participates in the strategy formulation process by supplying information** regarding the company's internal strengths and weaknesses. For example, IBM's decision to buy Lotus was probably prompted in part by IBM's conclusion that its own human resources were inadequate to enable the firm to reposition itself as an industry leader in networking systems, or at least to do so quickly enough. The strengths and weaknesses of a company's human resources can have a determining effect on the viability of the firm's strategic options. For example, "situations, where human resource capabilities serve as a driving force in strategy formulation, occur where there are unique human capabilities."

2. HR's Role in Executing Strategy

HR management can play a pivotal role in the successful execution or implementation of a company's strategic plan. For example, *Times of India's* the competitive strategy is to differentiate itself from its competitors by offering superior customer service and guaranteed on-time deliveries. Since basically the same technologies are available to other competitors, it is the human resource that necessarily provides TOI with a crucial competitive advantage. This puts a premium on the firm's HR processes, as discussed earlier, and on the firm's ability to create a highly committed, competent, and customer-oriented workforce.

HR management supports strategic implementation in numerous other ways. For example, HR is today heavily involved in the execution of most firms' downsizing and restructuring strategies, through out-placing employees, instituting pay-for-performance plans, reducing health-care costs, and retraining employees. And in an increasingly competitive global marketplace, instituting HR practices that build employee commitment can help improve a firm's responsiveness, as explained earlier.

Illustrations of HR's Role as a Strategic Partner

- Firms like **Fed Ex, John Deere, Saturn,** and **Toyota** are not the only ones that rely on HR to perform as a strategic partner in the development and execution of their strategic plans. Here are two others.
- **Colgate-Palmolive**: Colgate-Palmolive Company is a global manufacturing company with sales of over $5 billion that recently received new "marching orders." The company adopted a new strategy. Consistent with this new strategy, several major steps were taken almost at once. Four major businesses were divested, including two sports and recreation companies. A major reorganization took place that eliminated one level of senior management. Additional resources were diverted to new product development, and research and development. And the human resource programmes at Colgate-Palmolive got a new mandate to help Colgate achieve its new goals. The programmes laid out for Colgate HRM provide a glimpse of how HRM today is being pressed to get involved in strategic management. At Colgate-Palmolive, HRM was directed by the President to develop and execute programmes designed to create a company culture that would achieve the following:
  - (i) **Encourage a spirit of teamwork and cooperation** within and among business units in working towards common objectives, with an emphasis on identifying, acknowledging, and rewarding individual and unit excellence.
  - (ii) **Foster entrepreneurial attitudes among the managers** and innovative thinking among all employees.
  - (iii) **Emphasize the commonality of interest** between the employees and shareholders.

To that end, numerous HRM programmes had to be designed. For example, the company's executive incentive compensation plan was redesigned to place more emphasis on individual performance and achieving operating targets. Employee benefits were redesigned to make them more flexible and responsive to employees' needs. At the same time, cost controls and employee pay-for-performance plans were instituted, two changes that were accomplished by effectively communicating both the changes and the reasons for them. The bottom line was that by implementing a number of programmes (including those aimed at redesigning compensation and benefits), HRM helped refocus Colgate employees' efforts in a manner that contributed to the execution of Colgate's strategic plan.

- **Tandy Corporation:** Tandy Corporation is another example of how HR policies are formulated to support company's strategy. In the case of this electronics/computer firm, success depends largely on retail sales profitability. In turn, these sales depend on the ability of retail employees, most of whom are selling items (like computers and electronic instruments) that require solid product knowledge and an intelligent sales effort.

At Tandy, therefore, HR policies (regarding selection and compensation, for instance) are aimed at attracting, hiring, and motivating the people required for Tandy's success. For example, Tandy's selection policy emphasizes identifying candidates who will be successfully selling Tandy's products, since 80% of the company's employees are in direct sales. To this end, Tandy developed a computerized program to administer a skill assessment profile. This is aimed at determining a candidate's aptitude for activities like qualifying customers, making sales presentations, closing sales, and providing after-sales customer service. Similarly, its training policies emphasize effective sales training, and its compensation policy puts a heavy premium on sales performance: In fact, 75% of the management compensation plans at Tandy, including that of the Vice President of human resources, are tied to the company's profits.

RECENT TRENDS OR EMERGING ISSUES IN HRM

Changes are occurring today in the environment of HRM. These changes are quite complex and pose serious challenges for HRM. These changes also constitute as the recent trends or we may call these as emerging issues in HRM. The recent trends include the following:

1. Workforce diversity
2. Technological trends
3. Globalization
4. Changes in the nature of jobs and work
5. Other trends affecting HRM

1. Workforce Diversity

The composition of the workforce will continue to change dramatically in the next ten years; specifically, it will continue to become more diverse as women, minority group members, and older workers flood the workforce. Diversity has been defined as—any attribute that humans are likely to use to tell themselves, 'that person is different from me' and thus includes such factors as race, sex, age, values, and cultural norms.

In some respects these are among the more mundane diversity-related demands that HR will have to cope with. Health care and promotional options are probably relatively manageable compared to the tensions and pressures that cultural, attitudinal, and value-based differences can trigger. Diversity training and similar programmes aimed at creating a cohesive and collegial workforce out of a group of highly diverse individuals are thus increasingly a necessity.

Creating unanimity from a diverse workforce may be more of a challenge for HR than it might at first appear. As several experts recently put it, there are two fundamental and inconsistent realities operating today with regard to diversity. One is that organizations claim they seek to maximize diversity in the workplace and maximize the capabilities of such a diverse workforce. The other is that traditional human resources systems will not allow diversity, only similarity. These experts specifically refer to the fact that employers traditionally hire, appraise, and promote people who fit a particular employer's image of what employees should believe and act like, and there's a corresponding tendency to screen out those who don't fit. Establishing HR programmes that do more than just pay lip service to the goal of diversity may thus be a considerable challenge for many employers.

2. Technological Trends

Technological change will continue to shift employment from some occupations to others while contributing to a rise in productivity. For example, telecommunications already makes it relatively easy for many to work at home. Computer-aided design/computer-aided manufacturing systems plus robotics will also increase. Thus, General Motors has over 14,000 robots building automobiles. Manufacturing advances like these will eliminate many blue-collar jobs, replacing them with fewer but more highly skilled jobs. Similar changes are taking place in office automation, where personal computers, word processing, and management information systems continue to change the nature of office work.

Labour-intensive blue-collar and clerical jobs will decrease while technical, managerial, and professional jobs will increase. Job and organization structures will have to be redesigned, new incentive and compensation plans instituted, new job descriptions written, and new employee selection, evaluation, and training programmes instituted—all with the help of HR management.

Technology will also force firms to become more competitive. In the 70s, we went to the post office to pick up our orders. In the early 80s, we put in an 800 number. In the late 80s, we got a fax machine. In 1991, pressured by Target [stores], we added electronic data interchange. Now, just two years later, more than half of Inter Design's orders arrive via modem, straight into company computers. Errors in order entry and shipping have all disappeared.

Information technology has also hastened what experts call the "fall of hierarchy" in other words, managers depend less and less on yesterday's stick-to-the chain-of-command approach to organizing. For example, with distributed computing, every employee with a personal computer on his or her desk can tap into the firm's computer network and get the needed information. One manager at Goodyear Tire and Rubber Company says: "It used to be, if you wanted information, you had to go up, over, and down through the organization. Now you just tap in. That's what broke down the hierarchy. It's not why we bought computers, but it's what they did."

HR plays an integral role in any such changes. For example, empowering workers to make more decisions presumes that they are selected, trained, and rewarded to do so.

3. Globalization

Globalization refers to the tendency of firms to extend their sales or manufacturing to new markets abroad, and, for businesses everywhere, the rate of globalization in the past few years has been nothing short of phenomenal.

Production is becoming globalized too, as manufacturers around the world put manufacturing facilities where they will be most advantageous. This globalization of markets and manufacturing has vastly increased international competition. Throughout the world, firms that formerly competed only with local firms—from airlines to auto makers to banks—now find that complacency must give way to an onslaught of foreign competitors.

Such global competition is, of course, a two-way street. Ford and GM have huge market shares in Europe, while IBM, Microsoft, Apple, and countless smaller firms have major market shares around the world. As one international business expert puts it, "the bottom line is that the growing integration of the world economy into a single, huge marketplace is increasing the intensity of competition in a wide range of manufacturing and service industries."

4. Trends in the Nature of Work

Technological and globalization trends are in turn producing changes in the nature of jobs and work. Technological changes including fax machines, information technology, and personal computers have allowed companies to relocate operations to locations with lower wages. However, the most notable trends in the nature of work are the trends to service jobs, and to knowledge work and the stress on human capital.

(i) **A Service Society:** An enormous shift from manufacturing jobs to service jobs is taking place in North America and Western Europe. Today over two-thirds of the US workforce is employed in producing and delivering services, not products. Virtually all will be in such service industries as fast food retailing, and consulting, teaching and legal work. These jobs, in turn, will demand new types of "knowledge" workers and new human resource management methods to manage them.

(ii) **Knowledge Work and Human Capital:** Management expert Peter Drucker has said that the typical business will soon bear little resemblance to the typical manufacturing company of 30 years ago. As Drucker predicts it, "*The typical business will be knowledge-based, an organization composed largely of specialists who direct and discipline their own performance through organized feedback from colleagues, customers and headquarters. For this reason, it will be what I call an information-based organization.*" As a result, the distinguishing characteristic of companies today and tomorrow, say many experts, is the growing emphasis on human capital—the knowledge, education, training, skills, and expertise of a firm's workers—at the expense of physical capital like equipment, machinery, and the physical plant.

This growing emphasis on education and human capital reflects several social and economic factors. One is the increase in the service oriented nature of the economy. Another is the fact that manufacturing jobs are changing too. At the same time, even heavy manufacturing jobs are becoming more high tech. Jobs today thus demand a level of expertise far beyond that required of most workers 20 or 30 years ago, so that human capital is quickly replacing machines as the basis for most firms' success.

For managers, the challenge of fostering intellectual or human capital lies in the fact that such workers must be managed differently than were those of previous generations. As one expert puts this, "the centre of gravity in employment is moving fast from manual and clerical workers to knowledge workers, who resist the command and control model that business took from the military 100 years ago". Workers like these, in other words, cannot just be ordered around and closely monitored. New human resource management systems and skills will be required to select and train such employees and to win their self-discipline and commitment.

5. Other Trends Affecting HRM

(i) **Impact of new laws:** Other trends are shaping HR management as well. As new laws continue to be passed, the effect of which is to limit manager's actions. For example, equal employment opportunity laws bar discrimination on the basis of race, age, disability, religion, sex, or nationality. Virtually all managers are thus now legally bound to uncover and correct instances of discrimination. Mandated health benefits, occupational safety and health requirements, and union management relations laws are among the other legal constraints managers must deal with, generally with the assistance of HR management.

(ii) **Protection by government regulation:** Similarly, the protection provided by governmental regulation to thousands of businesses in dozens of industries around the world has been stripped away in country after country. In the United States, for instance, a dozen airlines including Eastern, Braniff, and People's Express have either been bought out or gone under as a result of the pressures for better service and lower costs resulting from US airline deregulation in the 1970s. Similarly, bank failures rose from fewer than ten in the 1970s to almost 200 annually in the early 1990s as banking deregulation exposed inefficiencies that less responsive competitors couldn't eliminate in time. The increased competitive intensity puts an added emphasis on the need for human capital and a highly committed workforce.

NEW HR STRATEGIES TO DEAL WITH THE CHALLENGES/TRENDS IN HRM

In the companies that have successfully responded to these challenges, new modes of organizing and managing have emerged. For example:

1. **The traditional, pyramid-shaped organization is giving way to new organizational forms:** At firms like AT&T the new ways of organizing stresses are cross-functional teams and boosting interdepartmental communications. There is a corresponding de-emphasis on "sticking to the chain of command" to get decisions made. At General Electric, Chairman Jack Welch talks of the boundary-less organization, in which employees do not identify with separate departments but instead interact with whoever they want to get the job done.
2. **Employees are being empowered to make more and more decisions:** Experts argue for turning the typical organization upside down. They say today's organization should put the customer on top and emphasize that every move the company makes should be towards satisfying the customer's needs. Management must therefore empower its frontline employees—the front desk clerks at the hotel, the cabin attendants on the Delta plane, and the assemblers at Saturn. In other words, employees need the authority to respond quickly to the customer's needs. The main purpose of managers in this "upside down" organization is to serve the frontline employees, to see that they have what they need to do their jobs—and thus to serve the customers.
3. **Flatter organizations are the norm:** Instead of the pyramid-shaped organization with its seven to ten or more layers of management, flat organizations with just three or four levels will prevail. Many companies (including AT&T and General Electric) have already cut the management layers from a dozen to six or fewer. As the remaining managers have more people reporting to them, they will be less able to meddle in the work of their subordinates.
4. **Work itself—on the factory floor, in the office, even in the hotel—is increasingly organized around teams and processes rather than specialized functions:** On the plant floor, a worker will not just have the job of installing the same door handle over and over again. He or she will belong to a multifunctional team, one that manages its own budget and controls the quality of its own work.
5. **The bases of power are changing:** In the new organization, says management theorist Rosabeth Moss Kanter, position, title, and authority are no longer adequate tools for managers to rely on to get their jobs done.
6. **Managers will not manage:** Yesterday's manager knew that the president and owners of the firm gave him or her authority to command and control subordinates. Today, most

managers realize that reliance on formal authority is increasingly a thing of the past. Peter Drucker says that managers have to learn to manage in situations where they do not have command authority, where "you are neither controlled nor controlling." Yesterday's manager thinks of himself or herself as a "manager" or "boss". The new manager increasingly thinks of himself or herself as a "sponsor," "team leader," or "internal consultant".

7. **Managers today must build commitment:** Building adaptive, customer-responsive organizations means that eliciting employees' commitment and self-control is more important than it has ever been. GE's Jack Welch put it this way: "*The only way I see to get more productivity is by getting people involved and excited about their jobs. You can't afford to have anyone walk through a gate of a factory or into an office who is not giving 120%.*"

THE CHANGING ROLE OF HR MANAGEMENT

Not surprisingly, the role of HR management is also changing, to adapt to these trends. In the early 1900s personnel people first took over hiring and firing from supervisors, ran the payroll department, and administered benefit plans. It was a job consisting largely of ensuring that procedures were followed. As technology in such areas as testing and interviewing began to emerge, the personnel department began to play an expanded role in employee selection, training, and promotion.

Today personnel is speeding through phase 4, and its role is shifting from protector and screener to planner and change agent. The metamorphosis of personnel into human resource management reflects the fact that in today's flattened, downsized, and responsive organizations, highly trained and committed employees—not machines—are often a firm's best competitive key.

The changing role of HRM is discussed in following five areas:

1. **HR and Boosting Productivity:** Productivity improvement is crucial in today's globally competitive environment, and HR plays a pivotal role in lowering labour costs. In the US government, for example, researchers found that using a personnel screening test to select high-potential computer programmers could produce savings of millions of dollars per year. For many firms, instituting tough headcount controls is the first line of attack on lowering labour costs; the HR department generally plays central role in planning and implementing corporate downsizings like those at IBM and Citicorp and then taking steps to maintain the morale of the remaining employees. At employers like pharmaceuticals firm Merck & Company, HR helps employees adapt to the increased pressures in their downsized departments by helping them learn to prioritize tasks and reduce job stress.
2. **HR and Responsiveness:** Making the enterprise more responsive to product innovations and technological change is the basic aim of many of the management changes listed previously. Thus, downsizing, flattening the pyramid, empowering employees, and organizing around teams are aimed at facilitating communications and making it easier for decisions to be made and for the company to respond quickly to its customers' needs and its competitors' challenges. HR plays a crucial role in accomplishing this. At Levi Strauss, HR helped create the firm's new team-based alternative manufacturing system.

This ties employees' compensation incentives to team goals and, along with Levi's new flexible-hours programme, helps inject more flexibility into the firm's production process.

3. **HR and Service:** Employee behaviour is particularly important in service firms like banks and retail establishments. If a customer is confronted by a salesperson who is tactless or unprepared to discuss the pros and cons of the different products or downright discourteous, the entire firm's other efforts will waste. Service organizations have little to sell but their good service, and that makes them uniquely dependent on their employees' attitudes and motivation and on HR management. Therefore, HR plays a crucial role in service companies. It has been noted, for instance, that there are "quite a few [employees] who lack the temperament, maturity, social skills, and tolerance for frequent contact" that customer service jobs require, and that the first step in avoiding this problem is screening and selection. This process is adopted by best managed IT companies such as Infosys, TCS, and Wipro in India.
4. **HR and Employee Commitment:** Intense global competition and the need for more responsiveness put a premium on employee commitment. As the vice president of human resources at Toyota Motor Manufacturing in Georgetown, Kentucky put it: "*People are behind our success. Machines don't have new ideas, solve problems, or grasp opportunities. Only people who are involved and thinking can make a difference ... Every auto plant in the US has basically the same machinery. But how people are utilized and involved varies widely from one company to another. The workforce gives any company its true competitive edge.*"

   Building employee commitment—creating a synthesis of employees' and employer's goals so that employees want to do their jobs as if they own the company takes a multipronged effort, one in which HR plays the central role. For example, two-way communications foster commitment, and firms like Federal Express and Toyota have long had programmes that guarantee two-way communications and fair treatment of all employees' grievances and disciplinary matters. High commitment firms also tend to engage in actualizing practices, which aim to ensure their employees have every opportunity to fully use all their skills and gifts at work and become all they can be. HR practices are crucial here, for instance, in establishing career-oriented performance appraisal procedures and open job-posting and transfer practices. Convincing employees that the company and all its managers care about them is important, too. Therefore, high-commitment companies like Federal Express in USA, Reliance India Ltd., Wipro, TCS, etc. in India are very careful about whom to promote as manager.
5. **HR and Corporate Strategy:** But perhaps the most striking change in HR's role is its growing importance in developing and implementing strategy. Traditionally strategy—the company's plan for how it will balance its internal strengths and weaknesses with external opportunities and threats in order to maintain a competitive advantage—was a job primarily for the company's operating (line) managers. Thus, Company X's president might decide to enter new markets, drop product lines, or embark on a five-year cost-cutting plan. Then the president would more or less leave the personnel implications of that plan (hiring or firing new workers, hiring outplacement firms for those fired, and so on) to be carried out by HR management.

Today things are different. Strategies increasingly depend on strengthening organizational responsiveness and on building committed work teams, and these put HR in a central role. In a fast-changing, globally competitive and quality oriented industrial environment, it's often the firm's employees themselves—its human resources—who provide the competitive key. It is thus now increasingly common to involve HR in the earliest stages of developing and implementing the firm's strategic plan, rather than letting HR just react to it. We thus turn next to strategic planning and HR's strategic role.

REVIEW QUESTIONS

1. What do you understand by human resource management? Why is it needed?
2. Why human resource management is essential for an organization?
3. Describe the scope of human resource management.
4. Are human resource development and personnel management same? Describe various functions of HRM.
5. Explain the duties and responsibilities of HR manager.
6. Human resource management plays a vital role in the whole system of an industrial organization. Explain.
7. Discuss the objection and process of human resources management.
8. What is strategic HRM? Discuss the key issues in strategic HRM? What is the difference between traditional HRM and strategic HRM?
9. Discuss the recent trends or emerging issue in HRM. How HR strategies can be used to deal with the challenges or emerging trends in HRM?
10. Discuss the changing role of HR management. In which particular business areas the HR can play its role?
11. Write notes on the followings:
    - Line and staff organization
    - Workforce diversity
    - HR's role as a strategic partner
    - HR and technology

CASE STUDY

1.1 Revolution at Work—Saturn

Few industrial changes anywhere have been as revolutionary as what GM has tried to do with its new Saturn car-manufacturing facility. As the video explains the Saturn approach is a "revolution in how workers think about their work." As the employees describe in the video, at Saturn "you call the shots," and it's no longer a case of "management is the enemy." Instead, says one worker, "I feel part of what we did here." One big difference in how Saturn operates, the video points out, is that Saturn employees "use their brains" and work in teams that decide which parts to use and whom to hire. These teams also measure the quality of their products.

Questions

1. How does Saturn's competitive strategy translate into specific HR policies at the Saturn plant?
2. On the basis of the video and the contents of Chapter One, what specific Saturn HR policies do you think will foster employee commitment at Saturn? Why?
3. Why do you think the plant's output is so far below its capacity? Do you think Saturn is emphasizing social skills too much, but productivity not enough?

Source: ABC News, Revolution at Work: Saturn, "ABC News Special," August 31, 1991.

1.2 Cashing in on the HR Advantage

B&B Company had been quite successful since its inception in 1950s, but had witnessed high turnover among its young staff in the last eight years. The managing director was convinced that the problem was not salary because a survey indicated that the firm's salary structure was competitive with that of other major firms. Driven by the need to find out the real reason, the managing director asked Mr. Malhotra, a senior executive to look into the matter. After interviewing the senior managers of the firm, he believed that the root of the problem was the absence of a HR department. He mentioned this idea to the managing director, who was not convinced. The managing director asked him to prepare a proposal advocating his case for a HR department.

Mr. Malhotra prepared a proposal highlighting the role of a HR manager in today's competitive environment. According to the proposal, the HR manager plays a crucial role in a company's growth and success. The HR professional often adorns the role of a strategic partner, an employee sponsor, an advocate, a change mentor and a key driver of the organizations strategies. HR plays a crucial role in the financial well-being of an organization. The financial health of a company is directly linked to the low employee turnover. Companies with good HR practices often outperform those with a poor record in people management. It is impossible, therefore, to imagine a company as anything but successful, if it is weak in HR management. Moreover, HR department will provide specialized services in areas like design of work positions, hiring, reward, recognition, strategic pay, performance development and appraisal systems, career and succession planning, and employee development. HR manager also challenges and manages conflicts and raises the performance bar. He concluded by saying that HR professionals are exceptionally valued. HR will know how to link changes to the strategic needs of an organization, which will minimize employee dissatisfaction and resistance to change.

Source: Gupta Shashi K., Rosy Joshi, "Human Resource Management", Kalyani Publishers, New Delhi.

Questions

1. Can Mr. Malhotra sell the idea of the HR department to the managing director?
2. If you were in Mr. Malhotra's place, which functions and roles of HR would you have stressed and why?
3. What type of organizational structure would be needed in this type of scenario?

REFERENCES

1. Subba Rao, P. (2007). "Essentials of Human Resource Management and Industrial Relations". Himalaya Publishing House, New Delhi.
2. Aswathappa, K. (2008). "Human Resource Management", Tata McGraw-Hill, New Delhi.
3. Gupta Shashi, K. and Rosy Joshi. (2007). "Human Resource Management", Kalyani Publisher, New Delhi.
4. Aquinas, P.G. (2008). "Human Resource Management", Vikas Publishing House (Pvt.) Ltd., New Delhi.
5. Dessler, Crary "Human Resource Management", 7th ed., Prentice-Hall of India, New Delhi.
6. Werther, William B. (1993). "Human Resource and Personnel Management", McGraw-Hill, New York.
7. Douglas, McGregor, "The Human Side of Enterprise", Tata McGraw-Hill Publishing Co., New Delhi.
8. Davis, Keith (1962). "Human Relations in Management".
9. Stoner, James A.F. "Management", Prentice-Hall of India, New Delhi.
10. Porter, Micheal (1980). "Competitive Strategy", The Free Press, New York.
11. Porter, Micheal (1985). "Competitive Advantage", The Free Press, New York.
12. Prahalad, C.K. and Crary Hamel, (1990). "The Core Competence of a Corporation", Harvard Business Review.
13. Truss Catherine and Lynda Gratton, (1994). "Strategic Human Resource Mgt. A conceptual approach." The Institutional Journal of Human Resource Management, vol. 5, no. 3.
14. Wright, P. and McMahan, G. (1992). "Theoretical Perspectives for Strategic Human Resource Management", *J. Mgt.*, vol. 18, no. 2.

CHAPTER

2 Human Resource Planning

CHAPTER'S OUTLINE

- Introduction
- Meaning of HRP
- Planning at Different Levels
- Integrated Strategic Planning and HR
- Need for Human Resource Planning
- Objectives of HRP
- Determinants of HRP
- Process of Human Resource Planning
- Strategies for HR Planners
- Benefits of HR Planning
- Limitations of HR Planning
- Guidelines for Making HRP Effective

INTRODUCTION

Human resource planning is the most important managerial function of an organization. It ensures three main things:

- It ensures adequate supply of human resources.
- It ensures proper quality of human resources.
- It ensures effective utilization of human resources.

Since there is always a shortage of suitable persons, the organization needs to plan for the same. If adequate supply of required manpower is not matching the requirement, the organization will face problems in production and marketing. In most developing and underdeveloped economies, there is shortage of trained persons. Hence, an organization has to plan in advance about its requirements and sources of human resources.

In this chapter an attempt has been made to discuss the meaning of HRP, Integrated Strategic Planning (ISP), its need, objectives, process and benefits. It must be noted here that HRP and manpower planning (MPP) are used interchangeably though manpower planning is a part of HRP.

MEANING OF HR PLANNING

HRP implies planning at the organization level about the future needs of manpower in the organization and also about the sources of human resources.

It is the predetermination of the future course of action for procuring, developing, managing, motivating, compensating, career planning, succession planning the human elements in an organization.

Definitions

According to **Eric W. Vetter,** "*Human resource planning is the process by which a management determines how an organization should move from its current manpower position to its desired manpower position. Through planning a management strives to have the right number and the right kinds of people at the right places, at the right time to do things which result in both the organization and the individual receiving the maximum long range benefit.*"

According to **Dale S. Beach,** "*Human resource planning is a process of determining and assuring that the organization will have an adequate number of qualified persons available at the proper times, performing jobs which meet the needs of the enterprise and which provide satisfaction for the individuals involved.*"

According to **Leon C. Meginson,** "*Human resource planning is an integration approach to performing the planning aspects of the personnel function in order to have a sufficient supply of adequately developed and motivated people to perform the duties and tasks required to meet organizational objectives and satisfy the individual needs and goals of organizational members.*"

According to **G. Stainer,** "*Manpower planning is the strategy for the acquisition, utilization, improvement and preservation of an organization's human resources. It is aimed at coordinating the requirements for and the availability of different types of employees.*"

According to **Bruce P. Coleman,** "*Manpower planning is the process of determining manpower requirements and the means for meeting those requirements in order to carry out the integrated plan of the organization.*"

According to **E. Geister,** "*Human resource planning is the process including forecasting, developing and controlling by which a firm ensures that it has the right number of people and the right kind of people at the right places at the right time doing work for which they are economically most useful.*"

From the above definitions, following general characteristics of human resource planning are discovered.

(i) Human resource planning must incorporate the human resource needs in the light of organizational goals.
(ii) Human resource planning must be directed towards clear and well-defined objectives.
(iii) Human resource plan must ensure that it has the right number of people and the right kind of people at the right time doing work for which they are economically most suitable.
(iv) Human resource planning should take into account the principle of periodical reconsideration of new developments and extending the plan to cover the changes during the given long period.
(v) Human resource planning should pave the way for an effective motivational process.
(vi) Adequate flexibility must be maintained in human resource planning to suit the changing needs of the organization.

HRP or MPP is essentially concerned with the process of estimating and projecting the supply and demand for different categories of personnel in the organization for the years to come.

HR PLANNING AT DIFFERENT LEVELS

Human Resource Planning (HRP) may be done at different levels and for different purposes. National planners may make a HR plan at the national level whereas the strategists at a company may make a HR plan at the unit level. The HR Planning thus operates at five levels.

1. ***HRP at National Level:*** HRP at the national level helps to plan for educational facilities, health care facilities, agricultural and industrial development and employment plans, etc. The government of the country plans for human resources at the national level. National plans for HR forecast the demand and supply of human resources at the national level. It also plans for occupational distribution, sectoral and regional allocation of human resources.
2. ***HRP at the Sectoral Level:*** HRP at the sectoral level helps to plan for a particular sector like agriculture, industry, etc. It helps the government to allocate its resources to the various sectors depending upon the priority accorded to the particular sector.
3. ***HRP at the Industry Level:*** HRP at the industry level takes into account the output/operational level of the particular industry when manpower needs are considered.
4. ***HRP at the Unit Level:*** HR Planning at the company level is based on the estimation of human resource needs of the particular company in question. It is based on the business plan of the company. A manpower plan helps to avoid the sudden disruption of the company's production since it indicates shortages of particular types of personnel, if any, in advance, thus enabling the management to adopt suitable strategies to cope with the situation.
5. ***HRP at the Departmental Level:*** HRP at the departmental level looks at the manpower needs of a particular department in an organization.

INTEGRATED STRATEGIC PLANNING AND HR

HRP like production planning, financial planning and marketing planning needs to be comprehensive, unified and integrated for the total corporation. HR manager provides inputs like key HR areas, HR environmental constraints, HR capabilities and HR capability constraints to the corporate strategists. Corporate strategists further communicate their needs and constraints to HR manager. The corporate strategic plan and HR plan, thus incorporates both HR and other functional plans.

Integrated strategic planning involves four steps.

Figure 2.1 shows these steps.

Step I

Development and knowledge of organization's overall purpose or mission or goals and objectives.

↓

Step II

Providing inputs by HR manager regarding key HR areas, capabilities and constraints of HR and environment to corporate strategists.

↓

Step III

The corporate strategists in turn communicate their needs and constraints to the HR manager.

↓

Step IV

Integration of HR and other functional plans.

Fig. 2.1. Integrated Strategic Planning and HR.

Corporate strategic planning involves four time spans.

(i) **Long period (5 or more years):** Strategic plans that establish company's vision, mission and major long-range objectives. The time span for strategic plans is usually considered to be five or more years.

(ii) **Intermediate period (3 years):** Intermediate-range plans cover about a three-year period. These are more specific plans in support of strategic plan.

(iii) **Operation period (1 year):** Operating plans cover about one year. Plans are prepared month-by-month in sufficient detail for profit, human resources, budget and cost control.

(iv) **Short period (day-to-day or week-by-week):** Activity plans are the day-to-day and week-by-week plans. These plans may not be documented. Table 2.1. presents the link between strategic plan and human resource plan.

Hence, the strategic plan vs. HR plan can be at four levels:

(i) Corporate-level plan: Top management formulates corporate-level plan based on corporate philosophy, policy, vision and mission. The HRM role is to raise the broad and policy issues relating to human resources. The HR issues are related to employment policy, HRD policies, remuneration policies, etc. The HR department prepares HR strategies, objectives and policies consistent with company's strategy.

(ii) Intermediate-level plan: Large-scale and diversified companies organize Strategic Business Units (SBUs) for the related activities. SBUs prepare intermediate plans and implement them. HR managers prepare specific plans for acquiring future managers, key personnel and total number of employees in support of company requirements over the next three years.

(iii) Operations plan: Operations plans are prepared at the lowest business profit centre level. These plans are supported by the HR plans relating to recruitment of skilled personnel, developing compensation structure, designing new jobs, developing, leadership, improving work life, etc.

(iv) Short-term activities plan: Day-to-day business plans are formulated by the lowest level strategists. Day-to-day HR plans relating to handling employee benefits, grievances, disciplinary cases, accident reports, etc. are formulated by the HR managers.

Integration of business planning and HRP is shown in Table 2.1 and Figure 2.2.

Table 2.1: Linking Business Planning and HR Planning

Planning Level and Horizon	**Business Planning Process**	**Link**	**Human Resource Planning Process**
Strategic planning (5 or more years)	Corporate philosophy value system, and policies. Goals and objectives. Key success factors. Product market scope competitive edge allocation of resources	Issues analysis	Analysis of issues raised by external factors Employment demand projection Manpower supply analysis and projection
Intermediate-range planning (3-5 years)	Organization evolution. Programmes required to implement strategy. Deployment of resources. Acquisitions, divestments, and internal development of product lines.	Programming requirements	Forecasting total staffing level. Forecasting number of managers and key personnel. Forecasting net changes in managers and key personnel year to year. Planning P/HR support programmes.
Operational planning (12 months)	Detailing of programmes to specify actions, responsibilities, cost-time schedule and organizational profitability	Integrated control requirements	Detailing of P/HR activities that are incorporated in the one-year business plan
Activities planning (daily and weekly)	Day-to-day and week-to-week plans and work schedule decentralized throughout the company.	Implementation actions	P/HR day-to-day and week-to-week assignment in support of the objectives and plans of the P/HR department.

Source: Klatt Murdick and Schuster.

Figure 2.2 presents strategic plan vis-à-vis human resource plan.

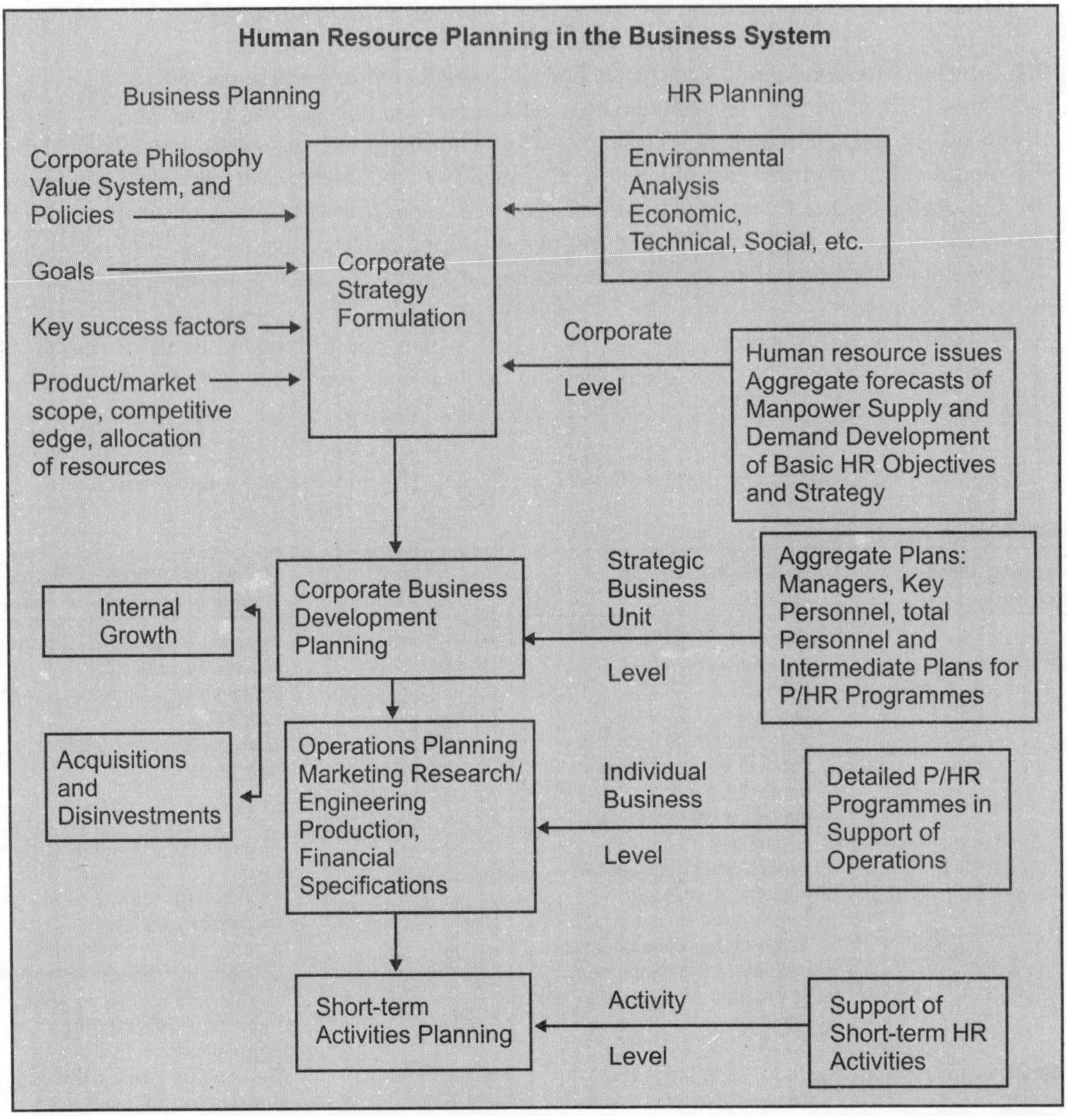

Fig. 2.2. HRP in the Business System.

Source: A. Klatt, Murdick and Schuster.

NEED FOR HUMAN RESOURCE PLANNING

Human resource planning is needed for foreseeing the human resource requirements of an organization and supply of human resources. Its need can be assessed from the following points:

1. **Replacement of Persons:** A large number of persons are to be replaced in the organization because of retirement, old age, death, etc. There will be a need to prepare persons for taking up new position in such contingencies.

2. **Labour Turnover:** There is always labour turnover in every organization. The degree of labour turnover may vary from concern to concern but it cannot be eliminated altogether. There will be a need to recruit new persons to take up the positions of those who have left the organization. If the concern is able to forecast turnover rate precisely, then advance efforts are made to recruit and train persons so that work does not suffer for want of workers.
3. **Expansion Plans:** Whenever there is a plan to expand or diversify the concern then more persons will be required to take up new positions. Human resource planning is essential under these situations.
4. **Technological Changes:** The business is working under changing technological environment. There may be a need to give fresh training to personnel. In addition, there may also be a need to infuse fresh blood into the organization. Human resource planning will help in meeting the new demands of the organization.
5. **Assessing Needs:** Human resource planning is also required to determine whether there is any shortage or surplus of persons in the organization. If there are less persons than required, it will adversely affect the work. On the other hand, if more persons are employed than the requirement, then it will increase labour cost, etc. Human resource planning ensures the employment of proper workforce.

OBJECTIVES OF HUMAN RESOURCE PLANNING

The following are the objectives of human resource planning:

1. Assessing manpower needs for future and making plans for recruitment and selection.
2. Assessing skill requirement in future for the organization.
3. Determining training and the development needs of the organization.
4. Anticipating surplus or shortage of staff and avoiding unnecessary detentions or dismissals.
5. Controlling wage and salary costs.
6. Ensuring optimum use of human resources in the organization.
7. Helping the organization to cope with the technological development and modernization.
8. Ensuring career planning of every employee of the organization and making succession programmes.
9. Ensuring higher labour productivity.

DETERMINANTS OF HRP

There are several factors that affect HRP. These factors or determinants can be classified into external factors and internal factors.

External Factors

- **Government Policies :** Policies of the government like labour policy, industrial relations policy, policy towards reserving certain jobs for different communities and sons-of-the-soils, etc. affect the HRP.
- **Level of Economic Development :** Level of economic development determines the level of HRD in the country and thereby the supply of human resources in future in the country.

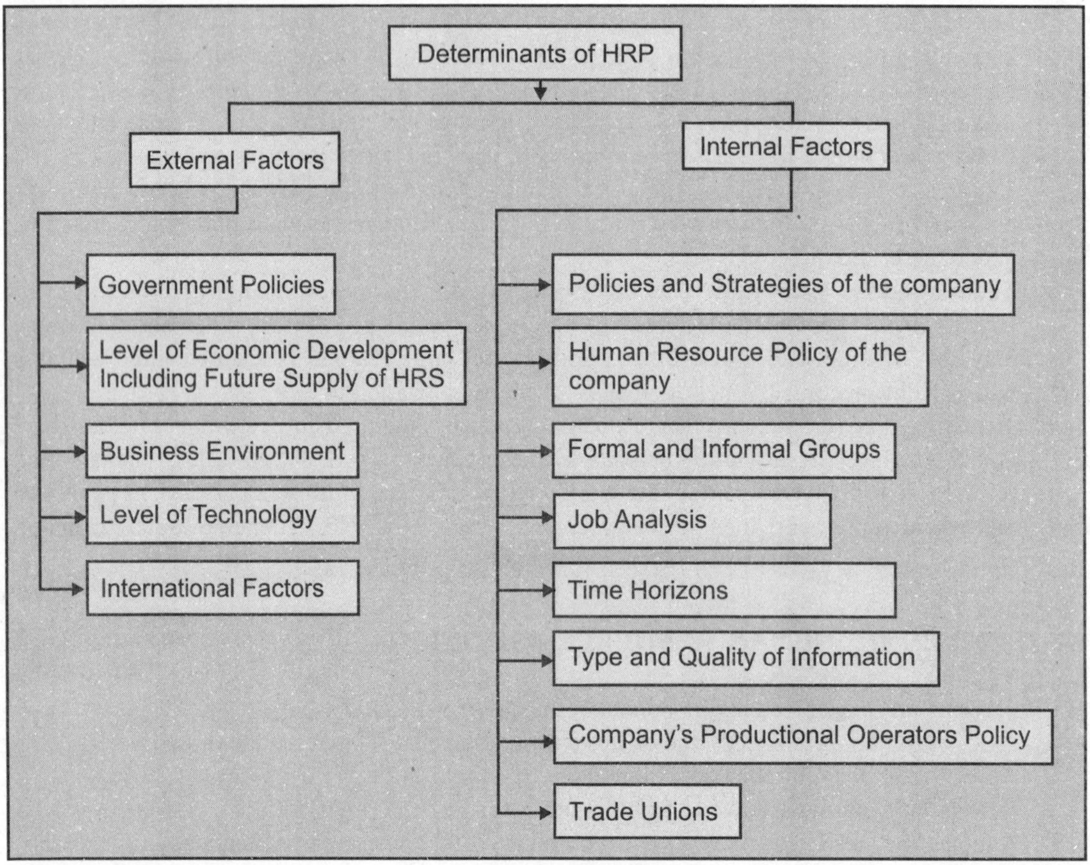

Fig. 2.3. Determinants of HRP.

- **Business Environment :** External business environmental factors influences the volume and mix of production and thereby the future demand for human resources.
- **Level of Technology :** Level of technology determines the kind of human resources required.
- **International Factors :** International factors like the demand for the resources and supply of human resources in various countries.

Internal Factors

- ***Company Policies and Strategies*:** Company's policies and strategies relating to expansion diversification, alliances, etc. determines the human resource demand in terms of quality and quantity.
- ***Human Resource Policies*:** Human resources policies of the company regarding quality of human resource, compensation level, quality of worklife, etc. influences human resource plan.
- ***Job Analysis*:** Fundamentally, human resource plan is based on job analysis. Job description and job specification determines the kind of employees required.
- ***Time Horizons*:** Companies with stable competitive environment can plan for the long run whereas the firms with unstable competitive environment can plan for only short-term range.

- ***Type and Quality of Information*** : Any planning process needs qualitative and accurate information. This is more so with human resource plan, strategic, organizational and specific information.
- ***Company's Production Operations Policy*** : Company's policy regarding how much to produce and how much to buy from outside to prepare a final product influence the number and kind of people required.
- ***Trade Unions*** : Influence of trade unions regarding number of working hours per week, recruitment sources, etc. affect the HRP.

PROCESS OF HUMAN RESOURCE PLANNING

With the expansion of business, adoption of complex technology and professional management techniques, the process of human resource planning has assumed great significance. HRP consists of the following stages.

1. Analyzing organizational plans and deciding objectives.
2. Analyzing factors for manpower requirements on demand side (demand forecasting)
3. Analyzing factors for requirements on supply side (supply forecasting). Obtaining the data and information about the present inventory of human resources and forecasting the future changes in present human resource inventory.
4. Estimating the net human resource requirement.
5. Developing employment plans.
6. Developing human resource plans.

1. Analyzing Organizational Plans and Deciding Objectives

Before undertaking the human resource planning of an organization, the short-term and long-term objectives should be analyzed. The process of human resource planning should start with analyzing the organizational plan. Analysis of organizational plans and programmes helps in forecasting the demand for human resources as it provides the quantum of future work activity. According to Sikula "the ultimate mission or purpose is to relate future human resources to future enterprise needs so as to maximize the future returns on investment in human resources."

The business plan would be a blueprint of desired objectives. These objectives stated in economic terms, would incorporate the growth rate of the company, diversification plans, market opportunities and government policies. Therefore, human resource planning should meet two requirements.

(i) It should be directly related to the essential nature of the organization.
(ii) The changes in the selected factors should be proportional to changes in the human resources required in the organization.

In a small organization, a human resource plan could be formulated to cover the whole organization. However, in a large organization, size may necessitate human resource planning by separate departments.

2. Analyzing Factors for Manpower Requirements on Demand Side (Demand Forcasting)

The existing job design and analysis may thoroughly be reviewed keeping in view the future capabilities, knowledge and skills of present employees. The job generally should be designed and analyzed reflecting the future human resources and based on future organizational plans. The factors for manpower requirements on demand side can be analyzed by making demand forecasting.

Demand forecasting is the process of estimating the future requirements of manpower, by function and by level of skills. It has been observed that demand assessment for operative personnel is not a problem but projections regarding supervisory and managerial levels is difficult. Two kinds of forecasting techniques are commonly used to determine the organization's projected demand for human resources. These are: (i) Judgemental forecasts, and (ii) Statistical projections.

(i) Judgemental Forecasts: Judgemental forecasts are also known as the conventional method. The forecasts are based on the judgement of those managers and executives who have intensive and extensive knowledge of human resource requirement. Judgemental forecasts could be of two types:

(a) ***Managerial Estimate*** : Under this method, the managers or supervisors who are well-acquainted with the workload, efficiency and ability of employees, think about their future workload, future capabilities of employees and decide on the number and type of human resources to be required. An estimate of staffing needs is done by the lower level managers who make estimates and pass them up for further revision.

(b) ***Delphi Method*** : A survey approach can be adopted with the Delphi technique. The Delphi process requires a large number of experts who take turns to present their forecast statement and underlying assumptions to the others, who then make revisions in their forecasts. Face-to-face contact among the experts is avoided.

(ii) Statistical Projection: Some forecasting techniques are based on statistical methods. Some of them are given below:

(a) ***Ratio-Trend Analysis*** : The ratio-trend analysis is carried out by studying the past ratios and the forecasting ratios for the future. The components of internal environmental changes are considered while forecasting the future ratios. Activity level forecasts are used to determine the direct human resource requirements. This method depends on the availability of past records and the internal environmental changes likely to occur in future.

(b) ***Econometric Model*** : Under the econometric model, the previous data is analyzed and the relationship between different variables in a mathematical formula is developed. The different variables affecting the human resource requirements are identified. The mathematical formula so developed is then applied to the forecasts of movements in the identified variables to produce human resource requirements.

(c) ***Work-Study Techniques*** : Work-study techniques are generally used to study work measurement. Under the workload analysis, the volume of workload in the coming years is analyzed. These techniques are more suitable where the volume of work is easily measurable. If the planners forecast expansion in the operations, additional operational workers may be required. If the organization decides to reduce its operations in a particular area, there may be decreased demand for the workers. If there is likely to be no change, present demand for workers will continue. The work-study method also takes into account the productivity pattern for the present and future, internal mobility of the workers like promotion, transfer, external mobility of the workers like retirement, deaths, voluntary retirements, etc.

3. Analyzing Factors for HR Requirements on Supply Side (Supply Forecasting)

Supply forecasting is concerned with human resources requirements from within and outside the organization. The first step of forecasting the future supply of human resource is to obtain the data and information about the present human resource inventory. The supply forecasting includes human resource audits; employee wastage; changes due to internal promotions; and changes due to working conditions.

Some of the steps are discussed below:

(i) ***Human Resource Audits*** : These are analysis of each employee's skills and abilities. This analysis facilitates the human resource planners with an understanding of the skills and capabilities available in the organization and helps them identify manpower supply problems arising in the near future. These inventories should be updated periodically otherwise it can lead to present employees being ignored for job openings within the organization.

(ii) ***Employee Wastage*** : The second step of supply forecasting is estimation of future losses of human resources of each department and of the entire organization. This is done to identify the employees who leave the organization and to forecast future losses likely to occur due to various reasons. Employees may leave the organization for reasons like retirements, layoffs, dismissals, disablement, ill health, death, etc. Reasons for high labour turnover and absenteeism should be analyzed and remedial measures taken. Management has to calculate the rate of labour turnover, conduct exit interview, etc. This helps to forecast the rate of potential loss, reasons for loss and helps in reducing the loss.

(iii) ***Internal Promotions*** : Analysis is undertaken regarding the vacancies likely due to retirements and transfer and the employees of particular groups and categories who are likely to be promoted. The multiple effect of promotions and transfers on the total number of moves should be analyzed and taken into consideration in forecasting changes in human resource supply of various departments. For example, if the personnel officer is promoted as personnel manager, 2 more employees will also get promotion. The senior clerk in the personnel department will become personnel officer and the junior clerk will become senior clerk. Thus, there are 3 moves for one promotion.

4. Estimating the Net HR Requirements

Net human resource requirements in terms of number and components are to be determined in relation to the overall human resource requirements (demand forecast) for a future date and supply forecast for that date. The difference between overall human requirements and future supply of human resource is to be found out.

5. Developing Employment Plans

After determining the number of personnel for each job in the organization, the human resource department has to determine the nature of job, i.e., job description and job specification.

(a) ***Job Description*** : A job description will generally describe the work performed, the responsibility involved, the skill or training required, conditions under which the job is done, relationships with other jobs and personal requirements on the job. According to The British Institute of Management — "a job description is not intended to catalogue all the duties involved with the result that an employee would feel justified in declining to perform any work not included in the description. It should be regarded as an outline of the minimum requirements of the job, thus preserving flexibility of operations."

(b) ***Job Specification*** : The job specification is an output of job description. It states the minimum acceptable qualifications that the newcomer must possess to perform the job satisfactorily and successfully. Job specifications serve as an important tool in the selection process and evaluation. They are developed by the human resource department in consultation with different line managers. The various elements of job specification are:

- (i) Minimum formal education necessary to perform the job
- (ii) Minimum experience required for performing the job.
- (iii) Manual/mental skill required for performing the job.
- (iv) Personality factors such as personal appearance, emotional stability, maturity, initiative, drive and sociability.
- (v) For high-level jobs, the ability to assume responsibility is an essential prerequisite.

6. Developing a Human Resource Plan

Net human resource requirements in terms of number and components are to be determined in relation to the overall human resource requirement. After estimating the supply and demand of human resources, the management starts adjustment. When the internal supply of employees is more than the demand, human resource surplus exists and the external recruitment is stopped. Besides the existing employees are encouraged to take voluntary retirement. It gradually reduces the surplus. If human resource deficit exists then the planners have to rely on the external sources. They, then proceed for scanning of the employment market for recruitment purposes. If future supply of human resources from all the external sources is estimated to be inadequate or less than the requirements, the manpower planner has to suggest to the management to alter or modify the organizational plan. In case of shortage of certain categories of employees, the organization has to take care not only of recruitment but also retention of existing employees. Thus, developing a HR plan, the management has to decide on the following issues:

- Forecasting future supply from all sources.
- Action plan for recruitment and development.
- Modify the organizational plan.
- Action plan for retrenchment.
- Action plan for retentions.

The process of HRP is depicted in Figure 2.4.

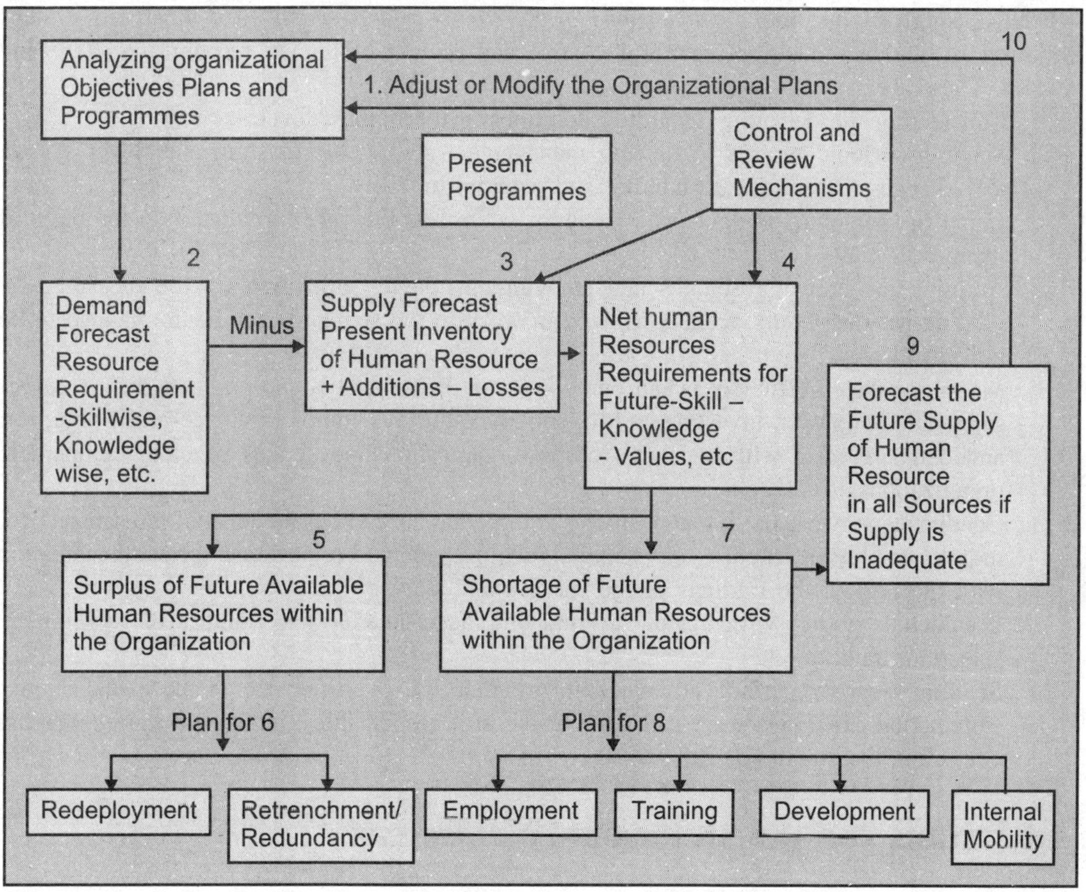

Fig. 2.4. Human Resource Planning Model.

CONTROL AND REVIEW MECHANISM

Human resource planning requires considerable amount of financial resources besides time and staff. Small firms may not go for it but large organizations prefer human resource planning as a means of achieving greater effectiveness and long-term objectives. J.W. Walker is of the opinion that, "In making a projection of manpower requirements, selecting the predictor — the business factor to which manpower needs will be related – is the critical first step. Selecting the right predictor in relation to the business is a difficult process. To be useful, the predictor should meet two requirements; first, it should be directly related to the essential nature of the business so that business planning is done in terms of the factor. The second requirement is that changes in the selected factor be proportional to changes in the manpower required in the business." Thus, the human resources structure and system should be controlled and reviewed with a view to keep them in accordance with the plan.

N.K. Singh in his book "*Dimensions of Personnel Management*" has identified 9 steps followed by Indian industries regarding control and review of human resource structure and system. These are:

1. Considering the decisions regarding additions at the highest level.
2. Sending periodic reports to the top management stating the existing manpower system and changes therein due to internal and external mobility.
3. Using the personnel budgets as a basis for control as they are formulated on the basis of manpower plans.
4. Auditing the human resources and studying manpower utilization can be measured by relating net man-hours actually utilized in work to the standard man-hours planned to be utilized in work.
5. Measuring the efficiency of labour periodically in the form of labour productivity, employee-sales ratio, employee-investment ratio, employee-turnover ratio, employee-profit ratio, etc. and compare them with standards of the organization and actuals of other comparable organizations.
6. Conducting surveys and research studies with a view to find out the level of job satisfaction, morale, employee attitudes, interpersonal relations, etc. and review and correct the situation with the help of the findings of the surveys and studies.
7. Conducting studies with a view to find out the efficiency and validity of recruitment, selection, training, etc.
8. Sending reports regarding absenteeism, irregularities, overtime, etc. to the management.
9. Conducting exit interviews; spotting out the area responsible, finding out the causes and correcting the situation.

STRATEGIES FOR HUMAN RESOURCE PLANNERS

The objective of manpower planning is to help the organization to achieve its goal. For this purpose, the manpower planners have to develop some strategies. Stainer has suggested nine strategies for the benefit of manpower planners:

1. They should collect, maintain and interpret relevant information regarding human resources.
2. They should periodically report manpower objectives, requirements and existing employment and allied features of manpower.
3. They should develop procedures and techniques to determine the requirements of different types of manpower over a period of time from the standpoint of organization's goals.
4. They should develop measures of manpower utilization as component of forecasts of manpower requirement along with independent validation.
5. They should employ suitable techniques leading to effective allocation of work with a view to improving manpower utilization.
6. They should conduct research to determine factors hampering the contribution of individuals and groups to the organization with a view to modifying or removing these handicaps.
7. They should develop and employ methods of economic assessment of human resources reflecting its features as income generator and cost and accordingly improving the quality of decisions affecting the manpower.

8. They should evaluate the procurement, promotion and retention of the effective human resources; and they should analyze the dynamic process of recruitment, promotion and loss to the organization and control these processes with a view to maximizing individual and group performance without involving high cost.

BENEFITS OF HR PLANNING

Manpower planning is a very important aspect of human resource management. A few benefits of manpower planning are as follows:

1. **Determining Future Personnel Needs.** Planning is significant as it helps determine future personnel needs. Surplus or deficiency in staff strength is the result of the absence of or defective planning. All public sector enterprises find themselves overstaffed now as they never had any planning of their personnel requirements. They went on a hiring spree upto the late 1980s. Since then, recruitment and selection have been almost banned, but the ban came too late. The private sector is no exception. As many as 76.5 per cent of our organizations have surplus labour and the excess varies between 10 and 20 per cent in as many as 47 per cent of the units. The problem of excess staff has become so heavy that many units are resorting to 'voluntary retirement schemes' (VRS) to remove the excess staff. *Such surplus labour or even shortage would not have been there if there were HRP.*
2. **Reduced Labour Costs.** With the help of HR planning management is able to anticipate shortage and/or surpluses of manpower. Thus, they are able to take the corrective action in time, before these unbalances become unmanageable and hence, expensive. All this leads to overall reduction in labour costs.
3. **Optimum Utilization of Manpower Force.** With the help of human resource planning there is optimum utilization of labour force in the organization. Workers are given those jobs to perform for which they are skilled (right person for the right job). It leads to overall development of the manpower in the organization.
4. **Part of Strategic Planning.** All the activities of HRM—planning, hiring, training, remunerating and maintaining—must be merged with strategic management.

   HR planning can become part of strategic planning at two ends. At the beginning of the strategic planning, HRP provides a set of inputs into the strategic formulation process in terms of deciding whether the types and numbers of people are available to pursue a given strategy. At the end of strategic planning process, HRP is relevant in terms of implementation concerns. Once the strategy is set, executives need to make resource allocation decisions, including those pertaining to structure, processes and human resources.

   In most successful companies there is virtually no distinction between strategic planning and HRP; the planning cycles are the same and HR issues are seen as inherent in the business management. HR managers are important facilitators of the strategic planning process and are viewed as important contributors to carve the organization's future.
5. **Creating Highly Talented Personnel.** As was mentioned earlier, jobs are becoming highly intellectual and the incumbents are getting vastly professionalized. L&T, an engineering giant, has MBAs, engineers and technicians who collectively constitute 75 per cent of the total employee strength of 20,000. The HR manager must use his/her ingenuity to attract and retain qualified and skilled personnel.

These people are known for job hopping, thereby creating frequent shortages in the organization. Manpower planning helps prevent such shortages. Furthermore, technology changes will often upgrade some jobs and degrade others. Indian Telephone Industries (ITI) had a stronger technology to ·start with, which later developed into crossbar telephone system. This was later changed to electronic technology. Jobs created and people hired when old technologies were in use became extinct, obsolete and redundant. ITI being a public sector undertaking, could not retrench its workers, and were subsequently retrained and redeployed to supervise the electronic system now in use. Jobs became highly technical necessitating hiring of engineers who had majored in electronics. So, ITI had no use of engineers with civil or mechanical engineering as major. Thus, ITI is in a tight spot so far as shop-floor workers are concerned, whose number is more than the demand for them. Even with regard to electronics engineers, the company is not in a comfortable position. With its existing compensation scheme, ITI is not in a position to attract talented people. This situation could have been avoided if ITI had done HRP.

Another facet of the high-talent personnel is management succession planning. Who will replace the retiring chief executive? From what pool of people will top executives be selected and how will these individuals be groomed for their increased responsibilities? HRP is an answer to these and other related questions.

6. **Identification of Gaps in Existing Manpower.** Human resource planning identifies gaps in existing manpower in terms of their quantity and quality with the help of suitable training and/or any other steps, these gaps can be filled in time. Existing manpower can also be developed to fill future vacancies.
7. **Career Succession Planning.** Manpower planning facilitates career succession planning in the organization. It provides enough lead time for internal succession of employees to higher position through promotions. Thus, manpower planning contributes to management succession as well as development.
8. **Improvement in Overall Business Planning.** Manpower planning is an integral part of overall business planning. Effective manpower planning will lead to improvement in overall planning also. No management can be successful in the long run without having the right type and right number of people doing the right jobs at the right time.
9. **Growth of the Organization.** Manpower planning facilitates the expansion and diversification of an organization. In the absence of human resource plans, the required human resources will not be available to execute expansion and diversification plans at the right time.
10. **Creates Awareness in the Organization.** Manpower planning leads to a great awareness about the effectiveness of sound manpower management throughout the organization. It also helps in judging the effectiveness of human resource policies and programmes of management.
11. **Beneficial to the Country.** At the national level manpower planning facilitates educational reforms, geographical mobility of talent and employment generation.

LIMITATIONS OF HR PLANNING

Manpower planning is not always successful, the main problems are described below:

1. **Accuracy of Forecasts.** Manpower planning involves forecasting the demand and supply of human resources. Thus, the effectiveness of planning depends upon the accuracy of

forecasts. If the forecasts are not cent per cent accurate, planning will not be hundred per cent accurate. Inaccuracy increases when departmental forecasts are merely prepared without critical review.

2. **Identity Crisis.** Many human resource specialists and the managers do not understand the whole manpower planning process. Because of this, there is generally an identity crisis. Till the specialists develop a strong sense of purpose, planning cannot be effective.
3. **Support of Top Management.** Manpower planning requires full and wholehearted support from the top management. In the absence of this support and commitment, it would not be possible to ensure the necessary resources, cooperation and support for the success of the manpower planning.
4. **Resistance from Employees**. Employees and trade unions resist manpower planning. They feel that this planning increases their overall workload and regulates them through productivity bargaining. They also feel that it would lead to widespread unemployment, especially of unskilled labour.
5. **Insufficient Initial Efforts**. Successful human resource planning flourishes slowly and gradually. Sometimes sophisticated technologies are forcefully introduced just because competitors have adopted them. These may not be successful unless matched with the needs and environment of the particular enterprise.
6. **Management Information System**. Effectiveness of planning depends upon the reliability of the information system. In most of the Indian industries, human resource information system has not fully developed. In the absence of reliable data it would not be possible to have effective planning.
7. **Uncertainties.** It is risky to depend upon general estimates of manpower in the face of rapid changes in the environment. Absenteeism, turnover, seasonal employment, technological changes and market fluctuations are the uncertainties which serve as constraints to manpower planning. Although discounts are made for these factors while preparing the plan, moreover these factors cannot be estimated correctly.
8. **Expensive and Time-consuming**. Manpower planning is an expensive and time-consuming process. Employers may resist manpower planning feeling that it increases the cost of manpower.
9. **Coordination with other Managerial Functions**. There is generally a tendency on the part of the manpower planners to remain aloof from other operating managers and to become totally absorbed in their own world. To be effective, manpower planning must be integrated with other management functions.
10. **Unbalanced Approach.** Many human resourcc experts give more importance on the quantitative aspect of the manpower to ensure that there is adequate flow of people in and out of the organization. They overlook the qualitative aspects like career development and planning, skill levels, morale, etc. are overlooked by them. Such unbalanced approach affects the effectiveness of manpower· planning. Thus, manpower planning suffers from two types of problems. One is inherent because of problems of forecasting and second comes from human weakness.

GUIDELINES FOR MAKING HRP EFFECTIVE

Some of the suggestions for making HR planning effective are as given below:

1. **Integration with Organizational Plans.** Human resource planning must be balanced with organizational plans. It must be based on the organizational objectives and plans. This requires development of good communication channels between organization planners and the human resource planners.
2. **Period of HR Planning.** Period of the planning should be appropriate to the needs and circumstances of the enterprise in question. The size and structure of the enterprise as well as the anticipated changes must be taken into consideration.
3. **Proper Organization.** To be effective, the planning function should be properly organized. If possible, within the human resource department. A separate cell or committee should be constituted to provide adequate focus and to coordinate planning work at various levels.
4. **Support of Top Management.** To be effective in the long run, manpower planning must have the full support of the top management. The support from top management is essential to ensure the necessary resources, cooperation and support for the success of the planning.
5. **Involvement of Operating Executives.** Human resource planning is not a function of manpower planners only. To be effective, it requires active participation and coordinated efforts on the part of operating executives. Such participation will help to improve understanding of the process and thereby reduce resistance.
6. **Efficient and Reliable Information System.** To facilitate human resource planning, an adequate database must be developed for human resources.
7. **Balanced Approach.** The human resource experts should give equal importance to both quantitative and qualitative aspects of manpower. Instead of matching existing people with existing job, stress should be laid on filling future vacancies with right people. Promotion should also be considered carefully. Career planning and development, skill levels, morale, etc. should be given due importance by the planners.

REVIEW QUESTIONS

1. What do you understand by human resource planning? Describe its characteristics.
2. Discuss the objectives of human resource planning. How is the planning carried at various levels in the organization?
3. Briefly discuss the steps involved in manpower planning in an industry.
4. Define HRP or manpower planning. Review its benefits and limitations. What steps can be taken by an organization to make manpower planning more effective?
5. What is manpower or HR planning? Why is it necessary? Discuss the various steps involved in integrated strategic planning and HR.
6. What are the basis of HR planning?
7. Describe the various steps in conducting HRP.

8. Define manpower planning. Why is it necessary? What are its various sequences? How far has it been adopted by Indian organizations?
9. What are the determinants of HRP?
10. Discuss the process of HRP. What are its stages?
11. Discuss the control and review mechanism in HRP.
12. What are the strategies for HR planners? Discuss the guidelines which are important for making HRP more effective.

CASE STUDY

Mother India Supermarket Ltd.

Mother India Supermarket Ltd. is a chain store having its branches in all major cities in India. At present it has 75 branches. The branch manager of the Mangalore branch reported the following data on 8-9-2004. The current employee strength revealed the following information.

Designation	No. of Employees
Branch Manager	1
(A. Offs.) Department Managers	3
(Officers) Assistant Manager (Sales)	6
Head Accountant	1
Accounts Officers	3
(Clerk) Counter Salesmen	10
Typists	2
Security personnel	2
Sub Staff	2

Two counter salesmen will be promoted and transferred to Udupi branch in October 2004 and three counter salesmen will be shifted to Chennai branch for 6 months in 2005 on a temporary basis. Two assistant managers (sales) have passed their C.A. examination and are planning to leave and join M.C.C. Bank, Mangalore in January 2005. One security personnel was shot by some robbers in October 2004 and was critically injured. Though he has completely recovered from the injury, he has been advised by doctors to take complete rest till March 2005.

The head accountant is due to retire in April 2005 and one accounts officer is due for promotion in April 2005.

The branch manager would be promoted as general manager (Mangalore Circle) in January 2005 but he would be retained in the Mangalore branch itself.

The branch wants to start three new divisions like cosmetic division, books and stationary division and toys division in January 2005. These divisions would require additional hands in the form of two assistant managers (sales), three counter salesmen and one sub-staff.

Prepare a comprehensive human resource planning for the year 2005.

Source: Aquinas, P.G. Human Resource Management, Vikas Publishing House, 2008, p. 48.

REFERENCES

1. Anthony, William P. (1993). "Strategic Human Resource Management", Dryden Press, New York.
2. Armstrong, Michael (1988). "A Handbook of Personnel Management Practice", Prentice Hall, New Jersey.
3. Beach, Dale S. (1980). "Personnel—The Management of People at Work", MacMillan, New York.
4. George Bohlander (2002). "Managing Human Resources", Therson, p. 24.
5. Jaffery, A. Mello (2003). "Strategic Human Resource Management", Thomson.
6. Rothwell, William J. (1988). "Human Resource Planning and Management", Prentice Hall, New Jersey.
7. Schuler Randall S. (1981). "Personnel and Human Resource Management", West Publishing. New York.
8. Werther, William B. and Keith Davis (1993). "Human Resources and Personnel Management", McGraw-Hill, New York.
9. Anthony, William P. (1993). "Strategic Human Resource Management", Dryden Press, p. 179, New York.

CHAPTER

3

Career Planning and Development

CHAPTER'S OUTLINE

- Introduction
- What is Career Planning?
- Objectives of Career Planning
- Factors Affecting Career Planning–Process of Career Planning
- Tips for Individual Career Planning
- Career Planning vs. Human Resource Planning
- Career Development
- Roles in Career Development
- Benefits of Career Planning and Development
- Limitations of Career Planning and Development
- Essentials for Effective Career Planning and Development
- Career Management Elements

INTRODUCTION

Career planning and development is the most important aspect of human resource management. Employees in the organization can prove to be a great asset provided the long-run interests of the employees are protected by the organization and that the employees are encouraged to grow and realize their full potential. Human resource management or personnel management protecting the interests of the employees and it is in the interest of the organization. **According to Richard**

Hackman and J. Lloyd Shuttle "*The basic assumption underlying this role of protecting long-run interests of the employees is that the employer has an obligation to utilize its employee's abilities to the fullest and to give all employees a chance to grow and to realize their full potential and to develop successful careers.*"

The role of the manager in fact has become more complex these days as recruiting, selecting and imparting training to the employees in a traditional role and ensuring growth of employees in their career is a new challenging role. Career planning and development for the employees is thus the main focus for HR managers. *Career planning and development is a deliberate process through which a person becomes aware of personal career-related attributes and the lifelong series of stages that contribute to his/her career fulfilment.*

In this chapter an attempt is made to discuss various aspects of career planning and development. Before proceeding, it would be useful to define some of the terms we will be using throughout this chapter. A *career* is a series of work-related positions, paid or unpaid, that help a person grow in job skills, success and fulfilment. Career development is the lifelong series of activities (such as workshops) that contribute to a person's career exploration, establishment, success and fulfilment. The concept of career planning is further explained in detail in the next section.

WHAT IS CAREER PLANNING?

Career planning is not an event or end in itself, but a continuous process of developing human resources for achieving optimum results. In simple language, career planning is a process by which one selects career goals and the path to these goals.

Definitions

According to **Richard Hackman and Lloyd Shuttle:** "*Career planning is the deliberate process through which a person becomes aware of personal skills, interests, knowledge, motivations and other characteristics; acquires about opportunities; identifies career related goals and establishes action plans to attain specific goals.*"

In the words of **Wrether and Davis,** "*Career planning is the process by which one selects goals and the path to these goals.*"

From these definitions following *characteristics* are identified in the meaning of career planning.

- Career planning is a deliberate process.
- Career planning is not an event or end in itself but a continuous process of developing HR for optimum results.
- Focus of career planning is on assessing the employees in the light of achieving organizational goals and providing an environment which allows the employees to grow in their career.
- Career planning involves growth of individual career as well as the growth of the organization.

OBJECTIVES OF CAREER PLANNING

The main objectives of career planning are as under:

1. To offer careers, not jobs to the employees so that talent can be attracted and retained in the organization.
2. To have effective utilization of human resources which will, in turn, lead to greater productivity.
3. To reduce employee turnover.
4. To motivate the employees and to boost their morals.
5. To meet the immediate and future human resource needs of the organization on a timely basis.

FACTORS AFFECTING CAREER PLANNING

It has been discussed that career planning is a continuous process by which career goals are identified and path is determined to achieve these goals. There are four main steps in planning a career for yourself or someone else.

1. Identify the Person's Career Stage—Step I

The first step in planning a career is to learn as much as possible about the person's interests, aptitude and skills. Each person's career goes through stages and the stage you are in will influence your knowledge of and preference for various occupations. The main stages of career cycle are as follows (Figure 3.1)

(i) Growth and Exploration Stage
(ii) Establishment Stage
(iii) Maintenance Stage
(iv) Decline Stage

(i) **Growth and Exploration Stage:** The **growth stage** lasts roughly from birth to age 14 and is a period during which the person develops a self-concept by identifying with and interacting with other people such as family, friends, and teachers. Towards the beginning of this period, role playing is important, and children experiment with different ways of acting; this helps them to form impressions of how other people react to different behaviours and contributes to their developing a unique self-concept or identity. Towards the end of this stage, the adolescent (who by this time has developed preliminary ideas about what his or her interests and abilities are) begins to think realistically about alternative occupations.

(ii) The **exploration stage** is the period (roughly from ages 15 to 24) during which a person seriously explores various occupational alternatives. The person attempts to match these alternatives with what he or she has learnt about them and about his or her own interests and abilities from school, leisure activities, and work. Tentative broad occupational choices are usually made during the beginning of this period. Then towards the end of this period,

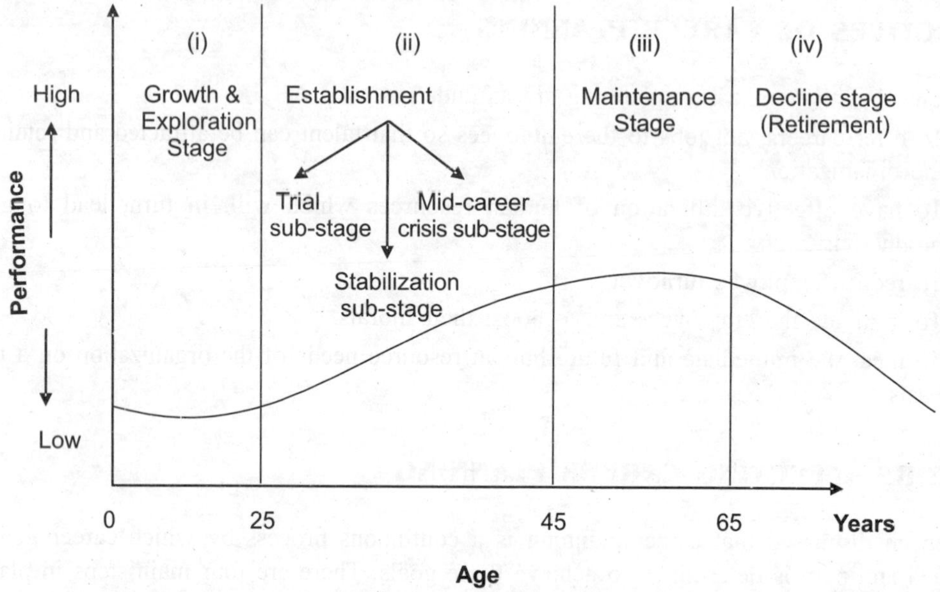

Fig. 3.1. Stages in Career Development.

a seemingly appropriate choice is made and the person tries out for beginning a job. Probably the most important task the person has in this and the preceding stage is that of developing a realistic understanding of his or her abilities and talents. Similarly, the person must make sound educational decisions based on reliable sources of information about occupational alternatives.

(iii) **Establishment Stage:** The establishment stage spans roughly from ages 24 to 44 years and is the heart of most people's work lives. During this period, it is hoped a suitable occupation is found and the person engages in those activities that help him or her earn a permanent place in it. Often and particularly in the professions, the person locks on to a chosen occupation early. But in most cases, this is a period during which the person is continually testing his or her capabilities and ambitions against those of the initial occupational choice. The establishment stage itself comprises three substages. The trial substage lasts from about ages 25 to 30 years. During this period, the person determines whether or not the chosen field is suitable; if it is not, several changes might be attempted. Roughly between the ages of 30 and 40 years, the person goes through a stabilization substage. Here firm occupational goals are set and the person does more explicit career planning to determine the sequence of promotions, job changes, and/or any educational activities that seem necessary for accomplishing these goals. Finally, somewhere between the mid-thirties and mid-forties, the person may enter the mid-career crisis substage. During this period, people often make a major reassessment of their progress relative to original ambitions and goals. They may find that they are not going to realize their dreams (such as being company president) or that, having been accomplished; their dreams are not all they were purported to be. Also during this period, people have to decide how important work and career are to be in their life. It is often during this mid-career substage that the person is faced for the first time with difficult choices between what he or she really wants, what really can be accomplished, and how much must be sacrificed to achieve it.

(iv) **Maintenance Stage**: Between the ages of 45 to 65 years, many people simply slide from the stabilization substage into the maintenance stage. During this latter period, the person has typically created a place in the world of work and most efforts are now directed at maintaining that place.

(v) **Decline Stage:** As the retirement age approaches, there is often a deceleration period in the decline stage. Here many people face the prospect of having to accept reduced levels of power and responsibility and learn to accept and develop new roles as mentor and confidante for those who are younger. There is then the more or less inevitable retirement, after which the person finds alternative uses for the time and effort formerly expended on his or her occupation.

2. Identify Occupational Orientation—Step-II

Career-counselling expert **John Holland** says that a person's personality (including values, motives, and needs) is another important determinant of career choices. For example, a person with a strong social orientation might be attracted to careers that entail interpersonal rather than intellectual or physical activities and to occupations such as social work. Based on research with his Vocational Preference Test (VPT), **Holland found six basic personality types or orientations.**

(i) **Realistic orientation.** These people are attracted to occupations that involve physical activities requiring skill, strength, and coordination. Examples include forestry, farming, and agriculture.

(ii) **Investigative orientation.** Investigative people are attracted to careers that involve cognitive activities (thinking, organizing, and understanding) rather than affective activities (feeling, acting, or interpersonal and emotional tasks). Examples include biologist, chemist, and college professor.

(iii) **Social orientation.** These people are attracted to careers that involve interpersonal rather than intellectual or physical activities. Examples include clinical psychology, foreign service, and social work.

(iv) **Conventional orientation.** A conventional orientation favours careers that involve structured, rule-regulated activities, as well as careers in which it is expected that the employee subordinate his or her personal needs to those of the organization. Examples include accountants and bankers.

(v) **Enterprising orientation.** Verbal activities aimed at influencing others are attractive to enterprising personalities. Examples include managers, lawyers, and public relations executives.

(vi) **Artistic orientation.** People here are attracted to careers that involve self-expression, artistic creation, expression of emotions, and individualistic activities. Examples include artists, advertising executives, and musicians.

Most people have more than one orientation (they might be social, realistic, and investigative, for example), and Holland believes that the more similar or compatible these orientations are, the less internal conflict or indecision a person will face in making a career choice. To help illustrate this, Holland suggests placing each orientation in one corner of a hexagon, as in Figure 3.2. As you can see, the model has six corners, each of which represents one personal orientation (for example, enterprising). According to Holland's research, the closer two orientations are in this figure, the more compatible they are. Holland believes that if your number-one and number-two orientations fall side by side, you will have an easier time choosing a career. However, if your orientations turn out to be opposite (such as realistic and social), you may experience more indecision in making a career choice because your interests are driving you towards very different types of careers.

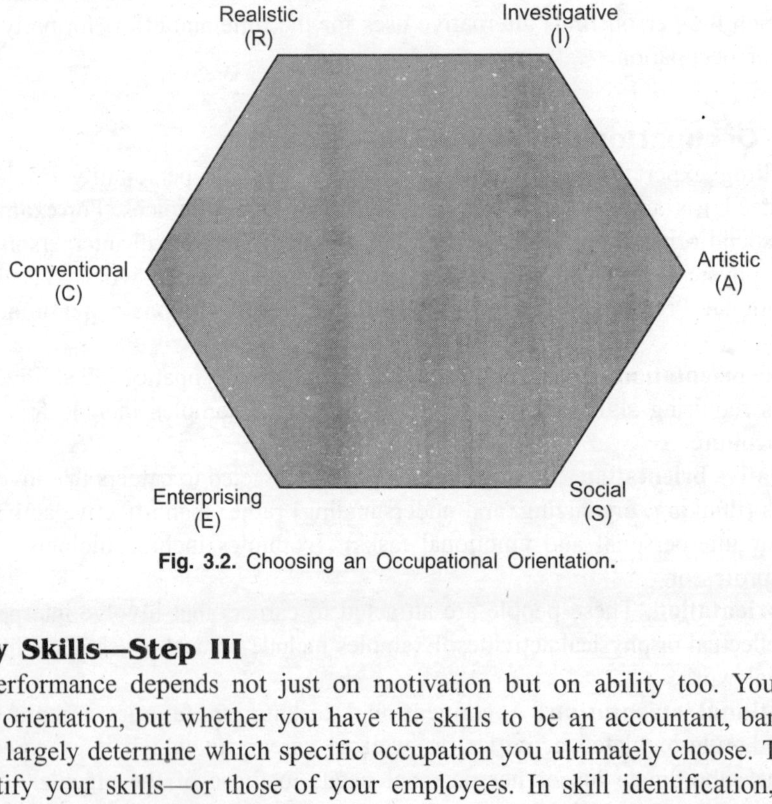

Fig. 3.2. Choosing an Occupational Orientation.

3. Identify Skills—Step III

Successful performance depends not just on motivation but on ability too. You may have a conventional orientation, but whether you have the skills to be an accountant, banker, or credit manager will largely determine which specific occupation you ultimately choose. Therefore, you have to identify your skills—or those of your employees. In skill identification, occupational skills and aptitudes need to be identified.

(i) Occupational Skills: The skills are needed to be successful in a particular occupation. According to the *Dictionary of Occupational Titles*, occupational skills break down into three groups depending on whether they emphasize data, people or things.

(ii) Aptitudes: Innate abilities which include intelligence, numerical aptitude, mechanical comprehension, and manual dexterity, as well as talents such as artistic, theatrical, or musical ability that plays an important role in career decisions.

4. Identify Career Anchors—Step IV

In choosing a career, the role of career anchors is also important. Career anchors, as their name implies, are the pivots around which a person's career swings; a person becomes conscious of them as a result of learning about his or her talents and abilities, motives and needs, and attitudes and values.

Based upon his study of MIT graduates, **Schein** identified five career anchors.

- **Functional Career Anchor**–They provide technical and financial guidance
- **Managerial Competence Anchor**–They guide on reading high responsibility management position.
- **Creativity Career Anchor**–They help in establishing our enterprises to produce new product or process?
- **Autonomy and Independence as Career Anchors**–They guide the students to become consultants working either alone or a part of small firm or proprietors of retail business.
- **Security as a Career Anchor**–These anchors help those students who are concerned with long-run career stability and job security.

For choosing an appropriate anchor, you are supposed to note the following:

(i) What is your major area of concern?
(ii) What is your first job?
(iii) What are your long-run goals?
(iv) What is your first change of job?
(v) What is your intention toward changing your job further?
(vi) Identify sometimes while looking back over your career when you had enjoyed.
(vii) Have you ever refused a job move or promotion and why?

After analyzing the answers of these questions, you can rate each anchor and make a final choice.

5. Identify High-Potential Occupations—Step V

Learning about oneself is only half the job of choosing an occupation. You also have to identify those occupations that are right (given your occupational orientations, skills, career anchors, and occupational preferences) as well as those that will be in high demand in the years to come.

There are two basic things you can and should do to improve the career decisions you make.

First, take charge of your own career by understanding that there are major decisions to be made, which require considerable personal planning and effort. In other words, you cannot leave your choices in the hands of others but must decide where you want to go in terms of a career and what job moves and education are required to get there.

Second, become an effective *diagnostician.* Determine through career counselling, testing, self-diagnostic books, and so on, what your talents or values are and how these fit with the sorts of careers you are considering. In other words, the key to career planning is self-insight into what you want out of a career, into your talents and limitations, and into your values and how they will fit with the alternatives you are considering. As **Schein** points out, "*Too many people* *never ask, much less attempt to answer, these kinds of questions. It was shocking to me when I conducted the interviews for the MIT panel study and discovered how many respondents said they had never in 10 years of their careers asked themselves the kinds of questions which I was asking just to fill in the details of their job history.*"

TIPS FOR INDIVIDUAL CAREER PLANNING

For successful career planning by an individual, apart from looking into five steps required in the process of career planning (discussed in the foregoing section), personal strategies need to be formulated so to overcome the weaknesses and flourish on the strengths. The main tips for individual career planning are as follows:

1. **Preparing Personal Profile:** It consists of various personality traits of the person. One should put some questions to oneself like attitudes towards work, nature, confidence, initiative, future expectations, etc. The answer to these and similar other questions will help in determining the direction of one's professional career.
2. **Formulating Personal and Professional Goals:** The personal goals will first enable a person to enter the profession and then professional goals will be needed for reaching higher heights. The setting of performance goals helps in identifying career goals. The career goals are not set once for all. There should be flexibility in career goals. With the change in circumstances and environment the goals should be revised. In order to support long-term objectives, there should be short-term objectives and action plans which can be a part of performance appraisal process. Continuing the previous example, if one aims to become a doctor then he should study medical courses for entering this line and then study various aspects of medicine and surgery. So short-term action plans are essential to achieve long-term goals.
3. **Analysis of Strengths and Weaknesses:** The strengths and weaknesses of a person should be matched with job requirements and environmental opportunities. Different jobs require different skills. One person may be more suitable at supervisory level only, while the other may go upto middle level management, and so on.
4. **Analyzing Environment Effect:** A good career planning by an individual requires a systematic analysis of the environment for opportunities. Both inside and outside environments influence career planning process. The stage of growth of the organization, future expansion plans, thinking of management, etc. should be considered while deciding about career strategy. For example, an expanding organization will provide more opportunities to its employees than a mature concern which is not expected to grow. The outside environmental factors such as economic, social, political, technological, etc. too need to be discussed for formulation of career strategy. Not only present, but future environment should also be considered. This requires forecasting. Since many factors need to be analyzed, planning the career necessitates being selective and concentrating on those factors which are critical to personal success.
5. **Developing Alternatives:** A good career planning requires the development of several alternatives. The alternatives are assessed in view of the environment and the opportunities available. One alternative may be suitable under particular conditions while

the other may benefit under other situations. Sometimes, efforts are made to overcome weaknesses to take advantage of opportunities. The strategies should be developed to meet the threats in the environment and cope with such situations. A person with excellent technical and managerial capabilities may like to join an expanding concern so that he benefits later on.

6. **Developing Contingency Plans.** The career plans are developed in the environment of uncertainty. Even though some future assumptions are made but these may not prove correct; so contingency plans should be formulated for facing the uncertain future situations. One may be happy while working in a growing concern because of more career opportunities but an assumption should be made if the venture fails then what is to be done.
7. **Monitoring Career Plan:** Monitoring of career plan is also an important requirement for good career planning for an individual. As required by a particular situation some adjustments may be needed. The monitoring should be done at the time of performance appraisal or when project or assignment is completed.

CAREER PLANNING VS HUMAN RESOURCE PLANNING

There cannot be effective manpower planning in the absence of effective career planning. Both career planning and manpower planning relate to the human resources in the organization, but these are totally different from each other. The main points of difference are:

1. Manpower or human resource planning is the process of determining manpower requirements and the means for meeting these requirements in order to carry out the integrated plan of the organization. Career planning is the process of finding those employees who could be groomed for higher level positions on the strength of their performance.
2. Human resource planning provides valuable information regarding the availability of human resources in case of expansion, growth, etc. of the organization. Career planning gives in a picture of who could succeed in case of any major developments leading to retirement, death, resignation of existing employees.

   Human Resource Planning is tied to the overall strategic planning efforts of the organization. Hence, there cannot be effective manpower planning in the absence of effective career planning.

CAREER DEVELOPMENT

Career development is essential to implement career plan. *Career development is the lifelong series of activities such as workshops that contributes to a person's career exploration, establishment, success, and fulfilment.*

Career development consists of personal improvements undertaken by the individual employee training, development and educational programmes by the organization and various institutes.

Steps and Tasks in Establishing a Career Development System

There are four steps in establishing a career development system. These steps are: conducting need assessment, vision, action plan and results. Table 3.1 shows the steps and tasks in establishing career development system.

Table 3.1: Steps and Tasks in Establishing a Career Development System

Step 1: Needs: Defining the Present System
- Establish roles and responsibilities of employees, managers, and the organization. Identify needs; establish target groups.
- Establish cultural parameters; determine organizational receptivity, support, and commitment to career development.
- Assess existing HR programmes or structures; consider possible links to a career development programme.
- Determine prior attempts at solving the problem or need.
- Establish the mission or philosophy of the programme.
- Design and implement needs assessment to confirm the data or collect more data.
- Establish indicators or criteria of success.

Step 2: Vision: Determining New Directions and Possibilities
- Create a long-term philosophy.
- Establish the vision or objectives of the programme.
- Design interventions for employees, managers, and the organization.
- Organize and make available career information needed to support the programme.

Step 3: Action Plan: Deciding on Practical First Steps
- Assess the plan and obtain support from top management.
- Create a pilot programme.
- Assess resources and competencies.
- Establish an advisory group.
- Involve advisory group in data gathering, programme design, implementation, evaluation, and monitoring.

Step 4: Results: Maintaining the Change
- Create long-term formalized approaches.
- Publicize the programme.
- Evaluate and redesign the programme and its components.
- Consider future trends and directions for the programme.

Source: Z.B. Leibowitze. C. Farren and B.L. Kaye, Designing Career Development Systems. San Francisco. CA: Jossey-Bass. 1986. p. 273.

Career Development Actions

There are five actions which are taken in career development:

(i) **Job Performance:** Employee must prove that his performance on the job is to the level of standards established, if he wants career progress.

(ii) **Exposure:** Employee's desire for career progress should expose their skills, knowledge, qualifications, achievements, performance, etc., to those who take the decision about career progress.

(iii) **Resignations:** Employees may resign the present job in the organization, if they find that career opportunities elsewhere are better than those of the present organization.

(iv) **Change the Job:** Employees who put organizational loyalty over career loyalty may change the job in the same organization if they find that career opportunities in other jobs in the same organization are better than those in the present job.

(v) Career Guidance: And counselling provides information, advice and encouragement to switch over to other career or organization, where career opportunities are better.

Career development actions are presented in Table 3.2.

Table 3.2: Career Development Actions

(a) Self-assessment tools
- Career planning workshops
- Career workbooks
- Individual counselling
- Information services
- Job posting systems
- Skills inventories
- Career ladders and paths
- Career resource centres

(b) Organizational assessment programmes
- Assessment centres
- Psychological testing
- Promotability forecasts
- Succession planning

(c) Developmental programmes
- Assessment centres
- Job rotation programmes
- Tuition refund plans
- Internal training programmes
- Mentoring programmes

(d) Programmes to address issues confronting employees at various career stages
- Early-career issues
- Anticipatory socialization programmes
- Realistic recruitment
- Employee orientation programmes
- Mid-career issues
    - Job rotation
    - Downward moves
    - Developmental programmes
- Late-career issues
    - Workshops on older worker issues
    - Pre-retirement programmes
    - Incentives for early retirement
    - Flexible work patterns
- Career programmes for special target groups
    - Fast-track or high-potential employees
    - Terminated employees (outplacement programmes)
    - Supervisors

(e) Women, minorities, and employees with disabilities; programmes to assist employed spouses and parents
- Policies on hiring couples
- Work-family programmes
- Job-sharing programmes
- Relaxed policies on transfers and travel flexible work arrangements
- Paid and unpaid leave (maternity, paternity)
- Childcare services

Source: J.E.A. Russell, Career Development Interventions in Organizations, *Journal of Vocational Behaviour,* 38, 1991, p. 244.

ROLES IN CAREER DEVELOPMENT

As summarized in Table 3.3, the individual, the manager, and the organization all have roles in the individual's career development. Ultimately it is the individual who must accept responsibility for his or her own career; assess interests, skills and values; seek out career information and resources; and generally take those steps that must be taken to ensure a happy and fulfilling career. Within the organization the individual's manager plays a role, too. The manager should provide timely and objective performance feedback, offer developmental assignments and support, and participate in career development discussions, for instance. The manager acts as a coach, appraiser, advisor, and referral agent, for instance, listening to and clarifying the individual's career plans, giving feedback, generating career options, and linking the employee to organizational resources and career options. This is also shown in Table 3.4.

Table 3.3: Roles in Career Development

Individual

- Accept responsibility for your own career.
- Assess your interests, skills, and values.
- Seek out career information and resources.
- Establish goals and career plans.
- Utilize development opportunities.
- Talk with your manager about your career.
- Follow through on realistic career plans.

Manager

- Provide timely performance feedback.
- Provide developmental assignments and support.
- Participate in career development discussions.
- Support employee development plans.

Organization

- Communicate mission, policies, and procedures.
- Provide training and development opportunities.
- Provide career information and career programmes.
- Offer a variety of career options.

Source: Fred L. Otte and Peggy G. Hutcheson, Helping Employees Manage Careers (Englewood Cliffs, NJ: Prentice-Hall, 1992), p. 56.

Table 3.4: Four Roles for Managers in Employee Development

Coach	Appraiser	Advisor	Referral Agent
Listens; Clarifies; Probes; Defines concerns	Gives feedback; Clarifies standards; Clarifies job; responsibilities	Generates options; Helps set goals; Recommends/advises	Links employee; to resources/people; Consults on action plan

Source: Fred L. Otte and Peggy G. Hutcheson, Helping Employees Manage Careers (Englewood Cliffs, NJ: Prentice Hall, 1992), p. 57.

It is thus evident that the employer plays a key role in career development. For example, it should provide career-oriented training and development opportunities, offer career information and career programmes, and give employees a variety of career options. Ultimately, as we will see, employers need not and should not provide such career-oriented activities purely out of selfless welfare of others. Most employees will ultimately grade their employers on the extent to which the organization allowed them to excel and to become the people they believed they had the potential to become. And that will help determine their commitment to their employers and their overall job satisfaction.

BENEFITS OF CAREER PLANNING AND DEVELOPMENT

Career planning and development is beneficial to the individual as well as to the organization. These benefits are as discussed below.

1. Benefits to the Individual

(i) It helps the individual to discover his own talents, needs and motives related to work.
(ii) It helps fulfil the individual's need to know what his position and future in the organization will be.
(iii) It provides a sense of affiliation with the organization and a feeling that the organization is interested in the individual's development.
(iv) It provides greater opportunity for the individual to obtain optimal return for his personal investment (contribution of talent, time, etc.) in the organization.
(v) It provides the individual with a greater awareness of his work environment and hence, promotes more intelligent decision-making with respect to careers and avoids frustration caused by lack of career information.
(vi) It helps fulfil the individual's need to retain a sense of control over his personal destiny in the increasingly complex and impersonalized modern industrial society.
(vii) It provides greater opportunities for change in the working environment that would otherwise lead to boredom.
(viii) It is conducive to job satisfaction by providing assignments most suited to the individual's needs and tastes.
(ix) It leads to optimal personal development by developing abilities and aptitudes to the full.

2. Benefits to the Organization

(i) It helps in increasing efficiency/productivity in jobs and in turn, effectiveness in meeting the organizational objectives through greater creativity, motivation and contribution of the staff.
(ii) It helps in reducing the turnover of high potential staff and absenteeism of all staff.
(iii) It facilitates staff mobility by planning assignments well enough in advance to avoid some of the obstacles which arise when staff is required to move at short notice.
(iv) It helps in providing greater assurance of an adequate supply of qualified· personnel for future openings in managerial technical and other key positions.
(v) It promotes continuity of organizational knowledge by drawing more upon internal personnel resources.
(vi) It helps in reducing pressure on job classification and other personnel system resulting from frustrated career.

(vii) It provides an added input in programme planning by offering more data on the capabilities of the workforce which, in turn permits a better judgement to be made of whether or in what manner the proposed programme objectives can be accomplished.

(viii) It prevents organizational chaos by helping to provide a more regulated, ordered and objective procedure for upward mobility of the staff members.

(ix) It promotes optimum utilization of human resources both at present by preventing instances of mismatched staff members and in the future by permitting longer term planning of the development of the employees' usefulness to the organization.

(x) It contributes significantly to the reduction of costs.

LIMITATIONS OF CAREER PLANNING AND DEVELOPMENT

There are some drawbacks in career planning and development also:

1. Career planning is not suitable for small units where the opportunities for vertical growth of the employees are very few.
2. Several environmental factors may upset career planning and development efforts of the organization, e.g. government policy, reservation policy, regional pressures, trade union demands, etc.
3. Problems may crop up, if the management fails to focus on any of the career related issues, e.g. minority groups, early career issues, retirement issues, late career issues, etc.
4. With the increase in career orientation among women, a number of female employees are on increase. With this the dual career families have also been on increase. Consequently, one of those family members might face the problem of transfer. This has become a complicated problem to organizations. Consequently other employees may be at disadvantage.

ESSENTIALS FOR EFFECTIVE CAREER PLANNING AND DEVELOPMENT

Systematic career planning offers a large number of benefits to the individual as well as to the organization. To ensure the success of such activity, a number of steps should be taken. A few of these steps are as follows:

1. **Support from the Top Management:** Career planning efforts to be effective must receive consistent support and help from the top management.
2. **Clear-cut Goals.** The corporate goals must be laid down clearly. It is not possible to develop appropriate goals for human resources if the management is not sure about the corporate goals.
3. **Rewards for Performance:** There must be appropriate rewards for employees as well as managers, who show promise. Employees must be made willing to expand their abilities and managers must be willing to coach, counsel and share their knowledge with the employees.
4. **Proper Placement:** Every effort must be made to put the employees on jobs for which they are best suited. If a talented employee is put on a job, below his standard, he will quit in frustration as soon as he gets the opportunity.

5. **Career Paths:** The career paths for different employees should be laid down clearly. Fast promotions should be available to talented people.
6. **Continuous Basis:** Career planning efforts should be carried out on a continuous basis keeping the changing needs of employees and the organization in mind. A record of career movements of employees must be kept and periodic assessment of who has gone where should be made.
7. **Awareness:** There should be publicity of the career opportunities in the organization, so that all the employees become aware of these opportunities.

CAREER MANAGEMENT ELEMENTS

Every management should have a policy to provide its employees with appropriate opportunities, encouragement and career growth. Career management has certain basic elements which are called career management elements. These are as under:

1. Preparation of an Up-to-date Inventory of Job Positions in the Organization

The first element in career planning is the preparation of an up-to-date job inventory, which will give complete information about the job positions. This inventory should contain the following information:

(i) Number of jobs at each level of career paths, number of vacancies likely to occur due to normal turnover and retirement and additional hands needed on account of implementation of development programmes.

(ii) Information about the duties, responsibilities and functions of each job.

(iii) Requisite academic qualifications, training, skills, experience and personality traits required for performing each assignment.

The above information will help in the development of career pattern, the placement of personnel who will best meet job requirements and the promotional opportunities in the organization.

2. Preparation of Personnel Inventory of Present and Anticipated Human Resources

The second element in career management is the preparation of inventory of human resources in the organization. This inventory will contain information about the currently employed manpower resources, their academic qualifications, training, and experience of various positions held and the appraisal of their performance. Further, an estimate will be prepared for the anticipated future manpower requirements based on job estimation. This manpower inventory will provide the basis for planning and development of manpower resources needed by the organization. It will lay a scientific base for planned career advancement and selection of eligible persons for career promotions.

3. Career Planning and Development

Till recently, majority of organizations are not aware of this element of career management. They are aware of the needs and aspirations of the employees. But research has proved that it is very essential for the organization to give consideration to the long-range and short-range goals and aspirations of the employees. Only then the management can devise career plans which will help the employees in moving towards their goals. The development of career plans will educate the employee in self-development. From the very stage of entry into the organization the employee should know, which career path he has to follow to reach the desired level in the organization. The management has to go through the following stages for an efficient and effective career management programme:

(i) **Matching of Management and Individual Career Plans:** While allocating jobs to the employees, the management should take into consideration their personal interests, goals, needs, aspirations and capabilities. If the management fails to do so, and the employees are not associated with their jobs, the employees will not display their real worth in their work and the management cannot make optimum utilization of manpower resources. Thus, the management should provide a flexible organizational structure which will match the career paths with the individual interests, capabilities, aspirations, attitudes on the one hand and the manpower needs of the organization on the other hand. Once the individual employee in assigned a specific career path, he will be allowed to continue unless it is felt that the particular path does not suit the employee or that he will do better in another career path.

(ii) **Management Development:** A very important segment of career management programme is the management development and introduction of development techniques which help in effective implementation of this programme. Development of the personnel should relate to the present and future needs of the organization. Moreover, the individual employee's abilities and potentialities as indicated by his performance appraisals will also have an impact on the development programme. The management should try to have a model plan for each career path, describing the skills required at specified points of time and devising techniques for enabling the employees to acquire or develop these skills. Thus, management development can be very important in career management in the following way:

   (a) Assessing manpower needs.
   (b) Ascertaining skills and capabilities required for effective performance.
   (c) Utilization of full potential and capabilities of employees.
   (d) Development of potential and capabilities of employees through training and coaching.

(iii) **Criteria in Development of Career Planning:** In the next stage, the management has to decide the criterion which is to be used for developing career planning. A number of criteria can be used by the management for this purpose such as:

   (a) Dialogue. Dialogues can generate the interest which will be advantageous to the organization as well as the individuals. Generally, this dialogue is between the individual employee and his immediate superior, but it can be between the individual and the top management of the organization.

   (b) Guidance. Within the framework of the career planning, individual employees can be guided to plan intelligently their own careers. They should be given information about options, opportunities and goals available.

(c) **Involvement and Participation.** Employees should be involved in setting of goals, time schedules, value system and other meaningful issues. This participation will give them a sense of belongingness to the organization.

(d) **Feedback.** There should be an effective feedback of information including employees' personal information as well as information about his career paths. This information is to be collected in a systematic way so that it can be used for knowing how many and what kind of human resources are available in the organization.

(e) **Dynamic.** The career planning programme should be dynamic because individuals are not static, they are changing entities.

(iv) **Career Planning System:** The career planning system will be effective only if the individual and organization are honest and informative about each other. Career planning system can generate data of great use in manpower planning process. The personnel department can play a very important role by organizing career planning workshops for employees which give them the basis for initiating career changes. Some of the important methods of career planning are:

(a) **Career Paths.** Career paths can be defined as the simply structured series of predetermined on the job experiences which result in job promotions within the organization itself. Career path can be a useful method, only when structured experience is a technical necessity. This method will not be suitable in the changing environment of individuals and the organization.

(b) **Job Posting.** Job posting as a method of career planning is an intra-organizational activity. In this method, the organization announces the various positions and vacancies in the classified section of a newspaper. Employees apply for these positions according to their aspirations and career plans. Thus, in this method, the employees opt themselves for promotion or job change.

(c) **Assessment Centre.** This method can be applied in almost all the situations. Under this method, miniature situations of job functions and processes are created under-controlled conditions, where individuals may be systematically observed by specialists and the candidates' readiness to advance in the organization is evaluated. The process of assessment can be carried out by a designated unit of the organization or a consultant. The assessment centre is an effective method to provide an objective evaluation of developed abilities, potential, strengths, weaknesses and motivation of the employees. This evaluation provides a basis of career planning and development.

CAREER MANAGEMENT GUIDELINES

Along with the employee, the person's manager and employer both have career management responsibilities. Guidelines here include:

- **Avoid Reality Shock:** Perhaps at no other stage in the person's career is it more important for the employer to be career development-oriented than at the initial entry stage, when the person is recruited, hired, and given the first assignment and boss. For the employee this is a period during which he or she has to develop a sense of confidence, learn to get along with the first boss and with coworker learn how to accept responsibility, and, most important, gain an insight into or her talents, needs, and values as they relate to initial career goals. For the new employee, in other words, this is (or should be) a period of reality testing during which his or her initial hopes and goals first confront the reality of organizational life and of the person's talents and needs. Reality shock refers to the rcsults of a period that may occur at the initial career entry when the new employee's high job expectation confronts the reality of a boring or unchallenging job.

- **Provide Challenging Initial Jobs:** Most experts agree that one of the most important things you can do is to provide new employees with challenging first jobs.
- **Provide Realistic Job Previews in Recruiting:** Providing recruits with realistic previews of what to expect once they begin working in the organization can be an effective way of minimizing reality shock and improving their long-term performance. Realistic job previews can boost the survival rate among employees who are hired for relatively complex jobs like management trainee, salesperson, or life insurance agent. They are also used successfully by firms such as Toyota and Saturn to show assembler recruits what their jobs will be like and how demanding the environments will be at these firms.
- **Be Demanding**: The more you expect and the more confident and supportive you are to your new employees, the better they will perform. Therefore, as two experts put it, "Don't assign a new employee to a 'dead wood' undemanding, or unsupportive supervisor. Instead choose specially trained, high-performing, supportive supervisors who can set high standards for new employees during their critical exploratory first year."
- **Provide Periodic Job Rotation and Job Pathing:** The best way new employees can test themselves and crystallize their career anchors is to try out a variety of challenging jobs. By rotating to jobs in various specializations—from financial analysis to production to human resource, for example—the employee gets an opportunity to assess his or her aptitudes and preferences. One extension of this is called job pathing, which means selecting care sequenced job assignments.
- **Do Career-Oriented Performance Appraisals:** Edgar Schein says that supervisors must understand that valid performance appraisal information is in the run more important than protecting the short-term interests of one's immediate subordinates. Therefore, he says, supervisors need concrete information regarding the employee's potential career path.
- **Provide Career Planning Workshops and Career Planning Workbooks:** Employers should also take steps to increase their employees' involvement and expertise in planning and developing their own careers. One option here is to organize periodic career planning workshops. A career planning workshop is defined as "a planned learning event in which participants are expected to be actively involved, completing career planning exercises and inventories and participating in career skills practice sessions". A career planning workbook may be distributed to employees either as part of a workbook or as an independent career planning aid. This is "a printed guide that directs its users through a series of assessment exercise, models, discussions, guidelines, and other information to support career planning."

REVIEW QUESTIONS

1. What is career planning? Discuss the objectives of career planning.
2. Discuss the factors affecting career planning. What are the stages in career development?

3. What are the various tips for individual career development?
4. Distinguish between career planning and human resource planning.
5. What are the steps and tasks in establishing a career development system?
6. Discuss the roles of individual, manager and the organization in individual's career Development.
7. Discuss the benefits and limitations of career planning development.
8. What is career management? What are its elements? Discuss career management guidelines.

CASE STUDY

The Career Planning Programme of Carter Cleaning Company

Career planning has always been a pretty low priority item for Carter Cleaning since "just getting workers to come to work and then keeping them honest is enough of a problem", as Jack likes to say. Yet Jennifer thought to what a career planning programme might involve for Carter. A lot of their employees had been with them for years in dead-end jobs, and she frankly felt a little bad for them: "perhaps we could help them gain a better perspective on what they want to do", she thought. And she definitely believed that the store management group needed better career direction if Carter Cleaning was to develop and grow.

Source: Gary Dessler, Human Resource Management, 1998, Prentice-Hall of India, New Delhi, p. 409.

Questions

1. What would be the advantages to Carter Cleaning of setting up such a career planning programme?
2. Who should participate in the programme? All employees? Selected employees?
3. Describe the programme you would propose for injecting a career planning and development perspective into the Carter Cleaning Centre.

REFERENCES

1. Bernardin, H.J., JEA Russel (1993). "Human Resource Management", McGraw-Hill, New York.
2. Ference, T.P., J A Stoner and E.K. Warrier (1977). "Managing the Career Plateau", Academy of Management Review.
3. Dessler, Gary "Human Resource Management", Prentice-Hall of India, New Delhi, p. 384-387.
4. Gran Haus, J.H (1987). "Career Management", Dryden, Chicago.
5. Gupta Shashi K. and Rosy Joshi, (2007). "Human Resource Management", Kalyani Publishers, New Delhi.
6. John Holland, (1973). "Making Vocational Choices: A Theory of Careers", Prentice-Hall.
7. Pareek Udai and T.V. Rao (1992). "Designing and Managing Human Environment System", Oxford & IBH.
8. Schein, Edgar (1978). Career Dynamics, Addison Wesley Reading Mass.
9. Schein, "Career Dynamics", p. 252-253.
10. Hackman Richard and Lloyd Shuttle, (1977). "Improving Life at Work".
11. Thomas, D.J. (1982). "Reexamining the Career Anchor Model", Personnel, May-June.
12. Subba Rao, P. "Human Resource Management", Himalaya Publication.

CHAPTER

4 Job Analysis and Job Description

CHAPTER'S OUTLINE

- Introduction
- Meaning of Job Analysis
- Nature and Objectives of Job Analysis
- Uses of Job Analysis
- Steps in Job Analysis—The Process
- Methods of Collecting Data for Job Analysis
- Job Description and Job Specification

INTRODUCTION

In the previous chapter on HRP, it was realized that it should be effective and for HRP to be effective, the duties involved and the skills required for performing jobs in an organization must be taken into consideration. This action is possible through the mechanism of Job Analysis. Job Analysis is a recent phenomenon as it was non-existent three decades ago. Nowadays Job Analysis is regarded as a detailed and systematic study of jobs to know the nature and characteristics of the people to be employed on various jobs. In this chapter several aspects of Job Analysis, Job Description and Job Specifications are studied. Job Description and Job Specifications are the immediate by-products of Job Analysis.

MEANING OF JOB ANALYSIS

Job Analysis is a detailed and systematic study of jobs to know the nature and characteristics of people to be employed for each job. It is a process of discovering and identifying the pertinent information relating to the nature of a specific job. It is the determination of the tasks which comprise the job and the skills, knowledge, abilities and attitudes required of the worker for successful performance of the job.

A few definitions of Job Analysis are discussed as under:

According to **Michael J. Jucius,** "*Job analysis refers to the process of studying the operations, duties and organizational aspects of jobs in order to derive specifications or as they are called by some, job descriptions.*"

According to **Edwin B. Flippo,** "*Job analysis is the process of studying and collecting information relating to the operations and responsibilities of a specific job.*"

According to **John A. Shbim**, "*Job analysis is the methodical compilation and study of work data in order to define and characterize each occupation in such a manner so as to distinguish it from all others.*"

According to **Richard Henderson**, "*Job analysis involves the identification and precisely identifying the required tasks, the knowledge and skills necessary for performing them and the conditions under which they must be performed.*"

According to **S.P. Robbins & D.A. De Cenzo**, "*Job analysis is the systematic exploration of activities within a job. It is a basic technical procedure. One that is used to define the duties, responsibilities and accountabilities of a job.*"

The **US Department of Labour** defined job analysis as, "*the process of determining, by observation and study, and reporting pertinent information relating to the nature of a specific job. It is the determination of the tasks which comprise the job and of the skills, knowledge, abilities and responsibilities required of the worker of a successful performance and which differentiate one job from all others.*"

The process of job analysis is essentially one of data collection and then analyzing that data. It provides the analyst with the basic data pertaining to specific jobs in terms of duties, responsibilities, skills, knowledge, degree of risk, etc. This data may be classified as follows:

(a) Job identification.
(b) Nature of the job.
(c) Operations involved in doing the job.
(d) Materials and equipment to be used in doing the job.
(e) Personal attributes required to do the job, e.g., education, training, physical strength, mental capabilities, etc.
(f) Relation with the other jobs.

The information relating to a job which is thus classified, if examined carefully, would suggest that some information relates to the job and some concerns the individual doing the job. The requirements of a job are known as Job Descriptions and the qualities demanded from the job-holder are termed Job Specifications. Thus, job descriptions and job specifications are the immediate by-products of job analysis. The detailed discussion of job description and job specification is given in the later sections of this chapter.

The emphasis in job analysis is upon determining the principal duties of a job.

- The nature and level of skills and aptitudes required to perform these duties, the relation of the job to other jobs in the organization, responsibilities involved, and working conditions.
- Its purpose is to describe and define the distinctions among various jobs.

- Considerable emphasis is placed upon an accurate listing of the human characteristics—physical and mental skills personality traits, and so on needed to adequately perform the job.
- This will facilitate the process of job evaluation which is concerned with determining the relative worth of various jobs.

NATURE AND OBJECTIVES OF JOB ANALYSIS

In order to describe nature and objectives of job analysis, it is essential to know the meaning of job itself.

A job is a bundle of related tasks, for example, vetting the C.V. of a job seeker is a task. Thus, the whole lot of tasks relating to recruitment constitutes job. Job or work involves physical and mental activity that is carried out at a particular place and time, according to instructions in return for money. Work is always rewarded in many terms. Job or work has two broad perspectives, i.e. psychological that relates to individual behaviour and sociological that relates to structural factors such as group dynamics and leadership, affecting people's experience at work.

The nature of job analysis comprises knowing the tool for collecting job related data expressed in terms of two sets of data.

(i) Job Description
(ii) Job Specification

These are the two by-products of job analysis. Figure 4.1 shows the distinction between the two.

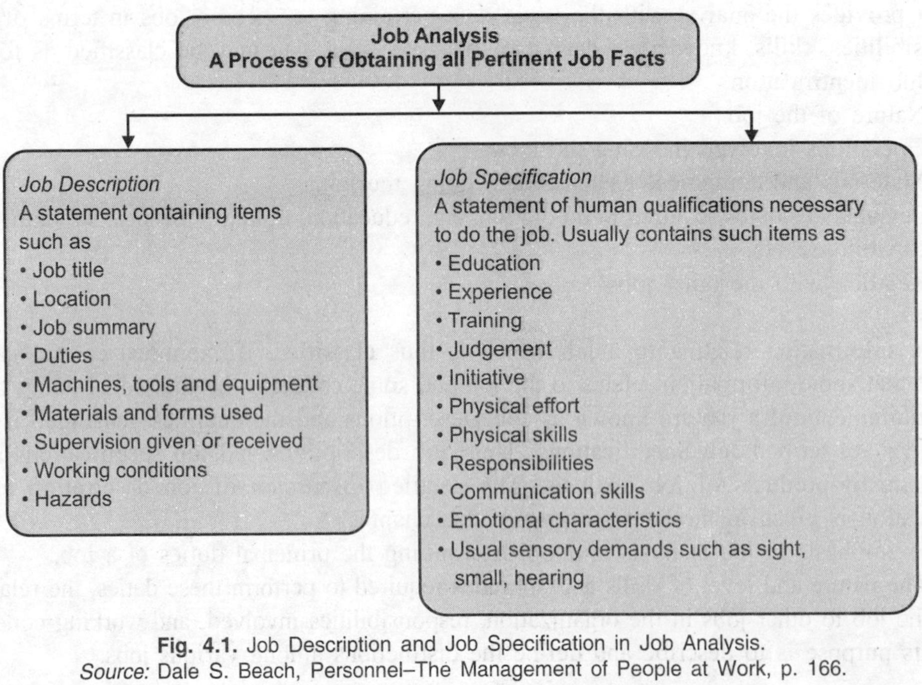

Fig. 4.1. Job Description and Job Specification in Job Analysis.
Source: Dale S. Beach, Personnel–The Management of People at Work, p. 166.

Job description reveals the job demand and job specification, determines abilities required to discharge the tasks. Any mismatch between the two leads to job dissatisfaction leading to low productivity and high absenteeism and turnover. The job analysis has to be consistent with the following objectives:

1. **Work simplification:** A job may be analyzed to simplify the process and methods involved in it. This will mean redesigning the job. Work simplification helps to improve productivity of the personnel.
2. **Establishment of standards of performance:** In order to hire the personnel on a scientific basis, it is very necessary to determine in advance a standard of performance with which applicants can be compared. This standard should establish the minimum acceptable qualities necessary for the effective performance of the job duties and responsibilities. These standards would be established with the help of job analysis only.
3. **Support to other personnel activities:** Job analysis provides support to other personnel activities such as recruitment, selection, training, development, performance appraisal, job evaluation, etc.

USES OF JOB ANALYSIS

Job analysis is useful for management of all personnel activities. The specific uses of job analysis are shown in the Figure 4.2.

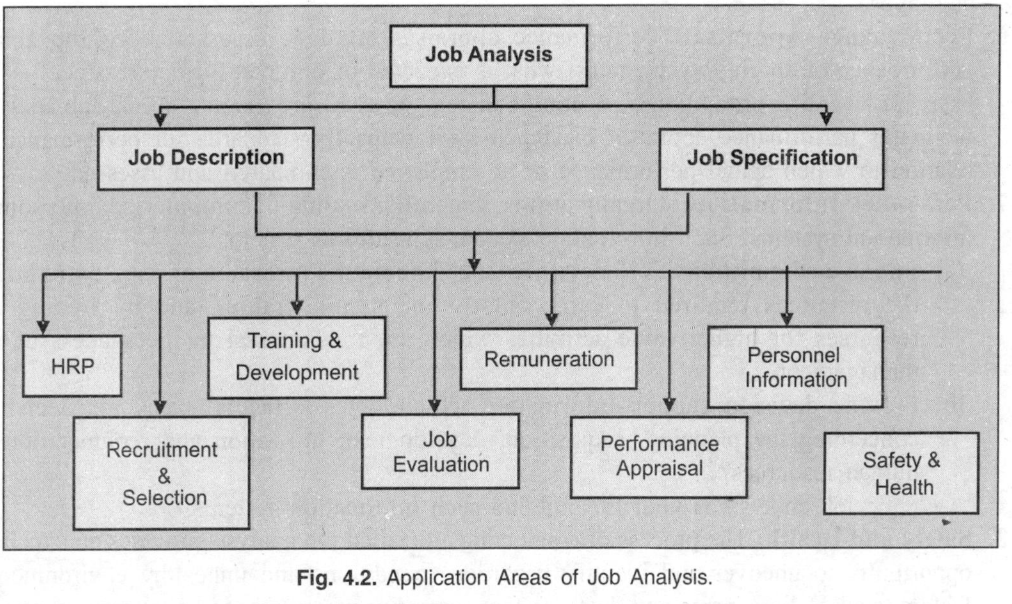

Fig. 4.2. Application Areas of Job Analysis.

1. **Human Resource Planning:** The number and the type of personnel are determined for the jobs which need to be staffed. Job related information is therefore, necessary for HRP.
2. **Recruitment and Selection:** Recruitment needs to be preceded by job analysis. Job analysis helps the HR manager to locate places to obtain employees for openings anticipated

in the future. An understanding of the types of the skills needed and a type of job that may open in the future enables managers to have a better continuity and planning in staffing their organization.

Similarly, selecting a qualified person to fill a job requires knowing clearly the work to be done and the qualifications needed to perform the work satisfactorily. Without a clear and precise understanding of what a job entails, the HR manager cannot effectively select someone to do the job.

The objective of employee hiring is to match the right people with the right jobs. The objective is too difficult to achieve without having adequate job information.

3. **Training and Development:** Job analysis is useful for an HRD manager inasmuch as it helps him/her know what a given job demands from the incumbent in terms of knowledge and skills. Training and development programmes can be designed depending on the job requirements. Selection of trainees is also facilitated by job analysis.
4. **Job Evaluation:** Job evaluation involves determination of relative worth of each job for the purpose of establishing wage and salary differentials. Relative worth is determined mainly on the basis of job description and job specification.
5. **Remuneration:** Job evaluation helps determine wage and salary grades for all jobs. Employees need to be compensated depending on the grades of jobs which they occupy. Remuneration also involves fringe benefits, bonus and other benefits. Clearly, remuneration must be based on the relative worth of each job. Ignorance of this basic principle results in inequitable compensation. A perception of inequity is a sure way of demotivating an employee.
6. **Performance Appraisal:** Performance appraisal involves assessment of the actual performance of an employee against what is expected of him/her. Such assessment is the basis for awarding promotions, effecting transfers, or assessing training needs. Job analysis facilitates performance appraisal inasmuch as it helps fix standards for performance in relation to which actual performance of an employee is compared and assessed.
7. **Personnel Information:** Organizations generally maintain computerized personnel information systems. Such information system is useful as it helps:
   (a) Improve administrative efficiency by speeding up the provision of data, by reducing the resources required to carry out routine administration, and by freeing the resources for higher-value activities which are fundamental to the success of the management.
   (b) Provide decision support-information which gives a factual basis for decisions concerning the planning, acquisition, development, utilization and remuneration of human resources?

   Job analysis is vital for building such information systems.
8. **Safety and Health:** The process of conducting a detailed job analysis provides an excellent opportunity to uncover and identify hazardous conditions and unhealthy environmental factors (such as heat, noise and dust), so that corrective measures can be taken to minimize and avoid the possibility of human injuries.

STEPS IN JOB ANALYSIS—THE PROCESS

Job analysis process is divided into six basic steps. These steps are shown in Figure 4.3.

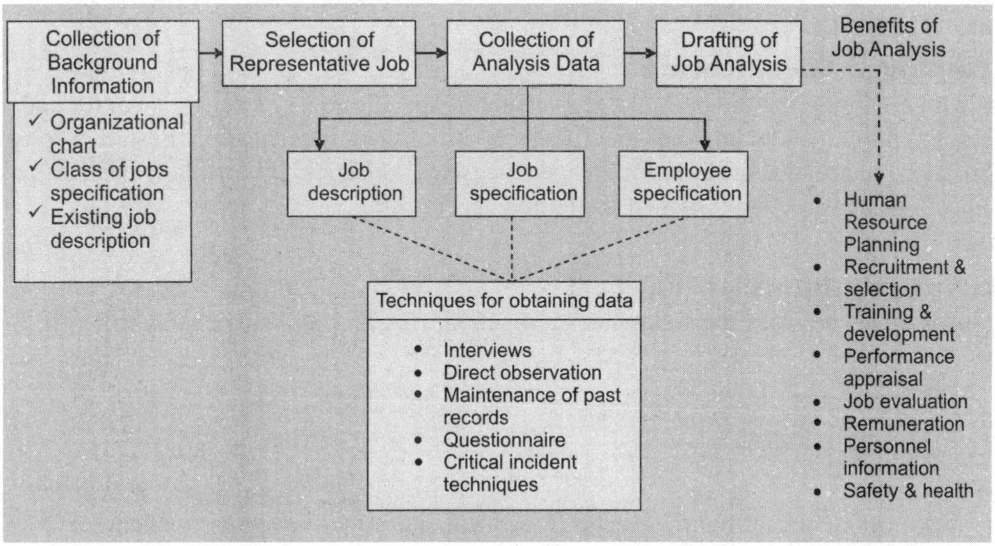

Fig. 4.3. Job Analysis Process.
Source: Adapted from P. Subba Rao, "Human Resource Management", p. 80.

1. Collection of Background Information

Background information consists of:

- Organizational charts, which show the relationship of the job with other jobs in the organization.
- Job class specifications, that describes the general requirements of the class of job to which this particular job belongs.
- Existing job descriptions, that provides a good starting point for job analysis.

2. Selection of Representative Jobs

It would be too difficult and time-consuming to analyze the jobs. So, the job analyst has to select some of the representative positions in order to analyze them.

3. Collection of Job Analysis Data

This step involves actually analyzing a job by collecting data on the features of the job, required employee behaviour and human requirements.

4. Job Description

This step involves describing or developing the contents of the job in terms of functions, duties, responsibilities, operations, etc.

5. Job Specification

The fifth step involves conversion of the job description statements into job specification. Job specification or job requirements describe the personal qualities, traits, skills, knowledge and background necessary for getting the job done.

6. Employee Specification

This is the final step that involves the conversion of specifications of human qualities under job specification into an employee specification. Employee specification describes physical qualification, educational qualifications, experience, etc., which specify that these qualities possess the minimum human qualities listed in the job specification.

Job Analysis Information

The job analysis provides the following information; (this has already been specified in Figure 4.3)

- Job title
- Locating the job
- Job summary
- Duties
- Machines, tools and requirements
- Materials and forms used
- Supervision given and received
- Working conditions and
- Hazards

This information reveals, what is to be done, how it is done and why? This is all job description information. The job specification information relates to the following human qualifications which are necessary to do the job:

- Education
- Experience
- Training
- Judgement
- Initiative
- Physical efforts
- Physical skills
- Communication skills
- Responsibilities
- Emotional characteristics
- Unusual sensory demands right smell, hearing, etc.

Leap and Crino, in their book HRM at page 127, brings out the elements to be gathered from a given job, Table 4.1.

Table 4.1: Types of Job Analysis Information.

I. Work Activities

A. Description of work activities (tasks)
   1. How is a task performed?
   2. Why is a task performed?
   3. When is a task performed?
   B. Interface with other jobs and equipment

C. Procedures used

D. Behaviours required on the jobs

E. Physical movements and demands of the jobs

II. Machines, Tools, Equipment and Work Aids Used

A. List of machines, tools etc. used

B. Materials processed with items listed in II-A

C. Products made with items listed in II-A

D. Services rendered with items listed in II-A

III. Job Context

A. Physical working conditions
   1. Exposure to heat, dust, toxic substances
   2. Indoor versus outdoor environment

B. Organizational context

C. Social context

D. Work schedule

E. Incentives (financial and non-financial)

IV. Personal Requirements

A. Specific skills

B. Specific education and training

C. Work experience

D. Physical characteristics

E. Aptitudes

Sources of Job Analysis Information

The most direct source of information about a job is the job holder. Still a number of other human and non-human sources are available, Table 4.2 shows these sources.

Table 4.2: Sources of Job Data.

Non-human Sources	Human Sources
Existing job descriptions and specifications	Job analysts
Equipment maintenance records	Job incumbents
Equipment design blueprints	Supervisors
Architectural blueprints of work area	Job experts
Films of employees working	
Training manuals and other job training materials	
Popular literature such as magazines and newspapers	

Source: Cynthia D. Fisher, et al., "Human Resource Management", Houghton Miffin, 1997, p. 140.

METHODS OF COLLECTING DATA FOR JOB ANALYSIS

The methods or techniques of collecting job related data are:

- Observation Method
- Interviews
- Questionnaire
- Checklists
- Technical Conferences
- Diary

Figure 4.4 shows these methods.

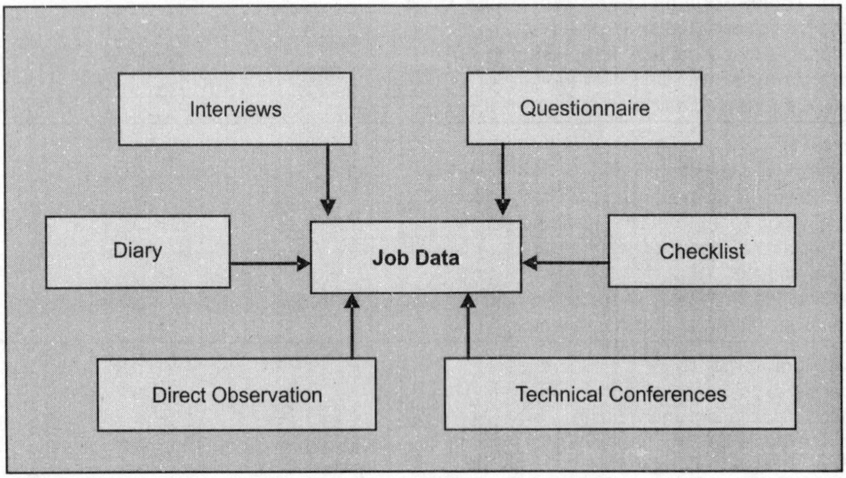

Fig. 4.4. Methods/Techniques of Collecting Job Data.

1. Direct Observation

Direct observation is particularly useful in jobs that consist primarily of observable physical activity like draftsman, mechanics, etc. One approach to this method is observing the worker on the job during a complete work cycle. In this process, notes should be taken regarding all the job activities observed. The next stage is interviewing, the worker and getting the additional information from him. The other approach is to observe and interview simultaneously.

2. Interviews

There are two types of interviews which can be used for collection of data for job analysis, viz., individual interviews (with groups of employees who do the same job) and supervisory interviews (with one or more supervisors who are thoroughly knowledgeable about the job being analyzed). The interviewer has to collect accurate and complete data and information by creating favourable attitude among employees and supervisors. There are several basic attitudes and techniques that will serve to secure maximum of accurate and complete information. These attitudes and techniques will also help to reduce the natural suspicion of both the employee and the supervisor towards the interviewer. Important among them are:

- The interviewer should introduce himself so that the workers know him, who he is, and why he is there?

- He has to show a sincere interest in the worker and the job being analyzed.
- He should not try to tell the employee how to do the job.
- He has to try to talk to the employees and supervisors in their own language.
- He should not confuse the work with the worker.
- He has to do a complete job study within the objectives of the programme.
- He has to verify the job information obtained by consulting the other employees doing the same job.

3. Questionnaire

Job holders fill in the given structured questionnaire, which are then approved by their supervisors. The filled-in questionnaires offer enough data on jobs. Standard questionnaires are available or these may be prepared for the purpose by the analysts. Standard or prepared, questionnaires should contain the following basic information:

1. The job title of the job holder.
2. The job title of the job holder's manager or supervisor.
3. The job titles and numbers of the staff reporting to the job holder (best recorded by means of an organization chart).
4. A brief description (one or two sentences) of the overall role or purpose of the job.
5. A list of the main tasks or duties that the job holder has to carry out as appropriate, these should specify the resources controlled, the equipment used, the contracts made and the frequency with which the tasks are carried out.

These basic details can be supplemented by questions designed to elicit from the job holder some information about the level of his/her responsibilities and the demand made upon him/her by the job. Such questions are difficult to phrase and answer in a meaningful way. The replies may be too vague or misleading and usually have to be checked with the job holder's supervisor. But these at least give the job holder an opportunity to express his/her feelings about the job and they can provide useful leads for further clarifications. These questions can cover such aspects of the job as:

1. The amount of supervision received and the degree of discretion allowed in making decisions;
2. The typical problems to be solved and the amount of guidance available while solving the problems;
3. The relative difficulty of the tasks to be performed; and
4. The qualifications and skills required to carry out the work.

The questionnaire method has its own advantages and limitations. The major advantage of the questionnaire method is that information on a large number of jobs can be collected in a relatively short period of time. But some follow-up observations and discussions are necessary to clarify inadequately filled-in questionnaires and interpretation problems. Further, the questionnaire method helps save time and the staff required to carry out the programme. Finally, all the job holders participate in the method unlike in an interview where one or two workers only would participate.

The accuracy of the information obtained through the questionnaire leaves much to be desired. Job analysis work requires specialized knowledge and training. The average employee, although, knows best what his/her duties are, he/she is not trained to identify the essential aspects of his/her work and often cannot express the information in a meaningful and clear fashion. To depend exclusively upon questionnaires as the source of job information is bound to create some errors in the programme.

4. Checklists

A checklist is similar to a questionnaire, but the response sheet contains fewer subjective judgements and tends to be either yes-or-no variety. Checklist can cover as many as 100 activities and job holders tick only those tasks that are included. Preparation of a checklist is a challenging job. The specialists who prepare the list must collect all relevant information about the job concerned. Such information can be obtained by asking supervisors, industrial engineers, and others familiar with the work. When a checklist has been prepared for a job, it is sent to the job holder. The job holder is asked to check all the listed tasks that he/she performs and indicate the amount of time spent on each task as well as the training and experience required to be proficient in each task. He/she may also be asked to write any additional tasks he/she performs which is not stated in the checklist. The checklist, thus answered, will be the basis for tabulating job-related data.

One advantage of the checklist method is that it is useful in large firms that have a large number of people assigned to one particular job. Also, this technique is amenable tabulation and recording on electronic data-processing equipment. The technique, however, is costly and, hence, not suitable for small firms.

5. Technical Conference Method

In this method, services supervisors who possess extensive knowledge about a job are used. It is from these experts that details about the job are obtained. The analyst initiates discussion which provides details about jobs.

6. Diary Method

This method requires the job holders to record in detail their activities each day. If done faithfully, this technique is accurate and eliminates errors caused by memory lapses, the job holder makes while answering questionnaires and checklists. This method, however, is time consuming because the recording of tasks may have to be done over a number of days. It also engages considerable time of a production worker. No wonder, the diary method is not much in practice.

The methods described above are not to be viewed as mutually exclusive. None of these is universally superior. The best results can be obtained by a combination of these methods.

JOB DESCRIPTION AND JOB SPECIFICATION

Job description and job specification are the two by-products of job analysis. Various aspects of these two are discussed as under:

(A) Job Description

A job description is an organized factual statement of job contents in the form of duties and responsibilities of a specific job. The preparation of description is necessary before a vacancy is advertised. It tells in brief nature and type of a job. In other words, it emphasizes the job requirement as the title indicates, the document is descriptive in nature and constitutes a record of job facts in an organized way.

Job description document discloses what is to be done, how it is to be done and why it is to be done. It must disclose at least the facts relating to the three points in detail. The data to be recorded on the job description document must be objectively determined by the job analyst. To make this document more meaningful, the personnel or human resource department may invite descriptions from workers, foremen and supervisors.

Definitions

According to **Edwin B. Flippo**, "*The first and immediate product of job analysis is job description. As its title indicates this document is basically descriptive in nature and constitutes a record of existing and pertinent job facts.*"

In the words of **Pigors and Myres**, "*Job description is a pertinent picture of the organizational relationships, responsibilities and specific duties that constitute a given job or position. It defines a scope of responsibility and continuing work assignment that are sufficiently different from that of other jobs to warrant a specific title*".

The contents of job description have been discussed below:

(i) **Job Title**. It is desirable that the job title should be short, definite suggestive of the nature of the job. Commerce and industry nomenclature wherever applicable, should always be considered in phrasing meaningful titles.

(ii) **Job Location.** It is necessary to give the location of the job. By location we mean the name of the department where the job under consideration exists.

(iii) **Job Summary.** A short paragraph succinctly summarizing the tasks performed by the employee is helpful for subsequent convenient identification of the job.

(iv) **Duties to be performed.** Each task performed should be written and estimate made of the percentage of the time that is devoted to performance of each task. This is the most important phase of the job description and should be carefully prepared.

(v) **Materials and Forms used:** The tools, machines, equipment, materials used in the performance of the job should also be included in the job description. This is necessary since these items tend to indicate the nature and complexity of the job.

(vi) **Relation to other jobs**. Clear-cut relation of the job consideration with other jobs in the organization will help to understand nature of the job well.

(vii) **Supervision given or received.** There are certain jobs, particularly unskilled jobs, which require intensive supervision, while other jobs require less supervision, because people manning these positions are more committed to the achievement of organisation's goals. Nature of supervision must be given in the job description.

(viii) **Working Environment.** The working conditions and other characteristics of the physical surroundings within the working area should be described to help in subsequent interpretation of job evaluation.

(ix) **Hazards.** The various hazards involved in the job are also described in job description.

Table 4.3: Job Description Form of a Supervisor.

Job Title	Job	Supervisor
Factor	Elements	Supervisor's Responsibility
(i) Manning	(a) Requisition for instructors	Act
	(b) Preparation of advertisements	Recommended
	(c) Interviewing candidates for instructor jobs–accept/reject	Act
	(d) Assessment of instructors performance/merit for pay purposes	Recommended
	(e) Discharging for misconduct	Recommended
	(f) Supervision of training centre instruction and ensuring that established performance standards are met	Act
	(g) Supervision of clerical and secretarial duties of training centre secretary	Act
(ii) Equipment	(a) Developing a system for safeguarding and distributing tools	Act
	(b) Operating a system for safeguarding and distributing tools	Delegate
	(c) Authorizing within the budget limitations the purchase of small items. Act of capital equipment, i.e., tools	Act
	(d) Purchase of major items, i.e., machines	Recommended
(iii) Safety	(a) Ensuring compliance with training centre safety regulations	Act
	(b) Preparation of accident reports	Act and delegate
	(c) Requisition and issue of protective clothing	Act
	(d) Ensuring the use of protective clothing.	Act and delegate
(iv) Cost of Control	(a) Preparation of annual cost budget for training centre	Prepare and recommend
	(b) Submission of reports on reason for monthly budget variances to superiors	Act
(v) Inspection	Receipt of inspection reports on below standard work	Advise instructors
(vi) Apprentice Trainees	(a) Instruction of apprentices in training school	Delegate
	(b) Placement of apprentices in appropriate course	Act
	(c) Examination of reports on apprentices and allocation of apprentices today; release for subsequent sessions	Act
	(d) Assessment from apprentice feedback of the value of specific course	Act
	(e) Selection of alternative courses if the existing ones are inadequate	Recommended
	(f) Preparation of documentation for rates for age rewards	Act
	(g) Authorization of rate for age rewards	Act
	(h) Assessment from the reports of instructor and foreman for additional annual merit awards	Recommended act with appropriate line supervisor
	(i) Placement of apprentices on completion of training	Act
	(j) Raising and processing documentation for those apprentices who resign	Act
	(k) Discharge of apprentices failing to meet 80% performance level	Recommended
	(l) Maintenance of apprentice records.	Delegate
	(m) Preparation of work rotation for apprentices	Act

Source: C.B. Mamoria, Personnel Management, pp. 194-195.

Sources of Job Description

The information necessary for the preparation of job descriptions can be obtained in one or more of the following ways:

(i) By observation of job being performed.
(ii) By discussion with the supervisor of the job.
(iii) By requesting the supervisor of the job to fill in a questionnaire describing the job.
(iv) By discussion with some of the employees working on the job.
(v) By requesting some of the employees working on the job to fill in the questionnaire describing the job.

The most practical method of getting information is through personal observation of the work performed, along with discussion with the supervisor of the job. It can also be prepared in the workshop itself. Questionnaire method is time-consuming and is recommended only in case of those jobs where the job contents are not completely known to the supervisor.

Characteristics of Good Job Description

A good job description must possess the following characteristics:

1. It should be kept up-to-date. Necessary adjustments and amendments should be made from time to time.
2. Job title should be short, definite and suggestive so as to indicate the nature of the work.
3. It should describe insufficient detail each of the duties and responsibilities.
4. Job specifications should clearly be mentioned.
5. It should be descriptive but short and concise.
6. Statement of opinion should be avoided.
7. Examples of work performed may be quoted.
8. It should ensure that a new employee can understand the job by reading the description.
9. All employees must know the contents of job description.

In order to make it up-to-date, a regular survey should be made in the organization and necessary changes should be incorporated in the existing job description.

(B) Job Specification

Job specification is also an important by-product of job analysis. Job specification is a statement of the minimum acceptable human qualities required for the proper performance of a job.

According to **Edwin B. Flippo,** "*A job specification is a statement of minimum acceptable human qualities necessary to perform a job properly.*"

According to **Dale Yoder,** "*The job specification, as such a summary properly described is thus, a specialized job description, emphasizing personnel requirement and designed especially to facilitate selection and placement.*"

It is clear from the above definitions that job specification is a statement of summary of personnel requirements for a job. It may also be called "standard of personnel for the selection".

Characteristics of Good Job Specification Information

A job specification should include:

(i) **Physical Characteristics** such as height, weight, chest, vision, hearing, health, age, voice, poise, etc.

(ii) **Psychological and Social Characteristics** such as emotional stability, flexibility, decision-making ability, analytical view, mental ability, pleasing manners, initiative, conversational ability, etc.

(iii) **Mental Characteristics** such as general intelligence, memory, judgement, ability to concentrate, foresight, etc.

(iv) **Personal Characteristics** such as sex, education, family background, and job experience, hobbies, extracurricular activities, etc.

All these characteristics must be classified into three categories:

(a) Essential attributes which a person must possess.

(b) Desirable attributes which a person ought to possess.

(c) Contraindicators which will become a handicap to successful job performance.

Preparation of Job Specifications

The job specifications should define the minimum acceptable standard for employment and performance on the job. Exceptional functions, which are of non-routine nature, should not be allowed to influence the overall description. Specifications should not be coloured by the personalities of special skills exhibited by particular people from whom job information may have been obtained.

Job specifications are generally developed with the cooperation of the personnel department and various supervisors throughout the organization. The personnel manager coordinates the writing of job descriptions and specifications. So he should see that useful information regarding the preparation of job descriptions and specifications is obtained by studying actual practice in the different jobs. There is no doubt that because of the supervisor's knowledge of the job, the personnel department will give a great deal of weightage to his suggestions while preparing job specifications, but it should also ensure that specifications are realistic, fair and designed to assist the organization in attaining its goals.

Accountability for Job Specifications: As an outgrowth of job descriptions, job specifications are typically developed with the cooperation of the personnel department and various supervisors throughout the organization. The personnel department coordinates the writing of job descriptions and job specifications and secures agreement on qualifications desired.

Because of the supervisor's knowledge of the job, the personnel manager will give a great deal of weightage to the suggestions of a supervisor concerning needed qualifications, but the personnel manager will like to make certain that specifications are realistic, fair, and designed to assist the organization in attaining its goals.

JOB SPECIFICATION VS. JOB DESCRIPTION

In contrast to job description, job specification is a measuring rod of a personnel and it combines qualities required for acceptable performance of a particular job like formal education, experience, psychological attitude, physical measurement, etc. The qualities as assessed and recorded on job specification document involve an element of subjectivity. Proper assessment of these qualities depends upon the value judgements of a number of people such as job analysis, job holder and his supervisor.

In fact, job specification includes two sections—job identification and human requirements. The exact list of human requirements will vary from firm to firm and according to the uses to which job specification is to be put.

REVIEW QUESTIONS

1. What do you understand by Job Analysis? Discuss its importance in the management of human resources?
2. Define Job Analysis. Discuss the reasons for growing interest in job analysis in recent times. State the uses of Job Analysis.
3. What is Job Analysis? What steps are involved in the process of job analysis?
4. What are the by-products of Job Analysis? Discuss the methods of collecting data for job analysis.
5. What is Job Description? How is it prepared? Explain with the help of a specimen.
6. Define Job Specification. How is it different from Job Description?
7. Trace out the role of job analysis in the human resource management system. How will you proceed for gathering data for job analysis?
8. Write notes on the following :
   a) Basic characteristics of a good Job Description
   b) Methods of collecting job information/data
9. What are the relative advantages of interview and questionnaire methods in collecting data for job analysis?
10. "Job analysis is the most basic personnel management function." Discuss.
11. Are job descriptions really necessary? What would happen if a company decides not to use any job description?

CASE STUDY

The Job Description Carter Cleaning Company of USA

Based on her review of the stores, Jennifer concluded that one of the first matters was to develop job descriptions for her store managers.

As Jennifer tells it, her lessons regarding job descriptions in her basic management and HR management courses were insufficient to fully convince her of the pivotal role job descriptions played in the smooth functioning of an enterprise. Many times during her first few weeks on the job, Jennifer found herself asking one of her store managers why he was violating what she knew to be recommended company policies and procedures. Repeatedly the answers were either "Because I didn't know it was my job" or "Because I didn't know that was the way we were supposed to do it." Jennifer knew that a job description, along with a set of standards and procedures that specified what was to be done and how to do it, would go a long way towards alleviating this problem.

In general, the store manager is responsible for directing all store activities in such a way that quality work is produced, customer relations and sales are maximized, and profitability is maintained through effective control of labour, supply, and energy costs. In accomplishing that general aim, a specific store manager's duties and responsibilities include quality control, store appearance and cleanliness, customer relations, bookkeeping and cash management, cost control and productivity, damage control, pricing, inventory control, spotting and cleaning, machine maintenance, employee safety, hazardous waste removal, human resource administration, and pest control.

The questions that Jennifer had to address follow.

Source: Gary Dessler, Human Resource Management, Prentice-Hall of India, New Delhi, p. 114.

Questions

1. What should be the format and final form of the store manager's job description?
2. Was it practical to specify standards and procedures in the body of the job description, or should these be kept separately?
3. How should Jennifer go about collecting the information required for the standards, procedures, and job description?

REFERENCES

1. Aswathappa, K. (2008). "Human Resource Management", Tata McGraw-Hill Publishing Company Ltd., New Delhi, pp. 115-118.
2. Dale S. Beach, (1980). "Personnel Management of People of Work", MacMillan, New York, pp. 169-170.
3. Flippo Edward, B. (1984). "Personnel Management", Tata McGraw-Hill, New York.
4. Dessler, Gary (1998). "Human Resource Management", Prentice-Hall of India Pvt. Ltd., New Delhi, pp. 83-87.
5. Armstrong, Michael (1988). "A Handbook of Personnel Management Practices", Kogan Paze Ltd., London, pp. 316.
6. Mamoria, C.B. (2008). "Personnel Management", Himalaya Publishing House, New Delhi.
7. Subba Rao, P. (2007). "Human Resource Management and Industrial Relations", Himalaya Publishing House, New Delhi, pp. 79-81.
8. Terry L. Leap and Michael D. Crino, (1990). "Personnel/Human Resource Management", MacMillan, New York, pp. 133-134.
9. Westher William, B. and Keith Davis, (1993). "Human Resource and Personnel Management", Tata McGraw-Hill, New York.

CHAPTER

5

Recruitment and Selection

CHAPTER'S OUTLINE

INTRODUCTION

Human resource planning and job analysis are used to determine the number and type of people required by a firm and specifies tasks and duties of jobs and qualifications of job-holders. This implies that HRP and job analysis determine the recruitment needs as is shown in Figure 5.1.

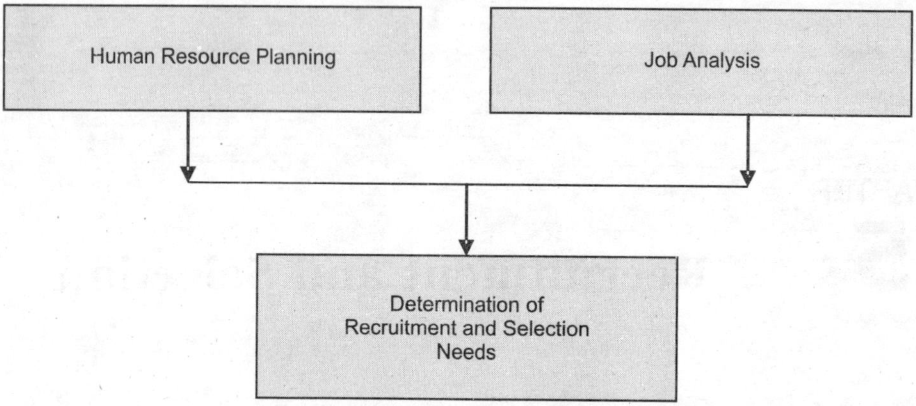

Fig. 5.1. Recruitment and Selection Needs.

Once the recruitment and selection needs are determined, the next logical step is the hiring process. Hiring involves two main activities:

1. Recruitment
2. Selection

The process of hiring is an ongoing process as employees leave the organization due to their retirement, change to better jobs or an account of death, etc. The hiring function stops only when the company or the firm ceases to exist. In this chapter, first we shall discuss the recruitment and selection process in general in brief and then examine various aspects of recruitment and selection separately.

THE STEPS IN RECRUITMENT AND SELECTION PROCESS—A GENERAL FRAMEWORK

The recruitment and selection process is a series of hurdles aimed at selecting the best candidate for the job. Figure 5.2 demonstrates that there are sequential steps in recruitment and selection. The steps are:

(i) Doing employment planning and forecasting to determine the duties of the positions to be filled.
(ii) Building a pool of candidates for these jobs by recruiting internal or external candidates.
(iii) Having the applicants fill out application forms and perhaps undergo an initial screening interview.
(iv) Utilizing various selection techniques such as tests, background investigations, and physical exams to identify viable job candidates.
(v) Sending to the supervisor responsible for the job one or more viable job candidates.
(vi) Having the candidate(s) go through one or more selection interviews with the supervisor and other relevant parties for the purpose of finally determining to which candidate(s) an offer should be made.

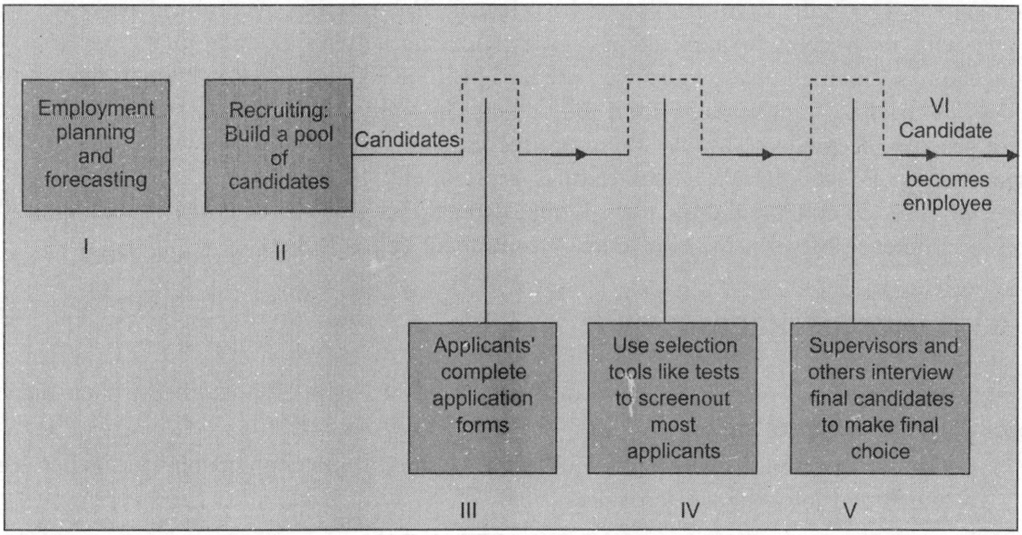

Fig. 5.2. Steps in Recruitment and Selection Process.

MEANING OF RECRUITMENT

Recruitment is a linkage activity bringing together those with jobs and those seeking jobs. Recruitment is the process of searching for prospective employees and stimulating them to apply for jobs in the organization. When more persons apply for jobs then there will be a scope for recruiting better persons. The job seekers too, on the other hand, are in search of organizations offering them employment.

Definitions

According to **Yoder,** "*Recruitment is a process to discover the sources of manpower to meet the requirements of the staffing schedule and to employ effective measures for attracting that manpower in adequate numbers to facilitate effective selection of an efficient working force.*"

In the words of **C.B. Mamoria,** "*Recruiting is the discovering of potential applicants for actual or anticipated organizational vacancies.*"

According to **Flippo,** "*Recruitment is the process of searching for prospective employees and stimulating and encouraging them to apply for jobs in an organization.*"

According to **Dale S. Beach,** "*Recruitment is the development and maintenance of adequate manpower resources. It involves the creation of a pool of available labour upon whom the organization can depend when it needs additional employees.*"

NATURE OF RECRUITMENT

Recruitment refers to the process of receipt of applications from job-seekers. In simple terms, recruitment is understood as the process of searching for and obtaining applications for jobs, from among whom, the right people can be selected. Theoretically, recruitment process is said to end with the receipt of applications, in practice the activity extends to the screening of applications so as to eliminate those who are not qualified for the job. Recruitment refers to the process of receipt of applications from job-seekers. In reality, the term is used to describe the entire process of employee hiring. There are recruitment boards for railways, banks and other organizations. B schools talk about campus recruitment. In newspapers too, recruitment is frequently used to connote the process of employment. But students of HRM should know that there is difference between the two terms—recruitment and selection.

IMPORTANCE OF RECRUITMENT

The general purpose of recruitment is to provide a pool of potentially qualified job candidates. Specifically the purposes are to:

(1) Determine the present and future requirements of the firm in conjunction with its personnel planning and job analysis activities.
(2) Increase the pool of job candidates at minimum cost.
(3) Help increase the success rate of the selection process by reducing the number of visibly underqualified or overqualified job applicants.
(4) Help reduce the probability that job applicants, once recruited and selected, will leave the organization only after a short period of time.
(5) Meet the organization's legal and social obligations regarding the composition of its workforce.
(6) Begin identifying and preparing potential job applicants who will be appropriate candidates.
(7) Increase organizational and individual effectiveness in the short term and long term.
(8) Evaluate the effectiveness of various recruiting techniques and sources for all types of job applicants.

PROCESS OF RECRUITMENT

The recruitment process comprises five interrelated stages.

(1) Recruitment Planning
(2) Strategy Development
(3) Searching
(4) Screening
(5) Evaluation and Control

According to **Herbert G. Heneman,** "*The ideal recruitment programme is the one that attracts a relatively larger number of qualified applicants who will survive the screening process and accept positions with the organization, when offered.*"

The recruitment process is shown in Figure 5.3.

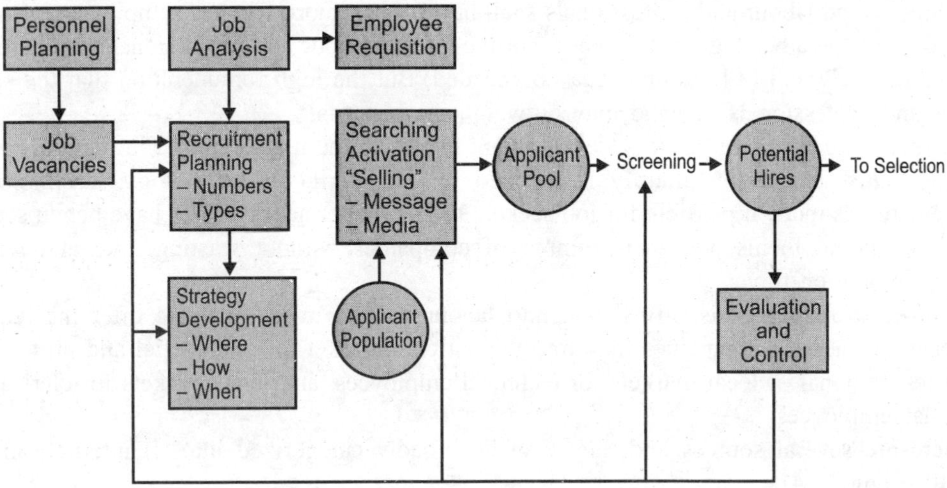

Fig. 5.3. Recruitment Process.
Source: Herbert G. Heneman III, et al., Personnel/Human Resource Management, p. 226.

1. Recruitment Planning

The first stage in the recruitment process is recruitment planning. It involves the translation of likely job vacancies and information about the nature of these jobs into a set of objectives or targets that specify the

- number, and
- type of applicants to be contacted.

Organizations, nearly always, plan to attract more applicants than they will hire. Some of those contacted will be uninterested, unqualified, or both. Each time a recruitment programme is contemplated; one task is to estimate the number of applicants necessary to fill all vacancies with qualified people. The type of people depends on the tasks and responsibilities involved and the qualifications and experience expected. These details are available through job description and job specification.

2. Strategy Development

Once it is known how many and what type of recruits are required, following serious consideration needs to be given in strategy development to

- 'make' or 'buy' employees;
- technological sophistication of recruitment and selection devices;
- geographical distribution of labour markets comprising job-seekers;
- sources of recruitment; and
- sequencing the activities in the recruitment process.

Firms must decide whether to hire less skilled employees and invest on training and education programmes, or they can hire skilled labour and professionals. Essentially, this is the 'make' (hire less skilled workers) or 'buy' (hire skilled workers and professionals) decision. Organizations which hire skilled labour and professionals shall have to pay more for these employees. 'Buying' employees has the advantage in the sense that the skilled labour and professionals can begin the work immediately and little training may be needed. But the high remuneration that the skilled workers and professionals demand may outweigh the benefits.

The second decision in strategy development relates to the methods used in recruitment and selection. This decision is mainly influenced by the available technology. Technological advancement has made it possible for job-seekers to gain better access. They have begun sending video tapes about themselves to a number of companies without wasting time and without spending money on travel.

In order to reduce costs, firms look into labour markets most likely to offer the required job-seekers. Generally, companies look into the national market for managerial and professional employees, regional or local markets for technical employees, and local markets for clerical and blue-collar employees.

There are several sources and they may be broadly categorized into (i) internal, and (ii) external. (Figure 5.4)

3. Searching

Once a recruiting plan and strategy are worked out, the search process can begin. Search involves two steps-(i) source activation, and (ii) selling.

Typically, sources and search methods are activated by the issuance of an employee requisition. This means that no actual recruiting takes place until line managers have verified that a vacancy does exist or will exist. If the firm has planned well and done a good job of developing its sources and search methods, activation soon results in a flood of applications and/or resumes. The applications received must be screened. Those who pass have to be contacted and invited for interview. Unsuccessful applicants must be sent letters of regret.

A second issue to be addressed in the searching process concerns communications. Here, organizations walk a tightrope. On one hand, they want to do whatever they can to attract desirable applicants. On the other hand, they must resist the temptation of overselling their virtues. In selling the company, both the message and the media deserve attention. Message refers to the employment advertisement. With regard to media, it may be stated that effectiveness of any recruiting message depends on the media. Media are several—some have low credibility, (employment exchanges, for example) while others enjoy high credibility (advertisements in business magazines, for example). Selection of medium or media needs to be done with a lot of care.

4. Screening

Screening of applications can be regarded as an integral part of the recruiting process, though many view, i.e.; as the first step in the selection process. Even the definition on recruitment, we quoted in the beginning of this chapter, excludes screening from its scope. However, we have included screening in recruitment for valid reasons. The selection process will begin after the applications have been scrutinized and shortlisted. Hiring of professors in a university is a typical situation. Applications received in response to advertisements are screened and only eligible applicants are called for an interview. Interview is conducted by selection committee comprising the Vice-Chancellor, Registrar and subject experts. Here, the recruitment process extends upto screening the applications. The selection process commences only later.

The purpose of screening is to remove from the recruitment process, those applicants who are visibly unqualified for the job. Effective screening can save a great deal of time and money. Care must be exercised, however, to assure that potentially good employees are not lost and that women and minorities receive full and fair consideration and are not rejected without justification.

In screening, clear job specifications are invaluable. It is both a good practice and a legal necessity that applicants' qualifications be judged on the basis of their knowledge, skills, abilities and interests required to do the job.

The techniques used to screen applicants vary depending on the candidate sources and the recruiting methods used. Interviews and application blanks may be used to screen walk-ins. Campus recruiters and agency representatives use interviews and resumes. Reference checks are also useful in screening.

5. Evaluation and Control

Evaluation and control is necessary as considerable costs are incurred in the recruitment process. The costs generally incurred are:

1. Salaries for recruiters.
2. Management and professional time spent on preparing job description, job specifications, advertisements, agency liaison, and so forth.
3. Cost of advertisements or other recruitment methods, that is, agency fees.
4. Cost of producing supporting literature.
5. Recruitment overheads and administrative expenses.
6. Costs of overtime and outsourcing while the vacancies remain unfilled.
7. Cost of recruiting suitable candidates for the selection process.

Questions should always be asked as to whether the recruitment methods used are valid and whether the recruitment process itself is effective.

The recruitment process has the objective of searching for and obtaining applications from job-seekers in sufficient numbers and quality. Keeping this objective in mind, the evaluation might include:

- Return rate of applications sent out.
- Number of suitable candidates for selection.
- Retention and performance of the candidates selected.
- Cost of the recruitment process.
- Time lapsed data.
- Comments on image projected.

The evaluation of recruitment methods might include:

- Number of initial enquiries received which resulted in completed application forms.
- Number of candidates at various stages of the recruitment and selection process, especially those shortlisted.
- Number of candidates recruited.

• Number of candidates retained in the organization after six months.

SOURCES OF RECRUITMENT

The sources of recruitment are broadly divided into two main sources:

I. Internal Sources
II. External Sources

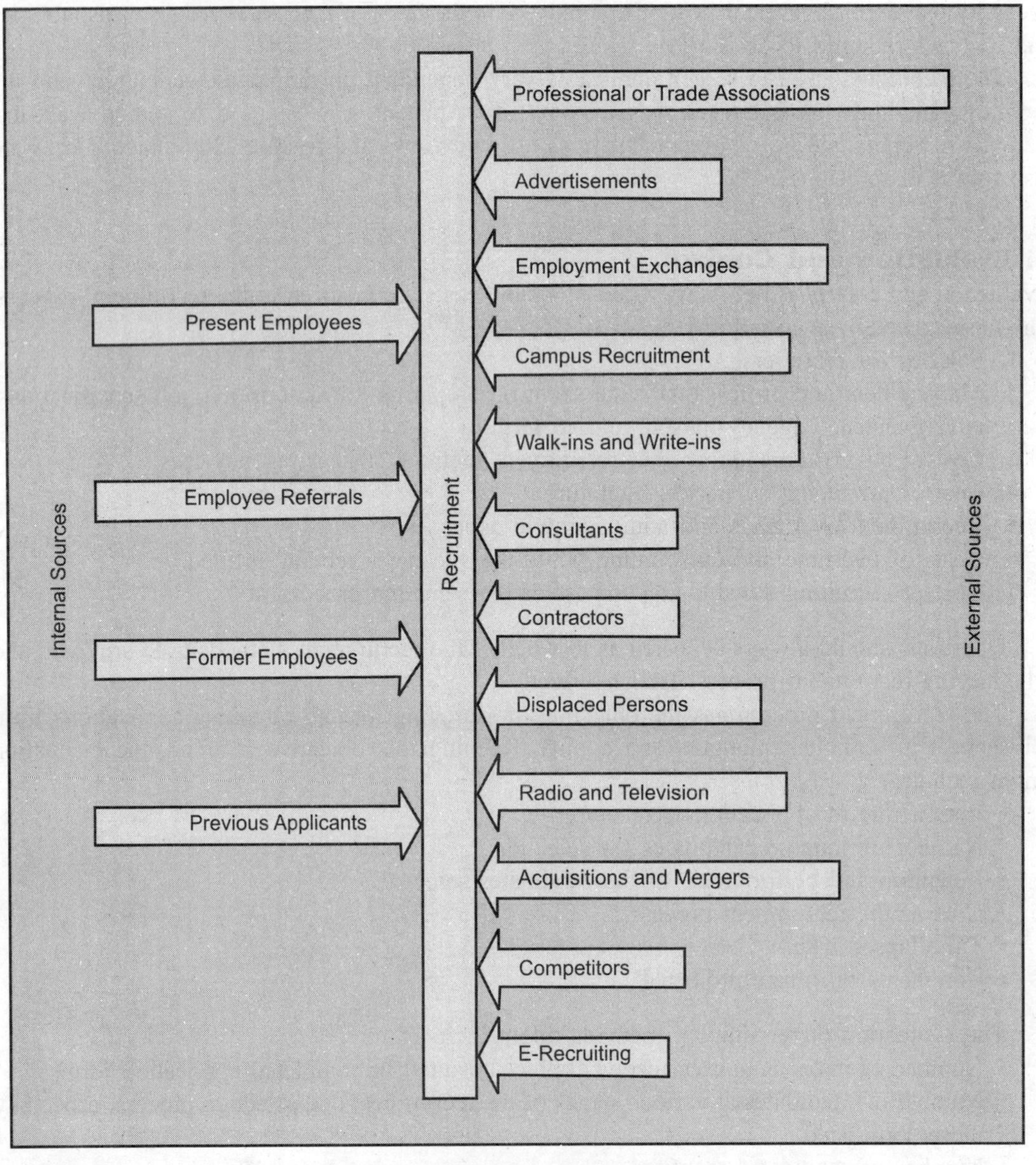

Fig. 5.4. Sources of Recruitment.

I. Internal Sources: Internal sources refer to the employees already working in the organization. This is a more reliable source. Internal sources include:
(a) present permanent employees,
(b) present temporary/casual employees,
(c) retrenched or retired employees,
(d) dependents of the deceased, disabled, retired and present employees.

(a) Present Permanent Employees: Organizations consider the candidates from this source for higher level jobs due to: (i) the availability of most suitable candidates for jobs relatively or equally to the external source, (ii) meet the trade union demands, (iii) the policy of the organization to motivate the present employees.

(b) Present Temporary or Casual Employees: Organizations find this source to fill the vacancies relatively at the lower level owing to the availability of suitable candidates or trade and pressures or in order to motivate them on the present job.

(c) Retrenched or Retired Employees: Generally, a particular organization retrenches the employees due to lay-off. The organization takes the candidates for employment from the retrenched employees due to obligation, trade union pressure and the like. Sometimes the organizations prefer to re-employ their retired employees as a token of their loyalty to the organization or to postpone some interpersonal conflicts for promotion, etc.

(d) Dependents of the Deceased, Disabled, Retired and Present Employees: Some organizations with a view to developing the commitment and loyalty of not only the employee but also his family members and to build up image provide employment to the dependent(s) of the deceased, disabled and present employees. Such organizations find this source an effective source of recruitment.

Why do Organizations Prefer Internal Source?

Organizations prefer this source to external source to some extent for the following reasons:

(i) Internal recruitment can be used as a technique of motivation.
(ii) Morale of the employees can be improved.
(iii) Suitability of the internal candidates can be judged better than the external candidates as "known devils are better than unknown angels."
(iv) Loyalty, commitment, a sense of belongingness, and security of the present employees can be enhanced.
(v) Employees' psychological needs can be met by providing an opportunity for advancement.
(vi) Employee's economic needs for promotion, higher income can be satisfied.
(vii) Cost of selection can be minimized.
(viii) Cost of training, induction, orientation, period of adaptability to the organization can be reduced.
(ix) Trade unions can be satisfied.
(x) Social responsibility towards employees may be discharged.
(xi) Stability of employment can be ensured.

But organizations do not excessively rely on internal source as too much consumption of even sugar tastes bitter. The excessive dependence on this source results in in-breeding, discourages flow of new blood into the organization, organization would become dull and back number without innovations, new ideas, excellence and expertise. Hence, organizations depend on internal source to the extent of motivating and then depend on external sources.

II. External Sources: External sources are those sources which are outside the organizational pursuits. Organizations search for the required candidates from these sources for the following reasons:

(i) The suitable candidates with skill, knowledge, talent, etc., are generally available.
(ii) Candidates can be selected without any preconceived notion or reservations.
(iii) Cost of employees can be minimized because employees selected from this source are generally placed in minimum pay scale.
(iv) Expertise, excellence and experience in other organizations can be easily brought into the organization.
(v) Human resources mix can be balanced with different background, experience, skill, etc.
(vi) Latest knowledge, skill, innovative or creative talent can also be flowed into the organization.
(vii) Existing will also broadens their personality.
(viii) Long-run benefit to the organization in the sense that qualitative human resources can be brought.

External sources include:

(a) Campus Recruitment,
(b) Private Employment Agencies/Consultants,
(c) Public Employment Exchanges,
(d) Professional Associations
(e) Data Banks,
(f) Casual Applicants,
(g) Similar Organizations,
(h) Trade Unions.

(a) Campus Recruitment: Different types of organizations like industries, business firms, service organizations, social or religious organizations can get inexperienced candidates of different types from various educational institutions like colleges and universities imparting education in Science, Commerce, Arts, Engineering and Technology, Agriculture, Medicine, Management Studies, etc., and trainee candidates in different disciplines like vocational, engineering, medicine from the training institutes like Vocational Training Institutes of State Governments in various trades, National Industrial Training Institutes for Engineers, etc. Most of the universities and institutes imparting technical education in various disciplines like engineering, technology, and management studies provide facilities for campus recruitment and selection. They maintain the bio-data and performance required of the candidates. Organizations seeking to recruit the candidates from this source can directly contact the institutes either in person or by post and stimulate the candidates to apply for jobs. Most of the organizations using this source perform the function of selection after completing recruitment in the campus of the institute itself with a view to minimizing

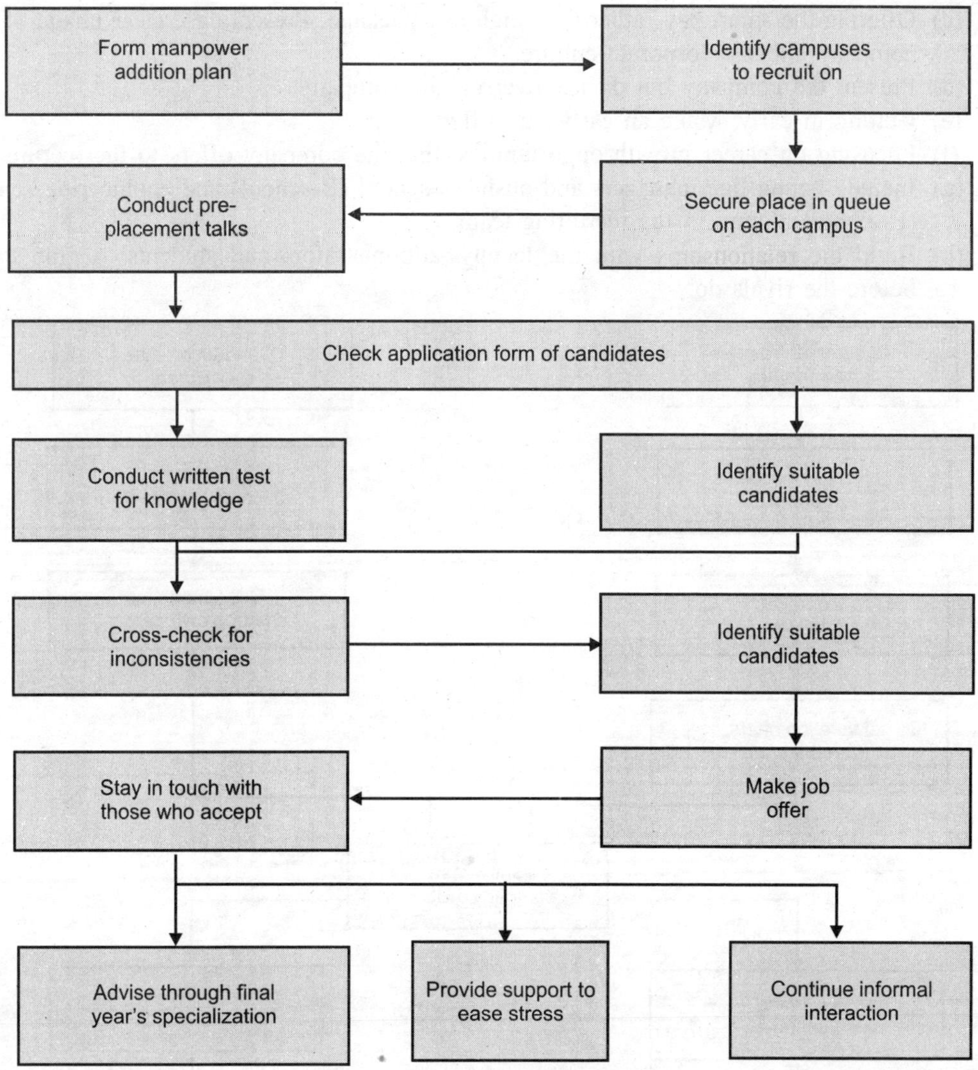

Fig. 5.5. Process of Campus Recruitment.
Source: Business Today, p. 64.

time lapse and to securing the cream before it is attracted by some other organizations. Figure 5.5 presents the process of campus recruitment.

(a) Campus Recruitment Techniques: Companies realize that campus recruitment is one of the best sources for recruiting the cream of the new blood. The techniques of campus recruitment include:

(a) Shortlisting the institutes based on the quality of students intake, faculty facilities and past track record.

(b) Selecting the recruiting team carefully.

(c) Offering the smart pay rather than high pay package. Presenting a clear image of the company and the corporate culture.
(d) Present the company but do not oversell the company.
(e) Getting in early. Make an early bird offer.
(f) Focusing on career growth opportunities, that the company offers to the recruits.
(g) Include young line managers and business school (B-school) and engineering school (E-school) alumni in the recruiting team.
(h) Build the relationships with the faculty, administrators and students to grab them before the rivals do.

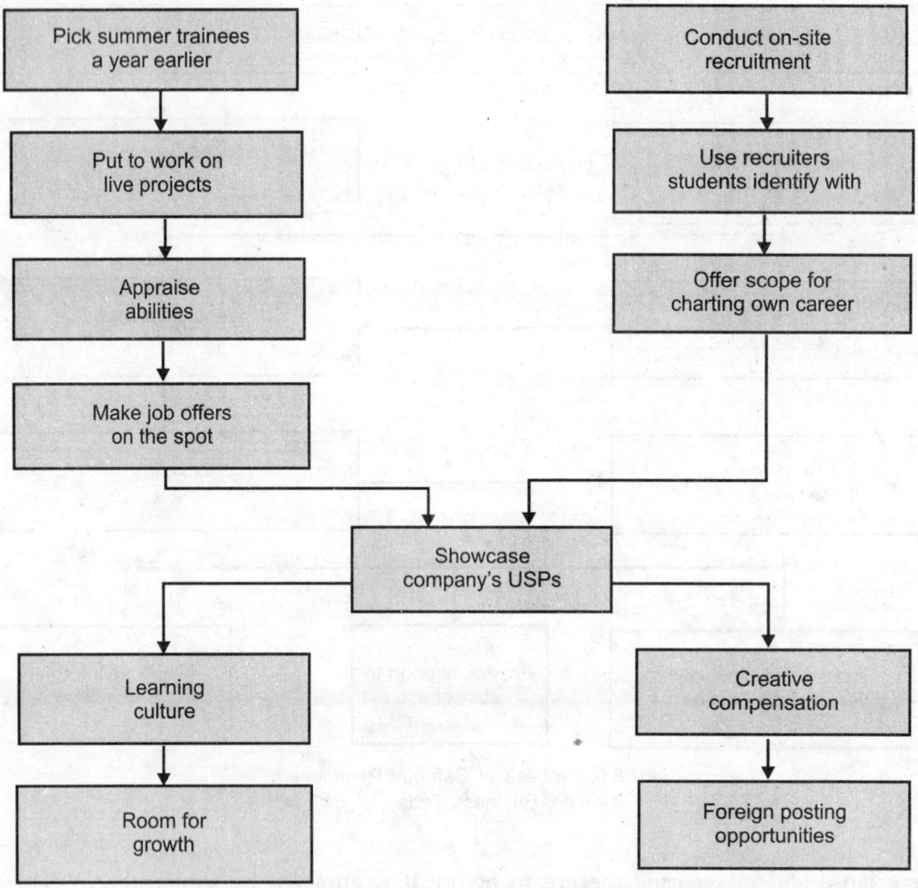

Fig. 5.6. Techniques to Winning on Campus.
Source: Business Today, p. 64.

(b) Private Employment Agencies/Consultants: Public employment agencies or consultants like ABC. Consultants in India perform the recruitment functions on behalf of a client company .by charging fee. Line managers are relieved from recruitment functions so that they can concentrate on their operational activities and recruitment functions are entrusted to a private agency or consultants. But due to limitations of high cost, ineffectiveness in performance, confidential nature of this function, managements sometimes do not depend on this source. However, these agencies function effectively in the recruitment of executives. Hence, they are also called executive search agencies. Most of the organizations depend on this source for highly specialized positions and executive positions.

(c) Public Employment Exchanges: The Government set-up Public Employment Exchanges in the country to provide information about vacancies to the candidates and to help the organizations in finding out suitable candidates. The Employment Exchange (Compulsory Notification or Vacancies) Act, 1959 makes it obligatory for public sector and private sector enterprises in India to fill certain types of vacancies through public employment exchanges. These industries have to depend on public employment exchanges for the specified vacancies.

(d) Professional Organizations: Professional organizations or associations maintain complete bio-data of their members and provide the same to various organizations on requisition. They also act as an exchange between their members and the recruiting firms in exchanging information, clarifying doubts, etc. Organizations find this source more useful to recruit the experienced and professional employees like executives, managers, engineers, etc.

(e) Data Banks: The management can collect the bio-data of the candidates from different sources like Employment Exchange, Educational Training Institutes, candidates, etc., and feed them in the computer. It will become another source and the company can get the particulars as and when it needs to recruit.

(f) Casual Applicants: Depending upon the image of the organization, its prompt response, participation of the organization in the local activities, level of unemployment, candidates apply casually for jobs through mail or hand over the applications in Personnel Department. This would be a suitable source for temporary and lower level.

(g) Similar Organizations: Generally, experienced candidates are available in organizations producing similar products or are engaged in similar business. The management can get most suitable candidates from this source. This would be the most effective source for executive positions and for newly established organizations or diversified or expanded organizations.

(h) Trade Unions: Generally, unemployed or underemployed persons or employees seeking change in employment put a word to the trade union leaders with a view to getting suitable employment due to latter's intimacy with the management. As such the trade union leaders are aware of the availability of candidates. In view of this, and in order to satisfy the trade union leaders, management enquires trade unions suitable candidates. Management decides about the sources' depending upon the type of candidates needed time lapse period, etc. It has to select the recruitment technique(s) after deciding upon the source.

TECHNIQUES/METHODS OF RECRUITMENT

The methods/techniques of recruitment can be discussed in two parts:

I. Traditional Methods/Techniques of Recruitment
II. Modern Methods/Techniques of Recruitment

I. Traditional Methods/Techniques of Recruitment

Recruitment techniques are the means or media by which the management acts prospective employees or provides necessary information or exchanges ideas or stimulates them to apply for jobs. The management uses different types of techniques to stimulate internal and external candidates. Techniques useful to stimulate internal candidates are:

(i) Promotions;
(ii) Transfers;
(iii) Present employees;
(iv) Scouting; and
(v) Advertising.

(i) Promotions: Most of the internal candidates would be stimulated to take up higher responsibilities and express their willingness to be engaged in the higher level jobs if the management gives them the assurance that they will be promoted to the higher level.

(ii) Transfers: Employees will be stimulated to work in the new sections or places if the management wishes to transfer them to the places of their choice.

(iii) Recommendations of the Present Employees: The management can contact, persuade the outsiders to apply for job in the organization through the recommendations to the candidates by the present employees, trade union leaders, etc.

(iv) Scouting: Scouting means sending the representation of the organizations to various sources of recruitment with a view to persuading or stimulating the candidates to apply for jobs. The representatives provide information about the company and exchange information and ideas and clarify the doubts of the candidates.

(v) Advertising: Advertising is a widely accepted technique of recruitment, though it mostly provides one-way communication. It provides the candidates in different sources, the information about the job and company and stimulates them to apply for jobs. It includes advertising through different media like newspapers, magazines of all kinds, radio, television, etc.

The technique of advertising should aim at: (a) attracting attention of the prospective candidates; (b) creating and maintaining interest; (c) stimulating action by the candidates.

The management in order to achieve these objectives of advertising has to:

(i) Analyze job requirements;
(ii) Decide who does what;
(iii) Write the copy;
(iv) Design the advertisement;
(v) Plan and select the media; and
(vi) Evaluate response.

The management after selecting the recruitment techniques has to decide upon the type of appeal in order to make the recruitment efforts effective.

II. Modern Sources and Techniques of Recruitment

A number of modern recruitment sources and techniques are being used by the corporate sector in addition to traditional sources and techniques. These sources and techniques include walk-in and consult-in, head-hunting, body shopping, business alliances, and tele-recruitment.

(i) **Walk-in:** The busy organizations and the rapid changing companies do not find time to perform various functions of recruitment. Therefore, they advise the potential candidates to attend for an interview dircctly and without a prior application on a specified date, time and at a specified place. The suitable candidates from among the interviewees will be selected for appointment after screening the candidates through tests and interviews.

(ii) **Consult-in:** The busy and dynamic companies encourage the potential job-seekers to approach them personally and consult them regarding the jobs. The companies select the suitable candidates from among such candidates through the selection process.

(iii) **Head-hunting:** The companies request the professional organizations to search for the best candidates particularly for the senior executive positions. The professional organizations search for the most suitable candidates and advise the company regarding the filling up of the positions. Head-hunters are also called search consultants.

(iv) **Body Shopping:** Professional organizations and the hi-tech training institutes develop the pool of human resources for the possible employment. The prospective employers contact these organizations to recruit the candidates. Otherwise, the organizations themselves approach the prospective employees to place their human resources. These professional and training institutions are called body shoppers and these activities are known as body shopping. The body shopping is used mostly for computer professionals.

(v) **Business Alliances:** Business alliances like acquisitions, mergers, and takeovers help in getting human resources. In addition, the companies do also have alliances in sharing their human resources on ad hoc basis. It does mean that, the company with surplus human resources offers the services of their employees to other needy organizations.

(vi) **Tele-Recruitment:** The technological revolution in telecommunication helped the organizations to use Internet as a source of recruitment. Organizations advertise the job vacancies through the World Wide Web (www) Internet. The job-seekers send their applications through e-mail or Internet. Alternatively, job-seekers place their CVs in the world wide web/Internet, which can be drawn by the prospective employers depending upon their rcquirements.

MEANING OF SELECTION

Selection, either internal or external, is a deliberate effort of the organization to select a fixed number of personnel from a large number of applicants. The primary aim of employee selection is to choose those persons who are most likely to perform their jobs with maximum effectiveness and remain with the company. Thus, in selection, an attempt is made to find a suitable candidate for the job. In doing so, naturally many applicants are rejected. This makes selection a negative function. In contrast, recruitment is a positive function because it attempts to increase the number of applicants applying for the job.

Selection is thus, the process of picking up individuals out of the pool of job applicants with requisite qualifications and competence to fill jobs in the organization.

According to **Dale Yoder,** "*Selection is the process in which candidates for employment are divided into two classes–those who are to be offered employment and those who are not.*"

According to **Thomas Stone,** "*Selection is the process of differentiating between applicants in order to identify (and hire) those with a greater likelihood of success in a job.*"

Thus, the selection process is a tool in the hands of the management to differentiate between the qualified and unqualified applicants by applying various techniques such as interviews, tests, etc. In this sense, it is a negative process of employment in which only a few who qualify for job are offered employment and others are denied the opportunities. A sound selection policy ensures the selection of suitable candidates.

STEPS IN SELECTION PROCESS

There is no short cut to an accurate evaluation of a candidate. A variety of methods are used to select personnel. The selection pattern, however, is not common for all organizations. It varies from one to another, depending on the situation and needs of the organization. Therefore, there is no standard selection procedure followed by all organizations.

The selection procedure consists of a series of methods or steps or stages by which additional information is secured about an applicant. At each stage facts may come to light which may lead to the rejection of an applicant. Selection procedure may be compared to a series of barriers which an applicant is required to cross before he is finally selected.

Requirements of a Good Selection Process

The procedure will be successful if it satisfies the following requirements:

- There should be sufficient number of applicants from whom the required number of candidates may be selected. The selection will not be proper if the number of candidates is less.
- There should be some person who is assigned the authority to select. The authority is given on the basis of type of persons to be selected and the nature of work they will take up.
- There should be some standard of personnel with which a prospective employee may be compared or there should be available beforehand a comprehensive job specification as developed by job analysis.

Significance of Selection Process

The success of an organization depends on the quality of personnel selected for the jobs. The importance of selection for the organization can be judged from the following factors:

(i) Procurement of Skilled Workers: Only the suitable candidates who are fit for the job are selected from among the prospective candidates for employment.

(ii) Reduction in the cost of Training: Proper selection of candidates reduces the cost of training because

a. Qualified personnel have better grasping power, they can understand the techniques of work better and in no time;

b. The organization can develop different training programmes for different persons on the basis of their individual differences, thus, reducing the time and cost of training considerably.

(iii) Solution to Personnel Problems: Proper selection of personnel reduces personnel problems in the organization. Many problems like labour turnover, absenteeism and monotony shall not be experienced in severity in the organization. Labour relations will be better because workers will be fully satisfied by their work.

Selection is a long process, commencing from the preliminary interview of the applicants and ending with the contract of employment. Figure 5.7 shows a generalized selection process in which there are several steps. In practice, the process differs among organizations and between two different jobs within the same company. Selection procedure for senior managers will be long-drawn and rigorous, but it is simple and short for hiring shop-floor workers.

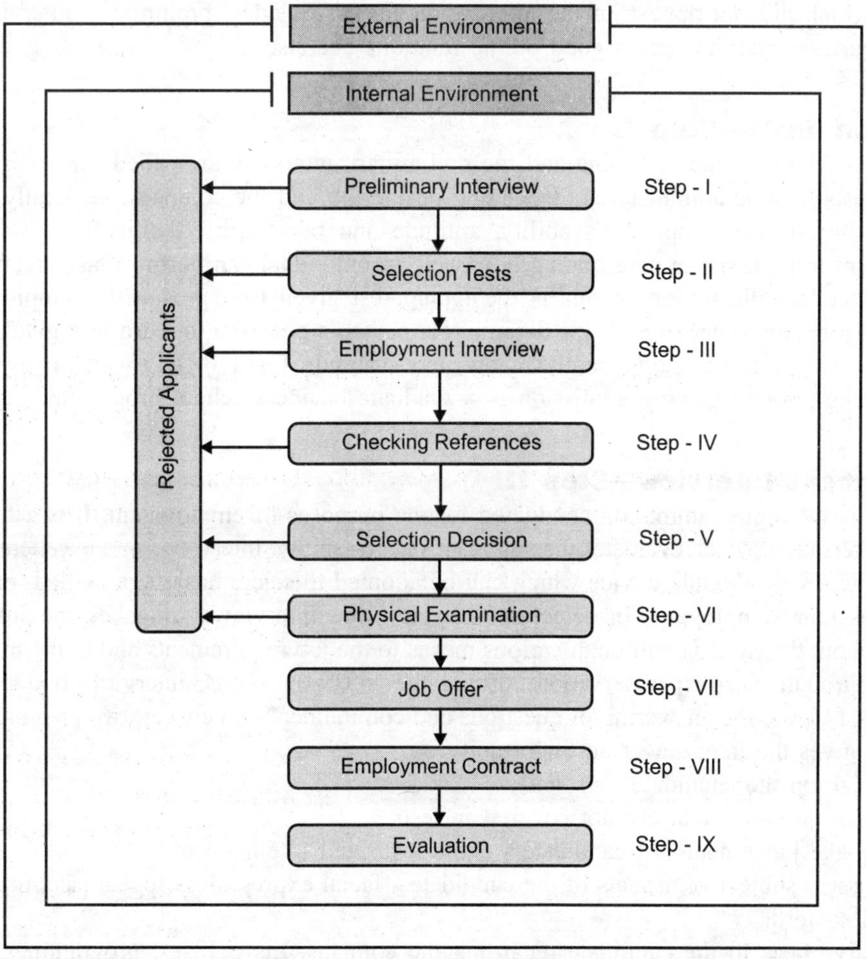

Fig. 5.7. Steps in Selection Process.

Source: Adapted from Personnel—The Management of Human Resources by R. Wayne Mondy and Robert M. Noe III, p. 156.

Environmental Factors Affecting Selection

Selection is influenced by several external and internal factors. More prominent among them are supply and demand of specific skills in the labour market, unemployment rate, labour-market conditions, legal and political considerations, company's image, company's policy, HRP, and cost of hiring. The last three constitute the internal environment.

Preliminary Interview—Step I

In the previous sections of this chapter, it was stated that the applications received from job seekers under recruitment process would be subject to scrutiny so as to eliminate unqualified applicants. This is usually followed by a preliminary interview, the purpose of which is more or less the same as scrutiny of applications, that is, elimination of unqualified applications. Scrutiny enables the HR specialists to eliminate unqualified job-seekers based on the information supplied in their application forms. Preliminary interview, on the other hand, helps reject misfits for reasons, which did not appear in the application forms. Besides, preliminary interview, often called 'courtesy interview', is a good public relations exercise.

Selection Tests—Step II

Job-seekers who pass the screening and the preliminary interview are called for tests. Different types of tests may be administered, depending on the job and the company. Generally, tests are used to determine the applicant's ability, aptitude and personality. Ability tests (also called achievement tests) assist in determining how well an individual can perform tasks related to the job. An excellent illustration of this is the typing test given to a prospective employee for a secretarial job. An aptitude test helps determine a person's potential to learn in a given area. An example of such a test is the General Management Aptitude Test (GMAT) which many business students take prior to gaining admission to a graduate business school programme.

Employment Interview—Step III

Interview is the oral examination conducted for the purposes of employment. It is a formal, in-depth conversation, which evaluates the applicant's acceptability. Interview is an excellent selection device. It is a very flexible device which can be adopted to select unskilled, skilled, managerial and professional employees. In selection interview the interviewer matches the information obtained about the candidate through various means to the job requirements and to the information obtained through his own observations during the interview. Thus, interview is a purposeful exchange of views, the answering of questions and communication between two or more persons. Interview gives the interviewer an opportunity:

- to size up the candidate personally
- to ask questions that are not covered in tests
- to make judgements on candidate's enthusiasm and intelligence
- to assess subjective aspects of the candidate—facial expressions, appearance, nervousness and so forth
- to give facts to the candidate regarding the company, its policies, programmes, etc. and promote goodwill towards the company.

However, interviews do have some limitations. Absence of reliability is one limitation. Due to personal and subjective judgements, no two interviewers offer similar scoring after interviewing an applicant. Lack of validity is another shortcoming. This is because, some departments use standardized questions upon which validation studies can be conducted.

Checking References—Step IV

Many employers request names, addresses, and telephone numbers or references for the purpose of verifying information and, perhaps, gaining additional background information on an applicant. Although listed on the application form, references are not usually checked until an applicant has successfully reached the fourth stage of a sequential selection process.

Previous employers, known public figures, university professors, neighbours or friends can act as references. Previous employers are preferable because they are already aware of the applicant's performance. But, the problem with this reference is the tendency on the part of the previous employers to over-rate the applicant's performance just to get rid of the person.

Companies normally seek letters of reference or telephone references. The latter is advantageous because of its accuracy and low cost. The telephone reference also has the advantage of soliciting immediate, relatively candid comments, and attitudes can sometimes be inferred from hesitations and inflections in speech. Reference checks serve two important purposes. One purpose is to gain insight about the potential employee from the people who have had previous experience with him or her.

The second purpose for reference checks is to assess the potential success of a prospect. Who else can give an objective assessment of an individual than his or her previous employer or a person known to him or her?

But one should guard against the following while considering employing a prospect:

- The prospect is likely to approach those persons who would speak well about him or her.
- People may write favourably about the candidate in order to get rid of him or her.
- People may not divulge the truth about a candidate, lest it might damage or ruin his or her career.

Selection Decision—Step V

Upto this stage selection is handled by personnel department or staff executives. Since the persons employed are to work under different line officers, the candidates are referred to them. Line officers will finally decide about the work to be assigned to them. If the line officer is a production manager or foreman he may assess on the job performance of the candidates. If the candidate is not suitable for one job then he is tried at some other. If candidate's performance is not upto the mark then he may be kept as apprentice for some time. Normally, a candidate is not rejected at this stage.

Physical Examination—Step VI

After the selection decision and before the job offer is made, the candidate is required to undergo physical fitness test. Candidates are sent for physical examination either to the company's physician or to a medical officer approved for the purpose. Such physical examination provides the following information:

(i) Whether the candidate is physically fit for the specific job or not?
(ii) Whether the candidate has health problems or psychological attitudes likely to interfere with work efficiency or future attendance?
(iii) Whether the candidate suffers from bad health which should be corrected before he can work satisfactorily?
(iv) Whether the candidate's physical measurements are in accordance with job requirements or not?

A job offer is, often, contingent upon the candidate being declared fit after the physical examination. The results of medical fitness test are recorded in a statement and preserved in the personnel records. Such records will protect the employer from worker's compensation claims that are not valid because the injuries or illnesses were present when the employee was hired.

Job Offer—Step VII

The next step in the selection process is the job offer to those applicants who have crossed all the previous hurdles. Job offer is made in the form of an appointment letter. Such a letter, generally, contains a date by which the candidate must report for duty. Reasonable reporting time is given to all the appointed candidates. This is particularly necessary when the appointed person is already in employment, in which case he has to give notice to the previous employer. Moreover, the job may require movement to another city which means considerable preparation and shifting of property and family members.

Some organizations also inform the rejected candidates about their non-selection. Their application may, however, be preserved for future use. The applications of selected candidates are always preserved for future references.

Employment Contract—Step VIII

After the job offer has been made and the candidate accepts the offer, a contract for employment is executed by the employer and the candidate. The basic information that is included in a written contract varies according to the level of the job. Generally, the following details and included in the contract:

(i) Job title
(ii) Details of duties
(iii) Date when the continuous employment starts
(iv) Remuneration and method of payments
(v) Hours of work including lunch break, overtime and shift arrangements
(vi) Holiday arrangements and details of holidays
(vii) Sickness leaves rules
(viii) Length of notice due to and from employee
(ix) Grievance procedure
(x) Disciplinary procedure
(xi) Work rules
(xii) Terms of termination of employment

(xiii) Terms for union membership
(xiv) Employer's right to vary terms of the contract subject to proper notification being given.

Great care is taken in drafting the contracts. Often services of law firms are obtained to get the contracts drafted and finalized. Employers, who belong to high employee turnover sectors, insist on agreements being signed by newly hired employees. The limitation of contracts is that it is almost impossible to enforce them. A determined employee will leave the organization, contract or no contract. It is for this reason that several companies have scrapped the contracts altogether.

Evaluation—Step IX

The selection process, if properly performed, will ensure availability of competent and committed personnel. A period audit, conducted by people who work independently of the human resource department, will evaluate the effectiveness of the selection process. The auditors will do a thorough the intensive analysis and evaluate the employment programme.

BARRIERS TO EFFECTIVE SELECTION

The main objective of selection is to hire people having competence and commitment. This objective is often defeated because of certain barriers. The impediments which check effectiveness of selection are perception, fairness, validity, reliability and pressure.

1. **Perception:** Our inability to understand others accurately is probably the most fundamental barrier to select the right candidate. Selection demands an individual or a group of people to assess and compare the respective competencies of others, with the aim of choosing the right persons for the jobs. But our views are highly personalized. We all perceive the world differently. Our limited perceptual ability is obviously a stumbling block to the objective and rational selection of people.
2. **Fairness:** Fairness in selection requires that no individual should be discriminated against on the basis of religion, region, race or gender. But the low numbers of women and other less-privileged sections of the society in middle and senior management positions and open discrimination on the basis of age in job advertisements and in the selection process, would suggest that all the efforts to minimize inequity have not been very effective.
3. **Validity:** Validity, as explained earlier, is a test that helps predict job performance of an incumbent. A test that has been validated can differentiate between the employees who can perform well and those who will not. However, a validated test does not predict job success accurately. It can only increase the possibility of success.
4. **Reliability:** A reliable method is the one which will produce consistent results when repeated in similar situations. Like a validated test, a reliable test may fail to predict job performance with precision.
5. **Pressure:** Pressure is brought on the selectors by politicians, bureaucrats, relatives, friends and peers to select particular candidates. Candidates selected because of compulsions are obviously not the right ones. Appointments to public sector undertakings generally take place under such pressures.

TYPES OF TESTS

In the selection process, employment test or selection test is an important step. If tests are properly conducted the selection cost is considerably reduced and good selection can be made. There are various types of tests which test is to be chosen depends upon the type of job, the skills required, etc.

Following are the various types of tests:

1. **Aptitude Test:** Aptitude or potential ability tests are widely used to measure the talent and ability of a candidate to learn a new job or skill. Aptitude tests measure ability and skills. They enable us to find out whether a candidate, if selected, would be suitable for a job. Specific aptitude tests have been designed for jobs that required clerical, mechanical and manual abilities and skills. Aptitude tests for medicine, law, painting, and other activities are also available. The disadvantage of aptitude tests is that they do not measure motivation. On the job motivation is often found to be more important than aptitude for the job. That is why, aptitude test is supplemented by interests test and personality tests.
2. **Interest Test:** Interest test is used to find out the type of work in which the candidate has an interest. An interest test only indicates the interest of a candidate for a particular job. It does not reveal his ability to do it. These tests aim at finding out the types of work in which a candidate is interested. They are inventories of the likes and dislikes of the people in some occupations. Therefore, they are useful in vocational guidance. Interest tests have been designed to discover a person's area of interest and to identify the kind of work that will satisfy him.
3. **Intelligence Test:** This test is used to find out the candidate's intelligence. By using this test, the candidate's mental alertness, reasoning ability, power of understanding, etc., are judged. Intelligence tests are generally aptitude tests, although there is some disagreement on this. Mental or intelligence tests measure the overall intellectual activity of a person and enable the employer to know whether he has the mental capacity to deal with new problems. The scores on intelligence tests are usually expressed as Intelligence Quotient (lQ); which are calculated as follows:

$$IQ = \frac{\text{Mental Age}}{\text{Actual Age}} \times 100$$

   Intelligence tests are useful for selection purposes and determine the future of an employee. Word fluency, memory, inductive reasoning and speed of perception are tested. There are various forms of intelligence tests for various age groups, the administration of these IQ tests calls for much preparation on the part of the organization and they are expensive and cumbersome as well. However, they are conducted on the assumption that intelligence testing gets bright and alert employees who can learn fast and can be trained fast.
4. **Performance Test:** This test is also called achievement test. This test is used to measure the candidate's level of knowledge and skill in the particular trade or occupation in which he will be appointed in case he is finally selected. Achievement tests measure the skill or

knowledge which is acquired as a result of previous experience or training secured by a candidate. These tests determine the admission feasibility of a candidate and what he is capable of doing. Achievement tests measure a person's potential in a given area. One example is the trade lest which involves the performance of a sample operation requiring specialized skill and believed to be satisfactorily answered by those who have some knowledge of the occupation and trade. A candidate for a driver's post may be asked to drive the vehicle.

Achievement tests are of two kinds:

(i) **Tests for Measuring Job Knowledge:** These tests are administered to determine proficiency. Such tests are useful for stenographers, salesgirls, etc.

(ii) **Work Sample Tests:** This test is administered on the actual job. A typing test for a typist tests the skill and accuracy of the candidate.

5. **Personality Test:** Personality test is used to measure those characteristics of a candidate which constitute his personality. Personality tests are very important in the selection process, particularly in the case of appointment to the posts of supervisors and higher executives. Personality tests have a wider use in industry because they provide a well-rounded picture of an applicant's personality and because managers have to realize the importance of emotional characteristics. They assess a candidate's motivation, interests, his ability to adjust himself to the stresses of everyday life and his capacity for interpersonal relations and self-image. Personality tests are of three types:
   (i) Objective tests are tests which measure self-sufficiency and self-confidence.
   (ii) Personality tests are tests which assess a candidate's interpretation for certain standard stimulus situations. They test a candidate's values—motives and personality.
   (iii) Situation tests: This test measures a candidate's reaction when he is placed in a peculiar situation.

In recent years, tests have become an integral part of the selection process in different types of organizations in the country. It is more so in a majority of government undertakings. Testing is an important stage of the selection process. If tests are properly conducted, they can reduce the selection cost by reducing the large groups of applicants to manageable levels.

Characteristics of a Good Test

Tests must be chosen based on the criteria of reliability, validity, objectivity and standardization. These are the characteristics of a good test.

(i) **Reliability:** It refers to standardization of the procedure of administering and scoring the test results. A person who takes a test one day and makes a certain score should be able to take the same the next day or the next week and make more or less the same score. An individual's intelligence, for example, is generally a stable characteristic. So if we administer an intelligence test, a person who scores 120 in March would score close to 120 if tested in July. Tests which produce wide variations in results serve little purpose in selection.

(ii) **Validity** is a test which helps predict whether a person will be successful in a given job. A test that has been validated can be helpful in differentiating between prospective employees who will be able to perform the job well and those who will not. Naturally, no test will be 100 per cent accurate in predicting job success. A validated test increases possibility of success.

There are three ways of validating a test. The first is concurrent validity. This involves determining the factors that are characteristic of successful employees and then using these factors as the yardsticks.

Predictive validity involves using a selection test during the selection process and then identifying the successful candidates. The characteristics of both successful and less-successful candidates are then identified. Synthetic validity involves taking parts of several similar jobs rather than one complete job to validate the selection test.

Benefits of a validated test are obvious from Figure 5.8. Individuals who score 40 and above are successful employees. Those who score less than 40 are unsuccessful. As noted from the figure, the test is not absolutely accurate. A small number of workers who score below 40 are good workers. Also, some applicants scoring above 40 are less successful.

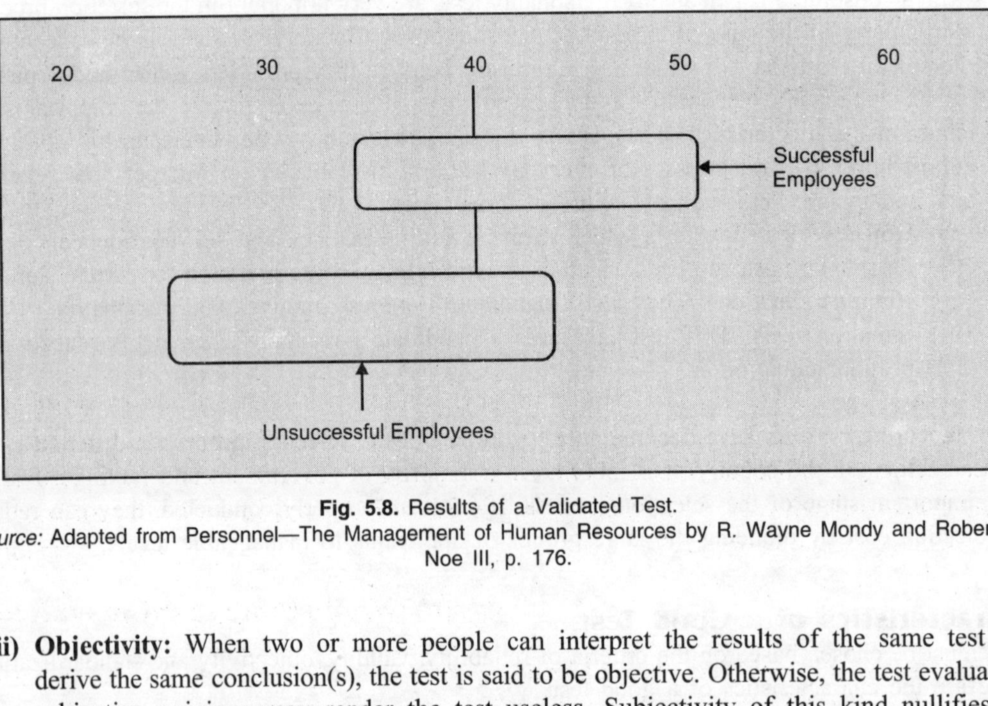

Fig. 5.8. Results of a Validated Test.
Source: Adapted from Personnel—The Management of Human Resources by R. Wayne Mondy and Robert M. Noe III, p. 176.

(iii) **Objectivity:** When two or more people can interpret the results of the same test and derive the same conclusion(s), the test is said to be objective. Otherwise, the test evaluators' subjective opinions may render the test useless. Subjectivity of this kind nullifies the purpose of objectivity and is the reason why some tests are not valid.

(iv) **Standardization:** A test that is standardized is administered under standard conditions to a large group of persons who are representatives of the individuals for whom it is intended. The purpose of standardization is to obtain norms or standards, so that a specific test score can be meaningful when compared to other scores in the group. When a test is standardized, it is administered to a large number of people who are performing similar tasks.

INTERVIEWING PROCESS

Another important step in the selection process is employment interview. An interview is conducted at the beginning and at the end of the selection process. The emphasis here is on the latter. Interview is a formal, in-depth conversation conducted to evaluate the applicant's acceptability. It is considered to be an excellent selection device. Its popularity stems from its flexibility. Interview can be adapted to unskilled, skilled, managerial and professional employees. It allows a two-way exchange of information, the interviewers learn about the applicant, and the applicant learns about the employer.

However, interviews do have shortcomings. Absence of reliability is one limitation. No two interviewers offer similar scoring after interviewing an applicant. Lack of validity is another limitation. This is because, few departments use standardized questions upon which validation studies can be conducted. Finally, biases of interviewers may cloud the objectivity of interviews.

Classification of Interviews

The types of interviews are:

(i) **One-to-One Interview:** (Figure 5.9(a)) there are two participants—one interviewer and other interviewee.

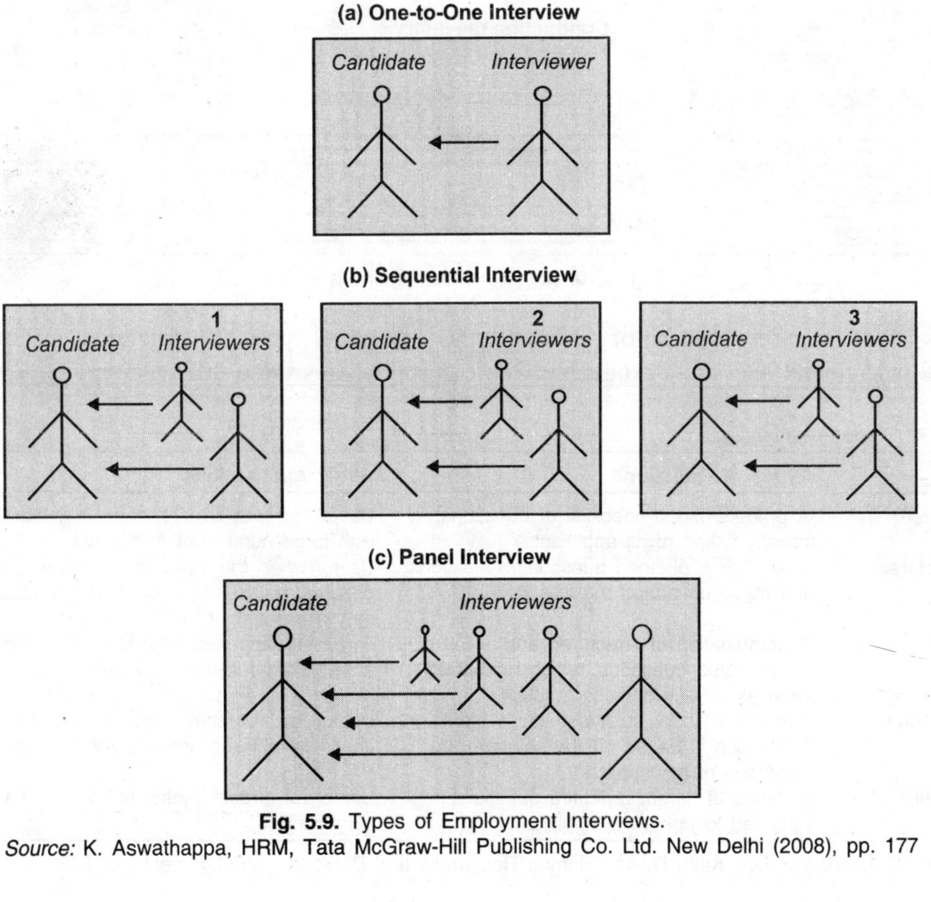

Fig. 5.9. Types of Employment Interviews.
Source: K. Aswathappa, HRM, Tata McGraw-Hill Publishing Co. Ltd. New Delhi (2008), pp. 177

(ii) Sequential Interview (Figure 5.9(b)): It involves a series of interviews where several interviewers are to interview the candidate in one-to-one form. The candidate moves from one room to another.

(iii) The Panel Interview (Figure 5.9 (c)): It consists of two or more interviewers and the figure may go up to as many as 15. Any panel interview is less intimate and more formal than the one-to-one, but if handled and organized well, it can provide a wealth of information. If not handled carefully, the panel interview can make the candidate feel ill at ease and confused about whose question to answer and whom to address. Interviewers themselves are likely to experience nightmare, not knowing who will ask which questions and in what order.

Steps in Interviewing Process

Figure 5.10 shows five steps which have been identified by HR experts for conducting interviews.

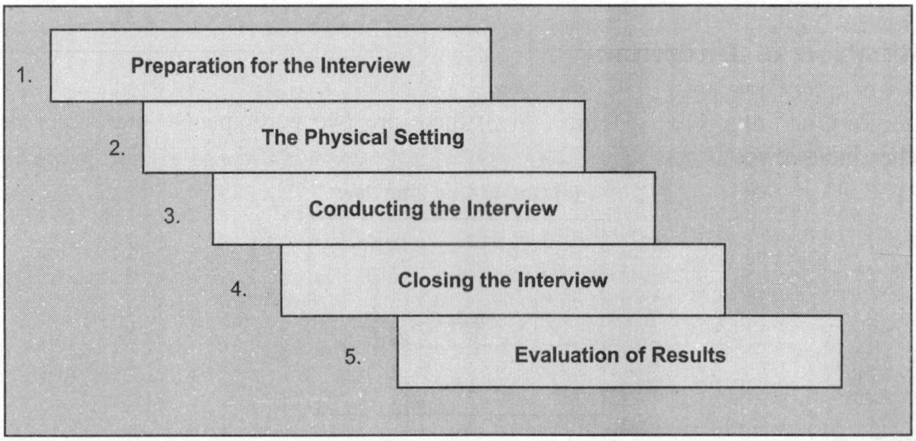

Fig. 5.10. Steps in Employment Interview.

Types of Interviews can be of different types. The usual types are structured, unstructured, mixed, behavioural and stress-producing. Table 5.1 compares these different types.

Table 5.1: Types of Interviewing

Type	Types of Questions	Usual Applications
Structured	A predetermined checklist of questions, usually asked of all applicants.	Useful for valid results, especially when dealing with large number of applicants.
Unstructured	Few, if any, planned questions. Questions are made up during the interview.	Useful when the interviewer tries to probe personal details of the candidate to analyze why they are not right for the job.
Mixed	A combination of structured and unstructured questions, which resembles what, is usually done in practice.	A realistic approach that yields comparable answers plus in-depth insights.
Behavioural	Questions limited to hypothetical situations. Evaluation is based on the solution and approach of the applicant.	Useful to understand applicant's reasoning and analytical abilities under modest stress.
Stressful	A series of harsh, rapid-fire questions intended to upset the applicant.	Useful for stressful jobs, such as handling complaints.

Source: William B. Werther, Keith Davis, "Human Resources and Personnel Management", p. 243.

(i) In a **structured interview**, the interviewer uses preset standardized questions which are put to all the interviewees. This interview is also called 'guided' or 'patterned' interview.

(ii) In an **unstructured interview**, also known as 'unguided' or 'unpatterned' interview, the interview is largely unplanned and the interviewee does most of the talking.

(iii) In **practice,** a blend of structured and unstructured questions is used by the interviewer while interviewing the job-seekers. This approach is called the mixed interview. The structured questions provide a base of information that allows comparisons between candidates. But the unstructured questions make the interview more conventional and permits greater insights into the unique differences between the applicants.

(iv) **Behavioural** interviewing focuses on a problem or a hypothetical situation that the applicant is expected to solve. Often, these are hypothetical situations, and the applicant is asked what she/he would do in the given circumstances. This interview technique has a limited scope. It primarily reveals the applicant's ability to solve the types of problem presented. Validity is more likely if the hypothetical situations match those found on the jobs.

(v) When the job involves much stress, **stress** interview attempts to learn how the applicant will respond to the pressure. This technique is more relevant in jobs involving stress, for example, in the police force. Since stressful situations are usually only a part of the job, this technique should be used along with other approaches.

LIMITATIONS OF INTERVIEWING PROCESS

Several problems are inherent in interviews. Selection specialists must be aware of these problems and need to be trained to overcome these.

- Interviewers do not seek applicants' information dimensions needed for successful job performance. Often, they do not have a complete job description or an accurate appraisal of the critical job requirements. In addition, the interviewer often does not know the conditions under which the job is performed.
- Interviewers may make snap judgements early in the interview. Consequently, they block out further potentially useful information.
- Interviewers permit one trait or job-related attribute to influence their evaluation of the remaining qualities of an applicant.
- Interviewers have a tendency to be influenced by negative information about the applicants.
- Information from interviews is not integrated or discussed in a systematic manner. This casual approach may save time and confrontation, but only in the short run. In the long run, everyone in the company will pay for poor hiring decisions.
- Interviewers' judgement regarding an applicant is often affected by the list of available applicants. For example, a good person looks better in contrast to a group of average or below-average applicants.

There is the problem of different cues used by interviewers. Some interviewers may place more weight on certain attributes than others, or they may combine attributes differently, as they make their overall decisions. For instance, some interviewers may give emphasis to educational experience while others give weightage to work experience.

Table 5.2: Do's and Dont's for Interviewers

Do's	Don'ts
• Plant the interview	• Start the interview unprepared
• Establish an easy and informal relationship	• Plunge too quickly into demanding questions
• Encourage the candidate to talk	• Ask leading questions
• Cover the ground as planned	• Jump to conclusions on inadequate evidence
• Probe where necessary	• Pay to much attention to isolated strengths or weaknesses
• Analyze career and interests to reveal strengths weaknesses, patterns of behaviour	• Allow the candidate to gloss over important facts
• Maintain control over the direction and time taken for the interview	• Talk too much

INTERVIEW QUESTIONS FROM THE EMPLOYER

Questions at the Opening

(i) May I see your resume?
(ii) What can I do for you?
(iii) Why are you interested in joining our company?
(iv) What do you think you can do for us?
(v) What attracts you to us?
(vi) Tell me about your experience.
(vii) What pay do you have in mind?

Questions Regarding Education

(i) Describe your educational qualifications.
(ii) What was your class standing?
(iii) What extra-curricular activities did you take part in?
(iv) What honours did you earn?
(v) What were your average grades?
(vi) Did your grades adequately reflect your full capability? If not, why?
(vii) What courses did you like best/least and why?
(viii) Have you had any special training for this kind of job?

Motivational Questions

(i) Is your present employer aware of your interest in a job change?
(ii) Why do you want to change your job?
(iii) What caused you to enter your job field?
(iv) Why do you want to change your field of work?
(v) What would you like to be doing five years from now when you retire?
(vi) What is the ideal job for you?
(vii) If you had complete freedom of choice to be a great success in any job field, which would you choose? Why?

Questions Regarding Experience

(i) Why should I hire you?
(ii) How do you fit the requirements for this job?
(iii) Who has exercised the greatest influence on you? How?
(iv) What duties performed in the past have you liked best/least and why?
(v) What are your greatest strengths/limitations for this job?
(vi) What are the strongest limitations you have found in your past supervisors?
(vii) Which supervisor did you like best and why?
(viii) What kind of people appeal most/least to you as work associates?
(ix) How many people have you supervised? What types?
(x) Why have you changed jobs so frequently?
(xi) What are your greatest achievements till date?
(xii) Describe the biggest crisis in your career.
(xiii) What were you doing during the period not covered in your resume?
(xiv) Why were you out of work for so long?
(xv) Why did you leave your previous jobs?
(xvi) Could I see samples of your work?

Questions Regarding Pay

(i) What do you require?
(ii) What is the minimum pay you will accept?
(iii) What is your pay record for the last five years?
(iv) Why do you believe you are qualified for so much more?
(v) We can't pay the salary you ask for. Would you be willing to start lower and work towards that figure?

REVIEW QUESTIONS

1. Discuss how recruitment and selection needs are determined. What are the steps involved in recruitment and selection process?
2. What is recruitment? Discuss its nature and importance.
3. What do you understand by recruitment process? Discuss various steps involved in it.
4. Discuss the internal and external sources of recruitment.
5. What are the methods of recruitment?
6. What is selection? Discuss the steps in selection process. What are the prerequisites of a good selection process?
7. What are the barriers to effective selection?
8. What are the types of tests which are used to select a candidate? Discuss the characteristics of a good test.
9. What is an interview? Discuss various types of interviews. What are the steps involved in interviewing process?
10. "Recruitment is generating application while selection is choosing some of them." Discuss.

11. Write notes on the following:
    (a) Aptitude tests
    (b) External sources of recruitment
    (c) Intelligence tests
    (d) Performance tests
    (e) Characteristics of a good test
    (f) Sequential interview
12. Distinguish between structured and unstructured interview. Discuss the limitations of interviewing process.

CASE STUDY

5.1 Info Tech Ltd.

Info Tech Ltd. is a Mangalore based company having a countrywide network. It is considered a leading software company having a turnover of Rs. 7500 crore. The company is growing rapidly and during the past year the number of employees has increased from 50 to 125. Most of the employees are graduate engineers having a B.E. degree in Computers, Information Systems or Electronics and Communications. The employees in the sales field are MBA degree holders having a basic degree in science or engineering. The work is highly pressured and result focused, in return for which large reward packages are available.

The sales force in particular needs strong presentation and negotiation skills since the market is very competitive. Recently, however, the company has had enormous difficulty in selecting the right calibre staff for the sales role (MBA degree holder) though they are able to attract candidates in sufficient numbers.

The HR manager analyzed the selection procedure to provide a more successful model for the selection of the sales force. The model should allow the selection process to:

- Identify differences between recruits that are important to the role.
- Carry out the identification of differences in a reliable and consistent manner.
- Make valid predictions about the future performance of recruits with confidence.

The findings revealed some interesting features relating to the basic skills and attitudes needed for such a role. These are:

1. The first of these factors was what is seen as 'professionalism' suggested as an ability to deal sensitively with prospective customers, being 'human' rather than 'clinical'.
2. Style of behaviour which was 'non-threatening' and 'non-arrogant' but also 'challenging' when required.
3. Skills like tolerance for ambiguity and a capacity to empathies with prospective customers.
4. Show 'pride' in working with Info Tech and their products.

Source: P.G. Aquinas, Human Resource Management, Vikas Publishing House, p. 65.

Questions

1. Which selection techniques could measure the attributes identified?
2. How would the HR manager operate the selection of sales force? Justify your answer.

5.2 Which is More Important: Recruiting or Retaining of an Employee?

Shine Electronics Ltd. is a pioneering and internationally reputed firm in the electronics industry. It is one of the largest firms in the country. It attracted employees, from internationally reputed institutes and industries by offering high salaries, perks, etc. It has advertised for the position of an Electronics Engineer recently. Nearly 220 candidates working in various electronics firms applied for the job. Mr. Rajesh, an Electronics Engineering graduate from Indian Institute of Technology with 6 years of working experience in a small electronics firm was selected from among the 150 candidates who took tests and interview. The interview board recommended an enhancement in his salary by Rs. 2000 more than his present salary at his request. Mr. Rajesh was very happy to achieve this and he was congratulated by a number of people including his previous employer for his brilliant interview performance and good luck.

Mr. Rajesh joined Shine Electronics Ltd. on 15 February, 1997 with a great enthusiasm. He also found his job to be quite comfortable and challenging and he felt it was highly prestigious to work with this company during the formative years of his career. He found his superiors as well as subordinates to be friendly and cooperative. But this climate did not live long. After one year of his service, he slowly learnt about a number of unpleasant stories about the company, management, the superior-subordinate relations, rate of employee turnover, especially at higher level. But he decided to stay on as he promised several things to the management in the interview. He wanted to please and change the attitude of the management through his diligent performance, firm commitment and dedication. He started maximizing his contributions and the management got the impression that Mr. Rajesh has settled down and will remain in the company.

After some time, the superiors started riding over Mr. Rajesh. He was overloaded with multifarious jobs. His freedom in deciding and executing was cut down to size. He was ill-treated on a number of occasions before his subordinates. His colleagues also started assigning their responsibilities to Mr. Rajesh. Consequently, there were imbalances in his family life, social life and organisational life. But he seemed to be calm and contented. The management felt that Mr. Rajesh had the potential to bear many more organisational responsibilities.

It was quite surprising to the General Manager to see the resignation letter of Mr. Rajesh along with a cheque equivalent to a month's salary one fine morning on 16th January, 1999. The General Manager failed to convince Mr. Rajesh to withdraw his resignation. The General Manager relieved him on 27th January, 1999. The General Manager wanted to appoint a committee to go into the matter immediately, but dropped the idea later.

Questions

1. What prevented the General Manager from appointing a committee?
2. What is wrong with the recruitment policy of the company?
3. Why did Mr. Rajesh resignation surprise the General Manager?

5.3 How to Select A New Employee?

Ramoji Rao is in charge of a bindery in Vijayawada, which employs fifteen people, five of whom work in the factory. Three of these employees run machines, one supervises, and the fifth moves the blank paper and finished print by handcar. This fifth position, which demands no skill other than driving a handcar, needs to be filled, and three applicants have responded.

The first is Mr. Matti Anjaiah who is thirty-five, unmarried, and a Navy veteran. Anjaiah has a poor work record. During his five years in Vijayawada he has worked only seasonal labour and occasional odd jobs. He drove a forklift in the Navy, while working at Visakhapatnam. He has a strong build, which could help, although the work is generally light.

Mr. Nehal Singh, age twenty-two, came to Vijayawada two years back from Punjab. He has done farm labour for many years and assembly-line work for one year. His command of English is poor (but can speak the regional language, Telugu, fluently). He resides with his mother and seems certain to remain in the area for some time. After having run farm equipment, he should have no trouble steering a handcar.

Mr. Vangaveeti Raja is a local boy who finished high school two years ago. Subsequently, he got a diploma from a local III and is currently employed as an assistant in Savani Transport Company, Vijayawada. His character references are excellent. Mr. Raja is small, but he seems quick and was track star in high school.

Source: P. Subba Rao, "Essentials of Human Resource Management and Industrial Relations", Himalaya Publishing House, p. 188.

Questions

1. How much consideration should be given to Mr. Anjaiah's poor work record? Should Mr. Ramoji Rao check to verify it?
2. How important is a command of English to the job? How quickly could Mr. Nehal Singh assimilate enough English to be effective?
3. Should Mr. Nehal Singh be passed over because of his status as a recent migrant?
4. Should Mr. Raja get the job? How heavily should his references be weighed against his inexperience?
5. Who should be hired? Why?

REFERENCES

1. Dale Yoder, (1958). "Handbook of Personnel Management and Labour Relations", Tata McGraw-Hill Book Company, New York.
2. Aswathappa, K. (2008). "Human Resource Management", Tata McGraw-Hill Publishing Company Ltd., New Delhi, pp. 144-160.
3. Dessler, Gary (1998). "Human Resource Management", Prentice-Hall of India, New Delhi, pp. 119.
4. Werther William, B. and Kaith Davis, (1993). "Human Resource and Personnel Management", Tata McGraw-Hill Publishing Company Ltd., New York.
5. Gatewood, R. and Field, H. "Human Resource Selection", Fort Worth Dryden.
6. Mamoria, C.B. and Gankar, S.K. (2008). "Personnel Management", Himalaya Publishing House, New Delhi.

CHAPTER

6 Placement and Induction

CHAPTER'S OUTLINE

- Introduction
- Meaning of Placement
- Employee Placement Process
- Principles of Placement
- Problems of Placement
- Meaning of Induction
- Objectives and Purpose of Induction
- Procedures of Induction
- Problems of Induction

INTRODUCTION

Once an offer of employment has been extended and accepted, the final stage in procurement function is to be concluded and it is the placement of the individual on the new job and inducting or orienting him to the organization. It means placement precedes induction process. In this chapter issues relating to placement and induction are discussed. The problem of placement arises when the candidate selected for the job comes to join the organization. Placing the right man at the right job is as important as hiring the right person. It is desirable to have a sound scheme of placement in the organization so that the employees feel comfortable on their new job.

MEANING OF PLACEMENT

Placement is understood as the allocation of people to jobs. It is the assignment or re-assignment of an employee to a new or different job. It can also be called the process of assigning a specific job to each one of the selected candidates. In simple words, by placement we mean sending the newly employed person to some department for work.

According to **Paul Pigors and Charles A Myres,** "*Placement is the determination of the job to which an accepted candidate is to be assigned and his assignment to that job. It is a matching of what the supervisor has reason to think he can do with the job demands, it is a matching of what he imposes (in strain working conditions) and what he offers in the form of payroll, companionship with others, promotional possibilities, etc.*"

This match is not easy as the new employee is still unknown to many. So the new employee is placed as a probationer until the trial period is over. If the employee's performance during the probation period is satisfactory, his services will be regularized and he will be placed permanently on the job.

EMPLOYEE PLACEMENT PROCESS

Placement, in fact, is a process. It involves certain steps. These steps have been discussed by **Cascio and Elios** in their book, *Human Resource Management*. The employee placement process is shown in Figure 6.1.

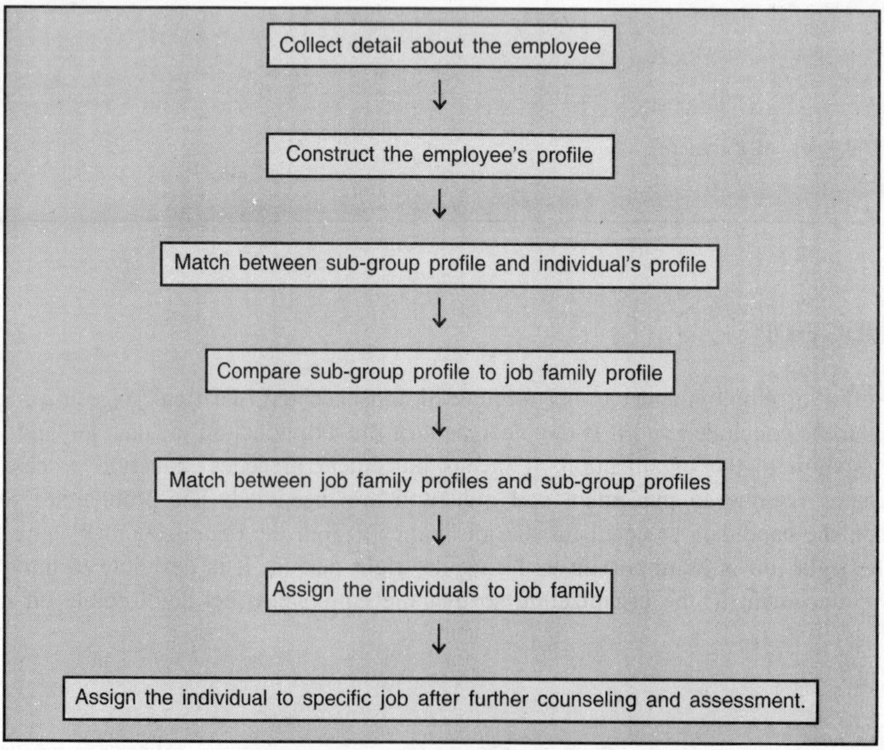

Fig. 6.1. Employee Placement Process.
Source: Wayne F Cascio and Elios M. Award, HRM, p. 25.

Figure 6.1 shows that once we establish the unique profile for each individual, people and jobs. It can be matched optimally within the constraints set by available jobs and available people. If the number of individuals is large in selection to the available jobs, only the best qualified persons can be selected and placed, thus the number of people and the number of jobs determine the placement process in any company.

Importance of Placement

A proper placement of a worker reduces employee turnover, absenteeism, accident rates; and improves the morale. If a candidate adjusts himself to the job and continues to perform as per expectations, it means that the candidate is properly placed.

PRINCIPLES OF PLACEMENT

A few basic principles have been evolved to be followed at the time of placement of a worker on the job. These principles are discussed as under:

1. **Principle of Job First, Man Next:** Man should be placed on the job according to the requirements of the job. The job should not be adjusted according to the qualifications or requirement of the man. Job First, Man Next, should be the principle of placement.
2. **Principle of Qualifications:** The job should be offered to the man according to his qualifications. The placement should neither be higher nor lower than the qualifications.
3. **Principle of Working Conditions:** The employee should be made conversant with the working conditions prevailing in the industry and all things relating to the job. He should also be made aware of the penalties if he commits a wrong.
4. **Principle of Loyalty and Cooperation:** While introducing the job to the new employee, an effort should be made to develop a sense of loyalty and cooperation in him so that he may realize his responsibilities better towards the job and the organization.
5. **Principle of Timely Preparation:** The placement should be ready before the joining date of newly selected person.
6. **Principle of Transfer:** The placement in the initial period may be temporary as changes are likely after the completion of training. The employee may later be transferred to the job where he can do better.

PROBLEMS OF PLACEMENT

The main difficulty or problem with placement arises when the recruiters look at the individual and not at the job. Often, the individual does not work independent of the others. Jobs in this context are classified into three categories:

1. **Independent Jobs:** In independent jobs, non-overlapping routes or territories are allotted to each employee, e.g. in field sales. In such situations, the activities of one employee have little bearing on the activities of other workers. Independent jobs do not pose great problems in the placement. Each employee has to be evaluated between his capabilities and interests and those required on the job:

(a) To fill the job with people who have at least minimum required qualifications.
(b) People should be placed on the job that will make the best possible use of their talents, given available job and HR constraints.

2. **Sequential Jobs:** Sequential or pooled jobs are also called dependant jobs. In sequential jobs, the activities of one employee are dependent on the activities of the fellow employee. Assembly lines are the best example of such jobs.

   In pooled jobs, there is high interdependence among jobs. The final output is the result of the contribution of all the workers. It is the team work which matters. Project teams, temporary task forces and assembly teams represent pooled jobs. In general the problems of placement are as under:

   (i) **Independent jobs do not pose great problems in placement excepting these jobs are rare:** The reason is that each employee is evaluated relative to the match between his/her capabilities and interests and those required on the job. The objective is to fill all jobs with the individuals who are best suited to the jobs under given HR constraints. These jobs are becoming rare and rare.
   (ii) **Sequential or pooled or dependent jobs pose great problems:** This is because in these cases for matching individuals with jobs, firms use the assessment classification model, which is complex as in this first, the details of employee's skills, interests, past performance and biographical details are collected and then each individual is placed in a specific sub-group. Here there is a problem of placing all individuals of equal characteristics in one sub-group.
   (iii) **Difficulty in categorizing jobs in sub-groups:** Just as it is difficult to prepare a sub-group of individuals of same characteristics, similarly it is difficult to put all jobs having similar characteristics in each sub-group.
   (iv) **Matching sub-group profiles with job-family profiles is again a problematic task:** This is because perfect match is very rare. Individual biases may be there. In fact assessment classification model is faulty and quite away from reality.

MEANING OF INDUCTION

It is observed that in most organizations the rate of turnover is very high among new employees compared to that among senior employees. These employees fail to adjust and adapt to the new surroundings and environment. Further, absence of information, lack of knowledge about the new environment, behavioural variations, cultural gaps, different levels of technology, variations in the requirement of the job, disturb the new employees. The obvious reason for such a state is the failure of the companies to understand the need and requirement of the induction programme for the new employees. The employees have to be educated about the job location surroundings and organizational surroundings. Hence, induction is essential as the newcomer may feel insecure, shy and hesitant. Induction is thus, very much essential to remove instability and turnover.

Induction, also called orientation, is designed to provide a new employee with the information; he/she needs to function comfortably and effectively in the organization. Induction is a planned introduction of new employees to their jobs, their peers and the company. It was introduced in US companies during early 1970s and is gaining popularity with prominent user companies IT companies, Taj Group of Hotels, P&G, HUL, Citibank and Colgate Palmolive.

Definitions

According to **Edwin B. Flippo,** "*Induction is the welcoming process to make the new employee feel at home and generate in him a feeling of belongingness to the organization.*"

According to **Michael Armstrong**, "*Orientation or induction is the process of receiving and welcoming an employee when he first joins a company and giving him the basic information he needs to settle down quickly and happily and start work*".

Induction or orientation provides information in three related areas:

(i) General information about the daily work routine.

(ii) Information about the firm's history, founding fathers, objectives, operations and products or services.

(iii) Detailed presentation of the organization's policies, work rules and employee benefits.

Table 6.1 demonstrates the topics covered in employee orientation programmes.

Table 6.1: Employee Orientation Programmes

Organizational Issues	
• History of employer • Organization of employer • Names and titles of key executives • Employee's title and department • Layout of physical facilities	• Probationary period • Product line or services provided • Overview of production process • Company policies and rules • Disciplinary regulation • Employee handbook • Safety procedure and enforcement
Employee Benefits	
• Pay scale and pay days • Vacations and holidays • Rest breaks • Training and education benefits • Counselling	• Insurance benefits • Retirement programme • Employer-provided services to employees • Rehabilitation programmes
Introduction	
• To supervisor • To trainers	• To coworkers • To employee counselor
Job Duties	
• Job location • Job tasks • Job safety requirements	• Overview of job • Job objectives • Relationship to other jobs

Essentials of Good Induction Programme

A good induction programme has three main elements:

1. **Introductory Information:** Introductory information regarding the history of the company and company's products, its organizational structure, policies, rules and regulations, etc. should be given informally or in group session in the personnel department. It will help the candidate to understand the company and the organizational policies and standards as well.

2. **On the job Information:** Further information should be given to the new employee by the department supervisor in the department concerned where he is placed on the job, about departmental facilities and requirements such as nature of the job, the extent of his liability and employee's activities such as recreational facilities, safety measures, job routine, etc.
3. **Follow-up Interview:** A follow-up interview should be arranged several weeks after the employee has been on the job by the supervisor or a representative of the personnel department to answer the problems that a new employee may have on the job.

OBJECTIVES OF INDUCTION

A large organization should have a systematic induction programme to achieve the following objectives:

(i) To promote a feeling of belongingness and loyalty to the organization among new comers so that they may not form false impression regarding the company because first impression is the last impression.

(ii) To build the new employee's confidence in the organization and in himself so that he may become an efficient employee.

(iii) To bring an arrangement between the organization goals and the personal goals.

(iv) To give the new employee information regarding company (its structure, products, policies, rules and regulations) and facilities provided by the company such as cafeterias, locker rooms, break time, leave rule etc.

(v) To introduce the new worker to the supervisor and fellow workers with whom he has to work.

(vi) To create a sense of security for the worker in his job by impressing upon the idea that fairness to the worker is the inherent policy of the organization.

(vii) To lessen or reduce the cost of replacing the worker in the early impressionable period because of the lack of information or incorrect business impressions.

PURPOSE OF INDUCTION

According to one important research study, there are specific purposes of induction or orientation programmes. These are discussed as under:

- Minimizing disturbance and anxious state of employees in the initial days of job.
- Minimizing anxieties of new employees by initiation practices of the peers.
- Avoid anxiety to interfere with the training process.
- Ensure that the new employee discuss their problems with their supervisors.
- Induction seeks to expose new employees to all areas of the company.
- The purpose of induction is to make new employees productive to the company quickly.
- To create a favourable impression of the firm and its work.
- Effectiveness of an orientation programme is to have a lasting effect on absenteeism and turnover.
- Induction programme is thus required to minimize the problems of new employees.

PROCEDURES OF INDUCTION

There is no set model of induction programme as each company develops its own procedure as per its needs and requirements. Many organizations develop formal orientation programmes which include tour of the offices, plant, talking about the history of the organization and discussion with the representative of personnel department. Some firms may opt for informal orientation programme in which a senior employee is assigned the job of introducing the new employee to the workers and show other things.

Before discussing the steps taken in orientation/induction process, it is essential to first discuss, in brief, the prerequisites of an effective induction programme.

Prerequisites of an Effective Orientation Programme

1. **Make Strategic Choices:** A firm needs to make four strategic choices before designing the induction programme, i.e. the programme is formal or informal individual or collective, serial or disjunctive and investiture or divestiture. Figure 6.2 shows these choices.
2. **HR Unit and Supervisor to Prepare for New Employees:** This is essential to make the new employees feel at home and comfortable. It would create an atmosphere of initial acceptance and trust.
3. **Determine Information Employees Want to Know:** This is to avoid overlapping of or missing out of any important information. The information that must be provided to the employees is shown in Figure 6.1. Some firms also use orientation checklist. Such checklists contain items to be covered by the HR unit and the line manager. Table 6.2 shows such a checklist.
4. **Determine How to Present Information:** Line managers and HR representatives should determine the most appropriate way to present the orientation information. For example, rather than telling an employee verbally, information on company sick leave and holiday policies may be presented on the first day in a handbook.
5. **Completion of Paperwork:** All essential paperwork should be completed during orientation so that the employee gets paid accurately and on time. Various tax and insurance forms as well as time cards and other items need to be completed in a timely fashion. There is nothing more agonizing for a new employee than to miss the first pay cheque or to be paid improperly because the correct forms were not completed accurately.

Steps in Induction Procedure

The induction procedure should basically follow the following steps shown.

- **Step I**–Knowledge of time and place to report to work.
- **Step II**–The supervisor or the immediate boss meet and welcome the employees to the organization.
- **Step III**–Administrative work should be completed (vacations, probation period, medical leaves, and suggestion system).
- **Step IV**–Conducting departmental orientation (introduction to department, functions of department, to whom the new employee should look for help in case of problem).

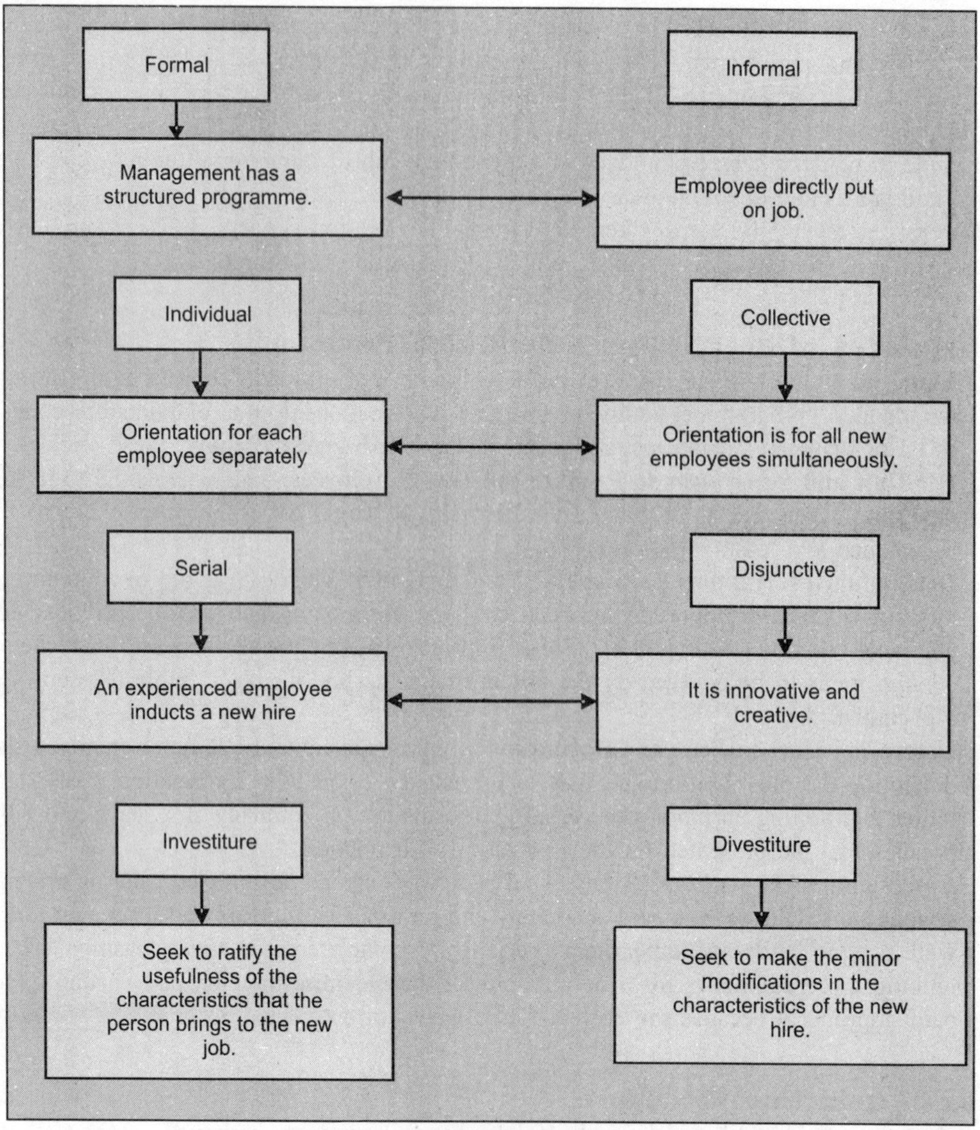

Fig. 6.2. Strategic Choices of Orientation.
Source: Adapted from David Decezo, Ed., Personnel/HRM, Prentice-Hall of India, 2000, p. 223.

- **Step V**–Supply of written material (employee handbooks, flyers, employee manuals, picture stories, short guide pictures, etc.)

The stages of induction process are also revealed in Table 6.3 that shows the employee orientation schedule.

Table 6.2: Orientation Checklist

Name of Employee
Starting Date
Department

HR Department

Prior to Orientation

- Complete Form A and give or mail to new employee
- Complete Form B
- Attach Form B to orientation
- Checklist-supervisor and give to the supervisor

Employee's First Day

Organization and Personnel Policies and Procedures

- History of XYZ Inc.
- Organization Chart
- Service to Community-Purpose of the Company
- Employee Classifications

Insurance Benefits

- Group Health
- Disability
- Life
- Workmen's Compensation

Other Benefits

- Holidays
- Jury and Election Duty
- Vacation
- Death in the Family
- Health Services
- Professional Discounts
- Appointments

End of Orientation—First Day

- Make Appointment for Second Day
- Introduce Employee to Supervisor

Other Items

- Job Posting
- Bulletin Board—Location and Use
- Safety
- No Drinking
- Where to get Supplies
- Employee's Records—Updating

Name of Employee
Starting Date
Department *Position*

Supervisor

Employee's First Day

- Introduction to Coworkers
- Tour of Department
- Tour of Company

Location of

- Coat Closet
- Rest Room
- Telephone for Personal Use and
- Rules Concerning it

Working Hours

- Starting and Leaving
- Lunch
- Breaks
- Overtime
- Early Departures
- Time Clock

Pay Policy

- Pay Period
- Deposit System

Other Items

- Parking
- Dress

During Employee's First Two Weeks

Emergencies

- Medical
- Power Failure
- Fire

Employee's Second Day

- Pension Retirement Plan
- Sick Leave
- Personal Leave
- Job Posting
- Confidentiality
- Complaints and Concerns
- Termination
- Equal Employment Opportunity

At the end of the employee's first two weeks, the supervisor will ask if the employee has any questions on the above items. After all questions have been satisfied, the supervisors will sign and date this form and return it to the HR Department.

Signature

Date ORIENTATION CONDUCTED BY

Source: Robert L. Mathis and John H. Jackson, Personnel—Contemporary Perspectives and Applications, West Publishing, New York, 1982, p. 225.

Table 6.3: A New Employee Orientation Schedule

New Employee	Mr. Niraj Mittal, M.B.A. (Human Resource Management), Bangalore University, 1999
Job Title	Human Resource – Executive
Department	Human Resource Development
Reporting Date	1st June 1999. 8.00 am Report to Ms. Roopa, HRD. Chief
8.00 a.m. to 9.00 a.m.	Ms. Roopa will: Distribute brochures describing the organization's history, Products and Philosophy Review the organization's overall structure, authority structure within the HRD department. Review HRM Policies and Practices.
9.30 to 10.30 a.m.	Mr. Rao will discuss company benefits; New employee is to fill out health, tax and other relevant forms.
10.30 to 11.30 a.m.	Tour to main building and auxiliary facilities with Ms. Roopa.
11.30 a.m. to 12.30 p.m.	Lunch with HR manager and with Ms. Roopa.
12.30 p.m. to 3.00 p.m.	Mr. Swaraj will:
·	Provide a detailed tour of the Production and Marketing Departments
·	Detailed discussions with Chief Executive-HRM about daily job routine and department policies and rules.
·	Explain job expectations. Introduce Mr. Niraj to his co-workers.
3.00 p.m. to 5.00 p.m.	New employee on his own to familiarize himself with his job.

Source: P. Subba Rao, HRM and Industrial Relations, pp. 185-186.

PROBLEMS OF INDUCTION

An orientation programme can go wrong for a number of reasons. The HR department should try to avoid such errors. Some of them are:

1. Supervisor who is entrusted with the job, is not trained or is too busy.
2. Employee is overwhelmed with too much information in a short time.
3. Employee is confused with so many forms to complete.
4. Employee is given only menial tasks that discourage job interest and company loyalty.
5. Employee is asked to perform tasks where there are high chances of failure that could needlessly discourage the employee.
6. Employee is pushed into the job with a sketchy orientation under the mistaken belief that 'trial by fire is the best orientation'.
7. Employee is forced to fill in the gaps between a broad orientation by the HR department and narrow orientation at the department level.
8. Employee is thrown into action too soon and his mistakes can damage the company.
9. Employee may develop wrong perceptions because of short periods spent on each job.

REVIEW QUESTIONS

1. What do you mean by placement? Discuss the placement process.
2. What is placement? What are the benefits of placement?

3. Discuss the principles of placement. How are employees placed on independent, pooled sequential jobs?
4. Distinguish between placement and induction. Are they substituting for each other?
5. What is induction? Discuss the objectives and purpose for induction.
6. "Induction is the guided adjustment of employees to the organization and his work environment". Discuss.
7. Discuss an ideal induction procedure for sales executives in an IT organization.
8. You need to hire three sales representatives for your company. Describe appropriate induction methods, you would like to use.
9. Explain briefly a few selection techniques in general. Outline those selection techniques which are used in India.
10. "If employees are properly selected, there should be no need for an orientation programme." Comment.

CASE STUDY

6.1 Introduction of Induction

Mrs. Sunita Devi worked for 15 years in the ABC Biscuit Ltd. She joined very recently the Parle G Company as the Production Manager. She was supposed to attend a routine departmental heads meeting last Monday at 5.30 p.m., which was presided over by the Managing Director of the company. She did not attend the meeting as there was no formal or informal communication to her. The managing director did not like her absence as there were many important items to be discussed regarding the production department. Mrs. Sunita Devi was called by the Managing Director on the next day and asked explanation for not attending the meeting. Mrs. Sunita Devi replied that there was no information. The secretary said that it was a routine meeting and as such information was not sending to any departmental head. But all other heads, except Mrs. Sunita Devi attended the meeting. Then, the Managing Director spent a lot of time to find out the man, who is responsible for the incident. But he could not succeed.

Questions

1. Who is responsible for occurrence of such a mistake?
2. Find out the reason for the incident. How do you propose to solve such problems in the future?

6.2 Naik AGM Materials Resignation

Naik, AGM Materials, is fuming and fretting. He bumped into Kamath, GM Materials, threw the resignation letter on his table, shouted and walked out of the room swiftly. Naik has reason for his sudden outburst. He has been driven to the wall. Perhaps, details of the story will tell the reasons for Naik's bile and why he puts in his papers, barely four months after he took up his present assignment.

The year was 1995 when Naik quit the prestigious SAIL plant at Vishakhapatnam. As a manager, materials, Naik enjoyed powers—he could even place an order for materials worth Rs. 25 lakh. He needed nobody's prior approval.

Naik joined a pulp-making plant located at Harihar in Karnataka, as AGM Materials. The plant is a part of the multi-product and multi plant-conglomerate owned by a prestigious business house in India. Obvious, perks, designations and reputation of the conglomerate lured Naik away from public sector steel monolith.

When he joined the eucalyptus pulp making company, little did Naik realize that he needed prior approval to place an order for materials worth Rs. 12 lakh. He had presumed that he had the authority to place an order by himself worth half the amount of what he used to do at the mega steel maker. He placed the order; material arrived, was received, accepted and used up in the plant.

Trouble started when the bill of Rs. 12 lakh came from the vendor. The accounts department withheld payment for the reason that the bill was not endorsed by Kamath. Kamath refused to sign on the bill as his approval was not taken by Naik before placing the order.

Naik felt fumigated and cheated. A brief encounter with Kamath only aggravated the problem. Naik was curtly told that he should have known company rules before venturing. Naik decided to quit.

Source: K. Aswathapa, Human Resource Management, p. 201.

Questions

1. Does the company have an orientation programme? If yes, how effective it is?
2. If you were Naik what would have you done.

REFERENCES

1. Aswathappa, K. (2008). HRM, Tata McGraw-Hill Publishing Company Ltd, New Delhi, pp. 115-118.
2. David A. DeCenzo and Stephen P. Robbins, (1989). "Personnel/Human Resource Management", Third edition, Prentice-Hall of India, New Delhi, p.111.
3. Michael Armstrong, (1988). "A Handbook of Personnel Management Practices", Third edition, Kogan Page, London, p. 316.
4. Lloyd L. Byars and Leasile W. Rue, (1997). "Human Resource Management", Irwin.
5. Subba Rao, P. (2007). "Human Resource Management and Industrial Relations", Himalaya Publishing House, New Delhi, pp. 182-183.
6. Terry L. Leap and Michael D. Crino, (1990). "Personnel/Human Resource Management", Macmillan, New York, p. 316.
7. William P. Anthony, et al., (1993). "Strategic Human Resource Management", Dryden Press, p. 208.

CHAPTER

7

Training and Development

CHAPTER'S OUTLINE

- Introduction
- Meaning of Training
- Need for Training
- Importance/Benefits of Training
- Methods of Training
- Types of Training
- Process/Steps in Training Programmes
- Executive or Management Development
- Management Development Process
- Need and Importance of Executive Development
- Methods/Techniques of Executive Development

INTRODUCTION

Organizations and individuals should develop and progress simultaneously for their survival and attainment of mutual goals. So, every modern management has to develop the organization through Human Resource Development (HRD). Employee training is one of the important techniques of HRD. It is a specialized operative function of Human Resource Management (HRM).

The techniques of HRD include:

(i) Performance Appraisal
(ii) Training and Development
(iii) Management Development
(iv) Career Development
(v) Workers' Participation
(vi) Organization Development
(vii) Quality Circles
(viii) Social and Spiritual Development

Among these techniques of HRD, the role of training and development is highly instrumental. In this chapter, besides, explaining the meaning of training, need, importance, methods and process of training, emphasis would be given on the need and methods of executives or management development.

MEANING OF TRAINING OF EMPLOYEES

After the newly appointed employees (new recruits), have joined the organization, the next phase of personnel programme is to impart necessary training to them to make them fit for the jobs they are supposed to handle. Every company must have a systematic training programme for growth and development of its employees. Training is equally necessary for old employees whenever new machines and equipment are introduced. In fact, training is an ongoing process and organized activity for improving, changing, moulding the employee's knowledge, skill, behaviour, aptitude and attitude towards the requirements of the job and organization. It refers to teaching and learning activities.

Training, bridges the gap between job requirement and employees' present job specification.

Definitions

According to **Edwin B. Flippo**, "*Training is the act of increasing the knowledge and skill of an employee for doing a particular job.*"

According to **Mathis and Jackson**, "*Training is a learning process whereby people acquire skills, concepts, attitudes or knowledge to aid in the achievement of goals.*"

According to **Michael Armstrong,** "*Training is the systematic modification of behaviour through learning which occurs as a result of education, instruction, development and planned experience.*"

According to **Wayne F Cascio**, "*Training consists of planned programme designed to improve performance at the individual, group, and/or organizational levels. Improved performance, in turn, implies that there have been measurable changes in knowledge, skills, attitudes, and/or social behaviour.*"

From the above definitions and meaning, the **following features of training** are highlighted:

- Increased knowledge and skills for doing a job.
- Bridges the gap between 'job needs' and employee skills, knowledge and behaviour, etc.
- Job-oriented process is vocational in nature.
- Short-term activity designed essentially for operations.

- Useful for employees.
- Useful for organization.
- Continuous process.
- Useful for old employees.
- Brings change in attitude of workers.

NEED FOR TRAINING

Every organization and individual need training due to following reasons:

1. **To match the Employee Specification with the Job Requirements and Organizational Needs:** Every organization finds deviations between employee's present specification and the job requirements and organizational needs. Training is needed to fill these gaps by developing and moulding the employees' skill, knowledge, attitude, behaviour, etc. to the tune of the job requirements and organizational needs.
2. **Technological Advancement:** Every organization in order to survive and to be effective should adopt latest technology, i.e., mechanization, computerization and automation. Adopting of latest technological means and methods, will not be completed until they are manned by employees possessing skill to operate them.
3. **Quality Conscious Customers:** The customers have become quality conscious and their requirements keep on changing. To satisfy the customers, quality of products must be continuously improved through training of the workers.
4. **Greater Productivity:** It is essential to increase productivity and reduce cost of production for meeting competition in the market. Effective training can help increase productivity of workers.
5. **Stable Workforce:** Training creates a feeling of confidence in the minds of the workers. It gives them a security at the workplace. As a result, labour turnover and absenteeism rates are reduced.
6. **Increased Safety:** Trained workers handle the machines safely. They also know the use of various safety devices in the factory. Thus, they are less prone to industrial accidents.
7. **Better Management:** Training can be used as an effective tool of planning and control. It develops skills among workers for the future and also prepares them for promotion. It helps in reducing the costs of supervision, wastages and industrial accidents. It also helps increase productivity and quality.
8. **Change in the Job Assignment:** Training is also necessary when the existing employee is promoted to the higher level in the organization and when there is some new job (assignments) or occupation due to transfer. Training is also necessary to equip the old employees with the advance technology or techniques.

So, training is necessary from individual viewpoint, as it will give them greater job security and an opportunity for advancement. Similarly, skill acquired through training is an asset for the organization.

Difference between Training and Development

The process of training and development are often confused. Mostly, we take the same sense of both. But training is the act of increasing knowledge for doing a particular job. Development, on the other hand, means growth of the individual in all respects.

Table 7.1: Difference between Training and Development

Training	Development
1. Training means learning skills and knowledge for doing a particular job. It increases job skills.	Development means the growth of an employee in all respects. It shapes attitudes.
2. The term 'training' is generally used to denote imparting specific skills among operative workers and employees.	The term 'development' is associated with the overall growth of the executives.
3. Training is concerned with maintaining and improving current job performance. Thus, it has short-term perspective.	Executive development seeks to develop competence and skills for future performance. Thus, it has a long-term perspective.
4. Training is job-centred in nature.	Development is career-centred in nature.
5. The role of a trainer or supervisor is very important in training.	All development is 'self development'. The executive has to be internally motivated for self-development.

IMPORTANCE / BENEFITS OF TRAINING

Training plays an important role in human resource development. It is necessary, useful and productive for all categories of workers and supervisory staff. It is vary important in the present age, as development in science and technology are introducing drastic changes in the industrial field. Trained personnel are like valuable assets of an organization. These personnel are responsible for the progress and stability or survival of an organization.

Expenditure on training is a profitable investment. The responsibility of imparting training to the employees rests on the employer. If there is no formal training programme in an organization, the workers will train themselves on the basis of trial and error or by observing others. But this process will take a lot of time and will result in higher cost of training. Moreover workers may not be able to learn the best operative methods.

Modern organizations arrange for the training of the human resources to achieve the following benefits:

(i) **Quick learning:** Training helps to reduce the learning time to reach the acceptable level of performance. The employees need not learn by observing others and waste time if the formal training programme exists in the organization. The qualified instructors will help the new employees to acquire the skills and knowledge to do particular jobs quickly.

(ii) **Higher productivity:** Training increases the skill of the new employee in the performance of a particular job. An increase in skill usually helps increase in both quantity and quality of output. Training is also great help to the existing employees. It helps them to increase their level of performance on their present job assignments and prepares them for future assignments.

(iii) **Standardization of procedures.** With the help of training, the best available methods of performing the work can be standardized and taught to all employees. Standardization will make high levels of performance rule rather than exception. Employees will work intelligently and make fewer mistakes when they possess the required know-how and have an understanding of their jobs and of the interdependence of one job on another.

(iv) **Less supervision:** If the employees are given adequate training, the need of supervision will be lessened. Training does not eliminate the need for supervision, but it reduces the need for detailed and continuous supervision. A well-trained employee is self-reliant in his work because he knows what to do and how to do. Under such situations, close supervision is ordinarily, not mandatory.

(v) **Economical Operations:** Trained personnel will be able to make better and economical use of materials and equipment. Wastage also will be low. In addition, the rate of accidents and damage to machinery and equipment will be kept to the minimum by the trained employees. These will lead to lower cost of production per unit.

(vi) **Higher morale:** The morale of employees is increased if they are given proper training. A good training programme will mould employees' attitudes towards organizational activities and generate better cooperation and greater loyalty. With the help of training dissatisfactions, complaints, absenteeism and turnover can also be reduced among the employees. Thus, training helps in building an efficient and cooperative workforce.

(vii) **Preparation of future managers:** When totally new skills are required by an organization, it has to face great difficulties in the selection process. Training can be used in spotting out promising men and preparing them for promotion. It is better to select and train from within the organization rather than seek skilled employees from the outside sources.

(viii) **Better management:** A manager can make use of training to manage in a better way. To him, training the employees can assist improving planning, organizing, directing and controlling. For instance, maintaining delegating authority and stimulating employees are all assisted by effective training.

METHODS OF TRAINING

There is wide range of training methods and techniques have been developed over the years by various organizations and training experts. Different training methods are suitable for different categories of employees in the organization, like, managerial and non-managerial, technical, administrative, skilled, unskilled, senior, and junior, and so on. Each organization has to choose those methods and techniques which are relevant for its training needs.

1. On-the-Job Training

This type of training is most effective for operative personnel. Under this method, the worker is given training at the workplace under the supervision and guidance of a trained worker or instructor. This trained worker may be a coach, immediate supervisor, senior person or expert in the organization; the worker learns in the actual environment. There are several types of on-the-job training methods; some of them are given as under:

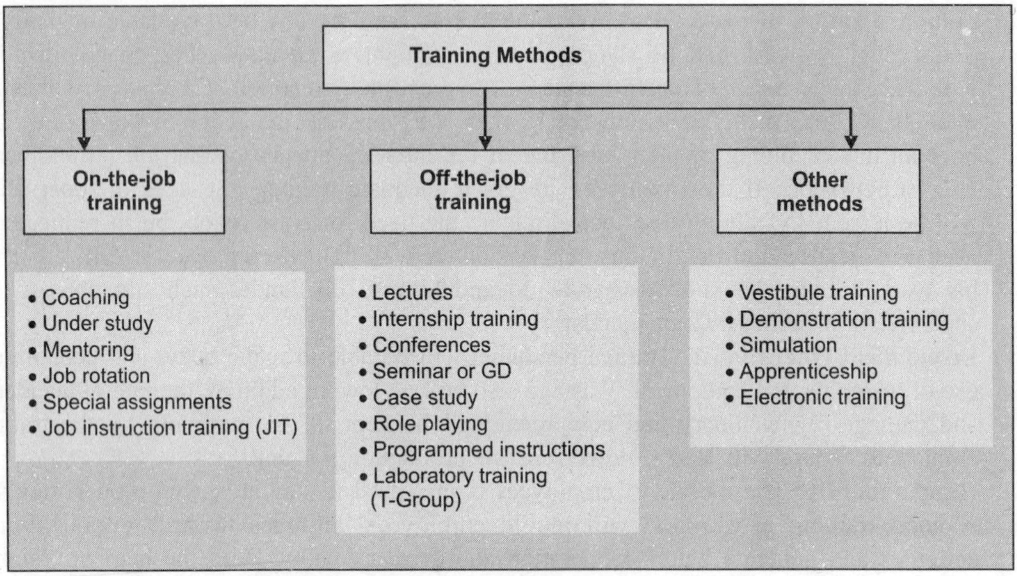

Fig. 7.1. Methods of Training.

(i) Coaching

Under this method, the supervisor imparts job-knowledge and skills to his subordinate. More emphasis is given on 'learning-by-doing'. Coaching involves direct personal instructions and guidance, usually with extensive demonstration and continuous critical appraisal and correction. This method is very effective if the superior has sufficient time to provide coaching to his subordinates.

(ii) Under-study

In this, the superior gives training to his subordinate who is under his study (assistant). The subordinate learns through 'experience and observation'. It prepares the subordinate to assume the responsibilities of the superior's job in case the superior leaves the organization.

The subordinate chosen for under-study is designated as the heir-apparent and his future depends upon what happens to his boss. The purpose of under-study is to prepare someone to fill the vacancy caused by death, retirement, promotion or transfer of superiors.

(iii) Mentoring

It is a somewhat different form of training method. In mentoring, senior person in the organization assumes the responsibility for training as well as grooming of a junior person. A mentor acts as a teacher, guide, counsellor, philosopher, exemplar, supporter and facilitator of the junior. The basic objective of mentoring is to help an employee gain psychological maturity and effectiveness and get integrated with the organization. Mentoring can take place both at formal and informal levels depending on the prevailing work culture and commitment from the management.

Mentoring in India is based on the time honored Guru-Shishya relationship where the guru would do everything to develop the personality of the Shishya, offering emotional support and guidance. Shishya, on the other hand, can do anything and everything for the guru. Companies like Coca-Cola, TISCO have used mentoring systems to good effect in recent times. A good mentor has to:

- Listen to the mentee and understand him
- Challenge his intellect and stimulate the learning process
- Coach
- Build self-confidence.
- Provide wise counselling
- Teach by examples
- Act as the role model
- Share experience
- Offer motivation

(iv) Job-rotation

This type of training involves the movement of the trainee from one job to another at a certain time intervals. However, sufficient time should be given to trainee on all the jobs to become an all-rounder and to get full knowledge of the jobs. The trainee gets knowledge of each job from his trainer or superior of each job. This method is common for managers for general management position and also for workshop jobs.

Merits

- Job rotation method is used by that organization who wants all-round workers.
- The employees get and learn new knowledge, skill and gain experience in handling different kinds of jobs.
- This method gives opportunities to the trainee to understand; the problems faced by the employees on other jobs and respect them.
- The trainee may come to know the interrelationship between different jobs.
- Job rotation is useful when there is any need (leave, transfer, etc.) in the organization, in that case the trainee can handle their task.

(v) Special assignment or committee assignment

Under the committee assignment, group of trainees are given and asked to solve an actual organizational problem. The trainee solves the problem jointly. It develops team work.

It is used for lower-level executives with first-hand experience in working actual problems.

(vi) Job-instruction training (JIT)—training through step by step

This method is very popular for preparing supervisors to train operatives. This method is also known as step-by-step learning. So, the list is made in proper sequence. Each step show "What is to be done" with 'key points' i.e. "how it is to be done and why". It is a four-step process:

Step I: Prepare the employee for instruction, it includes:
- Putting him at ease.
- Emphasizing importance of the task.
- Giving general description of job duties and responsibilities.
- Create interest in learning the job.

Step II: Presentation of the instructions, it includes:
- Telling and showing him each step of the job.
- Stressing why and how each step is carried out.
- Instruct clearly and patiently.

Step III: Let him try, it includes:
- Let him try, to show that he has understood the instructions.
- Correct errors or mistakes.
- Continue until you know, he knows.

Step IV: Follow through, it includes:
- Encouraging the questions and allow the trainee to work along and the trainer follow-up regularly.

The JIT method provides immediate feedback on results, quick correction of errors and provision for extra practice when required. But it demands a skill-trainer.

Advantages of on-the-job training method

1. The main advantage of on-the-job training is that the trainee learns on the actual equipment and in the true environment of his job. So, he gets practical knowledge.
2. It is highly economical, since no additional expert or facilities are required for training.
3. The trainee learns the rules, regulations and procedures by observing their day-to-day applications. So, can easily understand the management.
4. It is suitable for an organization where number of jobs are equal to number of employees.
5. It requires relatively short period, say, a few days or weeks.
6. It needs no school and training institutes, so cost is less.

Disadvantages of on-the-job training method

1. The disadvantage of on-the-job training is sometimes the instructions are disorganized and not properly supervised, may be because of less experienced trainer to impart skill to the trainee.
2. Learners are often subject to distractions of noisy shop or office.
3. There may be low productivity, if the trainee is unable to fully develop his skills.

However, on-the-job methods are generally given in a large number of organizations and are suitable for all levels of operatives, supervisors and executives.

2. Off-the-Job Training

In off-the-job training methods, the trainees have to leave their workplace and devote their entire time to the training. In this method, the trainee can place his entire concentration on learning the job rather than spending his time in performing it. There is an opportunity for freedom of expression for the trainees. Off-the-job training may be held in other institutions/ colleges, universities or associations, which have no connection with the company.

(i) Lectures

Lectures are regarded as one of the simplest ways of imparting knowledge to the trainees. In lecture, basic facts, concepts or principles, attitudes, theories and problem-solving abilities are to be taught. It is a formal organized talk (direct method) by the training specialist (outside expert), the formal superior or other individual on specific topic. The lecturer or instructor/ specialist seeks to communicate his thought at the level of trainee and create interest in the class and enable them to retain and engage. The trainee generally takes notes as an aid to learning. The lecture can make cheerful with discussion, film shows, case studies, role-playing, demonstrations, audio-visual aids, etc.

Merits

- It is direct communication and can be used for a large group of trainees. Thus, cost and time involved are reduced.
- It is a simple and efficient method and through it more material can be presented within a short time than by any other method.

Demerits

- It requires a lot of time for preparation for which management personnel often lack the time. Moreover, it requires substantial speaking skill.
- Listener's capacity to listen is generally limited to 15 minutes to 20 minutes. So, because of one hour or more, attention of listeners drifts.
- It will not be effective, if material is not the common level of knowledge.
- Too much explanation or information makes a lecture unpalatable to the listener.
- It is one-way communication as compared to other methods.

(ii) Internship training

In internship training, educational institutions and business firms have a joint programme of training. Selected candidates carry on regular studies for the prescribed period. They also work in some factory or office to acquire practical knowledge and skills. This method helps to provide a good balance between theory and practice. But due to its slow process, it requires long time period. Internship training is used in professional courses e.g. MBBS, MBA, CA, ICWA, etc.

(iii) The conference method

A conference is a group meeting conducted according to an organized plan, in which the members participate in oral discussion on a particular problem and thus develop their knowledge and understanding. It is an executive training device for conference members and conference leaders. Both learnt a lot from other views and compare their opinions with others. The conference leader may also learn how to develop their skill to motivate people through direction of discussion. Conference is of three types:

(a) Guided or directed conference
(b) Consultative conference or training conference
(c) Problem-solving conference (seminar conference)

For training purpose, guided or directed conference is used, in which trained guides the discussion in such a way that facts, principles or concepts are explained.

Merits of Conference Method

- There is two-way communication, which is more effective.
- The conference is ideally suited for purpose of analyzing problems and issues, and examining them from different point of view.
- The trainee actively participates and his interest in learning is maintained.
- It is an useful method in training clericals, professionals and supervisory personnel.

Demerits of Conference Method

- It is limited to a small group of 15-20 persons, because a large group often discourages the active participation of all the delegates.
- Sometimes, irrelevant issues are allowed to speak, which slows the progress.
- The conferees should have some knowledge of the subject to be discussed at the conference.
- Good and stimulating leaders are needed who give summarized material and help in analyzing and reach decisions.
- It should involve the problem which is currently faced by an individual.

(iv) Seminar or team discussion (GD)

This is an established method for training. A seminar is conducted in many ways:

- It may be based on a paper prepared by one or more trainees on a subject selected in consultation with the person in charge of the seminar. It may be a part of a study or related to theoretical studies or practical problems. The trainee reads his/her paper and this is followed by a critical discussion. The chairman of the seminar summarizes the contents of the papers and the discussions which follow their reading.
- It may be based on the statement made by the person in charge of the seminar or on a document prepared by an expert, who is invited to participate in the discussion.
- The person in charge of the seminar distributes in advance the material to be analyzed in the form of required readings. The seminar compares the reactions of thc trainees, encourages discussion, defines the general trends and guides the participants to certain conclusions.

- Valuable working material may be provided to the trainees by actual files. The trainees may consult the files and bring these to the seminar where they may study in detail the various aspects, ramifications and complexities of a particular job or work or task.

(v) Case studies

Case study method is generally used to teach law, Business Management, Human Relations, Market Management, etc. to let the trainee understand that there may be different solutions to a particular problem. Under this method a real or sometimes hypothetical problem or situation is presented in writing to the trainees. They are required to identify and analyze the problem, suggest and evaluate alternative courses of action and choose the most appropriate solution. The trainer guides the discussion and ensures that no relevant factor is overlooked. In India cases are prepared by the Administrative Staff College at Hyderabad and other institutes of higher learning in management.

Merits of Case Study Method

- It promotes analytical thinking and develops a problem-solving ability.
- It encourages open-mindedness.
- Although the trainee learns that there is no single answer or solution of a case problem yet they are expected to arrive at useful generalizations and principles.
- As because of case of real problem situations, the trainee takes great interest in them.

Demerits of Case Study Method

- It is taught from books at developing centres of learning. If we really took the case from the organization, perhaps we gave different solution.
- The preparation of cases is difficult; it needs time and money and also requires training from special training centres.
- The case becomes a permanent precedent in their minds and may be used indiscriminately.

(vi) Role playing

Under this a conflicting situation is artificially created and two or more trainees are assigned different roles to play. No dialogues are given in hand. The role players before playing are provided with either written or oral description of the situation and the role they are to play. After being allowed sufficient time to plan their actions, they must then act their parts spontaneously before the class.

So, it has been defined as a method of human interaction which involves realistic behaviour in the imaginary situations. The idea of role playing involves action, doing and practice. This is just like a stage programme related to management field. Role playing primarily involves employee-employer relationship like hiring, discussing a grievance procedure, conducting a post-appraisal interview or disciplining a subordinate, or salesman making a presentation to the prospective buyer or customer.

Merits of Role Playing Method

- Learning by doing is emphasized.
- Human sensitivity and interactions are stressed.
- Immediate knowledge of the result is possible.
- Trainee interest and involvement tend to be high.
- It is useful method to project the living conditions between learning in the classroom and working on the job and creating a live business situation in the classroom.
- It develops skill and ability to apply knowledge, particularly in areas like human relations.
- It brings about desired changes in behaviour and attitudes.

Demerits of Role Playing Method

- The role playing sometimes seems artificial, if not played properly and seriously.

(vii) Programmed instruction (Teaching by the machine method)

Programmed instruction involves a sequence of steps in the performance of a desired operation or series of operation. First, the learning material or course is divided into small units called steps. These are set up through the Central Panel of Electronic Computer. The trainee takes the information or study material step by step. Then questions, facts or problems are presented to the learner. Learner gives the answer and immediately gets the feedback, i.e., whether their answers are right or wrong. It includes two main features:

(a) Providing information to the learner
(b) Providing feedback whether the response is correct or not.

Merits

- Trainee learns themselves.
- Instructors are not a key part of learning
- The materials to be learnt are broken down in small units.
- Immediate feedback is available.
- Active participation of the learner in each step.

Demerits

- Instructions are not properly arranged.
- Advance study (machine study) is not possible until preliminary information has been acquired.
- Only factual subject matters can be programmed, technical or motor skill cannot be taught.
- Cost of creating such programmes is high.

So, this method is preliminary used in teaching factual knowledge, such as mathematics, physics, foreign language, etc.

(viii) Laboratory training

It is also called sensitivity training and T-Group training, as here experiments are made. Sensitivity training is an experimental approach to training. It provides participants an opportunity to actually experience some concepts of management just as a manager would experience them in his own organizational situation. Sensitivity training is a group training method that uses intensive participation and gives immediate feedback for self-analysis and change. This training has two advantages:

(a) Participants remain involved and enthusiastic.
(b) The responsibility for learning experience lies with the participants.

As the name suggests sensitivity training aims at developing sensitivity within people towards thought, feeling and behaviour of other persons and through this, improve upon one's human interactions. The effectiveness of sensitivity training depends upon the ability of the participant to apply concepts and awareness obtained in the laboratory or group to his job, the transfer of his knowledge to the organization is possible if the organization has an open culture, an atmosphere of open discussion, encourage conflict resolution and promote mutual trust.

(ix) T-Groups

One of the methods of sensitivity training is the T-Group. Bethel Maine of USA was the pioneer of the T-Group. It was considered necessary that to change behaviour imparting necessary skills is required. A change in variety of skills and experience like self-awareness, interpersonal relationships, team work, group, and organizational process and inter-group conflict resolution. Sensitivity training has developed to the status of an intervention in organizational development. T-Group training is process oriented and not content oriented where people operate a feeling level of communication, observing, revealing, listening, and unravelling messages.

3. Other Methods of Training

(i) Vestibule training (Training-centre training)

This method attempts to duplicate on-the-job situations in a company classroom. It is a classroom training which is often imparted with the help of the equipment and machines which are identical with those in use in the place of work. This technique enables the trainee to concentrate on learning the new skills rather than on performing an actual job. In other words, it is geared to job duties. Theoretical training is given in the classroom, while the practical work is conducted on the production line.

It is a very efficient method of training semi-skilled, personnel, particularly when many employees have to be trained for the same kind of work at the same time. It is often used to train clerks, bank tellers, inspectors, machine operators, testers, typists, etc. It is most useful when philosophic concepts, attitudes, theories and problem-solving abilities have to be learnt. Training is generally given in the form of lectures, conferences, case studies, role playing and discussion.

Merits of Vestibule Training

- As training is given in a separate room, distractions are minimized.
- Secondly, a trained instructor, who knows how to teach, can be more effectively utilized.
- Thirdly, the correct method can be taught without interrupting production.
- It permits the trainee to practise without the fear of supervisors'/co-workers' observation and their possible ridicule.

Demerits of Vestibule Training

- The splitting of responsibilities leads to organizational problems.
- An additional investment in equipment is necessary, though the cost may be reduced by getting some productive work done by trainees while in the school.
- This method is of limited value for the jobs which utilize equipment which can be duplicated. Finally, the training situation is somewhat artificial.

However, when the number of trainees is, large vestibule schools are generally utilized; but when the number is small, on-the-job training is preferred.

(ii) Demonstrations and examples

In the demonstration method, the trainer describes and displays something, as when he teaches an employee how to do something by actually performing the activity himself and by going through a step-by-step explanation of "shy" and "what" he is doing.

Demonstrations are very effective in teaching because it is much easier to show a person how to do a job than to tell him or ask him to gather instruction from reading material. Demonstrations are often used in combination with lectures, pictures, text materials, discussions, etc.

Teaching by example is effective in mechanical operations or interpersonal relationships, for job duties and responsibilities, for informal group standards, supervisory expectations, and the like.

Demonstrations are particularly effective in the training for the acquisition of skills; but their usefulness is limited when it is a question of training management personnel. In a demonstration, the emphasis is primarily on know-how, the principles and theory of a job must, therefore, be taught by some other method.

(iii) Simulation

Simulation is a technique which duplicates as nearly as possible, the actual conditions encountered on a job. So, it is the representative of real situation. Where experiment on actual situation is destructive and harmful, the simulation is used. The vestibule training method or the business-game methods are examples of business simulations. Simulation techniques have been most widely used in the aeronautical industry.

Trainee interest and employee motivation are both high in simulation exercise because the actions of a trainee closely duplicate real job conditions. This training is essential in cases in which actual on-the-job practice might result in a serious inquiry, a costly error, or the destruction of valuable materials or resources. It is for this reason that the technique is a very expensive one.

(iv) Apprenticeship

For training in crafts, trades and in technical areas, apprenticeship training is the oldest and most commonly used method, especially when proficiency in a job is the result of a relatively long training period of 2 years to 3 years for persons of superior ability and from 4 years to 5 years for others. The field in which apprenticeship training is offered are numerous and range from the job of a draughtsman, a machinist, a printer, a tool-maker, a fitter, an architect, a mechanic, carpenters, weavers, jewellers, diesinkers, engravers, and electricians. A major part of training time is spending on-the-job productive work. Each apprentice is given a programme of assignments according to a pre-determined schedule, which provides for efficient training in trade skills.

Merits of Apprenticeship

- A skilled workforce is maintained.
- Immediate returns can be expected from training.
- The hiring cost is lower because of reduced turnover and lower production costs.
- The loyalty of employees is increased and opportunities for growth are frequent.

(v) Electronic training

Computerized and Internet based tools have revolutionized the training process. Some electronic training methods are as follows:

(a) **Audio-Visuals**: Audio-visuals include television slides, overheads, films, power points videoconferencing, audio-video tapes, etc. These can be very effective and are widely used as training techniques. This method is more interesting but more expensive as compared to other traditional methods. Besides, there is lack of two-way communication, no flexibility according to the requirement from different audience.

(b) **Distance and internet:** Organizations use various forms of distance learning methods for training. Distance learning methods include traditional paper and pencil correspondence courses as well as tele-training, videoconferencing and Internet based classes.

In tele-training, a trainer in a central location teaches groups of employees at remote locations via television. Honda America corporate began by using satellite technology to train engineers and now it uses it for many other types of employee training. This method is very cost effective since the employees learn at home and the company does not have to pay for their travel, stay and training.

Videoconferencing is used by companies to train the employees who are geographically separated from each other or from the trainer. This method allows people in one location to communicate line via a combination of audio and visual equipment with people in another city or country or with groups on several cities.

Many firms need the Internet and their proprietary intranets to deliver computer based training. Employees can access the programmes, whenever they want. Distribution costs are zero and changes can be made in the programmes at the central location whenever need arises.

Many forms are using Business Portals nowadays. Training is often found and delivered through training oriented learning portals. These portals contract with employers and deliver training options to the firms employees (e.g. web based). Many forms are creating their own learning portals for their employees.

Relative Effectiveness of Different Training Methods

The relative effectiveness depends upon the extent each method satisfied the specified goals. For this a research is made. In this a questionnaire was issued to 200 training directors with a request to rank the above methods from "Highly Effective (5)" to "Not Effective (1)".

Result of the research was as under:

(i) Programmed instruction (computer technique), as the most useful in case of organizations, who gives the importance to the knowledge acquisition and knowledge retention.

(ii) Sensitivity training (group-experience), ranked highest where there is a need of changing attitudes and developing interpersonal skills.

(iii) Conference method is most successful in gaining participants' acceptance.

(iv) The case-study method is the most suitable in case of problem-solving.

Therefore, it is concluded that the relative effectiveness of different training methods depends upon the specified goal, nature of the organization, type of personnel who requires training, type of product or services rendered by the organization, training budget, etc.

Criteria for Evaluation of Training

Generally, the following criterion is used for evaluating training programmes:

1. **Reaction:** Evaluate the trainee's reaction to the programme. Potential questions to the trainee might include:
   - What were the goals of the Training Programme?
   - Did you achieve them?
   - Did you like the programme?
   - Would you recommend it to others who have similar learning goals?
   - What suggestions would you give for the improvement of programme?
   - Is it beneficial for the organization to continue these types of programmes?
2. **Learning**: Did the trainee learn the skills, principles and facts that the trainer wanted him to learn?
3. **Job Behaviour:** Whether the trainee's behaviour on the job changed because of the training programme? This evaluation includes the manner and extent to which the trainee has applied his learning to the job.
4. **Organization:** This evaluation measures the use of training, learning, and change in the job behaviour of the department in the form of increased productivity, quality, morale, sales turnover, etc.
5. **Ultimate value:** It is the measurement of the ultimate result of the contribution of training programme to the company goals like survival and social goals like maximizing social benefits.

TYPES OF TRAINING

On the basis of purpose, several types of training programmes are offered to the employees. It should be noted that these programmes are not mutually exclusive. They invariably overlap and employ many common techniques. The important types of training programmes are as follows.

1. Induction or Orientation Training

Induction is concerned with introducing or orienting a new employee to the organization and its procedures, rules and regulations. When a new employee reports for work, he must be helped to get acquainted with the work environment and fellow employees. It is better to give him a friendly welcome when he joins the organization, get him introduced to the organisation and help him to get a general idea about the rules and regulations, working conditions, etc. of the organization.

Employee orientation or induction training is nothing but introduction of the organization to the newly employed person. The purpose is to give a 'bird's eye view' of the organization where he has to work. It is a very short informative training given immediately after the recruitment. It creates a feeling of involvement in the minds of newly appointed employees.

2. Job Training

Job training relates to specific job which the worker has to handle. It gives information about machines, process of production, instructions to be followed, and methods to be used, and so on. It develops skills and confidence among the workers and enables them to perform the job efficiently.

Job training is the most common of formal in-plant training programmes. It is necessary for the new employees to acquaint them with the jobs they are expected to perform. It helps in creating interest of the employees in their jobs.

3. Apprenticeship Training

Apprenticeship training programme tends more towards education than merely on the vocational training. Under this, both knowledge and skills in doing a job or a series of related jobs are involved. The governments of various countries have passed laws which make it obligatory on certain classes of employers to provide apprenticeship training to the young. The usual apprenticeship programmes combine on the job training and experience with classroom instructions in particular subjects.

The trainees receive wages while learning and they acquire valuable skills which command a high wage in the labour market. In India, there are so many 'earn when you learn' schemes both in the private as well as public sector undertakings. This is also advantageous to the trainees. Some employers look upon apprentices as a source of cheap labour. Apprenticeship training is desirable in industries which require a constant flow of new employees expected to become all-round craftsmen. It is very much prevalent in printing trade, building and construction, and crafts like mechanics, electricians, welders, etc.

4. Internship Training

Under this method, the educational or vocational institutes enters into arrangement with an industrial enterprise for providing practical knowledge to its students. Internship training is usually meant for such vocations where advanced theoretical knowledge is to be backed up by practical experience on the job. For instance, engineering students are sent to big industrial enterprises for gaining practical work experience and medical students are sent to big hospitals to get practical knowledge. The period of such training varies from six months to two years. The trainees do not belong to the business enterprises, but they come from the vocational or professional institutions. It is quite usual that enterprises giving them training absorb them by offering suitable jobs.

5. Refresher Training or Retraining

As the name implies, the refresher training is meant for the old employees of the enterprise. The basic purpose of refresher training is to acquaint the existing workforce with the latest methods of performing their jobs and improve their efficiency further. In the words of **Dale Yoder,** "*Retraining programmes are designed to avoid personnel obsolescence.*" The skills with the existing employees become obsolete because of technological changes and because of the tendency of human beings to forget. Thus, refresher training is essential because of the following factors:

(a) The workers require training to bring them up-to-date with the knowledge and skills and to relearn what they have forgotten.

(b) Rapid technological changes make even the qualified workers obsolete in course of time because new technology is associated with new work-methods and job requirements. The workers need to learn new work methods to use new techniques in doing their jobs

(c) Refresher training becomes necessary because many new jobs which are created due to changes in the demand for goods and services are to be handled by the existing employees.

6. Training for Promotion

The talented employees may be given adequate training to make them eligible for promotion to higher jobs in the organisation. Promotion of an employee means a significant change in his responsibilities and duties. Therefore, it is essential that he is provided sufficient training to learn new skills to perform his new duties efficiently. The purpose of training for promotion is to develop the existing employees to make them fit for undertaking higher job responsibilities. This serves as a motivating force to the employees.

PROCESS/STEPS IN TRAINING PROGRAMMES

Training programmes are a costly affair, and a time consuming process. Therefore, these need to be drafted very carefully. Usually in the organization of training programmes, the following steps are required:

1. Identification of Training Needs

A training programme should be established only when it is felt that it would assist in the solution of specific operational problems. The most important step, in the first place, is to make

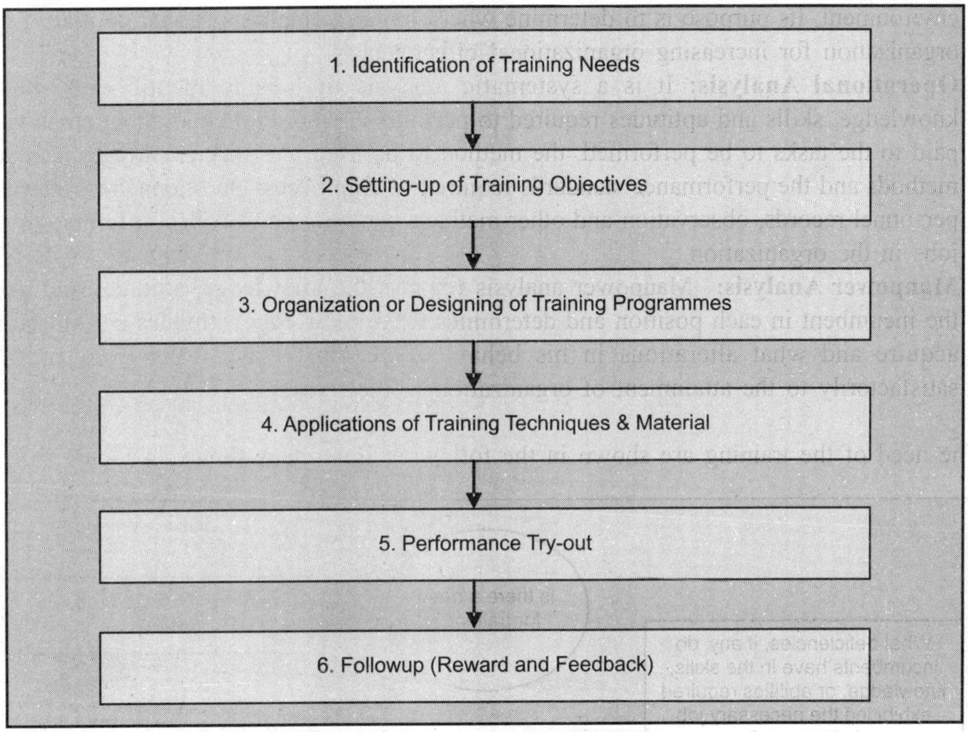

Fig. 7.2. Steps in Training Programmes.

a thorough analysis of the entire organization, its operations and manpower resources available in order to find out 'the trouble spots' where training may be needed. It should, however, be noted that training is not a cure-all, other factor may also involved.

For example, if the efficiency of an employee is low, or he cannot get the job done, it may be due to faulty raw materials and equipment or not getting their timely supplies, or a defective engineering design, or uncongenial work environment, or low wages, or tax supervision. In this case, these problems should be rectified.

Identification of training needs involves three types of analysis:

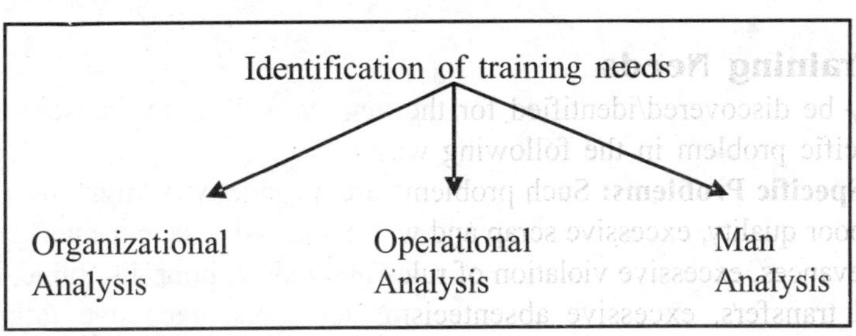

(i) Organizational Analysis: It is a systematic study of the organization in terms of its objectives, its resources, resource allocation and utilization, growth potential and its environment, its purpose is to determine where training emphasis should be placed in the organization for increasing organizational effectiveness.

(ii) Operational Analysis: It is a systematic analysis of jobs to identify job contents, knowledge, skills and aptitudes required to perform the job. Particular attention should be paid to the tasks to be performed, the method to be used, the way employees learn these methods and the performance standards required of employees. Questionnaires, interviews, personnel records, observation and other methods can be used to collect information about jobs in the organization.

(iii) Manpower Analysis: Manpower analysis reviews the knowledge, attitudes and skill of the incumbent in each position and determines what knowledge, attitudes or skill he must acquire and what alterations in his behaviour he must make if he is to contribute satisfactorily to the attainment of organizational objectives.

The need of the training are shown in the following flow chart shown in Figure 7.3.

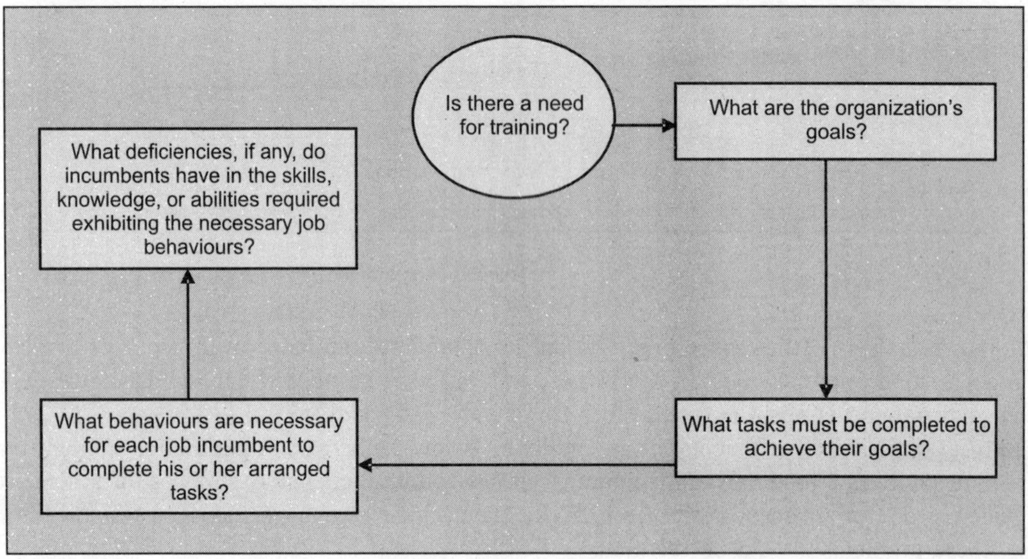

Fig. 7.3. Need for Training.

Determining Training Needs

Training needs may be discovered/identified for the new as well as the present employees and for solving the specific problem in the following ways:

(i) Identifying Specific Problems: Such problems are: productivity, high costs, poor material and control, poor quality, excessive scrap and waste, excessive labour-management troubles, excessive grievances, excessive violation of rules of conduct, poor discipline, high employee turnover and transfers, excessive absenteeism, accidents, excessive fatigue, fumbling, discouragement, struggling with the job; standards of work performance not being met, bottlenecks in production, deadlines not being met, and delayed production. Problems like these suggest that training may be necessary. For this the task and the workers should be closely observed and the difficulties found out.

(ii) **Anticipating Impending and Future Problems:** Bearing on the expansion of business, the introduction of new product, new services, new designs, new plant, and new technology and of organizational changes concerned with manpower inventory for present and future needs.

(iii) **Management Requests:** The supervisors and managers may make specific request for setting training programmes. Though this method is simple and a correct evaluation of the employees' performance deficiencies can be made, but often such recommendations may be built on faulty assumptions; and requests may not coincide with each other or organizational goals.

(iv) **Interviewing and Observing the Personnel on the Job:** Interviewing personnel and direct questioning and observation of the employee by his superiors may also reveal training needs.

(v) **Performance Appraisal:** An analysis of the past performance records of the perspective trainee and comparing his actual performance with the target performance may provide clues to specific interpersonal skills that may need development.

(vi) **Questionnaires:** Questionnaires may be used for eliciting opinions of the employees on topics like communication, satisfaction, job characteristics, their attitude towards working conditions, pay, promotion policies, etc. These will reveal much information about where an employee's skills and knowledge are deficient.

(vii) **Checklist:** The use of checklist is a useful supplement to interviews and observations. Through it, more reliable information can be obtained and the data got are quantifiable. This facilitates evaluating the training programme effectiveness.

(viii) **Morale and Attitude Surveys:** An occasional personnel audit may be conducted to forecast future promotions, skill requirements, and merit rating, to initiate informal discussions and an examination of records and statistics regarding personnel, production, cost, rejects and wastages. All these generally reveal the potential problems to be tackled through training programmes.

(ix) **Request from Top Management:** On the basis of employees' recommendation, the top management can assess the need of the training.

Survey Report (USA and India): In a survey of 150 firms in USA, it was found that training needs of an organization were determined generally by request from top management. In a survey of 13 private sector companies in India, it was found that training needs are determined generally by supervisory recommendations.

2. Objectives or Goals of Training

Once it has been determined that training is necessary, training goals must be established. The management should explicitly state what and how much change is required in employees. The overall aim of any training programme is to increase organizational effectiveness. However, each training programme must also have specific objectives such as increased productivity, improved quality, better human resource planning, better health and safety, prevention of organizational effectiveness. The relationship between specific objectives and overall purpose of training is shown in the figure below:

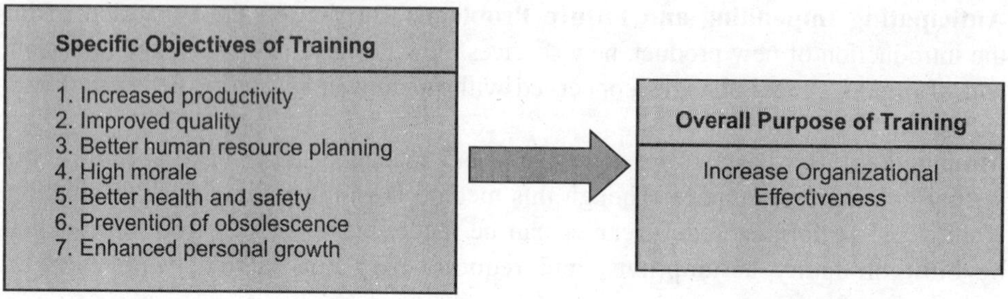

Fig. 7.4. Objectives of Training.

3. Organization or Designing of Training Programme

Every training programme includes trainees, trainers, a training period and training material. These constituents of training are discussed below:

(i) **Selection and motivation of the trainees:** It is necessary to decide who are to be trained—new or old employees, unskilled or semiskilled workers, supervisors or executives. Selection of candidates/trainee for training should be made only after careful screening of the prospective employees for effectiveness of the programme. It is necessary to create desire or interest for learning and trainee should be given proper background information before training.

(ii) **Preparation of the trainer/instructor:** The success of training programme depends upon the trainer or the instructor. Qualified instructors may be obtained from inside or outside the organization. The trainer needs professional expertise in order to fulfil his responsibility. Trainee needs many qualifications besides knowing how to do the work. He must be able to decide before hand how to divide the whole job/course into logical parts so that he may take up one part at a time without losing his perspective of the whole. He must be tolerant and patient. He must explain all course of material step by step and should allow the trainees to repeat these operations. He should also encourage questions from the trainees. Lastly he must link between training objective and organizational objectives.

(iii) **Training Period:** The length of the training period depends on the type of skill and capacity of trainees, purpose of the training, training methodology used, etc. On the basis of this decision can be taken regarding total period (6 months or one year), hours of training each day (one hour or two hours), how many days in a week or month the training will be provided, etc.

4. Training Methods and Material

There are several on-the-job and off-the-job methods. On-the-job methods like coaching, mentoring, job-rotation, job-instruction and off-the-job like, lecture, conferences, case studies, role playing, etc. The choice of any method to train the employee depends upon specific objective of the organization and type of employee to be trained. Similarly, training material includes study notes, case studies, pamphlets, charts, brochures, manuals, movie slides, etc. The decision regarding material required is taken with the help of supervisors.

5. Performance Try out

The trainee is asked to do the job several times slowly. His mistakes are corrected and if it is necessary, the complicated steps are explained again. All the steps are repeated again and again till the trainee demonstrates and accepts that he can do the job rightly. He is put on his own and the training is over.

6. Follow-up (Effectiveness of Training Programme)

In this step, effectiveness of a training programme is assessed. The feedback generated through follow-up will be helpful to reveal weaknesses or errors, if any. The supervisor must have constant eye on the person and performance. The following criteria may be used to measure the effectiveness of training:

- **Reactions:** Trainees' reactions to the objectives, contents and methods of training are good indicators of effectiveness. In case the trainees considered the programme worthwhile and liked it, the training can be considered effective.
- **Learning:** The extent to which the trainees have gained the desired knowledge and skills during the training period is a useful basis of evaluating training effectiveness.
- **Behaviour:** Improvement in the job behaviour of the trainees reflects the manner and extent to which the learning has been put to practice.
- **Results:** Productivity improvement, quality improvement, cost reduction, accident reduction, reduction in labour turnover and absenteeism are the outcomes of training which can be used for evaluating effectiveness.

EXECUTIVE OR MANAGEMENT DEVELOPMENT

The managers or executives are the most important and valuable assets of an organization. The manager has to deal not only with the staff but also with others outside his own group, and has a decided influence on the organization. The calibre and performance of the managers will largely determine the success of a business. So, managers should make self-development and organization is only to provide the necessary conditions for the development. If the organization wants to improve the quality of its managers, it must expend money and efforts and introduce imaginative and systematic development schemes for them.

Executives or management development is a long-term educational process utilizing a systematic and organized procedure by which managerial personnel learn conceptual and theoretical knowledge. Development is a related process. It covers not only these activities which improve job performance, but also those which bring about growth of the personality; help individuals in the progress towards maturity and actualization of their potential capacities so that they become not only good employees but also better human beings. In organizational terms, it is intended to equip persons to earn promotion and hold greater responsibility. Training a person for a bigger and higher job is development.

In brief, management development is a systematic process of growth and development by which the managers develop their abilities to manage and managers are those who perform all or some of the basic functions of the management.

Definitions

According to **Edwin Flippo,** "*Management development includes the process by which the managers and executives acquire not only skills and competency in their present jobs but also capabilities for future managerial tasks of increasing difficulty and scope.*"

According to **National Industrial Conference Board,** "*Management or executive development includes all those activities and programmes which have substantial influence on changing the capacity of the individual to perform his present assignment better and in so doing are likely to increase his potential for future management assignment.*"

From the above definitions, management development involves the following features:

- Executive development is a systematic, planned and organized process.
- It is a long-term process as managerial skills cannot be developed overnight or in one shot.
- It is an endless process throughout an executive's entire professional life.
- Executive development means self and overall development.
- Development includes knowledge, change, attitude change, behaviour change, performance change, end-operational results, etc.

MANAGEMENT DEVELOPMENT PROCESS

Contemporary organizations have realized the importance of human capital and increasingly finding it necessary to continuously train and develop human resources. The training and development needs of the employees cannot be looked at in isolation; any proactive organization has to view the individual training needs in the overall organizational context. The training and development processes are no longer adjunct to other departments but have become a part of organizational strategy and one of the key organizational objectives. The process of arriving at the developmental needs of the executives can be comprehensively analyzed through the process given in Figure 7.5.

The MDP comprises three steps.

Step I: In the step I, at the macro level, three key elements: a competitive advantage, organizational strategy and organizational objectives are considered. The analysis of competitive environment helps the organization to decide its competitive positioning in the marketplace, based on which the organizational strategy is drawn out in an attempt to transform or reposition of the organization. The macro view is broken down into specific organizational objectives for further dissemination to functional/departmental, group, and individual levels.

Step II: This step is the most important and crucial phase of executive development process. This step deals analysis on the competency mapping, identification of competency gap and career planning. In the competency step which helps to capture the competencies of all the employees of the organization which includes the capacities of the management also. In the second step, the organizational requirements and competency gap is analyzed. The third phase deals with identifying and verifying the organizational needs, individual growth and along with career planning of the executives.

Step III: This step consists of three levels. The first level deals with the activities involving training need assessment of individuals and of all employees based on which Annual Training

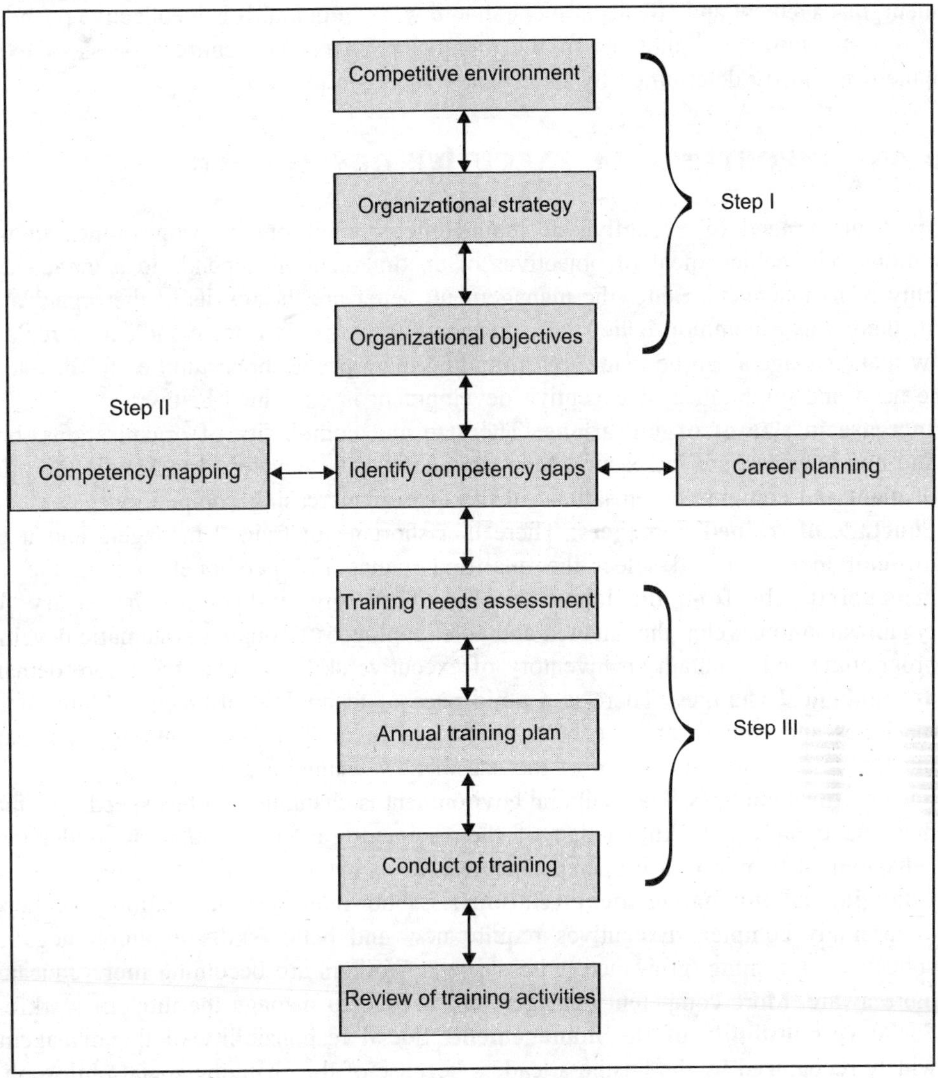

Fig. 7.5. Executive Development Process.

Plan (ATP) is drawn. Based on the annual training plan the employees are chosen to expose to either corporate training programme, for internal training programmes and external organizations. While deciding the venue and types and nature of the training programme the personnel department and training facilitator should consider the various issues like number of executives, cost, outsourcing and availability of technical expertise in the organizations. In case of organizational development related exercises, the combination of internal and external training programmes should be arranged for the all employee of the organization.

Though the money, infrastructure and finally the manpower to be utilized in the whole process keeping into this, the top management has to take decision in this regard. The training department, management and HR department should work in union. It is a collective phenomenon, which is mostly initiatives, motives of the top management. The entire process of executive development is mostly determined by its efficacy and its effectiveness.

NEED AND IMPORTANCE OF EXECUTIVE DEVELOPMENT

There is a great need of executive or management development programmes in modern organizations. The achievement of objectives of an organization depends to a great extent on the quality of its managers. Better the management, better are the results of the organization. In the past, there was a common belief that 'managers are born and not made', now replaced by the view that 'managers can be made' by providing them proper opportunities for development.

The need and importance of executive development is explained below:

1. **Increase in size of organisations:** The size and complexity of organisations, business and non-business, are increasing. Managers need to be developed to handle the problems of giant and complex organisations in the face of increasing competition.
2. **Shortage of trained managers:** There is a shortage of trained managers and it is very difficult to recruit and select the qualified managerial personnel to man the various managerial jobs from the labour market. Therefore, it becomes necessary for the organization to develop the talented and able employees through a systematic development programme and maintain an inventory of executive skills to meet the future demands.
3. **Technological changes:** There is a rapid pace of technological change. Many automatic machines and equipment have been introduced in modern organizations. The managers must have working knowledge of the use of new technology.
4. **Sociocultural changes:** Sociocultural environment is changing at a fast speed. The manager must have up-to-date knowledge of the sociocultural environment to understand the behaviour of people in a proper perspective.
5. **Changing labour-management relations:** Labour-management relations are becoming increasingly complex. Executives require new and better skills in union negotiations, collective bargaining, grievance redressal, etc. Workers are becoming more educated and more aware. More competent managers are needed to manage the modern workforce.
6. **Social responsibility of the management:** Social responsibility of the management is widely recognized by the business leaders because of the changing social philosophy. The increased management task and leadership responsibilities arising out of social and technological changes have made the executive development necessary.
7. **Shift in the nature of the management:** In the recent years, there is a noticeable shift from owner managed to professionally managed enterprises, even in family business houses executive development programmes are required to train and develop professional managers.
8. **Unending process:** Executives need education and training to understand and adjust to changes in socio-economic forces. Without management development programmes, executives may become obsolete. Executive personnel will not be able to survive in future unless they keep pace with modern management education, research, principles and practices; it is a continuous and unending process and not a one shot affair.

Without a systematic and planned programme of executive development, no organisation can be successful in the long run. According to **Peter Drucker,** *"An institution that cannot produce its own managers will die. From an overall point of view, the ability of an institution to produce managers is more important than its ability to produce goods efficiently and cheaply."*

METHODS/TECHNIQUES OF EXECUTIVE DEVELOPMENT

A large variety of methods of executive/management development have come into prominence these days. Today there is a shift towards development techniques that teach managers to learn and develop the competencies they need to cope with changes such as sizing up foreign markets and searching for new strategic opportunities. Different types of skills and knowledge needed by executives nowadays are as follow:

1. Decision-Making Skills

Today, the role of executives transformed from administrative to strategic leader. For that purpose, there is a need to increase decision-making abilities. These involve:

(i) In-Basket method

As the name indicates, in-basket training is structured around the familiar receptacle used for collecting incoming mail, memos and reports. Materials that require problem solving are put into an in-basket and the trainee plays the role of a manager responsible for solving the problems (decision-maker). The trainees are given background information on a simulated exercise about a company and its product, its organization and key personnel, they are providing with an in-basket of assorted memoranda. The trainee must make sense out of this mass of paperwork and prepare memos, make notes and delegate tasks within the limited period. The in-basket training includes:

In-basket training involves:

(a) Situational judgement in being able to recall details, establish priorities interrelated items and determine need for more information.
(b) Scheduling meetings with involved personnel and explaining reason for action taken.
(c) Willingness to make a decision and take action.

Merits of In-basket Method

- It is simple and easy to follow.
- It is inexpensive and can be organized easily.
- Trainees learn quickly as they have to list priorities, make assumption assign work to others and get things done within a time frame.

Since participants are from different departments, it is easy to put out interdepartment fires.

Demerits of In-basket Method

- This method is somewhat academic and removed from real life situations.
- The participants knowing fully well that they are handling an imaginary situation, may not be too excited about the whole exercise and may not fully commit themselves to the task.
- It discourages originality, since the teams have to adopt themselves to rigid situations.

(ii) Management games

A management game is a classroom exercise in which a number of teams of trainees compete against each other to achieve certain objectives. The game is designed to be a close representative of real-life conditions. The group of trainees may be allowed to decide about (1) how much to spend on advertising (2) how much to produce (3) how much inventory to maintain (4) how much investment is made (5) how much resources are allocated, etc. So, people learn best by getting involved in the activity itself. Business games help trainees to develop their problem-solving skills and for fostering cooperation and team work.

Under this method, the executives learn by analyzing problems and hold discussions by using some intuition and by making trial-and-error technique. In some games, players can even get a second chance to do something all over again if their first decision is wrong.

A management game may be either simple or complex. If it is simple, the trainee itself can calculate outcome. But if it is of complex type, then computer should be used.

Merits

- There is usually a great sense of excitement and enjoyment in playing the games. This helps to develop problem solving skills.
- These games compress time. Events that take painfully long periods of time are made to occur in a matter of hours.
- In these games, one can learn from mistakes. Participants can take a different course of action by looking at the consequences and improve performance.
- It helps in changing attitudes. Participants become more tolerant.
- Prompt feedback facilitates quick learning.
- These games focus on planning rather than just putting out fires.

Demerits

- The games can be very expensive to develop and implement particularly when the game itself is computerized.
- Business games are removed from reality. These force the decision-makers to choose his alternatives from a closed list, whereas in real life, managers may get, unlimited chances for creating new alternatives.
- No evidence is available which may indicate that those who are successful in business games will also be successful in a real job.
- Unorthodox strategies may be advanced by innovative participants. But when these strategies do not find acceptance from others, creativity may take a back seat.
- Participants may be so engrossed in getting ahead of all others that they fail to grasp the underlying management policies being taught.

(iii) Case-Study

Under this method, a written problem—real or hypothetical, collected from various business units is presented to a group of trainees for analysis and solution or for decision-making. The trainer guides the discussion, shows the right path and ensures that no relevant factor is overlooked. These cases may require written analysis and oral class discussion without any prior explanation of a particular concept and theory.

The case studies are extensively used in teaching Law, Personnel Management, Human Relations, and Marketing Management in various educational institutions. Trainee learns that there are various alternative solutions to a particular case. The answer of each trainee may differ. That is why, case studies are frequently used in supervisory and executive training in business.

Merits

(i) This method improves the problem solving skills of the participants.

(ii) This method is a way of learning by doing. Trainees can apply theory to practical problems and learn quickly.

(iii) Trainees get a feel of how others work at a problem and begin to appreciate and learn from each other.

(iv) If the case reflects a real life situation, trainees take keen interest and examine the cross currents with an open and inquisitive mind.

(v) Case study method can provide stimulating discussions among participants as well as excellent opportunities for individuals to defend their analytical and judgemental abilities.

Demerits

- It is a costly and time consuming method since the case studies do not originate easily.
- Cases, sometimes, are not sufficiently realistic to be useful.
- Examining the old case studies may fail to develop the analytical and reasoning abilities of the participants.
- Cases may contain information which may not be appropriate for the kind of decisions that the trainees would take in real-life situations.
- A trainee who is not skilled in this technique may undermine its usefulness.

2. Interpersonal Skills

There are various methods which develop interpersonal skills as discuss below:

(i) Role playing

Under this method, a conflicting situation is artificially created and two or more trainees are assigned different roles to play. No dialogues are given beforehand. The role players are provided with either a written or oral description of the situation and the roles they are to play. After being allowed sufficient time to plan their actions, they must then act their parts spontaneously before the class. For example, a role playing situation may be a salesman making his presentation to the prospective buyer.

Role playing technique is generally used for human relations and leadership training. The purpose is to give trainees an opportunity to learn human relations skill through practice and to develop an insight into one's own behaviour and its effect upon the other. Thus, is a laboratory method which can be used rather easily as supplement to other conventional training methods.

Merits

- In this method learning by doing is emphasized.
- Human interactions and sensitivity are stressed.
- Knowledge of results is immediate.
- Training interest and involvement tend to be high.
- It brings about desired changes in the behaviour and attitudes.
- Competitive atmosphere spurs active participation.

Demerits

- Realism is sometimes lacking in role playing so that the learning experience is diminished.
- It is not easy to duplicate the pressures and realities of actual decision-making on the job.
- Individuals act very differently in real life than they do in acting out a simulated exercise.
- Many trainees often feel uncomfortable in role playing situation.

(ii) Sensitivity, Laboratory or T-Group Training

Sensitivity training aims to increase participants' insights into their behaviour and the behaviour of others by encouraging an open expression of feelings in the trainer-guided T-Group "Laboratory." The assumption is that newly sensitized employees will then find it easier to work together amicably as a team. Sensitivity training seeks to accomplish its aim of increasing interpersonal sensitivity by requiring frank, candid discussion in the T-Group, discussions of participants' personal feelings, attitudes, and behaviour. Participants are encouraged to inform each other truthfully of how their behaviour is being seen and to interpret the kind of feelings it produces.

Merits

- Development of awareness and sensitivity of behavioural patterns of oneself and others.
- Through this, there is a greater concern for others that is how they react to others and how others react to them.
- Confront interpersonal problems directly, so that they may be solved and not try to avoid them rather smooth them over or seek a compromise.
- Enhance listening skills.
- Increase trust and support.

Demerits

- Role played by the trainee here is not a structured one as in role playing.
- It is a controversial method surrounded by heated debate and is used much less today than in the past.

- Sensitivity training makes the trainees so sensitive to the feelings of others that he is not in a position to take harsh decisions.
- Such training induces anxiety among participants. Such anxiety may cause the people to be highly frustrated, unsettled and upset.
- T-Group training when applied to technical professionals is often less effective as compared to the conventional method.

(iii) Behaviour modelling

It is a developmental technique in which trainees are first shown good management techniques in a film, and then asked to play roles in a simulated situation, and is then given feedback and admired by their supervisors. Lastly, the trainee is encouraged to try the behaviour at job. Behaviour modelling is used to train the following managerial personnel:

(a) Train first-line supervisors to handle common supervisor-employee interactions better. This includes giving recognition, disciplining, introducing changes and improving poor performance.

(b) Train middle managers to better handle interpersonal situations, for example, performance problems land undesirable work habits.

(c) Train employee and their supervisors to take and give criticism, ask and give help, and establish mutual trust and respect.

(iv) Multiple management

The idea of multiple management (also called Junior-Board), is to give trainees top-level analysis and policy making experience by having 10 to 12 trainees sit on a junior board of directors. They make recommendations regarding top-level issues like organization structure, executive compensation, and interdepartmental conflict to the official board of directors. This technique provides middle-management trainees with on-the-job training and experience in dealing with organization-wide problems.

Merits

This technique has several advantages:

- It gives the board members an opportunity to gain knowledge on various issues.
- It helps identify those who have executive talent. Multiple judgements are obtained on each individual through the board rating system.
- The members gain practical experience of group decision-making and of teamwork. As a result of the interaction process, they develop respect for the rights and views of their associates.
- It is relatively an inexpensive method of development.
- It permits a considerable number of managers to participate in certain activities within a reasonable period of time. Besides, the boards do make important contributions to efficiency, productivity, and a better human relations climate. In fact, they assist in a better administration in the organization.

Demerits

The demerits or limitations of this method are:

- It is only suitable for middle and senior-level managers.
- It does not permit any specific attention to training needs of the manager.
- The debates in these committees often tend to be discursive lacking authority. The deliberations often degenerate into academic discussions without the participants feeling committed to the conclusion.

(v) Transactional analysis (TA)

TA offers a model of personality and dynamics of self and its relationship to others that makes possible a clear and meaningful understanding of behaviour. It is used in industry as a method of analyzing and understanding interpersonal behaviour. When people interact, there is a social transaction in which one person responds to another. The study of these transactions between people is called 'Transactional Analysis'. It was originally developed by **Eric Berne**, a psychotherapist in 1950. He observed in his patients that it was as if there were several different persons inside one person. He also observed that these several selves transmitted with people in different ways. Later on the application of TA for ordinary transactions was popularized by **Harris and Jongeward** besides Berne.

Transactional analysis is a very popular method of executive development. By exposing their executives to courses in transactional analysis, the companies seek to improve their self-understanding, interpersonal effectiveness, and communication and leadership skills.

3. Job-Knowledge Method

In order to perform the particular job effectively in the organization, the executives may also have to adopt the following methods:

(i) Coaching

In coaching the trainee is placed under a particular supervisor who acts as an instructor and teaches job knowledge and skill to the trainee. He tells him what he wants him to do, how it can be done and follows up while it is being done and corrects errors.

Merits

The merits of coaching are:

- Increased motivation of the trainee, since coaching constitutes learning by doing.
- Minimization of the problems of transferring learning from theory to practice.
- Least centralized staff coordination is required, since every executive can coach his men even if no management development programme exists.
- Feedback on performance is received quickly.

Demerits

This method has the following demerits also:

- This method relies on the ability of the coach to be a good teacher, which he may not necessarily be.

- In many cases, the learner cannot develop much beyond the limits of his own boss's abilities.
- This technique is authoritarian, for a coach tends to familiarize his subordinates with his own work habits and beliefs, even though these may be faulty.
- The training atmosphere is not available in this method.

(ii) Understudy approach

In the understudy approach, the trainee works directly with the person he or she is to replace; the latter is in turn responsible for the trainee's coaching. Normally, the understudy relieves the executive of certain responsibilities, thereby giving the trainee a chance to learn the job. This helps ensure that the employer will have trained managers to assume key positions when such positions are vacated due to retirement, promotions, transfers or terminations. It also helps guarantee the long-run development of company-bred top managers.

Merits

The merits of understudy method are as follows:

- This method creates a practical and realistic situation in which the training is conducted.
- It is a practical and fairly quick way of training designated persons for greater management responsibilities.
- It emphasizes learning by doing.
- It relieves the boss of some of his workload by delegating some portion of the workload to the understudy.
- It ensures that the organisation will not be in a disadvantageous situation if an executive suddenly leaves his job. The understudy will be in position to hold that position.

Demerits

There are quite a few disadvantages of this method are as follows:

- Since the understudy has been specifically designated, it may spark off jealousy and rivalry among competing subordinates. The others may feel that the competition for promotion is over. This reduces the motivation level of both the one who is designated and the other personnel.
- The understudy may be picked up on the basis of his similarity in thinking and acting with those of his superior and then the understudy will learn the ways of his superior, who has learnt from his superior. Thus, understudy will perpetuate the existing practices, the bad as well as the good. Therefore, outside contacts through other development techniques are essential for the development of the person and for the well-being of the organization.

The effectiveness of understudy assignments depends upon the willingness and ability of the higher level manager to share experience and to transfer knowledge to the under study manager.

4. Organizational Knowledge

Besides, the job knowledge, the executives must have knowledge about the organization as a whole in which they are working. To get organizational knowledge two methods are used:

(a) Job Rotation

(b) Multiple management*

(a) Job rotation

Job rotation means moving management trainees from department to department to broaden their understanding of all the parts of the business. The trainee, often a recent college graduate, may spend several months in each department; this helps not only broaden his or her experience but also discover the jobs he or she prefers. The person may just be an observer in each department but more commonly get fully involved in its operations. The trainee thus learns the department's business by actually doing it, whether it involves sales, production, finance or some other function. According to **W.E. Benett,** "*Job rotation is a process of horizontal movement that widens the manager's experience horizon beyond the limited confines of his own.*"

Merits

Job rotation has many advantages:

- It works to bring down the feeling of superiority of one department over the others; since everyone is moved from one department to the other.
- It develops interdepartmental cooperation.
- Boredom and monotony are reduced.
- Job rotation injects new ideas into the different departments of the organization.
- Under this system, an executive is not destined to end up in just one spot but is equipped to step up into any of the several executive posts in any of various functional decisions.
- The trainee will learn the nature and significance of management principles by transferring learning from one job to another.
- Each executive's abilities and talents are best tested in a variety of jobs. So the organization can secure his best utilization in the ultimate assignment.

Demerits

The demerits of job rotation are:

- Productive work may suffer due to disruptions caused by changes and limitations of individuals to adjust to a new job. So it is better to lengthen the interval of rotation and to rotate fewer personnel at a time.
- The executives can't gain specialized knowledge in one particular branch of work during a short span of time.
- It upsets home and family life, since many a time transfers are done to different geographical areas.

---

* The discussion of "multiple management" has already been done in one of the previous sections of this chapter.

- It becomes difficult for the subordinates to adjust themselves to their new bosses. Interpersonal relationship takes time for adjustment and employees with frequent moves are apt to feel insecure.
- It develops friction, jealousy and other non-cooperative and dysfunctional forms of human behaviour.

5. Other Knowledge

Besides the knowledge about the job and about the organization as a whole, the executive must be and all-rounder and must have knowledge about the external environment. He should have knowledge about what is happening in national and international business world. He can acquire all those knowledge with the help of following methods:

1. **Special Courses.** The executives can attend the workshops or executive development programmes organized by the management institutes, universities, and colleges. These courses will help in improving their general knowledge.
2. **Special Meetings.** Some outside organisations like consumer forums, chambers of industry and commerce, and so many other voluntary organizations, organize special meetings from time to time. The executives can attend such meetings to acquire general knowledge.
3. **Specific Readings.** Specific articles published by various journals, specific portions of important books are provided to the trainees to improve their general knowledge.

6. Specific Individual Needs (Knowledge about Specific Area)

Some executives may have to be trained in some specific areas due to some specific needs or weaknesses. The methods of training for this aspect are:

(i) Special projects assignments

A special assignment is a high training device under which a trainee is assigned a project that is closely related to his job. Sometimes, a number of trainee executives are put together to work on a project directly related to their functional areas. The trainee studies the problems and submits the written recommendations upon it. It provides him a valuable experience in tackling the problem but would also have the other values of educating the trainees the importance of the problem and to understand the organizational relationship of the problem from different angles. When he works as a member of the team, he not only acquires knowledge, but also learns how to work with others having different points of view.

(ii) Committee assignments

This method is similar to project assignment. Under this system an ad hoc committee is constituted and is assigned a subject related to the business to discuss and to make recommendations. Through discussions in committee meetings, the executives get acquainted with different point of views and alternative methods of problem solving. They also learn interpersonal skills. Generally, the executives are selected from different departments having specialized knowledge in different areas.

(iii) Outside conferences/seminars

Many organizations offer special seminars and conferences aimed at providing skill-building training for managers. Thousands or hundreds of course areas are provided for discussion. The trainee can involve in his particular area and discussion. So, it is an organized plan in which the members participate in oral discussion of a particular problem and thus, develop their knowledge and understanding. It is an executive training device for conference members and conference leaders. Both learn a lot from others' viewpoint and compare their opinions with others. The conference leaders may also learn how to develop their skills to motivate people through direction of discussion. The conferences are of three types:

- Guided or directed conference
- Consultative conference and
- Problem-solving conference. For training purposes, guided or directed conference is used. It is ideally suited in developing conceptual knowledge, reducing dogmatism and modifying attitudes. The trainee actively participates and his interest in learning is maintained.

CONCLUSION

Various training methods of management have been discussed above. However, it is difficult to suggest which of the training methods/techniques will prove better. For the success of each method following parameters are considered:

- How it is employed?
- The instructor's ability and personality.
- The trainee's maturity, background and willingness to learn.
- Company atmosphere and the extent to which there is an opportunity and encouragement to the trainee to apply to the job what he learnt in the class or the programme.

It may only be said that some methods may suit some training objective or group of participants better than others; but the acceptance and adoption of one or other of these methods will have to be done with caution and careful thinking.

REVIEW QUESTIONS

1. What is employee training? Explain the need and objectives of training.
2. Define employee training. Explain different methods of training for the employees.
3. What are the major steps of a training programme? How you can design a training programme?
4. How do you identify the training needs of an organization?
5. Explain various types of training programmes.
6. What are the essential features of good training? Explain training methods.
7. Define development. What is the difference between training and development?
8. "No organization can choose today between training and development". Comment.
9. What do you understand by executive development? Explain its need and importance.
10. Explain various techniques of executive development.

11. Write notes on following:
    a. Job Rotation
    b. Job-Instruction training (JIT)
    c. Case Study method
    d. In-basket game method

CASE STUDY

7.1 Hotel Mangalore Private Ltd.

Hotel Mangalore Private Ltd. is located in Hampankatta, Mangalore. It is 1 km from Mangalore railway station. Though started about 2 years ago, it is now attracting business customers throughout the country. Mr. R.K. Shetty who has served in five-star hotels in Mumbai and Chennai wants to make this hotel the number one hotel in Mangalore.

The staff and employees of this hotel are recruited locally. Since most of them do not have experience of working in five-star hotels, they do not have the attitudes and skills to deal with the hotel's customers. In contrast, the supervisory staff are qualified, having a degree in hotel management and have undergone an intensive training in five-star hotels in Mumbai before joining Hotel Mangalore. They, however, found that their assistants in the front office, lobby, restaurant, kitchen and housekeeping, did not have any formal training in their respective jobs. The supervisory staff therefore found it difficult to give them suitable instructions. The employees and staff did not rise to the standards expected of them from the business customers, who compared the service at Hotel Mangalore with other five-star hotels. Often, there have been an increasing number of complaints about general cleanliness, housekeeping, room service and service at restaurants.

Mr. Shetty has called a number of meetings with departmental heads and supervisory staff. They have strongly recommended a formal training programme for staff and employees of the hotel. It was therefore agreed that suitable training be given to the staff and employees. However, the problem was that the supervisory staffs do not wish to relieve the staff during working hours and the staff is not willing to attend the training programme after the working hours.

You have been appointed the management consultant for Hotel Mangalore and have been asked to give a comprehensive training plan for the employees giving the needs, duration of the training, contents, methodology, resource persons, and a formal appraisal method to evaluate the effectiveness of the training programme.

Source: P.G. Aquinas, Human Resource Management, Vikas Publishing House, New Delhi, p. 78-79.

Questions

1. How will you commence your work of making a comprehensive training plan for all the staff that needs to be given training?
2. What would be the contents of the training programme?
3. How will you assess the training needs?
4. How will you motivate the staff for attending the training programme?

7.2 Reinventing the Wheel at Apex Door Company

Jim Delaney, president of Apex Door, has a problem. No matter how often he tells his employees how to do their jobs, they invariably 'decide to do it their way,' as he puts it, and arguments ensue between Jim, the employee, and the employee's supervisor. One example is the door-design department, where the designers are expected to work with the architects to design doors that meet the specifications. While it's not 'rocket science,' as Jim puts it, the designers invariably make mistakes such as designing in too much steel—a problem that can cost Apex tens of thousands of wasted dollars, once you consider the number of doors in, say, a 30-storey office tower.

The order processing department is another example. Jim has a very specific and detailed way he wants the order written up, but most of the order clerks don't understand how to actually use the multiple order form, and simply improvise when it comes to a detailed question such as whether to classify the customer as 'industrial' or 'commercial.'

The current training process is as follows. None of the jobs have training manuals per se, although several have somewhat out-of-date job descriptions. The training for new people is all on the job. Usually, the person leaving the company trains the new person during the 1- or 2-week overlap period, but if there's no overlap, the new person is trained as well as possible by other employees who have filled in occasionally on the job in the past. The training is basically the same throughout the company, e.g., for machinists, secretaries, and assembler and accounting clerks.

Source: Gary Dessler, Human Resource Management, 8th edn., Pearson Education, pp. 285-86.

Questions

1. What do you think of Apex's training process? Could it help to explain why employees 'do things their way' and if so, how?
2. What role do job descriptions play in training?
3. Explain in detail what you would do to improve the training process at Apex. Make sure to provide specific suggestions, please.

REFERENCES

1. Aquinas, P.G. (2008). "Human Resource Management" Vikas Publishing House (Pvt.) Ltd.
2. Armstrong "Management: A Handbook of Personnel Management Practice", Kogan Page Ltd. London.
3. Barnard, Chester I. "The Functions of the Executives", Cambridge, Harvard University Press.
4. Cascio, W.F. "Managing Human Resources", McGraw-Hill, New York.
5. Dale, Ernest, L.D. Michelon, "Modern Management Techniques", Penguin Books.
6. David A. Decenzo, and Stephen P. Robbins, "Human Resource Management", 7th edn., Wiley Publications.
7. Dessler, Gary, (1998). "Human Resource Management", Prentice-Hall of India, New Delhi.
8. Drucker, P.F. "Managing for the Future", Tata McGraw-Hill, New Delhi.
9. Aswathappa, K. (2008). "Human Resource Management", Tata McGraw-Hill, New Delhi.
10. Mamoria, C.B. and Gankar, S.V. (2008). "Personnel Management", Himalaya Publishing House, Mumbai, pp. 257-259.
11. Pigors, Paul Myres, "Management of Human Resources", McGraw-Hill, New York.
12. Snell Scott, George Bohlander, (2007). "Human Resource Management", Thomson-South Western Publication, New York.
13. Subba Rao P. (2007). "Essentials of Human Resource Management and Industrial Relations". Himalaya Publishing House, New Delhi.
14. Yoder, Dale, "Personnel Management and Industrial Relations", Sir Isaac Pitman and Sons Ltd., London.

CHAPTER
8

Managing Strategic Organizational Renewal

CHAPTER'S OUTLINE

- Introduction
- HR's Role in Organizational Change and Renewal
- Managing Organizational Change and Renewal
- Organizational Development and Objectives
- Organizational Targets for Change
- Organizational Development Process and Techniques
- Methods of Introducing Organizational Change and Renewal
- Total Quality Management Programmes
- HR's Role in Quality Management
- HR and Business Process Reengineering

INTRODUCTION

The environment, within which organizations operate today, is changing very fast. Hence, for survival and growth, the organizations need to adjust as per the changes. Resistance to change was quite common in the distant past but now it is a matter of history. Change is the law of nature. The organizations and personnel have become quite used to change. Organizations undergo strategic organizational change and renewal. Change is inevitable in the life of an organization. Organizations that learn and cope with change will thrive and flourish and others which fail to do so will be wiped out.

In strategic organizational renewal, HR should be made a "strategic" partner. Today, around the world, firms including GM, Sony, Reliance, Wipro, Procter and Gamble, Toyota, MCI,

WorldCom are undergoing organizational change and renewal to become more competitive. HR is more involved in bringing about these changes. In this chapter, we will discuss HR's role in organizational change and renewal, managing organizational change and development, TQM programmes and HR and business process reengineering.

HR'S ROLE IN ORGANIZATIONAL CHANGE AND RENEWAL

In order to explain the HR's role in organizational change and renewal, first we are supposed to discuss what is change and its nature?

What is Change?

According to **Stephen P. Robbins,** "*Change is concerned with making things different. Things must be different because they change constantly due to change in factors such as strategy, culture, structure tasks, technologies and the attitudes and skills of its people.*"

In a simple way it can be said that "*Change is defined as the disturbance in the organizational system by some internal or external force and it occurs frequently. Change as a process, is simply modification of the structure or process of a system. It may be good or bad. The concept is descriptive only.*"

Changes can be divided into two categories:

(i) Work change that includes changes in machinery, working hours, methods of work, job redesign or reengineering.

(ii) Organizational change, that is, change in the working hours like morning shifts, evening shifts, operation of organization on Sundays/holidays.

When changes take place in various aspects of the company as discussed above, the CEO of the company takes the help of HR department in dealing with these changes. HR professionals cannot ignore such changes. They are supposed to design and execute innovative mechanism of developing skills and competencies of human resources to prepare them to accept the emerging challenges. **HR's role in organizational change and renewal is discussed as under**:

1. Dealing with Strategic Change

Organizational change often starts with strategic change, a change in the firm's strategy, mission, and vision. Strategic change may then require other changes, for instance, in the firm's production, technology, structure, and culture.

Illustration: The strategic change initiated at Fuji-Xerox by President Yotaro Kobayashi provides an example. In response to declining market share, a dearth of new products, and increasing customer complaints, Kobayashi and his team formulated a new vision for the firm. It was called the—*New Xerox Movement* and was aimed at transforming Fuji-Xerox into a more cost-conscious, competitive and quality-control-based company.

2. Role in Bringing Cultural Change

As at Fuji, implementing a strategic change often requires changing the culture, the firm's shared values and aims. Fuji-Xerox took several steps to implement such cultural change. For example, it created a new set of "heroes," individuals and teams who were publicly congratulated whenever their behaviour reflected Fuji's new values of quality, teamwork, and customer focus.

HR plays an important role in changing culture. For example, one expert advocates five "primary embedding mechanisms" to change a company's culture, each of which requires HR's support and advice:

(i) **Make it clear to your employees what you pay attention to, measure, and control:** For example, direct the attention of your employees towards controlling costs or serving customers if those are the values you want to emphasize.

(ii) **React appropriately to critical incidents and organizational crises:** For example, if you want to emphasize the value that "we're all in this together," don't react to declining profits by laying off operating employees and middle managers, leaving your top managers intact.

(iii) **Deliberately role models, teach, and coach the values you want to emphasize:** For example, Wal-Mart founder **Sam Walton** embodied the values of "hard work, honesty, neighbourliness, and thrift" that he wanted Wal-Mart employees to follow. Although he was one of the richest men in the world, he drove a pickup truck, a preference he explained by asking, "If I drove a Rolls Royce, what would I do with my dog?"

(iv) **Communicate your priorities by the way you allocate rewards and status:** Leaders communicate their priorities and values by the way they award pay raises and promotions. For example, when the top management at General Foods decided several years ago to reorient its strategy from cost to diversification and sales growth, the HR department revised the compensation system so as to link bonuses to sales volume rather than just increased earnings as in the past.

(v) **Make your HR procedures and criteria consistent with the new values:** When he became Chairperson and CEO of IBM, **Louis Gerstner** brought in a new top management team, including a new HR head, whose values were consistent with shaking up IBM's traditionally bureaucratic and politicized culture. They then revised IBM's HR policies and procedures; for example, new incentive plans, promotion and appraisal criteria, and dismissal policies were instituted to support IBM's new performance-oriented strategies.

3. Helpful in Bringing Structural Change

Reorganizing or redesigning the organization's departmentalization, coordination, span of control, reporting relationships, or centralization of decision-making is a relatively direct and quick method for changing an organization. According to **Stewart Thomas**, "*At GE, for instance, Jack Welch of HR department collapsed the firm's management structure from nine layers to as few as four, reduced 29 pay levels to 5 broad bands, and reorganized 350 different product lines and business units into 13 big businesses.*"

HR plays a role in such structural change. As at GE, downsizings require performance reviews to decide who stays and who goes and an outplacement effort; reorganizing requires personnel planning, selection, and job analysis; and flattening the organization may require consolidating pay levels into fewer, broader bands. The tasks and authority assigned to individuals and teams within the organization are often changed as well. For example, traditional assembly-line jobs were abolished at Saturn. Instead, the work is now organized around work teams.

4. Support to Technological Change

Technological changes are modifications to the work methods the organization uses to accomplish its tasks. They may include new production technologies, new selection and screening procedures, and new performance appraisal techniques, for instance. The compensation plans and appraisal systems instituted by Fuji-Xerox illustrate HR-based technological changes, in this case implemented to support cultural and strategic changes.

5. Helpful in Bringing Changes in People, Attitudes and Skills

Sometimes the employees themselves must change. Techniques such as lectures, conferences, and on-the-job training are often used to provide new or present employees with the skills they need to perform their jobs adequately. HR-based organizational development interventions are aimed at changing employees' attitudes, values, and behaviour.

MANAGING ORGANIZATIONAL CHANGE AND RENEWAL—A 10 STEP PROCESS

Actually managing or implementing and leading an organizational change can be a tricky matter. The change may be complex and requires dozens or even hundreds of managers and supervisors to do their parts; resistance may be considerable; and the change may have to be accomplished while the company continues to serve its customer base. Change can be at individual, group or organizational levels.

Individual Level Change: At the individual level change is reflected in such developments as changes in a job assignment, physical move to a different location, or the change in maturity of a person which occurs overtime. It is said that changes at the individual level will seldom have significant implications for the total organization. This is not true because a significant change at the individual level will have its repercussions on the group which, in turn, might influence the wider organization. A manager, who desires to implement a major change at the individual level, transferring an employee for instance, must understand that the change will have repercussions beyond the individual.

Group Level Changes: Most organizational changes have their major effects at the group level. This is because most activities in organizations are organized on a group basis. The groups could be departments, or informal work groups. Changes at the group level can affect work flows, job design, social organization, influence and status systems, and communication patterns.

HR managers must consider group factors when implementing change. Informal groups can pose a major barrier to change because of the inherent strength they contain. Formal groups can resist change, as exemplified by the resistance demonstrated by unions to the changes proposed by the management.

Organisation Level Changes: Changes at this level involve major programmes that affect both individuals and groups. Decisions regarding these changes are generally made by senior management and are seldom implemented by only a single manager. Frequently, they occur over long periods of time and require considerable planning for implementation. Example of these changes would be reorganization of the organizational structure and responsibilities, revamping of employee remuneration system, or major shifts in an organization's objectives. Change at the organizational level is generally referred to as "*organization development*" which will be considered later in this chapter.

The relationship among the three levels of change is shown in Figure 8.1. It suggests that changes at any level affect the other levels. The strength of the effect will depend on the level or source of change.

	Source		
	Individual	Group	Organization
Individual	–	L	L
Group	M	–	L
Organization	S	M	–
	S = Small	M = Medium	L = Large

Fig. 8.1. Interaction Effects of Different Levels of Organizational Change.
Source: Gray and Starke, Organizational Behaviour, p. 571.

Psychologist **Kurt Lewin** formulated the classic explanation of how to implement a change. To Lewin, all behaviour in organizations was a product of two kinds of forces— those striving to maintain the status quo and those pushing for change. Implementing change thus meant either reducing the forces for the status quo or building up the forces for change. Lewin's process consisted of these three steps:

1. **Unfreezing.** Unfreezing means reducing the forces that are striving to maintain the status quo, usually by presenting a provocative problem or event to get people to recognize the need for change and to search for new solutions.
2. **Moving**. Lewin's second step aims to shift or alter the behaviour of the individuals in the departments or organization in which the changes are to take place. Moving means developing new behaviours, values, and attitudes, sometimes through organizational structure changes and sometimes through the sorts of HR-based organizational change and development techniques explained later in this chapter.
3. **Refreezing.** Lewin assumed that organizations tended to revert to their former ways of doing things unless the changes were reinforced. This reinforcement is accomplished by refreezing the organization into its new state of equilibrium. Lewin advocated instituting new systems and procedures (such as compensation plans and appraisal processes) to support and maintain the changes that were made.

These three phases or steps in managing the implementation of organizational change is shown in Figures 8.2 and 8.3.

For unfreezing, the manager must understand the causes for resistance to change. It is common knowledge that there are people who desire status quo and there are also individuals who push for change. And the two groups may be equal in their force as shown in Figure 8.3. The forces against change (labelled A) have strengths equal to those forces pushing for change (labelled F).

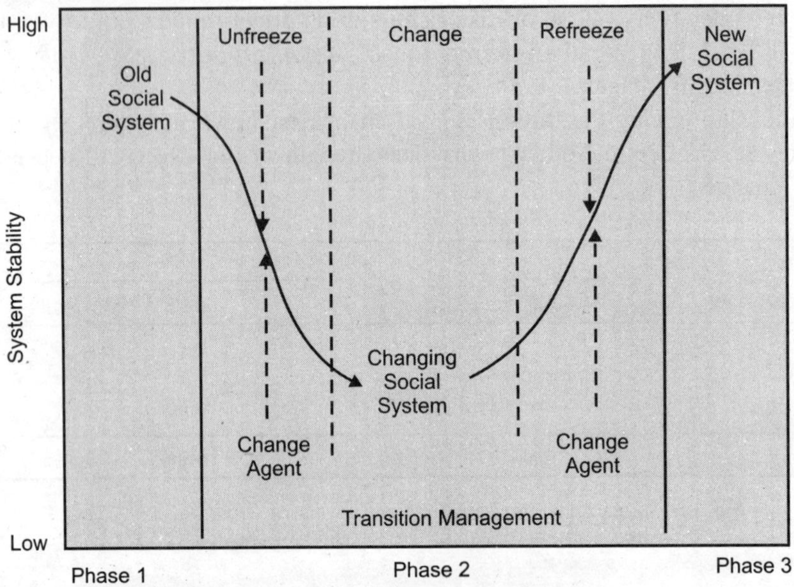

Fig. 8.2. Process of Organizational Change.
Source: Moorhead and Griffin, Organizational Behaviour, p. 675.

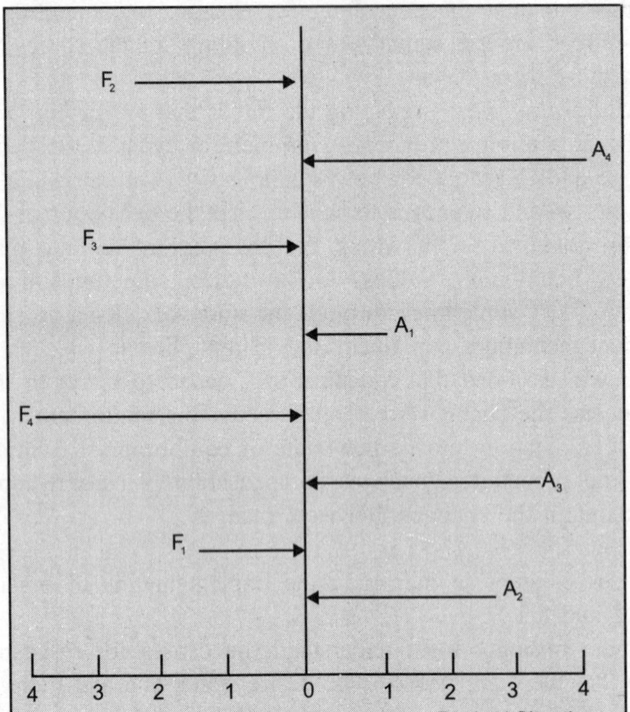

Fig. 8.3. Equal Forces for Change.
Source: Richard M. Hodgetts, Organizational Behaviour, MacMillan, 1991, p. 454

An example of four forces pushing in each direction is seen in the case of the organization that has announced the introduction of a new monthly cost report. After careful analysis, a top manager may find various reasons given by subordinates for resisting change, on the one hand, or for promoting change, on the other hand. Among the reasons given for resisting change might be:

- The old report is easy to fill out because the data are readily available.
- The old report takes very little time to think.
- Top management has never used this report in the past for control purposes.
- The new report will be very comprehensive and requires more time to fill out.

The reasons for advocating change might be:

1. An organizational streamlining of reporting forms is necessary.
2. Organizational control is getting out of hand.
3. If a report is going to be filled out, why not make it a meaningful one?
4. This new report is going to be analyzed by staff personnel, and useful recommendations will be forwarded to each manager who has filled one out.

In such a situation, the manager must unfreeze the equilibrium. In doing so, three courses of action are available: (a) increase the strength of forces that push for change; (b) decrease the strength of forces that resist change; and (c) change a resisting force into one supporting the change.

Based on several recent large-scale organizational renewal projects, a more detailed listing of the steps involved in such a process may be summarized as follows:

1. **Establish a Sense of Urgency:** Once they become aware of the need to change, most leaders start by creating a sense of urgency. When he took over electronics giant Philips, CEO **Jan Timmer** knew that to rouse his top managers out of their status quo thinking, he had to create a sense of urgency and he did this by presenting his top managers with a (fictitious) press announcement describing Philip's bankruptcy.
2. **Mobilize Commitment to Change through Joint Diagnosis of Business Problems:** Having established a sense of urgency, many leaders then create one or more task forces to diagnose the business problems. Such teams can produce a shared understanding of what can and must be improved and thereby mobilize the commitment of those who must actually implement the change.
3. **Create a Guiding Coalition:** Major transformationists: such as **Bill Gates** accomplished in the mid-1990s by transforming Microsoft into an Internet-oriented company are sometimes associated with just one highly visible leader, but no leader can really implement any such change alone. Many, therefore, create a guiding coalition of influential people, who act as missionaries and implementers.
4. **Develop a Shared Vision:** To transform an organization, a new vision is usually required, a general statement of the organization's intended direction that evokes emotional feelings in organization members.
5. **Communicate the Vision Change:** The real power of a vision is unleashed only when most of those involved in an enterprise or activity have a common understanding of its

goals and directions. In fact, fostering support for the new vision is virtually impossible unless the vision has been effectively communicated.

The key elements of effectively communicating a vision include:

- Keep it simple.
- Use multiple forums.
- Use repetition.
- Lead by example.

6. **Enable Employees to Facilitate the Change:** By now employees understand the vision and want to make it a reality, but may feel inadequate. Perhaps a lack of skills stands in the way; or policies, procedures and the organization chart make it difficult to act; or some bosses may actually discourage those actions aimed at implementing the company's new vision. It's the company's job to see to it that such barriers are removed.

   Doing so, requires considerable HR assistance. When he took over as CEO of Sony and its loss-making movie studios, **Nobuyuki Idei** proceeded, in a most un-Japanese way, to sweep the old studio executives out of office and to install a newly recruited team led by industry veterans, with a mandate to fix Sony's movie business.
7. **Generate Short-Term Wins:** Transforming a company can take time, but employees need reinforcement periodically. That's why building in '*short-term wins*' is important. For example, the guiding coalition in one company intentionally set its sights on producing one highly visible and successful new product about 20 months after the start of the organizational change effort. The new product was selected in part because they knew its introduction was doable.
8. **Consolidate Gains and Produce More Change:** The company can then use the credibility from such short-term wins to change all the systems, structures, and policies that don't fit well with the company's new vision. And, managers can continue to produce more change by hiring and promoting new people and by providing additional opportunities for short-term wins by employees.
9. **Anchor the New Ways of Doing Things in the Company's Culture:** Most organizational changes require a corresponding change in employees' shared values. For example, a 'team-based, quality-oriented, adaptable organization' is not going to happen if the values employees share still emphasize selfishness, mediocrity, and bureaucratic behaviour. We've already noted how to lead a change in organizational culture. In brief, it means crystallizing values that are consistent with your vision for the company and then modeling teaching, and communicating the values you want your employees to share.
10. **Monitor Progress and Adjust the Vision as Required:** Progress then must be monitored. Thus, one firm appointed an oversight team to monitor its new team-based organization and self-managing teams.

In ten steps process of managing organizational change and renewal is in fact a multi-dimensional process. Its short form is depicted in Figure 8.4 in the form of a model of implementation of change in an organization.

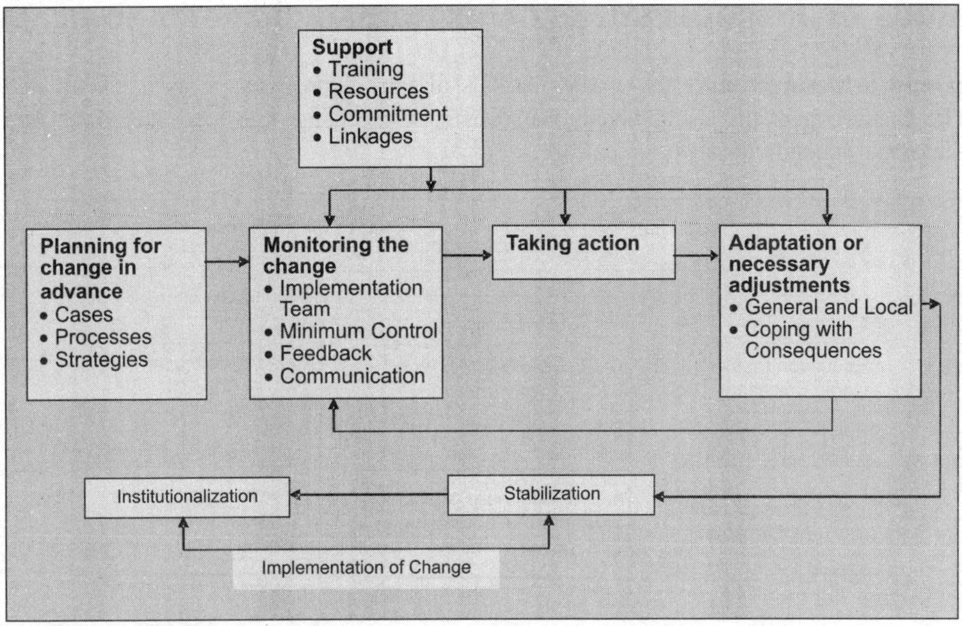

Fig. 8.4. The Model of Implementaiton of Change in an Organization.

Illustrations of Managing Change Implementation

SBI in 1971

In 1971, in response to its increasing size, and nationalization of the banking sector the State Bank of India embarked on an organization-wide restructuring exercise. Taking the help of external consultants, and through the involvement of a top management steering group, it managed to implement major changes in the organization: a shift from a functional structure to a market segment-based structure; introduction of a budgeting and performance review system; differentiation and strengthening of planning and staff functions; and creation of more unified channels of command of branches from the local head offices.

Steel Authority of India Ltd. in 1980-84

The Steel Authority of India (SAIL) suffered losses of Rs. 2760 million during 1980-84. When **V. Krishnamurthy** became the CEO, he met almost 25,000 employees, either individually or in groups and, based on the discussions with them prepared a list of priorities action. Company-wide discussions on these priorities were initiated by calling meetings and mailing the list to all its 2.5 lac employees. As a result, a great amount of decentralization was introduced, cost savings were made on overtime payments and fuel consumption, a flatter organizational structure was introduced at plant levels, more efforts were put in to develop human resources, and so on. In 1988-89, the company registered a profit of Rs. 3600 million.

METHODS OF INTRODUCING ORGANIZATIONAL CHANGE AND RENEWAL

Kotler and Schlesinger have given six methods of introducing change as is shown in Figure 8.5. The change agent must understand that resistance to change must be overcome. Approach to be adopted depends upon the situation.

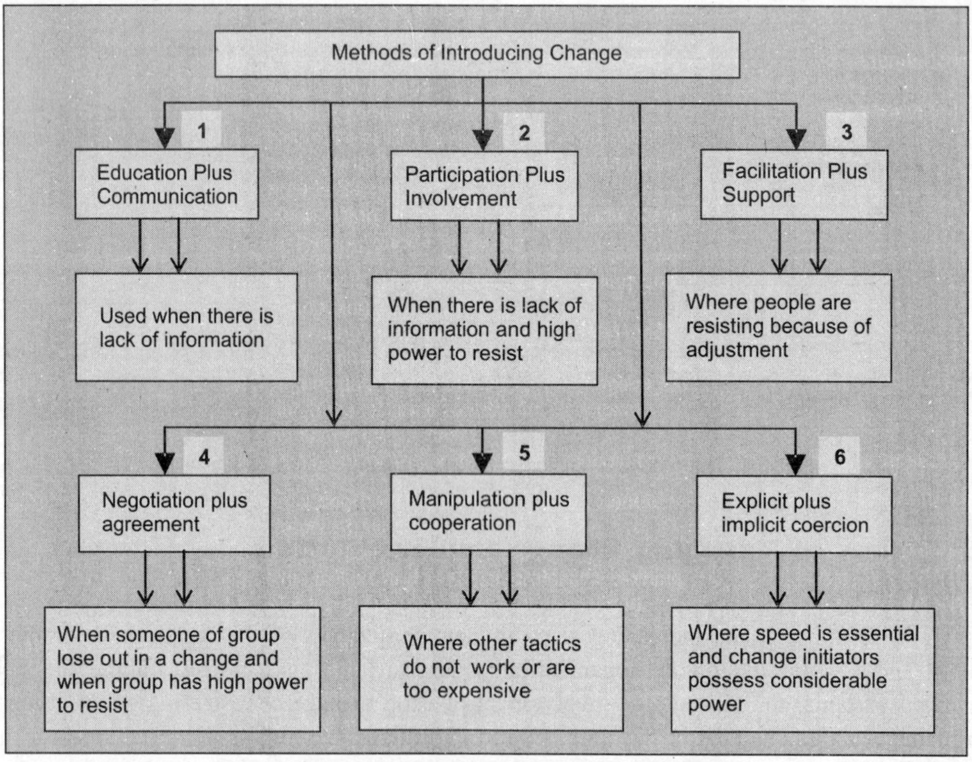

Fig. 8.5. Methods of Introducing Change or Dealing with Resistance to Change.
Source: Adapted from Kotler and Schlesinger, Choosing Strategies for Change, March-April 1979, Harvard Business Review.

↓ Indicates method of change

↓↓ Indicate situational factors for adopting the method

The six methods shown in Figure 8.5 are helpful in unfreezing changing the values and behaviours of the people and refreezing these values and behaviours.

Approaches to make the Change and Renewal Permanent

(1) **The Change Agent Must Change:** The HR managers involved in bringing change and going for renewal must be prepared to accept the new method. In this way he/she will be able to reinforce a psychological climate of support for change. Unwillingness of managers to give up traditional managerial practices is a serious barrier to the introduction of change and to make it permanent in the organization.

(2) **Use of Group Forces:** In making the change and renewal permanent, it is essential for change agent to use group force as group exercises considerable influence on the behaviour of members. The behaviour attitude, perceptions, belief and values of individuals are firmly rooted in the groups to which they belong.

(3) **Unions to be taken into Confidence:** The change agent must ensure that the trade unions are taken into confidence. Unions can act as change agent, if fully convinced of the change. Many union leaders do not accept modern technology as it is thought that it will displace the labour force. But if they are taken into confidence the change is easily introduced.

(4) **Build Support by Highlighting Shared Rewards:** An important way to build support for change is to ensure that the people affected will be benefited from the change and renewal. Benefits include increased pay, promotion, training, recognition, and so on.

(5) **Concern for Employees:** A change should not be introduced for the sake of it. Change needs to be introduced only when necessary and must ultimately benefit the employees. It must be by evolution and not by revolution.

(6) **Cautions and Slow Introduction:** The management should not introduce any change suddenly and abruptly. It must be an objective for the management to build in the organization an awareness of change and an ability to forecast it, and also to construct an attitude of welcoming change. Change must be introduced in sequential parts, if possible, the results must be reviewed, and required adjustments must be made in it.

(7) **Positive Motion:** The management should use the policy of positive motivation to counterpart negative resistance. It should be the attempt of the management to make the job easier and less exerting. The management should impart proper training to its employees in new techniques and work knowledge, etc. The leadership styles should also be supportive and human oriented. This policy will also bring down the resistance to change.

(8) **Career Planning and Development:** Organisation on the basis of change plans and redesigned jobs should plan for careers of employees, possibilities to move the employees to the higher levels and develop them. The developed employees for future careers demand the management to implement change.

(9) **Training and Development:** Management should plan for change. Based on the change plan, the job should be redesigned. Management should train the employee's before-hand and prepare the employees to invite change. Normally trained and developed employees will not resist change as they cannot keep quiet with enriched skill and knowledge.

ORGANIZATIONAL DEVELOPMENT AND OBJECTIVES

Organizational development (OD) is a special approach to organizational change in which the employees themselves formulate the change that is required and implement it, often with the assistance of a trained consultant. Particularly in large companies the OD process (including hiring of facilitators) is almost always handled through HR, whose staff has the special knowledge and networks required to implement this approach.

Various authors have given a variety of definitions about organizational development.

Definitions

Warren G. Bennis defines "*Organizational development as a complex educational strategy intended to change the beliefs, attitudes, values and structure of organizations so that they can better adapt to new technologies, markets and challenges and the dizzying rate of change itself.*"

Dale S. Beach defined OD "*as a complex educational strategy designed to increase organizational effectiveness and wealth through planned intervention by a consultant using theory and techniques of applied behavioural service.*"

Wendell L. French and Cecil H. Bell Jr. defined OD "*as a long-range effort to improve an organization's problem solving and renewal processes, particularly through a more effective and collaborative management of organization culture—with special emphasis on the culture of formal work teams—with the assistance of a change agent, or a catalyst and the use of the theory and technology of applied behaviour science, including action research.*"

It is clear from these definitions that OD has emerged in response to needs primarily because of the inadequacy of training and executive development programmes and secondly due to fast pace of change itself. The distinguishing features are:

1. It is usually based on **action research**, which means collecting data about a group, department, or organization and then feeding the data back to the employees so they can analyze it and develop hypotheses about what the problems in the unit might be.
2. It applies **behavioural science knowledge** for the purpose of improving the organization's effectiveness.
3. It **changes the attitudes, values, and beliefs** of employees so that the employees themselves can identify and implement the technical, procedural, structural, or other changes needed to improve the company's functioning.
4. It **changes the organization in a particular direction** towards improved problem solving, responsiveness, quality of work, and effectiveness.
5. OD is concerned with **problem-solving approach** as it seeks to solve the problems rather than merely discussing them.
6. OD is a **long-term approach** to improve the overall organizational effectiveness.
7. OD is **not a separate discipline** rather it draws from other disciplines like psychology, sociology, anthropology, etc.

Objectives of Organizational Development

Wendell L. French – an American expert has given the following objectives of OD:

- Increasing openness of communication among people.
- Increasing commitment, self-direction and self-control.
- To encourage the people who are at the helm of affairs or close to the point of actual action to make the decisions regarding their issues through collaborative effort.
- Involving the members in the process of analysis and implementation.
- To encourage the confrontation regarding organizational problems with a view to arriving at effective decisions.
- To enhance the personal enthusiasm and satisfaction levels.
- To increase the level of trust and support among employees.
- Developing strategic solutions to problems with higher frequency.
- Increasing the level of individual and group responsibility in planning and execution.

ORGANIZATIONAL TARGETS FOR CHANGE

Before discussing OD techniques, it is useful to know the organizational aspects which can be targets for change. Table 8.1 indicates the six targets and possible change methods. As shown in the table, the targets are objectives, strategy, tasks, technology, people and structure. Most often planned organizational change involves more than one of these targets.

Table 8.1 Organizational Targets and Methods of Change

Targets	Possible Change Methods
1. Purpose and Objectives	1. Clarify overall mission, modify existing objectives, use MBO
2. Strategy	2. Modify strategic plans, modify operational plans, modify policies and procedures
3. Tasks	3. Modify job designs, use job enrichment
4. Technology	4. Improve equipment and facilities, improve methods and work flows
5. People	5. Modify selection criteria
6. Structure	6. Modify job descriptions, modify organizational design, adjust coordination mechanisms, modify distribution of authority.

Source: Schermerhorn, *et al.*, "Managing Organizational Behaviour", New York, John Wiley & Sons, p. 634.

ORGANIZATIONAL DEVELOPMENT PROCESS AND TECHNIQUES

OD is a long run process as it takes several years to complete it. It is complex also as it is multidimensional involving top management, union, employees and other groups. There are various approaches to OD process. We have taken the typical process given by **William B. Wrether** which contains seven steps given as under:

1. **Initial Diagnosis:** It is necessary to find out the professional and competent people within the organization to plan and execute OD activities. If competent people are not available within the organization the services of the outside consultants to help in diagnosing the problem and developing OD activities are to be taken. The consultants adopt various methods including interviews, questionnaires, direct observation, analysis of documents and reports for diagnosing the problem.
2. **Data Collection:** Survey method is used to collect the data and information for determining organizational climate and identifying the behavioural problems.
3. **Data Feedback and Confrontation:** Data collected are analyzed and reviewed by various work groups formed for this purpose in order to mediate in the areas of disagreement or confrontation of ideas or opinions and to establish priorities.
4. **Action Planning and Problem Solving:** Groups prepare recommendations and specific action planning to solve the specific and identified problems by using data collected.
5. **Team Building:** The consultants encourage the employees throughout the process to form into groups and teams by explaining the advantages of the teams in the OD process, by arranging joint meetings with the managers, subordinates, etc.
6. **Intergroup Development:** The consultants encourage the intergroup meetings, interaction, etc., after the formation of groups/teams.

7. **Evaluation and Follow-up:** The organization evaluates the OD programmes, find out their utility, and develop the programmes further for correcting the deviations and/or improved results. The consultants help the organization in this respect.

OD Applications / Techniques

The number and variety of OD applications (also called OD interventions or techniques) have substantially over the past few years. OD got its start with what were called *human process interventions*. These were generally aimed at enabling employees to develop a better understanding of their own and others' behaviours to improve that behaviour for the growth of organization.

Today OD practitioners have become increasingly involved not just in changing participant's behaviours but also indirectly altering the finite structure practices, strategy, and culture. They are using four types of OD applications:

I. Human Process
II. Technostructural
III. Human Resource Management, and
IV. Strategic Applications

All these approaches are based upon getting the employees themselves to collect the required data and to create and implement the solutions. Table 8.2 illustrates a much wider range of applications.

Table 8.2: Examples of OD Interventions and the Organizational Levels

	Primary Organizational Level Affected		
Interventions	**Individual**	**Group**	**Organization**
Human Process			
T-Groups	X	X	
Process consultation		X	
Third-party intervention	X	X	
Team building		X	
Organizational confrontation meeting		X	X
Intergroup relations		X	X
Technostructural			
Formal structural change			X
Differentiation and integration			X
Cooperative union-management projects	X	X	X
Quality circles	X	X	
Total quality management		X	X
Work design	X	X	
Human Resource Management			
Goal setting	X	X	
Performance appraisal	X	X	
Reward systems	X	X	X
Career planning and development	X		
Managing workforce diversity	X		
Employee wellness	X		
Strategic			
Integrated strategic management			X
Culture change			X
Strategic change			X
Self-designing organization		X	X

Source: Gary Dessler, HRM, Pearson Education, Asia, 2002, New Delhi, p. 297.

Figure 8.6 reveals the particular techniques used in each of four major OD applications.

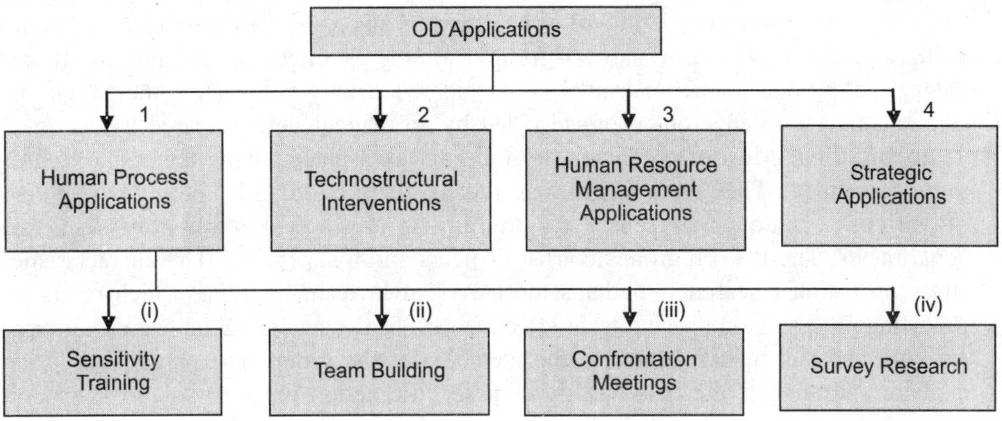

Fig. 8.6. OD Applications / Techniques.

These techniques along with some other techniques are discussed as under:

1. Human Process Application

Human process OD techniques generally aim first at improving employee's human relations skills. The goal is to give employees the insight and skills required to analyze their own and others' behaviour more effectively, so they can then solve interpersonal and intergroup problems. **Sensitivity training** is perhaps the most widely used technique in this category.

(i) Sensitivity Training: Sensitivity, laboratory, or T-group training (the T is for training) was one of the earliest OD techniques; although its use has diminished, it is still found today. Sensitivity training's basic aim is to increase the participant's insight into his or her own behaviour and the behaviour of others by encouraging an open expression of feelings in the trainer-guided T-group. Typically, 10 to 15 people meet, usually away from the job, and no activities or discussion topics are planned. The focus is on the here and now (specifically, the feelings and emotions of the members in the group). Participants are encouraged to portray themselves as they are in the group rather than in terms of past experiences or future problems. The T-group's success depends largely on the feedback process and in particular on participants' willingness to tell each another how their behaviour is being perceived. A climate of 'psychological safety' is therefore necessary if participants are to feel safe enough to reveal themselves, to expose their feelings, to drop their defenses, and to try out new ways of interacting. The objectives of this training are:

- To help people to understand themselves better.
- To create better understanding of others.
- To gain insight into the group process.
- To develop specific behavioural skills.

Sensitivity training is obviously quite personal in nature, so it's not surprising that it's a controversial technique the use of which has diminished markedly since its heyday 20 years ago. The personal nature of such training suggests that participation should be voluntary; some therefore view T-group training as unethical because participation 'suggested' by one's superior cannot be considered strictly voluntary. Others argue that it can actually be a dangerous exercise if led by an inadequately prepared trainer.

(ii) Team Building: Most of the laboratory training takes place among the employees of the same department. They work together as a team. Team building is nothing but application of various techniques of sensitivity training to the actual work groups in various departments. These work groups consist of peers and a supervisor. The characteristic OD stress on action research is perhaps most evident in team building, which refers to the following process of improving team effectiveness. Data concerning the team's performance are collected and then fed back to the members of the group. The participants examine, explain, and analyze the data and develop specific action plans or solutions for solving the team's problems. This is another example of a human process OD application.

According to experts **French and Bell**, the typical team-building meeting begins with the consultant interviewing each of the group members and the leader prior to the meeting. They are all asked what their problems are, how they think the group functions, and what obstacles are keeping the group from performing better. The consultant might then categorize the interview data into themes and present the themes to the group at the beginning of the meeting. The themes are ranked by the group in terms of their importance, and the most important ones become the agenda for the meeting. The group then explores and discusses the issues, examines the underlying causes of the problems, and begins working on some solutions. Table 8.3 shows the team building activities applicable to family and special groups.

Table 8.3: Team Building Activities

Activity	**Family Groups**	**Special Groups**
Diagnosis	Diagnostic meetings: "How are we doing?"	Diagnostic meetings: "Where would you like to go?"
Task accomplishment	Problem solving, decision-making, role clarification, goal setting, etc.	Special problems, role and goal clarification, resource utilization, etc.
Building and maintaining relationships	Focus on effective interpersonal relationships, including boss-subordinate and peer	Focus on interpersonal or inter-unit conflict and underutilization of other team members as resources.
Management of group processes	Focus on understanding group processes and group culture	Focus on communication, decision-making, and task allocations
Role analysis and role negotiations	Techniques used for clarification and definition	Techniques used for role clarification and definition

Source: Stoner, *et al.* Management p. 423.

(iii) Confrontation Meetings: Other human process interventions aim to bring about intergroup or organization-wide changes. Organizational confrontation meetings can help clarify and bring into the open intergroup misconceptions and problems so that they can be resolved. The basic approach here is that the participants themselves provide the input for the meeting. They then confront and thrash out misperceptions in an effort to reduce tensions.

(iv) **Survey Research:** Another human process OD technique requires that employees throughout the organization fill out attitude surveys. Data collection is through standardized questionnaires. The data are then used as feedback to the work groups as a basis for problem analysis and action planning. In general, such surveys are a convenient method for unfreezing an organization's management and the employees by providing a comparative, graphic illustration of the fact that the organization does have problems which should be solved.

2. Technostructural Interventions

OD practitioners are also increasingly involved in changing the structures, methods, and job designs of firms. Compared with human process interventions, these technostructural interventions generally focus more directly on productivity improvement and efficiency.

OD practitioners use a variety of technostructural interventions. For example, in a formal structure change programme the employees collect data on the company's existing organizational structures; they then jointly redesign and implement a new one, usually answering to HR.

3. Human Resource Management Applications

OD practitioners increasingly use action research to enable employees to analyze and change their firm's personnel practices. Targets of change here might include the firm's performance appraisal system and reward system, as well as installing diversity programmes.

4. Strategic Applications

Among the newest OD applications are strategic interventions, organization-wide programmes aimed at achieving a fit between a firm's strategy, structure, culture, and external environment. Integrated strategic management is one example of how OD can be used to create or change a strategy. This intervention consists of four steps:

(i) **Analyze current strategy and organizational design:** Managers and other employees analyze the firm's current strategy, as well as its organizational design.

(ii) **Choose a desired strategy and organizational design:** Based on the OD consultant assisted analysis, senior management formulates a strategic vision, objectives, and plan and an organizational structure for implementing them.

(iii) **Design a strategic change plan:** The group designs a strategic change plan, which "is an action plan for moving the organization from its current strategy and organizational design to the desired future strategy and design." The plan explains how the strategic change will be implemented, including specific activities as well as the costs and budgets associated with them.

(iv) **Implement the strategic change plan:** The final step is actually implementing the strategic change plan and measuring and reviewing the results of the change activities to ensure that they are proceeding as planned.

Some Other Approaches/Techniques of OD

One such technique usually adopted by the OD practitioners is Management by Objectives. Likewise another prominent technique used by the experts is quality of work life programmes. These two techniques are discussed as under:

1. Management by Objectives (MBO)

MBO is a process by which managers at different levels and their subordinates work together in identifying goals and establishing objectives consistent with the organizational goals and attaining them. The main objectives of MBO technique developed by Peter Drucker in 1954, are:

- To increase the precision of the planning process at the organizational level.
- To reduce the gap between employee and organizational goals.

As a result of MBO technique performance appraisal through a process of shared goal setting and evaluation is encouraged.

Elements / Steps in MBO Process

1. **Setting of Objectives at the Top:** The managers at the top level set the overall objectives of the organization by taking planning premises into account. These objectives set by the superiors are preliminary as they must be regarded as tentative and subject to modification as the entire chain of verifiable objectives is worked out by subordinates.
2. **Clarification of Organizational Goals:** The relationship between the results expected and the responsibility for attaining them should be established as every goal and sub-goal should be someone's clear responsibility and accountability.
3. **Setting of Subordinate Objectives*:*** The organization's objectives are accomplished by a number of individuals in the organization. Therefore, each individual should be assigned a specific task and he must know, in advance, what he is expected to achieve. In view of this, the subordinates' objectives should also be set in consultation, within the purview of the preliminary objectives of the organisation. In exceptional cases, the preliminary objectives may be modified or changed in view of abilities, strengths and weaknesses of the subordinates and their objectives.
4. **Recycling of Objectives*:*** In fact, the final objectives are neither set at the top nor at the bottom. As discussed earlier, they are set after thorough consultations and discussions between the superiors and subordinates. This joint process creates the feeling of commitment and involvement to the employees at various levels.
5. **Performance Appraisal*:*** Each employee should evaluate his accomplishment with the objectives set, with the help of his superior. This appraisal provides him the scope for correction and further improvement.

The full MBO cycle is depicted in Figure 8.7. The actual MBO cycle may vary from organization to organization but the overall results are uniform:

- High morale and positive attitude
- Improved level of performance and contribution
- Better understanding of overall organizational goals

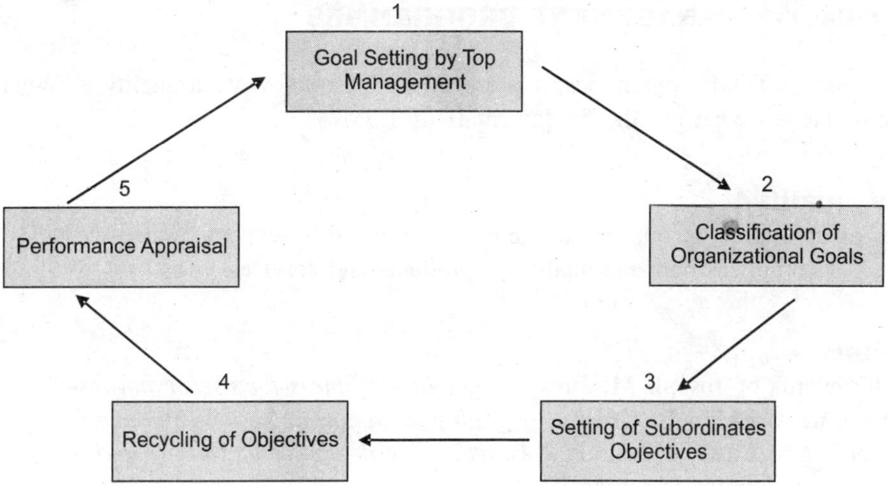

Fig. 8.7. The MBO Cycle.

2. Quality of Work Life Programmes

Quality of work life programmes have been designed by OD practitioners to create work situations that enhance employee's motivation, satisfaction, and commitment factors that may contribute to high levels of organizational performance, collectively called quality of work life (QWL) programmes, these are designed to remove drudgery associated with any work situation—the attempt is to humanize the workplace. There are two popular approaches to humanize the workplace.

(i) **Work Restructuring:** Work restructuring is the process of changing the way jobs are done to make them more interesting to workers. The most popular techniques of work restructuring include job enlargement and job enrichment. These two were already covered in the chapter on motivation. These techniques also help improve QWL of employees.

(ii) **Quality Circle:** These are small groups of employees who meet regularly; usually weekly on voluntary basis to identify and solve problems related to the quality of the work they perform, and the conditions under which people work on their jobs. An organization may have several QC operating at once, each dealing with a particular work area about which it has the most expertise. To help them work effectively, the members of the circle usually receive some form of training in problem solving.

Benefits of QWL

QWL programmes benefit organizations in at least three ways: (i) The most direct benefit is increased job satisfaction, organizational commitment, and reduced turnover among the workforce. (ii) A second benefit is increased productivity. (iii) Finally, organizations stand to gain in the form of profitability and goal attainment.

These benefits do not, however, accrue automatically. Two hurdles have to be crossed to realize the benefits. First, both management and labour must cooperate in designing the programme. Second, the plans agreed to by all concerned parties must be fully implemented. It is easy to forget QWL activities amidst the hectic pace of daily activities. This should not happen.

TOTAL QUALITY MANAGEMENT PROGRAMMES

In order to discuss TQM programmes, it is essential first to know what quality is. What is TQM and its importance? What are the fundamentals of TQM?

What is Quality?

A number of definitions of quality have been propounded by experts. When we talk of quality in business, it comprises both the quality of products and services.

Definitions

- In the words of **Joseph M. Juran**, "*Quality is fitness for use or purpose.*"
- According to **Philip B. Crosby**, "*Quality is conformance to requirement.*"
- According to **Edward Deming**, "*A predictable degree of uniformity and dependability at low cost and suited to market.*"
- According to **James Evans**, "*Quality measures how well a product or service meets customer needs.*"

Quality thus is expressed as the totality of features and characteristics of a product or service that bears on its ability to satisfy given needs. The basic consideration is thus always the extent to which the product or service meets the customer's expectations.

Quality standards today are international. Doing business in Europe often means the firm must show it complies with **ISO 9000**, the quality standards of European Community (EC). If required to do so by a customer, the vendor would have to prove that its quality manuals, procedures, and job instructions all comply with the ISO 9000 standards.

Improving quality is a necessity to companies all over the world. Globalization of competition has done more than just force firms to become more efficient; it has raised the quality bar too, by forcing competitors in industries ranging from cars to computers to phone service to meet and exceed the quality of the firms with which they compete HR plays a central role in proving product and service quality.

What is TQM?

Total quality management is a dynamic process which has been accepted as a necessary requirement throughout the world for attaining excellence in business and services. TQM calls for continuous improvement of quality with the cooperation of employees through innovation in product and technology so to meet the changing requirements of the customer. It refers to meeting the requirements of customers consistently by continuous improvement in the quality of work of all employees.

Definitions

According to **Prag Diwan**, "*TQM is defined as an all encompassing dynamic process in an organization to promote never ending involvement in the effectiveness and efficiency of all elements of a business.*"

According to **British Quality Association** (1989), "*TQM is a corporate business management philosophy which recognizes that customer needs and business goals are inseparable and it ensures maximum effectiveness and efficiency within industry and commerce.*"

According to **CII**, "*TQM is defined as meeting the requirements of the internal and external customers consistently by continuous improvement in the quality of work of all employees.*"

The Definitions Reveal Three Main Processes in TQM

1. Meeting customer's requirements;
2. Continuous improvement through management process; and
3. Involvement of all employees.

1. **Meeting Customer's Requirements:** TQM aims at satisfying the requirements of customers which never remain constant, but keep on changing with the change in time, environments, circumstances, needs, fashion, etc. Thus, meeting the changed requirements of customers is a continuous goal of the producer.
2. **Continuous Improvement:** The change in customer requirements may be in terms of desire for better quality product/services, bigger size, reduced cost, etc. So a product has to cope up with new requirements. A new process may have to be developed, or it may require a new design. The production process has thus to be attuned and accelerated to meet these changing requirements.
3. **Empowerment of Employees:** As said above, TQM requires a continuous improvement in quality of products. This calls for the improvement in the quality or competency of employees through training and development. The enhancement of skills of employees will not only improve quality, but also bring down the cost of production through efficient use of machines and materials and reduction of wastages. The employees must also be conscious about the need for improvement in quality of work. Quality circle is an outstanding example of quality in this regard. It is because of employees' involvement in improvement of quality that TQM is referred to as *people's process.* TQM should be the concern of all managers and workers in the organization if it is to serve its purpose fully.

TQM is a philosophy that calls for development of a company-wide culture for quality. TQM typically involves an increase of awareness through training and motivation. It requires every member of the organization to accept quality as his responsibility.

Significance of TQM

The following benefits can be derived from a sound TQM programme:

1. Total Quality Management brings quality consciousness in the enterprise which encourages the production of quality products.
2. TQM helps in providing greater satisfaction to the customers by meeting their requirements. If the customers are satisfied, the sales will increase. It creates a good public image of the enterprise by helping it to provide goods and services of higher quality to the society.
3. There is better utilization of materials, machines, capital, human resources, etc.

4. Wastages are reduced to the minimum. As a result, cost of production is reduced and profitability is increased. Even the customers could be provided goods at lower cost. The competitive position of the firm in the market is improved.
5. The employees are committed to higher quality and feel highly motivated. Their morale is high due to good image of the firm.

Fundamentals or Principles of TQM

TQM fundamentals/principles can be developed by examining those companies which have been successful or which are Quality Award winners.

Some Indian companies like Philips, Telco, Bharat Electronics, Kirloskar, SAIL, RIL have won Golden Peacock National Quality Award from Quality Council of India. In USA, Motorola and Federal Express are the winners of Malcolm Baldrige Award. Miami-based Florida Power & Light Co (FPL) won Deming Prize. Toyota also won Deming Prize. On examining these companies, common fundamentals or principles of TQM have been developed. Table 8.4 shows these principles or fundamentals.

Table 8.4: Fundamentals or Principles of TQM

	Fundamentals or Principles	Support
1.	Putting the Customer First	This principle supports the traditional view that customer is the king.
2.	Management by Factors	This principle shows that facts are better than opinions.
3.	Deming Wheel for Improvement	This principle of Plan-Do-Check-Act (PDCA) also known as Deming Wheel promotes continuous improvement.
4.	Focus on Prevention	This principle ensures solution of problems and reoccurrence is prevented.
5.	Employee Involvement	This principle creates respect for people and top employees' innovative and exciting ideas.
6.	Cross-functional Management	This principle promotes cooperation across functional organizational boundaries.

Prominent TQM Programmes

The prominent TQM programs adopted by the most Quality Award Winning Companies across the world have demonstrated the following four TQM programmes that are generally adopted for total quality improvement in organizations:

1. Quality Circles
2. Kaizen–Continuous Improvement
3. Statistical Process Control
4. Just-in-Time (JIT)

1. Quality Circles

The concept of Quality Circle emerged from quality control. Quality circles are quite popular in Japan. Looking at their success, many organizations in USA and India have also attempted to implement quality circles. It should be noted that quality circles provide a future-oriented approach. They seek high quality products in the current production run and in the future.

According to **William and Rose**, "*A quality circle is a small group of employees doing similar or related work who meet regularly to identify, analyze and solve product-quality problems and to improve general operations.*"

Definitions of QC reveals the following elements or features:

(i) Quality circles are voluntary or relatively autonomous units (ideally about 10 workers), usually led by a supervisor or a senior worker and organized as work units.

(ii) The circles intend to focus attention on the self-development of workers and the improvement of working conditions.

(iii) QCs are a group activity.

(iv) QCs are participative.

(v) Top management must play positive role by attending the orientation courses.

(vi) Proper coordination is required between top management and other participants. The structure of QCs is shown in Figure 8.8.

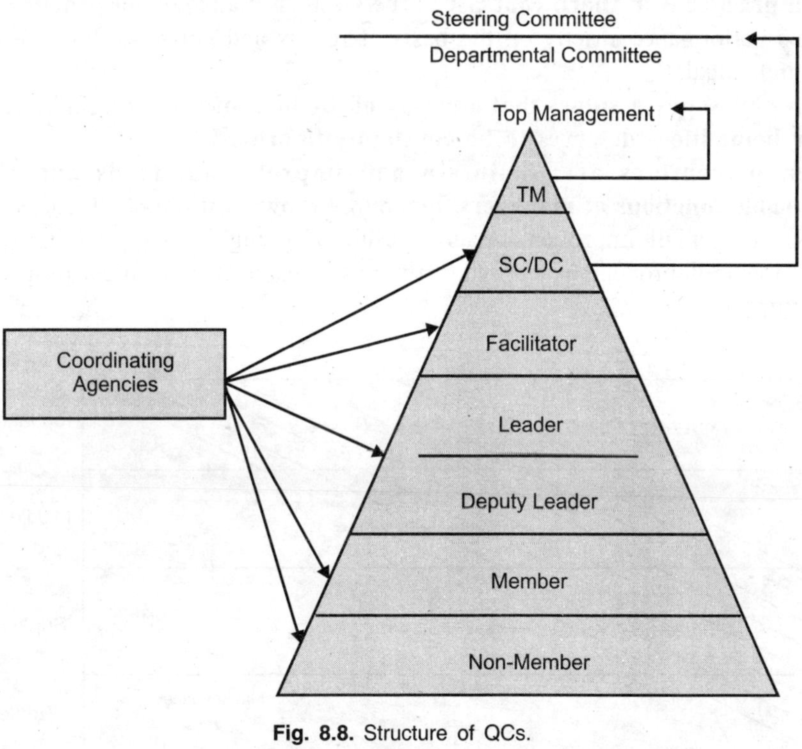

Fig. 8.8. Structure of QCs.

Objectives of QCs

The technique of quality circle has been refined over the years. It is now followed to achieve the following objectives:

1. Overall improvement of quality of products manufactured by the enterprise.
2. Improvement of production methods and productivity of the enterprise.

3. Self-development of the employees who take part in quality circles.
4. Encouragement of innovative ideas among the employees.
5. Building high morale of employees by developing team spirit in the organization.

2. Kaizen–Continuous Improvement

Kaizen is a Japanese word which means continuous improvement over improvement. Kaizen strategy is the single most important concept in Japanese management which is key to competitive success. It is regarded as the most important TQM programme.

The basic essence of this programme is: "*There will be no progress if you keep on doing things exactly the same way all the time.*"

Features of Kaizen TQM Programme

- **Kaizen has its emphasis on process oriented way of thinking and management system** that supports and acknowledges people's process-oriented efforts for improvement.
- **Kaizen practice is in sharp contrast to the western management practice** of reviewing people's performance strictly on the basis of results and not rewarding the efforts made by an individual.
- **Kaizen philosophy assumes that our way of life be it our working life, our social life, or our home life – deserves to be constantly improved.**
- **Kaizen perceptions are: maintain and improve standards and the two are inseparable functions of managers.** Figure 8.9 shows that improvement is broken down into Kaizen (small improvement as a result of going efforts) and innovation which means drastic improvement with status quo as a result of investment in new technology and equipment.

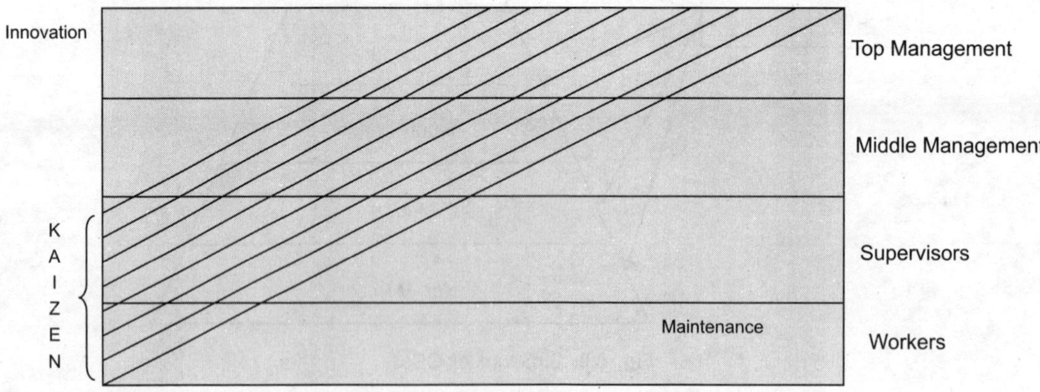

Fig. 8.9. Japanese Management Functions and Kaizen.

Features of Kaizen and Innovations

Table 8.5 shows the comparison of features of Kaizen and innovations.

Table 8.5: Features of Kaizen and Innovations

	Features	*Kaizen*	Innovations
1.	Effect	Long-term and long-lasting but undramatic	Short-term but dramatic
2.	Pace	Small steps	Big steps
3.	Time frame	Continuous and incremental	Intermittent and non-Incremental
4.	Change	Gradual and constant	Abrupt and volatile
5.	Involvement	Everybody	Select few "champions"
6.	Approach	Collectivism, group efforts, systems approach	Rugged individualism, individual ideas and efforts
7.	Mode	Maintenance and improvement	Scrap and rebuild
8.	Spark	Conventional know-how and state-of-the-art	Technological breakthroughs new inventions, new theories
9.	Practical requirements	Requires little investment but huge effort to maintain	Requires large investment but little effort to maintain it
10.	Effort orientation	People	Technology
11.	Evaluation criteria	Process and efforts for better results	Results for profits
12.	Advantage	Works well in slow-growth economy	Better suited to fast growth economy

Kaizen and Total Quality Control

TQC is a part of Kaizen movement in Japan. TQC activities are considered not simply concerned with quality control but also associated with the people. TQC is a system of control on the improvement of managerial performance at all levels. It deals with the following:

- Quality Assurance
- Cost Reduction
- Meeting Production Quotes
- Meeting Delivery Schedules
- Safety Measures
- New Product Development
- Productivity Improvement
- Improving SCM

3. Statistical Process Control for Quality Improvement

The statistical process control (SPC) is also regarded as an important TQM programme. The control process detects and takes action on quality problems and helps in improvement process.

SPC is a measure of improving processes by reducing their variability. It is application of statistical methods to the measurement and analysis of variation in any process which is a unique combination of machines, methods, materials, people, and software services.

Applications / Benefits of SPC—Stage-wise

SPC applications involve four stages:

1. **Identification of Process Failure Modes:** The application SPC commences with the developing as an understanding of the process, its parameters and defining the control

the mechanism. The technique used in initial phase is *failure mode effect analysis* (FMEA).

2. **Analyzing Process Data:** In order to determine normal variation the organizations must collect and analyze the process data.
3. **Evaluating Process Capability:** The third stage of SPC application is to determine the relationship between the natural variation of the process and the allowable specification limits. This relationship is known as the process capability.
4. **Charting of the Process Performance:** The going control of the process can be monitored using control charts which represent the final stage of the SPC application in manufacturing organizations. Figure 8.10 shows this process.

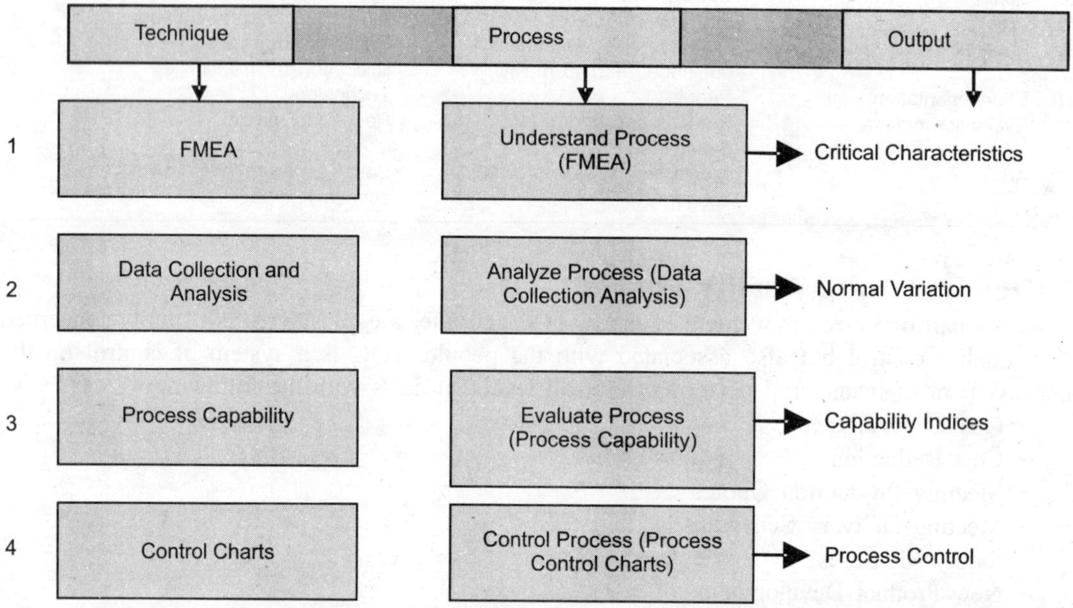

Fig. 8.10. Applications of SPC and a Control Process.

In a nutshell, we can say that the control of variation is an important element of quality improvement. *The implementation of statistical process control (SPC) can reduce the overall process cost.*

How Quality is Improved Through SPC?

In the control process, statistical control charts are used which detect the existence of special causes of variation which results in sporadic problems. The charts show this in the form of sample data falling beyond statistical control limits, i.e., the process is "*out of statistical control*". Conversely when a chart shows a process to be in statistical control, the process is in a state of stability and hence no quality variation. But stability does not always mean customer satisfaction with the result. A process thus, in statistical control can have serious quality problems here again change is required which affects the average or variation. Such a change which affects variation or average is the job of improvement. Process improvement is directed as the following set of problems:

- When process average of the process is too large
- When variability of the process is too large
- When the instrument is inadequate
- When there is a process drift
- When there are cyclical changes in the process
- When the process is erratic

This total quality management programme is not applicable to services but only to manufacturing.

4. Just-in-Time (JIT) Programme

The JIT programme of TQM is applicable only the quality issues in manufacturing and not the services sector. It is a Japanese technique which may be called philosophy as it goes beyond inventory control. It is also used as waste elimination approach. The JIT system results in much less inventory, lower costs and better quality than in Just-in-Case (JIC) approach.

Meaning of JIT: Just-in-Time is an approach to minimize waste in manufacturing in the form of time materials, energy and errors. It is a broad philosophy of pursing zero inventories, zero transactions and zero disturbances, i.e., execution of the schedule day-in-day-out. The major issue in any JIT system is maintaining flow times. JIT displays an excellent ability to adapt to the changes in demand and help reduction of work in processing industry.

Objectives of JIT

1. To reduce the set-up times and lot sizes.
2. Achieving zero defects, goal in manufacturing.
3. To focus on continuous improvement.
4. Using knowledge of the workers.
5. Minimizing travel distances and inventories between the machines.
6. To minimize inventory carrying costs.
7. To eliminate waste such as long set-up times, zigzag materials flow, scrap, machine breakdown, higher stocks, etc.
8. To cross-train the workers in multi-functions to maintain and enable them to run several machines at a time.

JIT Methods and Elements of JIT System

The main JIT methods: These include the following:

- Good housekeeping
- Waste elimination through problem exposure
- Lead time reduction
- Set-up time reduction
- Visual control
- Mistake proofing

- Process stopping for defect
- Production rule
- Total productive maintenance

The elements of JIT system: The major elements of the system are as under:

1. **Master Schedule** – drawn in advance
2. **Kanban** (Japanese Term) – pulling parts from one work centre to the next
3. **Set-up Time** – producing parts in a lot size of one
4. **Multiple Function Workers** – multifunctional workers
5. **Layout of Plant** – capable of adjusting inventory on shop floor
6. **Emphasis on Quality** – as defects are quickly detected by the next process
7. **Vendors Relations** – vendors are to make frequent deliveries.

The main theme of JIT system of TQM is that if we acquire higher stocks the productivity problems get hidden and never get exposed as shown in Figure 8.11. JIT *philosophy is to*

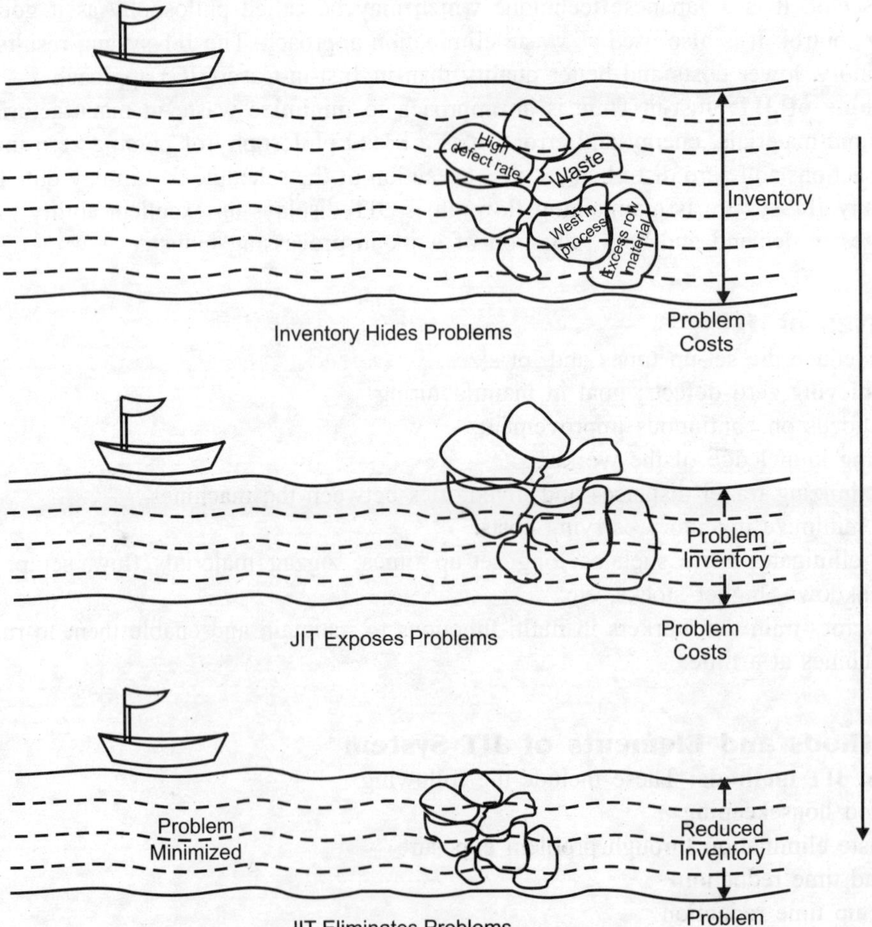

Fig. 8.11. JIT Exposes and Eliminates Problems.

expose these problems and involve all employees to remove them so that the necessity of higher stocks does not arise.

HR'S ROLE IN QUALITY MANAGEMENT

HR plays a central role in improving product and service quality in the organizations by improving the efficiency and productivity of employees and other personnel.

How can HR contribute to a company's quality improvement efforts? This question can be answered after studying the quality improvement experience of Florida Power & Light Company (FPL). It is given in Table 8.6.

Table 8.6: TQM at Florida Power & Light

Company Introduction

Miami-based Florida Power & Light Company (FPL), Florida's largest utility, was the first company outside Japan to win the Deming Prize, which is similar to America's Baldrige Award. Awarded annually (and since 1986 outside Japan), the prize recognizes outstanding achievement in quality control management. The steps FPL took to win the award help to illustrate the activities involved in implementing comprehensive company-wide total quality management programmes and **the role of HR management** in doing so.

Components/Phases of Quality Improvement Programmes of FPL

1. Policy Deployment

Policy deployment is the process through which the company focuses its resources on achieving customer satisfaction. Policy deployment provides direction. At FPL, the policy deployment process began by determining what FPL customers wanted and then compiling these needs in a customer needs table. Specifically, annual surveys were made of customer needs, and these were then summarized and prioritized into five or six main customer needs categories. At FPL, the needs emerging from the customer needs assessment included:

- Improve public confidence in safety programmes.
- Reduce the number of complaints to the Florida Public Service Commission.
- Improve the reliability of electric service.
- Continue to emphasize safe, reliable, and efficient operation of nuclear plants.
- Strengthen fossil fuel plant reliability and availability.

Such needs are then translated into more measurable goals, such as increase fossil plant availability to about 95% of total time. Measurable objectives like these, which FPL refers to as *policies,* are then distributed to all FPL employees via the *Annual Guide to Corporate Excellence.* This publication folds out into a wall chart, and, as the company puts it, "*Hung in offices throughout FPL, it reminds one and all to check whether their QI teams and daily work are contributing to the corporate vision.*" It is through policy deployment that the measurable quality objectives (or policies) of FPL are deployed throughout the company and its facilities, thus giving this process its name.

2. Quality Improvement Teams

At FPL and many other firms, most total quality efforts rely on quality improvement teams–groups of specially trained employees who meet at work for an hour or so once each week to spot and solve quality programmes at work. FPL used several types of teams: functional teams, cross-functional teams, task teams, and lead teams (about 1,700 teams altogether). (i) **Functional teams** are composed of volunteers who typically work together as natural work units on a daily basis. They generally choose their own problems and meet 1 hour every week. The basic aim here is to involve first-line employees in improving their daily work activities to enhance the quality of their work life and to develop their skills. (ii) **Cross-functional teams** are ongoing teams that are formed to address problems that cut across organizational boundaries. (iii) **Task team** members are appointed from one or more departments to work on specific high-priority assigned problems. When the problem is solved, the task team is disbanded.

Table 8.6: Contd.

Finally, (iv) **lead teams** are headed by a vice-president or other manager and serve as steering committees for all the teams that operate in their areas. It is the lead team, for instance, that decides how employees are assigned to serve on various teams and establishes guidelines regarding frequency and duration of team meetings.

The basic policies (such as 'improve reliability of service') produced by the policy deployment process provide the framework within which the quality improvement teams work. The teams then generally select their own problem topics (called themes) to study, but certain topics are off limits. (These include the company's union agreement, absenteeism, pay, salaries, promotions, the apprenticeship programme, and general safety rules produced by a joint safety committee).

Team members must be trained, and this is one area in which HR has a major impact. For example, Team Member Training is a 2-day programme focusing on special techniques such as statistical quality control and group decision-making techniques such as brainstorming.

About a thousand quality improvement recommendations are presented per year. For example, one team discovered that it was bird droppings, not inclement weather, that causes some of FPL's high-voltage lines to sort out so often.

3. Quality in Daily Work

In addition to policy deployment and quality improvement teams, FPL encourages *quality in daily work* (QIDW). Individual employees are urged to identify their customers and their needs, keeping in mind that 'customers' may be external or internal (that is, inside the company). The basic thrust of QIDW is to encourage individual employees to apply a quality improvement approach to their individual jobs.

Source: Gary Dessler. HRM, Pearson Education Asia, 2002, New Delhi, pp. 300-301.

(A) HR guidelines from FPL for Role in Quality Management on the basis of FPLs experience. Some HR guidelines or lessons from FPL are as under:

1. **Make sure all teams work within a policy**: Deployment process to ensure their efforts are consistent with the firm's goals.
2. **Do not institute quality improvement teams as separate, parallel organization structures**: Simply trying to superimpose such teams outside the normal chain of command elicited resistance from supervisors, many of whom made comments like "*I don't know what these people are doing: they're not helping me do my job.*" The teams should, to the greatest extent possible, be composed of natural work units.
3. **Do not treat the quality improvement programme as if it has an end:** It is important to emphasize that it is really a systematic and continuing way of doing business, one that has no end.
4. **Recognize that training is essential:** Quality improvement is successful largely because training continually upgrades the problem analysis and statistics skills of even first-line employees. This training is crucial both to provide the required analytical skills and also to emphasize the firm's commitment to the programme.
5. **Give employees the skills they need to analyze and solve problems:** Then get to analyze and solve the problem; and finally follow up on their suggestions.
6. **Remember that whether or not the company achieves its quality goals is important but almost secondary:** The new employee values that emerge are the heart of the programme.
7. **Don't focus exclusively on "boosting productivity" or assume that emphasizing quality means that productivity will necessarily fall:** In fact, FPL and other companies have often found that as quality rises, so does productivity.

8. **Recognize effort and encourage employees:** A main benefit of such a programme is the sense of satisfaction it can foster in employees. This results from encouraging employees to identify and devise countermeasures against problems and from giving them the tools required to get this job done.
9. **Reward individuals and team efforts in a concrete manner:** Not necessarily just with money but with rewards like merchandise or pins.
10. **Remember that the first steps need to be taken by top management:** "*From the board of directors to every supervisor, management must adopt the principles and language of quality, follow the processes, set examples and guide others. A substantial commitment is necessary for employee education, and for awareness and recognition programmes. These programmes require reallocation of budgets and personnel, and will take time to produce results but will be worth it.*"

(B) HR's Role in Winning the Quality Awards

HR similarly plays a big role in meeting the Malcolm Baldrige Quality Award – a top US quality awards world over Baldrige applicants are evaluated by a board consisting of quality experts. The experts examine seven basic areas: (i) ***senior executive leadership*** (top management's symbolic commitment to quality) (ii) ***information and analysis*** (an adequate system for collecting statistical data on matters such as product or service quality) (iii) ***strategic quality planning*** (the adequacy of the firm's planning process and how key quality requirements are integrated into the firm's overall business planning process) (iv) ***HRD and management*** (making moves for growth of HR and its management (v) ***management of quality*** (for example, rather than viewing design, production, and sales as separate entities, top firms usually recognize the integrated nature of their work so that the departments work together) (vi) ***quality and operational results*** (to show the firm is achieving continuous improvement in critical operational areas, such as in service quality levels); and (vii) ***customer focus and satisfaction*** (wherein the examiners look for objective, validated data regarding the applicant's success in satisfying the customer). Baldrige Award criteria framework is shown in Figure 8.12 which proves the crucial HR's role in quality improvement.

Note: Senior executive leadership is the "driver" of total quality management, with each of the other six elements, or Baldrige categories, playing a crucial role.

As part of this process, the applicant's human resource development and management is also evaluated. Specifically, judges evaluate the firm's achievements with respect to developing its employees potential to pursue the firm's quality objectives. In practical terms, examiners focus in this category on the extent to which HR management and related techniques (such as enrichment, empowerment, training, and career development) are used to tap each employee's potential. For example, judges expect that employees should be trained to use problem-solving tools and group decision-making skills.

HR practices are also an integral part of companies' efforts to achieve ISO 9000 certification: ISO 9000 refers to the International Organization for Standardization's basic written standards for quality management and assurance. Certification usually requires a five-step process: (i) ISO assessment reviewing the company's quality systems and procedures (ii) Quality assurance and policy manual preparation compiling the specific quality-oriented techniques and policies to

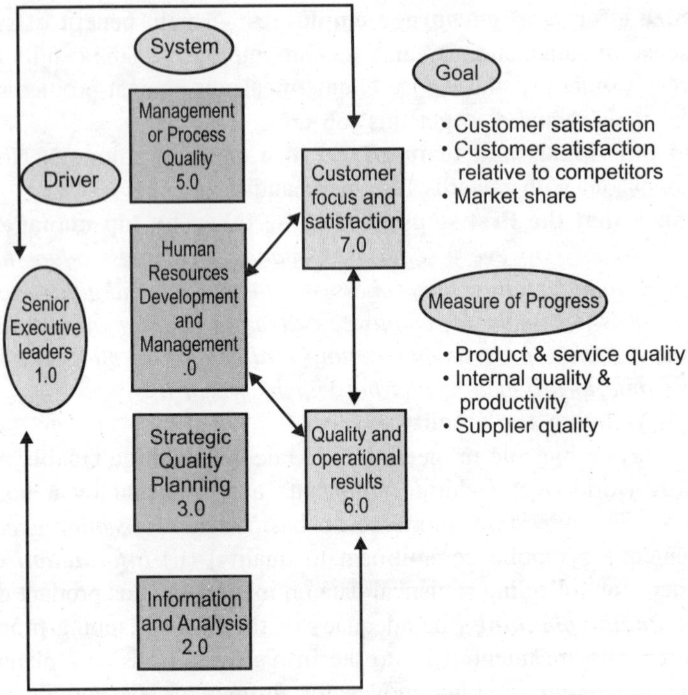

Fig. 8.12. Baldrige Quality Award Criteria Framework.
Source: U.S. Department of Commerce, 1992.

be followed (iii) Training of employees in ISO 9000 (iv) documentation of work instructions, documenting each new work procedure, for instance (v) and registration audit having the quality system reviewed by a special registrar who audits the company's quality efforts.

Employee training and related HR activities such as selection thus play an important role in gaining ISO 9000 certification.

(C) HR Helps to Build Productive Teams in the Organizations for Quality Improvement: According to Gary Dessler, "*Building productive teams for quality enhancement requires careful selection, training and motivation and all HR related activities.*"

HR's role in the context of building productive teams is as under:

1. **Establishing urgent, demanding performance standards:** All team members should believe the team has urgent and worthwhile purposes and they need to know what their performance standards are.
2. **Select members for skill and skill potential:** Select team members for their existing skills and for their potential to learn new ones.
3. ***Train leaders to "coach" not "boss":*** Self-directed work teams are empowered—they have the authority, tools, and information to manage themselves. HR must thus ensure that team leaders know their jobs are not to boss but to support and to coach.
4. **Challenge the group regularly with fresh facts and information:** New information (such as on how the company is doing) helps a team to understand the challenges it

and the company faces. Having HR supply such information thereby helps the team shape its common purpose, set clearer goals, and improve its approach.

5. **Exploit the power of positive feedback, recognition, and reward:** There are many ways HR can arrange to have team performance recognized and rewarded. For example, have a senior executive speak directly to the team about the urgency of its mission and use special awards to recognize the team's contributions.
6. **Choose people who like teamwork:** Companies like Toyota recruit and select employees who have a history of preferring to work in teams and of being good team members. Loners and antisocial types don't usually make good team members.
7. **Train, train, train:** Perhaps HR's major role here is to ensure team members have the training required to do their jobs. Training should cover topics such as the philosophy of doing work through teams, how teams make decisions, interpersonal and communications skills for team members, and the technical skills that team members will need to perform their jobs.
8. **Cross-train for flexibility:** Members of most teams also need cross-training, to learn the jobs of fellow team members either informally or through scheduled rotating assignments. This can help reduce disruptions due to absenteeism and can boost flexibility, since all team members are always ready to fill in when needed.

HR AND BUSINESS PROCESS REENGINEERING

Business process reengineering (BPR) is one of the most crucial concepts that has become an effective tool in the globally competitive dynamic environment of modern business. The concept of BPR is associated with the value-added processes in business organizations. It is redesigning of business processes to achieve improvements in measures of performance such as cost, quality, service and speed. **Michael Hammer and James Champy** are regarded as the fathers of reengineering.

What is Business Process Reengineering?

BPR means starting afresh in business discarding everything of the past course. It is a process of rethinking and redesigning which creates value to the customer.

In the words of **Michael Hammer and James Champy**, BPR is defined, "*as the fundamental rethinking and radical redesign of business processes to achieve drastic improvement in critical, contemporary measure of performance such as cost, quality, service and speed.*"

According to **William R. King and Vikram Sethi**, "*BPR is redesign and reorganization of business activities that results from questioning the status quo. It seeks to fulfil specific objectives and can lead to breakthrough improvement. It is often associated with significant cultural and technological changes.*"

These definitions reveal **five main elements** of BPR:

1. The main focus is on business processes.
2. A questioning of the status quo.
3. Stress on specific objectives
4. Breakthrough achievement
5. Significant cultural change

Illustrations of BPR

Two examples of BPR are given in the Boxes 1 and 2 to demonstrate the logic of BPR.

Box 1. An Example of BPR: The Ford·Mazda Story

The genesis of BPR can be traced to Ford Motors. In the mid-eighties, management of cash flow became a major problem for vendors supplying components to Ford. The suppliers approached Ford and requested the company to settle their invoices expeditiously. When Ford looked at why it took several weeks to send the payment, he discovered that some 500 people were employed in functions relating to accounts payable and a major portion of their time was being spent in reconciling various documents like purchase orders, goods received notes, vendor bills, etc.

By streamlining the process and reducing the work involved in such reconciliation, Ford was able to halve the process time. The company also achieved a 25% reduction in manpower. Ford felt happy over the performance improvement until it was discovered that Mazda of Japan employed just five people to manage the payment process.

In the case of Mazda, there were no purchase orders or bills. Vendors had a direct telelink to Mazda's computer. They picked up their delivery schedule directly from Mazda's system and supplied strictly in conformity with that. At the end of the day, the vendors' accounts were credited through Electronic Funds Transfer based on the total production in the Just-in-Time (JIT) line at Mazda. The system was elegantly simple.

This gave Ford the idea to dispense with the need for a bill from the vendor to make the payment. The process was changed from "*We pay on receipt of vendor invoice*" to "*We pay on receipt of goods*". Dispensing with the bills was a major breakthrough which led to the process time being dramatically reduced by a factor of four and a simultaneous (near 50%) reduction in staff strength.

What Ford achieved was not mere automation. The company had obliterated the unnecessary processes involving the vendor bills. Subsequently, Ford obliterated a lot of other redundant processes also. Thus, the quintessence of business process reengineering lies in Michael Hammer message. "*Do not merely automate, obliterate*".

Source: Jayaraman, M.S., Jayaraman *"Business Process Reengineering",* Tata McGraw-Hill Publishing Co. Ltd., New Delhi, 1996.

Box 2. An Example of BPR: The IBM Credit Corporation Story

One reengineering effort took place at IBM Credit Corporation, the IBM unit that finances the computers, software, and services sold by IBM. Before reengineering, the credit-checking and approval process took several weeks. A salesperson would call in to get credit for a prospective customer. A sequence of steps was then carried out by individual workers, each of whom logged in the request, carted the request upstairs to the credit department, entered the information into a computer system, checked the credit, and dispatched it to the next link in the chain.

When this process was assessed, IBM Credit made a monumental discovery. Specifically, if the person who got the financing request walked it through all the stages personally and at each stage did what needed to be done, the whole process took only 90 minutes rather than a week or more! Reengineering the process in this case involved substituting several generalists for all the specialists and letting a generalist do all the tasks for a request, rather than having the process carried out like a relay race.

> This IBM example illustrates some of the basic characteristics of business process reengineering. In business process reengineering several jobs are combined into one so that an assembly-line process is replaced by generalists who carry out all the tasks themselves. Another reengineering characteristic is, therefore, that workers make more decisions. For example, each of the new generalists at IBM Credit had to be solely responsible for deciding on a potential client's creditworthiness. Related to this checks and controls are reduced; instead, there's more emphasis on carefully selecting and training the new generalist. Reengineered processes also tend to take a 'case manager' approach to dealing with customers, in that each customer ends up with a single point of contact when checking on the status of an order or request.

Source: Gary Dessler, HRM, Pearson Education Asia, 2000, New Delhi, p. 309.

These illustrations/examples further reveal the following characteristics of BPR:

1. Several jobs in BPR are combined into one so that assembly-line process is replaced by generalists who carry all the tasks themselves.
2. Workers are making more decisions.
3. Checks and controls are reduced.
4. Emphasis on careful selecting and training the new generalists.
5. Benefit to customers as there is now a single point of contact to check status of an order.
6. BPR eliminates only unwanted work and not people.
7. BPR offers a radical new principle that the new design of work is based upon end-to-end processes and creation of new values for the customers.
8. It is a planned change in the system or process.

The BPR Process

The BPR framework, in a nutshell, is shown in Figure 8.13. The process is divided into four steps or components:

1. Business drivers of reengineering
2. The engineering process
3. Reengineering facilities
4. The reengineering end product

Figure 8.13 shows that:

- The key factors which lead to consider business redesigning are competitive environment, recent internal changes and IT infrastructure.
- The reengineering effects begin by articulating the strategic intent of the firm and defining the core competencies. According **to Hamel and Prahalad**, strategic intent in the firm's desired leadership position in its environment. Defining the strategic intent and core competencies establishes a target for the firm and identifies the capability of the firm that will be used to achieve that target.
- Reengineering facilitators are: effective change management; control mechanism; education and training of employees.
- The final "product" of the reengineered process, must be judged using two criteria:

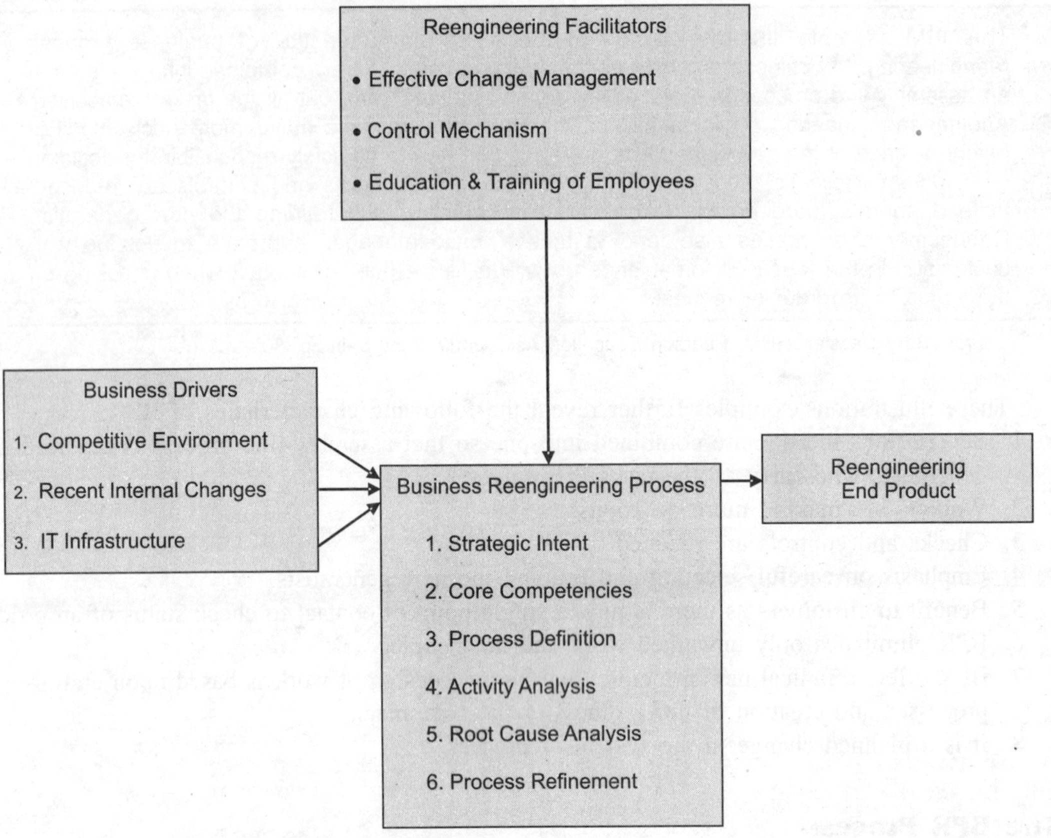

Fig. 8.13. A Framework for Business Reengineering.

(a) Has it met the goals of the reengineering effort?
(b) Is the process flexible enough to accommodate future changes?

After having examined the motivations for reengineering and the component parts in the framework we can examine the BPR process in six key steps. (Figure 8.14)

Components and Principles of BPR

Most successful reengineering initiatives share certain basic ingredients. Hamer, the father of BPR has given six principles/components of reengineering. Figure 8.15 shows these principles.

Goals and Benefits of BPR

Goals of BPR: The company can proceed in three directions in setting its goals.

1. **Process Improvement:** It can lead to dramatic cost reduction in non-core areas or processes.
2. **Best in Class:** It is aimed at attaining competitive parity with those who have set higher standards in the past.

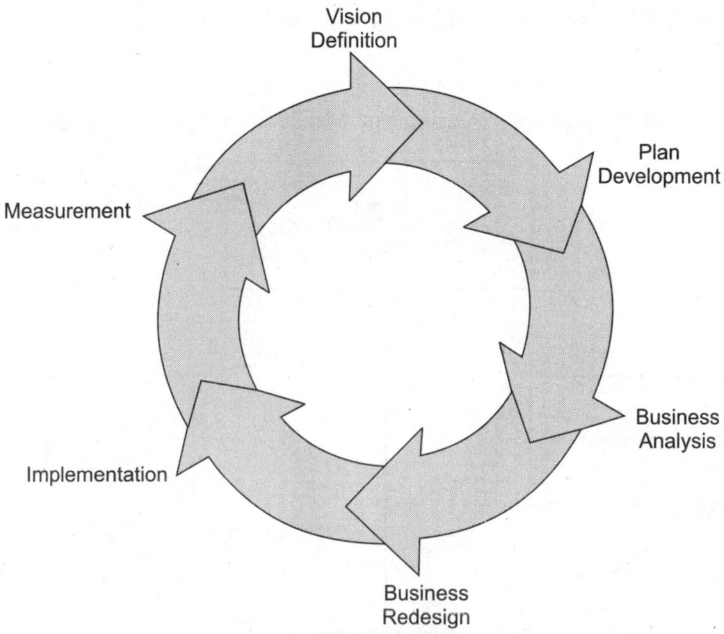

Fig. 8.14. Six Key Steps in the Reengineering Process.

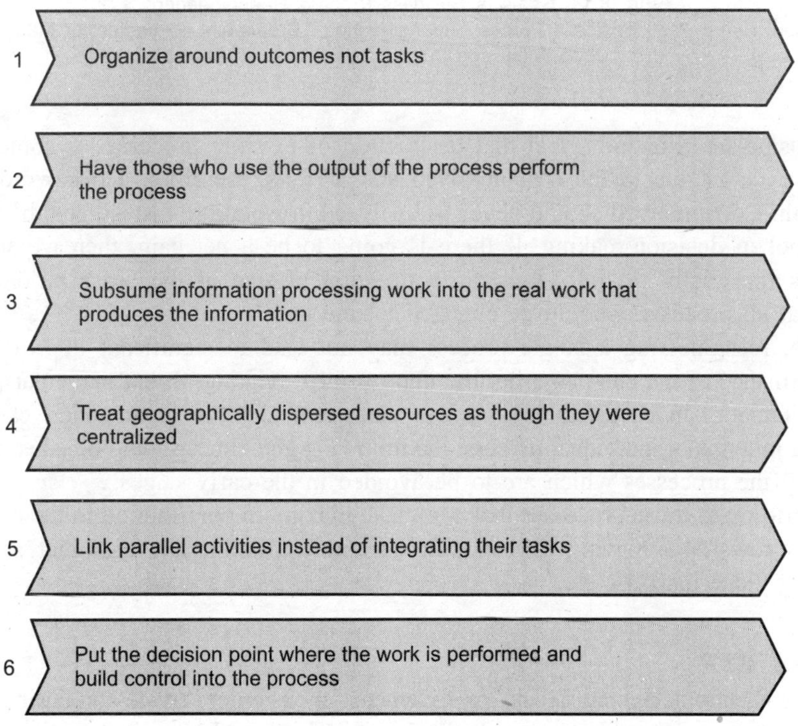

Fig. 8.15. Hammer's Six Principles of Reengineering.

3. **Break-Point BPR:** It means to find and implement break-points and create new definitions of best in class for others to attain.

Figure 8.16 shows these three directions in which the company can proceed.

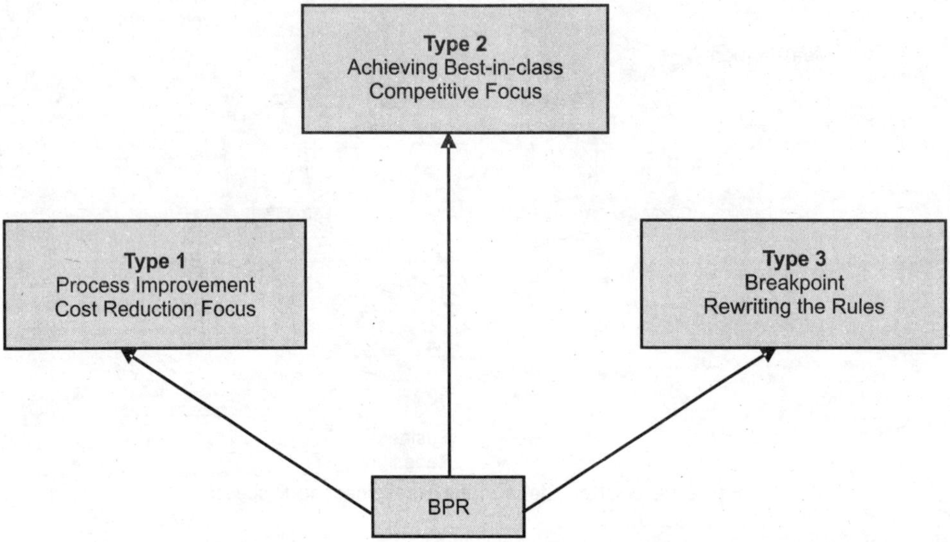

Fig. 8.16. Goals of Business Process Reengineering.
Source: Johnson, Henry et al. Business Process Reengineering : Breakpoint Strategies for Market Dominance, John Wiley and Sons Ltd., England, 1994.

Many businessmen in India feel that destruction of existing processes is something which they cannot think of due to the cost involved and BPR is, therefore, a buzzword for MNCs. This is a myth. Cost involved should never be analyzed in isolation, instead cost-benefit analysis is a better tool of decision-making. If there is going to be a net gain, then we should accept something as financially feasible. It is not a question of size of the organization as it is not necessary that all processes should be changed in one go.

Although, reengineering a single process may not lead to significant improvement in the overall performance of the company; but the improvement relating to that particular process may, indeed, be dramatic. In case, resources are a constraint and the organization can implement reengineering in terms of individual process, the following guidelines should be taken into account:

i. Identify the processes which are to be avoided in the early stages.
ii. Give priority to those processes that can make maximum contribution to the overall bottom line, or towards achieving any specific corporate mission like customer satisfaction or creating niche markets, etc.

Benefits of BPR

BPR is an approach to achieving radical improvements in customer service and business efficiency. It can bring substantial benefits, not only to the organizations but to its partners as well. The key internal benefits are shown in Figure 8.17.

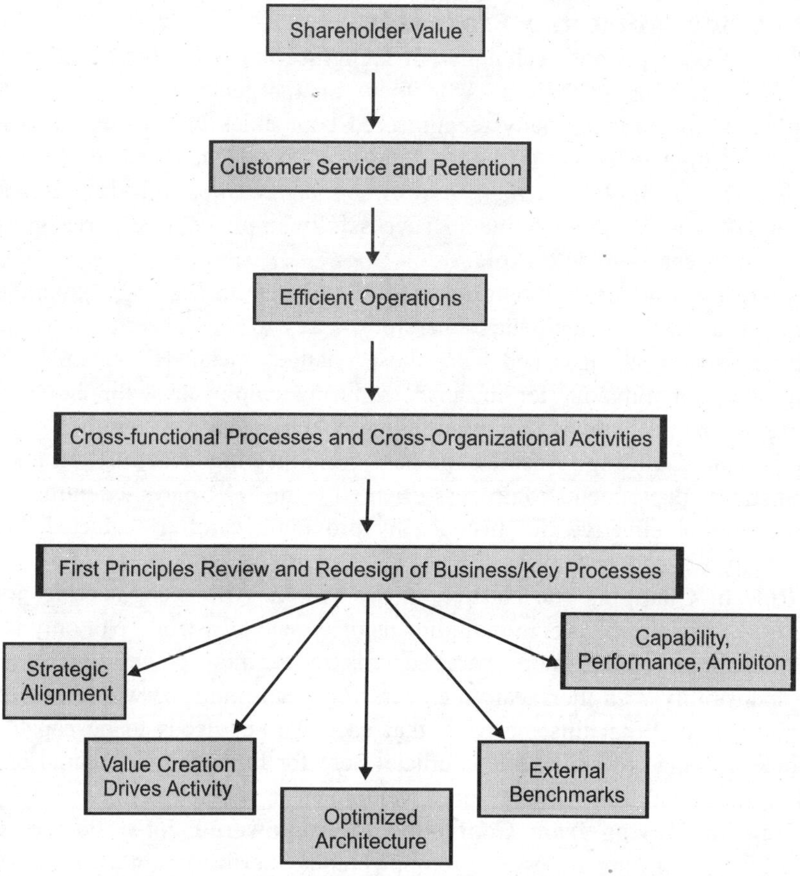

Fig. 8.17. Reengineering Approach to Corporate Transformation and Benefits.

Six categories of BPR tools used in the process are shown in Table 8.7.

Table 8.7: Six Categories of BPR Tools

	Tools	Usage of the Tools
1.	Project Management	Used for planning, scheduling, budgeting, reporting and tracking projects
2.	Coordination	Used to distribute plans and to communicate updated details of projects
3.	Modelling	Used to make a model of something in order to understand and its structure and workings.
4.	Business Process Analysis	Used for the systematic reduction of a business into its constituent parts and examination of the interactions among those parts and design
5.	Human Resource Analysis	Used for requisition, candidate tracking and position history
6.	System Development	Used to automate the engineered business processes

Source: Adapted from Vikram Sethi & William R. King, Organizational Transformation through Business Process Reengineering, Pearson Education, New Delhi, 2006, p. 246.

HR's Role in Reengineering Processes

Two years after the concepts and techniques of reengineering were introduced, it was obvious that something was lacking. In their quest to focus on reorganizing the work and eliminating unneeded duplicative operations, many reengineered companies had neglected to institute new HR practices. According to **Huge Willmott,** "*the firms had failed to win the commitment of their managers and employees to their new reengineered jobs.*" Today, experts therefore understand that HR plays a crucial role in successfully implementing a reengineering effort. Following are some aspects of HR's role.

1. **Building Commitment to Reengineering:** Reengineering is an ongoing, never-ending commitment to doing things better. Therefore, a key to reengineering is winning people's commitment to the changes and what those changes mean. HR can play a big role in winning such commitment, for instance by hiring employees with the right values, by providing the right incentives, and by installing effective two-way communications practices.
2. **HR and Team Building:** Business process reengineering generally means reorganizing from functional departments to process-oriented teams. HR plays a central role in making such teams more effective, for instance by providing carefully selected "*team players*" and the required technical training.
3. **HR's Role in Changing the Nature of the Work:** With reengineering, jobs generally change from specialized tasks to multidimensional generalist work. Not only is each worker responsible for a broader, more enriched job, but the new process team members share joint responsibility with their team members for performing the whole process, not just a small piece of it. What this means is that each worker needs to be capable of using a much broader range of skills. HR is crucial here for hiring high-potential employees and providing them with the training and development they require.
4. **HR's Role in Moving from Controlled to Empowered Jobs:** People working in a reengineered setting are necessarily empowered to perform a broader set of tasks with relatively little supervision. This means that HR in reengineered companies must stress values in selection. The two experts Hammer and Champy say, "*It is no longer enough merely to look at prospective employees' education, training, and skills; their character becomes an issue as well. Are they self-starting? Do they have self discipline? Are they motivated to do what it takes to please a customer?*"
5. **HR's Role in Moving from Training to Education:** Hammer and Champy say that in companies that reengineer, the emphasis necessarily shifts from training to education. In other words, it's no longer enough to give employees training that show them "how" to do the job such as how to turn the bolt on the left front fender. Instead the new generalist team members need education. They need the insight and understanding of how to analyze and solve problems and improve processes continuously, and must thus understand not just the "how" of the job, but the "why" of it.

Relationship between Reengineering and Total Quality Management

Total Quality Management involves continuous customer-centred employee driven improvements. *It refers to meeting the requirements of customers consistently by continuous improvements in the quality of work of all employees.* For achieving total quality, three things are essential:

(i) Meeting customers' requirements;
(ii) Continuous improvement through management process; and
(iii) Involvement of all employees.

Both BPR and TQM are similar in focusing on customer needs, process-orientation, and are committed to excellent performance. But still, the differences are:

- TQM seeks incremental and continuous improvements; BPR looks for quantum leaps in performance.
- TQM tries to improve something which is basically okay whereas BPR destroys redundant processes and starts afresh.
- TQM stresses structured problem-solving whereas reengineering emphasizes total process redesign
- Reengineering is the next step when TQM succeeds.

REVIEW QUESTIONS

1. Examine the role of Human Resource Manager in industrial organizations.
2. What is organizational change? Discuss how to manage an organizational change programme.
3. Define organizational development. Critically examine its techniques.
4. Discuss in brief the emerging issues in Human Resource Management.
5. Define the term change. Why is it important?
6. What do you understand by freezing the change? How can it be done?
7. Define the term "Total Quality Management" and describe its elements.
8. Write an explanatory note on Quality Circles.
9. What is Business Process Reengineering? What are its tools? What are its implications?
10. Discuss the relationship between Reengineering and Total Quality Management.
11. Discuss BPR process and the benefits and goal setting in BPR.
12. What is TQM? Discuss basic programmes of TQM.
13. Write notes on the following:
    (a) Role of HR Manager in organization renewal
    (b) Qualities of HR Manager
    (c) Role of human resources in TQM
    (d) Scope of Business Process reengineering

CASE STUDY

8.1 HR: A Strategic Partner in Creating Teams at Signicast Corp – A US Co.

The recent experience of Wisconsin-based Signicast Corp. helps illustrate HR's role in creating a team-based organization. The firm produces metal parts from what's known as the investment casting process: wax moulds are used to create ceramic moulds which in turn are used to cast the metal parts. In 1992, the company decided to expand by building a new, highly automated plant about 25 miles away. But it discovered that "in the real world, new automation technology requires a new kind of employee ......" **The firm's HR group therefore played a crucial role in the design, staffing, and start-up of the firm's new facility and strategy.**

HR's involvement began at the plant design stage. It invited employees from the existing facility to participate in several planning and design meetings; here their suggestions on matters ranging from how to design a new piece of equipment, to the work flow in the new plant were solicited: "Employees would come up with suggestions; we'd implement them, and bring them back to [employees] for confirmation."

As the new plant began to take shape, HR's task was to select and train a new kind of workforce. While the firm's original plant would continue to operate, the new automated plant would produce parts almost five times faster than the old plant, and this would leave no time for rework or errors. The new plant's employees would therefore have to have more responsibility, and in many ways be more highly trained and carefully selected than were their counterparts at the old facility.

The new plant's selection standards were thus tighter. At the old plant, no specific prior experience was sought, and the only hiring requirements were for a high school diploma and a good work ethic. The 135 employees at the new plant would require the same high school degree and work ethic plus team orientation, good trainability, good communication skills, and a willingness to do varied jobs over a 12-hour shift.

HR's role as strategic partner in building of this new plant was apparent in other ways, too. For example, **HR had to help create a cross-training programme, so that employees could do each other's jobs and be rotated amongst jobs**, so as not to become bored or tired during their 12-hour shifts. And, a new compensation plan was designed that paid workers not just for performance but also for knowledge and for the number of new jobs at which they became competent.

Questions

1. When Winconsin-based Signicast Corp. decided to expand by building a new automated plant, what role was played by HR department of the company at the designing stage?
2. What steps HR department took when the new plant began functioning?
3. What distinguishes between the old and new plant of the company in matters of selection standards for employees?
4. What were the bases of compensation at the new plant of the company?

8.2 No News is Good News

Coromandel Agricultural Inputs Ltd. was established in Vangalapudi, a rural centre in Andhra Pradesh, with a view to producing all types of agricultural inputs and, supply them to rural people at subsidized prices. The company was established with high values of serving the rural community, which is presently exploited by the business and industry. The company also initiated laudable values towards all people in the universe as the company was promoted by some religious organisations. The company published its policy towards the employees regarding participative management, creation and encouragement of congenial interpersonal relations, creation of opportunities for free interaction among various groups, cooperation, openness, etc.

The company has built quarter of apartment model very close to the factory and made it compulsory to all the employees to stay in the quarters. The company filled all the higher level jobs and only 20% of the secretarial and ministerial posts. Indirectly, the managers were forced to work on their own, regarding secretarial work.

The competent employees in various similar organizations joined this organization to have complete openness and to lead peaceful life. The religious organizations, which sponsored the company, employed their members in various departments to have strong communication network.

The company did not provide any other facilities or fringe benefits, except quarters, even after five years of its inception. Discontent among the employees started. Members used to compare and discuss the company's policy and practices regarding values, benefits and facilities. There was no trade union, either formal or informal, in the company. The wives of employees used to listen the news of dismissal of one or two employees everyday at 1.30 p.m., i.e., the time of lunch break. The family members of employees would be nervous at 1.30 p.m. everyday and for them; it was good news, if there was no news on any day.

Source: Subba Rao, "Essentials of Human Resource Management and Industrial Relations", Himalaya Publishing House, Mumbai, 2007, pp. 371-372.

Questions

1. Why do the family members of employees feel that no news was good news?
2. Identify the value of OD movement applicable to this case.
3. Why did the organization deviate its practices from its policies?
4. Do you think that OD programmes solve the problem in this case? If yes, how?

8.3 Attitude of Union

In a company called ABC Product Ltd. the following incident took place in the HR department. There was a supervisor who had risen to his position by his hard work and sincerity. In his good old days, when he worked as a clerk in this company for fifteen years, before becoming a supervisor, he had been a staunch, active and dynamic unionist.

After becoming a supervisor, in response to change in his responsibility, he was forced to drift away from union activities. However, it must be noted here, that his being promoted to a supervisory job was not politically motivated. He was promoted because he really deserved that. But the union leaders, for reasons best known to them did not like his promotion to the supervisory post.

Although with excellent inter-personal skills that the supervisor had, he could somehow manage to do his work satisfactorily. On one fine morning, he assigned some work to the clerk of the department, but the clerk refused to do the same. There was exchange of heated arguments, a lot of people gathered around and at a certain point of time; the supervisor offensively gesticulated towards the clerk.

The basic issue remained aside and every one around started accusing the supervisor for his offensive gesticulation. The whole of the department refused to work unless the supervisor apologized for this behaviour and the trade union was also brought into the picture.

Questions

1. Analyze the gravity of the situation.
2. Discuss the role, the HR manager is supposed to play in this situation.
3. If you were the Personnel Manager, how would you resolve the problem?

REFERENCES

1. Fred Luthans, (1981). "Organizational Behaviour", McGraw-Hill International Book Company, New York, p. 611.
2. Dessler, Gary (1998). "Management: Leading People and Organizations in the 21st Century", NJ, Prentice-Hall, p. 476-478.
3. Dessler, Gary "Human Resource Management", 7th edn., Prentice-Hall of India.
4. Hamel, Gary and Prahalad, C.K. (1989). "Strategic Intent", Harvard Business Review, May-June, pp. 63.
5. Hugh Willmott, (1994). "Business Process Reengineering and Human Resource Management", Personnel Review, Vol. 3, No. 3, p. 34.
6. James A.F. Stoner, "Management", Prentice-Hall of India, New Delhi.
7. James Champy, (1995). "Reengineering Management", Harper Business, New York, p. 104.
8. Aswathappa, K. (2001) "Organizational Behaviour", Himalaya Publishing House, Mumbai, p. 535.
9. Aswathappa, K. (2008). "Human Resource Management", Tata McGraw-Hill, New Delhi.
10. Keith Davis and Newstrom, (1981). "Human Behaviour at Work", New York, McGraw-Hill, p. 291. Relations in Managements", 1962.
11. Stephen P. Robbins, (1989). "Organizational Behaviour", New Delhi, Prentice-Hall of India, p. 527.
12. Subba Rao P. (2007). "Essentials of Human Resource Management and Industrial Relations". Himalaya Publishing House, New Delhi.
13. Theodore T. Herbert, (1976). "Dimensions of Organizational Behaviour: MacMillan, New York, p. 338.
14. Udai Pareek, (1988). "Implementing Change in Organization, Oxford & IBH Publishing Co. Pvt. Ltd., p. 72.
15. Warren G. Benis, (1969). "Organizational Development", Addison Wesley, Reading Mass, p. 2.
16. Wendell L. French and Cecil H. Bell Jr. (1978). "Organizational Development", Prentice Hall, Englewood Cliffs, NJ, p. 14.
17. William R. King and Vikram Sethi, (2006). "Organizational Transformation through Business Process Reengineering", Pearson Education, New Delhi, p. 19.

CHAPTER

9 Performance Appraisal and Managing Performance

CHAPTER'S OUTLINE

INTRODUCTION

Performance appraisal is important for employees at all levels throughout the organization. The parameters, the characteristics and the standards for evaluation may be different, but the fundamentals of performance appraisal are the same. The performance appraisal has become the heart of the human resource management system in the organizations. Performance appraisal defines and measures the performance of the employees and the organization as a whole. It is a tool for accessing the performance of the organization. It is a common practice among every organization whether big or small, organized or unorganized. Traditionally, performance appraisal has been used as just a method for determining and justifying the salaries of the employees. This approach was a *past-oriented* approach which focused only on the past performance of the employees. This approach did not consider the developmental aspects of the employee performance, i.e. his training and developmental needs or career developmental possibilities.

In 1950s, performance appraisal was recognized as a complete system in itself and the modern approach to it was developed. The modern approach to performance development has made the performance appraisal process more formal and structured. The modern approach is a *future-oriented* approach and is developmental in nature. In this chapter, we shall discuss meaning, objectives, process, methods and critical evaluation of performance.

MEANING OF PERFORMANCE APPRAISAL

Performance refers to the degree of accomplishment of the tasks and it is measured in terms of results. Performance appraisal is the process of evaluating the performance and qualification of the employee in terms of the requirement of job, for which he/she is employed. In other words, it is the process of determining and communicating the employees, how well they are performing the job.

A performance appraisal is a part of guiding and managing career development. An appraisal evaluates not only the employee's performance but also his potential for development. It is the process of obtaining, analyzing, and recording information about the relative worth of an employee to the organization. Performance appraisal is an analysis of an employee's recent successes and failures, personal strengths and weaknesses, and suitability for promotion or further training. Performance appraisal is an objective system to judge the ability of an individual employee to perform his tasks.

Definitions

A few definitions of performance appraisal are as follows:

According to **Flippo,** a prominent personality in the field of human resources, "*performance appraisal is the systematic, periodic and an impartial rating of an employee's excellence in the matters pertaining to his present job and his potential for a better job.*"

According to **Dale Yoder,** "*Performance appraisal includes all formal procedures used to evaluate personalities and contributions and potentials of group members in a working organisation. It is a continuous process to secure information necessary for making correct and objective decisions on employees.*"

According to **Randall S. Schuler,** "*Performance appraisal is a formal structured system of measuring and evaluating an employee's job related behaviour and outcomes to discover how and why the employee is presently performing on the job and how the employee can perform more effectively in the future so that the employee, organisation and society will benefit.*"

According to **Dale S. Beach,** "*Performance appraisal is the systematic evaluation of the individual with respect to his or her performance on the job and his or her potential for development.*"

According to **C. Heigal,** "*Performance appraisal is the process of evaluating the performance and qualifications of the employees in terms of the requirement of the job for which he is employed for purposes of administration including placement, selection for promotion, providing financial rewards and other actions which require differential treatment among the members of a group as distinguished from actions affecting all members equally.*"

From the above definitions of performance appraisal, the following features are highlighted:

1. Performance appraisal is *a systematic process* consisting of a number of steps to be followed for evaluating an employee's strengths and weaknesses.
2. It is a systematic and *objective description* of an employee's strengths and weaknesses in terms of the job.
3. The appraisal is *an ongoing and continuous process* where the evaluations are arranged periodically according to a definite plan. It is not a one shot deal.
4. The performance appraisal *seeks to secure information* necessary for making objective and correct decisions on employees.
5. Performance appraisal may *be formal or informal.* The formal system is more fair and objective.
6. This is *an interactive process* by which the employee can also speak about his problems to his superior.

OBJECTIVES OF PERFORMANCE APPRAISAL

An effective performance appraisal system should emphasise individual objectives, organizational objectives and also mutual objectives. From the **viewpoint of individual** objective the performance appraisal should talk about

(a) What task the individual is expected to do?
(b) How well the individual has done the task?
(c) How can his performance be further improved?
(d) What is his/her reward for doing well?

From the organizational viewpoint, a performance appraisal should generate manpower information, improve efficiency and effectiveness, serve as a mechanism of control and provide a rational compensation structure. In short, the appraisal system establishes and upholds the principle of accountability in the absence of which organization failure is the only possible outcome.

In general, the main objective of performance appraisals is to measure and improve the performance of employees and increase their future potential and value to the company. Other objectives include providing feedback, improving communication, understanding training needs, clarifying roles and responsibilities and determining how to allocate rewards. These are discussed as under:

1. **Measuring and Improving Performance:** The main purpose/objective of performance appraisals is to measure and improve the performance of employees and increase their future potential and value to the company.
2. **Provide Feedback:** The feedback received by the employee can be helpful in many ways. It gives insight to how superiors value your performance, highlights the gap between actual and desired performance and diagnoses strengths and weaknesses as well as shows areas for improvement.
3. **Improve Communication:** The method of performance appraisal helps superiors strengthen relationships and improve communication with the employees.
4. **Training Needed:** These appraisals also identify the necessary training and development the employee needs to close the gap between current performance and desired performance.
5. **Clarify Expectations:** Performance appraisals should clarify roles, responsibilities and expectations of all employees.
6. **Allocate Rewards:** Performance appraisals reduce employee grievances by clearly documenting the criteria used to make organizational decisions such as promotions, raises or salary hikes, etc.

PERFORMANCE APPRAISAL PROCESS

The performance appraisal is a process which is done on the basis of certain standards or norms. The standards need to be clear and sound, and justified. Performance appraisal, in fact, is a six step process (Figure 9.1) which is discussed as under:

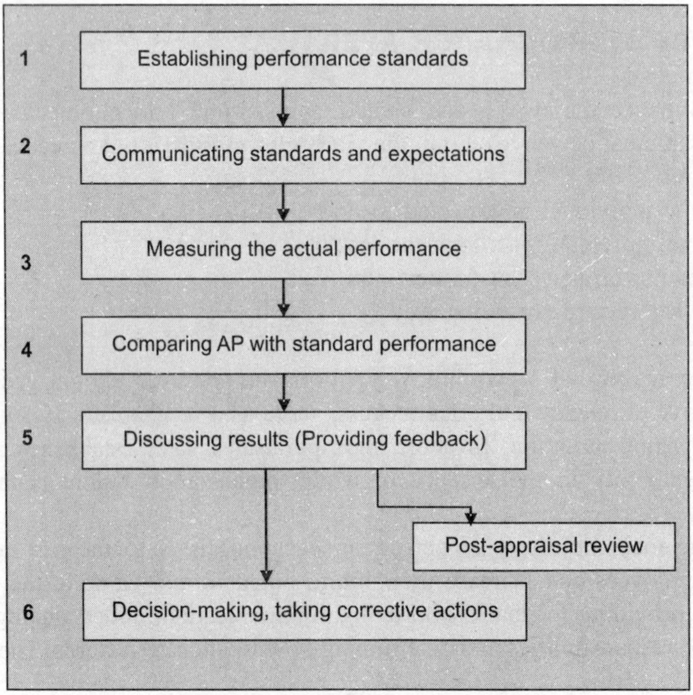

Fig. 9.1. Performance Appraisal Process.

1. Establishing Performance Standards (ESP)

Performance standards constitute the benchmark against which performance is measured. This is the first step in the process of performance appraisal, which will be used as the base to compare the actual performance of the employees. This step requires setting the criteria to judge the performance of the employees. The criteria may include quantity (output) as well as quality (work quality, honesty, cooperation and team work, job knowledge, initiative, leadership, safety consciousness, attendance, learning ability, adaptability, judgement, sense of responsibility, health and physical condition, etc.). These standards should be clear, easily understandable, and in measurable terms. In case the performance of the employee cannot be measured, great care should be taken to describe the standards. In fact, performance standards will depend upon the objectives of the appraisal, i.e. to appraise the actual performance on the present job or to judge potential for higher job. These standards will help in setting yardsticks for evaluating performance.

2. Communicating the Standards (CS)

Once set, it is the responsibility of the management to communicate the standards to all the employees of the organization. The employees should be informed and the standards should be clearly explained to them. This will help them to understand their roles and to know what exactly is expected from them. The standards should also be communicated to the appraisers or the evaluators and if required, the standards can also be modified at this stage itself according to the relevant feedback from the employees or the evaluators. For standard of performance, we can take help from Job Description and Job Specification.

3. Measuring the Actual Performance (AP)

The most difficult part of the performance appraisal process is measuring the actual performance of the employees, that is, the work done by the employees during the specified period of time. It is a continuous process which involves monitoring the performance throughout the year. This stage requires careful selection of the appropriate techniques of measurement, taking care that personal bias does not affect the outcome of the process and providing assistance rather than interfering in an employee's work.

Personal observations, written reports and face-to-face contact, feedback forms are the means of collecting data on performance. What is measured is more important than how it is measured.

4. Comparing the Actual Performance with the Standard Performance (CSP)

Actual performance is compared with the desired or the standard performance. The comparison tells the deviations in the performance of the employees from the standards set. The result can show the actual performance being more than the desired performance or, the actual performance being less than the desired performance depicting a negative deviation in the organizational performance. It includes recalling, evaluating and analysis of data related to the employee performance.

(+ or -) PA = AP (Actual performance) – SP (Standard Performance)
If AP > SP (+ve result)
If AP < SP (-ve result)

5. Discussing Results or Feedback (Post-appraisal Review)

Performance review sessions give employees feedback about their past performance or future potential. The result of the appraisal is communicated and discussed with the employees on one-to-one basis. The focus of this discussion is on communication and listening. The results, the problems and the possible solutions are discussed with the aim of problem solving and reaching consensus. The feedback should be given with a positive attitude as this can have an effect on the employees' future performance. The purpose of the meeting should be to solve the problems faced and motivate the employees to perform better. There are a few guidelines or precautions that are to be taken to make the performance evaluation system to be effective. These are shown in Box-1.

Box-1

- Emphasize positive aspects of employee's performance
- Tell each employee that the evaluation session is to improve performance, not to discipline
- Conduct the performance review session in private with minimum interruptions
- Review performance formally at least annually and more frequently for new employees or those who are performing poorly
- Make criticisms specific, not general and vague
- Focus criticisms on performance, not on personality characteristics
- Stay calm and do not argue with the person being evaluated
- Identify specific actions the employee can take to improve performance
- Emphasize the evaluator's willingness to assist the employee's efforts and to improve performance
- End the evaluation session by stressing the positive aspects of the employee's performance

6. Decision-Making (DM)

The last step of the process is to take decisions which can be taken either to improve the performance of the employees, take the required corrective actions, or the related HR decisions like rewards, promotions, demotions, transfers, etc. Training, coaching, counselling, etc. are examples of corrective actions that help to improve performance.

THE PERFORMANCE APPRAISAL METHODS

With the evaluation and development of appraisal system, a number of methods or techniques of performance appraisal have been developed. The important methods are classified into two categories as shown in Figure 9.2.

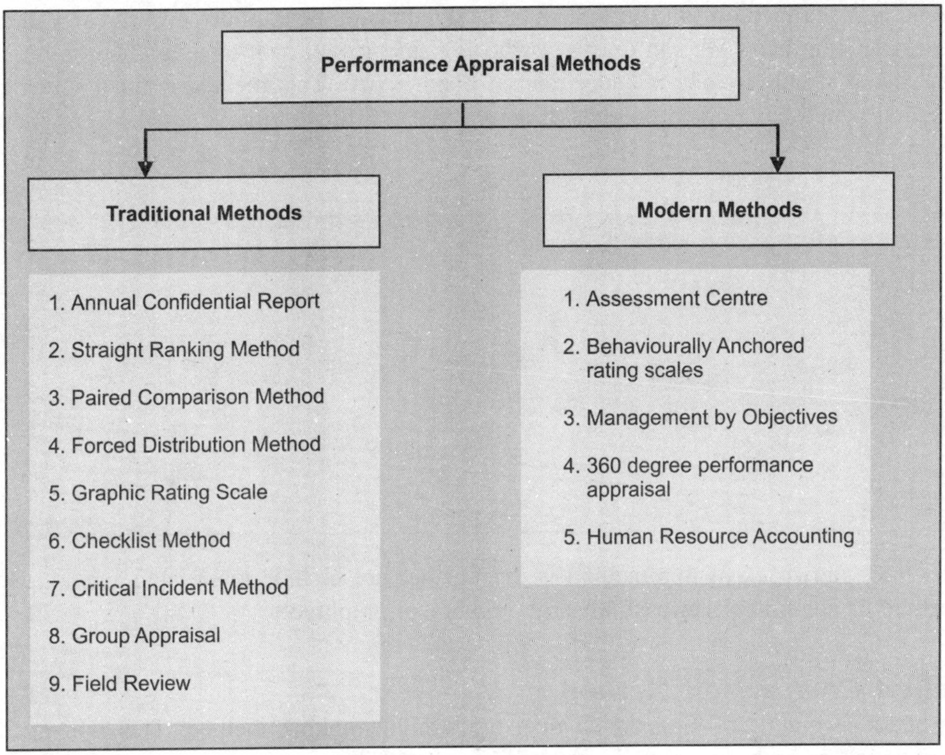

Fig. 9.2. Methods of Appraisal Methods.

A. Traditional Methods

These methods are also called past-oriented methods. Following methods are included in this category.

1. Annual Confidential Report

This is the traditional method of performance appraisal used in most of the government organizations. A Confidential Report (CR) prepared by the employee's immediate superior which covers the strengths and weaknesses, main achievements and failure, personality and behaviour of the employee. It is descriptive appraisal used for promotions and transfers of employees.

The main drawback of this method is that it involves subjectivity because the appraisal is based on overall impression and not on data. Further when feedback is provided, focus is on evaluation and not on development of the employee. In recent years, due to pressure from courts and trade unions, the details of a negative confidential report are given to the concerned employee.

2. Straight Ranking Method

This is one of the oldest and simplest techniques of performance appraisal. In this method, the appraiser ranks the employees from the best to the poorest on the basis of their overall performance. It is quite useful for a comparative evaluation. This method is also called man-to-man ranking. This method only tells about the standing of various persons and not the actual differences among them. We can only say who is number one, two, three, and so on but cannot say how much at number one is better than at number two. This method is most suitable in an organization which has limited number of employees. An illustration is given of this method in Box-2.

Box-2 Straight Ranking Method

Employee	Rank
A	3
B	1(best)
C	5(poorest)
D	4
E	2

The main drawback of this method is that it does not include job-related aspects. Besides, this method is not suitable in case of large number of employees.

3. Paired Comparison Method

It is a better technique of comparison than the straight ranking method. This is a method of comparison where each employee is first compared with the peers, one at a time, and when all the comparisons are done, the employees are given the final rankings. Here all the employees are compared with all the others in pairs one at a time. A range of plausible options is listed. Each option is compared against each of the other options. The results are tallied and the option with the highest score is the preferred option. The number of comparisons to be made can be decided on the basis of formulae N (N-1)/2. Illustration is given in the Figure 9.3.

Paired Comparison Method(N(N-1)/2

	A	B	C	D	E	Performance
A	-	A	A	A	A	100%
B	-	-	C	D	E	0%
C	-	-	-	C	E	50%
D	-	-	-	-	E	25%
E	-	-	-	-	-	75%

No. of +ve evaluation/Total no. of evaluations * 100

Fig. 9.3. Paired Comparison of Employees.

To compute employee's positive evaluations, as shown in Figure 9.3, we proceed as under:
Number of positive evaluations / Total number of evaluations × 100 = Employees' % superior evaluation

Employee A	Employee B	Employee C	Employee D	Employee E
4/4 × 100 = 100%	0/4 × 100 = 0%	2/4 × 100 = 50%	1/4 × 100 = 25%	3/4 × 100 = 75%

4. Forced Distribution Method

Forced distribution method is similar to grading on a curve. With this method, managers place predetermined percentages or rates into performance categories. The purpose is to eliminate the rater's bias of central tendency. Here also ranking technique is used. But here job related performance criterion is not used in rating. The rater after assigning the points to the performance of each employee has to distribute his ratings in a pattern to conform to normal frequencies distribution. For example, you may decide to distribute employees as follows:
15% high performance (in normal curve right side)
20% high average performance (in normal curve right side)
30% average performance
20% low average performance
15% low performance

This rating can be distributed in the form of normal frequency curve is shown in Figure 9.4.

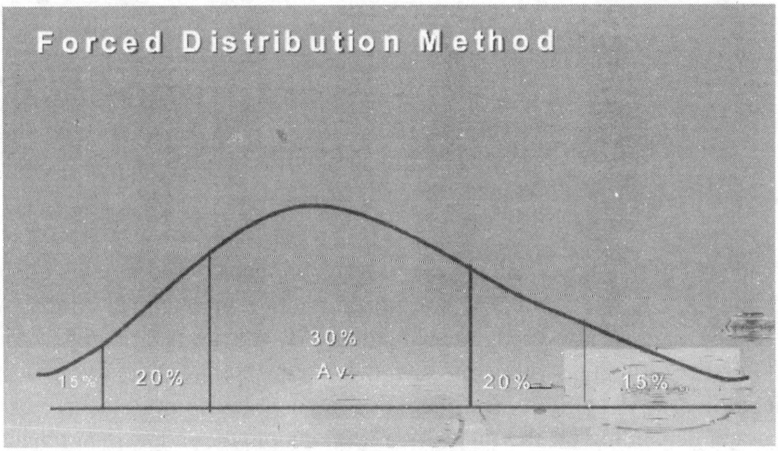

Fig. 9.4. Forced Distribution Method.

5. Graphic Rating Scale Method

The graphic rating scale method is the simplest and most popular technique for appraising performance. This method was introduced by Walter D. Scott to get the judgement of superiors on subordinates. Typically, a graphic scale assesses a person on the traits such as quality, quantity, dependability of his work and a range of performance values (is he outstanding, above average, average, or unsatisfactory) and on a variety of other traits that vary with the job but usually include personal traits like reliability and cooperation. It may also include specific performance items like oral and written communication. Subordinates are rated by circling of checking the score that best describes his or her performance for each trait. Then the total of assigned value is calculated for each employee.

Employee name.............. Job title......................
Department .... Rate...........................
Data................................

The format of this method is shown in Figure 9.5.

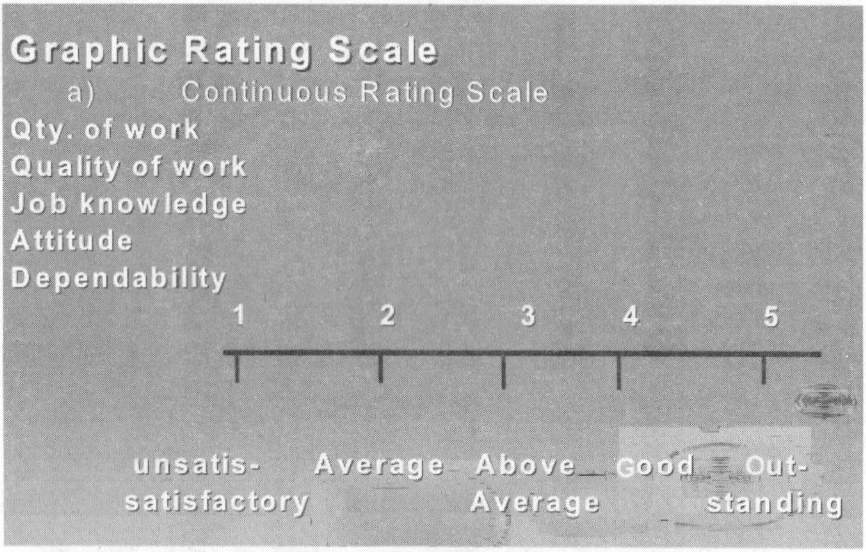

Fig. 9.5. Graphic Rating Scale.

The approach is multidimensional as several traits are considered in evaluation. It is an easy to understand and easy to use method where rating is done in a tabular form but is subjective because job related data is not used in evaluation. All the traits are given equal weightage which is not fair because high rating on one factor can compensate for low score on other factor, so rating will always be high. But then, this method is also not bias free as the supervisor may plot the graph depending on the rapport with the employee rather than objectively marking the performance.

6. Checklist Method

This is the simplest way of evaluation wherein the rater is given a checklist containing a description of the employee behaviour on the job. The duty of the superior is to find out which description best suits the employee. The checklist contains many statements which might be appropriate in describing the employees on the job performance. Each statement contains answers in form of Yes/No or Positive/Negative or Tick mark in the form of right and wrong.

There are two types of checklists that can be used:

(i) Simple checklist (equal weightage) and

(ii) Weighted checklist (unequal weightage)

(i) Simple Checklist Method: This checklist contains a large number of statements concerning employee behaviour. Figure 9.6 shows the details of the simple checklist method.

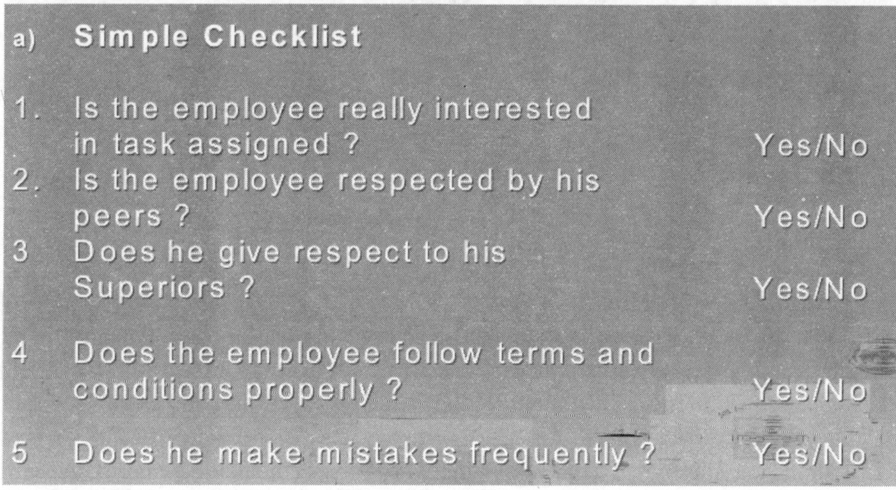

Fig. 9.6. Simple Checklist Model.

The rater checks to indicate if the behaviour of an employee is positive or negative to each statement. Employee's performance is rated on the basis of number of positive checks. The negative checks are not considered in this method.

(ii) **Weighted Checklist:** This method involves weighting different items in the checklist, having a series of statements about an individual to indicate that some are more important than others. The rater is expected to look into the questions relating to the employee's behaviour, the attached rating scale and tick those traits that closely describe the employee behaviour as shown in Figure 9.7. Often the weights are not given to the supervisors who complete the appraisal process, but are computed and tabulated by someone else, such as a member of the personnel unit. In this method performance ratings of the employee are multiplied by the weights of the statement and coefficients are added up to arrive at the cumulative coefficient as the weighted performance score of an employee.

The main advantage of the checklist method is that it is a descriptive technique and it provides concrete examples of evaluation. The flaw is that the checklist might not contain a certain statement which best describes the employee and is not free of the rater's bias. It is a time-consuming and an expensive method as separate checklists must be developed for each job category. Assigning of weights is a difficult task. Trained raters are required. However, this system is widely used and accepted.

b) Weighted checklist

	Traits (Characteristics)	Weights	Performance ratings (1-5)
1.	Attendance	0.5	
2.	Job Knowledge	1.0	
3.	Quantity	1.0	
4.	Quality	1.5	
5.	Dependability	1.5	
6.	Industrial relations	2.0	
7.	Organisational loyalty	1.5	
8.	Leadership quality	1.5	

Fig. 9.7. Weighted Checklist Method.

7. Critical Incident Method

In this traditional method of performance appraisal, the evaluator rates the employee on the basis of critical events and how the employee reacts in such events—essentially their behavioural patterns during those incidents. This includes both the positive and the negative traits of the employee. This method objectively discusses an employee's performance during such incidents. Under this method, the supervisor continuously records the critical incidents of the employee's performance or behaviour relating to all characteristics (+ve and -ve) in a specially designed notebook. This method is shown in Figure 9.8.

If some workers are badly injured at the workplace, etc. may be identified as critical incidents for the working of a factory. The behaviour of five workers during critical incidents is as follows:

However, this method has drawn a lot of flak as the superior has to make a record of critical incidents and the resulting employee behaviour as and when these happen, which is

Critical Incidents Method

Worker	Reaction	Score
A	Informed the supervisor/family	5
B	Immediately admitted to hospital.	4
C	Tried to discover the reas- -sons of accident.	3
D	Complaint of poor maintenance	2
E	Was happy to get rest.	1

Fig. 9.8. Critical Incidents Method.

difficult under the circumstances always. Again, the minor incidents might get precedence over the major ones as every individual tends to see things differently. Moreover, it is not very effective as every individual is different and reacts and performs very differently in similar circumstances. Similarly, quoting incidents after considerable time lapse may evoke negative emotions from employees.

8. Group Appraisal Method

In this a group of experts/evaluators assess employees' performance. The group consists of supervisor of the employee, other supervisors having close contact with employee's work, head of the department and personnel expert. The group identifies the standards of performance for the job, measures actual performance of an employee, analyses the causes of poor performance and offers suggestions for improvements in future. Due to multiple evaluators personal bias is minimized. But it involves more time.

9. Field Review Method

In this a training officer from the human resource department interviews line supervisors to evaluate their respective subordinates. The expert performs the field job in all the organizations. The expert prepares in advance the questions to be asked. By answering these questions a supervisor gives his opinions about the level of performance of his subordinate, the subordinate's work progress, his strengths and weaknesses, promotion potential, etc. The evaluator takes detailed notes of the answers which are then approved by the concerned supervisor. These are then placed in the employee's personal service file. But the success of this method depends upon the competence and sincerity of the interviewer.

Limitations of Traditional Methods of Performance Appraisal

1. **Managers generally are not qualified to assess personality traits**, and most mangers are even not properly trained to conduct evaluation and performance interviews. They have very vague notions of the purpose of evaluations. Hence, they do a poor job.
2. **Some managers discourage good performance by overemphasizing shortcomings** and almost neglecting good work. Others have little effect on poor workers because they tend to sugar-coat their criticism. Consequently the real message is lost.
3. Rater's personality also plays an important part in the effectiveness of evaluation programmes. **Some raters are by temperament, overly harsh and give low ratings** to all subordinates. Others are too lenient and give everyone a good rating; some raters play favourites, some are victims of 'halo' effect.
4. **The relative status of raters in their organization** is a factor that is important to the validity of performance appraisal. Using more raters or endorsements by a superior reduces rater bias and increases validity of performance appraisal.

B. Modern Methods

Modern techniques of performance appraisal include the following approaches:

1. Assessment Centre Method

This method was developed in USA and UK in 1943 and is gaining popularity in our country. Crompton Greaves, Eicher and HUL are using this technique successfully. An assessment centre is a group of employees drawn from different work units. This group evaluates all the employees, individually and collectively by using simulation techniques like role playing, business games and in-basket exercises. The traits taken are interpersonal skills, communicating ability, ability to plan and organize initiative ability. Paper and pencil tests are used to measure intellectual capacity.

An assessment centre for performance appraisal of an employee includes:

- **Social/Informal Events:** An assessment centre has a group of participants and also a few assessors which gives a chance to the employees to socialize with a variety of people and also to share information and know more about the organization.
- **Information Sessions:** Information sessions are also a part of the assessment centres. They provide information to the employees about the organization, their roles and responsibilities, the activities and the procedures, etc.
- **Assignments:** Assignments in assessment centres include various tests and exercises which are specially designed to assess the competencies and the potential of the employees. These include various interviews, psychometric tests, management games, etc. all these assignments are focused at the target job.

The following are the common features of all assessment centres:

- The final results are based on the pass/fail criteria.
- All the activities are carried out to fill the targeted job.
- Each session lasts from 1 to 5 days.
- The results are based on the assessment of the assessors with less emphasis on self-assessment. Immediate review or feedback is not provided to the employees.

So far, we have been talking about assessing past performance. What about the assessment of **future performance or potential?** In any placement decision, and even more so in promotion decisions, some prediction of future performance is necessary. How can this kind of prediction be made most validly and most fairly?

One widely used rule of thumb is that "*what a man has done is the best predictor of what he will do in the future.*" But suppose you are picking a man to be a supervisor and this person has never held supervisory responsibility? Or suppose you are selecting a man for a job from among a group of candidates, none of whom has done the job or one like it? In these situations, many organizations use assessment centres to predict future performance more accurately.

Typically, individuals from different departments are brought together to spend two or three days working on individual and group assignments similar to the ones they will be handling if they are promoted. The pooled judgement of observers—sometimes derived by paired comparison or alternation ranking—leads to an order-of-merit ranking for each participant. Less structured, subjective judgements are also made.

There is a good deal of evidence that people chosen by assessment centre methods work out better than those not chosen by these methods. The centre also makes it possible for people who are working for departments of low status or low visibility in an organization to become visible. In the competitive situation of an assessment centre; these people show how they stack up against people from more well-known departments. This has the effect of equalizing opportunity, improving morale, and enlarging the pool of possible promotion candidates. Some of the world known companies who adopted this method is shown in Box-3.

Box-3 Assessment Centre–Many Takers

- Ranbaxy retained the services of a team of psychologists from the UK-based Kelly & King to take the executives (of Ranbaxy) through an assessment centre. 20 star managers went through the exercise.
- Santrupt Misra, Director–Birla Management Corporation had plans for a similar exercise to be held at Gyanodaya, the Aditya Birla learning centre. Misra first used the assessment centre concept four years ago on 150 middle and senior level managers.
- Old timers like Tata have created their own assessment centres, and so have the talent-centric companies like Wipro and Cognizant.
- SHL, a HR consulting firm has worked with over 100 companies conducting close to 1,000 assessment centres.
- Consulting firm ECS (formerly known as Eicher Consulting Services) does a number of assessments in a month for a variety of clients like Tata Steel, ING Vysya and the host of BPO outfits.
- ICICI Bank uses assessment centre as a recruitment and selection tool to find the best talent, while GE India subsidiary GECIS has used it on 20% of its middle managers.

Limitations

(i) **The problem with the assessment centres is their cost:** Not only are the assesses away from their jobs while the company pays for their travel and lodging, but the evaluators are often company managers who are assigned to the assessment centre for short durations. These managers arc often supplemented by psychologists and HR specialists who run the centre and also make evaluations. **Hence, this approach is cost-effective only in large organizations.**

(ii) **Assessment-centre staff is often influenced by subjective elements, such as personality of the candidates:** Raters tend to evaluate the quality of the individual's social skills rather than the quality of the decisions he/she makes.

(iii) **The approach also involves real hazards:** One of the most obvious hazards is the examination-taking syndrome. Solid performers in day-to-day operations feel suffocated in the simulated environment. Another drawback is its potential adverse effect on those not selected to participate in the exercise.

(iv) **Employees who receive a poor report from the centre may react in negative ways:** Ideally, a rejected employee would return to his or her former job satisfied that he or she would not be promoted to a job he or she could not handle. However, a good performer at one level may leave the organisation in order to remove the bad assessment report from his or her work record. Thus, a poor report can demoralize an employee who was once an asset.

(v) **Other Problems:** Other problem include strong and unhealthy sense of competition among assesses is the difficulty of conducting the test frequently; and the possibility of overemphasizing the test performance.

But a well-conducted assessment centre can and does achieve better forecasts of future performance and progress than other methods of appraisal. Also, reliability, content validity, and predictive validity are said to be high in the assessment centres. The test also makes sure that the wrong people are not hired or promoted. Finally, the assessment-centre test clearly defines the criteria for selection and promotion.

2. Behaviourally Anchored Rating Scales (BARS)

Also known as the behavioural expectations scale, this method represents the latest innovation in performance appraisal. It is a combination of the rating scale and critical incident techniques of employee performance evaluation. The critical incidents serve as anchor statements on a scale and the rating form usually contains six to eight specifically defined performance dimensions. Table 9.1 represents an example of a sales trainee's competence and a behaviourally anchored rating scale.

Table 9.1: Behaviourally Anchored Rating Scale (BARS)

Performance	Points	Behaviour
Extremely good	7	Can expect trainee to make valuable suggestions for increased sales and to have positive relationships with customers all over the country.
Good	6	Can expect to initiate creative ideas for improved sales.
Above average	5	Can expect to keep in touch with the customers throughout the year.
Average	4	Can manage, with difficulty, to deliver the goods in time.
Below average	3	Can expect to unload the trucks when asked by the supervisor.
Poor	2	Can expect to inform only a part of the customers.
Extremely poor	1	Can expect to take extended coffee breaks and roam around purposelessly.

How to Construct BARS?

Developing BARS follows a general format which combines techniques employed in the critical incident method and weighted checklist ratings scales. Emphasis is pinpointed on pooling the thinking of people who will use the scales as both evaluators and employees being evaluated.

Step 1: Collect critical incidents: People with knowledge of the job to be probed, such as job holders and supervisors, describe specific examples of effective and ineffective behaviour related to job performance.

Step 2: Identify performance dimensions: The people assigned the task of developing the instrument cluster the incidents into a small set of key performance dimensions. Generally, between five and ten dimensions, account for most of the performance. Examples of performance dimensions include technical competence, relationships with customers, handling of paper work and meeting day-to-day deadlines. While developing varying levels of performance for each dimension (anchors), specific examples of behaviour should be used; which could later be scaled in terms of good, average, or, below average performance.

Step 3: Reclassification of incidents: Another group of participants who are knowledgeable about the job is instructed to retranslate or reclassify the critical incidents generated (in Step II) previously. They are given the definition of job dimension and told to assign each critical incident to the dimension that it best describes. At this stage, incidents for which there is not 75 per cent agreement are discarded as being too subjective.

Step 4: Assigning scale values to the incidents: Each incident is then rated on a one-to-seven or one-to-nine scale with respect of how well it represents performance on the appropriate dimension. A rating of one represents ineffective performance; the top scale value indicates very effective performance. The second group of participants usually assigns the scale values. Means and standard deviations are then calculated for the scale values assigned to each incident. Typically incidents that have standard deviations of 1.50 or less (on a 7-point scale) are retained.

Step 5: Producing the final instrument: About six or seven incidents for each performance dimension – all having met both the retranslating and standard deviation criteria – will be used as behavioural anchors. The final BARS instrument consists of a series of vertical scales (one for each dimension) anchored (or measured) by the final incidents. Each incident is positioned on the scale according to its mean value.

Advantages

(i) Because the above process requires considerable employee participation, its acceptance by both supervisors and their subordinates may be greater.

(ii) Proponents of BARS also claim that such a system differentiates among behaviour, performance and results and consequently is able to provide a basis for setting developmental goals for the employee.

(iii) Because it is job-specific and identifies observable and measurable behaviour, it is a more reliable and valid method.

(iv) The use of critical incidents may be more useful in providing feedback to the people being appraised.

Limitations

Researchers, after surveying several studies on BARS, concluded that "despite the intuitive appeal of BARS, findings from research have not been encouraging".

(i) It has not proved to be superior to other methods in overcoming rater errors or in achieving psychometric soundness.

(ii) A specific deficiency is that the behaviours used are activity oriented rather than results oriented.

(iii) This creates a potential problem for supervisors doing the evaluation, who may be forced to deal with employees who are performing the activity but not accomplishing the desired goals.

(iv) Further, it is time consuming and expensive to create BARS. They also demand several appraisal forms to accommodate different types of jobs in an organization. In a college, lecturers, office clerks, library staff, technical staff and gardening staff all have different jobs; separate BARS forms would be developed for each.

(v) There is lack of compelling evidence demonstrating the superiority of BARS over traditional techniques such as graphic rating scales.

Decotis concluded that: "*It may be time to quit hedging about the efficacy of behavioural scaling strategies and conclude that this method has no clear-cut advantages over more traditional and easier methods of performance evaluation.*"

3. Management by Objectives (MBO)

The concept of 'Management by Objectives' (MBO) was first given by **Peter Drucker** in 1954. It can be defined as a process whereby the employees and the superiors come together to identify common goals, the employees set their goals to be achieved, the standards to be taken as the criteria for measurement of their performance and contribution and deciding the course of action to be followed.

In the words of **Peter Drucker,** "*MBO is a process whereby the superior and subordinate managers of an organization jointly identify its common goals, define each individual's major areas of responsibility in terms of results expected of him and use these measures as guides for operating the unit and assessing the contribution of each of its members.*"

The essence of MBO is participative goal setting, choosing course of actions and decision making. An important part of the MBO is the measurement and the comparison of the employee's actual performance with the standards set. Ideally, when employees themselves have been involved with the goal setting and the choosing the course of action to be followed by them, they are more likely to fulfil their responsibilities.

MBO Process

The MBO process is shown in Figure 9.9.

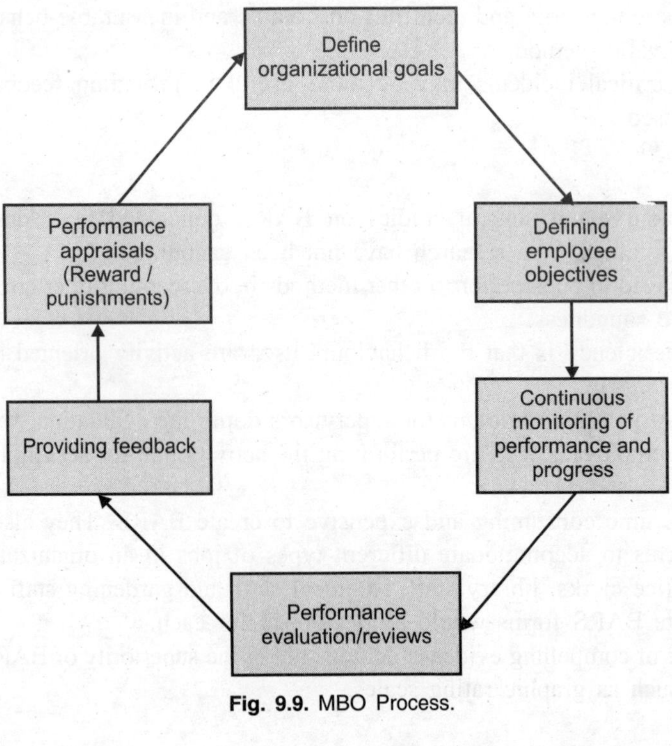

Fig. 9.9. MBO Process.

MBO represents a modern method of evaluating the performance of personnel. Thoughtful managers have become increasingly aware that the traditional performance evaluation systems are characterized by somewhat antagonistic judgements on the part of the rater. There is a growing feeling nowadays that it is better to make the superior work with subordinates in fixing goals. This would inevitably enable subordinates to exercise self-control over their performance behaviours. The concept of management by objectives is actually the outcome of the pioneering works of Drucker, McGregor and Odiorne in management science. MBO thus represents more than an evaluation programme and process. Practising management scientists view it as a philosophy of managerial practice. *It is a method by which managers and subordinates plan, organize, control, communicate and debate.*

Features

- MBO emphasizes anticipatively set goals that are tangible, verifiable and measurable.
- MBO focuses attention on what must be accomplished (goals) rather than how it is to be accomplished (methods).
- MBO, by concentrating on key result areas, translates the abstract philosophy of management into concrete phraseology. The technique can be put to general use. Further it is *"a dynamic system"* which seeks to integrate the company's need to clarify and achieve its profit and growth targets with the manager's need to contribute and develop him.
- MBO is a systematic and rational technique that allows the management to attain maximum results from available resources by focusing on achievable goals. It allows the subordinate plenty of room to make creative decisions on his own.

Importance / Benefits of MBO

(i) MBO increases employee motivation because it relates overall goals to the individual's goals; and helps to increase an employee's understanding of where the organization is and where it is heading.

(ii) Managers are more likely to compete with themselves than with other managers. This kind of evaluation can reduce internal conflicts that often arise when managers compete with each other to obtain scarce resources.

(iii) MBO reduces role conflict and ambiguity. Role conflicts exist when a person is faced with conflicting demands from two or more supervisors; and role ambiguity exists when a person is uncertain as to how he will be evaluated, or what he has to achieve. Since MBO aims at providing clear targets and their order or priority, it reduces both these situations.

(iv) MBO provides more objective appraisal criteria for evaluating the manager's performance.

(v) MBO identifies problems better and early because frequent performance review sessions in this technique make this possible.

(vi) MBO identifies performance deficiencies and enables the management and the employees to set individualized self-improvement goals.

(vii) MBO helps the individual manager to develop personal leadership, especially the skills of listening, planning, counselling, motivating and evaluating.

4. 360 Degree Performance Appraisal

360 degree feedback is also known as 'multi-rater feedback'. In this technique the opinions of customers, colleagues, peers, vendors, and subordinates are also taken to prepare the 360 review. Figure 9.10 is relevant in this context.

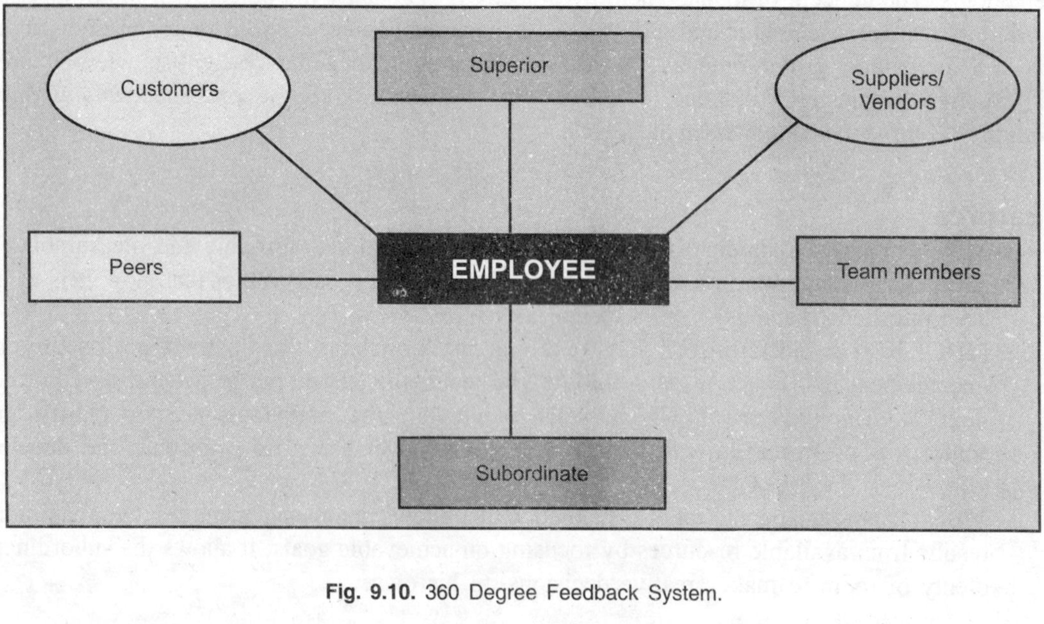

Fig. 9.10. 360 Degree Feedback System.

When you use the 360 method, collect customer feedback in the form of e-mails, phone calls or letters. The employee's colleagues must also be interviewed, either in person or through a feedback form. Finally, you, as the manager, must give your perspective of the employee's work to complete the review. Different forms with different formats are being used to obtain the information regarding the employee performance.

Components of 360 Degree Appraisal

360 degree appraisal has four integral components:

1. Self-appraisal
2. Superior's appraisal
3. Subordinate's appraisal
4. Peer appraisal.

Self-appraisal gives a chance to the employee to look at his/her strengths and weaknesses, his achievements, and judge his own performance. Superior's appraisal forms the traditional part of the 360 degree performance appraisal where the employees' responsibilities and actual performance is rated by the superior. Subordinate's appraisal gives a chance to judge the employee on the parameters like communication and motivating abilities, superior's ability to delegate the work, leadership qualities, etc. Also known as internal customers, the correct feedback given by peers can help to find employees' abilities to work in a team, cooperation and sensitivity towards others.

Benefits

(i) Self-assessment is an indispensable part of 360 degree appraisals and therefore 360 degree performance appraisal has high employee involvement and also has the strongest impact on behavior and performance.

(ii) It provides a '360 degree review' of the employees' performance and is considered to be one of the most credible performance appraisal methods.

(iii) 360 degree performance appraisal is also a powerful developmental tool because when conducted at regular intervals (say yearly) it helps to keep a track of the changes taking place in others' perceptions about the employees.

(iv) A 360 degree appraisal is generally found more suitable for the managers as it helps to assess their leadership and managing styles.

(v) This technique is being effectively used across the globe for performance appraisals. Some of the organizations following it are Wipro, Infosys, and Reliance Industries, etc.

Limitations

(i) Receiving feedback from multiple resources is difficult.

(ii) Selecting the rater and designing questionnaire and analyzing the data is time-consuming.

(iii) Beside, with the number of teams increasing in the organizations, it becomes difficult to measure and appraise the performance of the team. The question is how to separate the performance of the team from the performance of the employees. A solution to this problem that is being adopted by the companies is to measure both the individual and the team performance.

5. Human Resource Accounting

Human resources are a valuable asset of any organization. This asset can be valued in terms of money. When competent and well-trained employees leave an organization the human asset is decreased and vice versa. Under this method performance is judged in terms of costs and contributions of the employees. Costs of human resources consist of expenditure on human resource planning, recruitment, selection, induction, training, compensation, etc. Contribution of human resources is the money value of labour productivity or value added by human resources. Difference between cost and contribution will reflect the performance of employees. This method is under the transition stage and is, therefore, not popular at present.

USES OF PERFORMANCE APPRAISAL

Box-4 presents the uses of performance analysis.

Box-4 Uses of Performance Appraisal

- **Performance Improvement:** Performance feedback allows the employee, manager, and personnel specialists to intervene with appropriate actions to improve performance.
- **Compensation Adjustments:** Performance evaluations help decision-makers determine who should receive pay raises. Many firms grant part or all of their pay increases and bonuses based upon merit, which is determined mostly through performance appraisals.
- **Placement Decisions:** Promotions, transfers, and demotions are usually based on past or anticipated performance. Often promotions are a reward for past performance.
- **Training and Development Needs:** Poor performance may indicate the need for retraining. Likewise, good performance may indicate untapped potential that should be developed.
- **Career Planning and Development:** Performance feedback guides career decisions about specific career paths one should investigate.
- **Staffing Process Deficiencies:** Good or bad performance implies strengths or weaknesses of the personnel department's staffing procedures.
- **Informational Inaccuracies:** Poor performance may indicate errors in job analysis information, human resource plans, or other parts of the personnel management information system. Reliance on inaccurate information may have led to inappropriate hiring, training, or counselling decisions.
- **Job Design Errors:** Poor performance may be a symptom of ill-conceived job designs. Appraisals help diagnose these errors.
- **Equal Employment Opportunity:** Accurate performance appraisals that actually measure job-related performance ensure that internal placement decisions are not discriminatory.
- **External Challenges:** Sometimes performance is influenced by factors outside the work environment, such as family, financial, health, or other personal matters. If uncovered through appraisals, the human resource department may be able to provide assistance.
- **Feedback to Human Resources:** Good/bad performance throughout the organization indicates how well the human resource function is performing.

Source: William B. Werther and Keith Davis, Human Resources and Personnel Management, p. 339.

It is said that performance appraisal is an investment for the company which can be justified by following facts:

1. **Positive Work Environment:** It promotes a positive work environment which contributes to productivity. When achievements are recognized and rewarded on the basis of objective performance measures, there is improvement in work environment.
2. **Compensation Adjustments:** Performance appraisal helps in chalking out compensation packages for employees. Merit rating is possible through performance appraisal. Performance appraisal tries to give worth to a performance. Compensation packages which include bonus, high salary rates, extra benefits, allowances and pre-requisites are dependent on performance appraisal. The criteria should be merit rather than seniority.

3. **Informational Inaccuracies:** It helps to judge the effectiveness of recruitment, selection, placement and orientation systems of the organization.
4. **Basis of Personnel Decisions:** Performance appraisal provides valuable information for personnel decisions such as pay increases, promotions, demotions, transfers and terminations. So, the management gets an objective basis or logic for discussing salary increases and promotions with the staff. The performance appraisal serves as the basis of suitable personnel policies.
5. **Training and Development Needs:** Training needs can be assessed because performance appraisal reveals people who require further training to remove their weaknesses. It also identifies individuals with high potential who can be groomed up for higher positions.
6. **Career Planning and Development:** Performance appraisal helps the supervisors to chalk out the promotion programmes for efficient employees. In this regards, inefficient workers can be dismissed or demoted. So, it facilitates human resource planning, career planning and succession planning.
7. **Job Design Error:** A competitive spirit is created and employees are motivated to improve their performance. Systematic appraisal provides the management an opportunity to properly size up the employees.
8. **Avoidance of Discrimination:** Systematic appraisal of performance helps to develop confidence among the employees. Appraisal records protect the management from charges of discrimination levelled by trade union leaders. Employee grievances can be reduced.
9. **Effective Communication:** For an organization, effective communication between employees and employers is very important. Through performance appraisal, communication can be sought for in the following ways:
   (a) Through performance appraisal, the employers can understand and accept skills of subordinates.
   (b) The subordinates can also understand and create trust and confidence in superiors.
   (c) It also helps in maintaining cordial and congenial labour-management relationship.
   (d) It develops the spirit of work and boosts the morale of the employees.
   (e) All the above factors ensure effective communication.
10. **External Challenges:** Performance appraisals are a significant challenge for most new managers. However, it is possible to create a positive environment for appraisals by viewing them as a long-term and evolving process and not an event that occurs once a year, developing standards that are clear and objective, and using them as a tool for communicating with your employees about your expectations.

A recent survey shows (Figure 9.11) the purpose of performance appraisal in organizations. According to this survey, the percentage of organizations (out of the total organizations surveyed i.e. 50) using performance appraisal for the various purposes are as shown in the figure below:

The most significant reasons of using performance appraisal are:

- Making payroll and compensation decisions – 80%
- Training and development needs – 71%
- Identifying the gaps in desired and actual performance, and its cause – 76%
- Deciding future goals and course of action – 42%
- Promotions, demotions and transfers – 49%

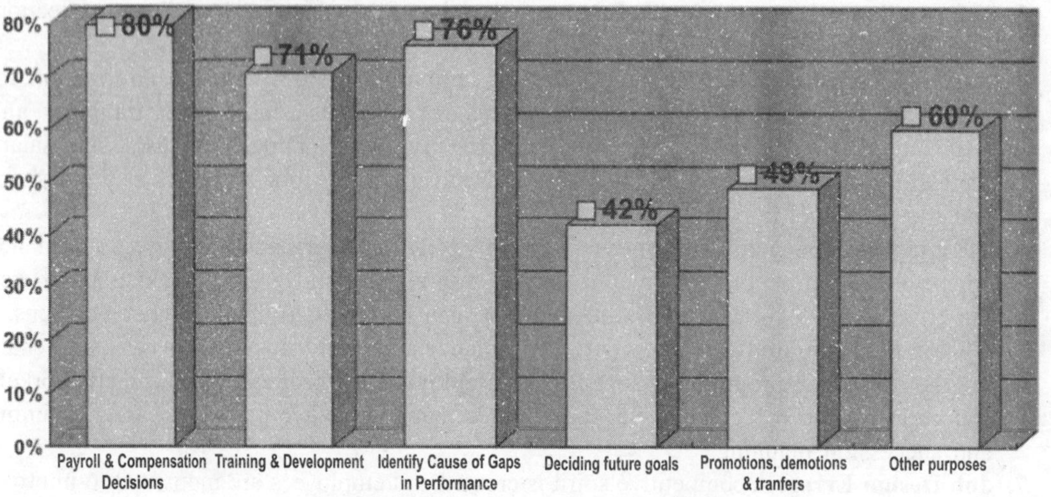

Fig. 9.11. Purpose of Performance Appraisal.

- Other purposes–6% (including job analysis and providing superior support, assistance and counselling).

LIMITATIONS OF PERFORMANCE APPRAISAL

In research studies various limitations or problems have come to light. The major problems in performance appraisal are discussed as under:

1. **Existence of Rating Biases**
   (i) **Halo Effect:** It is the tendency of the raters to defend excessively on the rating of one trait or behavioural consideration in rating all other traits or behavioural considerations. One way of minimizing the halo effect is appraising all the employees by one trait before going to rate on the basis of another trait.
   (ii) **The Error of Central Tendency:** Some raters follow play safe policy in rating by rating all the employees around the middle point of the rating scale and they avoid rating the people at both the extremes of the scale.
   (iii) **Personal Prejudice:** If the rater dislikes any employee or any group, he may rate them at the lower end, which may distort the rating purpose and affect the career of these employees.
   (iv) **The Recency Effect:** The raters generally remember the recent actions of the employee at the time of rating and rate on the basis of these recent actions rather than on the whole activities.
2. **Failure of the Superiors:** Failure of the superiors in conducting performance appraisal and post performance appraisal interviews.
3. **Elements of Subjectivity:** Most part of the appraisal is based on subjectivity.
4. **Limited Reliability:** Less reliability and validity of the performance appraisal techniques.

5. **Negative Ratings:** Negative ratings affect interpersonal relations and industrial relations system.
6. **Impact of Environment:** Influence of external environmental factors and uncontrollable internal factors.
7. **Punishment Rather than Development:** The management emphasizes on punishment rather than development of an employee in performance appraisal.
8. **Guess Work:** Some ratings particularly about the potential appraisal are purely based on guess work.
9. **Other Problems:** The other problems of performance appraisal reported by various studies are:
   (i) Relationship between appraisal rates and performance after promotions was not significant.
   (ii) Some superiors completed appraisal reports within a few minutes.
   (iii) Absence of inter-rater reliability.
   (iv) The situation was unpleasant in feedback interview.

ESSENTIALS OF AN EFFECTIVE APPRAISAL SYSTEM

According to **Mathis and Jackson**, "*Performance appraisal should be used primarily to develop employees as valuable resource. Only then it would show promising results. When management uses it as a whip or fails to understand its limitations, it fails. The key is not which form or which method is used.*"

Appraisal system to be effective must fulfil the following essentials/conditions:

1. **Reliability:** The top management must create a climate of reliable appraisal throughout the organization. Goal orientation, open communications, informal relationships, etc. are the basic elements of such a climate.
2. **Validity:** Appraisals must satisfy the condition of validity by measuring what they are supposed to measure. For example, if the appraisal is to be made for the potential of an employee for promotion, it should supply the information and data relating to potentialities of the employee to take up higher responsibilities and carry on activities at higher level.
3. **Specific Objectives:** The appraisal plan should be designed to achieve specific objectives. The objectives should be relevant, timely and open. The number of factors to be considered and the data to be collected should be tailor-made to achieve the objectives of the appraisal.
4. **Mutual Trust and Confidence:** An atmosphere of mutual trust and confidence in the organization is a must for an effective system of performance appraisal. Both the supervisor and the subordinate should be able to discuss matters frankly and offer suggestions which may be beneficial for the organization and lead to the improvement of the employees.
5. **Focus on Job Relatedness:** The evaluators should focus attention on job related behaviour and performance of the employees. The results of performance rather than personality traits should be given due weight. Suggestions for improvement should be directed towards the objective facts of the job. The individual as a person should never be criticized.

6. **Standardization Management:** Appraisal forms, procedures, administration of techniques, ratings, etc. should be standardized as appraisal decisions affect all the employees of the group. It will help to ensure uniformity and comparison of ratings. The appraisal techniques should measure what they are supposed to measure.
7. **Training to Appraisers:** The appraisers should be selected and trained properly so that they have no personal biases and possess the necessary capabilities for objective evaluation. It has been proved that appraisers who are trained in how to evaluate subordinates tend to be more effective appraisers than those who had not undergone such training.
8. **Focus on Feedback:** The results of the appraisal, particularly when they are negative, should be immediately communicated to the employees so that they may try to improve their performance.
9. **Post Appraisal Interview:** After appraisal, an interview with the employee should be arranged. It is necessary to supply feedback, to know the difficulties under which the employees work and to identify their training needs. A problem solving approach should be adopted in the interview and counselling should be provided for improving the performance of the employee.
10. **Review and Appeal:** There should be provision of appeals against appraisals to ensure confidence of the employees and their unions. A mechanism for review of ratings should be provided. The review may be made by a committee consisting of line executives and personnel experts.

PERFORMANCE MANAGEMENT

It has been discussed in the previous sections of this chapter that performance appraisal is a powerful tool which provides documented feedback on an employee's level of performance. This in turn, helps the employers in determining promotion, transfer, bonuses, pay raises, etc. The actual performance appraisal documents become part of an employee's permanent record and can greatly influence lives and careers. If performance evaluation management is poor, it can be used against the employer in the court. On the other hand, if performance management is efficient, it will strengthen the organizational structure for greater performance. Thus, managing performances in the organizations is a very important issue for the top management of the organizations.

What is Performance Management?

According to **Armstrong and Baron,** "*Performance management is a process which contributes to the effective management of individuals and teams in order to achieve high levels of organizational performance. As such, it establishes shared understanding about what is to be achieved and an approach to leading and developing people which will ensure that it is achieved.*"

Armstrong and Baron further points out "*Performance management is a strategy which relates to every activity of the organization set in the context of its human resource policies, culture, style and communications systems. The nature of the strategy depends upon the organizational context and can vary from organization to organization.*"

In the words of **Bourne M & Franco M**, "*Performance measurement is the process of assessing progress towards achieving predetermined goals while performance management is* *building on that process adding the relevant communication and action on the progress achieved against these predetermined goals.*"

These definitions of performance management reveal the following features of performance management:

1. Performance Management is *strategic* as it is about broader issues and long-term goals.
2. Performance Management is *integrated* as it involves linkage in business, people management and individuals and teams.
3. It should incorporate performance improvement for individual teams and organizational effectiveness.
4. It should incorporate development as unless there is continuous development of individuals and terms, performance will not improve.
5. Performance Management is a tool to ensure that managers manage effectively, i.e.
   - know and understand what is expected of them.
   - have the skills and ability to deliver on these expectations.
   - are supported by the organization to develop the capacity to meet these expectations.
   - are given feedback on their performance.
   - have the opportunity to discuss and contribute to individual and team aims and objectives.
6. **It is also about ensuring that the managers themselves are aware of the impact of their own behaviour** on the people they manage and are encouraged to identify and exhibit positive behaviours.
7. **Performance Management is about establishing a culture** in which individuals and groups take responsibility for the continuous improvement of business processes and of their own skills, behaviour and contributions.
8. **It is about sharing expectations.** Managers can clarify what they expect individuals and teams to do; likewise individuals and teams can communicate their expectations of how they should be managed and what they need to do their jobs.
9. It follows that performance management is about **interrelationships** and about improving the quality of relationships between managers and teams, between members of teams, and so on, and is therefore a **joint** process.
10. **It is also about planning**—defining expectations expressed as objectives and in business plans and about **measurement**; the old dictum is 'If you can't measure it, you can't manage it'.
11. **It should apply to all employees**, not just managers, and to **teams** as much as individuals.
12. **It is a continuous process, not a one-off event**.
13. Last but not the least, it is holistic and should pervade every aspect of running an organization.

PERFORMANCE MANAGEMENT PROCESS

Performance Management is a process, not an event. It operates as a continuous cycle. It involves four main steps:

1. Strategic Goal Setting or *Plan*	It is the starting point for business and development goals.
2. Agreement on Performance and development or *Do*	It is doing as per plan.
3. Continuous Monitoring and Feedback or *Review*	It is the third step in which the help of formal reviewers is taken.
4. Performance Improvement or *Revise*	It is revision on the basis of performance.

This performance management process has been further expanded and revised in seven steps which govern or overlap the **Plan-Do-Review-Revise Process** of performance management. It is shown in Figure 9.12.

Step I	Define performance
Step II	Plan performance and development
Step III	Meet development and support needs
Step IV	Monitor and give feedback
Step V	Assess performance
Step VI	Recognize and reward good performance
Step VII	Seek performance improvement

TOOLS OF PERFORMANCE MANAGEMENT AND CHALLENGES

Effective approaches to performance management operate at two levels:

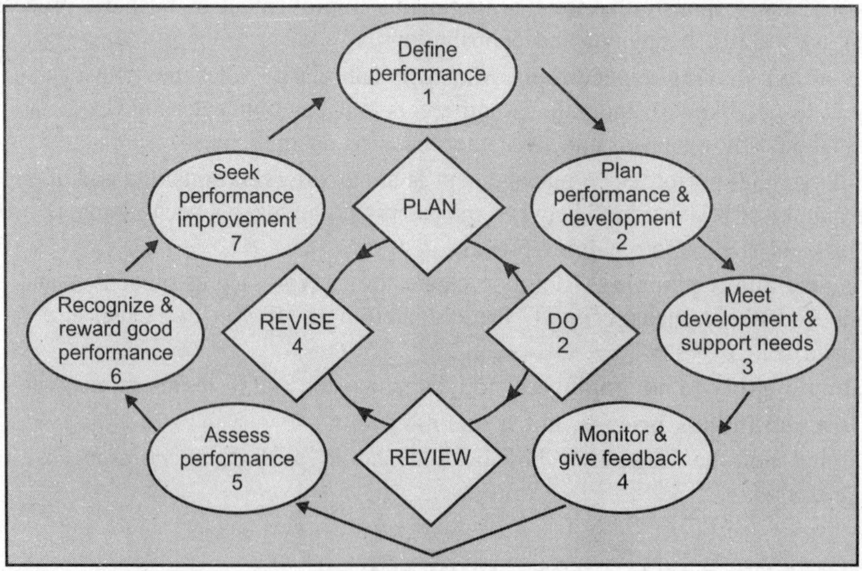

Fig. 9.12. Steps Involved in Managing People's Performance.
Source: Armstrong, M. and Baron, A. (2004) Managing Performance: Performance Management in Action. London: Chartered Institute of Personnel and Development.

- The organizational level, for example through the use of service or business planning and the cascading of organizational objectives.
- The individual and team level, for example, through the use of appraisals and training and development needs analysis and plans.

Managing the performance of people at work is about linking service and wider organizational plans and objectives to individual jobs and members of staff. Effective performance management requires an ongoing dialogue with employees and this, in turn, needs continual reinforcement. This is because people may not make the link between their day-to-day roles and achieving objectives.

Following tools are used for Performance Management:

1. **Appraisals and Performance Reviews**
   Many organizations without performance management systems operate 'appraisals', in which an individual's manager regularly, usually annually, records performance, potential and development needs in a top-down process. It can be argued that the perceived defects of appraisal systems led to the development of more rounded concepts of performance management. Nevertheless, organizations with performance management systems need to provide those involved with the opportunity to reflect on past performance as a basis for making development and improvement plans, and the performance and development review meeting provides this chance. The meeting must be constructive, and various techniques can be used to conduct the sort of open, free-flowing and honest meeting needed, with the reviewer doing most of the talking.

2. **Development Reviews**
   To keep development separate from performance and salary discussions, development reviews may be held at other times, e.g., anniversary of joining an organization. Increasing emphasis on talent management also means that many organizations are redefining performance management to align it to the need to identify, nurture and retain talent. Development programmes reflect the need of succession plans and seek to foster leadership skills. However, too much of an emphasis on talent management may be damaging to the overall development needs and every effort needs to be made to ensure that development is inclusive, accessible and focused on developing organizational capability.

3. **Coaching**
   Coaching is an important tool in learning and development. Coaching is developing a person's skills and knowledge so that their job performance improves, leading to the achievement of organizational objectives. Coaching is increasingly recognised as a significant responsibility of line managers, and can play an important part in a PDP. They will take place during the review meetings, but also and more importantly should be carried out throughout the year. For some managers coaching comes naturally, but for many it may not, and training may be needed to improve their skills.

4. **Objectives and Performance Standards**
Objectives describe something to be accomplished by individuals, departments and organizations over a period of time. They can be expressed as targets to be met (such as sales) and tasks to be completed by specified dates. They can be work-related, referring to the results to be attained, or personal, taking the form of developmental objectives for individuals. Objectives need to be defined and agreed.

Alongside objectives are performance standards which are used when it is not possible to set time-based targets, or when there is a continuing objective which does not change significantly from one review period to the next and is a standing feature of the job. These should be spelled out in quantitative terms if possible, for example, speed of response to requests or meeting defined standards of accuracy.

5. **Competence and Competencies**
Some organizations, but by no means all, use competence and competencies as components of performance management. Competence describes what people need to be able to do to perform a job well. Competencies are defined as the dimensions of behaviour that lie behind competent performance. There are various techniques for measuring competence (some organizations prefer to use 'capability') and once an analysis has been made, it provides a tool for measuring performance and, for providing development activities to help people meet the required standards.

6. **Measurement of Current Performance**
To improve performance, you need to know what current performance is. Measurement provides the basis for providing and generating feedback, and thus can build the platform for further success or identify where things are going less well so that corrective action may be taken. For measuring performance, the achievement of objectives, levels of competency, standards of performance, and work outputs are used but the emphasis varies according to the categories of staff, for example, a senior manager would be mainly measured by meeting objectives, but a production worker mainly by achieving outputs. Increasingly organizations are using more sophisticated measuring techniques such as balanced scorecards or return on investment (ROI).

7. **Pay**
Performance management is often linked with **performance-related pay** (PRP), although by no means all organizations claiming to use performance management have PRP. Nevertheless, PRP is an important element in many performance management schemes because it is believed to motivate. It is said to deliver the message that performance and competence are important, and it is thought to be fair to reward people according to their performance, contribution or competence. An alternative to PRP is **competence-related pay,** which provides for pay progression to be linked to levels of competence that people have achieved, using a competence profile or framework. The difficulty here is measuring competence, and some organizations use a mix of PRP and competence-related pay. Further possible pay systems are **team-based pay,** a kind of PRP for teams; and **contribution-related pay** which means paying for results plus competence, and for past performance and future success.

8. Teams

Team working has become an important part of life in many organizations, and where teams are permanent or for long-standing projects, measures can be based on team performance. They will mainly be concerned with output, activity levels or speed of servicing, customer service and satisfaction, and financial results. Indeed, team measures are not very different from those for individuals, and of course team members need to agree with their objectives and receive feedback in the same way as if they were not part of a team. Other team members can contribute towards this, in a process of peer review.

9. 360 Degree Feedback

360 degree feedback became increasingly talked about in the 1990s, is not widely used. It consists of performance data generated from a number of sources, who can include the person to whom the individual being assessed reports, people who report to them, peers (team colleagues or others in the organization), and internal and external customers. It can also include self-assessment. 360 degree feedback is used mainly as part of a self-development or management development programme, and is felt to provide a more rounded view of people, with less bias than if an assessment is conducted by one individual.

10. Performance Problem Solving

Performance management is a positive process, and good systems will create a culture in which success is applauded. Nevertheless, poor performance will exist. It may be a result of inadequate leadership, bad management or defective systems of work, and if so, remedies can be put in place. But individuals may under-perform and improvements can be achieved through continuing feedback and joint discussion between them and their managers, involving analyzing and identifying the problem, establishing the reasons for the shortfall, and deciding and agreeing to the action to be taken. If all this fails, disciplinary action may be taken.

The keys to the successful introduction and application of performance management are given in the Box 5.

Box-5

- being clear about what is meant by performance.
- understanding what the organization is and needs to be in its performance culture.
- being very focused on how individual employees will benefit and play their part in the process.
- understanding that it is a tool for line managers and its success will depend on their ability to use it effectively organization.

Challenges in Performance Management

In present-day organizations, the twin principles of motivating employees are common at all levels: acknowledge unique contributions and alleviate personal concerns that impact professional performance. To get the best out of people, the CEOs should:

- Create a culture of excellence that motivates employees at all levels.
- Match organizational objectives with individual aspirations.
- Equip people with requisite skills to discharge their duties well.
- Clear growth paths for talented employees.
- Provide new challenges to rejuvenate flattening corners.
- Empower employees to take decisions without fear of failing.
- Encourage team work and team spirit, and open communication.

CAREER MANAGEMENT

Career management is a process that includes both organizational actions and individual efforts aimed at setting career goals, formulating and implementing strategies and monitoring the results. *Career management is in fact, the appropriate long-term utilization and development of human talent in the work setting.*

A balanced approach to career management includes both individual career planning and organizational initiatives taken to balance career goals and organizational needs. The two strategies of career planning at individual level and organizational initiatives are complementary to each other and they reinforce each other. If individual employees have no career planning for their development, they may not be ready or willing to respond to opportunities presented through organizational career management activities. Likewise no amount of individual career planning and preparation will be effective if organizational opportunities for career movement are not available.

According to **Gutteridge**, "*Career development includes both career planning and career management.*"

Career management model as given by Gutteridge is shown in Figure 9.13.

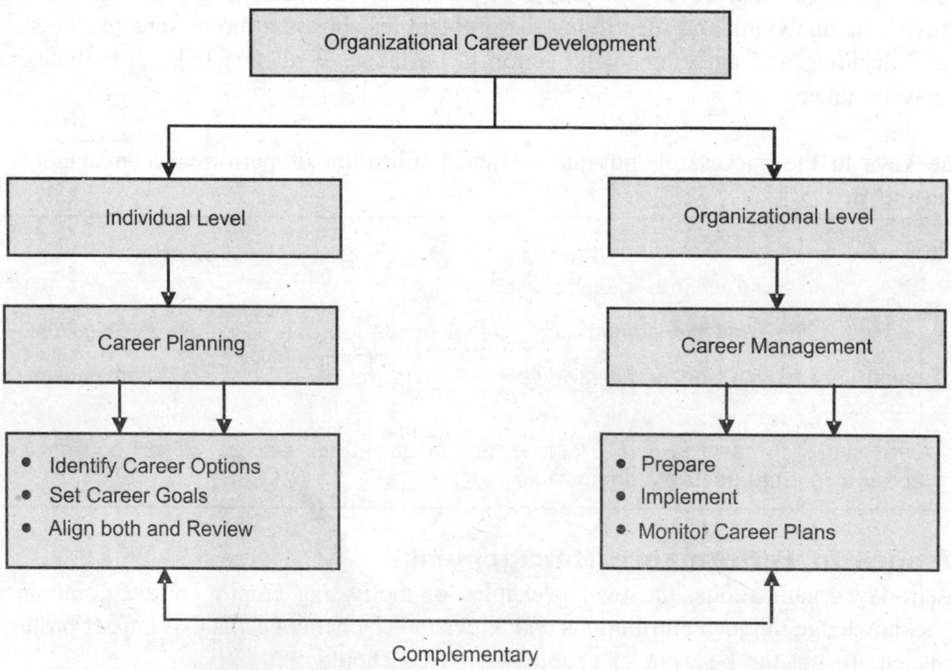

Fig. 9.13. Nature of Two Strategies that Complement and Reinforce/Career Management Model.

Another view is provided by Bernardin and Russel who integrate all the three concepts in a more refined manner as shown in Figure 9.14.

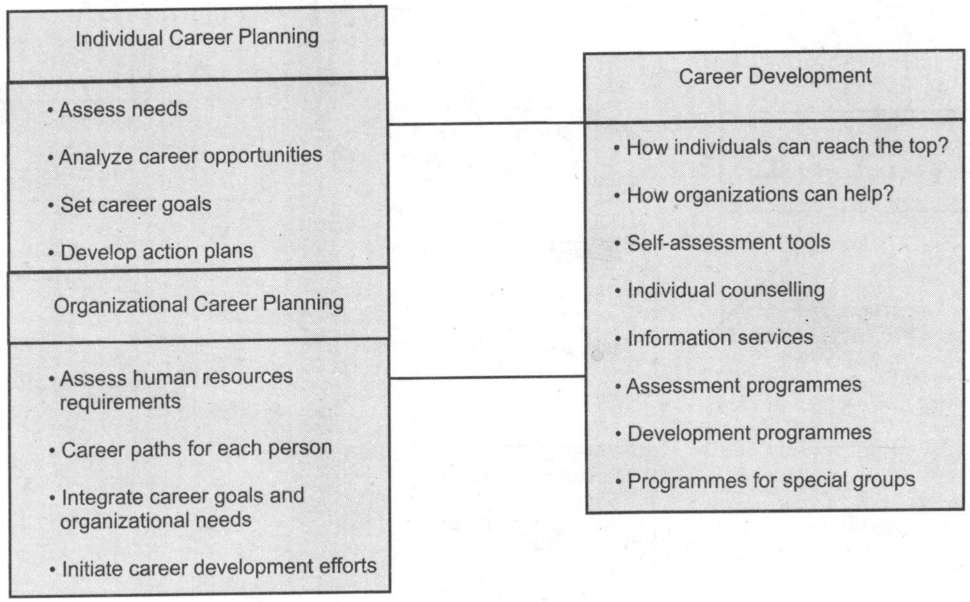

Fig. 9.14. Career Management Model (Bernardin and Russel).

CAREER MANAGEMENT PROCESS

Managing your career is not a one-time event; it is a continuous cycle of personal development. As goals are reached, new goals are established and development continues in a new direction. There are several steps in this process, as illustrated below in Figure 9.15.

Managing your career is a process that is very self-driven: it is up to you to determine your career goals and to plan for their achievement. To support employees in managing their careers through each of the steps in this process, the Public Service Commission offers a series of training courses through the Corporate Training Calendar.

These courses provide tools and resources which support potential and aspiring leaders at all levels throughout the Government of Nova Scotia to effectively manage their careers and help realize their career goals. The course offerings are designed to support employees at all different stages in the career management process: employees can choose whichever courses they require on an 'as needed' basis.

The Career Management courses offered focus on each step of the career management cycle and promote career management and advancement through targeted development, as illustrated in Figure 9.16.

How to Manage your Career?

Career Management courses are available through corporate training calendar. The Box = 6 demonstrates how can you manage your career? What are you supposed to do in each step?

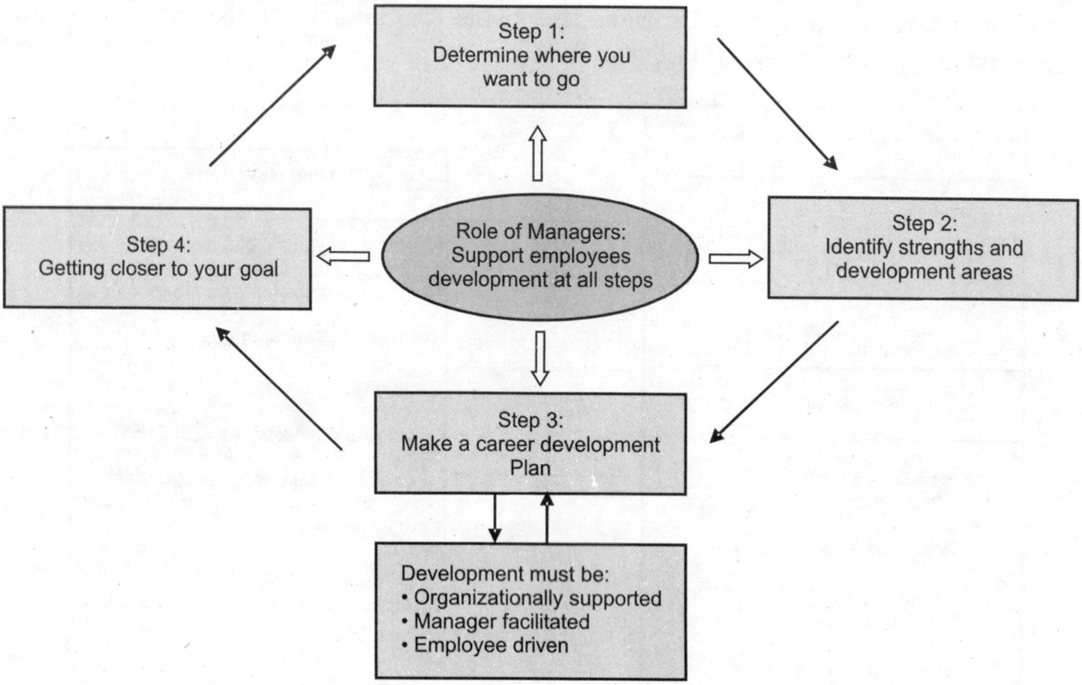

Fig. 9.15. Career Management Process/Cycle.

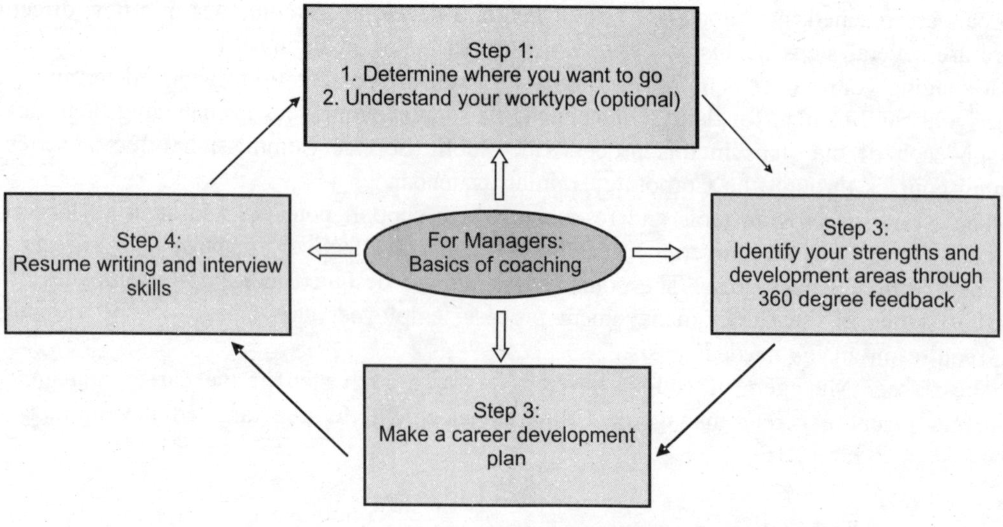

Fig. 9.16. Basics of Career Management Process.

Box-6 How to Manage Your Career?

Career Management Step 1(a): Determine Where You Want to Go

The first step in managing your career is, knowing yourself, and an important part of this self-insight is, knowing where you want to go in your career. Why do you pursue the work and the life you do? What activities are you drawn to? What keeps you engaged and energized? What gives you the greatest satisfaction and wanting to strive for excellence? These questions are at the heart of "knowing yourself." In this module, you will begin to identify your life interests, personality traits, and values that in turn drive your passions.

In this module you will identify the interests, values, and skills you already have and which allow you to contribute productively to your workplace. This will help you to see more clearly which competencies and life interests you want to continue to use in a work setting and those you may want to develop further. This self-reflection will guide you in determining career goals that are a good fit.

Career Management Step 1 (b): Understand Your Work type

The first step in managing your career is, knowing yourself, and a key piece of this self-insight is, understanding your work type. The Myers-Briggs Type Indicator (MBTI) is an indispensable tool in understanding your strengths and how to leverage these when planning your career path. This half-day course explores the relationship between personality types and the workplace. It is designed to increase self-understanding and appreciation of personal differences in order to improve one-on-one interactions and career success.

Career Management Step 2: Identify Your Strengths and Development Areas Through 360 Degree Feedback

The second step in managing your career is identifying your strengths and areas of development. The Hay Group 360º Tool will enable you to receive input from your manager, peers, people you manage, and other colleagues on the leadership competencies deemed critical to the provincial public service. A survey tool is administered online which allows participating individuals and their nominated colleagues to complete feedback in a secure, confidential and user-friendly environment. You will then meet individually with your Human Resources Development Consultant to review and discuss your feedback report.

Career Management Step 3: Make a Career Development Plan

The third step in managing your career is creating your own career development plan. Completing the plan will help you make the link between your career goals and the development that will help you move towards the achievement of your goals. Based on your past performance, strengths and career goals, you will prioritize your areas for development. You will then identify what types of opportunities will target your development areas and explore how to access these opportunities. You will also learn about the different available development resources.

Career Management Step 4: Resume Writing and Interview Skills

For many individuals, their career goal involves moving into a new position. Success in getting a job – externally or within government – is largely determined by gaining entry to the interview and then interviewing well. Good resumes are vital to getting an interview and strong interview skills are a must in selling the match between your qualifications and the job requirements. This workshop will provide you with the necessary skills to compete effectively for job opportunities.

For Managers

Supporting Others in their Career Management: Basics of Coaching

This course examines effective coaching in the workplace. You'll explore the different roles a coach may play: the coach as trainer, as mentor, and as counsellor. You'll examine the criteria and conditions that must exist in order to engage an individual and establish a climate of trust and commitment so that coaching may take place. Build on the skills that you have in the areas of leadership and communication by exploring how to adapt coaching to meet the needs of individuals and manage the process.

Source: Public Service Commission offering Additional Support in the Area of Career Management through Offering Courses at each Step in the Career Management Process.

HR'S ROLE IN CAREER MANAGEMENT

It has been accepted all over the world that HR structures relate to some of the essential aspects of the career management process. HR's role in career management is discussed in Figure 9.17.

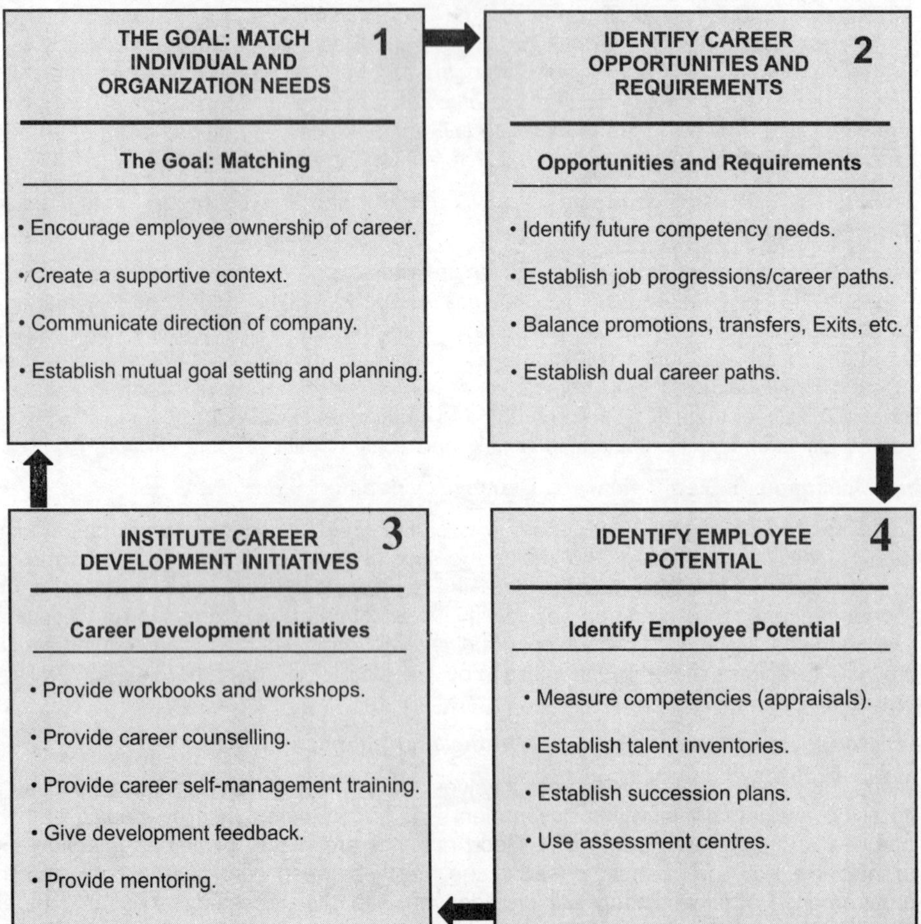

Fig. 9.17. HR's Role in Career Management.

1. Goal: Matching Individual and Organizational Needs for Career Management

In the final analysis a career development programme should be viewed as a dynamic process that matches the needs of the organization with the needs of employees.

Employee's Role

Although some firms play a role in the planning of their employees' careers, ultimately, employees are responsible for initiating and managing their own career planning. Because having a successful career involves creating your own career path—not just following a path that has been established by the organization—it is up to each individual to identify his or her own knowledge, skills, abilities, interests, and values and seek out information about career options in order to set goals and develop career plans.

Managers should encourage employees to take responsibility for their own careers, offering continuing assistance in the form of feedback on individual performance and making available information about the organization, the job, and career opportunities that might be of interest.

The organization is responsible for supplying information about its mission, policies, and plans and for providing support for employee self-assessment, training, and development. Significant career growth can occur when individual initiative combines with organizational opportunity.

Career development programmes benefit managers by giving them increased skill in managing their own careers, greater retention of valued employees, increased understanding of the organization, and enhanced reputation as people developers. As with other HR programmes, the inauguration of a career development programme should be based on the organization's needs as well.

Assessment of needs should take a variety of approaches such as surveys, informal group discussions, interviews, and so on and should involve personnel from different groups, such as new employees, managers, long-time employees, minority employees, and technical and professional employees. Identifying the needs and problems of these groups provides the starting point for the organization's career development efforts. As shown in Figure 9.6, organizational needs should be linked with individual career needs in a way that joins personal effectiveness and satisfaction of employees with the achievement of the organization's strategic objectives.

Organization's Role

If career development is to succeed, it must receive the complete support of the top management. For this, two steps are to be taken at the organization level.

(i) **Establishing a Favourable Context:** Ideally, senior line managers and HR department managers should work together to design and implement a career development system. The system should reflect the goals and culture of the organization, and the HR philosophy should be woven throughout. An HR philosophy can provide employees with a clear set of expectations and directions for their own career development. For a programme to be effective, managerial personnel at all levels must be trained in the fundamentals of job design, performance appraisal, career planning, and counselling.

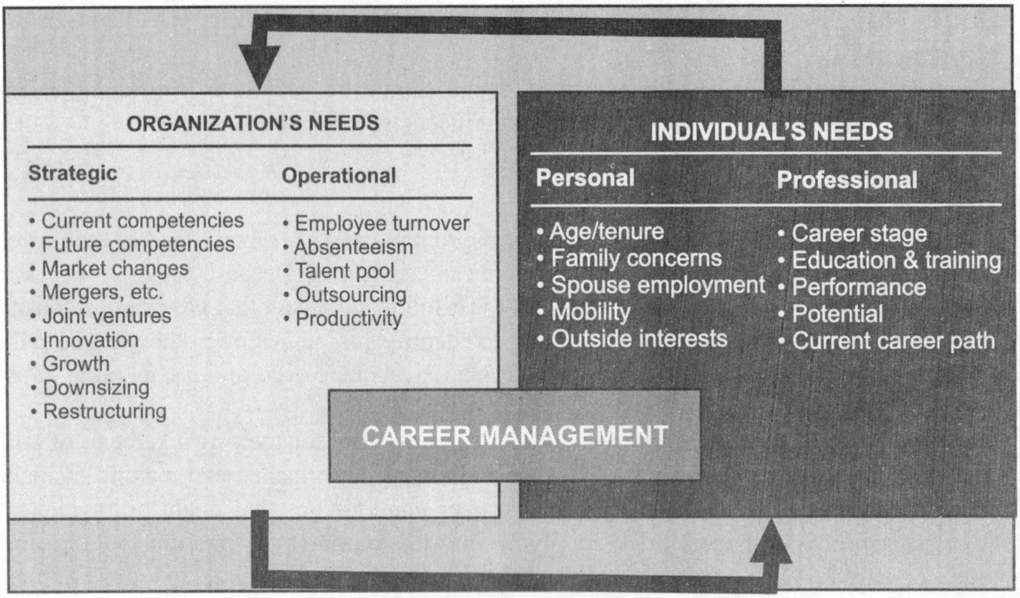

Fig. 9.18. Balancing Individual and Organizational Needs.
Source: Snell Scott, George Bohlander, "Human Resource Management", 2007, Thomson-South Western Publication, New York., p. 191.

One of the most important indicators of management support comes in the form of mentoring. This is true regardless of whether it is done formally as part of an ongoing programme or informally as merely a kind gesture to a less experienced employee. Dealing with uncertainty is one of the biggest challenges any individual faces in his or her career. Receiving advice and counsel from someone who has gone through similar experience can prove to be invaluable to employees. We devote an entire section to mentoring later in this chapter.

(ii) **Blending Individual and Organizational Goals:** Before individuals can engage in meaningful career planning, not only they have an awareness of the organization's philosophy, but they must also have a good understanding of the organization's immediate goals. Otherwise, they may plan for personal change and growth without knowing whether or how their own goals match those of the organization. For example, if the technology of a business is changing and new skills are needed, will the organization retrain to meet this need or hire new talent? Is there growth, stability, or decline in the number of employees needed? How will turnover affect this need? Clearly, an organizational plan that answers these kinds of questions is essential to support individual career planning.

At the same time, it would be unrealistic to expect that individuals can establish their career goals with *perfect* understanding of where they are going or—for that matter—where the organization is going. Individuals change over time, and because of that, their needs and interests change. Similarly, organizations also change their directions and adjust their strategies to cope with change. So while goal setting is critical, building in some flexibility is probably a good idea for proper matching of individual and organizational goals.

2. Identifying Career Opportunities and Requirements

HR also plays a crucial role in career management by keeping a steady watch on the needs and requirements of the organization. This involves an analysis of the competencies required for jobs, the progression among related jobs, and the supply of ready and potential talent available to fill those jobs and establish dual career paths.

(i) **Identify Future Competence Needs:** It is important for an organization to study its jobs carefully in order to identify and assign weights to the knowledge and skills that each one requires. This can be achieved with job analysis and evaluation systems such as those used in compensation programmes. The system measures three basic competencies for each job: (a) know-how, (b) problem solving, and (c) accountability. Know-how is broken down into three types of job knowledge: technical, managerial, and human relations. Problem solving and accountability also have several dimensions. Scores for each of these three major competencies are assigned to each job, and a total value is computed for each job.

(ii) **Identify Job Progressions** : Once the skill demands of jobs are identified and weighted according to their importance, it is then possible to plan **job progressions**. A new employee with no experience is typically assigned to a "starting job." After a period of time in that job, the employee can be promoted to one that requires more knowledge and skill. While most organizations concentrate on developing job progressions for managerial, professional, and technical jobs, progressions can be developed for all categories of jobs. These job progressions then can serve as a basis for developing **career paths**—the lines of advancement within an organization—for individuals.

Figure 9.19 illustrates a typical line of advancement in the human resources area of a large multinational corporation. It is apparent that one must be prepared to move geographically in order to advance very far in the human resources department of this firm. This would also be true of other career fields within the organization.

				Vice President, HR
			Corporate HR Director	
		Corporate HR Manager	Division HR Director	
		Asst. Division HR Director		
	Regional HR Manager	Plant HR Manager		
	Asst. Plant HR Manager			
Regional HR Associate	HR Supervisor			
HR Associate				

Fig. 9.19. Typical Line of Advancement in HR Management.

Many organizations prepare interesting and attractive brochures to describe the career paths that are available to employees. General Motors has prepared a career development guide that groups jobs by fields of work such as engineering, manufacturing, communications, data processing, financial, HR, and scientific. These categories give employees an understanding of the career possibilities in the various fields.

(iii) Balancing of Promotions, Transfers and Exits: HR policies have to be flexible enough to adapt as well as helpful enough to support the career change.

A **promotion** is a change of assignment to a job at a higher level in the organization. The new job normally provides an increase in pay and status and demands more skill or carries more responsibility. Promotions enable an organization to utilize the skills and abilities of its personnel more effectively, and the opportunity to gain a promotion serves as an incentive for good performance. The three principal criteria for determining promotions are merit, seniority, and potential.

A **transfer** is the placement of an employee in another job for which the duties, responsibilities, status, and remuneration are approximately equal to those of the previous job. Individuals who look forward to change or want a chance to learn more may seek out transfers. In addition, transfers frequently provide a broader foundation for individuals to prepare them for an eventual promotion. A transfer may require the employee to change work group, workplace, work shift, or organizational unit; it may even necessitate moving to another geographic area. Transfers make it possible for an organization to place its employees in jobs where there is a greater need for their services and where they can acquire new knowledge and skills. A downward transfer, or *demotion,* moves an individual into a lower-level job that can provide developmental opportunities. Such a move is ordinarily considered unfavourable.

Transfers, promotions and demotions require individuals to adjust to new job demands and to different work environment. The employee with a family has the added responsibility of helping family members adjust to the new living arrangements. Even though some employers provide all types of **relocation services**—including covering moving expenses, helping to sell a home, and providing cultural orientation and language training—there is always some loss of productive time.

Sometimes the employees decide to exit or may be forced to leave. HR policy should provide for assistance to be given them in finding more suitable career opportunities elsewhere. Jack Welch, chairman of General Electric, was one of the first executives to make a commitment to employees that while the company could no longer guarantee lifetime employment, it would try to ensure *employability.* That is, GE has committed to providing employees with the skills and support they would need to find a job in another organization.

(iv) Establishing Dual Career Paths: One of the most obvious places where career paths have been changing is in technical and professional areas. One of the ironies of organizations in the past has been that the most successful engineers, scientists, and professionals were often promoted right out of their area of specialization into management. Instead of doing what they were good at, they were promoted to a job they often didn't understand and often didn't enjoy. It has become apparent that there must be another way to compensate such individuals without elevating them to a management position. The solution has been to develop dual career paths, or tracks, that provide for progression in special areas such as information technology, finance, marketing, and engineering, with compensation that is comparable to that received by managers at different levels.

3. Identify Employee Potential

Career success was synonymous with ascending a corporate hierarchy over the course of a lifetime spent in a single firm. There are two categories of employees.

(i) Employees pursuing boundaryless careers
(ii) Employees pursuing traditional career.

Individuals pursuing *boundaryless careers* may prefer to see themselves as self-directed 'free agents' who develop a portfolio of employment opportunities by proactively moving from employer to employer, simultaneously developing and utilizing their marketable skills. Employees pursuing boundaryless careers develop their human capital along dimensions of industry and occupational knowledge. In contrast, individuals pursuing more traditional careers develop their knowledge in ways specific to a given firm.

HR's role here is to identify employee potential through:

(i) Appraisals for measuring competencies
(ii) Establishing talent inventories
(iii) Establishing successful plans
(iv) Using assessment centres.

Both approaches can be beneficial, but they are not the same. Under the boundaryless career model, success depends on continually learning new skills, developing new relationships, and capitalizing on existing skills and relationships. These individuals place a premium on flexibility and the capacity to do several different types of tasks, to learn new jobs, to adjust quickly to different group settings and organizational cultures, and to move from one firm, occupation, or industry to another. Their employment security depends on their marketable skills rather than their dedication to one organization over time. A number of studies have shown that people with boundaryless careers find them very satisfying. Organizations can also benefit from boundaryless careers because it allows them to attract top talent from all over the world on a project-by-project basis. One thing has to be seen is that HR's role must be to avoid career plateau.

A career plateau is a situation in which for either organizational or personal reasons the probability of moving up the career ladder is low. There are three types of plateaus: structural, content, and life. A *structural plateau* marks the end of promotions; one will now have to leave the organization to find new opportunities and challenges. A *content plateau* occurs when a person has learnt a job too well and is bored with day-to-day activities. A *life plateau* is more profound and may feel like a midlife crisis. People who experience life plateaus often have allowed work or some other major factor to become the most significant aspect of their lives, and they experience a loss of identity and self-esteem when there is no longer success in that area.

Organizations can help individuals cope with plateaus by providing opportunities for lateral growth when opportunities for advancement do not exist. Companies with international divisions can encourage employees to take assignments abroad to expand their horizons. Career enrichment programmes can help people learn more about what gives them satisfaction within a company, as well as what kinds of opportunities will make them happiest if they go elsewhere.

4. Institute Career Development Initiatives

HR's role in career management also involves taking career development initiatives. Following steps are required in this context:

(i) **Career-Planning Workbooks:** Several organizations have prepared workbooks to guide their employees individually through systematic self-assessment of values, interests, abilities, goals, and personal development plans. General Motors' *Career Development Guide* contains a section called 'What Do You Want Your Future to Be?' in which an employee makes a personal evaluation. General Electric has developed an extensive set of career development programmes, including workbooks to help employees explore life issues that affect career decisions.

(ii) **Career-Planning Workshops:** Workshops offer experiences similar to those provided by workbooks. However, they have the advantage of providing a chance to compare and discuss attitudes, concerns, and plans with others in similar situations. Some workshops focus on current job performance and development plans. Others deal with broader life and career plans and values.

As mentioned earlier, employees should be encouraged to assume responsibility for their own careers. A career workshop can help them do that. It can also help them learn how to make career decisions, set career goals, create career options, seek career planning information, and at the same time build confidence and self-esteem.

(iii) **Career Counselling:** Career counselling involves talking with employees about their current job activities and performance, their personal and career interests and goals, their personal skills, and suitable career development objectives. While some organizations make counselling a part of the annual performance appraisal, career counselling is usually voluntary. Career counselling may be provided by the HR staff, managers and supervisors, specialized staff counsellors, or outside consultants.

(iv) **Career Self-Management Training:** In response to the growing view that employees should assume greater responsibility for their own career management, many organizations are establishing programmes for employees on how they can engage in *career self-management.* The training focuses on two major objectives: (a) helping employees learn to continuously gather feedback and information about their careers, and (b) encouraging them to prepare for mobility.

The training is not geared to skills and behaviours associated with a specific job, but rather toward long-term personal effectiveness. Employees typically undertake self-assessments to increase awareness of their own career attitudes and values. In addition, they are encouraged to widen their viewpoint beyond the next company promotion to broader opportunities in the marketplace. For many, these external opportunities have not been seen as viable options, much less something the company would acknowledge.

Participants might be encouraged to engage in career networking or to identify other means to prepare for job mobility, such as hearing reports from employees who made transitions to new job opportunities both within and outside the organization.

(v) **Mentoring:** When one talks with men and women about their employment experiences, it is common to hear them mention individuals at work who influenced them. They frequently refer to immediate managers who were especially helpful as career developers. But they also mention others at higher levels in the organization that provided guidance and support to them in the development of their careers. These executives and managers who coach, advise, and encourage employees of lesser rank are called **mentors.**

Figure 9.20 shows a list of the most effective features of mentors as well as partners. In order to form an effective mentoring relationship, an employee seeking a mentor should follow a few general guidelines:

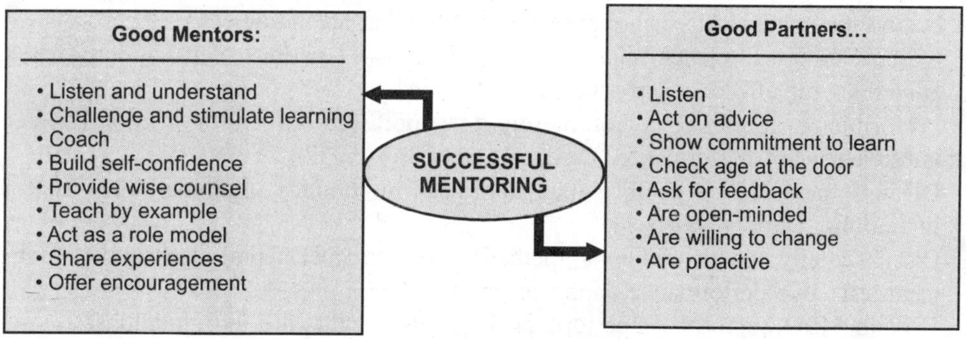

Fig. 9.20. Mentoring Functions.

- Research the person's background.
- Make contact with the person.
- Request help on a particular matter.
- Consider what you can offer in exchange.
- Arrange a meeting.
- Follow up.
- Ask to meet on an ongoing basis.

(vi) **Networking:** As the number of contacts grows, mentoring broadens into a process of **career networking.** As a complement to mentoring, in which relationships are more selective, networking relationships tend to be more varied and temporary. The networks can be internal to a particular organization or connected across many different organizations.

There are many ways to identify networking contacts. Some of the best places to consider are the following:

- Your college alumni association or career office networking lists
- Your own extended family
- Your friends' parents and other family members
- Your professors, advisors, coaches, tutors, and clergy

- Your former bosses and your friends' and family members' bosses
- Members of clubs, religious groups, and other organizations to which you belong
- All the organizations near where you live or go to school

Through networking, individuals often find out about new jobs, professional trends, and other opportunities.

CONCLUSION

The discussion of HR's role in career management clearly demonstrates that this role is indispensable to employees and managers for career growth.

REVIEW QUESTIONS

1. Define the concept of performance appraisal. What are its objectives?
2. Explain the performance appraisal process. Discuss various steps in it. What are the guidelines for effective performance evaluation?
3. Performance appraisal is not merely for appraisal but is for accomplishment and improvement of performance. Discuss.
4. Discuss the need of performance appraisal in modern organizations. What are its limitations?
5. Discuss briefly various traditional methods of performance appraisal. State the requirements of an effective performance appraisal programme.
6. Explain MBO approach to performance appraisal. What are its limitations?
7. Distinguish between straight ranking method and paired comparison method of performance appraisal. Which is better and why?
8. Explain modern methods of performance appraisal.
9. What is performance management? Give its fundamental characteristics.
10. Discuss performance management process. What are the tools of performance management?
11. Discuss the meaning of career management. Explain its process.
12. How to manage your career? What are the career management steps?
13. Explain HR's role in career management.
14. What are the essentials of a good appraisal system?
15. Write notes on the following:
    a. Checklist method of performance appraisal
    b. Field review method of performance appraisal
    c. 360 degree performance appraisal
    d. Challenges in performance management

CASE STUDY

9.1 Performance Rating of Employees

Ronak Finance Company Ltd. is a reputed finance company having 5 branches in different parts of the country. Its staff includes 140 operative employees and 32 executives. The company has a performance rating plan under which the staff members are rated at the end of each financial year by a committee of two executives by means of graphic scale. The qualities considered are the responsibilities, initiative, dependability, leadership potential, cooperative attitude and community service. After the performance is evaluated, the ratings are discussed with the concerned employees by their immediate boss and are used to counsel them and arrange further training for them. The ratings are also used for granting or withholding of increments and promoting of meritorious staff.

Recently, two employees working at the head office have been denied annual increments due to comparatively low ratings. They have made a representation to the Chief Executive of the company expressing their dissatisfaction with the appraisal system and insisting that community service is not a part of their job and it should not influence their ratings. The employees seem to organize a union and demand that annual increments should be granted automatically.

The Chief Executive Officer feels that performance appraisal is a dangerous source of friction and so it should be discontinued altogether.

Questions

1. If you were the Human Resource Manager, how would you defuse the problem?
2. How far do you agree with the CEO's view that performance appraisal should be discontinued?
3. What modifications would you like to suggest in the performance appraisal system of the company?

9.2 Politics and Performance Appraisal

Kalyani Electronics Corporation Ltd. recently diversified its activities and started producing computers. It employed personnel at the lower level and middle level. It has received several applications for the post of Commercial Manager–Computer Division. It could not decide upon the suitability of the candidate to the position, but did find that Mr. Prakash is more qualified for the position than other candidates. The Corporation has created a new post below the cadre of General Manager, i.e. Joint General Manager and asked Mr. Prakash to join the Corporation as Joint General Manager. Mr. Prakash agreed to it viewing that he will be considered for General Manager's position based on his performance. Mr. Anand, the Deputy General Manager of the Corporation and one of the candidates for General Manager's position was annoyed with the management's practice. But, he wanted to show his performance record to the management at the next appraisal meeting.

The management of the Corporation asked Mr. Sastry, General Manager of Televisions Division to be the General Manager in-charge of Computer Division for some time, until a new General Manager is appointed. Mr. Sastry wanted to switch over to Computer Division in view of the prospects, prestige and recognition of the position among the top management of the Corporation. He viewed this assignment as a chance to prove his performance.

The Corporation has the system of appraisal of the superior's performance by the subordinates. The performance of the Deputy General Manager, Joint General Manager and General Manager has to be appraised by the same group of the subordinates. Mr. Anand and Mr. Prakash is a stranger to the system as well as its modus operandi. Mr. Sastry and Mr. Anand were competing with each other in convincing their subordinates about their performance and used all sorts of techniques for pleasing them like promising them a wage hike, transfers to the job of their interest, promotion, etc. However, these two officers functioned in collaboration with a view to pull down Mr. Prakash. They openly told their subordinates that a stranger should not occupy the 'chair'. They created several groups among employees like pro-Anand's group, pro-Sastry's group, anti-Prakash and Sastry Group, anti-Anand and Prakash group.

Mr. Prakash has been watching the proceedings calmly and keeping the management in touch with all these developments. However, Mr. Prakash has been quite work-conscious and the top management found his performance under such a political atmosphere to be satisfactory. Prakash's pleasing manners and way of maintaining human relations with different levels of employees did, however, prevent anti-Prakash wave in the company. But in view of the polticalization, there is no strong pro-Prakash's group either.

The management administered the performance appraisal technique and the subordinates appraised the performance of all these three managers. In the end, surprisingly to the workers, assigned the following overall scores. Prakash: 560 points, Sastry: 420 points; and Anand: 260 points.

Source: P. Subba Rao, HRM and Industrial Relations, Himalaya Publishing House, New Delhi, pp. 239-240.

Questions

1. How do you evaluate the worker's appraisal in this case?
2. Do you suggest any techniques to avert politics creeping into the process of performance appraisal by subordinates? Or do you suggest the measure of dispensing with such appraisal system.

REFERENCES

1. Aquinas, P.G. (2008). "Human Resource Management", Vikas Publishing House (Pvt.) Ltd. pp. 82-90.
2. Armstrong "Management: A Handbook of Personnel Management Practice", Kogan Page Ltd., London.
3. Bourne, M., Franco, M. and Wilkes, J. (2003). "Corporate Performance Management", Measuring Business Excellence, p. 15.
4. Dale S. Beach, (1980). "Personnel–The Management of People at Work", 4th edn., MacMillan, p. 368.
5. Dessler, Gary, (1998). "Human Resource Management", Prentice-Hall of India, New Delhi.
6. Elmer H. Burack and Robert D. Smith, (1982). "Personnel Management–A Human Resource Systems Approach", NY, John Wiley & Sons, p. 531.
7. Mahapatro, B.B. HRM, New Age International Publishers, New Delhi, pp. 108-112.
8. Mamoria, C.B. and Gankar, S.V. (2008). "Personnel Management", Himalaya Publishing House, Mumbai, pp. 257-259.
9. Randall S. Schuler, *et al.*, (1989). "Effective Personnel Management", 3rd edn., West Publishing, NY, p. 389.
10. Snell Scott, and George Bohlander, (2007). "Human Resource Management", Thomson-South Western Publication, New York.
11. Subba Rao P. (2007). "Essentials of Human Resource Management and Industrial Relations". Himalaya Publishing House, New Delhi.
12. Thomas H. Stone, (1982). "Understanding Personnel Management", The Dryden Press, Chicago, p. 248.
13. William B. Werther and Keith Davis, (1993). "Human Resources and Personnel Management", 4th edn., McGraw-Hill, NY, p. 309.

CHAPTER

10

Job Evaluation and Compensation of Employees

CHAPTER'S OUTLINE

- Introduction
- Meaning of Job Evaluation
- Objectives and Importance of Job Evaluation
- Process of Job Evaluation
- Advantages of Job Evaluation
- Methods of Job Evaluation
- Principles of Job Evaluation Programme
- Limitations of Job Evaluation
- Meaning of Compensation
- Objectives of Compensation
- Importance of Ideal Compensation System
- Factors Influencing Compensation
- Strategic Pay Plans or Rate
- Compensation Trends
- Skill Based Pay
- Broad Bending

INTRODUCTION

For good industrial relations, job evaluation and compensation of employees are two interrelated activities that are performed in every organization. The primary objective of wage and salary administration programme is that each employee should be equitably compensated for the services rendered by him to the organization on the basis of the nature of job, the present worth of that type of job and the effectiveness with which the individual performs the job. These aspects are related to the process of job evaluation and compensation given in the form of wages and salaries to the employees.

In this chapter an attempt has been made to analyze the two interrelated concepts.

1. The concept and nature of job evaluation
2. The nature and concept of compensation principle

MEANING OF JOB EVALUATION

The essence of compensation administration is job evaluation and the establishment of a pay structure.

By job evaluation, we mean using the information in job analysis to systematically determine the value of each job in relation to all jobs within the organization. *In short, job evaluation seeks to rank all the jobs in the organization and place them in a hierarchy that will reflect the relative worth of each.*

It should be noted that job evaluation is ranking of jobs, not people. Job evaluation assumes normal performance of the job by a typical worker. Hence, job evaluation ignores individual abilities of the job holder. Job ranking is thus the product of job evaluation and it is used to determine the organization's pay structure. The external factors such as collective bargaining and individual skill differences may require a compromise between job evaluation ranking and the actual pay structure, yet even such compromises are necessary. Job evaluation can provide an objective standard from which modifications can be made.

Definitions

1. According to **Edwin B. Flippo** "*Job evaluation is a systematic and orderly process of determining the worth of a job in relation to other jobs.*"
2. According to **Wendell French** "*Job evaluation is a process of determining the relative worth of the various jobs within the organization, so that differential wages may be paid to jobs of different worth.*"
3. According to **Dale Yoder** "*Job evaluation is a practice which seeks to provide a degree of objectivity in measuring the organization value of jobs within organization and among similar organizations.*"
4. According to **Kimball and Kimball** "*Job evaluation is an effort to determine the relative value of every job in a plant to determine what the fair basic wage for such a job should be.*"
5. According to **Bureau of Labour Statistics** "*Job evaluation is the evaluation or rating of jobs to determine their position in the job hierarchy. The evaluation may be achieved*

through the assignment of points or the use of some other systematic method for essential job requirements, such as skills, experience and responsibility."

6. According to **ILO** "*Job evaluation may be defined simply as an attempt to determine and compare the demands which the normal performance of a particular job makes on normal workers without taking into account the individual abilities or performance of the workers concerned.*"

Features or the Nature of Job Evaluation

From the definitions given above following important characteristics of job evaluation are discovered:

- Job evaluation is to determine the value of each job in relation to all jobs within the organization.
- Job evaluation is ranking of jobs, not people.
- The standard of job evaluation is relative, not absolute.
- Job evaluation is done on the basis of information from job analysis.
- Job evaluation is also affected to some extent by external factors such as collective bargaining and individual skill differences.
- Job evaluation has some element of subjectivity.
- Job evaluation provides only the basis for evaluating a rational wage structure.

OBJECTIVES AND IMPORTANCE OF JOB EVALUATION

As per ***ILO*** *norms*, following are the main objectives of job evaluation:

(i) To *secure and maintain* complete, accurate and impersonal descriptions of each distinct job or occupation in the entire plant;

(ii) To *provide a standard procedure* for determining the relative worth of each job in a plant;

(iii) To *determine the rate of pay* for each job which is fair and equitable with relation to other jobs in the plant, community or industry;

(iv) To ensure that right *wages* are paid to all qualified employees for like work;

(v) To promote *a fair and accurate* consideration of all employees for advancement and transfer;

(vi) To *provide a factual basis* for the consideration of wage rates for similar jobs in a community and in an industry; and

(vii) To *provide information for work organization*, employees' selection, placement, training and numerous other similar problems.

In fact, the primary purpose of job evaluation is to set wages and salary on the basis of the relative work or jobs in the organizations.

Importance of Job Evaluation

Knowles and Thomson state, that job evaluation is useful in eliminating many of the evils to which nearly all systems of wage and salary payments are subject. Following are the points of importance for job evaluation:

(i) Payment of high wages and salaries of persons who hold jobs and positions not requiring great skill, effort and responsibilities;
(ii) Paying beginners less than they are entitled to receive in terms of what is required of them;
(iii) Giving a raise to persons whose performance does not justify the raise;
(iv) Deciding rates of pay on the basis of seniority rather than ability;
(v) Payment of widely varied wages and salary for the same or closely related jobs and positions;
(vi) Payment of unequal wages and salaries on the basis of race, sex, religion or political differences;
(vii) Job evaluation helps in keeping down the cost of recruitment and selection of workers; and
(viii) It helps in keeping down the rate of turnover as wages are determined systematically.

It may, however, be noted that a job evaluation system does not accomplish all the purposes: rather it facilitates them. Basically, it provides a systematic catalogue of the jobs in an organization, which is indispensable for management purposes.

PROCESS OF JOB EVALUATION

Job evaluation process starts with defining the objectives of evaluation and ends with wage and salary differentials as is shown in Figure 10.1.:

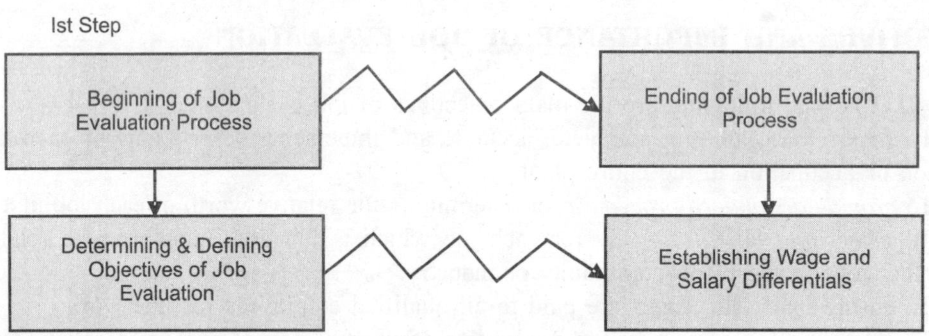

Fig. 10.1. Beginning and Ending of Job Evaluation.

In between the first and last stage there are many other steps. The main objective of job evaluation is to establish satisfactory wage and salary differentials. Several questions have to be answered in this process. These questions are:

- Which jobs are to be evaluated?
- Who should evaluate the jobs?
- What type of training is required?
- How much time is involved?
- What is the criteria of evaluation?
- What methods of evaluation to be employed?

Complete process of evaluation is shown in Figure 10.2.

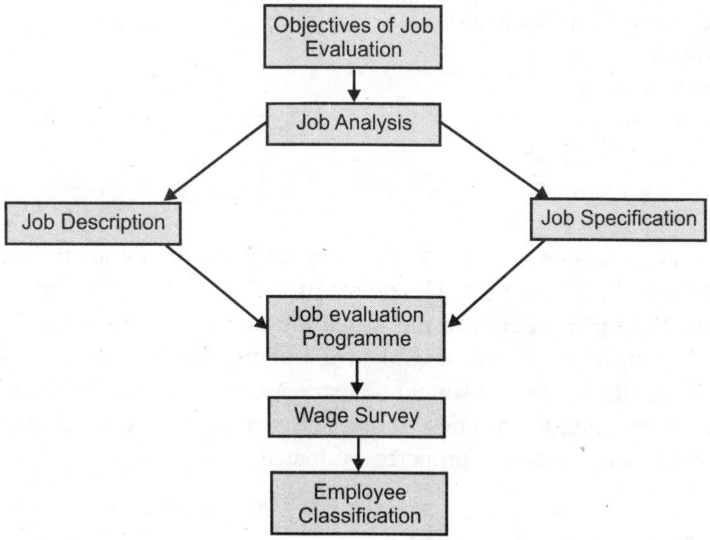

Fig. 10.2. The Process of Job Evaluation.

Following are the sequential steps in the job evaluation process:

1. **Step I: Selling the Guiding Objectives:** Before starting any programme of job evaluation, the top management must explain the aims and uses of the programme to the employees and unions. For this purpose, conferences, letters and booklets can be used for explaining the aims and benefits of job evaluation.
2. **Step II: Constituting Job Evaluation Committee:** As mentioned earlier, job evaluation is done by groups of individuals and not by individuals. Therefore, a committee consisting of experienced and respected representatives of management and workers and outside experts should be constituted, to set the ball rolling.
3. **Step III: Selection of Key Jobs for Evaluation**: It may not be possible to evaluate each and every job due to time and cost constraints. Thus, certain key jobs may be identified in each department. The key jobs are evaluated in detail and the other jobs are compared with the key jobs. While selecting the jobs, care must be taken to ensure that they represent the type of work performed in that department.
4. **Step IV: Job Description**: Job description is very useful in job evaluation process because it defines the title of the job analyses the job into its constituent tasks and records why, how and when these are done, states the responsibilities involved and conditions of employment for each job. Such grouping of information is very essential for evaluating the job.
5. **Step V: Selecting the Method of Evaluation**: Several methods of job evaluation are there, but the method most appropriate to the job and the organization is chosen in this step. More than one method may be used to increase the accuracy of evaluation.
6. **Step VI: Classification of Jobs:** The relative worth of various jobs in an organization may be found out after arranging jobs in order of importance. The criteria used may be:

- Skills—mental and manual
- Experience
- Efforts and initiative
- Working conditions
- Responsibilities involved
- Supervision required

Weights may be assigned to each such factor. When finally all the weights are added, the worth of a job is determined. The points may then be converted into monetary values.

7. **Step VII: Installing the Programme**: Once the evaluation process is over and a plan of action is ready, management must explain it to the employees and put it into operation.
8. **Step VIII: Periodic Review**: It should be made a permanent post of the evaluation process as it will keep updating the job description and can be used to satisfy the employees who believe that this work was not properly evaluated.

Job Evaluation Process in India

The National Institute of Personnel Management laid down the following five steps which should be taken to install a job evaluation programme:

1. **Analyze and Prepare Job Description:** This requires the preparation of a job description and also an analysis of job requirements for successful performance.
2. **Select and Prepare a Job Evaluation Plan:** This means that a job must be broken down into its component parts, i.e., it should involve the selection of factors, elements needed for the performance of all jobs for which money is paid, determining their value and preparing written instructions for evaluation.
3. **Classify Jobs:** This requires grouping for arranging jobs in a correct sequence in terms of value to the firm, and relating them to the money terms in order to ascertain their relative value.
4. **Install the Programme:** This involves explaining it to employees and putting it into operation.
5. **Maintain the Programme:** Jobs cannot continue without updating new jobs and job changes in obedience to changing conditions and situations.

ADVANTAGES OF JOB EVALUATION

An ILO, publication claims following advantages for job evaluation:

1. **Logical and Objective Methods of Job Ranking:** Job evaluation is a logical and, to some extent, an objective method of ranking jobs relative to one another. It may help in removing inequalities in existing wage structures and in maintaining sound and consistent wage differentials in a plant or industry.
2. **Job Fixation in Existing Wage Structure:** In the case of new jobs, the method often facilitates fitting them into the existing wage structure.
3. **Helpful in Removing Grievances:** The method helps in removing grievances arising out of relative wages; and it improves labour-management relations and workers' morale. In

providing a yardstick, by which workers' complaints or claims can be judged, the method simplifies discussion of wages to be explained and justified.

4. **Objective Basis of Negotiations:** The method replaces the many accidental factors, occurring in less systematic procedures, of wage bargaining by more impersonal and objective standards, thus establishing a clear basis for negotiations.
5. **Bring Uniformity and Simplification in Wage Administration:** The method may lead to greater uniformity in wage rates, thus simplifying wage administration.
6. **Improves Selection, Promotion and Transfer Procedures:** The information collected in the process of job description and analysis, may also be used for the improvement of selection, transfer, and promotion procedures on the basis of comparative job requirements.
7. **Ensures Efficient Use of Plant Labour:** Such information also reveals that workers are engaged in jobs requiring less skill and other qualities than they possess, thereby pointing to the possibility of making more efficient use of the labour.
8. **Sound Basis of Bonus Schemes:** It also helps in providing sound basis for bonus schemes and helps in job classification and work simplification.

METHODS OF JOB EVALUATION

Job evaluation methods are divided into two main categories and each category comprises two methods each as is shown in Figure 10.3.

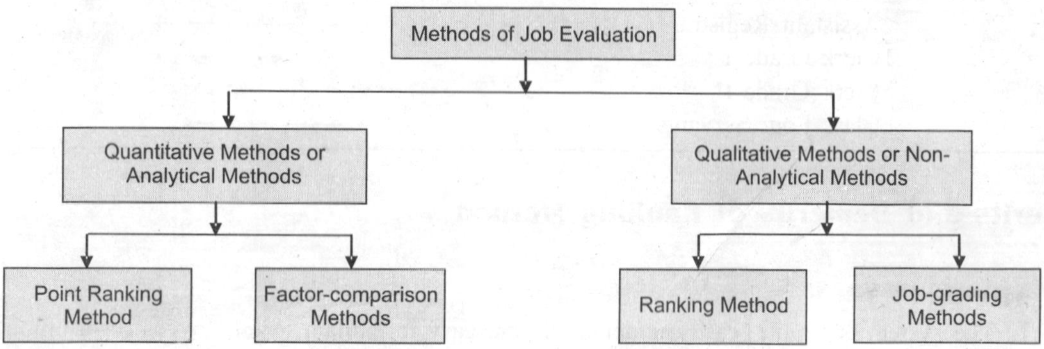

Fig. 10.3. Methods of Job Evaluation.

1. Point Ranking Method

In this analytical method all jobs are ranked in order of their importance and each successive job being higher or lower than the previous one in the sequence. A constituted committee ranks the jobs. Following five steps are involved in point ranking system:

Step 1: Preparation of Job Description: The first step is preparation of job description, particularly when the ranking of jobs is done by different individuals and there is disagreement among them.

Step 2: Selection of Raters: Jobs may be usually ranked by department or in 'Clusters' (i.e., factory workers, clerical workers, menials, etc). This eliminates need for directly comparing factory jobs and clerical jobs. Most organizations use a committee of raters.

Step 3: Selection of Rates and Key Jobs: Usually a series of key jobs or benchmark jobs (10 to 20 jobs, which include all major departments and functions) are first rated; then the other jobs are roughly compared with these key jobs to establish a rough rating.

Step 4: Ranking of all Jobs: Each job is then compared in detail with other similar jobs to establish its exact rank in the scale. For this each rater may be given a set of 'index card,' each of which contains a brief description of a job. These jobs are then ranked from 'the lowest to the highest' or from 'the highest to the lowest' are ranked first and then the next highest and the next lowest and so forth until all the cards have been ranked.

Step 5: Preparation of Job Classification from the Rating: The total ranking is divided into an appropriate number of groups or classifications, usually 8 to 12. All the jobs within a single group or classification receive the same wage or range of rates.

Illustration

Ranking of University Personnel

Ranking Order	Pay Scale Range
Professor	______
Associate Professors	______
Assistant Professors	______
Registrar	______
Dy. Registrar	______
Assistant Registrar	______
Clerk Grade I	______
Clerk Grade II	______
Class Four Servants	______

Merits and Demerits of Ranking Method

Merits

1. The system is simple, easily understood, and easy to explain to employees (or a union). Therefore, it is suitable for small organizations with clearly defined jobs.
2. It is far less expensive to put into effect than other systems, and requires little effort for maintenance.
3. It requires less time, fewer forms and less work, unless it is carried to a detailed point used by company.

Demerits

1. As there is no standard for an analysis of the whole job position, different bases of comparison between rates occur. The process is initially based on judgement and, therefore, tends to be influenced by a variety of personal biases.
2. Specific job requirements (such as skill, effort and responsibility) are not normally analyzed separately. Often a rater's judgement is strongly influenced by present wage rates.

3. The system merely produces a job order and does not indicate to what extent it is more important than the one below it. It only gives us its rank or tells us that it is higher or more difficult than another; but it does not indicate how much higher or more difficult.

2. Factor Comparison Method

Factor comparison method is a combination of ranking and point ranking method of job evaluation. It was first developed by **E.J. Benge** in 1926. Under this method the relative rank of the jobs is evaluated in relation to monetary scale. Some key jobs are selected at the first instance and then ranked by considering one factor at a time. In this method five factors are generally evaluated for each job. These factors are: *mental requirements, skill, physical requirements, responsibilities and working conditions.*

Following steps are taken under factor comparison method:

Step I: Factors to be used: The first thing to be done under this method is the selection of factors to be used for evaluation. The persons writing job descriptions should be given the proper definitions of these factors. Universally used factors are:

- mental requirements
- physical requirements
- skill requirements
- responsibility and
- working conditions

Step II: Selection of Key Jobs: The selection of key jobs is important in this method. These are to be taken as a standard and all other jobs are to be compared with key jobs evaluation. All key jobs should be exact and well understood and there should be no conflict between the management and the employees about them. The jobs so selected should cover the range from lowest to the highest paid ones. Generally, 10 to 25 jobs are picked up as key jobs.

Step III: Ranking of Key Jobs: All the members of job evaluation committee rank various jobs on the basis of each of the five factors given earlier. A meeting of the committee is called to evolve a consensus on each job.

Step IV: Valuing the Factors: Each factor of key job is then allocated a basic pay. The pay for such jobs should range from the lowest to the highest.

Step V: Comparison of Jobs: All jobs are compared with key job factor by factor to determine their relative importance and position in the scale of jobs. The money value of jobs is also determined with this comparison.

Step VI: Establishing Wage Structure: By assigning money value to each factor of various jobs, a wage structure is determined by summing up these values.

The following example in Table 10.1 will clearly show how the system works:

Suppose job E and job A are similar in skill (Rs. 3.00), job B in responsibility (Rs. 0.85); job C in effort (Rs. 1.40); and job D in working condition (Rs. 1.20); then its correct rate of pay will be Rs. 6.45, i.e., the sum total of all.

Table 10.1: Key Jobs, Job Factors and Correct Rates of Jobs

Job Facto	Job A Correct Rate: Rs. 20	Job B Correct Rate: Rs. 16	Job C Correct Rate: Rs. 14	Job D Correct Rate: Rs. 12	Job E Correct Rate: Rs. 24
1 Skill	10	8	7.50	5	11
2. Effort	5	3	4	4	6
3. Responsibility	3	1	1	1	4
4. Working Conditions	2	4	1.50	2	3

This system is usually used to evaluate white collar, professional and managerial positions.

Merits

1. It is a systematic, quantifiable method for which detailed step-by-step instructions are available.
2. Jobs are compared to other jobs to determine a relative value.
3. It is a fairly easy system to explain to employees.
4. There are no limits to the value which may be assigned to each factor.
5. The plan does not require a translation from points to money. It involves a comparative process wherein jobs are priced against other jobs rather than against some established numerical scale.
6. The reliability and validity of the system are greater than the same statistical measures obtained from group standardized job analysis plans.

3. Ranking Method

This is the most widely used method of job evaluation. It involves number of factors to be considered in each job. The degree of each factor is also determined for assigning points. The points of different jobs are then converted into money value or wage rates:

This method involves the following steps for job evaluation:

Step I: Type of Jobs to be evaluated: There are a number of jobs in every organization and these may range from top executive to unskilled ones. Similar jobs should be put in the same category for evaluation purpose. There should be separate evaluation programme for each class because the factors influencing them will be different. The job requirement of supervisor will be different from that of an unskilled worker.

Step II: Number of Factors to be used: It is very difficult to select the number of factors to be used for evaluating a job. The number of factors should be such that all aspects of a job are evaluated. The number of factors to be used varies from company to company, ranking from 3 to as many as 50. The common factors to be selected are education, training, skills, physical ability, mental requirement, responsibility, job conditions, etc.

Step III: Determination of Degrees: Each factor of evaluation should be further subdivided into degrees for example, experience which is a commonly used factor in each job may be subdivided into five degrees. The first degree may have experience of 2 to 6 months with 5 points, second degree points having experience from 6 months to 1 year with 10 points, 15 for experience between 1 and 2 years, 20 points for experience of 2 to 4 years and 25 points for experience of over 4 years.

Step IV: Assigning of Weights: Each factor may be assigned a weight as per its importance. For executives, mental requirements will have more weight than physical requirements.

Step V: Assigning Money Values to Points: The points assigned to each factor are added up for finding out the value of job. The values of jobs are translated into terms of money with a predetermined formula. The following type of formula may be used:

Point Range	Pay Scale	Rs. Grade
50-100	700-1600	1
100-150	1200-2000	2
150-200	1500-2500	3
200-250	2200-4000	4

Merits

1. It gives us a numerical basis for wage differentials.
2. The scale, once decided can be used for a fairly long time.
3. A job can easily be evaluated in money terms as these are assigned according to points.
4. The system of job evaluation being systematic and objective is more acceptable to workers.
5. The element of human bias is minimized.
6. The method is useful even if the number of jobs is very large. The system enjoys stability so far as the factors remain relevant.
7. The method is more accurate as compared to earlier methods.

Demerits

1. The use of this method involves high costs; it can be used only by giant concerns.
2. The task of defining job factors and then degree of factors is a time-consuming proposition.
3. The selection of factors and then sub-factors is a difficult task.
4. The allotting of marks to various factors and sub-factors is also a difficult task. The following example in Table 10.1 will clearly show how the system works: Suppose job E and job A are similar in skill (Rs. 3.00), job B in responsibility (Rs. 0.85); job C in effort (Rs. 1.40); and job D in working condition (Rs. 1.20); then its correct rate of pay will be Rs. 6.45, i.e., the sum total of all.

4. Job-Grading Method

The following steps are involved in the grading system:

1. **Preparation of Job Description:** It gives us the basic job information usually derived from a job analysis.
2. **Preparation of Grade Descriptions:** The first thing to be done in this method is to prepare grade description to evolve classification of jobs. A number of grades, different from each other, are selected. The grading should be done by considering the nature of duties of the job, supervising responsibilities, etc. Each job is then, attached to an appropriate grade. For grade description information about various jobs is collected through job descriptions.

3. **Selection of Grades and Key Jobs:** A number of jobs are graded, normally between 10 and 20, are selected. Key jobs are selected from important functions and major departments.
4. **Grading the Key Jobs:** Key jobs are assigned to an appropriate grade level and their relationship to each other studied.
5. **Classification of Fall Jobs:** For example, all menial jobs put in one class, clerical jobs in another class, and technical jobs in still other class, and so on. The jobs in one class receive the same wage rates.

Illustration

Job Classification Schedule

Grade	Description of Job Classification
I	Very simple tasks requiring minimum mental ability. Basically consisting of manual work.
II	Jobs requiring only clerical work and minimum manual work. Minimum training required.
III	Simple but requiring ability to apply established procedures and to guide others.
IV	Routine work but involving some element of responsibility for answering non-routine queries and exercising some measure of control over a small group of staff.
V	Jobs in this grade involve decision-making and administrative work. Professional qualifications are required.

Merits

1. This method is simple to operate and understand, for it does not take much time or require technical help.
2. The use of fully described job classes meets the need for employing systematic criteria in ordering jobs to their importance. Since many workers think of jobs in, or related to, clusters or groups, this method makes it easier for them to understand rankings.
3. If an organization consists of 400 people holding to different jobs, the jobs might be broken up into perhaps 4 classes, arranged in order of importance from high to low, and described class by class. This class description broadly reflects level of education, mental skill, profit impact or some combination of these.
4. The grouping of jobs into classifications, makes pay determination problems administratively easier to handle. Pay grades are determined for, and assigned to, all the job classification.
5. It is used in important government services and operates efficiently; but it is rarely used in an industry.

Demerits

This system suffers from the following defects:

1. Although it represents an advance in accuracy over the ranking method, it still leaves much to be desired because personal evaluations by executives (unskilled in such work) establish the major classes, and determine into which classes each job should be placed.

2. Since no detailed analysis of a job is done, the judgement in respect of a whole range of jobs may produce an incorrect classification.
3. It is relatively difficult to write a grade description. The system becomes difficult to operate as the number of jobs increases.
4. It is difficult to know how much of a job's rank is influenced by the man on the job.

PRINCIPLES OF JOB EVALUATION PROGRAMME

There are certain broad principles, which should be kept in mind before putting the job evaluation programme into practice. **According to A.L. Kress**, these principles are:

1. Rate the job and not the man. Each element should be rated on the basis of what the job itself requires.
2. The elements selected for rating purposes should be easily explainable in terms and as few in number as will cover the necessary requisites for every job without any overlapping.
3. The elements should be clearly defined and properly selected.
4. Any job rating plan must be shown to foremen and employees. The success in selling it will depend on a clear-cut explanation and illustration of the plan.
5. Foremen should participate in the rating of jobs in their own departments.
6. Maximum cooperation can be obtained from employees when they themselves have an opportunity to discuss job ratings.
7. In talking to foremen and employees any discussion of valve should be avoided.
8. Too many occupational wages should not be established. It should be unwise to adopt an occupational wage for each total of point valves.

LIMITATIONS OF JOB EVALUATION

Job evaluation system suffers from the following problems:

1. Human bias cannot altogether be eliminated from any job evaluation method even if efforts are made to make it systematic. The element of human judgement is present in all the methods of job evaluation.
2. The factors selected for job evaluation sometimes overlap. The weightage given to them and their reliability becomes questionable.
3. Job evaluation will have to be done regularly because the factors selected for it today may not remain valid tomorrow because of technological changes.
4. There are apprehensions in the minds of employees when job evaluation is introduced for the first time. It may create doubts in the minds of those whose jobs are evaluated.
5. Job evaluation programme takes long time and requires specialized technical personnel.
6. The introduction of job evaluation scheme may require substantial changes in the present set up. This change may be a costly affair and the concern may not be able to bear this financial burden.
7. This system is suitable to big concerns only because it is very expensive.

MEANING OF COMPENSATION

An extensive review of the literature indicates that important work related variables leading to job satisfaction include challenging work, interesting job assignments, equitable compensation, competent supervision and rewarding careers. Employees aspire a judicious compensation system that commensurates with their skills and expectations. Before exploring various aspects of compensation, let us first discuss what compensation is?

Compensation is the remuneration an employee receives in return for his or her contribution to the organization. Remuneration occupies an important place in the life of an employee. His or her standard of living in the society, motivation, loyalty, and productivity depend upon the remuneration he or she receives. For the employer too, employee remuneration is significant because of its contribution to the cost of production. Besides, many battles (in the form of strikes and lockouts) are fought between the employer and the employees on issues relating to wages or bonus. For HRM too, employee compensation is a major function. The HR specialist has a difficult task of fixing wages and wage differentials acceptable to employees and their leaders. Since employee remuneration is such an important subject, considerable space is devoted in books and periodicals for detailed discussion of wage-related and salary-related problems. This book is no exception.

Definitions

- According to **Thomas Patten,** "*Employee compensation refers to all forms of pay or rewards going to employees and arising from their employment.*"
- According to **Scott Snell & George Bohlander,** "*Employee compensation includes all forms of pay and rewards received by employees for the performance of their jobs. Direct compensation encourages employees' wages and salaries, incentives, bonuses and commissions. Indirect compensation comprises the benefits supplied by employers and non-financial compensation includes employees' recognition programmes, rewarding jobs, organizational support, work environment and flexible work norms to accommodate personal needs.*"
- In the words of **C.B. Mamoria,** "*Compensation may be defined as money received in the performance of work, plus many kinds of benefits and services that organization provides their employees.*"

Components of Compensation

Compensation may be classified into two forms:

(i) Base or primary compensation
(ii) Supplementary compensation

The primary compensation refers as to basic pay in the form of wages and salaries. It is a fixed and non-incentive payment on the basis of time spent on the job. Supplementary compensation consists of incentives and variable payments, based upon either individual output or output of the group as a whole.

The components of compensation or remuneration are as under:

1. **Wages or Salary**: Wages represent hourly rates of pay, and salary refers to the monthly rate of pay, irrespective of the number of hours put in by an employee. Wages and salaries are subject to annual increments. They differ from employee to employee and depend upon the nature of job, seniority, and merit.
2. **Incentives:** Also called 'payments by results', incentives are paid in addition to wages and salaries. Incentives depend upon productivity, sales, profit, or cost reduction efforts. There are:
   (i) Individual incentive schemes
   (ii) Group incentive programmes. Individual incentives are applicable to specific employee performance. Where a given task demands group effort for completion, incentives are paid to the group as a whole. The amount is later divided among group members on an equitable basis.
3. **Fringe Benefits:** These include such employee benefits as provident fund, gratuity fund, medical care, hospitalization, accident relief, health and group insurance, canteen uniform, recreation and the like.
4. **Perquisites:** These are allowed to executives and include company car, club membership, paid holidays, furnished house, stock option schemes and the like. Perquisites are offered to retain competent executives.
5. **Non-monetary Benefits:** These include challenging job responsibilities, recognition of merit, growth prospects, and competent supervision.

Figure 10.4 illustrates the various components of employee compensation.

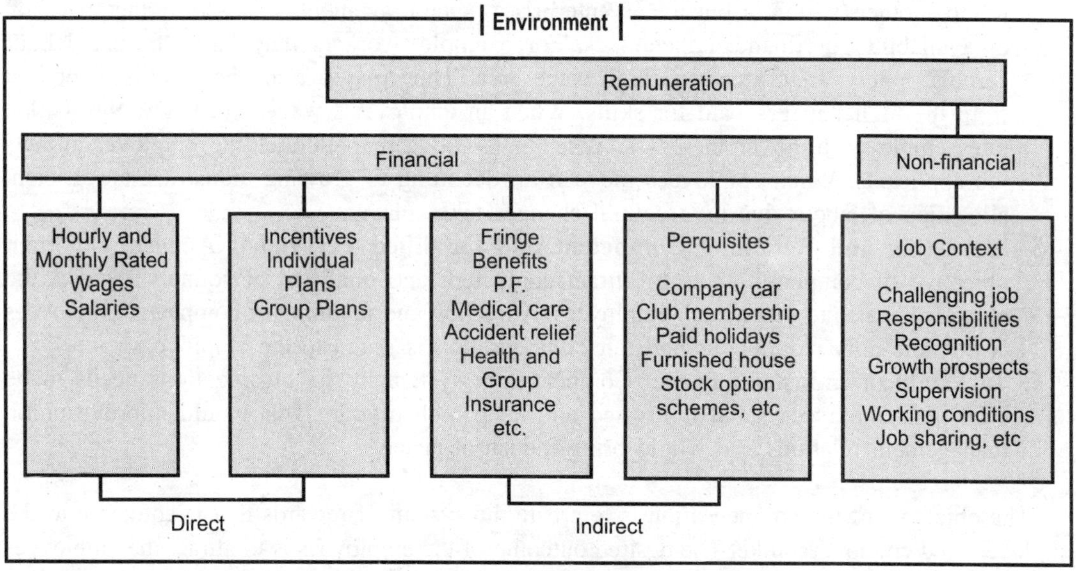

Fig. 10.4. Components of Employee Compensation.
Source: Adapted from K. Aswathappa, Human Resource Management, Tata McGraw-Hill Publishing Company Ltd., New Delhi, 2008, p. 286.

OBJECTIVES OF COMPENSATION

Compensation may have one or more objectives, which may often be in conflict with each other. The objectives can be classified as under:

1. **Establishing Equity:** The first important objective is equity, which may take several forms. They include income distribution through narrowing of inequalities, increasing the wages of the lowest paid employees, protecting real wages (purchasing power), the concept of equal pay for work of equal value. Even pay differentials based on differences in skills or contribution are all related to the concept of equity.
2. **Efficiency Objective:** A second objective is efficiency, which is often closely related to equity because the two concepts are fully consistent. Efficiency objectives are reflected in attempts to link a part of wages to productivity or profit, group or individual performance, acquisition and application of skills, and so on. Arrangements to achieve efficiency may be seen also as being equitable if they fairly reward performance or inequitable if the reward is viewed as unfair.
3. **Macroeconomic Stability:** A third objective is macroeconomic stability through high employment levels and low inflation, for instance. An inordinately high minimum wage would have an adverse impact on levels of employment, though at what level this consequence would occur is a matter of much debate. Though pay and pay policies are only one of the factors which impinge on macroeconomic stability, they do contribute to (or impede) balanced and sustainable economic development.
4. **Efficient Allocation of Labour:** A fourth objective is the efficient allocation of labour in the labour market. This implies that employees would move to wherever they receive a net gain; such movement may be from one geographical location to another or from one job to another (within or outside an enterprise). Such movement is caused by the provision or availability of financial incentives. For example, workers may move from a labour surplus or low wage area to a high wage area. They may acquire new skills to benefit from the higher wages paid for skills. When an employer's wages are below the market rates employee turnover increases. When it is above market rates the employer attracts job applicants. When employees move from declining to growing industries, an efficient allocation of labour due to structural changes takes place.
5. **Attracting and Retaining Competent and Qualified Personnel:** Another important objective of compensation is to attract competent and qualified personnel. Besides, the objective is also to retain such employees. Attracting and retaining of competent employees is possible only if judicious and fair compensation is given to the employees.
6. **To Establish Industrial Peace:** Compensation system in the organizations needs to be such that employees stand motivated and keep high morale. This would improve union management relations and would bring industrial peace.

The objective of the compensation is to create the system of rewards that is equitable to the employers and employees alike. The desired outcome of the employees is to attract the employees towards the tasks and motivated to do the good job for the employer. The compensation policy depends on certain criteria below:

1. **Adequate:** Minimal governmental, union and managerial levels should be met.
2. **Equitable:** Each person should be paid fairly, in the line with his or her effort, abilities and training.

Objectives According to D. S. Beach

- To recruit competent persons for a firm.
- To control payroll costs
- To satisfy people to reduce the incidence of quitting, grievances and fractions over pay and
- To motivate people to perform better.

Compensation Goals According to Scott Snell & George Bohlander

Increasingly, compensation specialists speak of value-added compensation. A value-added compensation programme, also called value-chain compensation, is one in which the components of the compensation package (benefits, base pay, incentives, and so on), both separately and in combination, create value for the organization and its employees. Using a value-added viewpoint, managers ask questions such as "*How does this compensation practice benefit the organization?*" and "*Does the benefit offset the administrative cost?*" Payments that fail to advance either the employee or the organization are removed from the compensation programme.

It is not uncommon for organizations to establish very specific goals for joining their organizational objectives to their compensation programme. Formalized compensation goals serve as guidelines for managers to ensure that wage and benefit policies achieve their intended purpose. The more common goals of a strategic compensation policy include the following:

- To reward employees' past performance
- To remain competitive in the labour market
- To maintain salary equity among employees
- To mesh employees' future performance with organizational goals
- To control the compensation budget
- To attract new employees
- To reduce unnecessary turnover

To achieve these goals, policies must be established to guide the management in making decisions. Formal statements of compensation policies typically include the following:

1. The rate of pay within the organization and whether it is to be above, below, or at the prevailing market rate.
2. The ability of the pay programme to gain employee acceptance while motivating employees to perform to the best of their abilities.
3. The pay level at which employees may be recruited and the pay differential between new and more senior employees.
4. The intervals at which pay raises are to be granted and the extent to which merit and/or seniority will influence the raises.
5. The pay levels needed to facilitate the achievement of a sound financial position in relation to the products or services offered.

IMPORTANCE OF IDEAL COMPENSATION SYSTEM

Compensation management is the most important factor in HRM. Sound compensation system is a prerequisite for industrial harmony and basis of attracting and retaining right personnel in right positions. For effective compensation policy, an organization has to balance fairly, financial and non-financial rewards. It must be consistent with the principle of equity and equity with job content. In countries like India, remuneration must fulfil the expectations and aspirations of employees and exploit their energies for the benefit of organizations. The following points are enough to highlight the importance of ideal compensation system.

1. Attractive remuneration/compensation enables organization to attract competent people. That is why Infosys, HUL, Reliance attract brilliant and talented MBA's and engineers.
2. Retention of competent personnel is also possible through sound compensation policy of the organization.
3. Loyalty towards an organization depends upon his or her perceptions about remuneration.
4. There is a sense of equity when the employees are paid remuneration equal or more than the remuneration received by others in the same category of jobs.

If adequate compensation is not given, the employees agitate, use foul language, turn violent, fall sick, etc. as is shown in Figure 10.5.

5. Employees get motivated to perform better when their past performance is rewarded adequately. Figures 10.5 and 10.6 show the performance model of motivation. Employees set expectations about rewards and compensation to be received if certain levels of performance are achieved. These expectations determine goals or levels of performance

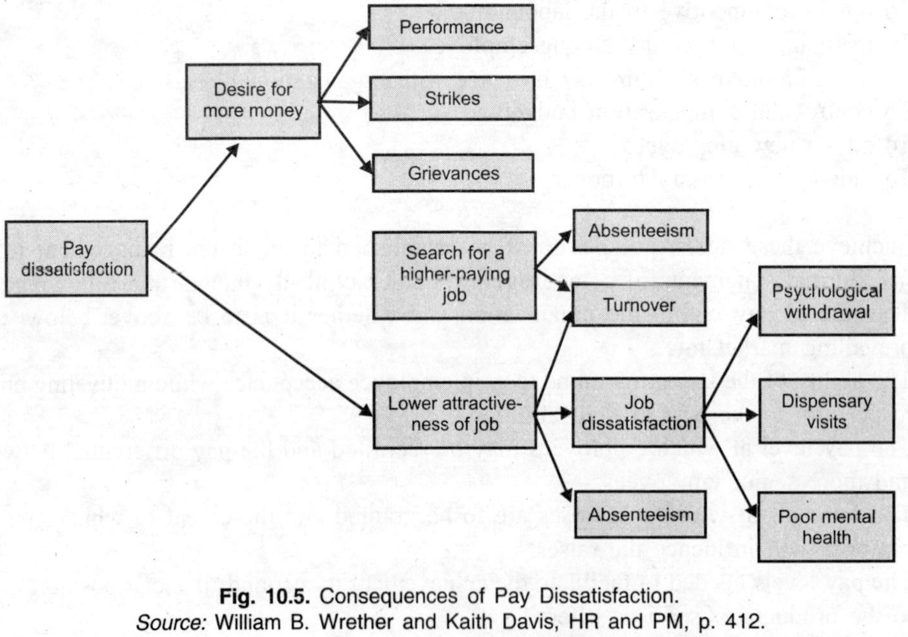

Fig. 10.5. Consequences of Pay Dissatisfaction.
Source: William B. Wrether and Kaith Davis, HR and PM, p. 412.

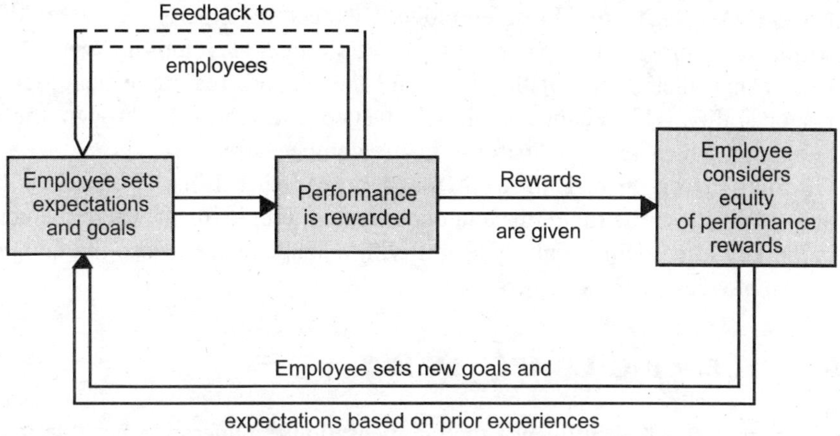

Fig. 10.6. Motivation and Performance Model.
Source: Michael R. Carrell, *et al.*, Personnel/Human Resource Management, p. 391.

for the future. Employees expect suitable compensation and management gives reward as per expectations employees further set higher future goals.

6. Effective compensation policy brings industrial peace as maximum industrial conflicts between employees and employers take place on remuneration related issues. Table 10.2 shows it clearly.

Table 10.2: Percentage of Remuneration Related Issues to Total Disputes

Year	Disputes Relating to Wages, Allowances and Bonus	Total Disputes	Percentage of Remuneration Related Issues to Total Disputes
1985	506	1755	28.83
1986	633	1892	33.45
1987	619	1799	34.40
1988	590	1745	33.81
1989	533	1786	29.84
1990	514	1825	28.16

Source: Labour Bureau, Indian Labour Year Books

7. Most HR practices such as performance appraisal training, career development and labour-management relations are closely related to compensation. This is explained as under:
   (i) Compensation and Performance Appraisal: Accurate performance appraisal is the key to effective merit pay programme. Or merit pay programme to succeed, the employees must know that their efforts towards meeting production quotas and quality standards may raise the pay of the employees. Moreover, the employees must have the strong relationship between attaining performance standards and receiving pay increases. Administering merit pay system requires a sound performance appraisal practices.
   (ii) Compensation and Training: When training is well designed, the employee should be able to learn the skills needed to increase their pay, as well as the skills necessary to each or coach other employees in the organization.

(iii) **Career Development:** Most employees expect to experience career development within their present companies. Employee's career develops in two different ways, i.e., change their focus of the work and the second, maintain their focus and more responsibility. This change exhibits advancement upwards through the company's hierarchy, which leads to increase in the compensation.

(iv) **Compensation and Labour-Management Relations**: Collective bargaining agreements describe the terms and conditions of employment where the compensation is the key issue. Unions always fight with management to raise the compensation of the employees in the organization.

FACTORS INFLUENCING COMPENSATION

There are several factors which influence the compensation/remuneration payable to employees. These factors can be categorized into two parts:

A. External Factors
B. Internal Factors

Figure 10.7 shows the details of these factors:

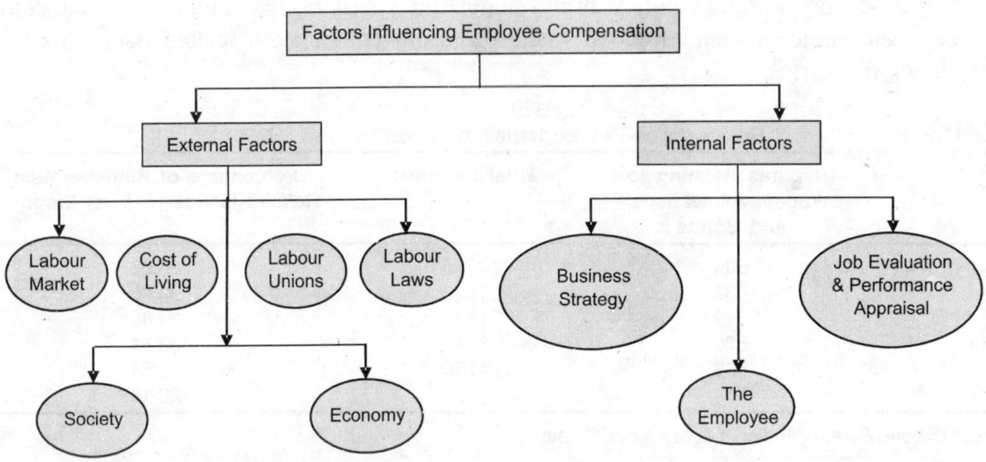

Fig. 10.7. Factors Influencing Employee Compensation.

A. External Factors

1. **Labour Market**: Demand and supply of labour influence wage and salary fixation. A higher wage has to be paid when the demand exceeds supply, in case of skilled labour. Going rate of pay is another labour-related factor influencing employee remuneration. The going rate system involves fixing wage/salary rates in tune with what is paid by different units of an industry in a locality. Going rates are generally paid in the initial stages of plant operations. Productivity of labour also influences wage fixation. This is when the productivity increases due to advanced technology better methods of production. But it is not acceptable that productivity will always increase if linked to remuneration.

2. **Cost of Living**: Next in importance to labour market is the cost of living. This criterion matters during periods of rising prices, and is forgotten when prices are stable or falling. The justification for cost of living as a criterion for wage fixation is that the real wages of workers should not be allowed to be whittled down by price increases. A rise in the cost of living is sought to be compensated by payment of dearness allowance, basic pay to remain undisturbed.
3. **Labour Unions**: The presence or absence of labour organizations often determines the quantum of wages paid to employees. Employers in non-unionized factories enjoy the freedom to fix wages and salaries as they please. Because of large-scale unemployment, these employers hire workers at little or even less than legal minimum wages. The employees' of strongly unionized companies too, have no freedom in wage and, salary fixation. They are forced to yield to the pressure of labour representatives in determining and revising pay scales.
4. **Labour Laws**: We have a number of labour laws at the Central as well as the State levels. Some of the Central laws which have a bearing on employee remuneration are the Payment of Wages Act, 1936; the Minimum Wages Act, 1948; the Payment of Bonus Act, 1965; Equal Remuneration Act, 1976; and the Payment of Gratuity Act, 1972. The Payment of Wages Act was passed to regulate payment of wages to certain classes of persons employed in the industry. It also seeks to protect workers against irregularities in payment of wages and unauthorized deductions by the employers. In addition, the Act ensures payment of wages in a particular form and at regular intervals. The Minimum Wage Act enables the central and the state governments to fix minimum rates of wages payable to employees in sweated industries. The Payment of Bonus Act provides for payment of a specified rate of bonus to employees in certain establishments. The Gratuity Act provides for payment of gratuity to employees after they attain superannuation. The Equal Remuneration Act provides for payment of equal remuneration to men and women workers for same or similar work. The Act stipulated stringent punishments for contravention of its provision.

   In addition to legal enactments, there are wage boards, tribunals and fair wages committees which aim at providing a decent standard of living to workers. In fact, ours is the only democratic country in the world which has attempted wage regulations on so large a scale through state-sponsored agencies.
5. **Society:** Remuneration paid to employees has social implications too. The Supreme Court has been keeping social and ethical considerations in adjudicating wage and salary disputes.
6. **The Economy**: Economy too constitutes an important external factor that has its impact on wage and salary fixation. In most cases, the cost of living will rise in an expanding economy. Since the cost of living is commonly used as a pay standard, the economy's health exerts a major impact upon pay decisions. Labour unions, the government, and the society are all less likely to press for pay increases in a depressed economy.

B. Internal Factors

Following internal factors too affect the compensation structure:

1. **Business Strategy**: The overall strategy which a company pursues should determine the remuneration to its employees. When the strategy of the enterprise is to achieve rapid

growth, remuneration should be higher than what the competitors pay. Where the strategy is to maintain and protect current earnings, because of the declining fortunes of the company, remuneration level needs to be average or even below average.

2. **Job Evaluation and Performance Appraisal**: Job evaluation helps establish satisfactory wage differentials among jobs. Performance appraisal helps award pay increases to employees who show improved performance.
3. **The Employee**: Several employee-related factors interact to determine his or her remuneration. These include performance, seniority, experience, potential, and even sheer luck.
4. **Performance is always rewarded with a pay increase**: Rewarding performance, motivates the employee to do better. Managements prefer performance to affect pay increases but unions view seniority as the most objective criterion for pay increases. Experience makes an employee gain valuable insights and should therefore be rewarded. Potential is useless if it is never realized. Yet, organizations do pay some individuals based on their potential. Young managers are paid more because of their potential to perform even if they are short of experience. Some people have luck to be at the right place at the right time.

STRATEGIC PAY PLANS OR RATE

The issue of strategic pay plans or rate is nothing but the strategic compensation planning which is instrumental in formulating a business strategy. The integration of remuneration plans with business strategy is found very rare as the general practice is to pay what competitors pay or to adhere to the corporate policy.

The strategic pay plan is not strictly a matter of what is being paid in the marketplace. Instead **compensation plans must derive from an assessment of what must be paid to attract and retain the right people**, what the organization can afford and what will be required to meet the organization's strategic goals. Thus, strategic compensation planning goes beyond determining what market rates to pay employees.

According to **Edward E Lawler,** "*Strategic pay plans refer to compensation of employees in ways that enhance motivation and growth while aligning their efforts with the objectives, philosophies and culture of the organization.*"

According to **Gerald Ledford and Elizabeth, Hawk—the two US compensation specialists,** "*Companies throughout the economy have begun to rethink their compensation systems in search of competitive advantage.*"

(i) **Attracting and Retaining Valued Employees:** According to an expert, "The linkage of pay levels to labour markets is a strategic policy issue because it serves to attract or retain valued employees while affecting the organization's relative payroll budget." For example, colleges such as IIMs, IITs and renowned universities in India and abroad know that they cannot attract or retain qualified professors unless their pay strategy is linked to competitive market rates.

Many fast-food restaurants in USA, such as Burger King, Taco Bell, and Blimpie's—traditionally low-wage employers—have needed to raise their starting wages to attract a sufficient number of job applicants to meet staffing requirements. If pay rates are high, creating a large applicant pool, then organizations may choose to raise their selection standards and hire better-qualified employees. This in turn can reduce employer's training costs. When employees perform at exceptional levels, their performance appraisals may justify an increased pay rate. For these reasons and others, an organization should develop a formal HR programme to manage employee compensation.

(ii) Linking Compensation to Organizational Objectives: Note that this aspect of strategic pay plans has already been discussed in one of the previous sections in this chapter while discussing "objectives of compensation".

(iii) The Pay-for-Performance Standards: According to another compensation specialist Edward E. Lawler III, pay-for-performance is a strategic pay practice. The pay-for-performance standard serves to raise productivity and lower labour costs in today's competitive economic environment. It is agreed that managers must tie at least some reward to employee effort and performance. Without this standard, motivation to perform with greater effort will be low and the costs to organization will be higher. Figure 10.8 shows the positive relationship between pay-for-performance and expectancy theory of motivation.

The term "*pay for performance*" refers to a wide range of compensation options, including merit-based pay, bonuses, salary commissions, job and pay banding, team/group incentives, and various gain sharing programmes. Each of these compensation systems seeks to differentiate between the pay of average performers and that of outstanding performers.

Unfortunately, designing a sound pay-for-performance system is not easy. Consideration must be given to how employee performance will be measured. For example, measuring an employee's output may be relatively easy and objective on an assembly line but more difficult and subjective when the employee works in a service environment.

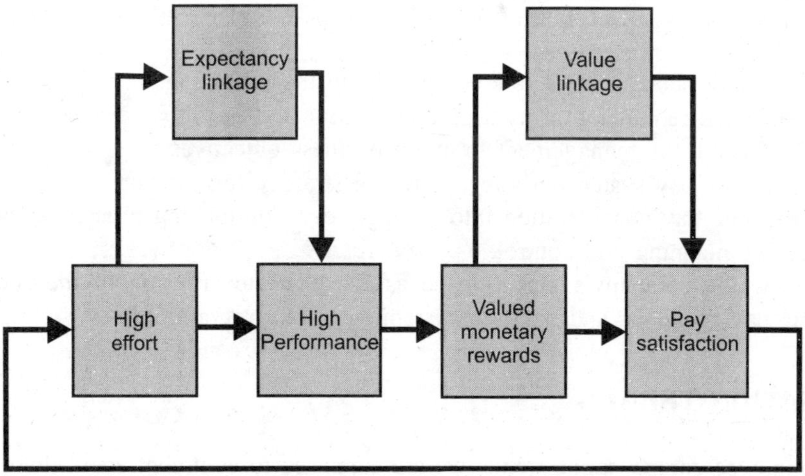

Fig. 10.8. Pay-for-Performances and Expectancy Theory.
Source: Scott Snell and George Bohlander, "Human Resource Management", 2007, Thomson-South Western Publication, New York, p. 383.

(iv) Motivating employees through Compensation: Pay constitutes a quantitative measure of an employee's relative worth. For most employees, pay has a direct bearing not only on their standard of living, but also on the status and recognition they may be able to achieve both on and off the job. Because pay represents a reward received in exchange for an employee's contribution it is essential, according to the equity theory, that the pay be equitable in terms of those contributions. It is essential also that an employee's pay be equitable in terms of what other employees are receiving for their contributions.

Table 10.3 illustrates the linkage of remuneration strategy to business strategy. It is evident from this table that the companies which are growing rapidly, business strategy tends to be focused on investing to grow. Hence, the compensation strategy to be consistent with business strategy should stimulate an enterprising and entrepreneurial style of management. For this purpose, the company should emphasize high cash payments with above average incentives.

Table 10.3: Linkage on Remuneration Strategy to Business Strategy

Business Strategy	Market Position and Maturity	Remuneration Strategy	Blend of Remuneration
Invest to grow	Merging or growth rapidly	Stimulate entrepreneurialism	High cash with above average incentive for individual performance. modest benefits.
Manage earnings–protect markets	Normal growth to maturity	Reward management skills	Average cash with moderate incentives on individual, unit, or corporate performance. Standard benefits.
Harvest earning–reinvest elsewhere	No real growth or decline	Stress on cost control	Below-average cash with small incentive tied to cost control. Standard benefits.

Source: Wayne F. Cascio, Managing Human Resources, McGraw-Hill, 1995, p. 352.

For strategic pay plans or rates, the companies do the following:

- They recognize remuneration as a pivotal control and incentive mechanism that can be used flexibly by the management to attain business objectives.
- They make the pay system an integral part of strategy formulation.
- They integrate pay consideration into strategic decision-making processes, such as those that involve planning and control.
- They view the company's performance as the ultimate criterion of the success of the strategic pay decisions and operational remuneration programmes.

COMPENSATION TRENDS

Regarding employee compensation trends we are supposed to comment about the evaluation of compensation programmes during the 21st century. The trends have to be predicted on the basis of present developments. The present developments are not very much encouraging as in majority of organizations employee compensation is based upon traditional job-oriented method and not on skill-based pay. Only a few well managed multinational companies have starting paying wages and salaries on the basis of skill or competence.

What shape employee compensation will take depends upon so many factors or forces which make the economic prediction difficult. The compensation field is affected by forces working in opposite directions. Employers seek to reduce labour costs to remain competitive in supplying goods and services, but at the same time may need to upgrade compensation programmes to attract and retain skilled workers. At the same time, however, a small supply of young workers may prompt employers to enhance compensation packages to compete for qualified staff.

These opposing forces will challenge efforts to maintain correct and relevant statistics on compensation in this new century. The voluntary nature of most data collection relies on the cooperation of employers and especially human resource professionals. As these individuals face the difficult task of developing competitive compensation packages while limiting costs, their ability to comply with requests for detailed data may be strained.

Three Major Trends

Three major trends characterized employee compensation in the last years of the 20th century, and these trends will probably shape employee compensation in the early years of the new century. As with the last century, however, it is unlikely that the ways employees are compensated will evolve along a straight path. Companies and governments will try many alternative programmes; some will work and become the paradigms of the 21st century whereas others will not and will be discarded or will be adopted in only a few workplaces.

I. **Aligning pay to organizational goals:** The first of these three major compensation trends is aligning pay to organizational goals. As our nation's economy becomes increasingly tied to world economic conditions, competitive pressures will prompt employers to seek ways to efficiently use their workforces. Employee compensation, in this environment, will increasingly be viewed as a tool for promoting increased productivity and innovation among workers. Compensation programmes are, thus, likely to be geared to employee performance or desired characteristics such as skills or knowledge. Examples of these compensation programmes include variable pay schemes that tie pay to individual or group performance and salary plans that reflect the possession or acquisition of knowledge or skills deemed critical to the success of the organization. Compensation in the 21st century is also likely to evolve in ways that tie employee pay and benefits to corporate performance. Examples include stock options and profit-sharing plans.

II. **Tailoring compensation to employee needs:** The second major trend is tailoring compensation to employee needs. This is a way of efficiently delivering compensation to employees by giving them a choice in what they want or need, rather than providing a universal programme that meets the needs of the average employee. Examples include choices among health care and within retirement savings plans, flexible work schedules and telecommunicating arrangements, and reimbursement accounts. Implicit in this flexibility is the increase of employee responsibility in making prudent choices. On the other hand, this flexibility may be constrained, particularly if significant numbers of employees make poor choices. Social policy concerns about the consequences of unwise choices, however, are less likely to stymie—than to shape—the evolution of this flexibility.

III. **Reconfiguring employee benefit plans:** The third major trend is reconfiguring employee benefit plans to provide for a defined level of employer contributions, rather than a defined level of ultimate benefit. This has been the trend in retirement plans over the 1980s and 1990s and may spread to other types of employee benefits plans. Examples include defined contribution employee health insurance plans, defined contribution retiree health insurance plans, and employer-funded reimbursement accounts. These arrangements give employers greater control over costs than in the past and greater ability to predict costs. On the other hand, employees are required to absorb more risks associated with insuring against future events than formerly. Coupled with the trend to charge employees with more responsibility for retirement savings and other benefits, the move towards defined contribution insurance arrangements may spur counter-measures to insulate employees from these risks. For example, a defined contribution health insurance plan might be required to include a core set of benefits that guards employees against catastrophic expenses.

In the 1990s, these three major compensation trends were seen as helping to meet the needs of a mobile workforce. With the expected labour shortages of the early years of the new century, however, these trends are likely to be tempered in ways thought to increase employee incentives for remaining with the organization. Employer drives to increase efficiency and curb costs may have to be balanced with one of the traditional goals of compensation programmes—to acquire and maintain an adequate supply of skilled labour.

Compensation Trends in India

In India, the traditional system of employee compensation was challenged during the last two decades by "money for the Job", "total cost to the company", "Flexible package", and "variable performance pay or bonus". This American compensation strategy conflicted with traditional British system.

The government, realizing the futility of very high taxation relaxed the compensation limits and provided an opportunity to companies to realign their compensation to suit the organizational needs.

The Y2K year opened the floodgates for Indian IT industry and personnel for lucrative overseas jobs. Hence, compensation plans in Indian IT sector too started amending. For knowledge workers in the organizations, changes in compensation strategies were needed that led to be extended to the traditional industry which had become very competitive. Despite differences in individual organizations, some general directions are evident in compensation strategy in India, i.e.

- **Salary, Basic Salary or Consolidated Salary continues to remain as the major component of compensation.** Though salary scales are often discarded these days, or used· only as guides. Individual salary is generally decided initially using the scale, but thereafter performance, contribution to targets or results generated determine the revisions periodically—which may vary widely from individual to individual. 'Salary broad banding' is therefore, getting recognition and acceptance.
- **Grade-wise flat allowances are being consolidated generally.** Except where tax exemption benefits are still available, when they continue as separate components.

Allowances may be linked to the salary as a percentage or by slabs, but preference is for flat amounts, which do not increase automatically, and therefore increases could be discretionary, and therefore controllable.

- **Reimbursements of expenses incurred on company work has become limited, and in line to conform to the tax laws.** Being actual in most cases, they are not considered a part of the compensation, unless it is provided towards personal benefits.
- **Annual payments, i.e., Bonus or Commission, and Leave Travel are common features.** Some tax relief does apply for the latter.
- **Benefits generally comprise medical coverage, retrial benefits covering Provident Fund, Pension or Superannuation and Gratuity, post-retrial medical assistance, easy loan schemes at low or zero interest rates for house building, cars or vehicles.** Furniture or utility items, etc. renting employee owned housing, club entrance fee reimbursement, etc. Minor benefits could be provision of security, driver or gardening assistance, sale of products or assets at a concessional rate, relocation and transfer expenses including admission, etc. fees for children, credit card fees, phones, etc.
- **Employee stock option schemes—which have been popular in IT industry—are not extensively used yet.** Not being tax advantageous to other industries, nor seen as being very attractive with lesser growth trends for their share values, especially in the well established older companies.
- **The "Total cost to the company" concept is used as basis by most companies, as against earlier visible costs.** Cost of most benefits are averaged or computed on actual basis, and included in the above. Greater openness is practised, and some permit individual flexibility within the system of the overall cost, but with greater compliance to tax laws, this 'basket concept' is on the wane.
- **As mentioned earlier, retirement benefits are important to many, whilst the younger generation and specially IT professionals, do not consider it as an advantage.** Unless the benefit value is available to them on moving to a new job. This is a complex issue, and may require attention. Periodic improvement in pensions or a guaranteed grade minimum pension is practised by some in recognition of the past external experience of pensioners, and to partly offset the inflation post-retirement.
- **The differential in performance is now being recognized.** Through very substantial and varying increases during the review to the very good performer, and often a salary freeze or loss of job is being used for poor performers! This strategy manages the rewards often within the same total cost.
- **Compensation review periods have become annual generally and sometimes oftener, as compared to every three to five years earlier.** In the fast changing market situation. The quantum of increment has jumped of late, and successful organization need to not only keep pace, but have to between and reputed to be amongst the best to attract talent. The employee cost increases have to be set off through productivity and greater contribution from the resources. This requires constant market data on compensation practices and benchmarks, and very pragmatic analysis for determining strategy.
- **Retention strategies employed are generally the attractive such as interest free or at low rates for loans.** On which market rate of interest may apply on early exit, renting employee owned property to set off repayment of loans, qualifying periods or attractive

service benefits added to the retrial benefits or post-retirement benefits, etc. Besides the terms, compensation and any special deals. Managers and teams having commitment require empowerment, lean and supportive structure, a healthy organizational climate—which are all great retention motivators, and also end up as a 'puller' from the external environment or the competition.

SKILL BASED PAY

Skill-based or competence-based pay is distinguished from job-based pay. **The Job-based pay** is shown in Figure 10.9 is the predominant approach to employee compensation and it is still prevailing in majority of the firms. In this traditional job-based system of pay, employees are paid on the basis of job they do.

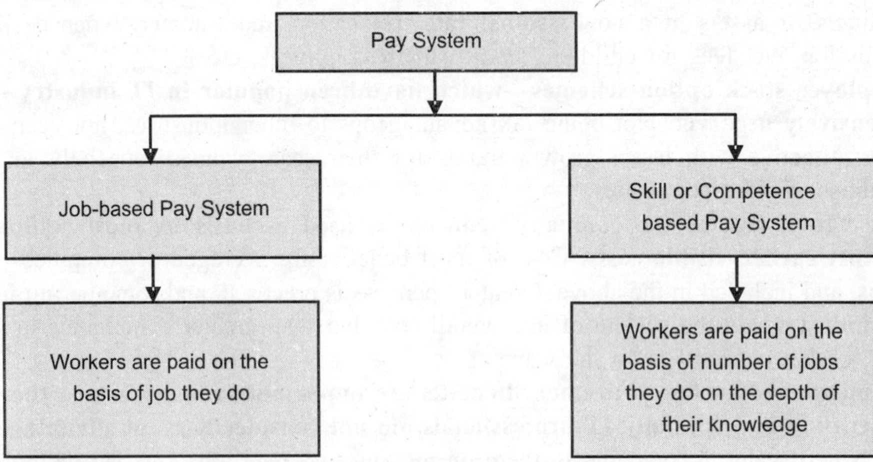

Fig. 10.9. Classification of Pay Systems.

Drawbacks of Job-based Pay

- Such a system often fails to reward employees for their skills and knowledge.
- This system fails to encourage them to learn new job-related skills.
- Job-based pay system may not reinforce an organizational culture stressing employee involvement.
- It fails to provide increased employee flexibility to meet overall production or service requirements. Due to these drawbacks, well managed organizations have introduced competence-based pay plans.

Figure 10.10 shows the job-based remuneration model.

Skill-based or Competence-based Pay

Competence-based pay, also referred to as skill-based pay or knowledge-based pay, compensates employees for the different skill or increased knowledge they possess rather than for the job

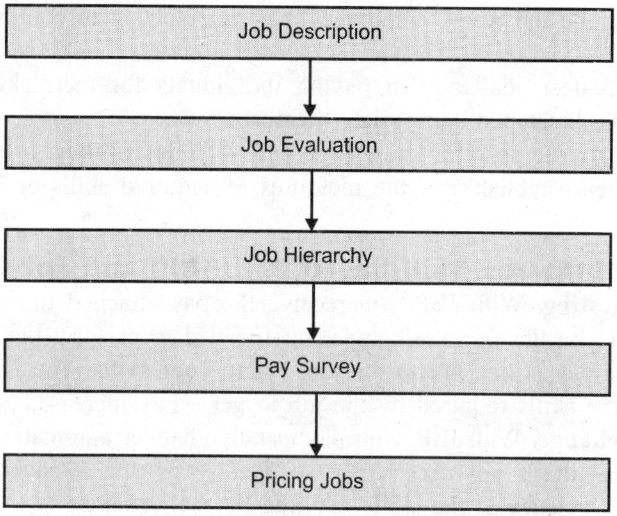

Fig. 10.10. Job-based Remuneration Model.

they hold in a designated job category. Regardless of the name, these pay plans encourage employees to earn higher base wages by learning and performing a wider variety of skills (or jobs) or displaying an array of competencies that can be applied to a variety of organizational requirements. For example, in manufacturing settings, new tasks might include various assembly activities carried out in a particular production system or a variety of maintenance functions. Within service organizations, employees might acquire new knowledge related to advanced computer systems or accounting procedures. Organizations will grant an increase in pay after each skill or knowledge has been mastered and can be demonstrated according to a predetermined standard.

Benefits of Skill-based Pay

1. It will encourage employees to increase their job-related knowledge and skills.
2. It brings change in the attitude of management regarding how work should be organized and how employees should be paid for their work efforts.
3. It enhances the productivity of the staff.
4. It improves employee learning and commitment to work.
5. It reduces the rate of absenteeism and turn over as manager can use employees where and when needed.
6. It improves staffing flexibility to meet production or service demands.
7. Skill-based pay also encourages employees to acquire training when new or updated skills are needed by an organization.

Limitations of Skill-based Pay

1. Some plans limit the amount of compensation employees can earn, regardless of the new skills or competencies they acquire.

2. After achieving the top wage, employees may be reluctant to continue their educational training.
3. Perhaps the greatest challenge in paying individuals for their skills, knowledge, and competencies is developed appropriate measures.
4. It is difficult to write specific knowledge and skill descriptions for jobs that employees perform and then establish accurate measures of acquired skills or knowledge.

Key Differences between Skill-based Pay (SBP) and Job-based Pay (JBP)

1. **Competence testing.** With JBP, you receive the pay attached to your job regardless of whether or not you develop the competence needed to perform the job effectively. With SBP, your base pay is tied not to the job, but to your skills. You have to be certified as competent in the skills required by the job to get a pay increase.
2. **Effect of job change.** With JBP, your pay usually changes automatically when you switch jobs. With SBP that's not necessarily so. Before getting a pay raise, you must first demonstrate proficiency at the skills required by the new job.
3. **Seniority and other factors.** Pay in JBP systems is often tied to 'time in grade' or seniority. In other words, the longer you're in the job, the more you get paid, regardless of how well you perform. SBP systems are based on skills, not seniority.
4. **Advancement opportunities.** Typically (but not always) there tend to be more opportunities for advancement with SBP plans than with JBP plans because of the company-wide focus on skill building. A corollary to this is that SBP enhances organizational flexibility by making it easier for workers to move from job to job because their skills (and thus their pay) may be applicable to more jobs and thus more portable. Table 10.4 compares skill-based pay with job-based operation.

Table 10.4: Comparison between Skill-based Pay and Job-based Operation

Factors	Job-based	Skill-based
Pay structure	Based on job performance	
Employer's focus	Job carries wage; Employee linked in job	Employee carries wages; Employee linked to skills
Employee's focus	Job promotion to earn greater pay	Skill acquisition to earn greater pay
Procedures required	Assess job content; Value jobs	Assess skills; Value skills
Advantages	Pay based on value of work performed	Flexibility; Reduced workforce
Disadvantages	Potential personnel bureaucracy; Inflexibility	Potential personnel bureaucracies; Cost controls.

Source: Raymond A. Stone, Human Resource Management, John Wiley & Sons, 1995, p. 324.

- It is believed that employees have the ability and motivation to perform well.
- Other programmes such as profit sharing, participative management, empowerment and job enrichment complement the skill-based pay system.
- Technology and organizational structure change frequently.
- There are opportunities to learn new skills.
- Employee turnover is relatively high.
- Workers value team work and opportunity to participate.

BROADBANDING

The trend for employers today is to reduce their salary grades and ranges from ten or more down to three to five. This process is called broadbanding.

In other words, broadbanding is defined as the process of collapsing salary grades and ranges them into just a few wide levels or "bands", each of which then contains a relatively wide range of jobs and salary levels.

Illustration—How to Broadband a Pay Plan

Let a firm has 10 salary grades each of which contains a salary range of say, Rs. 15,000. The firm might collapse the 10 grades into three broadbands each with a set of jobs such that the difference between the lowest and highest paid jobs might be Rs. 40,000 or more.

There are several steps in broadbanding a pay plan:

Step I: Setting Salary Ranges for Three Bands: The bands usually have wide salary ranges and also overlap substantially. As a result, there is much more flexibility to move employees from job to job within bands and less need to promote them to new grades just to get them higher salaries. Figure 10.8 shows the first step.

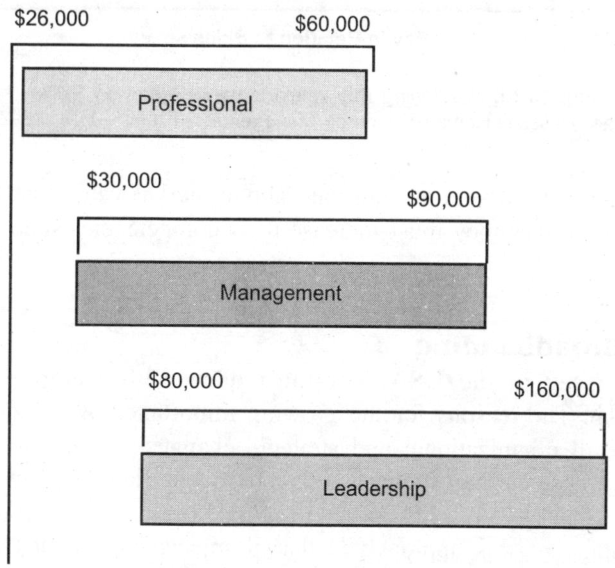

Fig. 10.11. Setting Salary Ranges for three Bands.
Source: Gary Dessler, Human Resource Management, Prentice-Hall of India, New Delhi, 1998, p. 414.

Step II: Assigning Market values to Jobs in a Band: The bands in the second step are subdivided into either specific jobs or skill levels. Figure 10.12 shows the subdivision into specific jobs and Figure 10.13 shows it into skill levels.

Figure 10.12 shows that a band may consist of a number of jobs, each assigned a market value. Figure 10.13 shows that bands are subdivided into several skill levels. The second approach

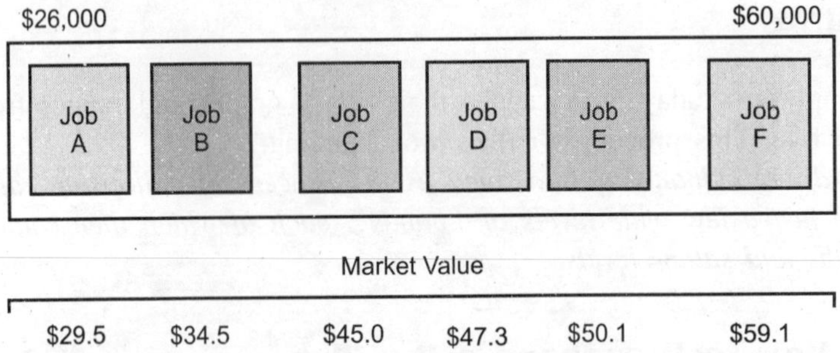

Fig. 10.12. Assigning Market Values to Jobs in a Band.
Source: Gary Dessler, Human Resource Management, Prentice-Hall, 1998, p. 414.

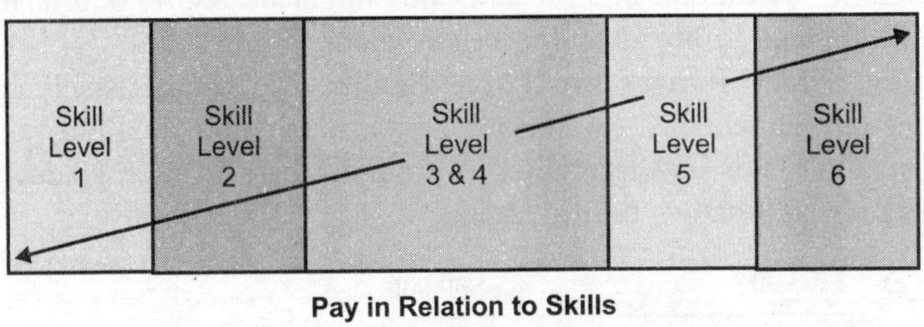

Fig. 10.13. Positioning Pay within a Band Based on Skills.
Source: Gary Dessler, Human Resource Management, Prentice-Hall, 1998, p. 414.

is considered better as in it workers are not paid above market value just for doing a job well or for having seniority. Rather they must increase their competencies such as skills, knowledge and abilities.

Importance of Broadbanding

According to one survey in the USA, one-third of the 3400 employees had adopted a broadbanding approach. The reasons for the growing importance of broadbanding are:

(i) It supports overall organizational and strategic changes. In one British company it was used to support cost cutting strategy and consequent flattening and downsizing of the organization.

(ii) Another advantage of this approach is that it injects greater flexibility into employee compensation.

(iii) It is more useful where firms want to flatten their hierarchies and organize into self-managing teams.

(iv) The salary bands can include both supervisors and subordinates and movement slightly up or down along the pay scale is possible with going into new salary range.

(v) The broadbanding approach is also useful for less specified and boundaryless job in such organizations which are being embraced by established firms like GE. In this organization routine duties of employees can be broadbanding so to improve the working of employees at routine jobs.

Application of Broadbanding Approach

General Electric and Toyota are two prominent employers who have broadbanded their pay scales.

At Toyota there are only three plant job classifications

(a) Division I includes all production members.
(b) Division II includes general maintenance team members.
(c) Division III includes all tie and dye members.

Likewise, General Electric was able to restructure its entire pay plan into five broad compensation bands.

REVIEW QUESTIONS

1. What is job evaluation? Discuss its main objectives and importance. What are the principles of job evaluation?
2. Discuss the process of job evaluation. Should the job evaluation depend upon an appraisal of the job holder's performance? Why?
3. What are the methods of job evaluation? In what respect is the factor comparison method similar to the ranking method? How do they differ?
4. Describe the use of job evaluation in practice. Why is there such a difference between theory and practice?
5. What is job evaluation? What are its uses? Discuss its limitations.
6. Define compensation. Discuss the objectives of compensation.
7. What is compensation? What are the main factors influencing compensation?
8. Discuss the importance of ideal compensation system.
9. What are the major compensation trends? Also discuss these trends in Indian context.
10. What is skill-based pay? How does it differ from traditional job-based pay? What are its benefits?
11. Compare the competence-based (skill-based) pay with job-based pay.
12. What are the pros and cons of broadbanding and would you recommend your current employer to use it? Why or why not?

CASE STUDY

10.1 Salary Inequities at Acme Manufacturing – A Job Evaluation Exercise

Joe Blackenship was trying to figure out what to do about a problem salary situation he had in his plant. Blackenship recently took over as president of Acme Manufacturing. The founder, Bill George, had been president for 35 years. The company was family owned and located in a small eastern Arkansas town. It had approximately 250 employees and was the largest employer in the community. Blackenship was a member of the family that owned Acme, but he had never worked for the company prior to becoming president. He had an M.B.A. and a law degree, plus 15 years of management experience with a large manufacturing organization, where he was senior vice president for human resources when he made his move to Acme.

A short time after joining Acme, Blackenship started to notice that there was considerable inequity in the pay structure for salaried employees. A discussion with the human resources director led him to believe that salaried employees' pay was very much a matter of individual bargaining with the past president. Hourly paid factory employees were not part of the problem because they were unionized and their wages were set by collective bargaining. An examination of the salaried payroll showed that there were 25 employees, ranging in pay from that of the president to that of the receptionist. A closer examination showed that 14 of the salaried employees were female. Three of these were front-line factory supervisors and 1 was the human resources director. The other 10 were of non-management.

This examination also showed that the human resources director appeared to be underpaid, and that the 3 female supervisors were paid somewhat less than any of the male supervisors. However, there were no similar supervisory jobs in which there were both male and female job incumbents. When asked, the HR director said she thought the female supervisors may have been paid at a lower rate mainly because they were women, and perhaps George did not think that women needed as much money because they had working husbands. However, she added the thought that they were paid less because they supervised less-skilled employees than did male supervisors. Blackenship was not sure that this was true.

The company from which Blackenship had moved had a good job evaluation system. Although he was thoroughly familiar and capable with this compensation tool, Blackenship did not have time to make a job evaluation study at Acme. Therefore, he decided to hire a compensation consultant from a nearby university to help him. Together they decided that all 25 salaried jobs should be in the same job-evaluation cluster, that a modified ranking method of job evaluation should be used, and that the job descriptions recently completed by the HR director were current, accurate, and usable in the study.

The job evaluation showed that there was no evidence of serious inequities or discrimination in the non-management jobs, but that the HR director and the three female supervisors were being underpaid relative to comparable male salaried employees.

Blackenship was not sure what to do. He knew that if the underpaid female supervisors took the case to the local EEOC office, the company could be found guilty of sex discrimination and then have to pay considerable back wages. He was afraid that if he gave these women an immediate salary increase large enough to bring them up to where they should be, the male supervisors would be upset and the female supervisors might comprehend the total situation and want back pay. The HR director told Blackenship that the female supervisors had never complained about pay differences, and they probably did not know the law to any extent.

The HR director agreed to take a sizable salary increase with no back pay, so this part of the problem was solved. Blackenship believed he had four choices relative to the female supervisors:

1. To do nothing.
2. To gradually increase the female supervisors' salaries.
3. To increase their salaries immediately.
4. To call the three supervisors into his office, discuss the situation with them, and jointly decide what to do.

Source: This case was prepared by Professor James C. Hodgetts of the Fogelman College of Business and Economics of the University of Memphis. It was quoted by Gary Dessler in his book, Human Resource Management, Prentice-Hall, 1998, p. 430.

Questions

1. What would you do if you were Blackenship?
2. How do you think the company got into a situation like this in the first place?
3. Why would you suggest Blackenship pursue the alternative you suggested?

10.2 Corporation Bank

The 1990s were a watershed for the Indian banking industry, and particularly for nationalized banks which hitherto have a monopoly in the industry. Following the deregulation of the financial sector, Corporation bank—a nationalized bank, have faced increasing competition from other financial institutions like Can Fin Homes Ltd., LIC Housing Corporation and foreign private sector banks. These specialized financial institutions were giving a tough competition to Corporation Bank resulting in an intense squeeze on profit margins and the need to make considerable efforts to retain its clientele. Under such pressure, Corporation Bank introduced new technology, new a financial products and new reward system for bank managers and staff. Information and communication technologies enabled the bank to process much larger volumes of business and just as importantly, the new ICTs themselves facilitated the development of new, technically based products and services such as home banking, smart cards and debit cards which Corporation Bank started to market to its customers.

Running parallel with these technical changes was the dismantling of the paternalistic human resource management system. In essence, Corporation Bank's bureaucratic culture and its associated belief system for managers and staff of appropriate behaviour being rewarded by steady promotion through the ranks was swept aside.

The new culture in the fast-changing environment, emphasized customer service, and the importance of measuring and rewarding staff according to their performance. The new performance-related reward system was introduced at the board meeting held in June 2002. Mr. N. K. Singh, chairman and managing director of the bank said that the proposed reward system would be a key strategy to 'maintain our reputation and market share'. He outlined that in future; the salary of bank managers would be tied to their leadership skills and the quality of customer service. Accordingly, the reward system would link a manager's pay to behaviour traits that relate to leadership and customer service. The variable pay for both managers and staff would be based on what is accomplished because customer service is central to Corporation. Bank's strategic plan, a three category rating system that involves 'not meeting' customer expectations, 'meeting' them or 'far exceeding' them; is the essence of the new reward system.

Questions

1. Outline the merits and limitations of Corporation Bank's proposed reward system for the managers and staff.
2. Develop an alternative reward system for Corporation Bank's employees and explain why it is superior to the proposed reward system.

REFERENCES

1. Belcher, David, (1974). "Compensation Administration", Prentice-Hall, Englewood Cliffs, N.J.
2. Dessler, Gary, (1998). Human Resource Management, Prentice-Hall of India, New Delhi.
3. French, Wendell, (1974). "The Personnel Management Process", Houghton Mufflin & Co.
4. George T. Milkovich and Jerry M. Newman, (2005). "Compensation", 8th edn., Boston: McGraw-Hill Irwin.
5. ILO, (1970). Job Analysis, New Delhi.
6. Subramanian, K.N. (1979). "Wages in India", Tata McGraw-Hill, New Delhi.
7. Kimbal, D.S., and Kimbal, Junior, (1971). "Principles of Industrial Organization", Vakils, Preffer & Simon Pvt. Ltd., Bombay.
8. Michel R. Currell, *et al.*, (1992). "Personnel/Human Resource Management", 4th edn., Maxwell, Macmillan, New York.
9. Personnel Management in India, Calcutta, 1973.
10. Richard Henderson, (2003). "Compensation Management in a Knowledge-based World", 9th edn., Englewood Cliffs, NJ, Prentice Hall.
11. Robert L. Mathis and John H. Jackson, (2003). "Human Resource Management", Thomson.
12. Scott Snell and George Bohlander, (2007). "Human Resource Management", Thomson-South Western Publication, New York.
13. Wayne F. Cascio, (1995). "Managing Human Resource", McGraw-Hill.
14. William B. Werther and Keith Davis, (1996). "Human Resources and Personnel Management", McGraw-Hill.

CHAPTER

11 Management of Employee Benefits and Services

CHAPTER'S OUTLINE

- Introduction
- What are Benefits and Services?
- Importance of Benefits and Services
- Types of Employee Benefits and Services
- Principles of Fringe Benefits and their Future
- Administration of Benefits and Services
- Requirements for a Sound Benefits and Services Programme
- Benefits and Services in India

INTRODUCTION

Employees are paid remuneration in terms of money as well as in kind. By and large remuneration for work done is paid in financial form. Hence, employee remuneration comprises both direct as well as indirect elements. Direct elements refer to wages and salaries or compensation paid to the employees in money form. In Chapter 10 compensation or remuneration in cash has been discussed. This chapter is devoted to discussion of the indirect benefits.

One of the greatest challenges in business today is attracting and retaining quality employees. Individuals expect more than wages or salary from their employers. Virtually all employers provide a variety of benefits and services to supplement the wages or salaries paid to their employees.

In this chapter, we shall discuss nature and types of benefits and services as well as their administration.

WHAT ARE BENEFITS AND SERVICES?

The terms benefits and services are often used interchangeably by some writers but some maintain distinction. According to the first view employee benefits and services are indirect compensation and include any benefit that the employee receives in addition to direct remuneration which can be ascertained in money. The common name for benefits and services, generally used is fringes. These are the cases of pension, medical insurance or holiday pay. According to the second view, service is different from benefit. The word Service applies to such items as a company newspaper, counselling, childcare, eldercare, etc. for which a direct money value for the individual employee cannot be readily established. Majority experts have preferred to treat the benefits and services as interchangeable terms.

According to **Scott Snell and George Bohlander**, "*Employee benefits and services constitute an indirect form of compensation intended to improve the quality of the work lives and the personnel lives of employees.*"

According to the **Glossary of Industrial Relations and Wage Terms** "*Fringe benefits are supplements to wages received by workers at a cost to the employers. The term encompasses a number of benefits—paid vacation, pension, and health insurance plans, etc.—which usually add up to something more than a 'fringe' and is sometimes applied to a practice that may constitute a dubious benefit for workers.*"

According to **D. Belcher**, "*Fringe benefits are any wage cost not directly connected with the employee's productive effort, performance, service or sacrifice.*"

According to **Werther and Davis**, "*Fringes embrace a broad range of benefits and services that employees receive as part of their total compensation package–pay or direct compensation—is based on critical job factors and performance. Benefits and services, however, are indirect compensation because they are usually extended as a condition of employment and are not directly related to performance.*"

According to researchers approximately 42 per cent of total payroll costs to employers are because of benefits and services provided to employees. In return employers expect employees to be supportive of the organization and to be productive.

However, it must be noted that, once viewed as a gift from the employer, benefits are now considered rights to which all employees are entitled.

IMPORTANCE OF BENEFITS AND SERVICES

Today, almost all organizations provide benefits and services to their employees. The chief objectives of most benefits programmes are as follows:

(i) Improve employee work satisfaction
(ii) Meet employee health and security requirements
(iii) Attract and motivate employees
(iv) Retain top-performing employees
(v) Maintain a favourable competitive position

The importance of these fringes is growing day by day. Several reasons are responsible for the growing importance. Perhaps these reasons constitute the growing importance of these benefits and services. Some of these reasons are discussed as under:

1. **Increased Earnings to Employees:** They represent increased earnings to employees. In fact, employees prefer indirect remuneration to direct pay. Any increase in direct pay only adds to one's taxable income. But most benefits are not taxed and hence are advantageous to employees. Furthermore, there are economic reasons why benefits are preferred by employees. Health and life insurance can generally be purchased by the employer at group rates, which are lower than those the employees would have to pay.
2. **Employers Prefer on Social Responsibility Ground:** Employers, too, prefer indirect remuneration to direct pay. Increase in benefits distorts salary structures less and are often easier to explain to shareholders as the social responsibility of the company. Besides, they often involve complex financial arrangements and underwritings so that their true cost may not be discernible by employees or unions.
3. **For Attracting and Retaining Competent Personnel:** More than salary structures and financial arrangements, there is a need to attract and retain competent personnel. An employee joins and stays with an organization which guarantees attracting fringe benefits.
4. **Increase in Productivity of Employees:** Besides, vacations along with holidays and rest breaks help employees mitigate fatigue and enhance productivity. Similarly, retirement, health care and disability benefits may allow workers to be more productive by freeing them of concerns about medical and retirement costs.
5. **Discourage Labour Unrest and Reduce Turnover:** The benefits and services are quite helpful in improving the industrial relations between employers and employees. Workers remain committed to such organizations which offer these fringes.
6. **Promote Good Corporate Image:** Fringe benefits help build up a good corporate image. Schemes like housing, educational institutions and recreational activities bring benefits to the society at large. In the case of some, the benefits are direct. For a religious programme or a sports event or a company school, the company draws its clientele not only from the employees but also from surrounding communities. In others, such as housing, there are indirect gains in terms of reduced pressure on the limited living accommodation and release on public funds for additional housing programmes. All these have wider dimensions than immediate gains of the employees.
7. **Importance according to Keith Davis:** These benefits are important because of the following reasons:
   - (i) Mitigate fatigue
   - (ii) Discourage labour unrest
   - (iii) Satisfy employee's objectives
   - (iv) Aid recruitment
   - (v) Reduce turnover
   - (vi) Minimize overtime costs

Thus, the organization, with the introduction of fringes, seeks to enhance employee morale, remain cost-effective, and introduce changes without much resistance.

TYPES OF EMPLOYEE BENEFITS AND SERVICES

The benefits and services provided by employers to their employees, for attracting and retaining competent employees include variety of programmes. These are classified into three categories as shown in Figure 11.1.

Types of Employee Benefits and Services *

1. Statutory Benefits and Services

- Social Security Insurance
- Unemployment Insurance
- Workers Compensation Insurance
- Family and Medical Leave Benefits

2. Discretionary Benefits and Services

- Health care Benefits
- Life Insurance
- Payment for time not worked
- Supplemental employment
- Benefits
- Long-term Care Insurance
- Retirement Programmes
- Pension Plans

3. Other Benefits and Services

- Employee Assistance Programmes
  - Knick-knacks
  - Office environment
  - Counselling services
- Counselling services
- Child and Elder care
- Treats and social acknowledgment
- Other services such as tokens
- Credit Unions
- Legal services
- Financial Planning
- Pay Cards
- Awards

Fig. 11.1. Types of Employee Benefits and Services.

*First two categories of benefits and services can be ascertained in money whereas the third category is not ascertainable in money.

1. Statutory Benefits and Services

These are legally required employee benefits and constitute nearly a quarter of the benefits package that employers provide. These benefits include employer's contribution to:

(i) Social security insurance
(ii) Unemployment insurance
(iii) Workers compensation insurance
(iv) Family and medical leave benefits

The Social Security Insurance provides an insurance plan designed to protect covered individuals against loss of earnings resulting from various causes such as retirement, unemployment, disability, death of workers, etc.

Employees who have been working in employment covered by the Social Security Act and who are laid off may be eligible for up to twenty-six weeks of *unemployment insurance benefits* during their unemployment. Eligible workers must submit an application for unemployment compensation with their state employment agency, resister for available work, and be willing to accept any suitable employment that may be offered to them.

Workers compensation laws typically provide that employees will be paid a disability benefit based on a percentage of their wages. Each state also specifies the length of the period of payment and usually indicates a maximum amount that may be paid. Benefits, which vary from state to state, are generally provided for four types of disability:

(1) Permanent partial disability
(2) Permanent total disability
(3) Temporary partial disability
(4) Temporary total disability

In addition to the disability benefits, provision is made for payment of medical and hospitalization expenses up to certain limits, and in all states, death benefits are paid to survivors of the employee. Commissions are established to resolve claims at little or no legal expense to the claimant.

The Family and Medical Leave Act (FMLA) in USA was passed and became effective on August 5, 1993. The FMLA applies to employers having fifty or more employees during twenty or more calendar workweeks in the current or preceding year. A covered employer must grant an eligible employee up to a total of twelve workweeks of unpaid leave in a twelve-month period for one or more of the following reasons:

(i) Birth of and care for a newborn child
(ii) Adoption or foster care placement of a child
(iii) Care for an immediate family member (spouse, child, or parent) with a serious medical condition
(iv) Serious health condition of the employee

2. Discretionary Benefits and Services

Discretionary benefits and services or voluntary benefits are those which are as per the willingness of the employers. There are a growing number of employees now, who regard that workers and other personnel are an asset to the organization. They need to be given other benefits and services besides direct compensation (wages or salaries). These include:

(i) Health care benefits
(ii) Life insurance
(iii) Payment for time not worked
(iv) Supplemental unemployment benefits
(v) Long-term care insurance
(vi) Retirement programmes
(vii) Pension plans

(i) Health care Benefits: The benefits that receive the most attention from employers today because of high costs and employee concern are *healthcare benefits*. In the past, health insurance plans covered only medical, surgical, and hospital expenses. Today, employers include prescription drugs as well as dental, optical and mental health care benefits in the package they offer their workers.

Since 1980, the employer cost of providing medical and dental costs has increased more than 250 per cent in USA. Health care spending in US economy has been steadily rising as a share of the economy, up from 5.29 per cent in 1950 to more than 16 per cent in 2004.

According to a US Chamber of Commerce study, medical and medical-related benefits costs (employer's share) average 15.2 per cent of payroll costs with the significant rise in health care costs, it is understandable that employers seek relief these expenses.

(ii) Life Insurance: One of the oldest and most popular employee benefits is group term life insurance, which provides death benefits to beneficiaries and may also provide accidental death and dismemberment benefits. The premium costs are normally paid by the employer, with the face value of the life insurance equal to two times the employee's yearly wages. These programmes frequently allow employees to purchase additional amounts of insurance for nominal charges. When employers operate a cafeteria benefits programme, selection of extra life insurance may be part of the choices offered employees.

(iii) Payment for Time Not Worked: The "*payment for time not worked*" category of benefits includes paid vacations, bonuses given in lieu of paid vacations, payments for holidays not worked, paid sick leave, military and jury duty, and payments for absence due to a death in the family or other personal reasons. These benefits constitute another large expenditure, i.e., 11.6 per cent of the employer's total payroll costs. (US Economy)

(a) Vacations with Pay: It is generally agreed that vacations are essential to the well-being of an employee. Eligibility for vacations varies by industry, locale, and organization size. To qualify for longer vacations of three, four, or five weeks, one may expect to work for seven, fifteen and twenty years, respectively. While vacations are a relatively easy benefit to manage, employers should, nevertheless, remember that vacation scheduling must meet the employer's state wage laws and state contract law principles.

(b) Paid Holidays: Both hourly and salaried workers can usually expect to be paid for ten holidays a year. The type of business tends to influence both the number and observance of holidays. Virtually all employers in the United States, however, observe and pay their employees for New Year's Day, Memorial Day, Independence Day, Labour Day, Thanksgiving Day, and Christmas Day. Many employers give workers additional two or three personal days off to use at their discretion.

(c) Sick Leave: There are several ways in which employees may be compensated during periods when they are unable to work because of illness or injury. Most public employees, as well as many in private firms, receive a set number of sick-leave days each year to cover such absences. Where permitted, sick leave that employees do not use can be accumulated to cover prolonged absences. Accumulated vacation leave may sometimes be used as a source of income when sick leave benefits have been exhausted. Group insurance that provides income protection during a long-term disability is also made available by some employers. As discussed earlier in the chapter, income lost during absences resulting from job-related injuries may be reimbursed, at least partially, through workers' compensation insurance.

(d) Severance Pay: A one-time payment is sometimes given to employees who are being terminated. Known as severance pay, it may cover only a few days' wages or wages for several months. The pay received usually depends on the employee's years of service. However, severance pay can also be based on the reason for termination, the salary or grade level of the employee, the title or level in the organization, or a combination of factors. Employers that are downsizing often use severance pay as a means of lessening the negative effects of unexpected termination of employees. Other triggers for severance pay include job elimination, voluntary separation programmes, or refusal of reassignment or relocation.

(iv) Supplemental Unemployment Benefits: While not required by law, in some industries unemployment compensation is augmented by supplemental unemployment benefits (SUBs), which are financed by the employer. These plans enable an employee who is laid off to draw, in addition to state unemployment compensation, weekly benefits from the employer that are paid from a fund created for this purpose. The amount of benefits is determined by length of service and wage rate. Employer liability under the plan is limited to the amount of money accumulated within the fund from employer contributions based on the total hours of work performed by employees.

(v) Long-Term Care Insurance: A small but growing number of employers are offering long-term care insurance as part of their benefits package. Long-term care insurance is designed to pay for nursing home and other medical-related costs during old age. An advantage of employer-sponsored long-term care insurance is that enrolled employees receive coverage automatically and do not need to pass a physical examination.

(vi) Retirement Programmes: A significant trend in workforce demographics is the increased age of US workers. A prominent cause of this change is the 'aging' of the baby boom generation. Therefore, retirement has become an important part of life for many individuals, requiring sufficient and careful preparation. In convincing job applicants, particularly older ones, that there is a good organization to work for, employers usually emphasize the retirement benefits that can be expected after a certain number or years of employment.

While most people eagerly anticipate retirement, many are bitterly disappointed once they reach this stage of life. Employers may offer pre-retirement planning programmes to help make employees aware of the kinds of adjustments they may need to make when they retire. These adjustments may include learning to live on a reduced, fixed income and having to cope with the problems of lost prestige, family problems, and idleness that retirement may create.

(vii) Pension Plans: Originally, pensions were based on a reward philosophy, which viewed pensions primarily as a way to retain personnel by rewarding them for staying with the organization until they retired. Because of the vesting requirements required by law, pensions are now based on an earnings philosophy. This philosophy regards a pension as deferred income that employees accumulate during their working lives and that belongs to them after a specified number of years of service, whether or not they remain with the employer until retirement. Since the passage of the Social Security Act of 1935, pension plans have been used to supplement the floor of protection provided by social security. However, the decision whether to offer a pension plan is up to the employer.

Types of Pension Plans

There are two major ways to categorize pension plans: **(1) according to contributions made by the employer and (2) according to the amount of pension benefits to be paid.** In a contributory plan, contributions to a pension plan are made jointly by employees and employers. In a non-contributory plan, the contributions are made solely by the employer.

When pension plans are classified by the amount of pension benefits to be paid, there are two basic types: The defined-benefit plan and the defined-contribution plan. Under a defined-benefit plan, the amount an employee is to receive on retirement is specifically set forth. This amount is usually based on the employee's years of service, average earnings during a specific period of time, and age at the time of retirement. While a variety of formulas exist for determining pension benefits, the one used most often is based on the employee's average earnings (usually over a three- to five-year period immediately preceding retirement), multiplied by the number of years of service with the organization.

A defined-contribution plan establishes the basis on which an employer will contribute to the pension fund. The contributions may be made through profit sharing, thrift plans, matches of employee contributions, employer-sponsored individual employees receive on retirement accounts, and various other means. The amount of benefits employees receive on retirement is determined by the funds accumulated in their account at the time of retirement and what retirement benefits (usually an annuity) these funds will purchase.

3. Other Benefits and Services

These benefits and services usually are those which are not monetary in nature or which cannot be ascertained in terms of money. These are popular employer-sponsored work/life benefits. Table 11.1 lists some of the more popular employer sponsored services and benefits to employees. This category of benefits and services include the following:

Table 11.1: Work/Life Benefits: Balancing Work and Home Needs

- Childcare/eldercare referral services
- Time off for children's school activities
- Employer-paid onsite or near-site childcare facilities
- Flexible work hours scheduling
- Employer-accumulated leave days for dependent care
- Customized training programmes
- Subsidized temporary or emergency dependent-care costs
- Extended leave policies for child/eldercare
- Sick-child programmes (caregiver on call)
- Work-at-home arrangements/telecommuting
- Partial funding of childcare costs
- Customized career paths

Source: Scott Snell and George Bohlander, HRM, Thomson, 2007 p. 473.

(i) **Employee Assistance Programmes:** These include assistance in improving office environment and on the job assistance (Table 11.2) .

(ii) **Counselling Services:** Sometimes employees may have problems that require the services of professional counsellors. Most organizations refer such individuals to outside counselling

Table 11.2: Examples of Fringes

1.	Legally required payments:
(i)	Old age, survivors, disability, and health insurance (commonly known as social security)
(ii)	Worker's compensation
(iii)	Unemployment compensation
2.	Contingent and deferred benefits
(i)	Pension plans
(ii)	Group life insurance
(iii)	Group health insurance
	(a) Medical expenses (hospitalization and surgical)
	(b) Disability income (short-term and long-term)
(iv)	Guaranteed annual wage
(v)	Prepaid legal plans
(vi)	Military leave and pay
(vii)	Jury duty and bereavement paid leave
(viii)	Maternity leave
(ix)	Childcare leave
(x)	Sick leave
(xi)	Dental benefits
(xii)	Tution aid benefits
(xiii)	Suggestion awards
(xiv)	Service awards
(xv)	Severance pay
3.	Payments for time not worked
(i)	Vacations
(ii)	Holidays
(iii)	Voting pay allowances
4.	Other benefits
(i)	Travel allowances
(ii)	Company car and subsidies
(iii)	Moving expenses
(iv)	Uniform and tool expenses
(v)	Employee meal allowances
(vi)	Discounts on employer's goods and services
(vii)	Childcare facilities.

Source: Terry L. Leap and Michael D. Crino, Personnel/Human Resource Management, Macmillan, 1990, p. 438.

services such as family counselling services, marriage counsellors and mental health clinics. The organizations may appoint experts in these areas.

(iii) Child and Elder Care: A growing benefit is offered to employees with children experiencing short illnesses is mildly-ill childcare. Medical supervision is the primary difference between mildly-ill facilities and traditional daycare arrangements. Mildly-ill care facilities serve children recovering from colds, flu, ear infections, soar throat, chickenpox, or other mild illnesses that temporarily prevent them from attending regular school or daycare. These facilities are either independently run, hospital based, or affiliated with childcare centres.

Responsibility for the care of aging parents and other relatives is another fact of life for increasing numbers of employees. The term, **eldercare,** as used in the context of employment, occurs when an employee provides care to an elderly relative while remaining actively at work. The majority of caregivers are women.

To reduce the negative effects of care giving on productivity, organizations may offer elder care counselling, educational fairs and seminars, printed resource material, support groups, and special flexible schedules and leaves of absence. Schering-Plough, a pharmaceuticals manufacturer, uses an 800 telephone line for elder care referrals, while IBM has a national telephone network of more than 200 community-based referral agencies. Employers may also band together for better elder care.

(iv) **Treats and Social Acknowledgement:** It includes treats such as free lunches with boss through activities like informal recognition, friendly greetings, and email company facility for personnel projects, etc. dinners, picnics and social acknowledgement.

(v) **Other Services Such as Tokens:** It includes movie tickets, vacation trips, anniversary and birthday celebrations, etc. These facilities induce the employees to be loyal to the organization.

(vi) **Credit Unions:** Credit unions exist in many organizations to serve the financial needs of employees. They offer a variety of deposits as well as other banking services and make loans to their members. Although the employer may provide office space and a payroll deduction service, credit unions are operated by the employees under federal and state legislation and supervision. At the end of July 2004, there were 9,542 credit unions in the United States with 85.6 million members and combined assets of $655 billion.

(vii) **Legal Services:** Legal service plans are generally of two types: access plans and comprehensive plans. Access plans provide free telephone or office consultation, document review, and discounts on legal fees for more complex matters. Comprehensive plans cover other services such as representation in divorce cases, real estate transactions, and civil and criminal trials.

Covered employees normally pay a monthly or an annual fee to be enrolled in the plan. When the need for legal assistance arises, the employee may choose an attorney from a directory of providers and incur no expenses for attorney fees. One benefits consultant remarked, "The whole idea behind prepaid legal plans is that the employer can use its purchase power and shift it to employees without incurring a lot of expense." Prepaid legal programmes are typically offered as part of an employer's cafeteria benefits plan.

(viii) **Financial Planning:** One of the newer benefits is financial planning. As mentioned previously, financial planning has become particularly important for employees making investment decisions regarding saving plans. Financial planning could also include (1) present position, (2) retirement planning, (3) protection planning, (4) tax planning, and (5) estate planning and related topics. Employers offer these programmes through multiple forums—seminars, online tools, pamphlets, and/or face-to-face advice.

(ix) **Pay Cards:** Pay cards, also known as PIN-based or stored-value cards, are an electronic way to pay employees. These cards are linked to an existing ATM or a point-of-service account. PIN-based cards may allow employees to purchase goods by phone, at stores, or on the Internet. Pay cards are helpful to organizations moving to a 100 per cent electronic payroll.

(x) **Awards:** This is also an important non-monetary reward. It includes trophies, citations, certificates and letter of appreciation.

The discussion given above shows that types of benefits and services include basically the monetary rewards, i.e. fringes and non-monetary rewards, i.e. by and large services. Table 11.2

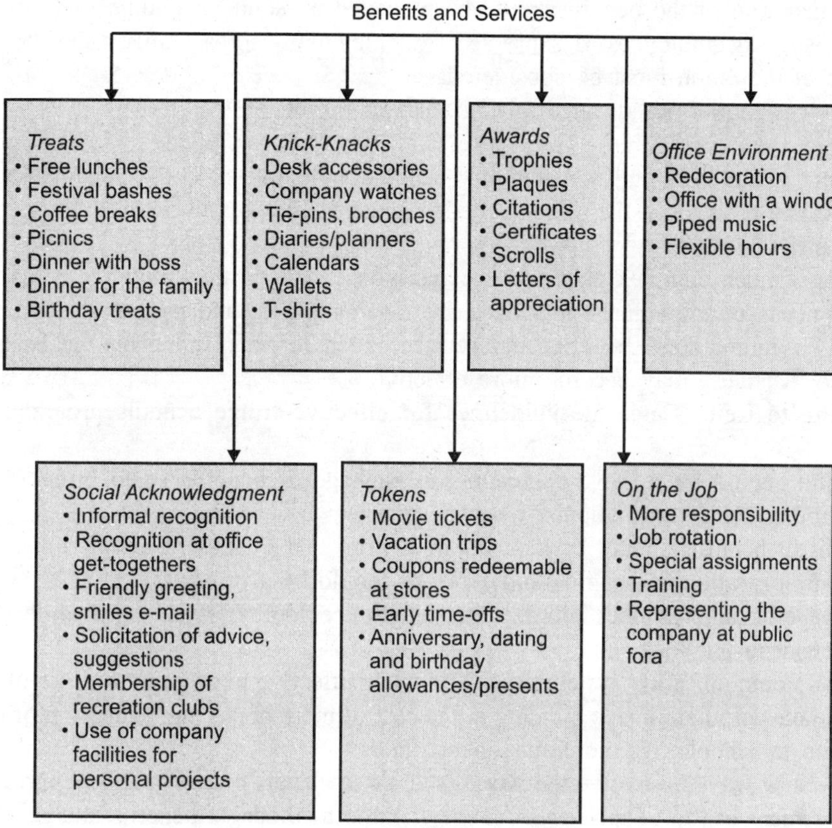

Fig. 11.2. Types of Non-Monetary Rewards.
Source: Business Today, Fourth Anniversary Issue, Jan. 7-21, 1996, p. 267.

contains list of fringes that includes statuary and discretionary benefits and services. Figure 11.2 shows non-monetary benefits and services made available to employees.

PRINCIPLES OF FRINGE BENEFITS AND THEIR FUTURE

According to **William B, Werther and Kaith Davis,** the following principles must govern the administration of fringe benefits:

(i) Benefits and services must be provided to the employees on the basis of a genuine interest in the protection and promotion of their well-being. The management should not feel that the fringes are thrust upon them. Nor should the management feel that they are providing the benefits as a matter of charity.

(ii) The benefit must satisfy a real need. Employees resist or are indifferent to any benefit which is not liked by them.

(iii) The benefit must be cost-effective.

(iv) The benefit should be as broad-based as possible.

(v) Administration of the benefit should be preceded by sound planning.
(vi) The wishes of employees as expressed by their union representatives and the bargaining power of the union must be considered.
(vii) Employees should be educated to make use of the benefits.

The future of statutory and non-statutory benefits and services in the organizations seem to be quite optimistic, as over the years benefit packages have evolved in India as well as in western countries like USA.

These days much complex patterns of plans with enhanced flexibility are being developed to meet the needs of individuals and these are costing public and private sector organization very dearly. In future these benefits and services need to be planned on the basis of some guidelines so that these may become more effective.

According to Keith Davis the guidelines for effective fringe benefits programmes are as under:

- The aim should be to have a meaningful package of benefits so to bring flexibility as inflexibility brings stagnation.
- The direct benefits should be kept separate from that of indirect programmes.
- The administration of benefits and services should be a priority.
- The benefits and services programmes should be looked at as worthwhile corporation instrument in HRM.
- Internal communication system should be made effective to promote welfare of the people to promote corporate image building at the cost of more bonus and admission of personnel's children to school with more and liberal funds.
- Devise new ways to involve the workers at all the levels of planning and implementation.
- Management has to adopt cost-effective flexible methods of benefits and services
- The cafeteria approach to benefits and services would be more effective as employees do have different preferences for benefits and services. According to this approach, the employees should be given the choice to choose the desirable benefits. Table 11.3 shows the advantages and disadvantages of flexible benefit programmes.

Table 11.3: Advantages and Disadvantages of Flexible Benefits Programmes.

Advantages	
1.	Employees choose packages that best satisfy their unique needs.
2.	Flexible benefits help firms meet the changing needs of a changing workforce.
3.	Increase involvement of employees and families improves understanding of benefits.
4.	Flexible plants make introduction of new benefits less costly. The new option is added merely as one among a wide variety of elements from which to choose.
5.	Cost containment – the organization sets the dollar maximum. Employee chooses within that constraint.
Disadvantages	
1.	Employees make bad choices and find themselves not covered for predictable emergencies.
2.	Administrative burdens and expenses increase.
3.	Adverse selection–employees pick only benefits they will use. The subsequent high benefit utilization increases its cost.
4.	Subject to non-discrimination requirements in section 125 of the internal revenue code.

Source: Milkovich and Newman, Compensation (Burr Ridge, IL: McGraw-Hill, 1998), p. 405.

ADMINISTRATION OF BENEFITS AND SERVICES

One serious problem relating to employee benefits and services is tough administration of these benefits. Administering satisfactorily is a great challenge. In order to make any suggestion for improving the administration of benefits and services, it is essential to pinpoint some of the serious problems in administration of benefits and services.

Problems in Administration

- **Lack of discretion for the employees:** This is the main problem in indirect remuneration. For example, the same pension programme to all workers. In fact, younger employees see pensions as distant and largely irrelevant. Older female workers feel that maternity benefits are not needed. Thus, uniformity of benefits, sometimes fails to recognize workforce diversity.
- **Little interest in benefits programmes by managers and unions:** Managers, too, have little interest in the benefits programmes and trade unions are almost hostile to the schemes. Managers are not even aware of the company's policy towards benefits and their contribution to the quality of corporate life. Trade unions entertain a feeling of alienation as the benefits are likely to erode their basis.
- **Unawareness about the benefits:** Since employees have little choice in their benefit packages, most workers are unaware of all the benefits to which they are entitled. This lack of knowledge often causes employees to request for more benefits to meet their needs. For example, older workers may want improved retirement plans, while younger workers seek improved insurance coverage for dependents. The result is often a proliferation of benefits and increased employer costs. And perhaps even worse, employee confusion can lead to complaints and dissatisfaction on about their fringe benefits packages, particularly when employees do not have to contribute financially.
- **Costly and time-consuming:** With the large number of benefits offered to employees today, administrating an organization's benefits programme can be both costly and time-consuming. Even for small employers, keeping track of each employee's use of a benefit or request for a change of benefits can be cumbersome. Tasks of monitoring such programmes become complex as the size of organization grows.

Precautions While Administration of Indirect Remunerations (Benefits and Services)

In the process of administration of indirect remunerations, i.e., benefits and services there are various precautions that need to be taken by the managers. Figure 11.3 demonstrates these precautions.

1. Establishing Objectives of Benefits & Services

It is essential for the management to establish objectives for its benefits & services programmes. In establishing objectives, the management may consider several factors. One such consideration is employee preference for benefits. Attendance, length of service, and performance should also receive the due attention in the objective-setting process.

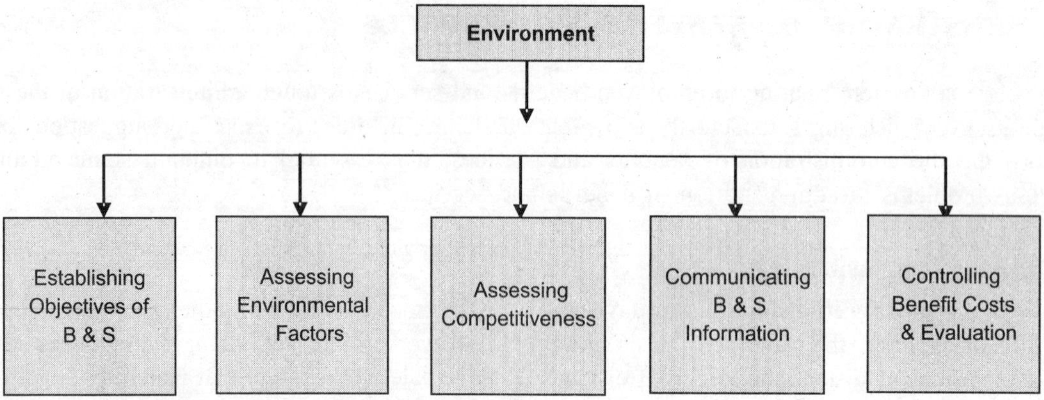

Fig. 11.3. Precautions in Administration of Benefits and Services.

Typically, benefits accomplish four objectives:
(i) fostering external competitiveness,
(ii) increasing cost-effectiveness,
(iii) meeting individual employee's needs and preferences, and
(iv) complying with legal compulsions.

Whatever the objectives, they must reflect the organization's ability to pay.

2. Assessing Environmental Factors

External as well as internal factors influence a company's indirect remuneration programmes.

(i) **External Factors:** Among the external factors are included such aspects as government policies and regulations, unions, and economic factors.

(a) The major government policies which influence employee benefits and services are wage regulations, tax policies, and specific benefit laws.

(b) Unions too are a dominant force to improve benefits and services. When labour unions and the management sit for a wage negotiation, benefits and services figure prominently in their discussion and the settlement reached invariably covers indirect remuneration to the advantage of the employees.

(c) Economic factors influence benefit decisions in conflicting ways. Struggling to achieve competitive prices for their products and services, managers look to reduce, increases in labour costs. As indirect remuneration constitutes a major chunk of labour costs, benefits and services receive top priority in the cost-reduction drive.

(d) Competition in the labour market to attract and retain production employees creates pressure to match the benefits offered by others.

(ii) **Internal Factors:** Organizational strategies and objectives, employee preferences and demographics constitute the internal environment of employee benefits and services.

(a) A large, well-established employer in a growing or mature industry, for example, may offer a relatively better benefits package. But a smaller, newly formed, emerging company may find that the high fixed costs attached to many benefits, particularly pensions, entail too great a financial burden.

(b) The preferences and demographics of a particular employee in an organization also affect indirect remuneration. Most employee benefits are tax free, and hence are likely to appeal to employees with higher incomes. A vast majority of workers may not be attracted by such tax-free benefits. For them, fewer tax advantages exist, or these employees may have more immediate needs which can be met only by cash benefits.

Similarly, employees having college-going children or marriageable daughters, have different benefit preferences than those who are newly hired with working spouses and children who have not reached the school-going age. Uniformity in benefits and services sometimes is not acceptable to employees because of their different preferences.

3. Assessing Competitiveness

More often than not, organizations offer benefits to match or outstrip those offered by competitors. How to ascertain the competitors' benefit packages? These are assessed through market surveys conducted by professional associations and consultants. These surveys provide data on the various benefits offered, their coverage, eligibility and costs. Thus, according to Randall S. Schuler, the data allow employers to assess the competitiveness of their benefits and costs, with those offered by others.

4. Communicating the Benefits and Services Information

Benefit programmes must be communicated to employees through booklets, brochures, slide presentations, and regular employee meetings. An effective technique is to use employee calendars which communicate the total remuneration components. Each month of the calendar shows a company employee receiving a benefit. For example, one month may feature a photo of an employee building a new home, made possible through the company's savings plan. Another month may feature the usefulness of the company's medical plan.

Communication helps remove ignorance of employees and of employers too about indirect remuneration. Further, employers might be able to increase the productivity and the advantages of good employee benefits by making employees aware of what the company does for them which does not appear on their pay slips.

5. Controlling Benefit-costs and Evaluation

Cost-benefit analysis is a reliable tool to evaluate the effectiveness of benefits and services programme. Assessing benefits and services real worth for the employees need to the present status of benefits and services with their plus and minus points. Cost of fringe benefits is a reliable test of their effectiveness and the employee benefit costs can be computed on the following lines:

- Total cost of benefits annually for all employees.
- Cost per employee per year.
- Percentage to annual payroll.

After having collected such cost data, **C.P. Thakur** recommends the steps in cost analysis.

- Examine the internal cost to the company of all benefits and services for pay roll classification.
- Compare the company's costs for benefits.
- Prepare a report for the decision-maker.
- Analyze the costs of the programme to employees and determine what each employee is paying for benefits, totally and by benefit.
- Compare the data in Step four with external survey data.
- Analyze how satisfied the individual is with the employer's programme as compared to the competitor's programme.
- This type of analysis will certainly be more effective, useful and long lasting for the employees and the organizations.

REQUIREMENTS FOR A SOUND BENEFITS AND SERVICES PROGRAMME

The soundness of a benefits programmes hinges on two factors:

(1) Selecting benefits that target important employee needs while promoting strategic organizational objectives, and

(2) Effective administration of benefits programmes.

Gone are the days of providing a particular benefit because other employers are doing it, because someone in authority believes it is a good idea, or because the benefit is 'popular' at the moment. Therefore, benefit specialists recommend paying attention to certain basic considerations.

1. Strategic Benefits Planning

Like any other component of the HR programme, an employee benefits programme should be based on specific objectives. The objectives an organization establishes will depend on many factors, including the size of the firm; its location, degree of unionization, and profitability; and industry patterns. Most important, these aims must be compatible with the organizations strategic compensation plan including its philosophy and policies.

The chief objectives of most benefits programmes are improving employee work satisfaction, meeting employee health and security requirements, attracting and motivating employees, retaining top performers and maintaining a favourable competitive position. Further, these objectives must be considered within the framework of cost containment.

2. Allowing for Employee Involvement

Before a new benefit is introduced, the need for it should first be determined through consultation with employees. Many organizations establish committees composed of managers and employees to administer, interpret, and oversee their benefits policies. Opinion surveys are also used to obtain employee input. Having employees participate in designing benefits programmes helps ensure that management is moving in the direction of satisfying employee wants.

3. Benefits for a Diverse Workforce

To serve their intended purpose, employee benefits programmes must reflect the changes that are continually occurring within our society. Particularly significant are changes in the diversity and lifestyles of the workforce. For example, recent figures from the US Census Bureau show that married-couple households have declined from nearly 80 per cent in the 1950s to approximately 51 per cent today. Unmarried people make up 42 per cent of the workforce. These demographic shifts, and others noted throughout the text, mandate that organizations design benefit packages that match the changing population. Fortunately, more employers have begun to tailor their benefit programmes to be family friendly.

Unfortunately, benefit plans sometimes provide little advantage to employees, limiting the organization's ability to attract or retain quality employees. For example, many employers provide unneeded medical benefits to the young and single in the form of dependents' coverage. Likewise, a well-designed-and costly-defined-benefits pension programme may not serve the needs of employees or the employer of a predominately younger workforce.

4. Providing for Flexibility

To accommodate the individual needs of employees, organizations may offer flexible benefits plans, also known as cafeteria plans. These plans enable individual employees to choose the benefits that are best suited to their particular needs. They also prevent certain benefits from being wasted on employees who have no need for them. Typically, employees are offered a basic or core benefits package of life and health insurance, sick leave, and vacation. Requiring a core set of benefits ensures that employees have a minimum level of coverage to protect unforeseen financial hardships.

5. Communicating Employee Benefits Information

Consider this research finding. A study on health care benefits by Towers Perrin found that many employees do not believe what their employers tell them about soaring benefits costs.

Employers use an array of methods to communicate benefits and services to employees, such as the following:

- In-house publications (employee handbooks and organizational newsletters)
- Group meeting and training classes
- Audio cassettes/video tapes
- Bulletin boards
- Payroll inserts/pay stub messages
- Speciality brochures
- Internet technology

Employee self-service (ESS) systems have made it possible for employees to gain information about their benefits plans, enrol in their plans of choice, change benefits coverage, and simply inquire about the status of their various benefit accounts without ever contacting an HR representative.

The technology of the Internet permits employees to access their benefits package, allowing both greater control and ownership of the benefits offered to them. Part of the advantage of an

Internet benefits system is that employees can obtain information on their own timetable. The web puts benefits information right in the hands of the people who need it. Employees want to track their claims, review their current coverage levels, and compare their options. They want to take responsibility for their health plan.

Online benefits programmes create a form of self-service benefits administration. An important advantage to an interactive benefits programme is the significant cost savings in benefits administration. Once an online system is operational, it is easy and inexpensive to adapt to employer and employee demands. However, while the Internet can be used effectively in benefits administration, security must always be a concern when transmitting benefits information.

Perhaps no part of the HR function is more technologically advanced than the administration of employee benefits programmes. A wide variety of commercially developed software packages facilitate benefits administration in such areas as pension, variable pay, workers' compensation, health benefits, and time-off programmes. Descriptions of and advertisements for a variety of benefits software programmes are readily found in HR journals such as Workforce and HR Magazine. Software programmes represent a cost-effective way to manage employee benefits programmes when employers lack the resources or expertise to manage such programmes. Table 11.4 demonstrates components of an effective benefit communication programme.

Table 11.4: Creating an Effective Benefits Communication Program

A well-designed benefits communication programme greatly enhances employees' appreciation of their benefits while ensuring that employers receive the intended value of these offerings. An effective programme provides frequent information to employees in a cost-effective and timely manner. Compensation specialists recommended the following points when administering a benefits communication programme.

In building an identity:

- Design materials that are eye-catching and of high interest to employees.
- Develop a graphic logo for all material.
- Identify a theme for the benefits programme.

In writing benefits materials:

- Avoid complex language when describing benefits. Clear, concise, and understandable language is a must.
- Provide numerous examples to illustrate benefit specifics.
- Explain all benefits in an open and honest manner. Do not attempt to conceal unpleasant news.
- Explain the purpose behind the benefit and the value of the benefit to employees.

In publicizing benefits information:

- Use all popular employee communication techniques.
- Maintain employee self-service (ESS) technology to disseminate benefits information and to update employee benefits selections.
- Use voice mail to send benefits information.
- Employ presentation software such as PowerPoint or Lotus Freelance to present information to group of employees.
- Maintain a benefits hotline to answer employee questions.

Source: Scott Snell and George Bohlander, HRM, Thomson, Delhi, 2007, p. 453.

6. Concerns of the Management

Managing an employee benefits programme requires close attention to the many forces that must be kept in balance if the programme is to succeed. Management must consider union demands, the benefits other employers are offering, tax consequences, rising costs, and domestic partner benefits.

Because many benefits represent a fixed rather than a variable cost, the management must decide whether it can afford this cost given the organization's financial position. As managers can readily attest, if an organization is forced to discontinue a benefit, the negative effects of cutting it may outweigh any positive effects that accrued from providing it.

A current trend (one not universally liked by employees) is for employers to require employees to pay part of the costs of certain benefits especially medical coverage. At all times, benefit plan administrators are expected to select vendors of benefit services who have the most to offer for the cost. Furthermore, besides the actual costs of employee benefits, these are the costs of administering them.

BENEFITS AND SERVICES IN INDIA

The benefits and services offered by various organizations in India are as under:

1. Payment for time not worked
2. Employee security
3. Safety and health
4. Workmen's compensation
5. Health benefits
6. Voluntary arrangements
7. Welfare and recreational facilities
8. Old age and retirement benefits.

1. **Payment for Time Not Worked**. This category includes the following:
    - **Paid Holidays.** According to the Factories Act, 1948, an adult worker shall have weekly paid holidays, preferably Sunday. When a worker is deprived of weekly holidays, he is eligible for compensatory holidays of the same number in the same month.
    - **Shift Premium.** Companies operating second and third shifts, pay a premium to the workers who are required to work during the odd hours' shift.
    - **Holiday Pay.** Generally, organizations offer double the normal rate of the salary to those workers who work during holidays.
    - **Paid Vacation.** Workers in manufacturing, mining and plantations who had worked for 240 days during a calendar year are eligible for paid vacation at the rate of one day for every 20 days worked in case of adult workers and one day for every 15 days worked in the case of child workers.
2. **Employee Security.** A minimum and continuous wage or salary gives a sense of security to the employees. The payment of Wages Act, 1936, The Minimum Wages Act, 1948, the payment of Bonus Act 1965, provide income security to the employees. In addition to this, the Industrial Disputes Act, 1947, provides for the payment of compensation in case of layoff or retrenchment.
3. **Safety and Health.** Employees' safety and health should be taken care of in order to protect the employees against accidents, unhealthy working conditions and to protect the workers productive capacity. In India, the Factories Act, 1948, stipulated certain conditions

and requirements regarding working conditions with a view to provide safe working environment.

4. **Workmen's Compensation.** In addition to health and safety measures, provision for the payment of compensation has also been made under Workmen's Compensation Act 1923. The Act is intended to meet the contingency of invalidity and death of a worker due to an employment injury or an occupational disease specified under the Act as the sole responsibility of the employer.
5. **Health Benefits.** Organizations provide various medical services like hospital, clinic and dispensary facilities to employees and their family members. Employees State Insurance Act, 1948 deals comprehensively about the health benefits to be provided. Benefits under this Act include:
   - Sickness benefit
   - Maternity benefit
   - Disablement benefit
   - Dependent benefit
   - Medical benefit
6. **Voluntary Arrangements.** Most of the large organizations provide health services over and above the legal requirements to their employees free of cost by setting up hospitals, clinics, dispensaries and homoeopathic dispensaries.
7. **Welfare and Recreation Facilities.** Welfare and recreational benefits include:
   - Canteens
   - Consumer Societies
   - Credit Societies
   - Housing
   - Legal aid
   - Employee counselling
   - Welfare organizations
   - Holiday homes
   - Educational facilities
   - Transportation
   - Parties and picnics
   - Miscellaneous.
8. **Old Age and Retirement Benefits.** Employers provide some benefits to the employees, after retirement and during old age, with a view to create a feeling of security about the old age. These benefits are called old age and retirement benefits and include:
   - Provident Fund
   - Pension
   - Deposit Linked Scheme
   - Gratuity and
   - Medical benefits.

The Employees Provident Fund Act provides for the institution of Provident Fund for employees in factories and establishments.

Employees Pension Fund Act provides family pension and life insurance benefits to the employees of various establishments. The payment of Gratuity Act, 1972 and Deposit Linked Insurance Scheme, 1976 under the PF Act, 1952, provide the respective benefits to the employees.

All organizations may not provide all the benefits discussed due to the financial stringencies. Moreover, the list of benefits given earlier is not an exhaustive one and some organizations provide different benefits which are not included in the list owing to their need and the financial ability of the organizations.

REVIEW QUESTIONS

1. Define benefits and services. Bring out their importance.
2. Bring out the various employees benefits and services. Describe each in brief.
3. Outline the principles of fringe benefits and services.
4. Explain the various steps in the benefits and services administration.
5. Explain nature of benefits and services. If you were establishing your own business, which benefits and services would you be legally required to pay and which would you choose to offer?
6. What are non-monetary rewards? Should employers provide childcare? Care for the elderly? Why?
7. What are the problems in administering employee benefits and services? What precautions should be taken to avoid these problems?
8. Discuss the requirements of a sound benefits and services programme.
9. Write notes on the following:
   a. Draw an effective communication programme about benefits and services.
   b. Benefit-cost and evaluation.

CASE STUDY

Revise Employee Benefits and Services Plan

"You HR people seem to have no other work than to talk about spending money", shouted Ms. Sarika, the Managing Director of E-Max Financial Services. "You keep coming with great ideas on how to spend money. Where is the money? Now get me thc hard facts on why we should change our benefit plan?" continued Sarika. She has reasons to lose his cool.

Mr. Gaurav, the HR manager, felt it was time to review the benefits and hence he mooted the idea before his boss.

Gaurav never expected Sarika to be so angry with his idea, but he was a bit comforted when he was asked to get back with facts to justify revision of benefits.

Back in office, Gaurav called in Ms. Veena, his deputy, for help in preparing the revision plan of benefits and services for an early submission to his boss.

Questions

1. Assume you are a part of the HR team assigned by Gaurav and Veena to survey the present range of benefits and services, offered by E-max Financial Services, Design the

questionnaire to survey the employee perception of the company's present benefits programme, ranking employees give to existing or alternative benefits, and any change employees want to be introduced to the present programme.

2. Using Maslow's hierarchy of needs, analyze the employee ranking of benefits.
3. Prepare a report for Gaurav and Veena on your findings.

REFERENCES

1. Dessler, Gary, (1998). "Human Resource Management", Prentice-Hall of India, New Delhi.
2. George T. Milkovich and Boudreau, (1990). "Personnel/Human Resource Management", 5th edn., Richard D. Irwin.
3. Scott Snell and George Bohlander, (2007). "Human Resource Management", Thomson-South Western Publication, New York.
4. William B. Werther and Keith Davis, (1993). "Human Resources and Personnel Management", McGraw-Hill.
5. David A. Decenzo, Stephen P. Robbins, "Human Resource Management", 7th edn., Wiley Publications.
6. Dale S. Beach, "Personnel—The Management of People at Work", 4th edn., MacMillan, p. 661.
7. Thakur, C.P. "Corporate Strategy on Fringe Benefits", Spectrum, Delhi.
8. Hermann, *et al.*, (1990). "Personnel/Human Resource Management", 5th edn., Richard D. Irwin.
9. Elmer H. Burack and Robert D. Smith, (1982). "Personnel Management—A Human Resource System Approach", John Wiley & Sons, New York.
10. Randell S. Schuler, *et al.*, (1989). "Effective Personnel Management", 3rd edn., West Publishing, St. Paul, p. 367.

CHAPTER

12 Promotions and Transfers

CHAPTER'S OUTLINE

- Introduction
- Meaning of Promotions
- Purpose of Promotions
- Basis of Promotions
- Principles of Promotion
- Meaning of Transfers
- Reasons for Transfers
- Types of Transfers
- Right Sizing of Workforce and its Need

INTRODUCTION

Promotions and transfers are the two key activities in every organization. It is through these activities, an adjustment in the size of workforce of an enterprise can be made to cope with the changing situations.

Such adjustments in the workforce are needed to meet the special situations such as:

- Changes in organizational structure involving grouping of jobs.
- Changes in the jurisdictions of the departments and relocation of individuals, jobs and departments.
- Fluctuations in volume of production and employment due to introduction of new or complete stoppage of old products, services, methods and processes.

The promotion and transfer functions provide workforce flexibility and mobility to suit the requirements of the organization. These functions can be performed in the organizations either formally or informally. Generally formal systems of promotion and transfer are adopted to secure operative consistency and efficiency.

MEANING OF PROMOTIONS

The term promotion covers a change and calls for greater responsibilities and usually involves higher pay and better terms and conditions of service. It means promotion involves a higher status or rank.

Promotion is always within an organization. It is an upward advancement of an employee from current job to another within the same organization with higher pay package, responsibility and status. If an employee shifts to a different job which has better working hours, better working conditions and location, it is not promotion. Promotion requires increased responsibilities and enhanced pay. It has been defined by different authors.

Definitions

According to **Scott and Spreigal**, "*A promotion is the transfer of an employee to a job that pays more money or that enjoys some preferred status.*"

According to **Pigors and Myres**, "*A promotion is the advancement of an employee to a better job—better in terms of greater responsibilities, more prestige or status, greater skill and especially, increased rate of pay or salary.*"

According to **Edwin B. Flippo**, "*A promotion involves a change from one job to another that is better in terms of status and responsibility.*"

The analysis of these definitions reveals the following **characteristics or elements of promotion:**

(i) Promotion is always within an organization.
(ii) It is an upward advancement of an employee from current job to another.
(iii) It involves higher salary and pay package.
(iv) It also involves better status.
(v) It involves increased responsibilities.
(vi) Promotion has higher job grade.

All these elements must be present in promotion. When a higher salary is given to an employee without corresponding change in the job grade it is not promotion rather it is upgrading or it may be called as dry promotion.

PURPOSE OF PROMOTIONS

Watkins, Dodd and others mention that purposes of promotion are:

(a) To furnish an effective incentive for initiative, enterprise and ambition
(b) To conserve proved skill, training and ability

(c) To reduce discontent and unrest
(d) To suggest logical training for advancement

As **Yoder** and others observe, "Promotion provides incentive to initiative, enterprise and ambition; minimizes discontent and unrest; attracts capable individuals; necessitates logical training of advancement and forms an effective reward for loyalty and cooperation, long service, etc.

Promotion is given to achieve the following purposes:

1. To put the worker in a position where he will be of greater value to the company and where he may derive increased personal satisfaction and income from his work.
2. To remove a worker from his job as an alternative to avoid the embarrassment of firing or demoting him.
3. To recognize an individual's performance and reward him for his work so that he may have an incentive to forge ahead. Employees will have little motivation if better jobs are reserved for outsiders.
4. To increase an employee's organizational effectiveness.
5. To build up morale, loyalty, and a sense of belonging on the part of the employees when it is brought home to them that they would be promoted if they deserve it.
6. To promote job satisfaction among the employees and give them an opportunity for unbroken, continuous service.
7. To provide a process of "*selective socialization*". Employees whose personalities and skills enable them to fit into an organization's human relations programme tend to stay on; while those whose personalities with those of the organization clash tend to leave.
8. To attract suitable and competent workers for the organization.
9. To create among employees a feeling of contentment with their present conditions, and encourage them to succeed in the company.

BASIS OF PROMOTIONS

Employees face a problem in deciding the basis to promote employees. The ways these decisions are made will affect the employee's motivation, performance and commitment. In this context four decisions have to be taken as is shown in Figure 12.1

The Figure 12.1 reveals that four important decisions are to be taken by the employees to determine the basis of giving promotion.

Decision 1: Is Seniority or Competence to be Made the Basis

Probably the most important decision is whether promotion will be based upon seniority or competence, or combinations of the two.

Seniority as the basis

Seniority means length of service in an organization. If seniority is adopted as the basis of promotion, the seniormost people in the lower grade shall be promoted as and when there is an opening in the higher position. The logic behind considering the seniority as a basis of promotion

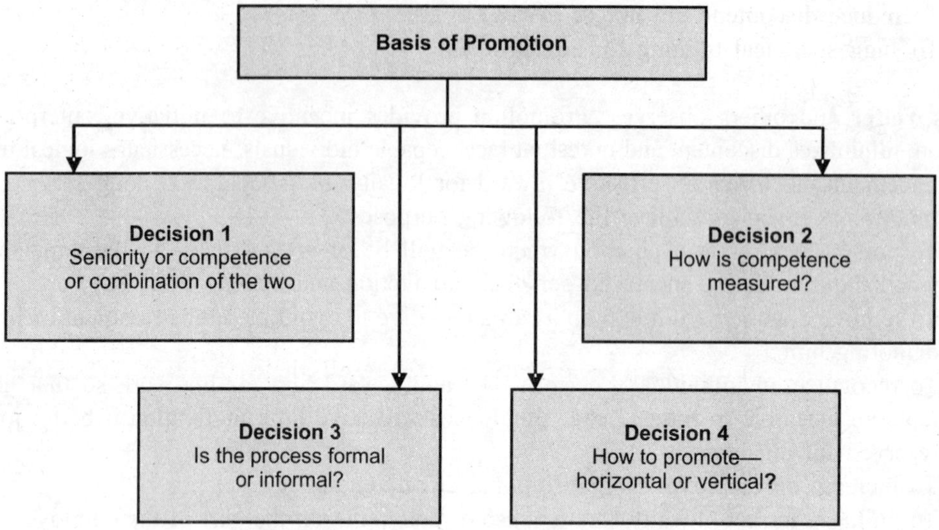

Fig. 12.1. Basis of Promotions—the Four Decisions.

is that there is a positive correlation between the length of service in the same job and the amount of knowledge and the level of skill acquired by an employee in an organization. Seniority on the basis of length of recognized service in the organization is decided by the organization and every employee knows his place in the promotion line. There will be no chance of favouritism or dispute regarding promotion. Seniority is widely recognized as the basis of promotion in almost all types of organizations, particularly in organizations where trade unions are strong. Often union agreements contain a clause such as – "*In the advancement of employees to higher jobs when ability, merit and capacity are equal, employees with the highest seniority will be given preference.*" The **advantages of seniority** as a basis of promotion are as follows:

- It is relatively **easy to measure the length of service** and to judge the seniority.
- **Trade unions generally emphasise on seniority** rather than merit as a basis of promotion.
- The employees trust this method as **there is no scope for favouritism**, discrimination and judgement.
- **Security and certainty is also a plus point in the use of seniority**. Employees can predict when and how he will be promoted. It increases employees' morale and gives them a sense of satisfaction.
- **It minimizes the scope for grievances** and conflicts regarding promotion.
- **Seniority basis of promotion helps in reducing labour turnover** because an employee will not easily give up his seniority in the organization.
- Organizations in the public sector are governed by civil service regulations that **emphasize seniority rather than competence** as the basis for promotion.

The **drawbacks in seniority system** of promotion are also pointed out. These are:

- Length of service and learning may fall beyond a certain age.
- Demotivation to young and more competent employees.
- It is against self-development.

- Judging seniority has problems like job seniority, company seniority, and service in different organizations, etc.

Competence as the basis

Competence means ability to work or employee's skill, knowledge, ability, efficiency and aptitude which is measured from educational, training and past employment record. On this basis, the most competent persons will be given promotion, irrespective of age and seniority. From the point of view of motivation, promotion based upon competence is the best. Merits of competence based promotion are:

- The competence of an employee can be better utilized at a higher level.
- Competent employees are motivated to exert all their energies and contribute to organizational efficiency and effectiveness.
- This system continuously encourages the employees to acquire new skills, knowledge, etc. for all-round development.

The system suffers from the following drawbacks:

- Measuring competence is not always easy.
- Many employees, particularly, trade unions distrust the management's integrity in judging competence.
- The techniques of competence measurement are subjective.
- The purpose of promotion may not be served if competence is taken as the sole criteria for promotion.

Security-cum-competence-basis

A combination of both seniority and competence may be considered the soundest basis for promotion as there is controversy whether promotions are given on the basis of seniority or competence. Managements generally prefer competence based promotions and trade unions prefer seniority as the basis of promotion. The best policy would be to combine both competence and seniority.

Decision 2: How is Competence Measured?

If promotion is to be based on competence, how will competence be defined and measured? Defining and measuring *past* performance is a fairly straightforward matter: The job is defined, standards are set, and one or more appraisal tools are used to record the employee's performance. But promotion also requires predicting the person's *potential;* thus, you must have a valid procedure for predicting a candidate's future performance.

Many employers simply use prior performance as a guide and extrapolate, or assume, that based on the person's prior performance he or she will perform well on the new job. This is the simplest procedure to use.

On the other hand, some employers use tests to evaluate promotable employees and to identify those employees with executive potential. Others use assessment centres to assess management potential.

Decision 3: Is the Process Formal or Informal

Next and particularly if you decide to promote based on competence, you have to decide whether the promotion process will be formal or informal. Many employers still depend on an informal system. Here the availability and requirements of open positions are kept secret. Promotion decisions are then made by key managers from among employees they know personally and also from among those who, for one reason or another, have impressed them. The problem is that when you don't make employees aware of the jobs that are available, the criteria for promotion, and how promotion decisions are made, the link between performance and promotion is cut and the effectiveness of promotion as a reward is thereby diminished.

Many employers therefore do establish formal, published promotion policies and procedures. Here employees are generally provided with a formal promotion policy statement that describes the criteria by which promotions are awarded. Formal systems often include a job-posting policy. This states that open positions and their requirements will be posted and circulated to all employees. The net effect of such actions is twofold: an employer ensures that all qualified employees are considered for openings; and promotion becomes more closely linked with performance in the minds of employees.

Decision 4: How to Promote—Horizontal or Vertical

Finally, employers increasingly have to deal with the question of how to 'promote' employees in an era in which higher-level jobs are less available. Worker empowerment and a related emphasis on technological expertise these days have created cadres of highly trained professionals, technicians, and first-line workers who aspire to higher-level positions but find their upward movement blocked by a dearth of openings.

Several options are available here:

(i) Some firms, such as the exploration division of British Petroleum, have created two parallel career paths, one for managers and another for "individual contributors" such as engineers. In that way individual contributors, such as highly accomplished engineers, can move up to non-supervisory but still more senior positions such as "senior engineer."

(ii) Another option is to provide career development opportunities for an individual, either by moving the person horizontally or even within the same position he or she currently holds. Horizontally, for instance, a production employee might be moved to HR in order to give him/her an opportunity to develop new skills and test and challenge aptitudes. And, in a sense, "promotions" are possible even leaving the person in the same job: for example, some job enrichment is usually possible, and the firm can provide training that increases the opportunity for assuming increased responsibility.

PRINCIPLES OF PROMOTION

Every organization aspires for a sound promotion system so that industrial peace is maintained and industrial relations become harmonious. Giving promotion is a delicate issue. It must be handled with great care by the management. Hence, a sound promotion policy is to be evolved and for this you are to take care of two things:

1 Criteria for sound promotion policy.
2 Principle or elements for sound promotion policy.

1. Criteria for Sound Promotion Policy

N.N. Chatterjee has points that a sound promotion policy must satisfy the following criteria:

(i) **Criterion of Consistency:** It should enjoy consistency, i.e., it will be applied irrespective of the persons concerned. Consistency demands that the policy should be so correlated to career planning that there should not be a sudden spurt of promotion in the organization conferring premature benefits on a number of persons, followed by a long period of absence of promotion.

(ii) **Criterion of Fairness and Impartiality:** It should be fair and impartial, i.e., the management should be able to remove all suspicion of arbitrariness, ad hocism, improvisation to suit particular individuals, nepotism, etc.

(iii) **Criterion of Planned Activity:** Promotion should be a planned activity, i.e., the management should make a correct assessment of the requirements or opportunities of promotion within the organization so that there is no phenomenon of 'bunching' or no period of 'promotional drought', i.e., no over-estimation or under-estimation.

2. Principles or Elements for Sound Promotion Policy

A sound promotion policy should be based on the following principles:

1. **Promotion Policy Statement**: **The promotion policy should be in writing** and must be understood by all employees to avoid any suspicion regarding line of promotion in the minds of employees.
2. **Establishing Plan of Jobs:** The promotion policy should lay down **what percentage of vacancies in higher levels of hierarchy are** *to be filled up by promotion* and it should be followed strictly. It is better to incorporate a statement of management intention that higher paid and better jobs will be filled by promotion from within, if possible, rather than by hiring from outside. If it is necessary to go outside to fill specific skilled or professional jobs. It should be notified in advance.
3. **Declaring Basis of Promotion**: The promotion policy should mention the **basis of promotion-seniority or competence**. A sound policy should be based on both the considerations, i.e., seniority and ability. Primarily it would emphasis the merit giving due weightage to seniority. If two persons are equal in merit and seniority, seniority should be the basis of promotion.
4. **Declaring Job Analysis Norms:** Job analysis decides the position of the jobs and their relationship to other positions. This should be charted to provide clear recognition of the natural movement from one job to another. Positions may be adjusted and arranged so that one position prepares workers for another and natural course of advancement throughout the organization or within each division or department may be provided. Employees should be fully aware of the plan so that they may prepare themselves for higher position.
5. **Promotion to be Linked with Training Programme:** Promotion programmes should be closely **allied to training** programme; which enables the employees to improve themselves for promotions.

6. **Promotion to be Linked with Performance:** A scientific procedure for **evaluating employee performance should be followed**. The assessment of employee and confidential reporting should be objective so that every employee has faith in the promotion policy and is motivated for better performance of work to get promotion.
7. **Principles of Recommendation: The supervisor or the immediate boss should recommend the promotion** which is subject to approval by his immediate superior in the line. Final decision in this respect should be taken by the top executive in line with the advice and assistance of the personnel department in a staff capacity. This serves as a check on the fairness of promotion and ensures that the policy will be consistently administered.
8. **Principle of Fairness:** The promotion policy should contain **a provision for the challenge of a particular promotion** by the employee or union within the limits of the promotion policy to ensure fairness in management decision.
9. **Principle of Advance Information: A vacancy or would be vacancy should be notified to employees in advance** so that interested employees may apply within a specified period. If possible, the candidate should be selected before the job actually becomes vacant.
10. **Principle of Probation: The promotion, at first, should be made on probation.** If he works satisfactorily during probation period, he should be made permanent.

MEANING OF TRANSFERS

The term 'transfer' refers to a change in job assignment without involving any substantial change in his duties, responsibilities, status and salary. Transfer does not imply promotion or demotion or change in status or responsibilities.

Transfers of employees are quite common in all organizations. A transfer may be defined as a change in job within the organization where the new job is substantially equal to the old in terms of pay, status and responsibilities. Transfers are possible from one department to another or from one plant to another.

Definitions

According to **Edwin B. Fippo**, "*Transfer is a change in job where the new job is substantially the equal to the old in terms of pay, status and responsibilities.*"

According to **Dale Yoder.** "*A transfer involves the shifting of an employee from one job to another without special reference to changing responsibility or compensation. Transfer may involve promotion, demotion or no change in status and responsibility.*"

Thus, transfer is a horizontal or lateral movement of an employee from one job, section, department, shift, plant or position to another at the same or another place, where his salary, status and responsibility are the same.

Attributes of Transfer

- Transfer is a change in job assignment
- Transfer involvers horizontal movement of an employee from one job, section, department or plant
- Salary status and responsibilities after the transfer remain the same

REASONS FOR TRANSFERS

The reasons for transfers are generally to build up a more satisfactory work team and to achieve the following purposes:

1. **To Satisfy the Needs of Organization**: To satisfy such needs of an organization as may arise out of a change in the quantity of production, fluctuations in work requirements and changes in the organizational structure; the introduction of new lines of production, the dropping of existing product lines, the reallocation of, or reduction in the workforce due to a shortage or a surplus in the same section so that lay-offs may be avoided; filling in of the vacancies which may occur because of separations or because of the need for suitable adjustments in business operations. Such transfers are known as production transfers, flexibility transfers or organizational transfers. The purpose of such transfers is to stabilize employment in an organization. They are generally controlled centrally through and by the personnel department.
2. **To Meet Employees' Request:** Sometimes, transfer is done at the request of the employer himself. Employee may need transfer in order to satisfy their desire to work under a different superior in a department/region where opportunities for advancement are bright, in or near their native place or place of interest, doing a job where the work itself is challenging, etc.
3. **To Have Better Utilization of the Employees:** An employee may be transferred because the management feels that he is not performing satisfactorily and adequately and when the management feels that he may be more useful or suitable elsewhere, where his capacities would be better utilized.
4. **To Adjust the Workforce:** Workforce may be transferred from a plant where there is less work to a plant where there is more work. Thus, the employees who have been in service of an organization are not thrown out of employment but adjusted elsewhere.
5. **For Improving Versatility of Employees:** Employees may be shifted from one job to another to expand their capabilities. Job rotation may prepare the employee for more challenging assignments in future.
6. **To Reduce Conflicts and Incompatibilities:** Where employees find it difficult to get along with colleagues in a particular section or department, they could be shifted to another place to reduce conflicts.
7. **For Providing Relief to the Employee:** Transfers may be made to give relief to employees who are overburdened or doing hazardous jobs for long periods. Transfer may also be made to break the monopoly of the employee. The climate of a place may be unsatisfactory for an employee's health. He may request a transfer to another place, where his health may not be affected by the climate.
8. **For the Maintenance of a Tenure System:** In senior administrative services of the government and also in industries or where there is a system of annual intake of management trainees, the employee holds a certain job for a fixed tenure but is made to move from job to job with a view to enable him to acquire variety of experience and skills and also to ensure that he does not get involved in politicizing informal groups.
9. **For Accommodating Family Related Issues:** Family related issues cause transfers, especially among female employees. When they get married, the female employees want to join their husbands and this fact necessitates transfers or resignations.

10. **To Penalize the Employees:** Transfers may be affected as disciplinary measures to shift employees indulging in undesirable activities to remote, far flung areas. In government organizations this practice is widespread.

TYPES OF TRANSFERS

Transfers may be classified on various bases as is shown is Figure 12.2.

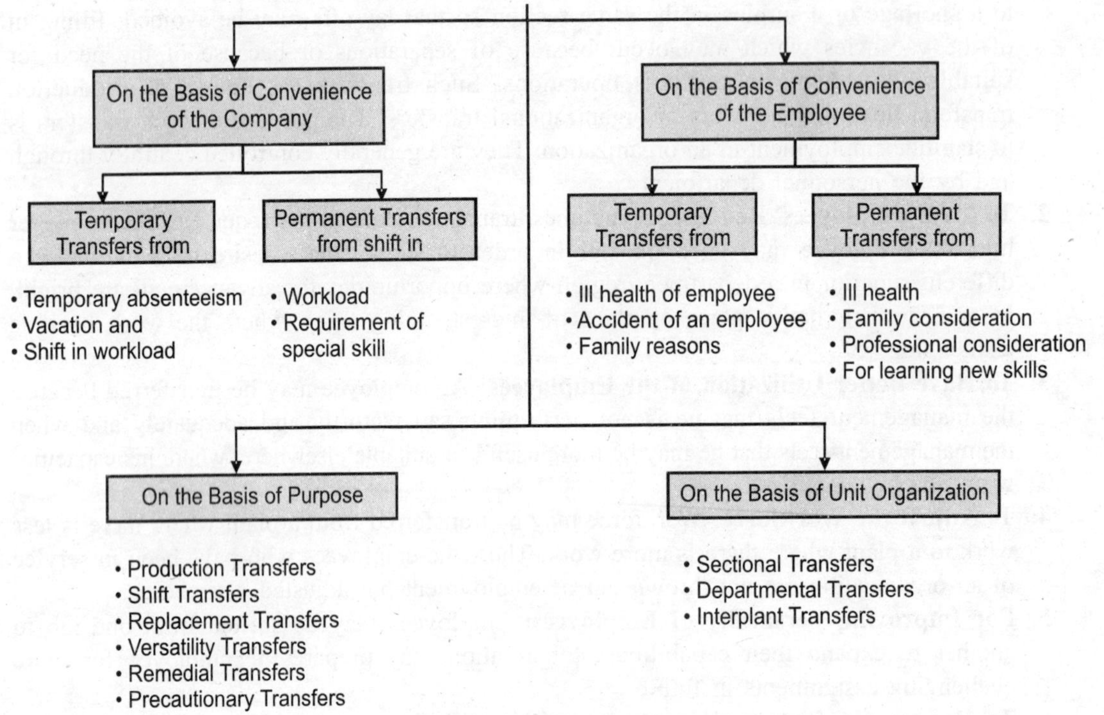

Fig. 12.2. Types of Transfer.

The transfers are effected on the basis of purpose and unit organization.

On the basis of Purpose

(i) **Production Transfers** are to deal with the shortage of surplus of workforce. A shortage or surplus of the workforce is common in different departments in a plant or several plants in an organization. Surplus employees in a department have to be laid off, unless they are transferred to another department. Transfers effected to avoid such inevitable lay-offs are called production transfers.

(ii) **Replacement Transfers** are the transfers of senior employees to replace the junior employees or new employees, when the latter are laid-off or shifted to other jobs. Sometimes, it is a temporary arrangement to make use of the services of the senior personnel.

(iii) **Versatility Transfers** are effected to make employees versatile and competent in more than one skill. It aims at giving training to the employees of various jobs of similar nature having different operations. It helps the employees to get them prepared for promotions and also helps the employer in developing the effective manpower prepared to handle the higher openings.

(iv) **Shift Transfers** are where employees are transferred from one shift to another on similar jobs. In some undertakings where shifts are operated regularly, employees may be recruited permanently for the shift, but in some cases they are rotated from one shift to another as a matter of practice, because many employees dislike second or third shift assignment as it interferes with their social or family engagements.

(v) **Precautionary Transfers** are made as a precautionary measure to avoid the misuse of office or misappropriation of funds by the employees. In some undertakings, where there are chances of misuse of office or misappropriation of funds. Generally, it is mentioned in the transfer policy of the organization that an employee cannot stay at one post for more than 3 years or so.

(vi) **Remedial Transfers** are effected at the request of the employees and are, therefore, called personal transfers. Personal transfers take place because the initial placement of an employee may have been faulty or the worker may not get along with his supervisor or with other workers in the department. He may be getting too old to continue his regular job or working conditions may not be well adapted to his personal health. If the job is repetitive, the employee may stagnate and would benefit by transfer to a different kind of work.

On the Basis of Unit

(i) **Sectional Transfers** are made within the department from one section to another. The main purpose of such transfers may be to train the workers and prepare them to handle the operations of the different sections of the department.

(ii) **Departmental Transfers** are transfers from one department to another department within the plant. Such transfers are made if the nature of work is same or substantially the same in both the departments such as clerical or routine jobs.

(iii) **Inter-Plant Transfers** are more than one plants under the control of same management; transfer may be made from one plant to another on varied reasons. Such transfers are called inter-plant transfers.

RIGHT SIZING OF WORKFORCE AND ITS NEED

For every organization, there is need to have the right or an appropriate size of workforce. It should be as per the requirements of the organization. The process of matching the supply of requisite workforce with need of the organization is called right sizing of the workforce. The right sizing of workforce in the organization can be done by adopting a suitable transfer policy.

Why Need for Right Sizing of Workforce?

There are circumstances and occasions which arise in day to day functioning of organizations, when there is need to keep the size of workforce right or in order as per requirement. Need for this purpose arises due to the following reasons:

- When quantity of production increases
- When work requirements fluctuate
- When organizational structure changes
- Introduction of new lines of production
- Dropping of existing product lines
- For suitable adjustments in business operations
- Reallocation of workforce due to a shortage or surplus in the same section

So for right sizing, production transfers, flexibility transfers and organizational transfers are required.

For right sizing of workforce impartial transfer policy is needed. For successful transfer policies, it is necessary to have a proper job description and job analysis. Care should be taken to ensure that frequent or large-scale transfers are avoided by laying down adequate selection and placement procedures for the purpose.

- Specifically clarify the types of transfers and the conditions under which these will be made;
- Locate the authority in some officer who may initiate and implement transfers;
- Indicate whether transfers can be made only within a subunit or also between departments, divisions/plants;
- Indicate the basis for transfer, i.e., whether it will be based on seniority or on skill and competence or any other factor;
- Decide the rate of pay to be given to the transferee;
- Intimate the fact of transfer to the person concerned well in advance;
- Be in writing and duly communicated to all concerned;
- Not be made frequently and not for the sake of transfer only.

In making transfers, the usual policy that is followed is to pay to the employee the actual cost of moving the household to the place of transfer.

REVIEW QUESTIONS

1. What is promotion? Explain the basic features of a sound promotion policy.
2. Discuss the purpose or benefits of promotion. Should it be based on seniority or merit? Give arguments.
3. Define promotion. Discuss the basis of promotions. What important decisions are taken in this respect?
4. What are the criteria for the sound promotion policy? Discuss principles or elements for sound promotion policy.
5. What is meant by transfer? Discuss the main attributes of transfer.
6. What do you mean by transfers? What are the reasons for transfers?
7. Discuss types of transfers on the basis of purpose and on the basis of unit organization.

8. Write short notes on :
   (a) Types of transfers on the basis of convenience of the company
   (b) Types of transfers on the basis of convenience of the employee
   (c) Need for right sizing of workforce
   (d) Transfer policy

CASE STUDY

Promotion Criteria

Mr. Bal Krishan is the Chairman of XYZ Limited. Recently, it was decided by the Board of Directors that it would be profitable for the corporation to open its own HR Department. Mr. Bal Krishan has been directed to pick up a person who he feels in capable of heading the department, and then putting this person in-charge of getting the department on its feet. After considering a number of good men, Mr. Bal Krishan has narrowed the field down to two possible choices: Vijay Bhatia and Om Verma.

Vijay Bhatia has a good track record with the company. He was hired seven year ago, and through the years he has shown a good ideal of drive and initiative in all of his endeavours. He is an aggressive young man, and has received the nickname of go-getter in his department. Although Vijay seems to be more concerned at times with ends rather than means, he is very efficient and he is considered a good leader by those who work under him. Vijay is also credited with accepting full responsibility, in all cases, and making quick decisions when action is called for.

Om Verma has been with the company for ten years. He is well liked by all in his department, and his work is first rate. Om's leadership style differs from Vijay's in that Om is not as aggressive and quick to act as Vijay. Before Om makes a decision, he generally consults others who he feels can contribute further information on a given subject. This often includes those who work under him. Those who work under Om consider him a good leader, and state that the atmosphere of participation produced by him really encourages their utmost individual output while on the job. This can be seen by the production increase which soon occurred when Om became the head of his workforce.

Questions

1. If you were Mr. Bal Krishan, whom would you select as the head of the HR Department? Why?
2. Will you give any weightage to the length of service in the organization? Why?

REFERENCES

1. Yoder, D. Heneman, Turnball, H.G. and Stone C.H. (1958). "Handbook of Personnel Management and Labour Relations", McGraw-Hill Book Co., New York, pp. 9.5.
2. Watkins, G., et al. (1950). "The Management of Personnel Relations", pp. 446-450.
3. Mamoria, C.B. and Gankar, S.V. (2008). "Personnel Management", Himalaya Publishing House, Mumbai, pp. 257-259.
4. Dessler, Gary, (1998). HRM, Prentice-Hall of India, New Delhi.
5. Mahapatra, B.B. (2010). HRM, New Age International Publishers, pp. 84-86.
6. Chatterjee, N.N. (1980). "Management of Personnel in Indian Enterprises", Allied Book Agency, Calcutta, pp. 130-131.

CHAPTER

13 Human Resource Development

CHAPTER'S OUTLINE

- Introduction
- Meaning of Human Resource Development
- Strategic Roles of HRD Professionals
- Objectives and Mechanism of HRD
- Human Resource Development Strategies
- Distinction between HRM and HRD
- Role of Training in HRD
- Knowledge Resources
- Knowledge Management
- Impact of Globalization on HRM
- Problems of HRM—Transnational and Multinational

INTRODUCTION

Human resources constitute the only active factor of production. The factors like land, capital, and technology are passive. No matter what quantity and quality of these passive factors you have. These factors cannot assure you of high growth of your organization as their utilization depends upon human resources. For the growth of the organizations proper human resource management (HRM) is not enough, rather human resource development (HRD) too is essential. HRD involves the upgrading of skills, extending the knowledge resources, and competencies of human resource.

HRD is a new concept that has evolved in the last decade. HRD in USA is identified with training and development and it is only in the recent years that other components of HRD are being included under the term HRD. In India, some organizations have taken the lead of evolving and implementing an integrated HRD system. So HRD is an integrated and multidisciplinary approach to development of human resources in the organization. HRD, in fact, is a positive concept in HRM.

Development of human resources is essential for any organization that would like to be dynamic and growth oriented. Unlike other resources, human resources have rather unlimited potential capabilities. The potential can be used only by creating a climate that can continuously identify, bring to surface nurture and use the capabilities of people. HRD system aims at creating such a climate. A number of HRD techniques have been developed in recent past years to perform the above task based on certain principles. This unit provides an understanding of the concept of HRD system, related mechanisms and the changing boundaries of the HRD.

MEANING OF HUMAN RESOURCE DEVELOPMENT

In order to define HRD, let us first discuss human resources and development separately.

HRD

Human resources can be viewed as the sum of knowledge, skills, attitudes, commitment, values and the life of the people of an organization.

Development is acquisition of capabilities that are needed to do the present job or the future expected job.

HRD is thus defined as the process to enhance an employee's capacity to successfully handle greater responsibilities through formal and informal means. In other words, *HRD may be defined as a continuous process to ensure the development of employee competencies, dynamism, motivation and effectiveness in a systematic and planned way.* HRD brings about all round development of the people so that they can contribute their best to the organization, society and nation.

Definitions

According to **T.V. Rao**, HRD is a process in which the employee's of organization are continually helped in a planned way to:

(a) acquire or sharpen capabilities required to perform various functions associated with their present or expected future roles.

(b) develop their general capabilities as individuals and discover and exploit their own inner potentials for their own organizational purposes.

(c) develop an organizational culture in which superior-subordinate relationships, team work and collaboration among subunits are strong and contribute to the professional well-being, motivation of employees."

According to **C. Leon Magginson**, "*HRD may be defined as development of people by providing the right environment where each individual may grow to his fullest potentialities. Human resources are viewed as total knowledge skills, creative abilities, talents and aptitudes of an organization's workforce as well as values, attitudes and beliefs of individuals involved.*"

According to **Udai Pareek**, "*Broadly there are three meanings attached to the concept of HRD:*

(a) In the first place, persons working in the organization is regarded as a valuable resource implying that there is a need to invest time and effort in their development.
(b) Secondly, they are human resources which mean that they have their own special characteristics and, therefore, cannot be treated like material resources. The approach focuses on the need to humanize organizational life and introduce human values in the organization.
(c) And thirdly, the term human resource does not merely focus on employees and individuals, but also in other social realities, units and processes in the organization. These include the role of a job a person has in the organization, the dyadic unit, the various teams in which people work, the inter-team processes and the entity of total organizations."

According to **Ishwar Dayal**, "*HRD involves:*

(a) ways to better adjust the individual to his job and the environment;
(b) the greatest involvement of an employee in various aspects of his work; and
(c) the greatest concern for enhancing the capabilities of the individual."

According to **L.P. Singh**, "*HRD refers to improvement in the capacities and capabilities of the personnel in relation to the needs of that particular sector. It involves the creation of a climate in which the flower of human knowledge, skills, capabilities, creativity can bloom .... HRD seeks to provide a package of systems and processes through which these can be cultivated and enhanced among the people forming part of the network of roles in that sector.*"

Features or Nature of HRD

On the basis of the above given definitions, the following features of HRD may be identified:

1. **Continuous and Dynamic Process:** HRD is a continuous and dynamic process which believes in the need for continuous development of personnel to face the innumerable challenges in the functioning of an organization. It is based on the belief that there is no end to the development of an individual and the learning process can continue throughout the life.
2. **Planned and Systematic Approach:** HRD is a planned and systematic approach to the development of people. HRD is a system consisting of several interdependent and interrelated subsystems, e.g., performance appraisal, training, job enrichment, etc. While designing a HRD system, enough attention should be paid to building linkages between the various subsystems.
3. **Interdisciplinary Approach:** HRD is an interdisciplinary approach. It involves collection of ideas for many sciences. It makes use of principles and concepts of behavioural sciences for the development of people. It uses knowledge drawn from psychology, sociology, anthropology, economics and political science for planning and implementing various programmes for the development of individuals, groups and the organization.
4. **Micro and Macro Aspects:** HRD has both micro and macro aspects. At the macro level, HRD is described as the core of all development activities in the sense of improvement of quality of life of people of a nation. At the micro level, HRD involves the improvement in the quality of managers and workers so as to achieve greater quality and higher levels of productivity.

5. **HRD improves quality of life:** HRD enables the employee discovers and utilizes his capabilities in service of organizational goals. He finds a new meaning in work, when managers support such initiatives through incentive plans and challenging work assignments. The whole effort of HRD, thus, is focused on improving the quality of life of employees working at various levels in an organization.

Thus, HRD is the essential ingredient of any human resource system poised to achieve productivity, quality, efficiency and effectiveness.

STRATEGIC ROLES OF HRD PROFESSIONALS

In the article on HRD competencies and future trends in HRD, **Pat McLagan** (1996) identified nine important roles for HRD practitioners to perform. As HRD practitioners create rather than just respond, they will seek leverage and ways to help managers, teams, and individuals take charge of their own human resource practices. **According to McLagan**, "*HRD may be the only function in a clear position to represent human ethics and morality*". It is in the following roles shown in Table 13.1 that the present HRD professionals are challenged to create new ways to address the human resources issues:

Table 13.1: Strategic Roles of HRD Professionals in Organization Activities

S. No.	Roles	Activities
1.	HR strategic advisor	In this role the issues and trends concerning an organization's external and internal people are brought to the attention of the strategic decision-makers.
2.	HR systems designer and developer	This role involves designing and preparing HR systems for implementation so that HR systems and actions are mutually reinforcing and have maximum impact on organizational performance, development and endurance.
3.	Organization change consultant	This role means facilitating the development and implementation of strategies for transforming organization.
4.	Organization design consultant	This role involves identifying the work required to fulfil organizational strategies. It also involves organizing the work so that it makes efficient and effective use of resources.
5.	Learning programme specialist	In this role learning needs are identified to design and develop structured learning programmes and materials in a variety of media formats for self-study and workshop or electronic delivery.
6.	Instructor/facilitator	This is an increasingly difficult role. In it information is presented, structural learning experiences are led and group discussions and group processes facilitated.
7.	Individual development and career consultant	This role involves helping people assess their competencies, values and goals so they can identify, plan, and implement development actions.
8.	Performance consultant	This role means assisting a group or individuals to add value in the workplace. It's a coaching and consulting role in which HRD people perform both analytical and systems design work.
9.	Researcher	This role involves assessing HRD practices and programmes and their impact empirically. It also means communicating results so that the organization and its people accelerate their change and development.

Source: McLagan Pat (1996), Great Ideas Revisited. Training and Development, January 1996, pp. 60-65.

OBJECTIVES AND MECHANISM OF HRD

Objectives

HRD, basically aims at developing:

1. The capabilities of each employee as an individual;
2. The capabilities of each individual in relation to his or her present role;
3. The capabilities of each employee in relation to his or her expected future roles;
4. Strengthen the superior relationship between each employee and his or her employer;
5. The team spirit and functioning in every organizational unit;
6. Collaboration among different units of the organization;
7. The organization's overall health and self-renewing capabilities, which, in turn, increase the enabling capabilities of individuals, dyads, teams and the entire organization; and
8. Develop and maintain high motivation level of employees.

Mechanism

Various thinkers and professionals have given divergent views and designed the mechanism in different ways. There is unanimity of opinion among HRD practitioners regarding the following instruments of HRD:

1. **Performance Appraisal:** Performance appraisal is an important instrument in HRD. It is the process of assessing the performance and progress of an employee or of a group of employees on a given job and his potential for future development. The objective of performance appraisal is to determine the present state of efficiency of an employee in order to establish the actual need for training. The process of performance appraisal consists of setting standards for performance, communicating the standards to the employees, measuring the performance and comparing the actual performance with the standards set.
2. **Instrument of Potential Appraisal:** Potential appraisal is used for providing necessary data which helps in preparing career plans for individuals. This technique aims at development of latent abilities of individuals. This is a process of developing in the employees, capacities to perform new roles and responsibilities. This need is generally, felt when the organization is diversifying or introducing changes. The major objective of potential appraisal is to ensure a good match between the employees and the job.
3. **Counselling and Monitoring:** Counselling is a two-way process in which a counsellor, provides advice and assistance to his subordinates. Performance counselling means the help given by a superior to his subordinate in improving the performance. It is in fact, a process of guiding a subordinate to adjust better with his work environment and to better understand others so that his dealings with them can be effective and purposeful.
4. **Motivation among the Employees of an Organization:** It has been, generally, noticed that the performance of the personnel either as individuals or members of a group is less as compared to their capabilities in terms of skills, abilities and capacities. A climate of creativity must be developed and maintained by the management so that the performance levels must come upto the mark and growth becomes a way of life in the organization. This is possible only with proper motivation of employees.
5. **Training Tool:** Training is an investment in the HRD process which gives dividends both in short and long run. The ultimate goal of training is improving competence of the

employees for raising the standards of organizational performance. An organization can do better if it invests in technology development and improvement of human systems, training is crucial for both of these. Lack of training may result in poor work performance, low production, demotivation and customer dissatisfaction. But it must be ensured by the HRD section that training is translated into practice. If one acquires knowledge but does not practise it, it will be useless.

6. **Building of Team Work:** The HRD section must try to develop a habit of team work among the human resources. Team work requires among other things, that the members have an image of their own team mates, which coincides as precisely as possible with reality. In addition, each member must have a self-image which adjusts to reality as much as possible and thus, coincides with the image the other members have of him.
7. **Creating Effective HRD Climate:** HRD climate is one of the prerequisites of effective HRD process implementation. It is an integral part of organizational climate. HRD climate creates interest and motivation among the employees to stay long in an organization. It creates growth opportunities and recognition. Its success is vitally based on the top management's confidence in employees which will propel them to take initiative and meet challenging responsibilities for the organization. Employees' dignity and individuality is boosted when an effective HRD climate is created. A dynamic HRD climate can be conducive to development of both the individual as well as the organization.
8. **Use of Quality Circle Technique:** A quality circle is a small group of employees doing similar or related work who meet regularly to identify, analyze and solve product related problems and to improve general relations. The quality circles are generally, autonomous units, usually led by a supervisor or a senior worker and organized as work units. The workers, who have a shared area of responsibility, meet periodically to discuss, analyze and propose solutions to ongoing problems.
9. **Quality of Working Life:** The quality of the workers' conditions, both working and living, influences the workers' satisfaction and job satisfaction to a large extent. Inadequate working and living conditions produce adverse mental and physical effects on the employees, which leads to decline in their efficiency and ultimately in the overall productivity of the organization. The HRD system should take care of employee's health and well-being of their families by providing them with better living and working conditions. Quality of working life generally promotes a healthy atmosphere of development and motivation among employees.
10. **Developing Emotional Intelligence:** Human resources are considered to be the greatest assets in any organization. It is, thus, essential to understand the role of emotional intelligence in enhancing the productivity of the human resources to achieve the overall success. Emotions of the employees play an important role in determining their productivity and output. HRD should thus focus on enhancing the emotional intelligence of the organization.
11. **Emphasis on Excellence:** Excellence is a state of mind which prepares the employees to perform duties with dedication. It also creates self-reliance and helps him to have a vision and an urge to do better and better. HRD approach should include, continuous training and development for all, performance planning and objective appraisal, emergence of self managing groups with less supervision, flexible attitude towards work and enriched job

contents, meaningful participation of workers in management, and creation of a will to work.

12. **Emphasis on Flexibility:** The HRD administrative machinery must become flexible and be able to respond quickly and effectively to a changing environment as rigid and inflexible systems will not be able to deal with the changing situations. An immediate need is an appropriate HRD approach at the micro level with an in-built system of training, career development, job enrichment, job rotation, and employee participation in the management.

HUMAN RESOURCE DEVELOPMENT STRATEGIES

Some new trends have been taking place in the field of HRD in the recent years. Some of the strategies of HRD are explained as follows:

1. **Total Quality Management (TQM):** TQM is a dynamic concept like HRD. TQM aims at continuous improvement in the quality of products, which calls for the improvement in the quality of work of employees through training and development. Total quality management can succeed only if it has the support of total quality people. TQM cannot work without TQL because processes cannot work till people work.

   The Total Quality Human Resource Management approach involves:

   (i) **Philosophy:** Shared responsibility, commitment and rewards.

   (ii) **Business Objectives:** Increased quality, productivity, customer satisfaction, employee satisfaction and loyalty.

   (iii) **Quality Objectives:** Total quality management and continuous improvement at and across every level.

   (iv) **Business Information Sharing:** Open books, share board information on profits, productivity, quality, costs, capital spending plans.

   (v) **Major Constituents:** Major constituents are shareholders, customers and all employees.

   (vi) **Education and Training:** Quality and economic education, multiple skill- training, problem solving and group process.

   (vii) **Reward Structure:** Reward structure designed and adjusted by the management employee committee, formal, early union involvement.

   (viii) **Job Security:** Job security ensured by formal commitment, a key consideration in all decisions.

2. **Kaizen:** Kaizen as a Japanese word which means continuous improvement with the involvement of everybody in the organization so as to generate value for customers. The message of Kaizen strategy is that not a day should go without some kind of improvement being made somewhere in the organization. It involves small improvements on ongoing basis. A Kaizen programme can be divided into three segments:

   (i) **Management Oriented Kaizen.** This segment concentrates on the most strategic and logistic issues and provides the momentum to keep up progress and morale.

   (ii) **Group Oriented Kaizen.** The group oriented kaizen is a permanent approach and is represented by quality circles and other small group activities.

   (iii) **Individual Oriented Kaizen.** Individual oriented kaizen is manifested in the form of suggestions. It is a morale booster.

There are five steps in kaizen programme:

1. Straighten up
2. Put things in order
3. Clean up
4. Personal cleanliness
5. Discipline

Kaizen practitioners view quality as an endless journey, not a final destination. They are always experimenting, measuring, adjusting and improving. Rather than naively assuming that zero defects means perfection, they search for potential and actual trouble spots for improvement of product design and processes.

3. **Just in Time Production:** Just in Time (JIT) production is also called hand-to-mouth approach to production. JIT focuses attention on eliminating waste by purchasing or manufacturing just enough of the right items just in time. JIT attacks the problem of bloated inventories that hamper productivity and profitability. JIT approach when applied to human resources implies multifunctional workers. These workers are a key factor in designing of streamlined process. The processes are designed in such a way that each worker can handle two or more machines and move from one centre to another. Development of such workers not only decreases the number of workers and increases productivity but also increases teamwork and morale among the workers. The potential benefits of JIT include quality improvement, higher productivity, lower cost, less work in process, less inventory of raw materials, finished goods, saved space, increased team-work, higher workers' morale and motivation. However, implementation of JIT will require considerable cooperation between the management and the workers.
4. **Empowerment:** This strategy is based on the philosophy that more power you give to the lower levels the more you have in terms of productivity and performance. This technique is seen by the traditional authoritarian managers as a threat to their authority. But nowadays the issue is not whether to give empowerment to workers or not, rather the issue is how empowerment should take place. Empowerment can take place when the employees are adequately trained, provided with all relevant information and the best possible tools, fully involved in key decisions and are fully rewarded for results.
5. **Benchmarking:** Benchmarking is the practice of identifying, studying and building upon best practices in the industry or in the world. Benchmarking helps establish quality targets which lead to a competitive advantage. The benchmarkers guide includes the following points:
   (i) Pick a specific area you want to improve. Study your own procedures thoroughly and choose a company or companies to benchmark that handle the process well.
   (ii) Send out the people who will have to make the changes. It won't help if senior executives or consultants do the benchmarking, then come back and tell the concerned workers of a process what to do.
   (iii) Be prepared to exchange information.
   (iv) Avoid legal problems and respect the confidentiality of the data you obtain.
6. **Learning Organization:** Learning is the organizational capability to recognize and nurture the development of skills, abilities and knowledge base. It is exemplified by company-

wide training, foundational knowledge, process knowledge, educational development, continuous self-improvement and managerial learning which are the well recognised mechanisms of HRD. TQM is a positive step towards developing learning organization.

In the current dynamic business environment, the learning organizations alone will survive because of their competence to learn, create, codify and use knowledge faster than their rivals. The future organization must be built as a complex institution in which thinking, learning and knowledge creation takes place, constantly generating ideas that will permit the transformation of the organization by its people. The above-mentioned strategies may bring drastic changes in the outlook and approaches towards management of human resources.

DISTINCTION BETWEEN HRM AND HRD

There has been an increasing trend in large organizations appointing HRD managers. However, many people are not clear as to what is the difference between HRM and HRD functions. As a result we find instances of personnel managers being re-designated HRD managers. We also find cases of HRD manager being expected to handle the personnel functions in addition to HRD. Human resource development efforts aim at providing conditions in which the employees can improve their skills, knowledge, energy and talents, which in turn may improve productivity. Human resource development differs from Personnel/Human Resource Management in respect of the following:

1. **Meaning.** Personnel management is the recruitment, selection, development, utilization, compensation and motivation of human resources by an organization. Human Resource Development is concerned with the development of human resources in an organization. It means improving the existing capabilities of the human resources in the organization and helping them to acquire new capabilities required for the achievement of the organizational and individual goals.
2. **Responsibility.** The personnel function is supposed to be the responsibility of the personnel department whereas human resource development is regarded as the concern of all managers in the organization. Every manager is concerned with developing the competencies of all those working under his guidance and supervision.
3. **Orientation.** The traditional personnel function is regarded as mainly a service function responding to the demands of the organization. But HRD is regarded as a proactive function. The function of HRD is not merely to cope with the needs of the organization but also to anticipate them and to act on them in advance.
4. **Mechanisms.** The traditional personnel function considers salary and other economic benefits, as important motivators. HRD emphasizes the importance of higher needs in motivating individuals. It considers autonomous work groups, job enrichment, job challenge and creativity as the main motivating forces.
5. **Emphasis on Culture.** The emphasis in the traditional personnel function is on increasing people's efficiency. The emphasis in HRD is on building the right type of culture in the organization—a culture which has many characteristics as mutual trust, openness, collaboration, clarity of goals and risk-taking capacity.

HRD MODEL FOR ORGANIZATIONAL EFFECTIVENESS

An HRD mechanism is the most important element in organizational effectiveness. Other resources like capital assets, technology cannot ensure long-term survival and growth of the organization. It is possible only through the HRD mechanism. HRD in this context can contribute for organizational effectiveness.

1. Optimizing the use of employees for the long-run growth of the organization.
2. Enabling employees to grow with the organization.
3. Helping in matching individual aspirations and organizational expectations.
4. Promoting collaboration and team spirit by establishing a climate of trust, openness and interdependence.
5. Maximizing managerial effectiveness by having an involved, committed and highly motivated team of managers.
6. Building the skills necessary to meet existing and long-term organizational needs.
7. Providing a favourable work environment and consciously fostering an open, largely participative management style based on trust and cooperation.
8. Achieving good employer-employee relations through regards for basic human values.

Organizational effectiveness results from trained and developed employees working in a healthy organization climate which results from both individual development interventions and organizational development plans.

Figure 13.1 shows the HRD model of organizational effectiveness.

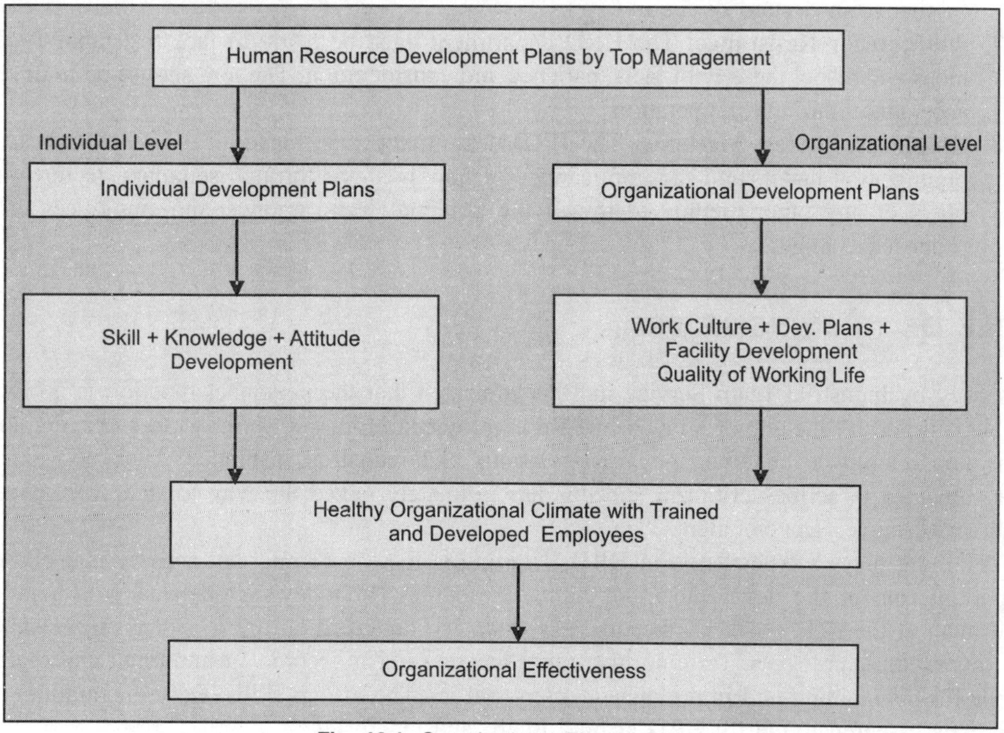

Fig. 13.1. Organizational Effectiveness.

The role of top management is very important in implementation of HRD plans for developing committed human resources and the work-environment committed to human resources.

Essentials of Effective Human Resource Development

HRD is an effort to develop capabilities and competencies among employees as well as create organizational environment conducive to the employees' development. While introducing HRD in an organization, the following essentials have to be kept in view:

1. **Will to Improve:** An urge and desire on the part of the human resources to find better methods to improve quality and productivity.
2. **Removing Hurdles:** Removal of hurdles and irritants from the organization affecting productivity of the employees.
3. **Competent Members of HRD Team:** Requisite skills, attitudes and ability in the persons engaged in HRD.
4. **Proper Coordination:** Proper rapport between the HRD members and the key personnel in the organization. Involvement of the personnel of the organization to get a lot of unwritten information for understanding the dynamics of the organization for developing an HRD programme.
5. **Appropriate Methods:** The need for suggesting the introduction of only such indigenous methods which can be implemented by the HRD division without much cost and resistance.
6. **Effective HR Information System:** Strengthening of human resource information system to keep continuous track of every employee and use performance appraisal, training, etc. to change in desired direction.
7. **Solution for Resistance:** The HRD department must be ready to face resistance to their ideas and dispel these with facts, patience and consideration. The aim should be to develop acceptance through cooperation.
8. **Emphasis on New Methods:** The HRD department must make all the employees in the organization understand the implications of new methods through seminars, lectures, role plays or any other method to thwart the potential fears amongst the employees of the proposed changes.

ROLE OF TRAINING IN HRD

A survey by Industrial Team Service in 1969 indicated that the personnel function is no longer viable if it doesn't include or allow scope for employment, training, welfare measures, employee education, employee benefits, industrial relations and industrial insurance. Thus, the concept was subjected to serious criticism and this has ultimately paved the way for the emergence of Human Resources Development.

Training plays a crucial role in HRD. Training is the most important activity that plays an important role in the development of human resources. In today's globalized world, putting right man at the right place has become essential. No organization has a choice on whether or not to develop employees. Training, therefore, has nowadays become an important and required factor for maintaining and improving interpersonal and intergroup skills. Before examining this role, it is essential to clarify HRD at both micro and macro levels.

HRD as stated earlier is mainly concerned with developing the competencies of people. When we call it a people-oriented concept then several questions come to mind like: should the people be developed in the larger and national context or in the smaller institutional context? Is it different at the macro level and micro level? As things stand now, HRD applies to both institutional (micro) as well as national (macro) issues. The main objective, however, is to develop the newer capabilities in people so as to enable them to tackle both present and future challenges while realizing organisational goals. However, it is useful both at macro and micro levels.

Macro Level: At the macro level HRD is concerned with the development of people for the nation's well-being. It takes health, capabilities, skills, attitudes of people which are more useful to the development of the nation as a whole. While calculating the national income and economic growth, the prospective HRD concept examines the individuals' potentialities, their attitudes, aspirations, skills, knowledge, etc. and establishes a concrete base for economic planning. However, HRD's contribution at macro level has not gained popularity as yet.

Micro Level: HRD has concern for grass root development in the organizations. Small wonder, then, that HRD was well received by companies' managements as they realized its importance and foresaw its future contribution for the individual and organizational development. Generally, HRD at micro level talks of the organization's manpower planning, selection, training, performance appraisal, development, potential appraisal, compensation, organizational development, etc. HRD's involvement in all these areas is mainly with an objective to develop certain new capabilities in people concerned to equip them to meet the present job challenges and to accept future job requirements.

Top management for HRD, both at micro and macro levels requires training for its employees as it is only through well-trained personnel, that an organization can achieve its goals.

Methods of Training*

The training of employee can be (i) on-the-job training and (ii) off-the-job training. In the first case, worker is trained under the guidance of a superior whereas off-the-job training is usually through lectures, conferences, case studies, audio visual, etc.

The role of training in HRD is explained below in terms of need for manpower training:

1. **Updating Knowledge:** Technological advancement, business environmental changes and new management philosophies have now made it imperative for the organization to renew and update the knowledge and skills of the employees so that they do not become redundant for obvious functional incompetence. The first and foremost need for manpower human resource training therefore, is to renew and update knowledge and skills of employees to sustain their effective performance and so also to develop them for future managerial positions.
2. **Avoiding Obsolescence:** Recent economic liberalization programmes of Government of India are necessitating organizational restructuring, which inter alia, calls for training the employees, irrespective of their functional level, for their redeployment in restructured jobs. Therefore, the second important need for training in HRD is to avert functional obsolescence.

* For the detailed discussion of the methods of training, refer Chapter 7 of this book.

3. **Improving Performance:** Continuous training being required to renew and update knowledge and skills of employees, it makes them functionally effective. The third need is, therefore, to make employees effective in their performance through continuous training.
4. **Developing Human Skills:** Apart from emphasizing on technical and conceptual skills, new training programmes also emphasize on developing human skills of employees. Such human skill is necessary for effective interpersonal relations and sustaining healthy work environment. This need for training therefore also cannot be altogether ignored.
5. **Imparting Trade-specific Skills:** In industrial employment, the convention is to recruit workers and employees through compulsory apprenticeship training. Such apprenticeship training enables an organization to impart industry and trade specific skills to workers. This also, therefore, is an important need for manpower training in HRD.
6. **Stabilizing the Workforce:** Throughout the world the importance of training is now increasingly felt for stabilizing the workforce to withstand the technological change and for making the organization dynamic in this changed process. Management theorists now unanimously agree that it is the responsibility of the organization to train and develop their manpower on a continuous basis.

Classification of Training Programmes Required for HRD

Depending on the functional level and occupational categories of employees, an organization can classify training programmes as shown in Table 13.2.

Table 13.2: Classification of Training Programmes

Level	Nos.	Types of Training
1. Workers	(i)	Introduction
	(ii)	Job Training
	(iii)	Craft Training
	(iv)	Special Purpose Training
2. Supervisors	(i)	Induction
	(ii)	Foremanship/Shop Floor Supervision
	(iii)	Manpower Management
3. Staff Members	(i)	Introduction
	(ii)	Professional
	(iii)	Technical
	(iv)	Human Relations
4. Managers and Executives	(i)	Induction
	(ii)	Executive Training
	(iii)	Training in Executive Development

Apart from the above routine training programmes for different levels, training on total quality awareness and training encompassing all aspects of total quality management have now become almost compulsory for all functional levels.

Role of Training Needs in Different Strategies for HRD

Table 13.3 shows four business strategies and highlights the implication of each for training practices:

- Concentration
- Internal growth
- External growth
- Disinvestment

Focus of each strategy differs. Amount and type of training also differs. Key issues in each strategy also differ. The end result of training for HRD is always positive and inspiring.

1. **A concentration strategy** focuses on increasing market share, reducing costs, or creating and maintaining a market niche for products and services. Southwest Airlines has a concentration strategy. It focuses on providing short-haul, low-fare, and high-frequency air transportation. It utilizes one type of aircraft (the Boeing 737), has no reserved seating, and serves no meals. This concentration strategy has enabled southwest to keep costs low and revenues high.
2. **An internal growth strategy** focuses on new market and product development, innovation, and joint ventures. For example, the merger between two publishing companies, McGraw-Hill and Richard D. Irwin, created one company with strengths in the US and the international college textbook markets.
3. **An external growth strategy** emphasizes acquiring vendors and suppliers or buying businesses that allow the company to expand into new markets. For example, General Electric, a manufacturer of lighting products and jet engines, acquired the National Broadcast Corporation (NBC), a television and communications company.
4. **A disinvestment strategy** emphasizes liquidation and divestiture of businesses. For example, General Mills sold its restaurant businesses.

Preliminary research suggests a link between business strategy and amount and type of training. Table 13.3 shows that training issues vary greatly from one strategy to another. **Divesting companies** need to train employees in job-search skills and to focus on cross-training remaining employees who may find themselves in jobs with expanding responsibilities. **Companies focusing on a market niche** (a concentration strategy need to emphasize skill currency and development of their existing workforce). **New companies formed from a merger** or acquisition need to ensure that employees have the skills needed to help the company reach its new strategic goals. Also, for mergers and acquisitions to be successful, employees need to learn about the new, merged organization and its culture. The organization must provide training on systems such as how the phone, e-mail, and company intranet work. Managers need to be educated on how to make the new merger successful (e.g., dealing with resistance to change).

Table 13.3: Implications of Business Strategy for Training

Strategy	Emphasis	How Achieved	Key Issues	Training Implications
Concentration	• Increased market share • Reduced operating costs • Market niche created or maintained	• Improve product quality • Improve productivity or innovate technical processes • Customize products or services	• Skill currency • Development of existing workforce	• Team building • Cross-training • Specialized programmes • Interpersonal skill training • On-the-job training
Internal Growth	• Market development • Product development • Innovation • Joint ventures	• Market existing products/add distribution channels • Expand global market • Modify existing products • Create new or different products • Expand through joint ownership	• Creation of new jobs and tasks • Innovation	• High-quality communication of product value • Cultural training • Development of organizational culture that values creative thinking and analysis • Technical competence in jobs • Manager training in feedback and communication • Conflict negotiation skills
External Growth (Acquisition)	• Horizontal integration • Vertical integration • Concentric diversification	• Acquire firms operating at same stage in product market chain (new market access) • Acquire business that can supply or buy products • Acquire firms that have nothing in common with acquiring firm	• Integration • Redundancy • Restructuring	• Determination of capabilities of employees in acquired firms • Integration of training systems • Methods and procedures of combined firms • Team building • Development of shared culture
Disinvestment	• Retrenchment • Turnaround • Divestiture • Liquidation	• Reduce costs • Reduce assets • Generate revenue • Redefine goals • Sell off all assets	• Efficiency	• Motivation, goal setting, time management, stress management, cross-training • Leadership training • Interpersonal communications • Outplacement assistance • Job-search skills training

Source: Raymend A. Noe and Amitabh Deo Kodwani, Employee Training and Development, Fourth edition, Tata McGraw-Hill Education Pvt. Ltd., New Delhi, 2008, pp. 60-62.

CONCLUSION

The discussion of the training need in HRD as given above boils down to the conclusion that training gives the following inspiring and productive results:

1. Growth, expansion and modernization cannot take place without trained manpower
2. It increases productivity and profitability, reduces cost and finally enhances skill and knowledge of the employee
3. Prevents obsolescence
4. Helps in developing a problem-solving attitude
5. Gives people awareness of rules and procedures
6. Training thus makes people more competent
7. Personnel become committed to their job resulting in proactiveness
8. People trust each other more

Finally, our approach to training must be to increase productivity and profitability and secondly to initiate personal growth and development.

KNOWLEDGE RESOURCES

Knowledge is regarded as power. It may revolutionize knowledgeable people, knowledge resources and the organizations.

Rapid changes in business and technology are forcing organizations to learn at an unprecedented rate. Many are realizing that unless knowledge resources are mobilized and transfer occurs at an equally rapid rate, their competitiveness is affected, leading them to focus more intensively on their knowledge assets or resources.

Knowledge Resources (Employee Knowledge + Process Knowledge + Stored Knowledge): Knowledge resources also known as knowledge assets, generally include databases, documents, policies and procedures as well as previously unarticulated expertise and experience residing in individual workers. Although the full specification of set of these knowledge resources/assets is evolving, there seems to be a consensus that they include employee knowledge, structure, culture and processes.

Employee Knowledge: Of these knowledge assets, the employee knowledge is greatly emphasized as it is tacit knowledge or unarticulated knowledge which is more personal, experiential, context specific and hard to formalize. It is difficult to communicate or share with others and is generally in the heads of individuals and teams. Knowledge in fact resides in employees. This viewpoint is valid and useful. Knowledgeable employees can be retained and attracted from other organizations to maximize their profitability, and market share.

Process Knowledge: Process knowledge is also an essential part of organizational knowledge. It has tremendous significance from a knowledge management point of view. Organisations have made a sizeable intellectual investment in the form of formalizations of processes. Descriptions of manufacturing processes, for instance, include the raw material and equipment used the appropriate environmental conditions to be realized. Knowledge resources or assets also include information and media, computer science, public health, and public policy. It is *explicit knowledge* which can easily be written down and codified. These descriptions are essential for training employees, establishing standards and communicating best practices within the organization. But these are by no means static. They keep on changing so knowledge resources are dynamic and need continuous system of tapping or collecting these resources and transfer to employees further establishing revised and modified standards and communicate for the benefit of organization.

Stored Knowledge: The third important knowledge resource is stored knowledge i.e. manuals, books, databases, intranets, magazines, etc.

Table 13.4 and Figures 13.2 and 13.3 further clarify the composition of knowledge resources.

Table 13.4: Where does KM Come From?

- Technology
    - Infrastructure, Database, Web, Interface
- Globalization
    - Worldwide markets, North American integration
- Demographics
    - Aging population, workforce mobility, diversity
- Economics
    - Knowledge economy
- Customer relations
    - Quality
- Increase in information
    - Specialization, Volume, Order

Sources: Brown J.S. and Duguid, P. (1991). Organizational Learning and Communities-of-Practice, *Organizational Science.* O'Dell C. and Grayson Jr., C.J. (1998). *If only we knew what we know.* Stewart, T. (2002).

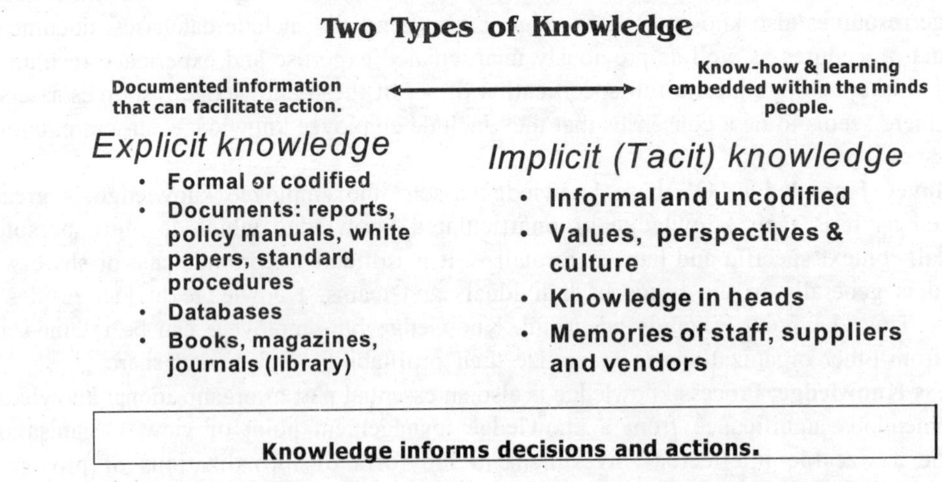

Fig. 13.2. Two Types of Knowledge.

Source: Polanyi, M. (1967). *The Tacit Dimension.* Leonard, D. and Sensiper, S. (1998). The Role of Tacit Knowledge in Group Innovation. *California Management Review.*

Layer of Knowledge

Implicit (Tacit)		Explicit
In people's heads.	Individual	Personal documents on my C:\
• Undocumented ways of working in teams, teaching. • Cultural conventions known and followed but not formalized.	Organizational	• Formalized process for developing curriculum. • Corporate polices and procedures.

Fig. 13.3. Layers of Knowledge.

Source: Luan, J. and Serban, A. (2002, June). Knowledge management concepts, models and applications. Paper presented at Annual AIR Forum, Toronto.

In this process of tapping of knowledge resources and proper knowledge management benefit not only the organization but also the employee of the organization and customers as their satisfaction increases.

A comprehensive explanation of knowledge resources can be discussed in the form of components which create knowledge. It is shown in Box-1. This is an alternative approach to knowledge resources in comparison to the approach given above.

Box-1 Components of Knowledge Resources

1. Experienced People. Experienced people have the historical perspective with the help of which they can view current situations; a newcomer does not have this advantage. As the experience grows, people are able to use short-cut solutions for similar problems they faced earlier. When they are faced with a new situation, they match it to make connections with what might have occurred earlier and evaluate decision in that light. Experienced employees can thus, analyze a situation accurately, quickly and efficiently. Experience is a very important source of knowledge.

2. Technical or Professional Education. Education, basic as well as technical and/or professional, is another important resource of knowledge. Knowledge is related to facts which can be learnt through formal as well as informal education. Because of this minimum qualifications are fixed for different jobs and posts in the organization.

3. Correct Judgement. Proper and correct judgement is another source of knowledge. Proper judgement of a situation helps in taking correct decisions. With judgement, knowledge can rise above and beyond an opinion and is refined every time it is applied and acted upon.

4. Values and Beliefs. Values and beliefs are so deeply ingrained into minds of the people who hold them that they find their way into most of decisions they make. The beliefs and values of key persons, thus, shape working of the organizations. Values followed by people also affect their attitude towards work. Values, assumptions and beliefs are important components knowledge.

5. Intelligence Quotient. Intelligence quotient of a person affects analytical abilities and decision-making powers. It also helps in improving performance or results. An intelligent person can understand things quickly accurately and can take appropriate decisions. Intelligent people are considered more knowledgeable since they can make optimum utilization of their knowledge.

6. Understanding of Ground Realities and Assumptions. Ground realities and their proper understanding helps in taking proper decisions. In business, so many assumptions are to be made regarding future situations. Ability to analyze these assumptions properly helps in knowledge management system.

KNOWLEDGE MANAGEMENT

What is Knowledge Management?

Knowledge management is the process by which the organizations generate wealth from its intellectual and other knowledge based assets. Knowledge management was first applied in the profit seeking enterprises to improve the operations to gain competitive advantage and make profits. Now, knowledge management can also be applied to non-profit-making institutions such as government and society at large.

Knowledge management has become the hottest subject of discussion today.

Definitions

According to **Michael J**, "*The knowledge management refers to the basic elements that include assessing, evaluation, and managing, organizing, filtering and distributing information in a manner that is useful to end users.*"

According to **Sviby Karl**, "*Knowledge management can be defined as an art of creating value from an organization's intangible assets.*"

According to **Roger Clarke**, "*Knowledge management is defined as the process of collecting, organizing, storing and disseminating knowledge.*"

Again in the words of **Roger Clarke**, "*The term knowledge is often referred to a body of facts and principles accumulated by mankind in the course of time.*"

According to **Keeler,** "*Knowledge management is the engine that transforms ideas into business value. It is a systematic process for creating, acquiring, synthesizing, sharing and using information, insights and experiences to achieve organizational goals*".

Objectives of Knowledge Management

The following objectives can be set in terms of the process within the context of knowledge management:

1. **Effective and Efficient Development of Ideas**: Ensure an effective and efficient development of new knowledge and improvement of existing knowledge with a view to the strategy of the organization and the individual objectives of the employee.
2. **Effective Capturing of Knowledge**: Ensure an effective securing of knowledge, which is also easily accessible to the whole organization.
3. **Ensure Effective Distribution of Knowledge**: Ensure a specific distribution of new knowledge to other departments and transfer of knowledge to new employees through knowledge transfer or relocation of knowledge bearers.

4. **Effective Combination of Available Knowledge:** Ensure the effective and efficient combination of the best knowledge available within an organization or its network. In terms of the dimensions of knowledge, the following objectives can be using knowledge management.
5. **Correct Record Keeping:** Keep the content of knowledge bearers up-to-date and correct under changing circumstances, apply the best knowledge.
6. **Optimal Location of Knowledge Bearers**: Make the location of knowledge bearers optimal in the context of service process; apply knowledge at the best location.
7. **Matching Knowledge Bearers and Users:** Improve the form of knowledge bearers in relation to the users and the expected use of it; apply knowledge in the best form.
8. **Accurate Adaptability in Knowledge Management:** Adapt availability of knowledge to the time that the knowledge is needed, apply knowledge when required.

Knowledge Management Process

Knowledge management is a process. It is dynamic process and a continuous process for the growth of organizations. The knowledge management process basically involves main steps as is shown in Figure 13.4.

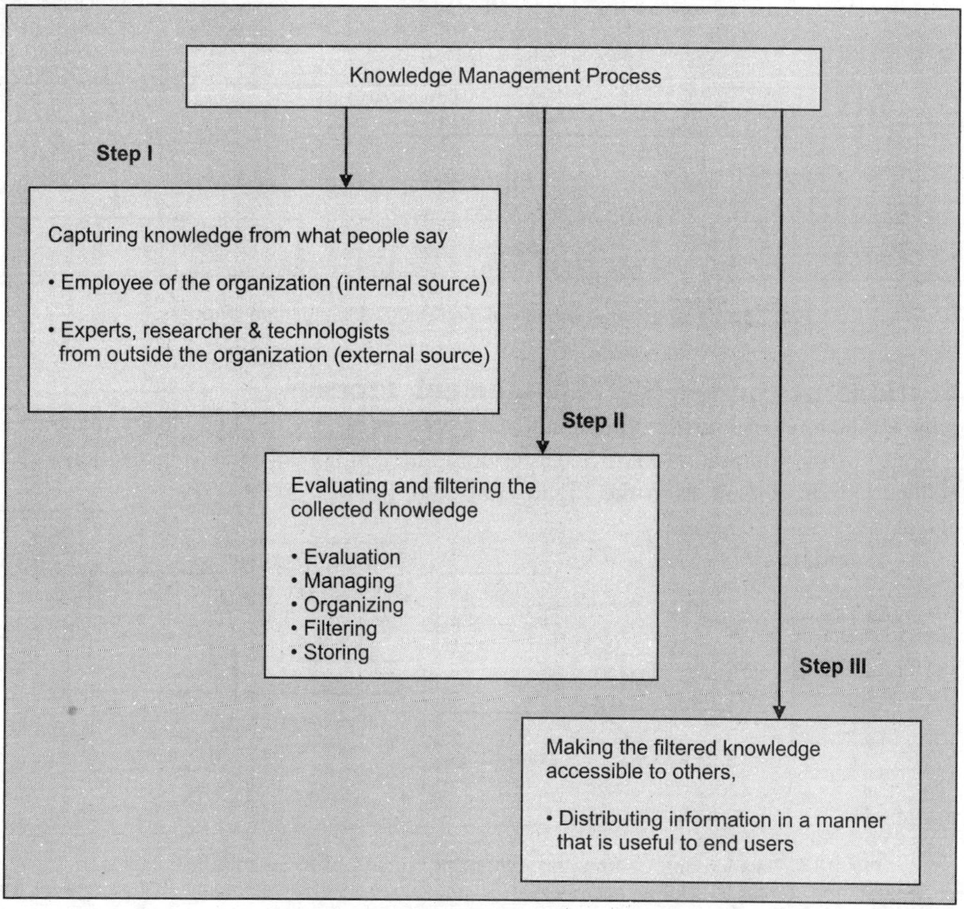

Fig. 13.4. Knowledge Management Process.

Step I : Capture knowledge from what people say.

Step II: Evaluate and filter the collected knowledge.

Step III: Make the filtered knowledge accessible to others.

The process of knowledge management can also be shown in Figure 13.5 which is an alternative approach.

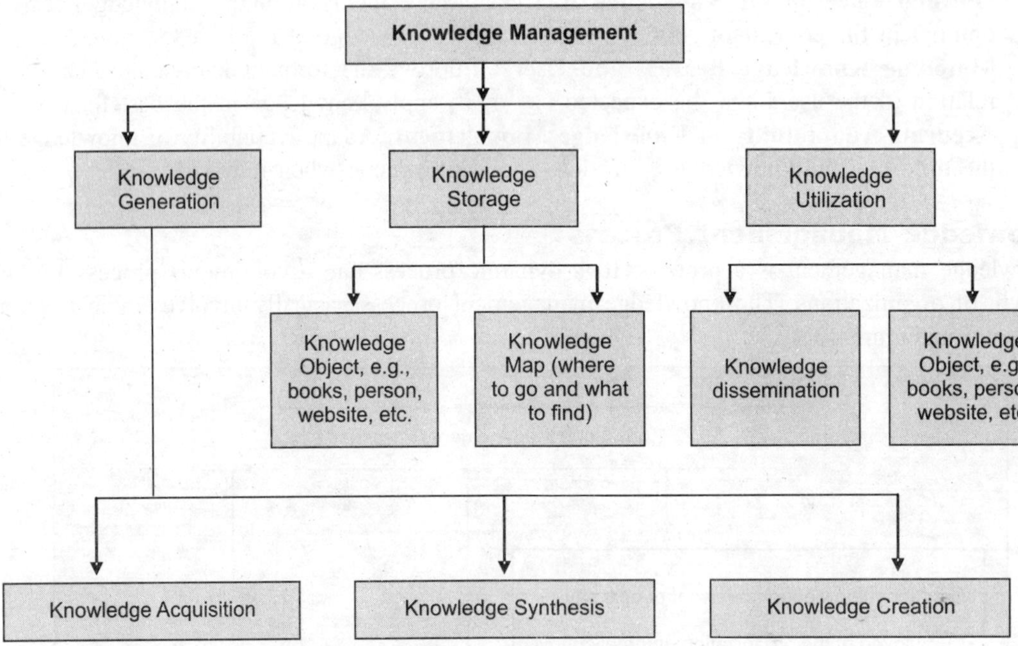

Fig. 13.5. Alternative Approach of Knowledge Management Process.

Implications of Knowledge Management Process

The main implication of knowledge management process is that the knowledge management is a continuous of data-information-knowledge-wisdom into component of an organization's customer satisfaction. This is evident from the Figure 13.6 and Table 13.5.

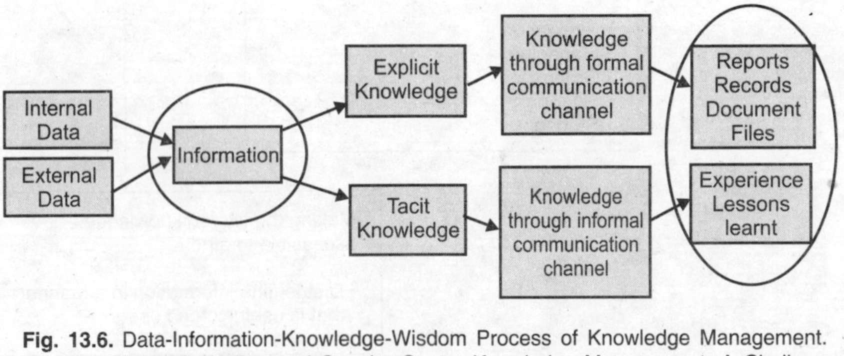

Fig. 13.6. Data-Information-Knowledge-Wisdom Process of Knowledge Management.

Source: Adapted from Giriraj, G. Halkar and Sangita Gupta, Knowledge Management: A Challenge for the 21st Century, published in IJTD Indian Journal of Training and Development, vol. XXXV, No. 1, Jan-March, 2005.

Table 13.5: Data Information and Knowledge

	Data	Information	Knowledge
Definition	Raw facts, figures and records contained in a system.	Data placed into a form that is accessible, timely and accurate	Information in context to make it insightful and relevant or human action.
Reason	Processing	Storing/Accessing	Insight, innovation improvement.

Source: Luan, J. and Serban, A. (2002, June). Knowledge management concepts, models and applications. Paper presented at Annual AIR Forum, Toronto.

Data, both internal and external, is an event or entity represented in some symbolic form and capable of being processed.

Information is when data is organized according to some preferences and in context.

Knowledge is the organized body of information or facts and principles accumulated by mankind in the course of time and knowledge.

Wisdom is the application of knowledge to produce the desired result

Data → Information → Knowledge → Wisdom sequence, as a matter of fact, reveals that knowledge can be sourced, stored, disseminated and used. *So the biggest challenge today is not only to capture knowledge but also to make it accessible to others after properly analyzing the captured knowledge.*

Another important implication of knowledge management process is that training should be provided to knowledge workers on how to utilize knowledge to get optimal results and why transfer of knowledge is required. Hence, the key challenge of the knowledge-based economy is to foster innovation.

Why is KM Crucial?

Knowledge management is crucial for the following reasons:

- Competitive marketplace.
- Accelerating rate of innovations that need to be assimilated at an even faster rate.
- Increasing mobility among employees leading to loss of knowledge.
- Majorities of the employees have less and less time to acquire knowledge.
- Competitive pressures leading to reduction in the size of the workforce holding special and strategic knowledge.

Knowledge management ought to be framed as follows:

- Conceptualizing organizational vision and communicating it to all the members of the organization.
- Creating organizational culture that motivates promotes and rewards people to create, share and use knowledge.
- Recognizing employee's personal efforts for taking challenges, finding innovative ideas for doing the task in different ways and rewarding them accordingly.

- Drafting compensation structure that supports special arrangement of bonuses and incentives for those who seek or generate ongoing information flow.
- Designing information systems that take regular feedback to guarantee ongoing information flow.
- Chalking out a performance management system that is based on evaluation of employee's performance as well as learning.
- Conducting education programmes for training and development.
- Encouraging employees to perform multifunctional responsibilities.
- Facilitating a work environment and culture that would render employees a feeling of freedom, trust and empowerment.
- Cultivating an organizational culture, wherein employees at all levels understand the importance of both learning and doing.

Importance of Effective Knowledge Management Programme

Knowledge revolution is the new revolution in information related areas. Today every organization needs to know what their knowledge assets are, and how to manage and make use of these assets to get maximum returns. It serves the users with ample information through tools, techniques and methods of KM. The practice of knowledge management can create wonderful results in any organizational context. Customers can be delighted with every transaction, becoming richer and more productive. Knowledge is the key driver, for those films who are keen to innovate and change the rules of the game. Consequently an effective knowledge management programme should help a company/organization do one or more of the following:

1. Foster innovation by an encouraging the free flow of ideas.
2. Improve customer service by streamlining response time.
3. Boost revenues by getting products and services to market faster.
4. Enhance employee retention rates by recognizing the value of employee's knowledge and rewarding them for it.
5. Streamline operations and reduce costs by eliminating redundant or unnecessary processes.
6. Involve collaboration, organized learning, best practices, workflow, IP management, document management, customer focus and using data meaningfully (data mining).

Lessons from Knowledge Management Experience of USA & Canada

Figure 13.7 and Table 13.6 show the knowledge experiences of western countries like USA and Canada which are considered the best knowledge management countries in the world.

Table 13.6: What are Organizations doing in Canada?

1. Knowledge capture and acquisition
   - E.g., environmental scanning.
2. Developing strategies for implicit K sharing:
   - E.g., CoPs, virtual teams, list of experts and mentoring.
3. Using technologies to store, analyze and distribute explicit K.
   - Corporate portals, business K base, process control inventories, CRM.

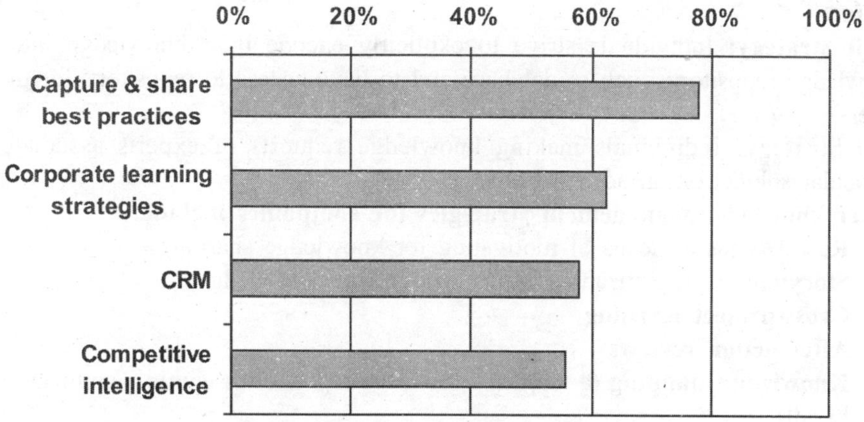

Fig. 13.7. Activities of US Companies in KM.

In USA 81% of businesses with KM solutions see productivity improvements. They capture and share best practices. 60% businesses use corporate learning strategies. In Canada environmental scanning is used for capturing and acquiring knowledge. The organizations build teams, involve experts and do mentoring for implicit knowledge sharing. Besides, Canadian organizations use corporate portals, business knowledge base, process control inventories for using technologies to store, analyze and distribute to explicit knowledge.

Tools and Strategies of Knowledge Management

Tools

1. **Intranet/Extranets:** Which allow the seekers to access the organization's information without any geographical boundary?
2. **Groupware:** This offers a platform for intercommunication between the employees in a organization. e.g. Lotus Notes, Netscape.
3. **Electronic Document Management**: This technology, meant for managing the knowledge, contends documents electronically mainly online in the knowledge management system.
4. **Information Retrieval Tools:** Information retrieval offers searching the required knowledge through free text search and search with advanced algorithms so that all the related knowledge can be found.
5. **Data Analysis:** Generally used methods of data analysis are pattern recognition, classification and forecasting.
6. **Data Warehousing:** Data warehousing and data mining are the technologies where the structured knowledge can be stored.
7. **Metadata:** Metadata is simply information added to a document that makes it easier to access and reuse that content. It is also referred to as simply "data about data".
8. **Help Desk Technologies:** It is primarily concerned with routing requests for help from information seekers to the right technical resolution person within an organization.

Strategies

1. **Push Strategy:** Individuals strive to explicitly encode their knowledge into a shared knowledge repository, such as database and to have access to repository for the ideas of others.
2. **Pull Strategy:** Individuals making knowledge requests of experts associated with a particular subject on an ad hoc basis.
3. **Other knowledge management strategies for companies include:**
   (i) **Rewards** (as a means of motivating for knowledge sharing)
   (ii) **Storytelling** (as a means of transferring tacit knowledge)
   (iii) **Cross-project learning**
   (iv) **After action reviews**
   (v) **Knowledge mapping** (a map of knowledge repositories within a company accessible by all)
   (vi) **Expert directories** (to enable knowledge seeker to reach to experts)
   (vii) **Competence management** (systematic evaluation and planning of competences of individual organization members)
   (viii) **Proximity and architecture** (the physical situation of employees can be either conducive or obstructive to knowledge sharing)
   (ix) **Collaborative technologies** (groupware, etc.)
   (x) **Knowledge brokers** (some organizational members take on responsibility for a specific "field" and act as first reference on whom to talk about a specific subject).

Essentials for Successful Managing of Knowledge

Successful managing of knowledge requires instilling the culture and helping people find ways to share and utilize their cooperative knowledge. Figure 13.8 shows five important tasks needed to display successful management of knowledge. These are five essentials for successful managing of knowledge.

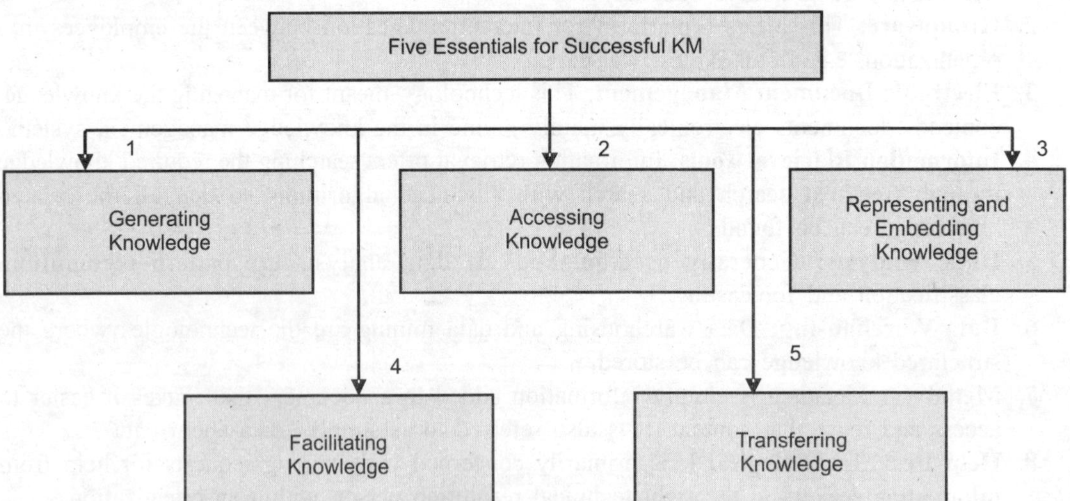

Fig. 13.8. Essentials for Successful Managing of Knowledge.

On the basis of surveys and search studies conducted all over the world during last fifteen years or so, it is revealed that **attributes of successful** KM programmes are common everywhere. These are shown in Box-2.

Box-2 Attributes of Successful KM Programmes

1. Information is widely disseminated throughout the organization. Wherever it is needed, it is accessible.
2. Accessible at a fast rate of speed.
3. Virtual communities of practice share what is known in a global fashion, independent of time zones and other geographic limitations.
4. Business boundaries are broad, and often virtual in nature.
5. Collaboration to support continuous innovation and new knowledge creation.

CONCLUSION

The discussion given above clearly demonstrates that knowledge resources have to be tapped and managed in an effective manner so that it becomes useful for organizations, employees and customers. To make the future of KM bright and to achieve the sustainability of a KM endeavour, focus is needed on the:

- Where are we going? What are we here for?
- People need awareness of the whole: in what direction is the organization going?
- To have a goal to reach in the future can provide great incentive for a KM initiative.
- Effective leveraging lies within an organization's capacity for rethinking and recreating. Scenario thinking can help us to see the blind spots, and help to create the future we want.
- Developing networks of committed people
- Improving business results
- Enhancing personal results
- To achieve sustainability, there must be a focus on learning, and learning how to harness the learning capabilities that lead to innovation.

IMPACT OF GLOBALIZATION ON HRM

Globalization that is taking place at a breathtaking pace has affected the international business in its all departments. It has thrown a great challenge to HRM. The theory and practice of HRM at national level is not applicable to international business. In fact, there is need for global HRM. Many globalization trends such as growth of trading blocs, the opening up of national boundaries for trade, and increasing instances of international strategic alliances have significantly influenced the theory and practice of HRM. It is increasingly being recognized that effective management of HR is a major determinant of success or failure in the international business.

The impact of globalization on human resource development may have favourable impact on HRM practices and adverse impact on HRM.

Favourable Impact of Globalization on HRM

1. **HR practices followed by globalized companies differ from company to company and need to be revised:** A survey conducted by Price Water House and Cranfield in 1993 across Europe found that there are significant variations in HRM practices, such as integration of HR and corporate strategy, education and training of HR manager, recruitment and selection, industrial relations, employee communication, and flexible working practices, etc.
2. **Need to appoint people of variety of culture:** Globalization leads to appointment of people from a variety of ethnic, racial, and cultural background. Hence, the problem for HRM is to positively exploit diversity and synergize different skills to achieve more successful outcomes.
3. **Need for Outsourcing:** Outsourcing concept has come into existence and the HRM department is to be downsized and will have to outsource a number of services. Development of HRM to line manager will be on the rise and line managers are to be involved in design and implementation of HRM system.
4. **Shortage of International Managers:** There is a shortage of international managers and a need to nurture this cadre is important.
5. **Need for Global Integration and Local Responsiveness:** HRM needs to ensure that the organizational structure and system enhances global effectiveness and enables the organizations to achieve both global integration and local responsiveness.

Adverse Impact of Globalization on HRM

The adverse effects of globalization on HRM are listed below:

1. **Loss of Jobs**: Around the world millions of people have lost their jobs due to imports or production shifts abroad. Most of them find jobs that pay less.
2. **Fear of Losing Jobs**: Millions of others fear losing their jobs, especially with those companies operating under competitive pressure.
3. **Pay Cut**: Workers face pay cut demands from employers who often threaten to export jobs.
4. **White Collar Jobs become Risky**: Service and white collar jobs are becoming vulnerable as they are moving their operations offshore.
5. **Loss of Competitive Advantage by Employees**: Employees in advanced countries such as USA, UK, and Japan can lose their competitive advantage when companies build advanced factories in low wage countries making them as productive as those at home.

Many people in developed countries like USA are angry with globalization, because the American jobs and wages levels are severely affected by the influx of cheap imports and shifting of production to low cost overseas locations.

Restructuring of HRM Practices in the Context of Globalization

The following are certain areas of HRM that needs to undergo a process of transformation to suit the globalized environment.

1. **Incorporating International Standards in Recruitment and Selection:** The globalized organizations need to maintain international standards in recruitment and selection processes. A universally compatible procedure needs to be evolved to make recruitment effective. Use of objective tests and assessment centre methods can be encouraged. In order to facilitate the recruitment of scarce skills, new techniques such as flexi-time and job-sharing may be introduced.
2. **Reorientation of Training and Development**: Development process can be upgraded by shifting it from traditional skill upgradation to organizational learning. Training method needs to be reoriented to include web-based training and net-based knowledge dissemination. Application of computers can be extensively encouraged to make the training and development programmes more effective.
3. **Evolve New Methods of Career Development:** As globalization gains momentum the traditional paths of career advancement in the organization will undergo drastic change. Hence, HR professionals need to evolve new methods of career management.
4. **Redesign Compensation:** Motivating the employees through properly structured compensation schemes is also an important demand raised by the globalized environment. The compensation scheme must be designed to include profit sharing share option, merit or performance related to pay, etc. Compensation scheme must recognize individual differences in the performance.
5. **Performance Appraisal:** The performance appraisal system must incorporate personal psychological factors such as sensitivity and adaptability, cross-cultural skills and interpersonal skills. Appraisal must be carried out as an ongoing process at regular intervals rather than annually.
6. **Direct Communication Practices:** Direct communication practices must be encouraged in a globalized environment. Use of internet, Intranet and LAN system allows the manager to send to all the employees a personalized copy of letters, memos, reports and other communications.
7. **Adoption of Flexi-working Practices**: The end result of these flexible working practices is cost reduction. Flexi-time concept allows for shift working, weekend work, subcontracting, home working, part-time working and temporary/casual/ fixed term employment.
8. **Need for Global Leadership**: A need to nurture global leadership is felt in a globalized organization. The global leader has talent to interact with managers from diverse cultural backgrounds that populate his/her multinational company.

It is concluded that HRM in the globalized era has to move across boundaries of culture, geography, and language. HRM practices such as training and development, performance appraisal; communication and participation need to be restructured in order to attain world class standards. Leadership must be developed to face global challenges effectively and HR professionals should create a work culture that is capable of motivating and satisfying all sections of employees in the globalized environment.

PROBLEMS OF HRM—TRANSNATIONAL AND MULTINATIONAL

In the previous section of this chapter, it has been discussed that due to intense globalization of business, the organizations are facing various HR problems which are both transnational and multinational. Primarily the HR problems relate to

- Staffing
- Performance Appraisal
- Compensation
- Training and Development

These crucial problems have different nature for HR people within the country than those in other countries. The organization operating within a country does not pose serious problems pertaining to the issues of staffing, performance appraisal, compensation, and training and development. However, it is the case of the organization which is transnational or multinational; the HR problems become highly complex and need wider international mechanism to overcome the said problems. Before discussing the HR problems and how are they tackled at international setting, it is essential to distinguish the concept of transnational and multinational.

Transnational Corporation (TNC): Transnational corporations are incorporated or unincorporated enterprises comprising parent enterprise and their foreign affiliates where a parent enterprise is deemed as an enterprise that controls assets of other entities in countries other than its home country through equity capital stake. A foreign affiliate is an enterprise in which an investor who is a resident in another country owns a stake.

To measure the extent of transnationalization of firms, the World Investment Report has been constructing a transnationality index which is the average of three ratios, shows the foreign dimension of the overall activities of a firm.

1. Foreign Assets/Total Assets
2. Foreign Sales/Total Sales
3. Foreign Employment/Total Employment

Multinational Corporation (MNC): There is no single universally agreed definition of MNC as it has several dimensions. Although MNC took birth in early 1860s, it was after the Second World War that MNCs have grown rapidly. USA is the home of the MNCs. One prominent MNV from USA is GE, from Japan is Toyota and from South Korea is Samsung. According to ILO report, MNC is one with significant investment and operations in a number of countries, generating significant share of the total revenue from foreign markets.

Distinction between a Transnational and a Multinational Corporation

A Multinational Corporation (MNC) is a corporation with extensive ties in international operations in more than one foreign country. Examples are General Electric, Exxon, Wal-Mart, Mitsubishi, Daimler Chrysler, etc.

A **transnational corporation** is a MNC that operates worldwide without being identified with a national home base. It is said to operate on a borderless basis. TNC is characterized by interdependence and integration between the overseas units. In transnational corporations resources and human capabilities are dispersed among the various operating units globally.

As a matter of fact the difference between the two, i.e., TNC and MNC is only a matter of degree. For the purposes of HRM and HRD both may be regarded as the same HR problems, these corporations are also the same. The only difference is that for MNCs the degree of severity in staffing, training, performance appraisal and compensation is much higher as compared to those in TNCs.

The Main HR Problems in Relation to TNC & MNC

Multinational and transnational companies are penetrating India and China so we can examine the HR problems being faced by TNCs and MNCs in these countries. The main problems that have been identified are four, i.e., Staffing, Performance Appraisal, Compensation, Training and Development. These are discussed below by taking the instances of China and India.

After introducing economic reforms in 1978, the Chinese government liberalized its trade, resorted to open-door policy for trade and investment. HRM issues in China were dealt as underline with new challenges. Likewise India too, after introducing economic reforms had to face HR problems in these four areas.

1. **Problems in Staffing:** In staffing activities, the two countries are facing the problem of cultural differences. Whether the staffing policy is
   - **(a) Geocentric**—seeking best people, regardless of nationality or
   - **(b) Polycentric**—requiring host country nationals to be recruited to manage subsidiaries or
   - **(c) Ethnocentric**—filling all key management positions by parent company nationals, all have problems due to difference in culture, tastes and preferences.

     Most of the time, managers appointed in other countries leave and return back to their own countries due to homesickness and due to limited opportunities to gain experience.
2. **Problems in Performance Appraisal:** Prior to economic reforms in China and India performance appraisal was mainly for promotion or transfer with the main criteria being political loyalty and seniority. Performance appraisal was usually conducted annually by HR department. After inducing economic reforms, the new scheme was introduced which was based upon the socialist principle of distribution. New criteria focused on four broad areas.
   - (a) Good moral practice
   - (b) Adequate competence
   - (c) Positive working attitude
   - (d) Strong performance record

But research studies in China show that there are problems with performance appraisal as the emphasis is still given to political considerations, inconsistent measurement, subjectivity, static rather than forward-looking attitudes and lack of communication.

3. **Problems in Compensation:** Before economic reforms, compensation in two countries was regardless of performance but after reforms compensation was linked to performance. Since the economic liberalization in the early 1990s, it has become more difficult for foreign multinationals to find and retain high-quality local staff, as the rapid rise in the level of foreign and local investments in India has led to a shortage of skilled people. This, in turn, is placing pressure on the compensation packages of qualified managers. According to a recent survey, an average Indian manager's annual real-salary increase is one of the highest in the world. Consistent with this report, a recent study found that continuous pay increases, along with a commitment to improve working conditions, are two preconditions to retain experienced staff, particularly in high-growth industries such as telecommunications and computer software development. Pressure is also being brought to bear on the minimum wage level, and this will increase the cost of labour over the longer term.

Problems Regarding Training and Development: Training aims to improve current work skills and behaviour, whereas development aims to increase abilities in relation to some future position of job. International training and development is shown in Figure 13.9.

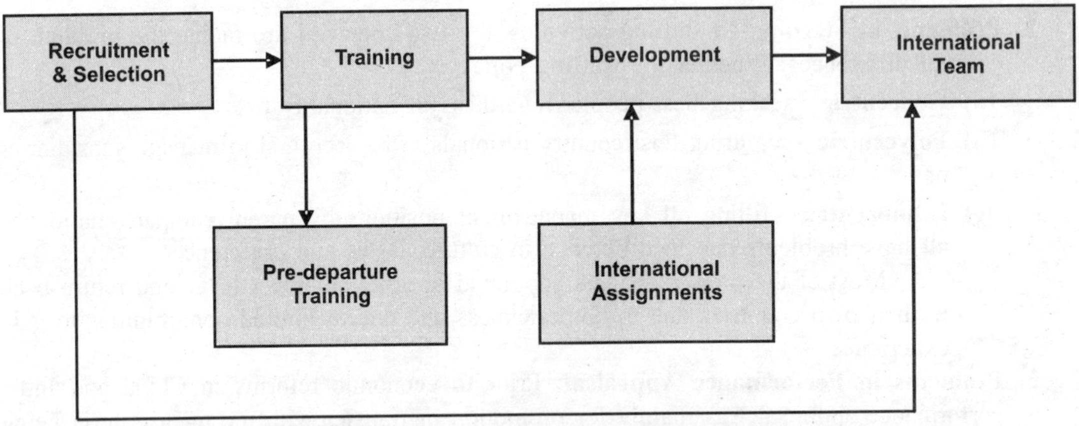

Fig. 13.9. International Training and Development.
Source: Peter J. Dowlling, Denice E. Welch and Randall S. Schuler International HRM, Managing People in A Multinational Context, Thomson, 2002 Singapore, p. 155.

Figure 13.9 shows that there is close relationship between recruitment and selection and internationally oriented personnel. Hence, training is important. In international setting multinationals establish their own universities and training centres. For example, Motorola, McDonald's Hamburger and Dinney universities are good in-house training centers. Several examples of these Korean, European and Japanese firms have similar arrangements.

The main problem that has been found is that most of the employees after seeking training leave the job or do not join. We can examine the problems related to training and development in the context of China and India.

Because the lack of adequately trained management had been identified as a major impediment to its reforms, the government established institutions for further education for professional and management training. A nationwide programme of management training has supported these institutions and the government has collaborated with institutions from several countries, including the United States, United Kingdom, Australia, Canada, Japan, and the European Union nations, to conduct courses, including MBA programmes. In spite of the progress achieved in employee and management training and development many inadequacies and limitations remain.

(i) The results from a 1994 survey disclosed that 34 per cent of 1,508 respondents in China had not received any training opportunities in the enterprises.

(ii) Researchers have also found that Chinese enterprises usually only emphasize technical training rather than behavioural training.

(iii) Many foreign managers may regard training as costly and risky, because they may not receive immediate returns and employees may leave the enterprise after training.

As far as the case of India, it has been observed that in transnational and multinational corporations people are hired from the home and host countries. Firms are focusing more on the role of HR as a critical part of their core competence and a source of competitive advantages.

Despite the availability of cheap labour, low productivity is a common complaint among manufacturers in India. As a consequence, a multinational may have to provide extensive training programmes for its local staff. The introduction of new production equipment and concepts such as just-in-time, quality management, and so on, require additional training. Developing and retraining the workforce so that the multinational has a pool of managerial talent to draw on is also a challenge.

It is evident from above (experience of China and India) that the HR problems in relation to TNCs and MNCs are basically concerning the recruitment and selection, performance appraisal, compensation and training and development. Although efforts are being made to solve these problems at international level by improving the HR practices, yet there are certain questions to be answered.

- How can foreign firms develop effective HRM strategies to enhance the productivity of their workforce?
- To what extent can foreign multinationals transfer their home-countries HR practices to their subsidiaries in other countries?
- What are the future HRM issues relating to developing a retaining quality staff?
- How to develop performance-based work culture in host countries?
- How to create harmonious relationship among the three types of employees of an international firm, i.e., host country nationals (HCNs), parent country nationals (PCNs) and third country nationals (TNCs)?

HR Problems in Relation to MNCs and TNCs—What and Why

Box-3 clarified this state.

Box-3 HR Problems in Relation to MNCs and TNCs—What and Why

- **Wider Scope of Globalization**

The MNCs and TNCs in addition to the basic human resources activities have to take into consideration host country laws and regulations, language, transaction services, international taxation, international orientation and relocation and administrative services for expatriates.

- **Wider Designing and Administrating Programmes**

HR managers working in the global environment face the problem of designing and administrating programmes for more than one country. People in different countries have different perceptions about different things. MNCs operating in these countries have to be aware of the varied perceptions. They have to modify some of their policies to suit the local sentiments. For example, in Australia and Singapore, if the work load increases, firms are most likely to add more staff, whereas, in Korea and Japan firms prefer that the existing employees work longer hours.

- **Need to Maintain International HR Services Centre**

Majority of MNCs have to maintain international human resource services section to provide services to the parent company and third country nationals such as handling of the banking, investments, housing arrangements, health care and coordinating home units, etc.

- **Enhancing HR Activities**

The need to enhance emphasis on HR activities as the MNC develops, broadens the responsibilities of the local HR activities. For example, in the initial stages, the MNCs use the employees from the home country or the third nation and the emphasis of HR activities is on expatriates, their relocation, orientation, welfare, etc. But as the MNC matures, trained locals become available and the emphasis shifts to selection, training and development. Thus, with the development of MNCs, the emphasis on HR activities keeps on changing.

- **Threatening Risks**
  - Physical safety of the employees is a major concern for the HR managers as well as for headquarters.
  - Terrorism poses a great risk to international operations.
  - The risk associated with wrong selection decisions is very high.
  - Another risk is that of expropriation or seizure of MNC's assets in a foreign country by the government of that country.

- **Political Hindrances**

MNCs occupy an important and more visible place in the host countries, particularly in the developing countries. The HR managers of these companies have to deal with ministers, political leaders and other important people in the society. Host country government can dictate the selection procedures also. The HR managers also need to learn and interpret the local ways of doing business and the general code of conduct regarding various other activities, e.g. giving gifts, etc.

Suggestions to Overcome the HR Problems in TNCs and MNCs

HR professionals in multinationals may be required to take the following steps:

- Minimize the exposure of employees to corrupt conduct by assisting in the development, publication, and implementation of appropriate codes of conduct;
- Ensure training programmes cover areas of ethical concern such as bribery, human rights, justice, and the common good in a manner consistent with the multinational's objectives in this regard;
- Align performance appraisal and compensation systems so that they support the ethical stance taken;
- Be conversant with the type of requests that may be made of staff operating internationally not just expatriates but also those who visit foreign markets in various capacities and provide the necessary training so that they have the requisite negotiating skills to handle problem situations that may arise;
- Ensure that employees understand the difference between corrupt bribery payments, gifts, and allowable facilitation payments. Given the strong positions taken by governments on ethical behaviour, it is important that all staff is fully briefed on their responsibilities in this regard.

REVIEW QUESTIONS

1. Explain the concept of human resource development. What are the objectives of HRD?
2. Distinguish between HRD and HRM. Discuss the strategic roles of HRD professionals in an organization.
3. Explain the various instruments of HRD. How can HR managers contribute towards TQM?
4. Discuss the role of training in HRD. What are the steps involved in the successful implementation of HRD?
5. What is knowledge management? How can HRD professionals manage knowledge resources in an organization?
6. What is HRD? Discuss its nature and the impact of globalization of HRD.
7. Discuss the problems in relation to transnational and multinational.
8. "HRD is not HRM". Comment and bring out the scope of HRD and HRM.
9. Explain the various instruments of HRD. What are the essentials of effective HRD in an organization?

CASE STUDY

13.1 HRD Scheme: A Bone of Contention

Innovative Technologies Limited (ITL) is a medium sized engineering company situated at Hyderabad, manufacturing telecom equipment. Its customers were primarily government departments (Railways, Post and Telegraph, Department of Telecommunications, etc.) and private telecom operators in the country. The company made rapid progress in recent years, thanks to the rising income levels, Internet boom and growth in infrastructure sector all over India. To encourage a culture of innovation and creativity, which is essential for the company's own survival in a highly competitive field, the company has all along been encouraging its employees numbering over 1000 mainly engineering graduates, to upgrade their knowledge and skills in their own fields of specialization. It had always encouraged employees to go for workshops, seminars, conferences and even volunteered to pay the tuition fee of employees if they are able to secure admission in prestigious Information Technology and Telecommunication Schools in India and abroad. With a view to promote managerial talent internally, the company wanted both engineering (600 in number) and non-engineering professions (390 in number) to go for MBA, PGDBA courses as well, offered by reputed business schools.

Since admission procedures in most reputed business and technology schools are quite tough consisting of entrance test, group discussion and interview, the field naturally is wide open only for the competent and bright people. The company's engineering graduates invariably got through these tests and were always utilizing a major portion of the funds earmarked by the company for this purpose. The non-engineering people, somehow, could not run the race and get benefited by the company's scheme. May be they lacked the will, or the quantitative and analytical skills needed to get through the competitive entrance examinations. But they were reluctant to admit this and instead targeted the engineering professionals for their own poor show. They, in fact, requested management to revise (a) the guidelines, suggesting a quota system (3 from engineering and 2 from non-engineering category every year, if selected in any business school) for selecting internal candidates for educational benefits. They even wanted the management to extend the scheme to all employees securing admission (b) to any professional course on the basis of seniority.

Meanwhile Mr Raj Pal (31) a brilliant computer professional working in the Telecom Software division for the past 4 years has been selected by IIM (A) for their PGDBA course. He is the fourth candidate who secured admission in business schools in 1999. From the non-engineering stream, two persons got selected but in lesser-known business schools.

Raj Pal's selection news came after the company has finalized the names of employees who are going to be sponsored under the HRD scheme in 1999. In addition to pressures from non-engineering candidates whose names are yet to be finalized, the company is facing lot of criticism from the Software Division also where seniors are of the opinion that the young professionals who get sponsored will either not return to the company or will be given preference ahead of seniors in case of internal promotions. In future, they, therefore, want the company to secure an undertaking from sponsored candidates to serve the company in the same category for at least three years before becoming eligible for promotion. If the sponsored ones decide to leave the company, they have to pay back the money with 12% p.a. interest.

The company is not very sure whether the quota system be introduced or the present scheme of picking up candidates on the basis of merit should be allowed to continue. The growing popularity of the scheme has in fact led the management think about certain guidelines for its implementation without any operational problems in future.

Source: VSP Rao, Human Resource Management, 2nd edn., Excel Books, New Delhi, p. 287.

Questions

1. What is the main problem in the case?
2. Should the quota system be introduced while selecting people under the HRD scheme?

3. Should ITL insist on execution of a 3-year bond by the employees who avail benefits under the HRD scheme?
4. Should ITL enlarge the scope of the scheme to include undergraduate and non-engineering graduate employees for taking admission in management diploma/ degree courses offered by various national institutions?

13.2 The Absentee Employee at NTC

The National Transport Corporation (hereafter referred to as NTC), a leading transport organisation with a fleet strength of 200 vehicles, is engaged in Parcel Service in South India has its headquarters at Madras and branches in important locations in Tamilnadu and other southern states.

Madhavan, a load man of NTC at Salem was transferred from Salem Madura, for long absence from work in the beginning of 1995, though the Corporation could have discharged him from service for long absence without permission for a period of two months because according to the company policy for such misconduct, company may fine, warn, demote, stop the increment, suspend, or dismiss the guilty employee. The Branch Manager of Salem NTC requested the Head of the HR Division to transfer the employee to another location to enable the employee to correct himself in future. Madhavan has been in NTC from the beginning of 1992.

Madhavan reported for duty at Madura, and again after six months started absenting from work as before. The Branch Manager of Madura counselled him several times, but Madhavan did not show any real change in his attitude. A written warning was given to him in October 1995. He again absented himself from duty for ten days from 17 December, 1995 and after joining duty, he was again absent for 20 days which led to initiation of disciplinary action.

At the departmental enquiry held in February 1996 the delinquent employee pleaded that he was suffering from jaundice and that he rushed to his village near Salem for taking Ayurvedic treatment and rest. No medical certificate was produced. He admitted mistake in not applying for leave, and requested for mercy. Based on the admission of the misconduct, the enquiry officer gave the findings that he was guilty. The Branch Manager, Madura was informed about the findings. He recommended dismissal of Madhavan. The Chief Executive of NTC, the final authority however again directed a transfer to Madura, rather than passing an order of dismissal. This was done to enable the employee to correct himself.

After issue of orders, the delinquent approached the Chief Executive of NTC and requested for mercy. The Chief Executive was not in favour of changing the order of transfer. He however, referred the matter to the Manager of the HR Division for proper disposal.

The Manager HRD called Madhavan and asked for the reasons for absence. He asked the delinquent how the company would tolerate such absenteeism, why he failed to produce medical certificates, if he was really sick. Was he not given an opportunity twice to correct himself, once by Branch Manager, Salem and later by Branch Manager, Madura? Madhavan had no answer to these questions. He however, requested the Manager to give him one last chance. He had no complaints against the Branch Managers. The HRD Manager assured support to him if his version was convincing. Madhavan then narrated his family background.

Madhavan's Family Background

Madhavan had two elder sisters, four elder brothers and another brother younger to him. His sisters and two brothers were living separately after marriage. Another unmarried brother was also living separately. He got the job as a loadman in NTC in 1992 at Salem. He was living with his parents; a disabled brother aged 35 at Kamandapatti till the end of 1994 in the family house. He was the bread winner of the family. Madhavan was now living at Omalur, with his wife Madhavi aged 22.

Madhavi's is a divorcee and before her marriage with Madhavan she was getting an alimony of Rs. 2000/-. This helped her to establish a small grocery shop at Omalur. Here Madhavan developed intimacy with Madhavi. Another person Gunapalan, a person known to Madhavan wanted to marry Madhavi, despite Madhavi's disliking. Gunapalan posed serious problems to Madhavi especially after Madhavan's transfer to Madura. He told her twice that she will have to forget Madhavan, or else she will have to blame herself for the consequences. Threats followed. Madhavan got a letter from Madhavi asking for protection.

Madhavan married her and later went on a pilgrimage for a fortnight. He neither informed the NTC officials about his marriage nor applied for leave. What followed were the disciplinary action against Madhavan and his plea against transfer.

HRD Manager's Decision

Madhavan gave a definite undertaking to the Manager that he would be diligent in the work in future and may be terminated upon any complaint in future. The Manager (HRD) contacted the Branch Managers of Madura and Salem and family background was fully explained to them. It transpired that Madhavan had never explained his problems to either of them. Both managers agreed to wide by the decision of the Manager (HRD) to help Madhavan. Both promised to counsel Madhavan as well if he were posted either at Madura or Salem. The Manager (HRD) taking into account his family background passed an order transferring Madhavan to Salem.

Questions

1. What would be your stand on this issue as the Head of HRD Division of the organisation?
2. Do you think that the employee cannot be corrected as he has absented continuously for long periods while at Salem and Madura and that sympathy shown to him will amount to a premium on indiscipline, adversely affecting the corporate image of the organization?
3. Are you of the view that it is possible to correct him by the theory of constructive discipline and, if so, how?
4. Are you of the view that you will have to adopt the stick method to prevent the disease of absenteeism spreading to other employees?
5. Are you of the view that if you transfer him to his home town, Salem, Madhavan would prove himself to be a good performer?

Source: Adapted from MBA, IGNOU, June 1996.

REFERENCES

1. Benjamin Schneider and Rover A. Synder, (1975). "Some Relationships between Job Satisfaction and Organizational Climate", *J. Appl. Psychology*, 60, No. 3, p. 318.
2. Brown J.S. and Duguid, P. (1991). "Organisational Learning and Communities-of-Practice", Organizational Science. O'Dell C. and Grayson Jr., C.J. (1998). If only we knew what we know. Stewart, T. (2002).
3. Clark, Roger, Knowledge. http://www.anu.edu.au/people/Roger.Clarke/Sos/Know.html.
4. Earl Michael, J. (1996). "Information Management: The Organizational Dimension", Oxford University Press, Oxford.
5. Giriraj G. Halkar and Sangita Gupta, (2005). "Knowledge Management: A Challenge for the 21st Century", published in Indian Journal of Training and Development, vol. 35, No. 1.
6. Gupta, S.K. (2010). HRM, Kalyani Publishers, New Delhi.
7. Luan, J. and Serban, A. (2002). "Knowledge Management Concepts, Models and Applications". Paper presented at Annual AIR Forum, Toronto.
8. Pareek, U. and Rao, T.V. (1981) "Designing and Managing Human Resource Systems", Oxford and IBH, New Delhi.
9. Pathak Deepti, (2009). "Knowledge Management, Managing Knowledge Workers across Different Stages of Employment", published in HRM Review.
10. Peter J. Dowling, Denice E. Welch and Randall S. Schuler, "International Human Resource Management", 3rd edn., Thomson South Western Publications.
11. Polanyi, M. (1967). The Tacit Dimension. Leonard, D. and Sensiper, S. (1998)." The Role of Tacit Knowledge in Group Innovation". California Management Review.
12. Radjamanogary Resource, (2006). HRM Review, ICFAI University Press, Hyderabad.
13. Rao, T.V. *et al.* (1988). "Alternative Approaches and Strategies of HRD", Rawat Publications, Jaipur.
14. Rao, T.V. and Periera, D.F. (1988). "Recent Experiences in HRD", Oxford and IBH, New Delhi.
15. Rao, V.S.P. (2005). HRM, Excel Books, pp. 270-275.
16. Sharma, Bharti, (1998). "Perspective on HRD Measures for Effective Governance". IJPA, July-Sept.
17. Singh, B.D. (1997). "HRD Dimensions of Industrial Relations in Selected Readings in HRD", Tata McGraw-Hill, New Delhi.
18. Sveiby, Karl-Eric. What is Knowledge Management? http://www.sveiby.com.au/knowledge management.html dated 5th March 2000.

CHAPTER
14

Industrial Relations, Trade Unions: Employee Welfare and Empowerment

CHAPTER'S OUTLINE

- Introduction
- Meaning of Industrial Relations
- Objectives of Industrial Relations
- Importance of Harmonious Industrial Relations
- Approaches to Industrial Relations
- Essential Conditions for Sound and Harmonious Industrial Relations
- Objectives and Functions of Trade Unions
- Trade Union Movement in India
- Employee Welfare
- Employee Empowerment

INTRODUCTION

Since Industrial Revolution, the industrial environment has been changing and has remained unstable. For a long time particularly upto the end of 20th century, it remained highly volatile and disturbed due to intense and militant attitude of trade unions and neglect of employee or labour welfare activities. There was exploitation of labour as the workers were paid low salaries and were made to work for longer hours. The gap increased between management and labour and it led to disharmonious industrial relationship between the labour and the employers. Industrial progress was adversely affected.

However, with the beginning of 21st century when globalization occurred at a very fast speed and with the emergence of HRM and HRD, the focus shifted to the need for harmonious relationship. Although initially, the HRD movement covered the managerial employees, its application to non-managerial employees has gained momentum over the years. Industrial relations, trade unions, labour welfare and employee empowerment are essential part of management system.

In this chapter, we will discuss the issues relating to industrial relations, trade unions, employee welfare, and employee empowerment.

MEANING OF INDUSTRIAL RELATIONS

The term "***Industrial Relations***" refers to relationship between management and labour or among employees and their organizations that grow out of employment. Theoretically speaking, there are two parties in the employment relationship—labour and management. So the parties need to work in a spirit of cooperation, adjustment and accommodation.

Various authors have defined the term industrial relations differently.

According to **Dale Yoder** "*The term industrial relations refers to the relationship between management and employees or among employees and their organization that arise out of employment.*"

According to **ILO** "*Industrial relations deal with either the relationships between the state and the employers and the workers' organization or the relation between the occupational organizations themselves.*"

According to **R.A. Lester** "*Industrial relations involve attempts to have workable solutions between conflicting objectives and values, between incentive and economic security, between discipline and the industrial democracy, between authority and freedom and between bargaining and cooperation.*"

According to **V.B. Singh** "*Industrial relations are an integral aspect of social relations arising out of employer-employee interaction in modern industries, which are regulated by the state, the legal system and the workers and employers' organizations at the institutional level and of the patterns of industrial organization (including management), capital structure (including technology), compensation of the labour force and a study of market forces—all at the economic level.*"

The following **important facts** about the industrial relations are revealed from the above given definitions:

1. Industrial relations involve two parties—employers and employees. (Figure 14.1)
2. Industrial relations, in the broader sense, include relations between employers' associations and trade unions as well as the role of the state in regulating these relations. (Figure 14.1)
3. Industrial relations is a dynamic and developing concept. It undergoes change with changing structure and environment of industry.
4. Industrial relations are multidimensional in nature and are conditioned by two sets of determinants – the institutional factors and economic factors. These are also an integral part of social relations.
5. The main purpose of industrial relations is to maintain harmonious relationship between the management and the labour.
6. Every industrial relations system creates a complex set of rules, regulations and procedures to govern the workplace.

Government, courts and tribunals are also actively involved in creating congenial environment for harmonious industrial relations (Figure 14.1).

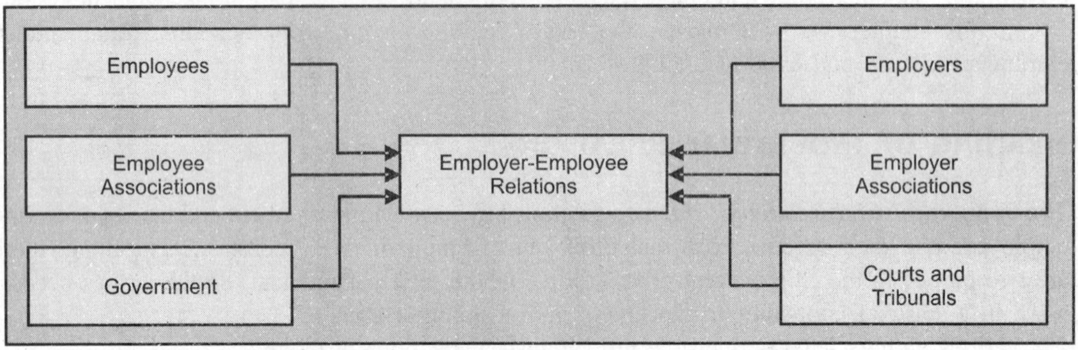

Fig. 14.1. Parties to Industrial Relations.

OBJECTIVES OF INDUSTRIAL RELATIONS

1. **Safeguarding the Interests of Labour and the Management:** The main objective is to safeguard the interests of labour as well as the management by securing the highest level of mutual understanding and goodwill among all those parties in the industry which participate in the process of production.
2. **Avoiding Industrial Conflict:** Another objective is to avoid all forms of industrial conflict so as to ensure industrial peace by providing better working conditions and living standards to workers.
3. **Raising Productivity:** To raise productivity to a higher level which is the need of the day to contribute to the economic development of the country.
4. **Reducing Rate of Turnover:** To reduce the tendency of higher labour turnover and absenteeism by providing job satisfaction to the workers is also a fundamental objective.
5. **Maintaining Industrial Democracy:** To establish and maintain industrial democracy based on the participation of labour in the management and profits is also an important objective. As a result individual's personality may grow to its full stature for the benefit of the industry and of the country as well.
6. **Ensuring Balanced Healthy Social Order:** In the end one more important objective is to ensure a healthy and balanced social order through recognition of human rights in industry and adaptation of complex social relationships to the advancement in technology.
7. **Establishing Government Control:** One of the objectives is to establish government control over such plants and units, which are running at loss, for protecting employment or where production needs to be regulated in public interest.
8. **Eliminating Strikes and Lockouts:** To eliminate as far as possible and practicable, strikes, lockouts and gheraos by providing reasonable wages and fringe benefits.
9. **Encouraging Trade Unions:** Still another objective is to encourage and develop trade unions in order to improve workers' collective strength.

IMPORTANCE OF HARMONIOUS INDUSTRIAL RELATIONS

There has been a phenomenal growth in employment, wages, benefits, working conditions, status of the worker, educational facilities, etc. with the growth and spread of industry. Moreover, career patterns have also changed widely by providing change for wide varieties of jobs to the working communities. This has been possible only through fast industrial development which, in its turn, depends on good industrial relations. Thus, for achieving the objectives of rapid national development and increased social justice there must be harmonious relationship between the labour and the management. The importance of good industrial relations can be judged from the following facts:

1. **Need for Industrial Peace:** Good industrial relations reduce the industrial disputes. Disputes are reflections of the failure of basic human urges or motivations to secure adequate satisfaction, which are fully cured by good industrial relations. Strikes, lockouts, go slow tactics, gherao and grievances are some of the reflections of industrial unrest which do not spring upon an atmosphere of industrial peace. It helps promoting cooperation and increasing production.
2. **Mental Revolution**: IR, if good, brings positive change in attitude of the employees. Industrial relations completely transform the outlook of employers and employees. The process of joint consultations paves the way for individual democracy. This motivates the workers to give their best to the organization and share the fruits of progress jointly with the management.
3. **High Morale:** Industrial relations have moral dimensions too good industrial relations improve the morale of the employees. Employees work with great zeal with the feeling in mind that the interests of employer and employees are the same, i.e., to increase production. Every worker feels that he is a co-owner in the organization and every employer realizes that the gains of industry are not for him alone but are to be shared equally and generously with workers. Complete units of thought and action are the main achievement of industrial peace. It naturally increases production because cooperative efforts produce great results.
4. **Reduced Wastage:** Good industrial relations are maintained on the basis of cooperation and recognition of each other. It helps in increasing production. Wastages of man, material and machines are reduced to the minimum which lead to fall in cost of production and thus national interest is protected.
5. **Benefits to Workers:** New programmes for workers development are introduced in an atmosphere of peace such as training facilities, labour welfare facilities, etc. It increases the efficiency of workers resulting in higher and better production at lower costs.

It is thus evident from above that good IR is the basis of higher production with minimum cost and high profit. Harmonious IR lead to rapid national development and increased social justice.

APPROACHES TO INDUSTRIAL RELATIONS

HRM and HRD are the two disciplines which are playing a good role in creating good industrial relations which is an essential condition for industrial growth and development of a nation. The approaches to IR are classified in two categories—one providing theoretical understanding for the role of HRM and HRD and the other providing practical outlook. These are discussed as under:

A. Theoretical Approach to IR

The three popular theoretical approaches to IR are unitary approach, pluralistic approach, and Marxist approach as is shown in Figure 14.2.

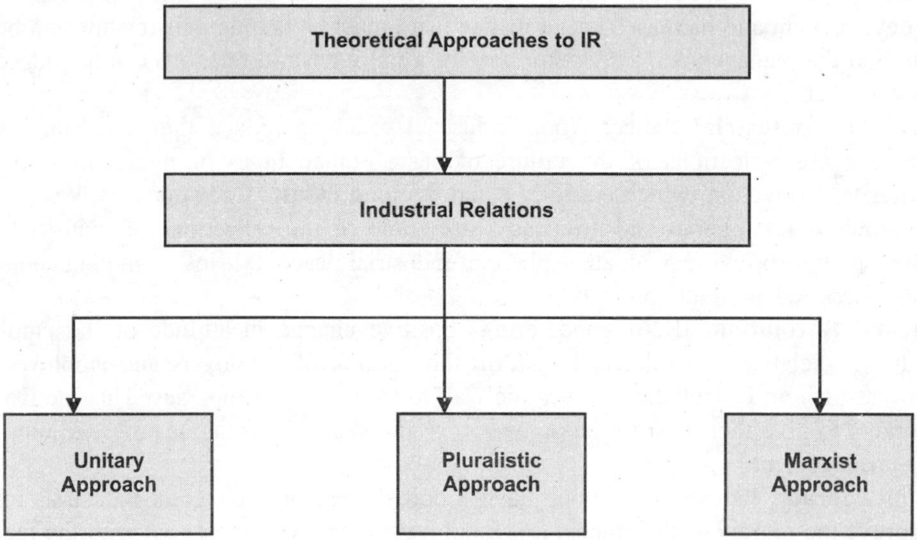

Fig. 14.2. Theoretical Approaches to IR.

1. **Unitary Approach:** According to this approach workplace conflict is temporary, resulting from poor management, and from workers who do not mix well with organizations' culture. So under this approach, IR is grounded in mutual cooperation, individual treatment, team work and shared goals. So the focus should be on common interest. The conflict in the form of strikes is not only regarded as unnecessary but destructive. Box-1 shows this viewpoint.

> **Box-1 Goodbye to Strikes and Lockouts**
>
> It is goodbye to strikes and an end to bitter negotiations at the Alwar factory of Eicher Tractors. The employees' union has given up its right to negotiate its wages, voluntarily. The management is now free to fix annual remuneration for workers. In return, workers can look forward to a fair treatment from the management.
>
> Workers' productivity, as was stated above, has gone up considerably. Not just productivity, the work culture has undergone a metamorphosis. The workers are highly motivated and they who needed supervisors to meet targets do it without them. There is fair treatment, mutual trust, transparency and, open communication.
>
> The environment of the workplace is so pleasant that the union leaders have to work to earn their salaries, so uncommon in industries.
>
> *Source:* Based on The Economic Times, 20th March, 1998.

Advocates of the unitary approach emphasize on a reactive IR strategy. They seek direct negotiations with employees. Participation of government, tribunals and unions are not considered necessary for achieving harmonious employee relations.

2. **Pluralistic Approach:** According to this approach conflict between employers and employees is inevitable. Employees join unions to protect their interests and influence decision-making by the management. Unions thus balance the power between the management and employees. In the pluralistic approach, therefore, a strong union is not only desirable but necessary. Similarly, society's interests are protected by state intervention through legislation and industrial tribunals which provide orderly process for regulation and resolution of conflict.
3. **Marxist Approach:** According to this approach too conflict is inevitable but it is the product of the capitalist society. Conflict arises not just because of competing interests within the organization, but because of the division within the society between those who own or manage the means of production and those who have only their labour to offer. Trade unions focus on improving the position of workers within the capitalist system and not to overthrow. For the Marxists, all strikes are political.

B. Practical Approach to IR

These approaches are practical oriented and are used to explain the multidimensional nature of industrial relations. These approaches include psychological approach, sociological approach, V.V. Giri's approach, Gandhian approach and HRD approach as shown in Figure 14.3.

1. **Psychological Approach:** To a psychologist, industrial conflict means the conflicting interests, aspirations, goals, motives and perceptions of different groups of individuals operating within and reacting to a given socio-economic and political environment. The perceptions of employers, workers and trade unions are different from one another. They view and interpret situations and issues involved in industrial conflicts in different ways. These differences in the perceptions of employers and workers give rise to problems of industrial relations.
2. **Sociological Approach:** The social and cultural changes shape behavioural patterns and cause adjustments in industrial relations. There cannot be harmony and peace in industry when the society is in turmoil. Industry is a part of society and the value systems, customs, status symbols and institutions of the society affect relations between the parties involved. Different family backgrounds, education level, personalities, attitudes, behaviour, etc. create problems of conflict and cooperation in industry. Various social problems cause stress and strain among workers which affect their industrial relations as well.
3. **V.V. Giri Approach:** Sh. V.V. Giri, the late President of India, gave an approach to settle industrial disputes. This approach, to industrial relations implies the encouragement of mutual settlement of disputes, collective bargaining and voluntary arbitration. The essence of this approach is internal settlement in preference to compulsion from outside and voluntary arbitration and collective bargaining rather than compulsory arbitration.
4. **Gandhian Approach:** Gandhian approach to industrial relations is based on the fundamental principles of truth, non-violence and non-possession. If the employers follow the principal of trusteeship, there is no scope for conflict of interests between them and labour. Workers can resort to Satyagraha in place of strikes to have their grievances

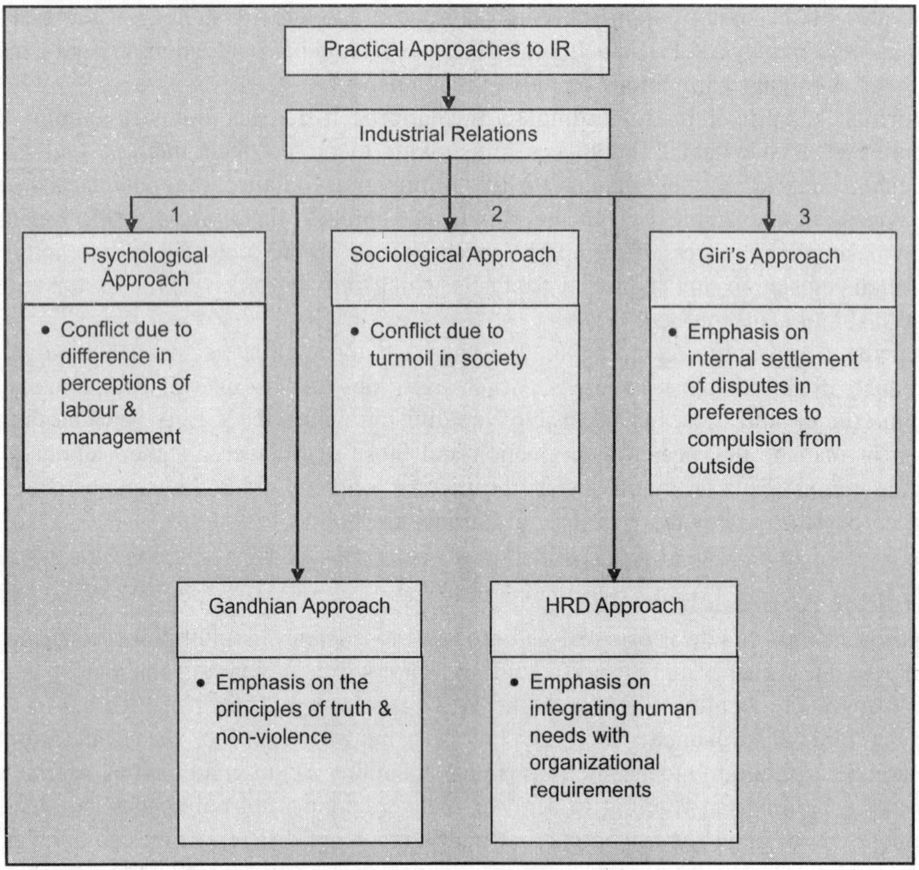

Fig. 14.3. Practical Approaches to IR.

redressed. Workers should resort to strike for just and reasonable cause and after the employers fail to respond to their moral appeals.

5. **HRD Approach.** The HRD approach recognizes employees as the greatest assets in an organization, believes that they can be developed to an unlimited extent with proper incentives, atmosphere and treatment. It is possible to integrate human needs with organizational requirements. The HRD approach can help in improving industrial relations in business organizations in multiple ways. The management, in its own self-interest, must create a motivating climate so that employees commit themselves to assigned tasks wholeheartedly. The management must provide safe and healthy working conditions, promote growth and development of employees, encourage participative spirit and motivation, ensure career development of employees and facilitate personal fulfilment of workers and their job satisfaction.

The methodology used in HRD approach to Industrial Relations includes diagnosis of the problem and design of interventions to bring about the necessary changes. A few possible interventions in tackling specific problems are given in Table 14.1.

Table 14.1: HRD Approach to Improve IR

Industrial Relations	**Possible HRD Interventions**
Demotivated and stagnated employees	Training Personal growth lab Work redesign Job enrichment and Job enlargement
Lack of leadership qualities	Leadership training Assertiveness training Role efficacy lab
Mistrust between the management and union	Union-management Interface team building exercise Role negotiation exercise
Indiscipline	Counselling Review of disciplinary Action machinery
Policy of appeasement	Conflict management Union and management interface

ESSENTIAL CONDITIONS FOR SOUND AND HARMONIOUS INDUSTRIAL RELATIONS

It is not easy to promote and maintain sound industrial relations. Certain conditions should exist for the maintenance of harmonious industrial relations. They are:

1. ***Existence of strong, well organized and democratic employees' unions:*** Industrial relations will be sound only when the bargaining power of the employees' unions is equal to that of management. A strong trade union can protect the employees' interest relating to wages, benefits, job security, etc.
2. ***Existence of sound and organized employers' unions:*** These associations are helpful for the promotion and maintenance of uniform personnel policies among various organizations and to protect the interests of weak employers.
3. ***Spirit of collective bargaining and willingness to resort to voluntary negotiations:*** The relationship between an employee and the employer will be congenial only when the differences between them are settled through mutual negotiation and consultation rather than through the intervention of a third party. Collective bargaining is a process through which employee issues are settled through mutual discussions and negotiations.
4. ***Maintenance of industrial peace:*** Permanent industrial peace in an organization can be ensured through the following measures:
   (i) Establish machinery for prevention and settlement of industrial disputes. This includes legislative and non-legislative measures. Preventive measures include works committees, standing orders, welfare officers, shop councils, joint councils and joint management councils. Settlement methods include voluntary arbitration, conciliation and adjudication.
   (ii) Government should be provided with requisite authority for settling the industrial disputes wherever necessary.
   (iii) Provision for the bipartite and tripartite committees in order to evolve personnel policies, code of conduct, code of discipline, etc.

(iv) Provision for the various committees to implement and evaluate the collective bargaining agreements, court orders and judgements, awards of voluntary arbitration, etc.

Functional requirements for sound Industrial Relations Programme are shown in Box-2.

Box-2 Functional Requirements for Sound Industrial Relations Programme

(1) *Top-Management Support:* Since industrial relations is a functional staff service, it must derive authority from the line organization. This is accomplished by having the industrial relations director report to the top line authority—the president, chairman or vice-president. Besides, top management must also set an example for others.

(2) *Sound Personnel Policies:* They constitute a business philosophy for the guidance of the human relations decisions of the enterprise. The purpose of such policies is to decide ahead of emergency need what shall be done with a large number of problems that may arise daily. Policy can be successful only when it is followed at all levels from top to bottom.

(3) *Adequate Practices:* Adequate practices should have been developed by professional in the field to assist the policies of the units. A system of procedures is necessary to translate intention into action. The procedures and practices of industrial relations are the "tools of management" which keep the supervisor ahead of his job; the work of time-keeping, rate adjustments, grievance reporting and merit rating.

(4) *Detailed Supervisory Training:* To carry out the policies and practices by the industrial relations staff the job supervisors must be trained in detail, and the significance of the policies must be communicated to the employees. They must be trained in leadership and communication.

(5) *Follow-tip of Results:* Constant review of the industrial relations programme is necessary not only to evaluate existing practices but also as a check on certain undesirable tendencies. Follow-up of turnover, absenteeism, departmental morale, grievances, employee suggestions, wage administration, etc., must be supplemented with continuous research to make certain that the policies pursued are those best fitted to company needs and employee wishes. Hints of problem areas may also be found in exit interviews, in union demands and in management meetings, as well as in formal social science research.

Source: Mamoria, C.B., Personnel Management, Himalaya Publishing House Pvt. Ltd., Mumbai, 2008, pp. 837-838.

OBJECTIVES AND FUNCTIONS OF TRADE UNIONS

Over the years trade unions have emerged as a dominating force to protect the workers from exploitation at the hands of employers and to struggle for seeking improved working conditions and better terms for the growth of workers in future. In modern era, trade unions activities are not confined to mere securing the economic benefits but also to perform political and welfare activities for the benefits of its members.

What is a Trade Union?

A trade union is defined as an organization of employees formed on a contractual basis for the purpose of securing diverse range of benefits. Few definitions of trade union are given as under:

Definitions

According to **Sec. 2(b) of the Trade Unions Act, 1926.** "*A trade union is any combination of persons, whether temporary or permanent, primarily for the purpose of regulating the relations between workers and employers, or between workers and workers, and for imposing restrictive conditions on the conduct of any trade or business and includes the federation of two or more trade unions.*"

According to **Dale Yoder.** "*A trade union is a continuing, long-term association of employees, formed and maintained for the specific purpose of advancing and protecting the interest of members in their working relationships.*"

According to **S.D. Punnekar.** "*A union is a continuous association of persons in industry—whether employees or independent workers – formed primarily for the purpose of the pursuit of the interests of its members of the trade they represent.*"

According to **V.V. Giri.** "*Trade union is a voluntary organization of workers formed to promote and protect their interests by collective action.*"

According to **Edwin B. Flippo.** "*A trade union is an organization of workers formed to promote, protect and improve through collective action, the social, economic and political interests of its members.*"

On the basis of the above definitions the following **characteristics** of a trade union are revealed:

1. Trade union is an association of employers, employees or independent workers.
2. Trade union is generally a permanent and not a combination.
3. The main aim of a trade union is to protect and further the economic, vocational and other interests of their members.
4. Members of a trade union have common interests and problems, will motivate them to unite.
5. Trade unions always act collectively, i.e., through united action of members.
6. The unions are ready to adapt according to technological and environmental changes that are taking place.

Objectives of Trade Unions

According to the **Trade Unions Act, 1926,** "*A trade union must work to protect and promote the interests of the workers and the conditions of their employment.*" In short the trade unions generally pursue the following objectives:

1. **Wages and Salaries:** The subject which drew the major attention of the trade unions is the wages and salaries of the workers. This item relates to the policy matter of the enterprise. However, differences may arise in the process of their implementation. In the case of unorganized sector, trade unions play a crucial role in bargaining the pay scales.
2. **Aims at Improving Working Conditions:** Trade unions aim to improve working conditions by securing shorter working hours, better leave facilities, adequate social security, better housing and education and other welfare benefits.

3. **Rationalization of Personnel Policies for Economic Security:** The economic security of an employee is determined not only by the level of wages and duration of his employment but also by the management's policies in respect of recruitment, selection, promotions, transfers, training, etc. Trade unions ensure fair treatment by the employers.
4. **Creating Harmonious Relations:** A trade union should also strive for harmonious relations between the employees and employer. Trade union, being the representative of all the workers, may carry out continuous negotiations with the management with a view to promote industrial peace.
5. **Recognition and Participation for workers:** Another objective that unions seek to achieve is winning recognition for workers that they are equal partners with management in the task of production. The unions try to secure for workers to put their views to the management and industrial democracy thereby bringing about a new social order.
6. **To Provide Legal Sanctions to Demands:** To provide legal sanctions to its demands, the unions attempt to get these framed in the form of Acts so that they become permanent features of the contract between the employers and the workers. For this purpose, the unions may take recourse to political action in terms of supporting some political party or forming their own political party.
7. **To Provide Educational, Medical and Other Facilities:** Modern trade unions also engage in providing educational, medical and other facilities for the development and welfare of their members, if they have sufficient funds at their disposal.

Principles of Trade Unionism

The trade union functions are performed on the basis of three cardinal principles:

- **Unity is Strengths:** The strength of trade unions is their unity. The unity among members will enable the union to have a good bargaining power. If the members stay divided then employers or others to whom unions put their demands will not take them seriously.
- **Equal Pay for Equal Work:** The unions strike on the principle of equal pay for equal work of the same type. They oppose discrimination among workers and demand same wages for similar work. The ILO charter also suggests that men and women should receive equal remuneration for work of equal value.
- **Security of Service:** The security of service of employees is the other principle of trade unions. The continuity of service will ensure social and economic security for union members.

Why Workers Join Unions?

The trade union movement is gaining momentum with the passage of time. Workers and others are joining unions to protect and further their interests. Why workers join unions? The working class is increasingly depending upon to take up its issues with the managements. The main reasons for the workers joining unions are as follows:

1. To get economic security as they want steady employment and proper income. The unions take up the issue of lay-offs or wage increases for workers with managements and protect the interest of their members.

2. To restrain management from taking any action which is irrational, discriminatory or, prejudicial to the interest of labour. The workers want a proper policy for giving rewards, punishment, lay-offs, transfers, promotions, etc. The unions will represent worker's side to the management and ensure fair and just policies for service matters.
3. To communicate their views, aims, ideas, feelings and frustrations to the management.
4. To get a job through the good offices of a trade union.
5. To secure protection to workers against economic hazards such as accident, illness, death, disability, etc.
6. To get along with their fellow-workers in a better way and to gain respect in the eyes of their peers.

The factors leading to unionization have been given by Randall S. Schuler in Figure 14.4.

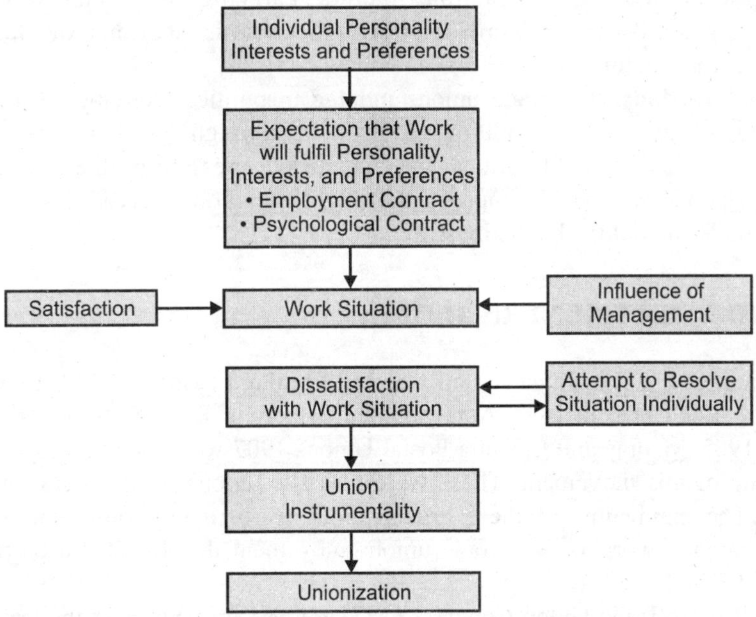

Fig. 14.4. Factors Leading to Unionization.
Source: Randall S. Schuler, *et al.*, Effective Personnel Management, p. 562.

Functions of Trade Unions

The functions of modern unions are comprehensive and these functions are classified into four categories:

1. Intramural functions or militant functions
2. Extramural functions or welfare functions
3. Social functions
4. Political functions

1. **Intramural Functions:** These functions are known as militant functions too because unions may resort to strikes and other pressure tactics to get their demands fulfilled.

Intramural functions include wage rises, proper working conditions, sanitation, safety, continuity in employment, and so on. The unions try to resolve these issues through collective bargaining. If discussions and meetings do not help in resolving these issues then unions use strike and other pressures as tools in getting these demands accepted.

2. **Extramural Functions:** Trade unions also undertake functions which are required for the welfare of their members. These functions include provision of educational, recreational and housing facilities. The unions raise funds in the form of subscription from members and spend them for the welfare of workers. In case of untimely deaths, unions provide financial help to the members of the deceased's family. Extramural functions are very important as they inculcate· the spirit of cooperation against members.
3. **Social Functions:** These functions include carrying out social service activities, discharging social responsibilities through various sections of the society like educating the customers.
4. **Political Functions:** The trade unions indulge in political activities in order to help in improving the economic conditions of workers through legislative and administrative measures. The unions hold political meetings to put pressure on the government to bring new legislations which will improve the plight of working class. The unions may also collect funds for political functions.

TRADE UNION MOVEMENT IN INDIA

The trade union movement in India started with the forming of Bombay Mill Hands Association in 1890 by N.K. Lokhands. In 1897, Amalgamated Society of Railway Servants, Printers Union of Calcutta in 1905, Madras and Calcutta Postal Unions 1907 were the other associations formed in the beginning of this movement. These were no trade unions in true sense but rather social organizations. The main aims of these organizations were to promote welfare activities and spread literacy among workers. The trade unions movement developed fast particularly during and after World War I.

In 1920, All India Trade Union Congress (AITUC) was formed under the leadership of Lala Lajpat Rai. There was a split in AITUC in 1926-27 and All India Trade Union Federation (AITUF) was formed under N.M. Joshi. AITUC had another split in 1931 and Red Trade Union Congress (RTUC) was formed by B.T. Ranadive and S.V. Deshpande. In 1935, RTUC merged into AITUC. After nine years of split NTUF also merged with AITUC (1940) making it again a sole representative of the organized labour.

Those favouring the ideals of socialism and sharing the views of Indian National Congress separated from AITUC and formed Indian National Trade Union Congress (INTUC) in 1947. The socialists later formed Hind Mazdoor Sabha (HMS). In 1962, a new organization called Confederation of Indian Trade Unions (CITU) was formed. The growth of registered trade unions and their membership in India is shown in Table 14.2.

Table 14.2: Growth of Registered Trade Unions and their Membership, 1991 to 2002

Year	No. of registered Trade Unions	No. of Unions submitting returns	Membership of Unions submitting Returns					Average membership per union
			Men Number ('000)	Percentage to total	Women Number ('000)	Percentage to total	Total Membership ('000)	
1	2	3	4	5	6	7	8	9
1991	53535	8418 (15.7)	5507	90.3	594	9.7	6100	725
1992	55680	9165 (16.5)	5148	89.6	598	10.4	5746	627
1993	55784	6806 (12.2)	2636	84.1	498	15.9	3134	460
1994	56872	6277 (11.0)	3239	79.1	856	20.9	4095	652
1995	57952	8162 (14.1)	5675	86.8	863	13.2	6538	801
1996	58988	7242 (12.3)	4250	75.9	1351	24.1	5601	773
1997	60660	8872 (14.6)	6504	87.8	905	12.2	7409	835
1998	61992	7403 (12.0)	6104	84.2	1145	15.8	7249	979
1999	64817	8152 (12.6)	5190	81.0	1218	19.0	6407	786
2000	66056	7253 (11.0)	4510	83.2	910	16.8	5420	747
2001	66624	6531 (9.8)	4392	74.8	1481	25.2	5873	900
2002	68544	7812 (11.4)	5102	73.2	1871	26.8	6973	893

N.B. (1) Figures in brackets in column 3 denote percentages of Unions submitting returns to total number of registered Unions.
(2) The figures of Trade Unions are exclusive of Federations in all the Statements.
(3) Figures in Col. 2 are estimated by incorporating the latest available information of the non-responding States.
Source: http://labourbureau.nic.in/TU%202k2%20Statement%202.1.htm

Present Position

There are a few central organizations which dominate the trade unions in India. These organizations are briefly discussed here:

1. **The Indian National Trade Union Congress (INTUC).** This organization which was formed by Congress party in 1947 has over 3153 affiliated trade unions with a total membership of over 30 1akh workers. It has strong roots in West Bengal, Assam, Gujarat, Bihar and Maharashtra. The largest number of workers in this organization belongs to textile, jute, tea plantation, hosiery, transport and mining industries.
2. **The All India Trade Union Congress (AITUC).** AITUC which is affiliated to Communist Party of India is considered to be the second largest federation of trade unions with over 26 lakh members. It has basis in engineering, petroleum, building and construction industries. AITUC is strong in West Bengal, Kerala, Tamil Nadu, Andhra Pradesh, Punjab and Delhi.

3. **The Hind Mazdoor Sabha (HMS).** HMS is the labour wing of Praja Socialist Party. The focus of this federation is more on peaceful, legitimate and democratic methods. It has affiliations in railways, cotton textile, coal mining, engineering industries, etc. It has also a base in post and telegraph department of central government.
4. **The United Trade Union Congress (UTUC).** Some socialist leaders formed UTUC in April 1949 with an objective to establish a workers' and peasants' state in India. It has influences in West Bengal, Bihar, Kerala and Tamil Nadu. Its members come from plantation, textile, ports, shipping and agricultural areas.
5. **The Centre of Indian Trade Unions (CITU).** It was formed by CPM members in 1970. CITU believes that the exploitation of the working class can be ended only be socializing all means of production, distribution and exchange and establishing a socialist state. CITU claims a membership of over 12 lakh workers.

Problems of Trade Unions

Indian trade unions suffer from many problems. These are discussed as under:

1. **Concentrated in Big Cities:** Trade unions are concentrated more or less in major metropolitan cities in India and traceable only in large-scale units especially in cotton textile industry. The degree of unionism also varies from industry to industry, iron and steel, tobacco, railways, cement, banking, insurance, etc. There is very little trade union activity in small-scale sector, agricultural sector and domestic sector.
2. **Low Membership of Unions:** Most of the unions have low membership. Though the number of unions and union membership are increasing, average membership is inadequate. Because of their small size, unions suffer from lack of adequate funds and find it difficult to engage the services of experts to aid and advise members in times of need. They can't bargain with employers effectively on their own.
3. **Poor Financial Position:** Most of the trade unions in India suffer from inadequate funds. This unsound financial position is mostly due to low membership and low rate of membership fee. Trade Union Act, 1926 prescribed the membership fee at 25 p. per member per month. But the National Commission on labour recommended the increase of rate of membership subscription from 25 paisa to Re. 1 in the year 1990. But the Government did not accept this recommendation. Due to the financial weakness, most of the unions are not in a position to undertake welfare programmes for their workers.
4. **Dominance of Political Leadership:** Most of the trade unions in India have professional political leadership. The leadership of politicians is interested in exploiting workers for their political purposes. Strikes are organized and prolonged for personal prestige and negotiations with employer's breakdown due to political considerations. The interest and welfare of the workers are very often ignored.
5. **Inter-Union Rivalry:** Due to the multiplicity of unions, inter-union rivalry takes place. Unions try to play down each other in a bid to gain greater influence on the workers. In the process, they do more harm than good to the cause of unionism as a whole. Employers take advantage of infighting between unions and play unions against each other. They can also refuse to bargain on the plea that there is no representative union. Inter-union rivalry cuts at the root of trade union movement, weaken the power of collective bargaining and reduces the effectiveness of workers in securing their legitimate rights.

6. **Multiple Unions:** Multiple unions both at the plant and industry levels are responsible for unhealthy growth of trade union movement. There exist several unions in the same establishment or industry. The existence of this phenomenon can be attributed partly to the domination of outside leaders and partly to the labour laws. Trade Unions Act encourages a small sector of workers to form separate unions. Political outsiders establish unions of their own to increase their political influence. In some cases, employers encourage split in unions to undermine their bargaining power.
7. **Heterogeneous Nature of Labour:** Workers come to the factories with varying backgrounds; therefore, it is difficult for them to put a joint front in case of trouble. Employers exploit the situation, under the circumstances, by dividing workers on the basis of race, religion, language, etc.
8. **Lack of Interest by Members:** In order to make the trade union movement succeed, the members of the trade unions should take keen interest in the union affairs. But majority of workers do not take interest in union activities. The attendance at the general meetings of unions is very poor. Under such circumstances, trade unionism cannot be expected to make much progress and outside political leaders exploit the situation to serve their own personal agenda.
9. **Neglect of Welfare Activities:** Many unions in India undertake only limited welfare activities. They feel that their major activity is to fight with the employer for more wages and allowances. Moreover, paucity of funds also hampers the welfare activities of the unions. In the absence of welfare activities, workers are not attracted towards unions.
10. **Absence of Paid Office Bearers:** Weak finances and political leadership do not permit unions to engage the services of full time, paid office bearers. Union activists, who work on a part-time basis, neither have the time nor the energy to take up union activities sincerely and diligently.
11. **Employers Refuse Recognition:** Many a times, the employers refuse recognition to trade unions on the contention that unions consist of only a small number of workers or because of multiplicity of union. Employers are under no obligation to give recognition to unions.

EMPLOYEE WELFARE

Employee or labour welfare work is undertaken by various groups within and outside of an organization to improve the living conditions of workers. The objective is to make the worker happy, healthy, committed and loyal. Employers with a progressive outlook have always invested heavily in enriching the life of workers. Employee welfare activities benefit not only the workers but also the management in the form of greater industrial efficiency.

Meaning of Employee Welfare

Employee welfare is a very comprehensive term which may include any activity which is connected with the social, moral and economic betterment of workers, provided by any agency such as governments, employers, trade unions and other welfare agencies.

Definitions

According to **Dr. Parandikar**, "*Labour welfare work is work for improving the health, safety and general well-being and the industrial efficiency of the workers beyond the minimum standards lay down by labour legislation.*"

According to **Arthur James Todd**, "*Labour welfare means anything done for the comfort and improvement, intellectual or social, of the employees over and above the wages paid which is not a necessity of the industry.*"

According to **ILO report**, "*Workers welfare should be understood as including such services, amenities and facilities which may be established in or in the immediate vicinity of undertakings to enable the persons employed in them to perform their work in healthy and peaceful surroundings and to avail of facilities which improve their health and bring high morale.*"

According to **the Committees on Labour Welfare (1969)**, "*Labour welfare includes such services, facilities and amenities as adequate canteen, rest and recreation facilities, sanitary and medical facilities, arrangements for travel to and from work and for the accommodation of workers employed at a distance from their homes and such other services, amenities and facilities including social security measures as they contribute to improve the condition under which workers are employed.*"

According to **the Labour Investigation Committee (1946)**, "*Employee welfare means anything divine for intellectual, physical, moral and economic betterment of the workers, whether by employers, government or by other agencies, over and above what is laid down by law or what is normally expected on the part of the contracted benefits for which workers may have bargained.*"

On the basis of the above-mentioned definitions, the following features of labour welfare can be identified:

- Labour welfare is a comprehensive term that includes various services, facilities and amenities provided to workers for improving their health, efficiency, economic betterment and social status.
- Welfare measures are in addition to regular wages and other economic benefits available to workers under legal provisions and collective bargaining.
- Employee welfare is **dynamic** in nature varying from country to country, region to region and organization to organization.
- Labour welfare is a **flexible** concept as new welfare measures are added from time to time to the existing measures.
- Employee measures may be introduced by the agencies such as employers, government, employees or by any social or charitable agency.
- The basic objective of labour welfare is to improve the lot of the working class, bring about the development of the whole personality of the worker and to make him a good citizen.

Importance of Employee Welfare

Employee welfare is always beneficial to the worker, employers and the society. How these are benefited is shown as under in Box-3.

Box-3 Employee Welfare and Benefits

Benefits to the Workers:

- Welfare activities provide better physical and mental health to the workers and make them happy.
- Welfare activities like housing, medical benefits, education and recreation facilities for the workers' families help to create contended workers.
- Improvement in material, intellectual and cultural conditions of life protects workers from social evils like drinking, gambling, etc.

Benefits to the Employers:

- Labour welfare activities help to **increase employee productivity** or efficiency by improving their physical and mental health.
- Welfare measures help to improve the **goodwill and public image** of the enterprise.
- Welfare services serve to maintain some peace with the employee's unions. Employee welfare also helps to improve industrial relations **and industrial peace.**
- Employees absenteeism and turnover are reduced due to the provision of welfare facilities. Employees take active interest in their jobs and work with a feeling of involvement and satisfaction.

Benefits to the Society:

- Employee welfare is also in the interest of the larger society because the health, efficiency and happiness of each individual represents the general well-being of all. Well housed, well fed and well looked after labour is not only an asset to the employer but serves to raise the standards of industry and labour in the country.

Principles of Employee Welfare

The following principles should be borne in mind while setting up a labour welfare service:

- **Principles of Determining Employee Real Needs:** First **determine the employees' real needs.** The welfare service should satisfy the real needs of the workers.
- **Principle of Mix of Benefits:** Due to differences in sex, age, income levels of employees, a mix of benefits is suggested so that the choice is left to each individual employee.
- **Principle of Cost:** The cost of the service should be calculated and its financing established on a sound basis.

Agencies of Employee Welfare in India

There are several agencies involved in labour welfare work. Besides central and state governments, employers, unions and social organizations work as agencies for extending welfare facilities to the workers.

1. **Central Government:** The Central Government tries to extend its helping hand through various Acts covering the safety, health and welfare of workers. The Factories Act, 1948, Mines Act, 1952, Shipping Act, 1948, Plantation Labour Act, 1951, Motor Transport Workers Act, 1961, Employees State Insurance Act, 1948, etc., provide for canteens,

crèches, restrooms, washing facilities, etc. Labour welfare officers are to review the welfare activities closely and ensure justice to workers. Statutory welfare funds are created to provide housing, educational, recreational and medical facilities to workers.

2. **State Governments:** Governments in different states and union territories offer welfare facilities to workers. In Assam, a statutory welfare fund is there for offering medical, educational, recreational and other facilities to plantation workers. In Gujarat, Maharashtra, Punjab, and Karnataka, Labour Welfare Centres are administered by welfare boards. However, the number of these welfare centres is inadequate to serve the growing needs of workers at various places. These centres do not have adequate funds and dedicated staff to carry out welfare work.
3. **Employers:** Enlightened employers like TISCO, Hindustan Lever, Godrej, L&T, Siemens, Voltas, Bajaj, Birlas, Sandoz, Philips, HMT, LIC, BHEL, Air India, Hindustan Zinc, Hindustan Copper, RCF, RIL, Wipro, etc. have undertaken welfare activities in the interest of workers. The management of TISCO runs a well equipped hospital in Jamshedpur, supported by health centres and dispensaries in different residential localities. Family planning clinics, credit societies, gymnasiums, clubs, creches, canteens, schools are also set up by TISCO for the benefit of workers. Employees Associations have also joined hands with employers in doing some welfare work for their workers. The Indian Jute Mill Association, The Bombay Mill Owners Association are worth mentioning here. Medical, educational, recreational facilities are also extended in paper, sugar, steel cement, engineering industries also, by the employees and employees' associations.
4. **Trade Unions:** The contribution of trade unions in India towards labour welfare activities is not significant. Poor finances, multiple unionisms, often come in the way of undertaking labour welfare work enthusiastically. There are certain exceptions to this—like the Ahmedabad Textile Labour Association, Mazdoor Sabha of Kanpur, Railwaymen's Union and the Indian Federation of Labour. These labour organizations have provided welfare facilities to workers such as running schools, libraries, sports centres, cooperative stores, recreation and cultural centres, legal cells, labour journals, etc. Though we cannot expect much from the trade unions in the field of welfare, they can at least identify the minimum facilities needed by workers and bring the same to the notice of the Government and the employers. They can act as a representative of the workers and secure the implementation of statutory measures.
5. **Other Agencies:** In addition to the above several social service agencies such as the Bombay Social Service League, Seva Sadan Societies of Bombay Women's Institute in West Bengal, Assam Seva Samity, YM.C.A. etc., also provide services to the working class on a voluntary basis. These agencies provide medical and educational facilities, scholarships, etc.

Types of Employee Welfare Services

Welfare services may broadly be classified into two categories: (i) Intramural services which are provided within the establishment such as latrines and urinals, crèches, rest centres, canteens, uniforms, library, medical aid, subsidized food, shift allowance, etc; (ii) Extramural services which are undertaken outside the establishment such as family planning, child welfare, cooperative stores, credit societies, vocational guidance, holiday homes, leave travel facilities, transport to and from the place of work, etc. Box-4 shows these services.

Box-4 Intramural and Extramural Welfare Activities: ILO

Intramural	Extramural
• Drinking water	• Housing
• Toilets	• Education facilities
• Crèches	• Maternity benefits
• Washing and bathing facilities	• Transportation
• Rest shelters	• Sports facilities
• Uniforms and protective clothing	• Leave travel
• Recreation facilities	• Vocational training
• Canteens	• Holiday homes
• Subsidized food	• Cooperative stores
• Medical aid	• Fair price shops
	• Social insurance

Labour welfare work may also be divided into two categories: (i) statutory welfare work comprising the legal provisions in various pieces of labour legislation (ii) Voluntary welfare work includes those activities which are undertaken by employers for their workers voluntarily.

Many employers, nowadays, offer the following welfare facilities voluntarily:

1. ***Education:*** A scheme of workers' education was envisaged on all India basis by the Government of India in 1957 with the objective to develop leadership from the rank and file and to promote, among workers, a greater understanding of the problems of their economic environment and their privileges and obligations as union members and officials and as citizens.

   The Committee on Labour Welfare (CLW), 1969, recommended that trade unions should assume an active role in educating workers and run schools for promoting literacy among the children of workers. To be effective, the programme of workers' education should be formulated, administered and implemented by the trade unions themselves. Education facilities for worker's children are usually in industrial townships in the form of schools, colleges set up by the government or by employers. Many employers so far have been generous in meeting the cost of books, annual fee, etc., on a voluntary basis. There is however no statutory obligation in respect of education for workers' children in any industry except in plantation.

2. ***Housing:*** Housing is the primary need of a worker's family in civilized life. Without a roof to cover his head, the worker naturally feels frustrated about his poor standard of living in big cities. Recognizing the need for housing accommodation, an Industrial Housing

Scheme was introduced in 1952. Under this scheme, the Central Government offers loans to industrial workers for constructing houses at concessional rates. The low income group housing scheme (1954), subsidised housing scheme for economically weaker sections of society (1952), rural house-sites-cum-hut construction scheme for landless workers (1971) have also been introduced to reduce the housing shortage to workers. The government has also introduced housing schemes for miners and plantation workers in early 50s. Housing schemes for dock workers was drawn up in 1964. The NCL recommended that the Government should assume major responsibility for housing, with active help from employers. It suggested that housing boards should be set up in other states as in the case of Uttar Pradesh, Maharashtra, Tamilnadu, Andhra Pradesh, Karanataka and that a Central Housing Board should oversee all housing boards with a 50% subsidy and 50% loan with interest. The problem of housing, of course, is of such a vast dimension that no single agency can reasonably be expected to solve it.

3. ***Transportation:*** The Committee on Labour Welfare, 1969, recommended the provision of transport facilities to workers so that they can reach the workplace punctually and comfortably. Most employers have, however, recognized the workers' need for transport services and therefore responded favourably by providing company owned/leased vehicles to workers in major industrial centres—especially in the private sector. They have also introduced innovative financing schemes in recent times enabling workers to buy their own bicycles, scooters, motor cycles, etc.
4. ***Recreation:*** Though there is no statutory stipulation in this area, progressive employers both in the public and private sector (like the Tatas, HUL, Air India, BHEL, Infosys technologies, Hughes Software systems, NUT, Cadbury, Ranbaxy, Railway and Defence Services have) consciously offered facilities for recreation sports and cultural activities. For example, companies like NUT and TISCO have appointed a Chief Fun Officer to take care of parties and functions held on every Friday. Sprawling food courts, basketball courts; tennis, golf, billiards, swimming sauna; jacuzzi, jogging tracks, beauty centres, spacious gyms, ATMs, gift shops are to be found in most software companies—such as Infosys, Wipro, Hughes Software systems, in India.
5. ***Other facilities:*** To improve the comfort level of workers while at work there are some other facilities that are provided by the welfare agencies:
   - *(i)* ***Canteen, restrooms and lunchroom:*** Canteens established inside factories generally offer food at subsidised rates. In modern organizations, food courts offering a variety of continental and intercontinental cuisine have become quite popular in recent times.
   - *(ii)* ***Washing facilities, medical aid, leave travel concessions:*** Most factories have first-aid facilities to take care of minor injuries. Reimbursement of medical expenses actually incurred is also increasingly favoured nowadays.
   - *(iii)* ***Consumer cooperative stores:*** The Indian Labour Conference in 1963 recommended the setting up of consumer cooperative stores in all industrial establishments including plantations and mines employing 300 or more workers. The employer is expected to extend help in the form of share capital, working capital, loans at concessive rates, etc. The Industrial Truce Resolution, 1962 aimed at keeping prices of essential items low by opening a sufficient number of fair price shops for workers.

Statutory Provisions Concerning Employee Welfare

Employers are required to offer welfare facilities to workers under different labour laws. These are discussed as follows:

The Factories Act, 1948

The Act provides the following services to workers:

- Washing facilities to male and female workers separately
- Facilities for storing and drying clothes
- Facilities for occasional rest for workers who work in a standing position for long hours
- First-aid boxes or cupboards—one for every 150 workers and the ambulance facility if there are more than 500 workers
- Canteens, where there are more than 250 workers
- Shelters, restrooms and lunch rooms where over 150 workers are employed.
- Creche, if 30 or more workers are employed
- Welfare officer, if 500 or more workers are employed

The Plantation Labour Act, 1951

The Act provides for the following:

- A canteen if 150 or more workers are employed
- Creche if 50 or more women workers are employed
- Recreational facilities for workers and their children
- Educational arrangements in the estate if there are 25 or more children of workers, between the age of 6 and 12
- Housing facilities for every worker and his family residing in the estate
- Medical aid to workers and their families; sickness and maternity allowance
- Providing umbrellas, blankets, raincoats to workers as a protection against rain or cold—as prescribed by the State government
- Welfare officer, if 300 or more workers are employed.

The Mines Act, 1951

The Act provides for the following:

- Shelters for taking food and rest if 50 or more workers are employed
- First-aid boxes and first-aid rooms if 150 or more workers are employed
- A canteen if employing 250 or more workers
- A creche if employing 50 or more females
- Pit-head baths equipped with showers, sanitary latrines
- Welfare officer if 500 or more workers are employed.

The Motor Transport Workers Act, 1961

The Act contains the following provisions:

- First-aid equipment in each transport vehicle
- Medical facilities at the operating and halting centres

- Canteen if employing 100 or more workers
- Comfortable, clean, ventilated and well-lighted restrooms at every place where motor transport workers are required to halt at night
- Uniforms, raincoats to conductors, drivers, and line checking staff for protection against cold and rain
- Prescribed amount of washing allowance to the above staff members.

The Contract Labour (Regulation and Abolition) Act, 1970

The Act requires the contractor to extend the following benefits to workers:

- Canteen, if employing 100 or more workers
- Rest rooms or other suitable alternative accommodation where contract labour is required to halt at night in connection with the work of an establishment
- Washing facilities
- First-aid boxes equipped with prescribed contents.

Labour Welfare Officer

The Factories Act, 1948, the Plantation Labour Act, 1951 and the Mines Act, 1951 provide for the appointment of a Labour Welfare Officer if the number of workers employed within a unit exceeds 500 (300 as per the Plantation Act). The post has been created specifically to (i) eliminate the malpractices of the jobber system in the recruitment of labour; (ii) improve labour administration in factories and (iii) serve as liaison with the State Labour Commissioner. The Labour Welfare Officer was also expected to discharge the functions of a policeman, with respect to law and order situation within an organization. In each case the respective state governments may prescribe duties, qualifications and conditions of service of such officers.

The Labour Welfare Officer should possess a university degree, degree or diploma in social service/social work from a recognized institution and adequate knowledge of local language of the area where the factory is situated.

The duties and responsibilities of a Labour Welfare Officer may be summarized thus (Central Welfare Officers Rules, 1951):

(i) ***Advising Management:*** He can advise and suggest the formulation of company labour policies; promote training programmes, promote welfare schemes; secure housing, recreational and educational facilities for workers, etc.

(ii) ***Counselling Services:*** He can offer help to workers in solving family and personal problems, in adjusting to work environment, in understanding their rights and privileges, in forwarding application for leave, etc. He can offer help to management by making workers understand various problems.

(iii) ***Supervisory Services:*** He can supervise, inspect and regulate welfare, health and safety programmes, working of joint committees and paid vacations.

(iv) ***Liaison Services:*** He can forward workers' grievances to management, can influence industrial relations climate when disputes arise, can restrain workers and management from resorting to illegal strikes and lockouts.

(v) ***Services as Mediators:*** He can mediate and build harmony between the labour and the management, secure speedy redressal of workers' grievances, settle disputes through

in resolving troubling issues peacefully.

persuasive efforts, maintain a neutral stance during strikes and lockouts and thereby help in resolving troubling issues peacefully.

Labour welfare officers are thus to act as advisors, counsellors, supervisors, mediators and liaison offers.

EMPLOYEE EMPOWERMENT

The concept of "***Employee Empowerment***" is not new. It is in fact, the concept of participative management. The focus on its importance has increased with the Industrial Revolution and advent of large enterprises.

Employee Empowerment or participative management in narrow sense refers to the constitution of consultative councils and committees, comprising representatives of employees and employers, to recommend steps for improving productivity, job loading, safety, etc. According to **Michael Armstrong**, "In broader and real sense participative management or employee empowerment exists when employees are involved in decision-making process, not in mere job related activities, but at all levels of management.

In the words of **Conger**, "*Empowerment is the act of strengthening an individuals' in his or her sense of effectiveness. It is not simply a set of external actions rather it is a process of changing the beliefs of people internally and they would more powerful if management succeeds in increasing their sense of self-determination.*"

According to **Ford and Fottler**, "*Empowerment is a process that provides greater autonomy to employees through sharing of relevant information and the provision of control over factors affecting job performance. Empowerment helps remove the conditions that cause powerlessness while enhancing employee feelings of self-efficacy.*"

Features of Employee Empowerment

1. It is mental and emotional involvement of employees rather than mere physical presence.
2. It is collective participation as a group through representatives rather than participating individually.
3. It involves a system of communication and consultation.
4. It involves various levels of participation.
5. There are different degrees of employee empowerment.
6. Employee empowerment allows individuals to identify and use their potential in helping the organization achieve its goals.
7. Empowered employees believe that they are competent and valued, that their jobs have meaning and impact and that they have opportunities to use their talent.
8. Empowered employees are energetic and passionate as empowerment enhances their intrinsic work motivation.

Process of Employee Empowerment

Empowerment authorizes employees to cope with situations and enables them to take control of problems as they arise. Five broad approaches to empowerment have been suggested:

1. Helping employees achieve ***job mastery*** (giving proper training, coaching, and guided experience that will result in initial successes).
2. Allowing more ***control*** (giving them discretion over job performance and then holding them *accountable* for outcomes).
3. Providing successful ***role models*** (allowing them to observe peers who already perform successfully on the job).
4. Using ***social reinforcement and persuasion*** (giving praise, encouragement, and verbal feedback designed to raise self-confidence).
5. Giving ***emotional support*** (providing reduction of stress and anxiety through better role definition, task assistance, and honest caring).

When managers use these approaches, employees begin believing that they are competent and valued, that their jobs have meaning and impact, and that they have opportunities to use their talents. In effect, when they have been legitimately empowered, their efforts are more likely to payoff in both personal satisfaction and the kind of results that the organization values. This chain of events is illustrated in Figure 14.5.

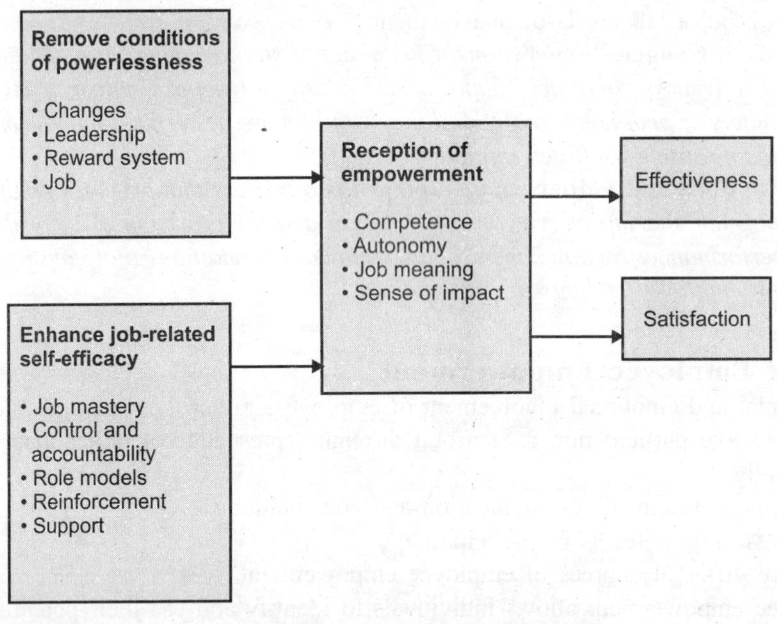

Fig. 14.5. Process of Empowerment.

Managers have many behavioural tools available to them to attack the powerlessness problem. Some of these tools, such as mutual goal setting, job feedback, modelling, and contingent reward systems, have already been discussed in previous chapters. A major approach, however, lies in the use of various programmes for participative management. Such programmes provide employees with varying degrees of perceived ownership, input into various steps in the decision-making process, and the key feeling of choice in their work environment.

Essential Components and Strategies of Employee Empowerment

Essentials

According to **Bowen and Lawler,** the essential components of employee empowerment are:

- Power
- Information
- Knowledge
- Rewards

Empowerment can be expressed in terms of an equation.

$$\text{Empowerment} = \text{Power} \times \text{Information} \times \text{Knowledge} \times \text{Rewards}$$

Empowerment Strategies

In today's competitive, global business environment, organizations are required to be optimally responsive to continuous change. Many organizations that were listed among the *Fortune* 500 companies in the 1980s and 1990s are no longer in business because of their failure to adapt to the changing marketplace. Thus, in an attempt to increase their success, business enterprises are employing various tools and techniques. It has been found that there is a general improvement on both the financial performance of a firm, as well as in its people through change processes, that is based on an empowerment approach.

As we are increasingly entering into the digital age, the compelling combination of knowledge and technology makes it possible to position the right information in the hands of the right people at the right time. Empowerment success requires an organizational commitment to strategies that support it. The following support strategies are required:

1. Position descriptions must be rewritten to identify, not only performance expectations but also outline the level and type of empowerment for every employee position;
2. Training reinforces the organization's empowerment objectives and must include elements that build, support and maintain organization-employee trust;
3. Recruitment and selection processes must identify and select candidates who are not only capable of performing the tasks, but also have the skills to handle empowerment responsibilities; and
4. Performance evaluation must be redesigned to accurately identify and reflect the evaluated employee's true measure of the facts. It may either be a two-way performance measurement or 360-degree measurement.
    - The forms of empowerment used depend on the managerial meaning of empowerment. For Example:

    (i) Empowerment through Participation (through Autonomous Work Groups).
    (ii) Empowerment through Involvement (through Quality Circles).
    (iii) Empowerment through Commitment (through Quality of Working Life Programmes).
    (iv) Empowerment through Delayering (through Job Redesign).

How to Implement Successfully Empowerment Strategies

The following steps may be followed by any organization that seeks to successfully implement empowerment.

> **Box-5 The Form, State and Outcomes of Empowerment**
>
> Managerial Intentions → Forms of Empowerment → Change in Working Arrangements → The State of Empowerment → Change in Work Behaviour → Organizational Objectives.

1. The organization should first identify what is needed from the empowerment process and ascertain the precise level of empowerment expectations, authority and responsibility;
2. Ensuring that information is readily available and would answer potential employee concerns. This can be achieved through formal training, disseminating information via the organizational intranet, and mentoring between the manager and the subordinates; and
3. Finally, empowerment strategies should be equally and fairly shared throughout the organization.

Outcomes of Empowerment Strategies

Empowerment is a comprehensive strategy as it brings about considerable improvements in macro and micro level of work process. The empowerment programmes that are implemented should suitably have the manifold objectives of improving skill utilization, information sharing, and decision-making. **Wilkinson and Sewall** have rightly pointed out that, although it may bring about positive results like increased productivity, the efficient operation of the task may be undermined by the employees.

Thus, real empowerment can only be achieved through the management's commitment for openness to new ideas, willingness to hand over control and command, team building and through open lines of communication.

In this era of intense competition, when employees are empowered to take decisions, it enhances the employees' motivation and also makes them work towards a common goal of organizational effectiveness. In knowledge organizations nowadays, significant investment in decision-making authority and empowerment provides employees with more control over their work. Employee empowerment leads to job satisfaction, employee motivation and loyalty. These have a profound impact on the organization and can thus benefit employees in the bottom line.

Conclusion: Employee empowerment strategies must be initiated by organizational leadership; cost and other considerations must be kept in mind. Managers are accountable for the success of empowerment programmes. The outcome of empowerment is good for the employees, organizations and society.

REVIEW QUESTIONS

1. What do you mean by industrial relations? What measures would you suggest to improve industrial relations in a firm?

2. Explain the concept of industrial relations. What is the significance of good industrial relations and what are its objectives?
3. Discuss the various approaches to industrial relations.
4. Explain the HRD approach to industrial relations. What are the functional requirements for sound IR programme?
5. Explain the various parties involved in industrial relations.
6. Discuss the various theoretical and practical approaches to industrial relations.
7. Define the term industrial relations. Explain how does the concept of industrial relations differ from the concept of human resource management?
8. Explain the necessary conditions for the maintenance of sound industrial relations.
9. Define a trade union. Why do employees join unions?
10. Write a detailed note on trade movement in India.
11. What is a trade union? Discuss the problems of trade unions.
12. What do you mean by employee welfare? Bring out the need for providing welfare facilities to workers.
13. State the agencies involved in labour welfare work in India. Are the services offered by these agencies in your opinion, satisfactory or not?
14. The government needs to play an active role in matters relating to labour welfare. Comment.
15. Comment on the adequacy of welfare provisions contained in the following Acts:
    - The Factories Act.
    - The Mines Act.
    - The Plantation Labour Act, 1951.

CASE STUDY

14.1 Mohan Lal—The Head Strong Employee

Mr. Raj Khurana, the Member of Managing Committee of a reputed institution of Yamuna Nagar district, is sitting in the meeting of the Management. Sitting there, sipping a cup of coffee, he started recollecting events of the year 2001 when he was the principal of the same institution. Later, after his retirement he became the member of the management committee, besides, heading a professional institute being run by the same management. This meeting of the office bearers of the governing body was called for discussing the case of Mr. Mohan Lal, an employee of the institution. Mr. Raj was also invited in the meeting. Raj Khurana was instrumental in the appointment of Mr. Mohan Lal as lecturer, despite of his poor personality. Reason behind this was that he being the only male member among other five successful candidates. In the early years of his career Mohan was quite and humble till he was confirmed.

The scene changed after his confirmation and especially after the retirement of Mr. Raj as Mohan started becoming vocal on petty issues and started taking interest in the union activities. Mr. Ramanpreet Singh was appointed as the new principal of the institution who happened to be from the same institution. Mohan was not in good books of Mr. Singh, because as colleague, he did not have good opinion of Mohan. But as principal, he tried to make him to do some fruitful work. Mr. Mohan started taking undue favour from the principal, did not take much interest in teaching, never bothered to motivate the students to attend his classes.

In due course, circumstances compelled Mr. Singh to leave the institution as he opted for VRS. As an alternative arrangement, Mr. Sridhar, a senior person from the faculty of the institution, was promoted as officiating principal. During the tenure of Mr. Sridhar, Mohan's role was passive and his academic performance was also not good as the bottom line of his results became red and growing thicker. Moreover, he was not considered a popular teacher and most of the students of his class did not give a positive feedback.

In the meanwhile, Mr. Sridhar retired from the institution. Again the same procedure was adopted as an alternative arrangement. This time Mr. Chander Verma was appointed as officiating principal. Mr. Mohan became vocal and starting complaining against the practices adopted by former principals. Rather he started inciting other staff members to build pressure on the officiating principal regarding the matters of promotion of the staff members. There was a farewell party for a senior faculty member on his retirement. Mohan along with others threatened to walkout from the party because the earlier principals did not arrange such parties when a few other staff members retired or left the institution.

He started violating the glorious traditions of the institution. Moreover, the academic environment of the institution deteriorated. The pass percentage in the subjects taken by Mohan was below the standard set by the management continuously for two years. So the management served him a show cause notice through the officiating principal. In reaction of this notice, Mohan wrote in reply a letter which was full of counter allegations and its wording too was quite insulting. In place of giving a calm reply, he criticized the officiating principal and demanded that on what grounds he had been served with this notice.

Since then the process of issuing letters and replies continued. Mr. Mohan was never expected to be so rude in his behaviour towards senior persons of the institution and members of the management. So, the management constituted a committee to find out the real facts. The committee comprised two former principals and the seniormost staff members of the teaching department of the institution.

Enquiry was conducted and Mohan was asked to appear before the committee. On the day of hearing, the members of the committee tried to convince Mohan to be polite and asked him to give an undertaking that he will behave rationally in future but his attitude remained the same. He did not agree to settle things in a cordial manner. He insisted that the principal should withdraw all the letters served to him and he has not done anything wrong.

The problem is still going on.

Questions

1. In your opinion what is the real cause of the problem?
2. If you were the principal of the institution, what would you do in this case?
3. The policy of providing undue favour to an employee like Mr. Mohan to make him work is justifiable or not. Give your views.
4. Do you think it was justifiable on the part of the principal to use his influence in getting him selected as a faculty member despite his poor personality?
5. What type of policy should be adopted to make sound relations between Mohan, the principal and the management?

14.2 "Whose Side are you on, Anyway"?

It was past 4 p.m. and Purushottam Kshirsagar was still at his shopfloor office. The small but elegant office was a perk he was entitled to after he had been nominated to the board of Horizon Industries (P) Ltd., as workman-director six months ago. His shift generally ended at 3 p.m. and he would be home by late evening. But that day, he still had long hours ahead of him.

Kshirsagar had been with Horizon for over twenty years. Starting off as a substitute mill-hand in the paint shop at one of the company's manufacturing facilities, he had been made permanent on the job five years later. He had no formal education. He felt this was a handicap, but he made up for it with a willingness to learn and a certain enthusiasm on the job. He was soon marked by the works manager as someone to watch out for. Simultaneously, Kshirsagar also came to the attention of the president of the Horizon Employees' Union who drafted him into union activities. Even while he got promoted twice during the period to become the head colour mixer last year, Kshirsagar had gradually moved up the union hierarchy and had been thrice elected secretary of the union.

Labour-management relations at Horizon were not always cordial. This was largely because the company had not been recording a consistently good performance. There were frequent cuts in production every year because of go-slows and strikes by workmen—most of them related to wage hikes and bonus payments.

With a view to ensuring a better understanding on the part of labour, the problems of company management, the Horizon board, led by chairman and managing director Avinash Chaturvedi, began to toy with the idea of taking on a workman on the board. What started off as a hesitant move snowballed, after a series of brainstorming sessions with executives and meetings with the union leaders, into a situation in which Kshirsagar found him catapulted to the Horizon board as workman-director.

It was an untested ground for the company. But the novelty of it all excited both the management and the labour force. The board members—all functional heads went out of their way to make Kshirsagar comfortable and the latter also responded quite well. He got used to the ambience of the boardroom and the sense of power it conveyed. Significantly, he was soon at home with the perspectives of top management and began to see each issue from both sides.

It was smooth going until the union presented a week before the monthly board meeting, its charter of demands, one of which was a 30 per cent across-the-board hike in wages. The matter was taken up at the board meeting as part of a special agenda.

"Look at what your people are asking for," said Chaturvedi, addressing Kshirsagar with a sarcasm that no one in the board missed. "You know the precarious finances of the company. How could you be a party to a demand that simply can't be met? You better explain to them how ridiculous the demands are," he said.

"I don't think they can all be dismissed as ridiculous," said Kshirsagar. "And the board can surely consider the alternatives. We owe at least that much to the union." But Chaturvedi adjourned the meeting in a huff, mentioning, once again to Kshirsagar that he should "advise the union properly".

When Kshirsagar told the executive committee members of the union that the board was simply not prepared to even consider the demands, he immediately sensed the hostility in the room. "You are a sell out," one of them said. "Who do you really represent—us or them?" asked another.

"Here comes the crunch," thought Kshirsagar. And however hard he tried to explain, he felt he was talking to a wall.

A victim of divided loyalties, he himself was unable to understand whose side he was on. Perhaps the best course would be to resign from the board. Perhaps he should resign both from the board and the union. Or may be resign from Horizon itself and seek a job elsewhere. But, he felt, sitting in his office a little later, "none of it could solve the problem".

Source: R. Chandrasekhar, The Buck Stops Here, Macmillan, p. 75-76.

Questions

1. What should he do?

14.3 Is Empowerment Always Beneficial?

Gaurav manages the customer relations department of Fortune Ltd., a Bangalore based company. The department is responsible for replying to customer requests for information and to customer complaints. There are ten typists in the department who handle the correspondence to customers dictated by the staff.

Gaurav recently promoted Sheetal to office supervisor. Sheetal had been a typist in the department for twelve years. She was considered the fastest and most accurate typist who had ever worked for Gaurav. Sheetal had the best attendance record in the department and Gaurav considered her his most dependable employee. She was very well liked by all the typists and they considered her to be a good personal friend.

As a supervisor, Sheetal does a good job of handing out work assignments, but she does little else to supervise the typists. She does not like to criticize the typists and does not enforce office rules. No matter what a typist does, Sheetal will not take any disciplinary action. She makes no attempt to check the work of the typists for compliance with quality standards or to see that work is completed on time. In fact, she spends most of her time typing to reduce the work load of the other typists.

Gaurav has been receiving an increasing number of complaints from the department staff about the poor quality of the typing and about the slow turn around time for work. He has also received complaints about the typists taking excessively long coffee breaks and spending time on personal phone calls.

When Gaurav talked to the typists, they told him that Sheetal frequently invites them to her house for dinner. It appears to Gaurav that the typists all like Sheetal as a friend, but they are becoming concerned about her lack of supervisory skills. Gaurav mentioned to Sheetal that she should focus her effort on improving the work of the typists. She replied, "These women are my friends and I don't feel right about cracking down on them."

Questions

1. Can an individual effectively manage a group and be a close personal friend with group members?
2. What should Gaurav do to ensure that the work of the typists will improve?

3. Should Sheetal have been promoted to office supervisor?
4. If you were Sheetal, what would you do? Would you quit the supervisor's job? Would you no longer be friends with the typists?

REFERENCES

1. Armstrong, Michael, (1988). "A Handbook of Personnel Management Practice", Kogan, London.
2. Best Employers in India, Annual Summary, 2002, 2003, 2004, Business Today.
3. Mamoria, C.B. and S. Mamoria, (2000). "Dynamics of Industrial Relations in India", Himalaya Publishing House, New Delhi.
4. Ramaswamy, E.A. (1986). "From IR to HRD", Business India.
5. Great Places to Work, annual summary, 2003 and 2004, Business World.
6. http://labourbureau.nic.in/TU%202k2%20Statement%202.1.htm
7. Dayal, I. (1989). "Management Training Organizations", Prentice-Hall of India, New Delhi.
8. Newstrom, John W. (2008). "Organization Behaviour", Tata McGraw-Hill Publishing Company Ltd., New Delhi, pp. 182-183.
9. Raymond J. Stone, (1995). "Human Resource Management", John Wiley & Sons, p. 415.
10. Report of the Committee on Labour Welfare, 1969.
11. Report of the National Commission on Labour, 1969.
12. Robert, C. Ford and Myron D. Fottler, (1995). "Empowerment: A matter of degree", Academy of Management Executive, vol. 9, no. 3, pp. 21-31.
13. Punekar, S.D. *et al.*, (1978). "Labour Welfare, Trade Unions, Industrial Relations", Himalaya Publishing House, Bombay.
14. Srivastava, C.S. (1983). "Industrial Relations Machinery", Deep and Deep, New Delhi.
15. Singh, V.B. (1968). "Climate for Industrial Relations, A study of Kanpur Cotton Mills", Allied Publishers, Mumbai, p. 1.
16. Giri, V.V. (1972). "Labour Problems in Indian Industry", Asia Publishing House, Bombay.
17. Yoder Dale, (1969). "Personnel Management and Industrial Relations", Prentice-Hall, New York.

CHAPTER

15 Industrial Disputes and Management of Grievances

CHAPTER'S OUTLINE

- Introduction
- Meaning and Nature of Industrial Disputes
- Causes of Industrial Disputes
- Preventions and Settlement of Industrial Disputes
- Meaning of Grievance
- Forms of Grievances
- Causes of Grievances
- Steps in Grievances Handling

INTRODUCTION

The conflict or dispute between labour and management is very common. Divergent views, opposite stands, contrasting demands characterize labour management relations. Employees want more jobs, high wages; better working conditions whereas the management wants to reduce staff, raise productivity, pay fewer wages, etc. On account of technological advancement and, computerization, requirement of labour force falls which is opposed by the trade unions. In such an environment of opposite interests, dispute or conflict arises. The disputes manifest in the form of strikes and lockouts. The consequences of disputes are loss of production, loss of profit, loss of market and even closure of the plant.

In this chapter, we shall answer a few pertinent questions, such as:

- What are these disputes?

- Why do they occur?
- How can they be resolved?

MEANING AND NATURE OF INDUSTRIAL DISPUTES

According to Industrial Disputes Act, 1947, "*Industrial disputes mean any dispute or difference between employers and workmen, or between workmen and workmen, which is connected with the employment or non-employment or terms of employment with the conditions of labour of any person.*"

The definition is too broad and includes conflicts even among employers under the term 'dispute'. In practice, disputes mainly relate to the strife between employers and their employees.

Thus, the term is characterized by the following factors:

(i) There should be a difference or dispute. For example, labour demands something, management does not grant the same.

(ii) The dispute could be between employer-employer, employee-employee or employer-employee.

(iii) The dispute must pertain to some work related issues.

(iv) Dispute between one or two workmen and their employers is not a dispute, instead, it must be raised by a group or class of workmen.

Forms of Industrial Disputes

The various forms of industrial disputes may be stated thus:

1. **Strikes:** A strike is a spontaneous and concerted withdrawal of labour from production temporarily. It is a collective stoppage of work by a group of workers for pressuring their employers to accept certain demands. The Industrial Disputes Act, 1947 has defined strike as "an assertion of work by a body of persons" employed in industry acting in combination, or a concerted refusal or a refusal under a common understanding of any number of persons who are or have been so employed to continue to work or to accept employment. Strikes are of several types:

   (i) Sympathetic Strike: When a strike is undertaken to show sympathy with workers in other industries, it is called sympathetic strike.

   (ii) General Strike: It is a strike by all or most of the unions in a industry or a region.

   (iii) Unofficial Strike: It is strike undertaken without the consent of unions.

   (iv) Sectional Strike: It is the refusal of a section of a given class of workers to perform their normal duties.

   (v) Bumper Strike: It is the strike when the unions plan to paralyse the industry, firm by firm, the order being chosen by the union. Such strikes are supported by the contributions of those who are still at work.

   (vi) Sit down Strike (also called stay-in, tool down, pen down strike): It is a strike in which the workers cease to perform their duties but do not leave the place of work.

   (vii) Slow down Strike: Known as a 'go-slow' tactic, the workers do not stop working but put breaks to the normal way of doing things.

(viii) ***Lightening Strike:*** Out of provocation, workers may go on strike without notice or at a very short notice. There is an element of surprise in such wildcat strikes.

(ix) ***Hunger Strike:*** To gain sympathy from the public and to get noticed by the employers, workers may decide to forego food for a specified period. Small batches of workers may also go on a relay hunger strike in a sequential order. Such non-violent protests generally bring moral pressure on employers to iron out the differences with labour quickly.

2. Lockouts: Lockout is the counterpart of strike. It is the weapon available to the employer to close down the factory till the workers agree to resume work on the conditions laid down by the employer. The Industrial Disputes Act, 1947 defined it as "The closing of a place of an employment, or the suspension of work or the refusal of an employer to continue to employ any number of persons employed by him". If it is impossible to meet the demands of the workers, employers may decide to go for lockout. An employer may also pull down the shutters so as to bring psychological pressure on the workers to agree to his conditions of face closure of the unit.

3. Gherao: Gherao means to surround. In this method a group of workers initiate collective action aimed at preventing members of the management from leaving the office. This can happen outside the factory premises too. The person who are 'gheraos' are not allowed to move for a long time, sometimes even without food or water. The National Commission of Labour, while refusing to accept it as a form of Industrial Protest, opined that gheraos tend to inflict physical duress (as against economic pressure) on the persons affected and endanger not only industrial harmony but also create problems of law and order.

4. Picketing and Boycott: When picketing, workers often carry/display signs, banners and placards (in connection with the dispute), prevent others from entering the place of work and persuade others to join the strike. Boycott aims at disrupting the normal functioning of an enterprise. Through forceful appeals and negative behavioural acts, striking workers prevent others from entering the place of work and persuade them not to cooperate with the employer.

CAUSES OF INDUSTRIAL DISPUTES

The causes of industrial disputes are many and varied. The major ones relate to wages, allowances, working conditions, union rivalry, political interference, unfair practices and multiplicity of labour laws, etc.

The main cause of industrial disputes may be classified into four groups: (i) Economic (ii) Managerial (iii) Political and (iv) others. These causes are discussed as follows:

1. **Economic Causes**: The most important cause of industrial disputes are economic causes. These include:
   (i) **Wages and Allowances:** Demand for increase in wages and allowances are the most important cause of industrial disputes. Due to inflation and high cost of living, workers and their unions periodically put up a demand for increase in their remuneration so as to maintain their real income. Employers do not accept the demand easily and fully, leading to strikes and other types of disputes in industry.

(ii) **Bonus:** Both the quantum and the method of bonus payment has led to a number of disputes. Workers and trade unions want a share in the profits of industry, employers sometimes oppose.

(iii) **Working Conditions and Working Hours:** The working conditions in Indian industries are not hygienic. Ample provisions of water, heating, lighting, safety, etc. are not available. Working hours are also greater. The demand for good working conditions and shorter hours of work are also responsible for the labour disputes.

(iv) **Modernization and Automation:** The attempt at modernization and introduction of automatic machinery to replace workers has been another cause of disputes in India. Workers go on strike, off and on, to resist rationalization and automation.

(v) **Demand for Medical, Education and Housing:** Demand for other facilities for meeting out their basic needs such as medical, education, housing, etc. encourage the workers to resort to direct action because such facilities are denied by the employers.

2. **Managerial Causes:** These causes include autocratic managerial attitude and defective labour policies, etc:

(i) **Failure to Recognize the Trade Unions:** Failure on the part of employers to recognize the trade unions, insult of trade union leaders by the employers is some of the examples of autocratic managerial attitude. The attitude of the employers leads to conflicts between management and labour.

(ii) **Defective Recruitment and Promotion Policies**: The recruitment practice in most of the industries is defective. Recruitment is generally made through the contractors who exploit the workers and suppress their individuality. The defective promotion, demotion, transfer and placement policies encourage dissatisfaction among workers.

(iii) **Irregular Layoff and Retrenchment:** Layoff and retrenchment are the reasons to be mentioned for encouraging industrial disputes. Some employers follow the policy of 'Hire and Fire'. As a matter of practice, workers are not made permanent for a pretty long time to deprive them of their legitimate rights.

(iv) **Defiance of Agreements and Codes:** The employers regularly defy the provisions of collective bargaining agreements, code of conduct and code of discipline for with a view to harass or exploit the employees. All this encourages strikes.

(v) **Inefficient Leadership:** Inefficient leadership is also one of the causes for industrial disputes. Defective management leadership ignores the labour problems and inefficient labour leadership cannot coordinate the efforts of their fellow members, so disputes arise.

(vi) **Weak Trade Unions:** Weak trade unions also lead to industrial interest. In some undertakings, there is no union and in some other undertakings, there is multiplicity of unions. Both the situations weaken the trade union movement. The workers in non-union undertakings resort to direct action instead of collective bargaining which can be a better course of action if there is a proper trade union.

3. **Political Causes:** Political leaders have used unions as powerful weapons to build tensions inside a plant/industry with a view to satisfy their own private ends on a number of occasions.

4. **Other Causes:** In addition to the causes mentioned above there are several other reasons of industrial disputes worth mentioning. These are:
   - Multiplicity of Labour Laws.
   - Inter-union Rivalry
   - Misbehaviour
   - Lack of Proper Communication

PREVENTION AND SETTLEMENT OF INDUSTRIAL DISPUTES

Whatever may be the cause of industrial disputes, the consequences are harmful to all the stakeholders—management, employees, economy and the society. For management, dispute results in loss of production, revenue, profit and even sickness of the plant.

Employees would be hard hit as the disputes may lead to lockouts and consequent loss of wages and even jobs. Industrial establishments are the pillars of the economy and the economy is bound to collapse, if industries are torn by industrial strike. The cumulative effect of all these is felt by society.

A dispute, therefore, needs to be settled as soon as possible. Basically two types of steps are taken:

1. The steps which further prevents the occurrence of disputes.
2. The steps which are required to settle or resolve the disputes.

Figure 15.1 shows the important measures taken to prevent and resolve the disputes.

Various methods are available for resolving disputes. More important of them are:

1. Workers' participation in management
2. Collective bargaining
3. Code of discipline
4. Grievance procedure
5. Arbitration
6. Conciliation
7. Adjudication
8. Consultative machinery

1. Workers' Participation in Management

This is an approach in which workers are associated with management in decision-making. This approach is considered important in preventing fresh disputes. It includes the following schemes:

(i) Works Committees: Every industrial undertaking employing 100 or more workers is under an obligation to set up a works committees consisting of representatives of employer and employees. The main purpose of such committees is to promote industrial relations.

(ii) Joint Management Councils: Just to make a start in labour participation in management, the Government suggested in its Industrial Resolution 1956 to set up joint management councils.

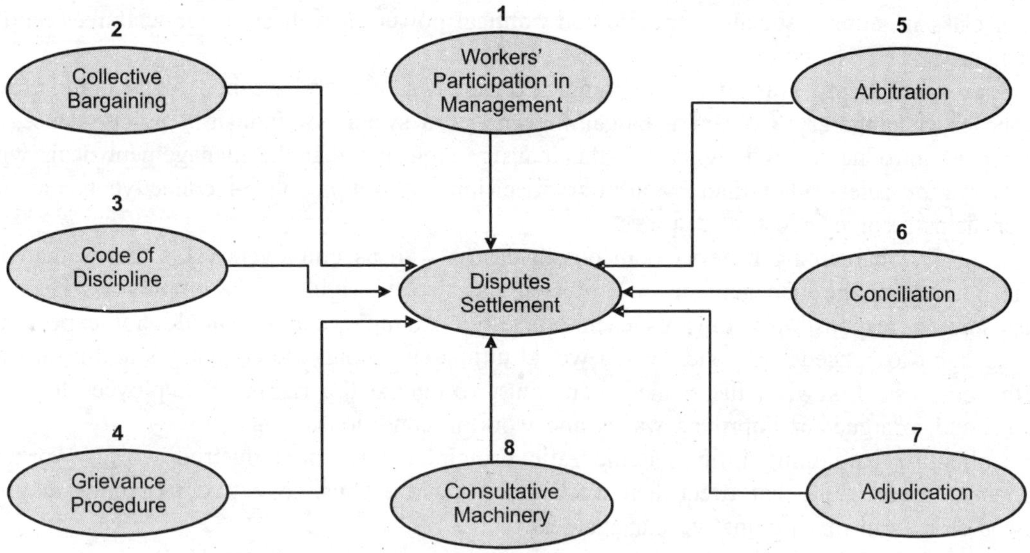

Fig. 15.1. Disputes Prevention and Settlement Mechanisms.

(iii) **Shop Council:** Shop councils have been established in the manufacturing and mining industries employing 500 or more workers in private, public and joint sectors. These councils assist the management in achieving production targets, improving production, productivity and efficiency, eliminating wastage and in achieving optimum utilization of machinery and manpower. They enforce safety measures and render assistance in the maintenance of general discipline on the shop floor.

(iv) **Joint Councils:** Joint councils are set up for the whole unit and deals with matters relating to optimum production and efficiency and the fixation of productivity norms for man and machine for the unit as a whole. They are also concerned with the development of the skills of the workers, provisions of adequate facilities for training, preparation of schedules for working hours and holidays, optimum use of raw material, quality of finished products, safety measures and general health and welfare of the workers.

2. Collective Bargaining

According to Michael J. Jucius. *"Collective bargaining refers to a process by which employers on the one hand and representatives of the employees on the other, attempt to arrive at agreements covering the conditions under which employees will contribute and be compensated for their services."*

Collective bargaining has been viewed:

(i) As a process of social change

(ii) As a peace treaty between conflicting parties.

(iii) As a system of industrial jurisprudence

As a process of social change, collective bargaining is understood as a technique of bringing about a change in the balance of power between employers and employees. It helps the inferior social class in gaining social, economic and political power as well as better welfare, security and liberty.

As a peace treaty, collective bargaining is regarded as a useful weapon for bringing peace but peace is temporary. Collective bargaining creates a system of industrial jurisprudence—a method of introducing civil rights into the industry requiring that the management deals with the labour by rules rather than by arbitrary decisions. It is this role of collective bargaining which helps resolve industrial disputes.

Collective bargaining benefits both employees as well as employers. This means that the basic interests of the management are protected and also the rights of the employees. The two sides have a responsibility towards each other. For example, unions should not expect the management to concede on issues which would ultimately impair the company's ability to stay in the business. Likewise, the management must recognize the rights of employees to form unions and to argue for improved wages and working conditions.

Collective bargaining infuses democratic principles into the industrial world. Workers participate in decisions that affect their work and work life. Thus, collective bargaining may be viewed as a form of participative management.

The process of collective bargaining involves six major steps (Figure 15.2):

(i) Preparing for negotiation
(ii) Bargaining issues
(iii) Negotiating
(iv) Reaching the agreement
(v) Ratifying the agreement
(vi) Administration of the agreement

Figure 15.2 shows that the environment influences the collective bargaining process. This includes bargaining structure and union-management relationship.

(i) Preparing for Negotiations: From the management side the negotiators are required to:

- Prepare specific proposals for changes in the contract language,
- Determine the general size of the economic package the company proposes to offer,
- Prepare statistical displays and supportive data for use in negotiations, and
- Prepare a bargaining book for company negotiations, a compilation of information on issues that will be discussed, giving an analysis of the effect of each case, its use in other companies, and other facts.

From the employees' side, the union should collect information on at least three areas:

- The financial position of the company and its ability to pay.
- The attitude of the management towards various issues, as reflected in past negotiations or inferred from negotiations in similar companies.
- The attitudes and desires of the employees.

The other arrangements to be made are selecting the negotiators from both sides and identifying a suitable site for negotiation.

(ii) Identifying Bargaining Issues: The major issues discussed in collective bargaining fall under the following four categories:

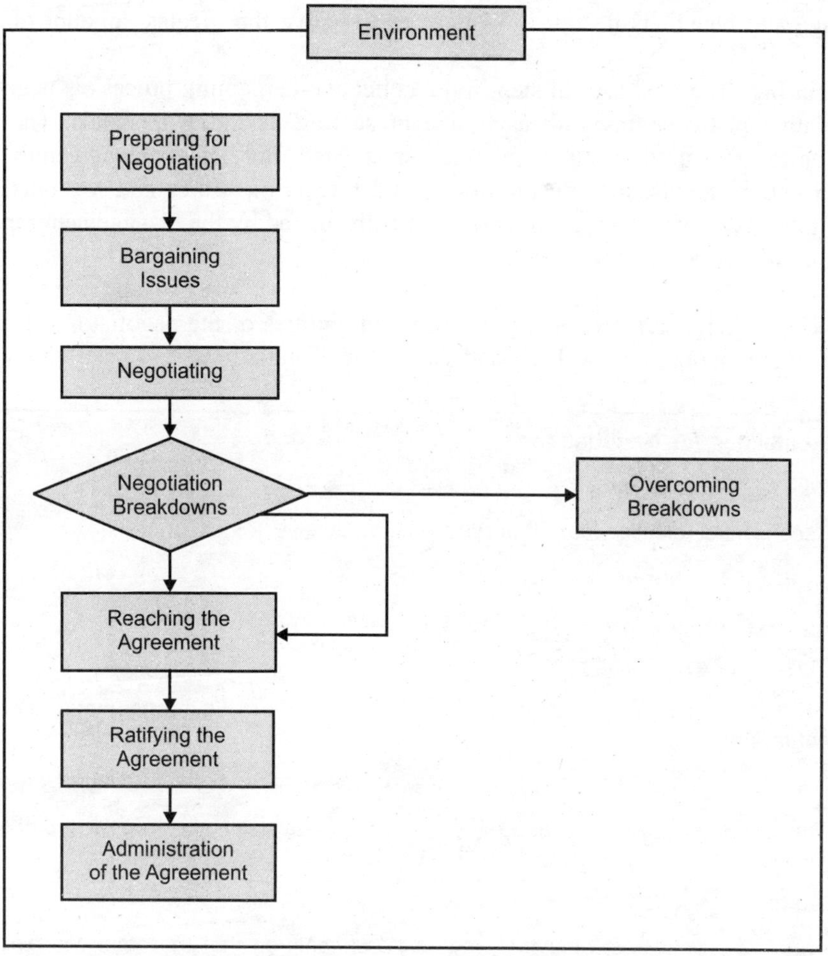

Fig. 15.2. The Collective Bargaining Process.
Source: Adapted from R. Wayne Mondy and Robert M. Noe III, Personnel: The Management of Human Resources, p. 407.

1. **Wage-Related Issues** such as how basic wage rates are determined, cost of living adjustments, wage differentials, overtime rates, wage adjustments, etc.
2. **Supplementary Economic Benefits** such as pension plans, paid vacations, paid holidays, health insurance plans, retrenchment pay, unemployment pension, and the like.
3. **Institutional Issues** These consist of the rights and duties of employers, employees, unions, employees' stock ownership schemes, and QWL programmes.
4. **Administrative Issues** such as seniority, employee discipline and discharge procedures, employee health and safety, technological changes, work rules, job security, training, and the like.

The wage and benefit issues are important and receive the greatest amount of attention at the bargaining table.

(iii) Negotiating: The next logical step in the collective-bargaining process is negotiation. The negotiating phase begins with each side presenting its initial demands. The negotiation goes on for days until the final agreement is reached. But before the agreement is reached, it is a battle of wits, playing on words, and threats of strikes and lockouts. It is a big relief to everybody when the agreement is finally signed by the management representatives and the union.

The success of negotiation depends on skills and abilities of the negotiators. Box-1 contains guidelines for negotiations or the Do's and Dont's of Negotiations.

Box-1 Guidelines for Negotiations

The "Dos" of Negotiations:

1. Do seek more (or offer less) than you plan to receive (or give).
2. Do negotiate in private not through the media.
3. Do let both sides win. Otherwise the other side may retaliate.
4. Do start with easy issues.
5. Do remember that negotiations are seldom over when the agreement is concluded. Eventually the contract will be renegotiated.
6. Do resolve deadlocks by stressing past progress another point or counter proposals.
7. Do enlist the support of the federal mediation and conciliation service if a strike seems likely.

The "Don'ts of Negotiations:

1. Do not make your best offer first; that is so uncommon that the other side will expect more.
2. Do not seek unwanted changes; you my get them.
3. Do not say "no" absolutely; unless your organization will back you up absolutely.
4. Do not violate a confidence.
5. Do not settle too quickly. Union members may think a quick settlement is not a good one.
6. Do not let the other side bypass your team and go directly to the top management.
7. Do not let the top management actually participate in face-to-face negotiations. They are often inexperienced and poorly informed.

Source: William B. Werther and Keith Devis, Human Resources and Personnel Management, New York, McGraw-Hill 1993, p. 574.

At times, negotiations may break down even though both the labour and the management may sincerely want to arrive at an amicable settlement. In order to get negotiations moving again, there are several measures that may be used:

1. Through third party intervention such as arbitration, and adjudication,
2. Unions tactics like strikes and boycotts, and
3. Management strategies such as lockouts, splitting the union, bribing union leaders, and using political influence.

(iv) Settlement and Contract Agreement: After an initial agreement has been made, the two sides usually return to their respective constituencies to determine whether what they have informally agreed upon is acceptable. A particularly crucial stage is ratification. In this stage, the union-negotiating team explains and puts the agreement to the union members for a vote. If voted, this agreement is formalized into a contract. It is important that the contract must be clear and precise. Any ambiguity leads to grievances or other problems.

(v) Administration of the Agreement: Signing the agreement is not the end of collective bargaining; rather it is the beginning of the process. The agreement must be implemented according to the letter and spirit of the provisions of the agreement. But in day-to-day stress of the work environment, strict adherence to the provisions may not always be easy. Moreover, it may be difficult to draft a flawless agreement, notwithstanding the exacting efforts of the most experienced negotiators and lawyers specialized in Industrial Relations.

The management is primarily responsible for implementing the agreement, which must be communicated to all affected levels. This could include meetings or training sessions not only to point out significant features, but also to provide a clause-by-clause analysis. Supervisors, in particular, need to know their responsibilities and what to do when disagreements arise. Additionally, managers can be encouraged to notify the top management of any contract provisions that are causing problems so that they can be considered when preparing for the next round of negotiations.

The HR manager plays a crucial role in the day-to-day administration of the contract. He or she advises on matters of discipline and works to resolve grievances arising out of the agreement. In addition, he or she works, with the line management to establish good working relationship with all employees affected by the terms and conditions of the agreement.

3. Code of Discipline

It is also a dispute prevention strategy. It defines duties and responsibilities of employees. It lays down specific obligations for the management and the worker with the objective of promoting constructive promotion between their representatives at all levels, avoiding stoppages, litigation, securing negotiation, conciliation and voluntary arbitration.

The code of discipline in the industry has been evolved by the ministry of labour and employment:

- To maintain discipline in the industry, and
- To ensure better discipline in industry

But this code does not have any legal sanction.

4. Grievance Procedure

Grievance procedure is a method of settling or resolving disputes. All labour agreements contain some form of grievance procedure. And if the procedure is followed strictly, any dispute can be easily resolved.

In the meanwhile, a grievance may be understood as an employee's dissatisfaction or feeling of personal injustice relating to his or her employment relationship. A grievance is generally well-defined in a collective-bargaining agreement. It is usually restricted to violations of the terms and conditions of employment. Other conditions which may give rise to a grievance are:

- A violation of law,
- A violation of the intent of the parties as stipulated during contract negotiations,
- A violation of company rules,
- A change in working conditions or past company practices, and
- A violation of health and/or safety standards.

When an employee believes that the labour agreement has been violated, he or she files a grievance. The grievance needs to be resolved according to a set procedure.

Grievance procedures generally establish the following:

1. How the grievance will be initiated?
2. The number of steps in the process.
3. Who will represent each party?
4. The specified number of working days within which the grievance must be taken to the next step in the hearing.

A typical grievance procedure followed in a Bangalore-based public sector unit is shown in Figure 15.3. It comprises four stages.

First Stage: The aggrieved employee shall, first submit his grievance in writing to his 'Sectional Head' in the prescribed form. The sectional head should study the grievance carefully with the least possible delay and the aggrieved employee should be given an opportunity to present his case in person if he requests for the same. If the employee so desires, he may take the assistance of a co-worker or a union representative. A written reply shall be given to the employee before the end of the fifth working day, if reply is not given before the end of the fifth working day, the concerned officer should record reasons for the delay which should be communicated to the aggrieved employee.

Second Stage: In case the said employee is not satisfied with the reply of the sectional head, or if the sectional head fails to give a reply within the stipulated time as in the first stage above, he shall be free to register his grievance in writing in the prescribed form with his departmental head (nominated by the management from time to time for this purpose). departmental head shall, after a careful study, give an opportunity to the concerned person to present his case before him, if the employee expresses a desire to be heard in person. The employee may be permitted to take the assistance of a co-employee or a union representative of his choice at the time of personal hearing. The head of the department should study the grievance and the points brought out by the employee in the personal hearing and give a reply at the end of the fifth working day from the day of the receipt of such complaint.

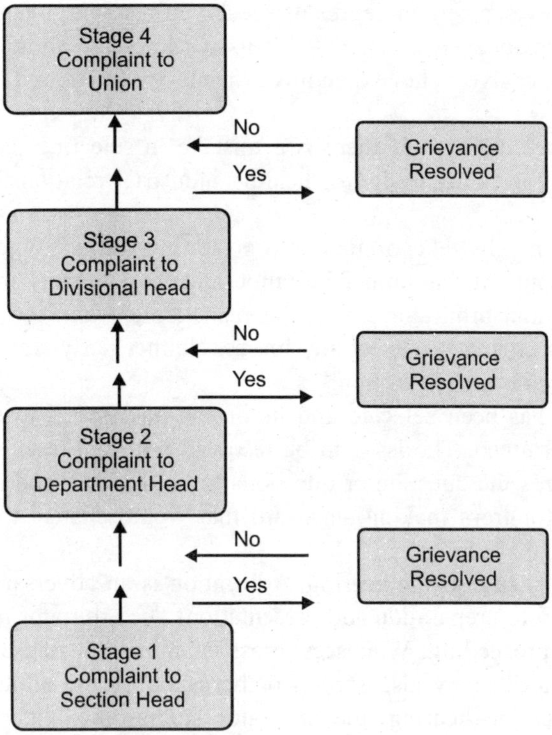

Fig. 15.3. Grievance Procedure.

Third Stage: If the employee is not satisfied with the decision of the departmental head or if the latter fails to give any decision within the stipulated period, the employee will be entitled to lodge an appeal to the divisional head or any other officer nominated by the management for this purpose. This officer should also follow the same procedure as prescribed in Stages 1 and II and a reply should be given before the end of the tenth working day. If the employee so desires, he may be permitted to take the assistance of a co-employee of his choice or an office bearer or executive committee member of the union at the time of personal hearing.

Fourth Stage: If the aggrieved employee is not satisfied with the decision of the divisional head, he can refer the case to the employees' union within 10 days. The union may discuss the subject if they deem fit, in the periodical management-union meetings which will be held within one month from the day, such reference is made by the union to the management.

5. Arbitration

Arbitration is a procedure in which a neutral third party studies the bargaining situation, listens to both the parties and gathers information, and then makes recommendations that are binding on the parties. Arbitration is effective as a means of resolving disputes because it is established by thc parties themselves and the decision is acceptable to them, and relatively expeditious when compared to courts or tribunals. Delays are cut down and settlements are speeded up.

Arbitration has achieved a certain degree of success in resolving disputes between the labour and the management. However, it is not without its weaknesses. Some weaknesses are:

(i) Arbitration is expensive. The expenditure needs to be shared by the labour and the management.
(ii) Judgement becomes arbitrary if there is a mistake in selecting the arbitrator.
(iii) Too much arbitration is not a sign of healthy industrial relations.

The labour union generally takes initiative to go for arbitration. When the union so decides, it notifies the management. At this point, the union and the company must select an arbitrator. When considering potential arbitrators, both the management and the labour will study their previous decisions in an attempt to detect any biases. Neither party wants to select an arbitrator who might be unfavourable to its position.

After the arbitrator has been selected and he or she has agreed to serve, a time and place for hearing will be determined. The issue to be resolved will be presented to the arbitrator in a document that summarizes the question or questions to be decided, and any contract restrictions that prohibit the arbitrator from making an award that would change the terms of the existing contract.

Each side presents its case at the hearing. Arbitration is an adversary proceeding, so a case may be lost because of poor preparation and presentation. The arbitrator may conduct the hearing much like a courtroom proceeding. Witnesses, cross-examination, transcripts, and legal counsel may all be used. The parties may also submit or be asked by the arbitrators to submit formal written statements. After the hearing, the arbitrator studies the materials submitted and the testimony given, and reaches a decision within 30 to 60 days. The decision is usually accompanied by a written opinion giving the reasons supporting the decision.

6. Conciliation

Conciliation is a process by which representatives of workers and employers are brought together before a third party with a view to persuading them to arrive at an agreement by mutual discussion between them. The third party may be one individual or a group of people. The alternative name for the third party is mediators. The Industrial Disputes Act, 1947 provides for the appointment of conciliators. Section 4 of the Act states that the appropriate government shall appoint such number of persons as it thinks fit as conciliation officers. The main duty of a conciliation officer shall be:

(i) To mediate in and promote the settlement of industrial disputes,
(ii) To hold conciliatory proceedings,
(iii) To investigate the dispute,
(iv) To send a report and memorandum of settlement to the appropriate government, and
(v) To send a full report to the appropriate government setting forth the steps taken, in case no settlement is arrived at.

The conciliation officer shall submit the report within 14 days from the date of commencement of the conciliation proceedings. The Act prohibits a strike or a lockout when the conciliation proceedings are in progress.

It may be stated that the conciliator has no power to force a settlement, but can work with the parties separately to determine their respective positions, explains a position more fully to the opposition, points out bases for agreement that may not have been apparent previously, helps in the search for solutions, and generally facilitates the reach of an agreement.

7. Adjudication

Adjudication means a mandatory settlement of an industrial dispute by a labour court or a tribunal. Generally, the government refers a dispute for adjudication depending on the failure of conciliation proceedings. Section 10 of the Industrial Disputes Act, 1947, provides for reference of a dispute to labour court or tribunal. The Act also lays down rules regarding the composition and powers of labour courts and tribunals.

Disputes are generally referred to adjudication on the recommendation of the conciliation officer who had dealt with them earlier. However, the government has discretionary powers to accept or reject recommendations of the conciliation officer. It is obvious that once a dispute is referred for adjudication, the verdict of a labour court or tribunal is binding on both the parties.

The system of adjudication is the most significant instrument of resolving disputes. But, it has been criticized because of the delay involved in resolving conflicts. Continued dependence on adjudication deprives the trade unions of their right to recognize and consolidate their strength.

Under the provisions of the Act, labour courts and industrial tribunals can be constituted by both central and state governments but the national tribunals can be constituted by the central government only.

(i) **Labour Court:** The labour court consists of one independent person (called presiding officer) who is or has been a judge of a High Court, or has been a district judge or additional district judge for not less than 3 years or has held any judicial office in India for not less than 7 years. The labour court deals with disputes relating to the propriety or legality of an order passed by employer under the standing orders, the application and interpretation of standing orders, discharge or dismissal of workers including reinstatement of, or grant of relief to wrongly dismissed persons, withdrawal of any statutory concession or privilege, illegality or otherwise of a strike or lockout and all matters except those reserved for industrial tribunals.

(ii) **Industrial Tribunal:** This is also a one-man ad hoc body (presiding officer) appointed by the government. It has a wider jurisdiction than the labour court. The government concerned may appoint two assessors to advise the presiding officer in the proceedings. An industrial tribunal can adjudicate on the following matters: (a) wages including the period and mode of payment; (b) compensatory and other allowances; (c) hours of work and rest periods; (d) leave with wages and holidays; (e) bonus, profit sharing, provident fund and gratuity; (f) shift working, otherwise then in accordance with the standing orders; (g) classification by grades; (h) rules of discipline; (i) rationalization; (j) retrenchment and closure of establishments; and (k) any other matter that may be prescribed.

(iii) **National Tribunal:** This is the third one-man adjudicatory body to be appointed by the Central government to deal with disputes of national importance or issues which are likely to affect the industrial establishments in more than one state.

8. Consultative Machinery

Towards the end, it is essential to refer to the consultative machinery set by the government to resolve conflicts. The main function of the consultative machinery is to bring the parties together for mutual settlement of differences in a spirit of cooperation and goodwill. Consultative machinery operates at the plant, industry, state and the national levels. At the plant level, there are works committees and joint management councils. Being essentially bipartite in character, works committees are constituted as per the provisions of the Industrial Disputes Act, 1947, and joint management councils are set up following the trust laid down in the Industrial Policy Resolution, 1956. At the industry level, there are wage boards and industrial committees.

Labour advisory boards operate at the state level and at the all India level there are the Indian Labour Conference (ILC) and the Standing Labour Committee (SLC). The bodies operating at the state and national levels are tripartite in character, representing the government, the labour and the management. Important legislative proposals are discussed and recommended by the ILC and SLC.

MEANING OF GRIEVANCE

Every company or industrial organization is required to develop a procedure for redressal of the grievances of the employees against employers and that of employers against employees. The complaints or disputes are a common thing in industries.

What is a Grievance?

It is very difficult to define a grievance. Personnel experts, however, have attempted to distinguish between dissatisfaction, complaint and grievance. Dissatisfaction is feeling of dissatisfaction. When dissatisfaction is made known to another, it becomes a complaint. A complaint becomes a grievance when this dissatisfaction, which is mostly related to work, is brought to the notice of the management. Various definitions have been given by different experts.

Definitions

According to **Dale S. Beach**, "*Grievance is any dissatisfaction or feeling of injustice in connection with one's employment situation that is brought to the attention of management.*"

According to **Michael J. Jucius**, "*Any discontentment or dissatisfaction whether expressed or not and whether valid or not, arising out of anything connected with the company that an employee thinks, believes or even feels is unfair, unjust or inadequate.*"

According to **Keith Davis**, "*Grievance is any real or imaginary feeling of personal injustice which an employee has concerning his employment relationship.*"

According to **Dale Yoder**, "*Grievance is a written complaint filed by an employee and claiming unfair treatment.*"

According to **International Labour Organization**, "*A grievance is a complaint of one or more workers in respect of wages, allowances, conditions of work and interpretation of service stipulations, covering such areas as overtime, leave, transfer, promotion, seniority, job assignment and termination of service.*"

According to **National Commission on Labour**, "*Complaints affecting one or more individual workers in respect of wage payments, overtime, leave, transfer, promotion, seniority, work assignment and discharge constitute grievances.*"

Broadly speaking, grievance is any dissatisfaction, which an employee may have with regard to his employment situation that adversely affects the production of the employees.

From these definitions of grievances, we can draw the following characteristics of a grievance:

- A grievance reflects feeling of dissatisfaction with any aspect of the organization.
- A grievance can arise out of real or imaginary reasons. The reasons may be valid or invalid, legitimate or irrational, justifiable or ridiculous.
- A grievance arises only when an employee feels that injustice has been done to him.
- The grievance results from perceived non-fulfilment of one's expectations from the organization.

Grievances, if not redressed in time tend to lower morale and productivity of employees.

FORMS OF GRIEVANCES

1. Factual

The employer-employee relationship depends upon the job contract in any organization. This contract indicates the norms defining the limits within which the employee expects the organization to fulfil his aspirations, needs or expectations. When these legitimate needs of expectations or aspirations are not fulfilled, the employee will be dissatisfied with the job. Such dissatisfaction is called factual grievance. For instance, when an employee is not given promotion which is due to him or when work conditions are unsafe, grievances of employee relating to these issues are based on facts. In other words, these grievances reflect the drawbacks in the implementation of the organizational policies.

2. Imaginary

When the job contract is not clear-cut and does not indicate the norms defining the limits within which the employee expects the organization fulfil his needs or aspirations, the employee develops such needs which the organization is not obliged to meet. Here, grievances are not based on facts. Even then the employee feels aggrieved. Normally, the organization does not feel any kind of responsibility for such grievances and their redressal, because they are based not only on wrong perceptions of the employee but also on wrong information. However, such grievances can have far-reaching consequences on the organization because the employees are likely to develop an altogether negative attitude towards the organization which decreases their effectiveness and involvement in work.

3. Disguised

In general organizations consider the basic requirements of their employees. Psychological needs of the employees such as need for recognition, affection, power, achievement, etc., are normally unattended and ignored. For instance, an employee complaining very strongly about the working conditions in the office may in turn be seeking some recognition and appreciation from his or her colleagues. Hence, disguised grievances should also be considered since they do have far-reaching consequences in case they are unattended and ignored.

CAUSES OR SOURCES OF GRIEVANCES

Grievances may occur for a number of reasons. These sources are classified into the following categories:

1. Grievances Resulting from Working Conditions

- Poor physical conditions of workplace
- Mismatch of workers with the job
- Unplanned changes in schedules or procedures
- Non-availability of proper tools, machines and equipment
- Tight and highly rigid production standards
- Failure to maintain proper discipline
- Poor relationship with immediate boss.

2. Grievances Resulting from Personal Maladjustment

- Over ambition
- Excessive self-esteem
- Impractical attitude to life
- Poor self-esteem

3. Grievances Resulting from Management Policy

- Wage rates and methods of wage payment
- Leave, overtime and transfers
- Promotion, demotion and discharge
- Lack of opportunities for career growth
- Lack of role clarity
- Penalties imposed for misconduct
- Hostile attitude towards trade union

4. Grievances Resulting from Violations

- Collective bargaining agreement
- Central or state laws
- Responsibilities of management
- Company rules and regulations

S. Chandra in his studies found the following causes of employee grievances shown in Box-2.

Box-2 Causes of Employee Grievances

- Promotions
- Amenities
- Continuity of services
- Compensation
- Disciplinary action
- Fines
- Increments
- Leave
- Medical benefits
- Nature of the job
- Payments of wages
- Acting promotion
- Recovery of dues
- Safety appliance
- Superannuation
- Suppression
- Transfer
- Victimization
- Conditions of work

Two American experts **Cruden** and **Sherman** are of the view that there are three main factors which contribute to grievances of the employees.

1. Management policies and practices
2. Trade union policies
3. Personality traits

Table 15.1 also reveals the causes of grievances given by **P.C. Tripathi**.

Table 15.1: Causes of Grievances

(a) Grievance Resulting from Working Conditions:
- Improper matching of the worker with the job
- Changes in schedules or procedures
- Non-availability of proper tools, machines and equipment for doing the job
- Tight production standards
- Bad physical conditions at workplace
- Failure to maintain proper discipline (excessive discipline or lack of it, both are equally harmful)
- Poor relationship with the supervisor

(b) Grievance Resulting from Management Policy:
- Wages payment and job rates
- Leave
- Overtime
- Seniority
- Transfer
- Promotion, demotion and discharges
- Lack of career planning and employment development plan
- Hostility toward a labour union

(c) Grievance Resulting from Alleged Violation of:
- The collective bargaining agreement
- Central or State Laws
- Past practices
- Company rules
- Management's responsibility

(d) Grievance resulting from Personal Maladjustment:
- Over-ambition
- Excessive self-esteem
- Impractical attitude to life, etc.

Source: P.C. Tripathi "Personnel Management and Industrial Relations" Sultan Chand and Sons, New Delhi, 1999, p. 365.

STEPS IN GRIEVANCES HANDLING

Every organization has to make a provision for setting up a grievance handling procedure to handle employee grievances.

Need for a Grievance Procedure

Without an analysis of their nature and pattern, the causes of employee dissatisfaction cannot be removed. The HR manager should help the top management and the line managers, particularly foremen and supervisors, in the formulation and implementation of the policies, programmes and procedures which would best enable them to handle employee grievances. These policies, programmes and procedures are generally known as the grievance redressal procedure. The grievance redressal procedure is a device by which grievances are settled, generally to the satisfaction of the trade union or employees and the management. The adoption of the grievance handling procedure is essential for a variety of reasons. They are given in Table 15.2.

Table 15.2: Reasons for Adoption of a Grievance Handling Procedure

1. Most grievances seriously disturb the employees. This may affect their morale, productivity and their willingness to cooperate with the organization. If an explosive situation develops, this can be promptly attended to if a grievance handling procedure is already in existence.
2. It is not possible that all the complaints of the employees would be settled by first-line supervisors, for these supervisors may not have had a proper training for the purpose, and they may lack authority. Moreover, there may be personality conflicts and other causes as well.
3. It serves as a check on the arbitrary action of the management because supervisors know that employees are likely to see to it that their protest does reach the higher management.
4. It serves as an outlet for employee gripes, discontent and frustrations. It acts like a pressure valve on a steam boiler. The employees are entitled to legislative, executive and judicial protection and they get this protection from the grievance redressal procedure, which also acts as a means of upward communication. The top management becomes increasingly aware of employees' problems, expectations and frustrations. It becomes sensitive to their needs, and cares for their well-being. This is why the management, while formulating plans that might affect the employees – for example, plant expansion or modification, the installation of labour-saving devices, and so on, should take into consideration the impact that such plans might have on the employees.
5. The management has complete authority to operate the business as it sees fit – subject, of course to its legal and moral obligations and the contracts it has entered into with the workers or their representative trade union. But if the trade union or the employees do not like the way the management functions, they can submit their grievances in accordance with the procedure laid down for that purpose.

Source: C.B. Mamoria and S.V. Gankar "Personal Management: Text and Cases", Himalaya Publishing House, 2001, p. 745-746.

What a Well-designed Grievance procedure should provide?

According to **Armstrong T.O.**, a well-designed and a proper grievance procedure provides:

1. A channel or avenue by which any aggrieved employee may present his grievance;
2. A procedure which ensures that there will be a systematic handling of every grievance;
3. A method by which an aggrieved employee can relieve his feelings of dissatisfaction with his job, working conditions or with the management; and
4. A means of ensuring that there is some measure of promptness in the handling of the grievance.

Table 15.3: Basic Elements of a Grievance Procedure

1. The existence of a sound channel through which a grievance may pass for redressal if the previous stage or channel has been found to be inadequate, unsatisfactory or unacceptable. This stage may comprise three, four or five substages.
2. The procedure should be simple, definite and prompt, for any complexity or vagueness or delay may lead to an aggravation of the dissatisfaction of the aggrieved employee.
3. The steps in handling a grievance should be clearly defined. These should comprise.
   (a) Receiving and defining the nature of the grievance;
   (b) Getting at the relevant facts about the grievance;
   (c) Analyzing the facts, after taking into consideration the economic, social, psychological and legal issues involved in them;
   (d) Taking an appropriate decision about the aggrieved employee; and
   (e) Communicating the decision to the aggrieved employee.
4. Whatever the decision, it should be followed up in order that the reaction to the decision may be known and in order to determine whether the issue has been closed or not.

Source: C.B. Mamoria and S.V. Gankar "Personal Management: Text and Cases", Himalaya Publishing House, 2001, p. 749-750.

Grievance Procedure Steps

A grievance procedure is a formal process which is preliminary to an arbitration which enables the employees involved to attempt to resolve their differences in a peaceful, orderly and expeditious manner.

The Code of Discipline adopted by the Indian Labour Conference in 1957 laid down that the management and unions should establish, upon a mutually agreed basis, grievance procedure which would ensure a speedy and full investigation leading to a settlement. At present, the Model Grievance Procedure in India provides for five, successive time bound steps, each leading to the next unless the aggrieved employee prefers an appeal. These steps are shown in Figure 15.4.

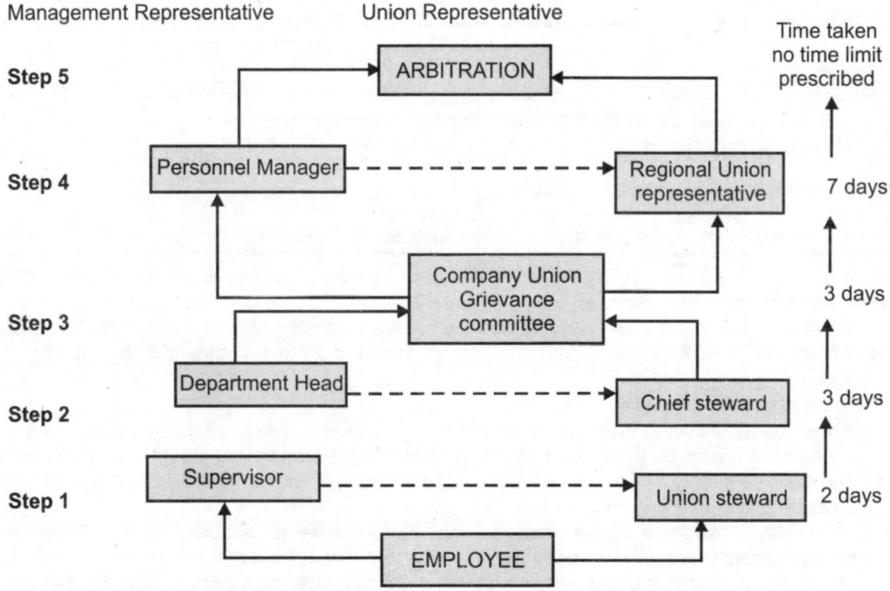

Fig. 15.4. Grievance Procedure—A 5 Step Process.

Step I: The aggrieved employee verbally explains his grievance to his immediate supervisor or in a conference or a discussion specifically arranged for the purpose. The employee seeks satisfaction from his supervisor. The supervisor must give his answer within forty-eight hours of the presentation of the complaint. The grievance can be settled if the supervisor has been properly trained for the purpose, and if he adheres strictly to a basic problem-solving method.

Step II: The second step begins when the grievance is not settled by the supervisor. If the employee does not receive an answer within the stipulated time or he is not satisfied with the answer, he shall either in person or with his departmental representative present his grievance to the head of the department designated for this purpose. The head of the department is generally the chief business manager, a superintendent or an industrial relations officer who goes into the grievance and gives his decision on the matter. He is required to furnish his answer within three days of the presentation of the grievance.

Step III: If the employee is not satisfied with the answer, he can approach the grievance committee which shall evaluate the case and make its recommendations to the management within seven days of presentation of the case. The grievance committee is composed of some fellow-employees, the shop steward or a combination of the union and the management representatives. The committee may suggest anyone of the possible solutions:

- It may call upon the grievant to accept the employer's proposed settlement.
- It may advise him that the trade union will not press for anything more than what has already been suggested.
- In some cases, it may recommend that the issue be submitted for arbitration.

The employee would be informed about the recommendation with three days.

Step IV: If the committee fails to a take decision within the stipulated period or if the employee is not satisfied with the decision, he can make an appeal for revision to the management. The management is supposed to communicate its decision within seven days of the worker's revised petition.

Step V: If the employee is dissatisfied with the management's decision, the union and the management may refer the grievance for voluntary arbitration within a week of the receipt of the management's decision by the aggrieved employee. The parties may agree beforehand that the arbitrator's award will be final and binding on both the parties.

The Indian Institute of Personnel Management, Calcutta, has summarized the grievance procedure. These steps are given in Table 15.4.

Table 15.4: Grievance Procedure Suggested by Indian Institute of Personnel Management

1.	In the first instance, the grievance should be settled at the lowest level, that is, the employee should raise his grievance with his immediate superior.
2.	It should be made clear to the employee that he may appeal if he does not get satisfaction from his immediate superior. He should know who the next person in the echelon of the management is to whom he should refer his grievance.
3.	The grievance should be speedily dealt with.
4.	If the grievance is against any instructions issued by the superior, the employee should clearly understand that in the interest of discipline, the instructions must first be carried out before the grievance can be considered and decided upon. It is only when this has been done that the employer will register his protest and set the grievance handling procedure in motion.
5.	It should be clearly understood by the employee that there will be no recourse to any official machinery till the grievance redressal procedure has been set in motion and that in the event the employee is still dissatisfied, there will be no direct action by either party which might prejudice the case or raise doubts while the grievance is being investigated.

Source: Indian Institute of Personnel Management, "Personnel Management in India", 1973, pp. 188-189.

BENEFITS OF A GOOD GRIEVANCE PROCEDURE

The benefits of a good grievance procedure are as under:

- It highlights the grievances so that the management can learn about them and try to settle them.
- It helps the management to solve a grievance before it becomes a dispute.
- It provides the workers an opportunity for expressing their fears, anxiety and dissatisfaction.
- It builds within the employees a sense of emotional security.
- It helps to maintain cordial relations in the industry by enabling both the parties to settle the grievances to their mutual satisfaction.
- The management knows that its arbitrary and biased action can be reviewed and challenged and therefore becomes more careful when dealing with its subordinates.
- Through grievance procedure the management comes to know the attitudes and feeling of employees regarding rules and practices of the organisation, this helps them to frame rules which are more acceptable to the workers.

Do's and Don'ts in Handling Grievances

When the employees and employers pass through the grievance handling procedure, they experience hard situations and hence careful understanding of the whole system is required. Experts have identified certain things which we must do and certain things which we must not do. The do's and don'ts in grievance handling are given in Box-3.

Box-3 Do's and Don'ts in Handling Grievances

Do's	Don'ts
• Investigate and handle each and every case as though it may eventually result in an arbitration hearing.	• Discuss the case with the union steward alone; the grievance should definitely be there.
• Talk with the employee about his grievance; give him a good and full hearing.	• Make agreements with individuals that are inconsistent with the labour agreement.
• Get the union to identify specific contractual provisions allegedly violated.	• Apply the grievance remedy to an improper grievance.
• Enforce the contractual time limits.	• Hold back the remedy if the company is wrong.
• Comply with the contractual time limits for the company to handle a grievance.	• Admit the binding effect of a past practice.
• Determine whether all the procedural requirements, as dictated by the agreement, have been complied with.	• Relinquish your authority to the union.
• Visit the work areas where the grievance arose.	• Settle grievances on the basis of what is fair. Instead, stick to the labour agreement which, after all, should be your standard.

• Determine if there were any witnesses.	• Make mutual consent agreements regarding future action.
• Examine the relevant contract provisions, and understand the contract thoroughly.	• Bargain over items not covered by the contract.
• Determine if there has been equal treatment of employees.	• Concede implied limitations on your management's rights.
• Examine the grievant's personal record.	• Argue grievance issues off the work premises.
• Fully examine prior grievance records.	• Treat as 'arbitrable' claims demanding the disciplining or discharge of the management members. Commit the company in areas beyond your limits of responsibility or familiarity.
• Evaluate any political connotations of the grievance.	• Give away your copy of the written grievance.
• Permit a full hearing on the issues.	• Discuss grievances of striking employees during an illegal work stoppage.
• Identify the relief the union is seeking.	• Settle a grievance when you are in doubt.
• Treat the union representative as your equal.	• Support another supervisor in a hopeless case.
• Command the respect of the union representatives.	• Refer a grievance to a different form of adjudication.
• Hold your grievance discussions privately.	• Overlook the precedent value of prior grievance settlement.
• Provide the grievance process to non-union members as well.	• Give long written grievance answers.
• Satisfy the union's right to relevant information.	• Trade a grievance settlement for a grievance withdrawal (or try to 'make up' for a bad decision in one grievance by 'bending over backwards' in another).
• Demand that proper productivity levels be maintained during the processing of incentive grievances.	• Negate the management's right to promulgate plant rules.
• Fully inform your superior of grievance matters.	• Deny grievances on the premise that "your hands have been tied by the management".
	• Agree to informal amendments in the contract.

Source: Baer Walter, "Grievance Handling", AMA, New York, 1970.

REVIEW QUESTIONS

1. What is an industrial dispute? What are the causes for disputes?
2. What is collective bargaining? Discuss the collective bargaining process in resolving disputes.
3. What is arbitration? How does it help resolve industrial conflict?
4. How does arbitration differ from grievance procedure? Bring out the respective roles in resolving disputes.
5. What is negotiation? What are the do's and don'ts of negotiation?

6. Define grievance. Why do grievances arise?
7. Why are grievances caused in an organization? How can these be redressed?
8. What are the desirable features of a grievance procedure? Which points should be remembered when handling the grievance?
9. What is grievance? Why should a manager be concerned about employee's grievances?
10. An effective grievance handling procedure is preventive rather than curative. Explain.
11. Write notes on the following:
    (a) Code of discipline
    (b) Unfair labour practices
    (c) Adjudication
    (d) Consultative machinery

CASE STUDY

15.1 Protest over Job Losses

Bitter it may taste, shrill it may sound, and sleepless nights it may cause, but it is true. In a major shake up, Airbus–the European aircraft manufacturer—has thrown a big shock to its employees. Before coming to the details of the shock, a peep into the company's resume.

Name: Airbus
Created: 1970
President, CEO: Louis Gallois
Employees: 57,000
Turnover (2006): 26 bn (Euro)
Total aircraft sold (Feb. 2007): 7187
Delivered: 4598
Headquarters: Toulouse (France)
Facilities: 16
Rival: Boeing

Airbus announced on February 27, 2007, that it would shed 10,000 jobs across four European countries and sell six of its units. On the same day the hapless workers did what was expected of them—downed tools and staged protests. The protesting workers at Airbus's factory at Meaulte, northern France, were seen picketing outside the factory gate after holding up production a day earlier. To be fair to Airbus, its management entered talks with unions before the job loss and the sale was formally announced. But the talks did not mollify the agitated workers.

Job shedding and hiring of units are a part of Power8 restructuring plan unleashed by Airbus to save itself from increasing loss of its ground to the arch rival, Boeing Co.

Airbus's Power8 strategy was first mooted in October 2006, but sparked a split between France and Germany over the distribution of job losses, and the placement of future ones. Later, the two countries agreed to share both job losses and new technology.

The Power8 plan, if finalized, would mean a 9 per cent reduction to Airbus's 55,000 employee strength.

Source: K. Aswathappa, "Human Resource Management", 5th ed., The McGraw-Hill, p. 591.

Questions

1. Why should Power8 focus on shedding jobs to save on cost? Are there no alternative strategies?
2. Will the proposed shedding of jobs and sale of six units help Airbus survive the intense competition from Boeing?

15.2 Adjustment Problem

Twenty female employees of a large company were grouped together daily in an area measuring forty feet by forty feet to perform semi-skilled assembly work. Though the layout was far from ideal, it was accepted as 'livable' at least as temporary quarters until construction of the new manufacturing facility was completed, and these women enjoyed their work. Their pleasure came mostly from the fact that they could talk freely about any subject that came to mind and still be able to do their jobs. They worked elbow to elbow and rarely failed to assemble their daily quota. When the new manufacturing facility finally opened, the women were assigned to an area several times as large as their former quarters. The new plant was equipped with superior lighting, water fountains, windows and, piped-in music. On the surface, these work conditions appeared ideal; no employee sat less than six feet away from any other. The management, however, became perplexed over the performance of this group of women after a few weeks in the new facility. Absenteeism increased, production lagged, complaints and grievances were numerous, and two women quit their jobs.

In a closed door conference with the Production Supervisor, the Plant Engineer and the Manufacturing Manager, the Personnel Director voiced his opinion about the unforeseen problems in the assembly department. In his opinion, the women missed the personal contact with each other; missed the continuous conversation and other accustomed forms of social interaction and basically were resisting the change to the new location. The Personnel Director recommended that the Plant Engineer should do something about redesigning the layout to bring the women closer together even if it meant spending several thousand rupees to do it.

Source: Adapted MBA, IGNOU, June 1999.

Questions

1. Analyze the problem in this case.
2. If you were the Personnel Director, how would have you dealt with the grievance of the worker?
3. If the employees were men, would the same situation have arisen? Why or why not?

REFERENCES

1. Armstrong, Michael, (1988). "A Handbook of Personnel Management Practice", Kogan, London.
2. Baer Walter, (1970). "Grievance Handling", AMA, New York.
3. Dale S. Beach, (1980). "Personnel–The Management of People at Work", 4th edn., Macmillan.
4. Ramaswamy, E.A. (1986). "From IR to HRD", Business India.
5. Indian Institute of Personnel Management, (1973). "Personnel Management in India", pp. 188-189.

6. Aswathappa, K. (2008). "Human Resource Management", Tata McGraw-Hill, New Delhi.
7. Mamoria, C.B. and Gankar, S.V. (2008). "Personnel Management", Himalaya Publishing House, Mumbai, pp. 544-550.
8. Tripathi, P.C. (1999). "Personnel Management and Industrial Relations", Sultan Chand and Sons, New Delhi, p. 365.
9. Randall S. Schuler, *et al.*, (1989). "Effective Personnel Management", 3rd edn., West Publishing, NY.
10. Raymond J. Stone, (1995). "Human Resource Management", John Wiley & Sons.
11. Subba Rao P. (2007). "Essentials of Human Resource Management and Industrial Relations". Himalaya Publishing House, New Delhi.
12. Werther, William B. and Keith Devis, (1993). "Human Resources and Personnel Management", McGraw-Hill, New York, p. 574.

CHAPTER

16 Global Human Resource Management

CHAPTER'S OUTLINE

- Introduction
- What is IHRM?
- Nature of IHRM
- Factors Affecting IHRM
- HRM Functions
- Strategic Functions of IHRM
- Staffing Policies (Recruitment and Selection)
- Staffing Policy Determinants
- Training and Development
- Management Development and Strategy
- Global Performance Management
- Knowledge Management Performance Framework
- International Compensation Strategy and its Determinants
- International Labour Relations
- HRM Competencies—An Exercise

INTRODUCTION

In international business, the big challenge is putting the right person into the right job, in the right place at the right time for the right salary. This challenge is met by the international human resource management. HRM has an important strategic component for international business which reduces costs and adds value to the customers.

The need to have highly qualified people to staff the organization cannot be overemphasized. Any company must determine its personnel needs, hire people to meet those needs, motivate them to perform well and upgrade their skills for higher demanding tasks. In this chapter, factors affecting international human resource management (IHRM), nature and structure of IHRM and staffing policy are discussed.

WHAT IS IHRM?

International human resource management (IHRM) is much broader in nature and scope in comparison to HRM.

According to **John D. Daniels**, "*IHRM refers to the range of activities that a global company takes to staff its organization—determining its human resource needs, hire people to meet these needs, motivate them to perform well, upgrade their skills so to perform more challenging tasks and finally retaining them.*"

In the words of **Cynthia D. Fisher**, "*The process of procuring, allocating and effectively utilizing human resource in an international business is called international human resource management.*"

International HRM thus involves ascertaining the corporate strategy of the company and assessing the corresponding recruitment, staffing and organizational strategy.

Characteristics of IHRM

- Ascertaining the corporate strategy of the company and assessing the corresponding human resource needs.
- Involves determining the recruitment, staffing and organizational strategy at international level.
- Involves induction, training and developing, and motivating the personnel to perform well.
- Involves upgrading the skills of the personnel so that they may perform more challenging tasks at international level.
- The strategic role of HRM is more complex in an international business than that in domestic business.

NATURE OF IHRM

IHRM involves the interplay among the three dimensions:

(i) Human Resource Activities
(ii) Types of Employees
(iii) Countries of Operations

These dimensions reveal the nature of IHRM. It is also explained in Figure 16.1.

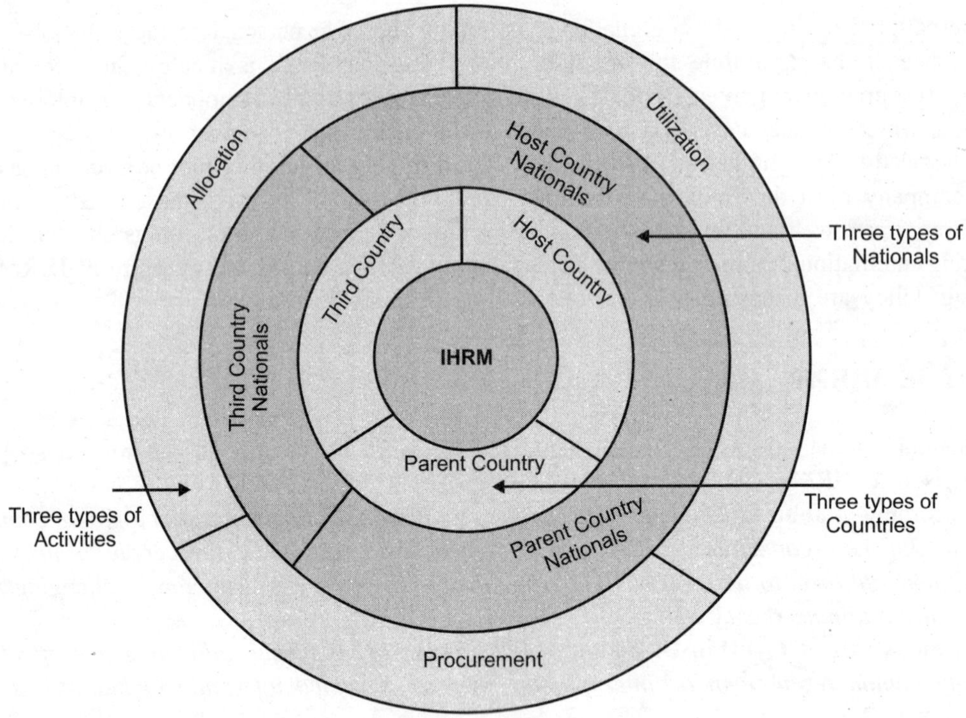

Fig. 16.1. Model of International HRM.
Source: Peter J. Dowling, IHRM, South Western College Publishing Co., 1999.

1. **Three Types of Activities:** The three broad activities of IHRM, namely, procurement, allocating, and utilizing, cover all the six activities of domestic human resources management (HRM). The six functions of domestic HRM are: human resource planning, employee hiring, training and development, remuneration, performance management, and industrial relations. These six functions can be dovetailed with the three broad activities of IHRM.
2. **Three Types of Countries:** The three national or country categories involved in IHRM activities are: the host-country where a subsidiary may be located, the home-country where the company is headquartered and 'other' countries that may be the source of labour or finance.
3. **Three Types of Employees:** The three types of employees of an international business include host-country nationals, parent-country nationals, and third-country nationals. Thus, for example, IBM employs Australian citizens in its Australian operations, often sends US citizens to Asia-Pacific countries on assignment, and may send some of its Singaporean employees of an assignment to its Japanese operations.

An alternative approach to model of IHRM is shown in Figure 16.2.

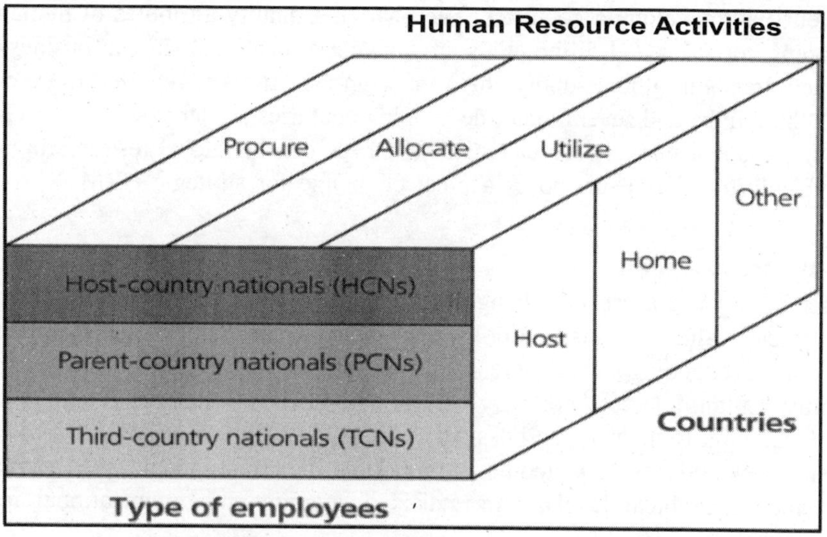

Fig. 16.2. A Model of IHRM—An Alternative Approach.

- **Host-country National (HCN):** Belongs to the country where the subsidiary is located.
- **Parent-country National (PCN):** Belongs to the country where the firm has its headquarters.
- **Third-country National (TCN):** Belongs to any other country and is employed by the firm.

FACTORS AFFECTING IHRM

According to **Charles W.L. Hill**, "*The strategic role of HRM is complex enough in a purely domestic firm, but it is more complex in an international business, where staffing management development, performance evaluation and compensation activities are complicated by profound differences in labour markets, culture, legal system, economic systems and the like.*"

The following are some of the important factors which make international HRM complex and challenging.

1. Differences in Labour Market Characteristics

The skill levels, the demand and supply conditions and the behaviour characteristics of labour vary widely in various countries. While some countries experience human resource shortage in certain sectors, many countries have it in abundance. In the past, developing countries were regarded, generally, as pools of unskilled labour. Today, however, many developing countries have abundance of skilled and scientific manpower as well as unskilled and semiskilled labour. This changing trend is causing significant shift of location of business activities. Hard disk drive manufacturers are reported to be shifting their production from Singapore to cheaper locations like Malaysia, Thailand and China. While in the past unskilled and semi-skilled labour-intensive activities tended to be located in the developing countries, today sophisticated activities also find favour with developing countries. The changing quality attributes of human resources in the developing countries and differentials are causing a locational shift in business activities, resulting in new trends in global supply chain management. India is reported to be emerging as a global R&D hub. India and several other developing countries are large sources of IT personnel. In short, changing labour market characteristics have been causing global restructuring of business processes and industries. And this poses a great challenge for strategic HRM.

2. Cultural Differences

Cultural differences cause a great challenge to HRM. The behavioural attitude of workers, the social environment, values, beliefs, outlooks, etc. are important factors, which affect industrial relations, loyalty, productivity, etc. There are also significant differences in aspects related to labour mobility. Cultural factors are very relevant in inter-personal behaviour also. In some countries it is common to address the boss Mr. so and so but in countries like India addressing the boss by name would not be welcome. In countries like India people give a great value to designations and hierarchical levels. This makes delayering and organizational restructuring difficult.

3. Differences in Regulatory Environment

A firm operating in different countries is confronted with different environments with respect to government policies and regulations regarding labour.

4. Attitude towards Employment

The attitude of employers and employees towards employment of people shows variations among different nations. In some countries hire and fire is the common thing whereas in a number of countries the ideal norm has been lifetime employment. In countries like India workers generally felt that while they have the right to change organizations as they preferred, they had a right to lifetime employment in the organization they were employed with. In such situations it is very difficult to get rid of inefficient or surplus manpower. The situation, however, is changing in many countries, including India.

5. Difference in Conditions of Employment

Besides the tenancy of employment, there are several conditions of employment the differences of which cause significant challenge to international HRM. The system of rewards, promotion, incentives and motivation, system of labour welfare and social security, etc. vary significantly between countries.

HRM FUNCTIONS

The following are the main functions of HRM:

1. Planning for Organizations, Jobs, and People
    - The Strategic Management of Human Resources
    - Human Resource Planning

2. Acquiring Human Resources
    - Selection
    - Recruitment
    - Integration
3. Building and Motivating Performance
    - HR Development
    - Performance Appraisal
    - Compensation Systems
4. Maintaining Human Resources
    - Benefits
    - Safety & Health
    - Collective Bargaining
    - Organizational Exit
    - Employment transitions
5. Multinational Human Resource Management

STRATEGIC FUNCTIONS OF IHRM

Research confirms and anecdotes suggest a powerful relationship between HRM process management productivity and strategic performance. The following figure shows the strategic decisions and their implications for human resource management.

CEO and Chairman of General Electric once said, "*Success is truly about people, not about where the buildings are. You have got to develop people so they are prepared for leadership jobs and then promote them. That is the most effective way to become more global.*"

The Chairman Unilever in 1990 said, "*The singlemost important issue for us has been and will continue to be, organization and people.*"

Research confirms these views, showing that superior human resources can sustain high productivity competitive advantage and value creation for international company.

Superior IHRM can sustain:

1. **High Productivity:** On the basis of the Human Capital Index study, it was found that superior HR practices are positively correlated with the firm's financial returns. Hence, superior HRM was a stronger determinant of a firm's financial performance. Collectively research regularly reports that while executives acknowledge that the effectiveness of HR practices materially affects firm's performance—many firms fail to achieve their HRM goals.
2. **Competitive Advantage:** A study of the role of HRM to enhance competitiveness at more than 300 multinationals reported that effectively developing HRM has positive effect on competitive advantage as through better HRM practices the right persons are placed in the right jobs in the right place at the right time for right salary. GE in 1990s globalized its intellect seeking learning and transferring ideas throughout its global operations. This is transnational strategy which has been successful due to the application of reused HRM philosophy.
3. **Value Creation for International Company:** The Human Capital Index, based upon a comprehensive global study of over 2000 companies found that superior human resource

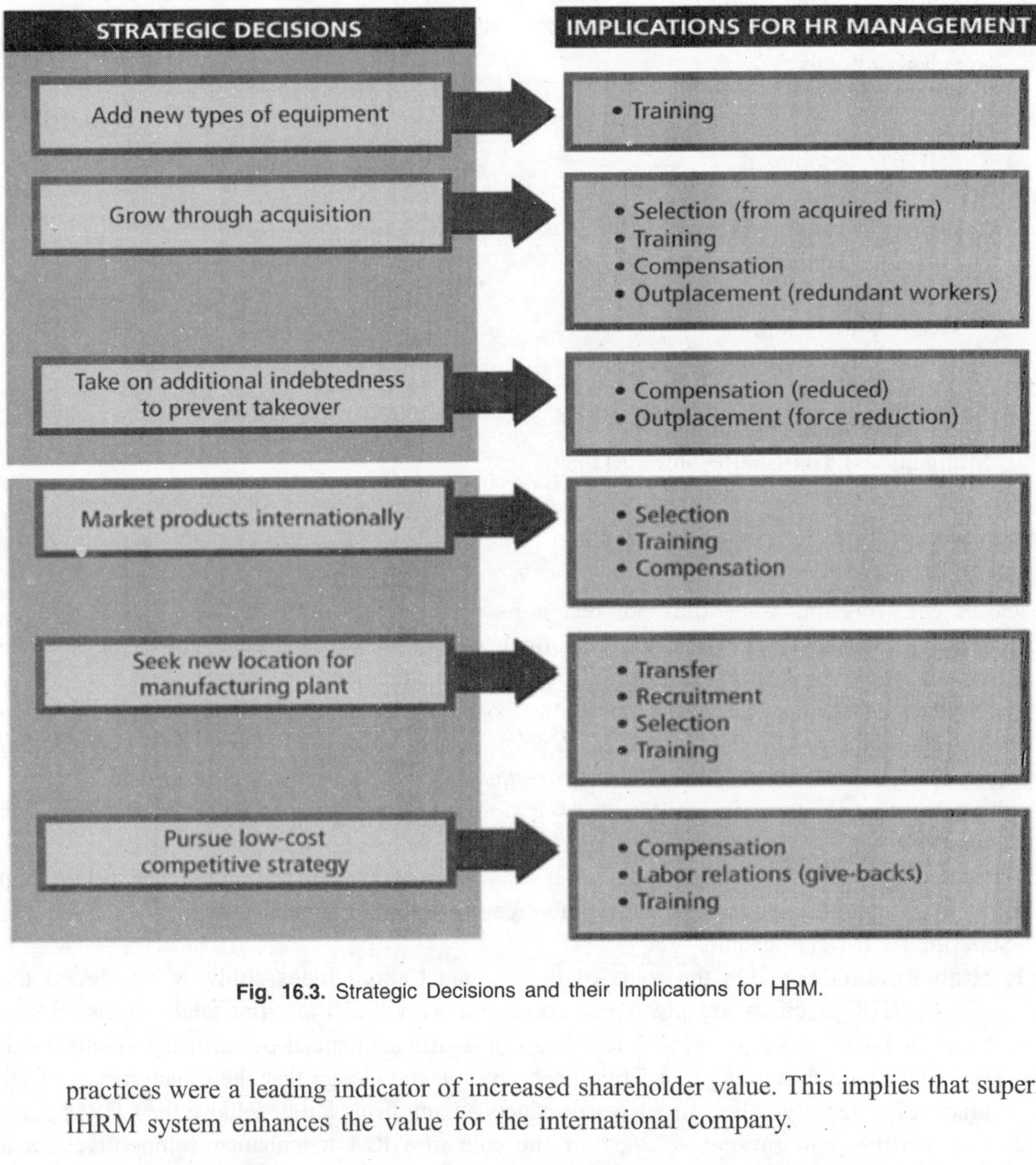

Fig. 16.3. Strategic Decisions and their Implications for HRM.

practices were a leading indicator of increased shareholder value. This implies that superior IHRM system enhances the value for the international company.

STAFFING POLICIES (RECRUITMENT AND SELECTION)

Staffing policy is concerned with the selection of employees for particular jobs. At one level, this involves selecting individuals who have the skills required to do particular jobs. At another level, staffing policy can be a tool for developing and promoting the desired corporate culture of the firm. By corporate culture, we mean the organization's norms and value systems. A strong corporate culture can help a firm to implement its strategy. General Electric, for example, is not just concerned with hiring people who have the skills required for performing particular jobs; it wants to hire individuals whose behavioural styles, beliefs, and value systems are consistent with those of GE. This is true whether an American is being hired, an Italian, a German, or an Australian and whether the hiring is for a U.S. operation or a foreign operation. The belief is that if employees are predisposed towards the organization's norms and value systems by their personality type, the firm will be able to attain higher performance.

Types of Staffing Policy

Research has identified three types of staffing policies in international businesses—the ethnocentric approach, the polycentric approach, and the geocentric approach. We will review each policy and link it to the strategy pursued by the firm. The most attractive staffing policy is probably the geocentric approach, although there are several impediments to adopting it.

1. The Ethnocentric Approach

An ethnocentric staffing policy is one in which all key management positions are filled by parent-country nationals. This practice was very widespread at one time. Firms such as Procter & Gamble, Philips NV, and Matsushita originally followed it. In the Dutch firm Philips, for example, all important positions in most foreign subsidiaries were at one time held by Dutch nationals who were referred to by their non-Dutch colleagues as the Dutch Mafia. In many Japanesc and South Korean firms; such as Toyota, Matsushita, and Samsung; key positions in international operations have often been held by home-country nationals. According to the Japanese Overseas Enterprise Association, in 1996 only 29 per cent of foreign subsidiaries of Japanese companies had presidents who were not Japanese. In contrast, 66 per cent of the Japanese subsidiaries of foreign companies had Japanese presidents.

Firms pursue an ethnocentric staffing policy for three reasons.

(i) The firm may believe the host country lacks qualified individuals to fill senior management positions. This argument is heard most often when the firm has operations in less developed countries.

(ii) The firm may see an ethnocentric staffing policy as the best way to maintain a unified corporate culture. Many Japanese firms, for example, prefer their foreign operations to be headed by expatriate Japanese managers because these managers have been socialized into the firm's culture while employed in Japan. Procter & Gamble until recently preferred to staff important management positions in its foreign subsidiaries with US nationals who had been socialized into P&G's corporate culture by years of employment in its US operations. Such reasoning tends to predominate when a firm places a high value on its corporate culture.

(iii) If the firm is trying to create value by transferring core competencies to a forcign operation as firms pursuing an international strategy are, it may believe that the best way to do this is to transfer parent-country nationals who have knowledge of that competency to the foreign operation. Imagine what might occur if a firm tried to transfer a core competency in marketing to a foreign subsidiary without supporting the transfer with a corresponding transfer of home-country marketing management personnel. The transfer would probably fail to produce the anticipated benefits because the knowledge underlying a core competency cannot easily be articulated and written down. Such knowledge, often a

> significant tacit dimension; it is acquired through experience. Just like the great tennis player who cannot instruct others how to become great tennis players simply by writing a handbook, the firm that has a core competency in marketing or anything else cannot just write a handbook that tells a foreign subsidiary how to build the firm's core competency anew in a foreign setting. It must also transfer management personnel to the foreign operation to show foreign managers how to become good marketers for example. The need to transfer managers overseas arises because the knowledge that underlies the firm's core competency resides in the heads of its domestic managers and was acquired through years of experience, not by reading a handbook. Thus, if a firm is to transfer a core competency to a foreign subsidiary, it must also transfer the appropriate managers.

Despite this rationale for pursuing an ethnocentric staffing policy, the policy is now on the wane in most international businesses for two reasons. First, an ethnocentric staffing policy limits advancement opportunities for host-country nationals. This can lead to resentment, lower productivity, and increased turnover among that group. Resentment can be greater still if, as often occurs, expatriate managers are paid significantly more than host-country nationals.

Second, an ethnocentric policy can lead to "cultural myopia," the firm's failure to understand host country cultural differences that require different approaches to marketing and management. The adaptation of expatriate managers can take a long time, during which they may make major mistakes. For example, expatriate managers may fail to appreciate how product attributes, distribution strategy, communications strategy, and pricing strategy should be adapted to host-country conditions. The result may be costly blunders. They may also make decisions that are ethically suspected simply because they do not understand the culture in which they are managing. In one highly publicized case in the United States, Mitsubishi Motors was sued by the Federal Equal Employment Opportunity Commission for tolerating extensive and systematic sexual harassment in a plant in Illinois. The plant's top management, all Japanese expatriates, denied the charges. The Japanese managers may have failed to realize that behaviour that would be viewed as acceptable in Japan was not acceptable in the United States.

2. The Polycentric Approach

A polycentric staffing policy recruits host-country nationals to manage subsidiaries while parent-country nationals occupy key positions at corporate headquarters. In many respects, a polycentric approach is a response to the shortcomings of an ethnocentric approach. One advantage of adopting a polycentric approach is that the firm is less likely to suffer from cultural myopia. Host-country managers are unlikely to make the mistakes arising from cultural misunderstandings to which expatriate managers are vulnerable. A second advantage is that a polycentric approach may be less expensive to implement, reducing the costs of value creation. Expatriate managers can be very expensive to maintain.

A polycentric approach also has its drawbacks. Host-country nationals have limited opportunities to gain experience outside their own country and thus cannot progress beyond senior positions in their own subsidiary. As in the case of an ethnocentric policy, this may cause resentment. Perhaps the major drawback with a polycentric approach, however, is the gap that can form between host-country managers and parent-country managers. Language barriers, national loyalties, and a range of cultural differences may isolate the corporate headquarters staff from the various foreign subsidiaries. The lack of management transfers from home to host countries, and vice versa, can exacerbate this isolation and lead to a lack of integration between corporate headquarters and foreign subsidiaries. The result can be a "federation" of largely independent national units with only nominal links to the corporate headquarters. Within such a federation, the coordination required to transfer core competencies or to pursue experience curve and location economies may be difficult to achieve. Thus, although a polycentric approach may be effective for firms pursuing a localization strategy, it is inappropriate for other strategies.

The federation that may result from a polycentric approach can also be a force for inertia within the firm. After decades of pursing a polycentric staffing policy, food and detergents giant Unilever found that shifting from a strategic posture that emphasized localization to a transnational posture was very difficult. Unilever's foreign subsidiaries had evolved into quasi-autonomous operations, each with its own strong national identity. These "little kingdoms" objected strenuously to corporate headquarters' attempts to limit their autonomy and to rationalize global manufacturing.

3. The Geocentric Approach

A geocentric staffing policy seeks the best people for key jobs throughout the organization, regardless of nationality. This policy has a number of advantages. First, it enables the firm to make the best use of its human resources. Second, and perhaps more important, a geocentric policy enables the firm to build a cadre of international executives who feel at home working in a number of cultures. Creation of such a cadre may be a critical first step towards building a strong unifying corporate culture and an informal management network, both of which are required for global standardization and transnational strategies. Firms pursuing a geocentric staffing policy may be better able to create value from the pursuit of experience curve and location economies and from the multidirectional transfer of core competencies than firms pursuing other staffing policies. In addition, the multinational composition of the management team that results from geocentric staffing tends to reduce cultural myopia and to enhance local responsiveness. Thus, other things being equal, a geocentric staffing policy seems the most attractive.

A number of problems limit the firm's ability to pursue a geocentric policy. Many countries want foreign subsidiaries to employ their citizens. To achieve this goal, they use immigration laws to require the employment of host-country nationals if they are available in adequate numbers and have the necessary skills. Most countries (including the United States) require firms to provide extensive documentation if they wish to hire a foreign national instead of a local national. This documentation can be time-consuming, expensive, and at times futile. A geocentric staffing policy also can be very expensive to implement. Training and relocation costs increase when transferring managers from country to country. The company may also need a compensation structure with a standardized international base pay level higher than national levels in many countries. In addition, the higher pay enjoyed by managers placed on an international "fast track" may be a source of resentment within a firm.

Comparison of Staffing Approaches

The advantages and disadvantages of the three approaches to staffing policy are summarized in Table 16.1. Broadly speaking, an ethnocentric approach is compatible with an international strategy, a polycentric approach is compatible with a localization strategy, and a geocentric approach is compatible with both global standardization and transnational strategies.

Table 16.1: Comparison of Staffing Approaches

Staffing Approach	Strategic Appropriateness	Advantages	Disadvantages
Ethnocentric	International	• Overcomes lack of qualified managers in host nation; • Unified culture; • Helps transfer core competencies	• Produces resentment in host country; • Can lead to cultural myopia
Polycentric	Localization	• Alleviates cultural myopia • Inexpensive to implement	• Limits career mobility; • Isolates headquarters from foreign subsidiaries
Geocentric	Global Standardization and Transnational	• Uses human resources efficiently; • Helps build strong culture and informal management networks	• National immigration policies may limit implementation; • Expensive

While the staffing policies described above are well known among both practitioners and scholars of international businesses, some critics have claimed that the typology is too simplistic and that it obscures the internal differentiation of management practices within international businesses. The critics claim that within some international businesses, staffing policies vary significantly from national subsidiary to national subsidiary; while some are managed on an ethnocentric basis, others are managed in a polycentric or geocentric manner. Other critics note that the staffing policy adopted by a firm is primarily driven by its geographic scope, as opposed to its strategic orientation. Firms that have a very broad geographic scope are most likely to have a geocentric mindset.

Dependence on Expatriate Managers

Two of the three staffing policies we have discussed—the ethnocentric and the geocentric—rely on extensive use of expatriate managers. Expatriates are citizens of one country who are working in another country. Sometimes the term expatriates is used to identify a subset of expatriates who are citizens of a foreign country working in the home country of their multinational employer. Thus, a citizen of Japan who moves to the United States to work at Microsoft would be classified as an expatriate. With an ethnocentric policy, the expatriates are all home-country nationals who are transferred abroad. With a geocentric approach, the expatriates need not be home-country nationals; the firm does not base transfer decisions on nationality. A prominent issue in the international staffing literature is expatriate failure—the premature return of an expatriate manager to his or her home country. Research suggests that between 16 and 40 per cent of all American employees sent abroad to developed nations return from their assignments early, and almost 70 per cent of employees sent to developing nations return home early.

According to the study of US, European and Japanese multinationals made by **R.L. Tung** for US multinationals, the reasons for higher expatriate failure, in order of importance, were:

1. Inability of spouse to adjust.
2. Manager's inability to adjust.
3. Other family problems.
4. Manager's personal or emotional maturity.
5. Inability to cope with larger overseas responsibilities.

Managers of European firms gave only one reason consistently to explain expatriate failure: the inability of the manager's spouse to adjust to a new environment. For the Japanese firms, the reasons for failure were

1. Inability to cope with larger overseas responsibilities.
2. Difficulties with new environment.
3. Personal or emotional problems.
4. Lack of technical competence.
5. Inability of spouse to adjust.

Figure 16.4 shows the model of the life cycle of an expatriate assignment which involves a process of determining the need for an expatriate assignment, selecting the candidate's pre-assignments training, departure, post-arrival orientation and training crisis and adjustment or crisis and failure, reassignment abroad or repatriation and adjustment.

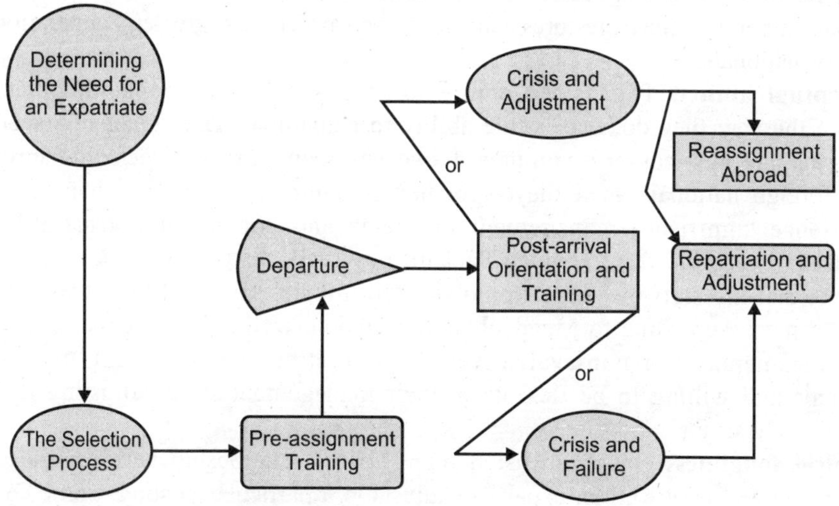

Fig. 16.4. The Expatriate Assignment Life Cycle.
Source: Cynthia D Fisher, *et al.*, Human Resource Management, Houghton Miffin, Co., 1997, p. 781.

How to Reduce Expatriate Failure Rates?

Expatriate Selection

One way to reduce expatriate failure rates is by improving selection procedures to screen out inappropriate candidates. In a review of the research on this issue, **Mendenhall and Oddou** state that a major problem in many firms is that HRM managers tend to equate domestic performance with overseas performance potential. Domestic performance and overseas performance potential is not the same thing. An executive who performs well in a domestic setting may not be able to adapt to managing in a different cultural setting. From their review of the research, Mendenhall and Oddou identified four dimensions that seem to predict success in a foreign posting: self-orientation, others-orientation, perceptual ability, and cultural toughness.

1. **Self-orientation:** The attributes of this dimension strengthen the expatriate's self-esteem, self-confidence, and mental well-being. Expatriates with high self-esteem, self-confidence, and mental well-being were more likely to succeed in foreign postings. Mendenhall and Oddou concluded that such individuals were able to adapt their interests in food, sport, and music; had interests outside of work that could be pursued (e.g., hobbies); and were technically competent.
2. **Others-orientation.** The attributes of this dimension enhance the expatriate's ability to interact effectively with host-country nationals. The more effectively the expatriate interacts with host country nationals, the more likely he or she is to succeed. Two factors seem to be particularly important here: relationship development and willingness to communicate. Relationship development refers to the ability to develop long-lasting friendships with host-country nationals. Willingness to communicate refers to the expatriate's willingness to use the host-country language. Although language fluency helps an expatriate need not be fluent to show willingness to communicate. Making the effort to use the language is what is important. Such gestures tend to be rewarded with greater cooperation by host-country nationals.
3. **Perceptual ability.** This is the ability to understand why people of other countries behave the way they do; that is, the ability to empathize. This dimension seems critical for managing host-country nationals. Expatriate managers who lack this ability tend to treat foreign nationals as if they were home-country nationals. As a result, they may experience significant management problems and considerable frustration. As one expatriate executive from Hewlett-Packard observed, "It took me six months to accept the fact that my staff meetings would start 30 minutes late, and that it would bother no one but me." According to Mendenhall and Oddou, well-adjusted expatriates tend to be non-judgemental and non-evaluative in interpreting the behaviour of host country nationals and willing to be flexible in their management style, adjusting it as cultural conditions warrant.
4. **Cultural toughness.** This dimension refers to the relationship between the country of assignment and how well an expatriate adjusts to a particular posting. Some countries are much tougher postings than others because their cultures are more unfamiliar and uncomfortable. For example, many Americans regard Great Britain as a relatively easy foreign posting, and for good reason the two cultures have much in common. But many Americans find postings in non-Western cultures, such as India, Southeast Asia, and the Middle East, to be much tougher. The reasons are many, including poor health care and housing standards, inhospitable climate, lack of Western entertainment, and language difficulties. Also, many cultures are, extremely male dominated and may be particularly difficult postings for female Western managers.

STAFFING POLICIES DETERMINANTS

According to **Taggart** and **M.C. McDermott**, the important factors influencing the staffing policy are the following:

(i) The Cultural Dimension: It should be pointed out, however, that, given the need to coordinate activities worldwide, and therefore the necessary ability of foreign subsidiary top executives to communicate directly with corporate headquarters, MNCs from some countries (e.g., Japan, South Korea, Taiwan) may need to depend more heavily upon home-country nationals because relatively few foreigners are fluent in the mother tongue of the home country. In contrast, language is less likely to prove a major restricting influence on the staffing policies of MNCs where English is the mother tongue. Japanese MNCs have been accused of adopting very ethnocentric staffing policies, and limiting job opportunities for non-Japanese nationals.

(ii) Subsidiary Characteristics: When an MNC establishes a new subsidiary or plant, it is likely to ensure that someone already very familiar with corporate culture heads the operation. Thus, initially the staffing policy is likely to be ethnocentric but become less so as host-country nationals are socialized into corporate culture.

(iii) Parent Company Characteristics: As indicated under the subsection staffing policy, the strategic predisposition of the MNC, in terms of its EPRG (ethnocentric, the polycentric, regiocentric, geocentric) profile, will influence staffing policy.

(iv) Host-Country Characteristics: Host-country characteristics like the social environment; government policies, host country human resource characteristics, government policies, etc. may also influence the staffing policy.

(v) Costs: The cost is also an important consideration in formulating the staffing policy when there are significant variations between nations the salary revels.

TRAINING AND DEVELOPMENT

Once selection of right persons is completed, the next step in IHRM is to train and develop new hires. In the meanwhile, it is desirable to have an understanding of the terms—training and development. Training aims at improving current work skills and behaviour, whereas development seeks to increase overall skill levels of managers through a mix of ongoing management education and rotations of managers through a number of jobs within the firm to give them varied experience. These are attempts to improve the overall productivity and quality of the firm's management resources. Historically, most international businesses have been focusing more on training than on managerial development. In addition, they tend to focus their training efforts on preparing home country nationals for foreign postings. Recently, however, the shift towards greater global competition, and rise of MNCs have changed the perspective. It is now common for firms to provide management development programmes in addition to training for particular posts. In many international businesses, the explicit purpose of management development programmes is strategic. Management development is seen as a tool to help the firm achieve its strategic goals.

We will examine the type of training imparted to managers for international postings. Later, we will discuss the connection between management development and strategy in the international business.

Expatriate Training: An expatriate needs pre-departure training before leaving for a foreign assignment. Typically, the expatriate needs to be taught about the host country's culture, language, food habits, socializing and other nuances. Popularly called cross-cultural-training (CCT), the training for the expatriate comprises the above inputs and more. Table 16.2 brings out the advantages and disadvantages of CCT.

Table 16.2: Benefits and Drawbacks of CCT

Merits	Demerits
• Increases chances of success in global assignment	• Develops a false sense of confidence among employees
• Provides a comprehensive global perspective for managers	• May not remove cultural biases and prejudices
• Instills a sense of confidence into people	• May not be taken seriously by the recipients
• Foreign employees can be managed better	• May not make a visible difference in business volumes
• Reduces culture shock due to frequent travels abroad	• Can never fully prepare an assignee to face real problems

Cultural Training: Cultural training seeks to foster an appreciation for the host country's culture. The belief is that understanding a host country's culture will help the manager empathies with the culture, which will enhance his or her effectiveness in interacting with host country citizens. An expatriate should receive training in the host country's culture, history, politics, economy, religion, and social and business practices. If possible, it is also advisable to arrange for a familiarization trip to the host country before the formal transfer, as this is likely to ease culture shock. Given the problems related to spouse adaptation, it is important that the spouse, and perhaps the whole family, be included in the training programmes. Often cultural training includes counseling on return to home base to prevent reverse culture shock.

Cultural training is essential for Indians who migrate mainly to the US in search of greener pastures. Majority of Indians who seek postings are software professionals who are from middle class, conservative, and religious families. Many of them are from South India which is known for deep religious sentiments and vegetarianism. They are reserved and almost shy with the opposite sex even after experiencing western winds of liberalism. The food, weather, and behaviour are all new to them. The venerable cow may have to be seen as meat in a burger, women may have to be accepted as being more masculine and freer in their interaction with men. The idea of a friendly kiss or a hug and bikinis and frocks need to be got used to. The absence of family and friends leads to loneliness and frustration. Thus, an Indian has number of reasons for failure in an alien culture. He or she should be trained to overcome all the obstacles.

It is not just Indians only need training. Every expatriate needs to be trained in language, culture, historical and local etiquette, personal imperatives, and food and dress habits. Dealing with racial discrimination in some countries and survival tips for vegetarians in countries like Japan, China, and Eastern Europe are other inputs in training. Cultural training is receiving considerable attention now as more and more managers are required to globe-trot on business deals. In 1994, the Japanese spent $17 million in business etiquette training. Nearer to home, firms which have recognized the importance of cultural training are the Mafatlal, OP Jindal Group. Reckitt & Coleman, and Ranbaxy.

Language Training: Language training is a seemingly obvious, desirable component of a pre-departure programme. One weakness of many international businesses is that they do not give sufficient attention to the importance of language training. English is the primary language of international business, and most expatriates from all countries can converse in English. Those who can speak only English are at a distinct disadvantage when doing business in non-English speaking countries like China. It may be reiterated that a willingness to communicate in the host country language will help build rapport with local employees and improve the expatriate's effectiveness.

In addition to English, an expatriate needs to know language of the host country. The ability to speak a foreign language can improve the expatriate's effectiveness and negotiating ability. It can also improve manager's access to information regarding the host country's economy, government and market.

Practical Training: Practical training seeks to help the expatriate manager and family feel 'at home', in the host country. The sooner the expatriate settles down, better are the prospects that he and his family will adapt successfully. One important need is for a support network of friends for the expatriate. Where an expatriate community exists, firms often devote considerable effort to ensuring that the new expatriate family is quickly integrated into that group. The expatriate community can be a useful source of support and information and can be valuable in helping the family adapt to an alien culture.

Training expatriates before their departure to overseas assignment cannot be over-emphasized. An extreme and tragic case highlights the importance of exposure and training for international areas. Management staff of an oil company operating in the Pacific assigned young local workers to supervisory roles over considerably older workers. Within one week all supervisors were discovered dead. Their throats were slit. The expatriate managers had been unaware that in this region status is related to age. As a result of this supervisory policy older workers were grossly insulted. This tragedy could have been avoided by training managers to reorientate their perspective when appointing locals in a foreign culture, and providing them with careful monitoring.

MANAGEMENT DEVELOPMENT AND STRATEGY

As stated earlier international businesses use management development as a strategic tool. This is particularly true for firms pursuing a multinational strategy which is common a feature among firms nowadays. Such firms need strong unifying corporate culture and informal management networks to assist in coordination and control. In addition, MNCs need to be able to detect pressures for local responsiveness. This obviously demands knowledge about host country culture.

Management development programmes help build unifying corporate culture by socialising new managers into the values and norms of the firm. In-house training programmes and intense interaction during off-site training can foster esprit de corps-shared experiences, informal networks, perhaps a company language or jargon, as well as develop competencies. These training courses often include songs, picnics, and sporting events that promote feelings of togetherness. These rites of integration may include "initiation rites" wherein personal culture is stripped, company uniforms are donned, and humiliation is inflicted. All these activities aim to strengthen a manager's identification with the company.

Bringing managers together in one location for extended periods and rotating them through different jobs in several countries help the firm build an informal management network. An example to be stated in this context is Ericsson, the Swedish telecommunications company. Inter-unit cooperation is extremely important at Ericsson, particularly for transferring know-how and core competencies from the parent to subsidiaries from subsidiaries to parent, and among subsidiaries themselves. To facilitate cooperation, Ericsson transfers large numbers of people back and forth between headquarters and subsidiaries. Ericsson sends a team of 5 to 100 engineers and managers from one unit to another for a year or two. This establishes a network of interpersonal contacts. This philosophy is effective for both solidifying a common culture in the company and coordinating the firm's globally dispersed operations.

GLOBAL PERFORMANCE MANAGEMENT

An expatriate's performance or performance global level needs to be assessed to effect his or her promotions, assess training and development needs, and introduce pay rises. Though the objective of performance assessment is appreciable, the task of evaluation is fraught with several difficulties. Unintentional bias makes it difficult to evaluate the performance of expatriate managers objectively in most cases, two groups evaluate the performance of expatriate managers, host-nation and home-country manage and both are subject to biases. Biases occur because of distances, different cultural backgrounds, and lack of experience in working in a foreign setting. Environmental conditions vary across countries. Political upheavals may reduce the capacity of expatriates to perform. The condition in some countries may be very difficult so that expatriates and third-country nationals may spend considerable effort simply adapting to daily living. This would affect job performance. Managers of relatively unskilled employees may spend much of their time training workers and supervising the most basic activities within their subsidiary. Objective indicators of subsidiary performance may be low, even though the manager is doing an excellent job, given what he or she has to work with.

Factors Influencing Performance

Figure 16.5 demonstrates the four factors that influence performance in a foreign assignment.

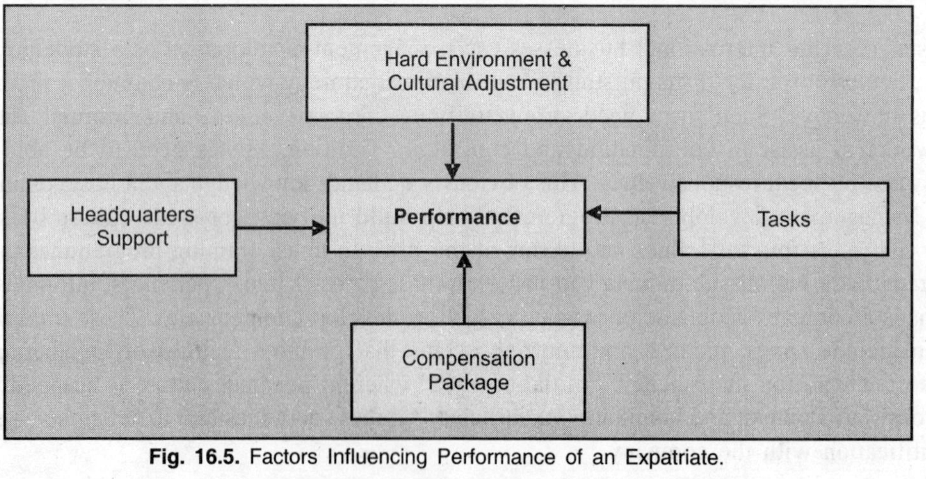

Fig. 16.5. Factors Influencing Performance of an Expatriate.

1. **Compensation Package:** Financial benefits, along with career prospects, motivate an individual to accept a foreign assignment. If these expectations are not met during the assignment, motivation declines and performance suffers.
2. **Task:** As stated above, the mission of an expatriate may be to act as trouble-shooter, operator, or executive officer. Whatever the assignment, task influences performance considerably.
3. **Headquarters Support:** Home office support is crucial in expatriate performance. An assignee has accepted overseas assignment, no doubt with the objective of making extra money or improving career prospects. But there are other motives—loyalty to the organization and commitment to make the firm successful. It is these altruistic motives which make assignees agree to work even in hostile environments. It is necessary that the home office extends support and offers moral courage particularly in times when the expatriate is passing through culture shock. Following are the specific support facilities required from the headquarters.
    - Organizational support in managing the practical problems of setting up home in a new culture is essential for enabling an expatriate to settle down.
    - The provision of timely psychological counselling for expatriates encountering problems of adjustment can contribute to their mental health and performance.
    - The families of employees should also be assisted in their efforts to find their feet in a new culture.
4. **Host Environment and Cultural Adjustment:** Environment yields considerable influence on performance, particularly of the expatriate. If the host environment is hostile, expatriates are under constant pressure and often there is threat to the life itself. We have lost two brilliant men while on duty in Afghanistan. Expecting enhanced performance from expatriates operating in such an environment is unrealistic. The form of ownership of the subsidiary is important too. For instance, it may be relatively easier to perform in a wholly owned subsidiary than in a joint venture with a state-owned enterprise in China. Conflicting goals between the parent companies are a common problem within international joint venture and can make the expatriate's job more difficult. Similarly, the stage of the international business will influence the success of the expatriate. An assignee overseeing the establishment of a new facility in a foreign country, especially in a developing market, will face different challenges and constraints to one who is posted into a mature operation.

The discussion given above shows the difficulty of evaluating expatriate performance. Here we can also discuss what to be assessed and who to conduct the assessment. Three types of criteria are used to assess the effectiveness of an expatriate manager—hard criteria, soft criteria, and contextual criteria. Hard criteria are objective, quantifiable, and can be directly measured such as return on investment (RGI), market share, and the like. Soft criteria tend to be relationship or trait-based, such as leadership style or interpersonal skills. Contextual criteria attempt to take into consideration factors that result from the situation in which performance occurs. Situational considerations deserve serious consideration inasmuch as the host country environment, as told earlier, plays a major role in expatriate performance. To the question who should evaluate expatriate performance, the simple answer is the immediate superior.

However, in the case of expatriate managers, the direct superior is often someone at the firm's headquartering several thousand kilometres away. Since the immediate superior may have little opportunity to observe the expatriate's performance information about the expatriate must be provided to those in a position to evaluate his or her activities. As with performance evaluations handled in domestic situations, many different individuals may be able to provide useful information about the performance of a particular employee.

KNOWLEDGE MANAGEMENT PERFORMANCE FRAMEWORK

A common theme in contemporary organizations is the concern of managers for achieving cultural change through radical management approaches. Knowledge management is one such management approach, and is portrayed in the popular business literature as an innovation with the potential to affect the whole of an organization's business, especially its processes and information systems. The issue as how to measure the success of a knowledge management approach is one which is still being explored by organizations, researchers and management consultants.

Knowledge is regarded as an important commodity used by an organization (BHEL in the public sector). Knowledge is created by employees through research and policy making and used for the benefit of the organization. Good information technology infrastructure is used to support knowledge flow. At BHEL, the problem remained of developing a performance management framework for measuring the impact of initiatives taken under knowledge management strategy. The main task at BHEL was in two main areas.

- Linking knowledge management to the overall business performance framework
- Linking knowledge management to organizational culture change.

On the basis of existing models used in public sector undertaking such as BHEL, a workable model is emerged which comprises two frameworks.

1. Knowledge Management Performance Scorecard
2. Knowledge Management Behaviour Framework

1. Knowledge Management Performance Scorecard

Assumptions are—

- A knowledge management performance framework is not in isolation from the organization's business performance framework.
- There is clear and direct alignment between individual work plans, team goals, business unit objectives and the organization's key result areas.
- There are clear benchmarks against which performance can be measured.
- Performance indicators are unambiguous.
- Knowledge management is a business principle and is embedded in all aspects of the organization's work.

The steps used in the model are:

Step I

The knowledge management performance scorecard adapts the balanced scorecard approach in which an organization measures its performance in four key result areas:

- Financial performance;
- Internal business processes;
- Customers; and
- Growth.

Table 16.3 shows balanced scorecard for public sector performance management.

Table 16.3: Balanced Scorecard for Public Sector Performance Management

Financial Performance	Internal Business Processes	Stakeholders	People
What do we need to do to succeed financially?	What business processes do we need to excel at?	How should we appear to our stakeholders?	How will we sustain our ability to learn and develop?

Step II

The next step in formulating a performance management framework involves mapping the key result areas for knowledge management across the scorecard. The key result areas were considered to be:

- strategy;
- products and services;
- information infrastructure (technology and content);
- processes;
- relationships; and
- culture and behaviour.

The final framework on this basis is given in Table 16.4.

Table 16.4: Mapping the Key Result Areas for Knowledge Management

Financial Performance	Internal Business Processes	Stakeholder	People
What do we need to do to succeed financially?	What business processes do we need to excel at?	How should we appear to our stakeholders?	How will we sustain our ability to learn and develop?
Knowledge management key result areas			
Strategy Products and services	*Strategy* information infrastructure (technology and content) processes	*Strategy* relationships product and services	*Strategy* culture and behaviour

Step III

The third step is setting objectives, expected outcomes, initiatives and performance indicators for each of the knowledge management key result areas. The expected outcomes for each of the defined objectives were grouped under the BHEL's public policy performance indicators. This provides a clear connection between the policy performance framework and knowledge management objectives. An example of this is given in Table 16.5.

Table 16.5: Knowledge Management Performance Objectives.

Key Result Area			
Objectives	**Expected Outcome**	**Initiatives**	**Performance Indicators**
		Stakeholders: relationships	
To increase the capacity for integration and collaboration	Changed behaviours % increase in inter-organizational communications	Encourage more formal and informal networks using team rooms	No. of team rooms and particulars in each
		Internal business processes: Information infrastructure (technology and content)	
To build awareness amongst all staff of knowledge management tools, processes and practices	Awareness and understanding All staff are familiar with the concepts and practices of knowledge management Use of tools, information, knowledge Increase in use of knowledge management tools and adoption of knowledge management practices	FAQ page on knowledge management is placed on intranet All staff attend awareness training in knowledge management tools Knowledge management team room is established and attracts growing number of members	Metrics on use of FAQ page and refreshment rate of its contents No. of staff trained No. of participants in and contributions to knowledge management team room discussions and documents

The design allows for high detail at the business unit and individual level. This is its major advantage that it can be cascaded clearly down from the organizational level to divisional, group and individual work plans. Its major disadvantage is that people's behaviour and organizational culture cannot be realistically framed in terms of such a rational planning model. Another approach was needed for this. This is the function of the Knowledge Management Behaviour Framework.

2. Knowledge Management Behaviour Framework

The second framework designed for the BHEL identifies and describes the use of knowledge management tools, systems, resources and practices as behaviours to be learnt when individuals progressively adopt knowledge management in their work. The behavioural framework, defined in terms of learning and learned behaviours, is directly linked to the key result area *people, culture and behaviour* in the Knowledge Management Performance Scorecard.

The Concerns Based Adoption Model (CBAM) developed by Gene Hall and his associates at the University of Texas at Austin in the early 1970s has been used to integrate knowledge and adoption of the knowledge in the organizations. CBAM has two dimensions to its system of describing how organizations and individuals adopt innovations. One is that individuals feel various concerns about adopting new ways of doing things, and that secondly their behaviour will reflect these concerns through differing levels of use they make of the new innovation or change.

The CBAM makes several *assumptions* about change. It assumes that change is a process, not an event, is made by individuals first then organizations, is a highly personal experience, and entails developmental growth in feelings and skills.

CBAM asserts that people go through predictable stages in adopting an innovation. These stages are shown in Table 16.6.

Table 16.6: Levels of use in the CBAM

Order	Level	
Last	6	Renewal
|	5	Integration
|	4b	Refinement
|	4a	Routine
|	3	Mechanical use
|	2	Preparation
|	1	Orientation
First	0	Non-use

Individuals exhibit a progressive order of adoption from non-use to renewal. Non-use might arise because individuals do not have the time to learn about the new way of doing things, or perhaps because they are concerned that the new way is counterproductive. When individuals begin to take action in learning more about the changes to be adopted, they are exhibiting a new level of use, that of orienting themselves to what the change has to offer. In deciding to begin using a changed practice or innovation, individuals are preparing themselves for more fully adopting the new. A person who begins to use the innovation has to grapple with organizing and managing her or his programme of work in order to establish a basic effectiveness. This is coined as mechanical use in the CBAM system. At the routine level, individuals have attained a degree of stabilization, and it is a small step from here to developing some refinements by which the impact of the innovation can be modified to suit specific needs of the work. The final stages describe individuals engaged in integrating the innovation within a team or larger group context, and finally, having fully integrated the innovation or change, individuals begin to seek modifications in response to the need for improved business performance.

What is especially attractive about this system of describing levels of use is that it legitimizes the learning that people experience when adopting organizational change. Too often, the implementation of change in organisations is accompanied by an implicit expectation that individuals will leap from non-use to integration in one rapid step. Another feature that makes this model attractive for assessing the adoption of knowledge management by individuals is that it is directly linked to the development of a person's knowledge. This builds an inherent integrity into the framework: learning and knowledge are directly linked.

How the CBAM system was adapted for describing knowledge management behaviours within a performance management framework?

- It was assumed that knowledge management was an innovation to be adopted throughout the whole organization by every individual.
- The levels of use were described in terms that related to people's skills in knowledge management. The order from 0-6, representing first to last stages, was retained. Table 16.7 shows these levels.

Table 16.7: Levels of Skill in Adopting Knowledge

Level	Knowledge Management Skills
0	Awareness but non-use of knowledge management tools or practices
1	Seeks information about knowledge management
2	Personal experimentation with knowledge management tools and practices
3	Personal implementation of knowledge management practices
4	Engaged with impact and consequences of knowledge management behaviour
5	Actively collaborates in all aspects of work
6	Refocussing knowledge management skills on new business opportunities

- It was beneficial to describe what role an individual might take up at each level, and what behaviours would characterize both the level and the role. Table 16.8 outlines these.

Table 16.8: Roles and Behaviours for the Levels of Knowledge Management Skill

Level	Knowledge Management Skills	Possible Role for Someone at this Level	Typical Behaviours
0	Awareness but non-use of knowledge management tools or practices	Maintainer of current competency and behaviour	Has little concern and low awareness about knowledge management tools or practices Interest may or may not be present Needs to understand how knowledge management will directly benefit individual's interests
1	Seeks information about knowledge management	Early learner	Wants descriptive information and opportunities to see knowledge management tools in use Explores realistic expectations about benefits and costs in acquiring knowledge management skills
2.	Personal experimentation with knowledge management tools and practices	Follower	Establishes rapport with people more skilled in knowledge management practices Accesses and uses knowledge management resources and tools provided by others Seeks personal support through access to facilitators and other help

Table 16.8: Contd.

Level	Knowledge Management Skills	Possible Role for Someone at this Level	Typical Behaviours
3.	Personal implementation of knowledge management practices	Implementer	Begins to focus more on team issues and collaborative opportunities Clarifies how knowledge management can be applied to other aspects of individual's work is continually building skill and increasing use of knowledge management tools, probably on a daily basis Identifies knowledge resources, creates and contributes own knowledge to organization's knowledge systems
4.	Engaged with impact and consequences of knowledge management behaviour	Problem-solver	Independently and routinely applies knowledge management practices Competent in capturing and organizing knowledge for others' use Clearly demonstrates collaborative knowledge behaviours Encourages other people to share expertise and participate in group problem-solving
5.	Actively collaborates in all aspects of work	Leader	Advocates and promotes collaboration to others Models knowledge management practices, especially learning and feedback into business processes
6.	Refocusing knowledge management skills on new business opportunities	Investigator/ Innovator	Engages in creative inquiry and analysis of business outcomes and strategies

The framework as it is presented in Table 16.8 bears a close relationship to the kind of competency models found in many organizations that have implemented employee performance management systems. An element missing in these systems, and one which is considered critical when implementing change, is the role supervisors or managers adopt in assisting staff to learn and adapt their work to the changes expected of them.

This relationship between a supervisor and supervisee is a critical success factor in both implementing change and assessing its effectiveness. The Knowledge Management Behaviour Framework includes this element, and is what gives it further integrity.

Knowledge management is defined specifically within the Public Sector as those actions which support collaboration and integration. Clearly collaborative action in the relationship between a manager and her or his staff establishes a core practice of knowledge management at its most critical interface. The Knowledge Management Behaviour Framework specifically defines this interface. Table 16.9 describes the roles and behaviours anticipated of managers.

Table 16.9: Roll and Behaviour for Managers

Level	Role for Manager in Response to Someone at this Level	Typical Behaviours of Manager
0	Provide vision	Focus on the individual Acknowledge that little concern and low awareness is legitimate Make individuals aware in a positive way Use promotional tools
1	Information provider	Focus on the individual Get them in touch with an enthusiastic person competent in knowledge management Help the early learner clarify needs and identify training opportunities
2	Counsellor	Focus on the individual supported by group processes Answer all questions, listen to problems, build success expectancy Establish milestones and realistic timelines in developing knowledge management behaviours: celebrate and reward achievement
3	Leader	Focus on team development and performance Establish consulting pairs or support groups Use demonstration projects to increase personal confidence and skill Provide lots of opportunities for group discussions, especially informal ones, to allow cross-fertilization of ideas
4	Supervisor	Encourage cross-functional working parties for identifying problems and exploring solutions Put individuals in contact with others who are ahead and behind them in their levels of competency with knowledge management
5	Mentor	Encourage collaborative problem-solving with customers and suppliers Give opportunities to go outside the organization for learning and sharing expertise
6.	Coach and sponsor	Allow considerable scope for individual to explore other ways of doing things Provide resources for testing new ideas

All of these actions are supported by the knowledge management tools, systems, resources and practices of the organization. In public sector these include:

- tools such as Lotus Notes team rooms; an intranet system that enables access to internal and external information;
- resources of an electronic library storing departmental documents and objects;
- communities of practice; and,
- personal practices in which knowledge resources are identified, created, contributed, captured and organized, accessed, shared, applied, weeded and archived by each individual in the normal course of daily work.

CONCLUSION

Implementation of the frameworks is still at an early stage. The design is to be trialled within one divisional group, then evaluated and refined before full implementation.

By distinguishing between organizational performance and individual behaviour, the design of these frameworks provides for "hard" business measures to be linked to "fuzzy" social measures in a coherent way. Importantly, learning, which is a fundamental activity within knowledge processes, is explicitly acknowledged and included in knowledge management performance.

INTERNATIONAL COMPENSATION STRATEGY AND ITS DETERMINANTS

Another important activity that receives considerable attention from the IHR manager is to design an attractive remuneration package to the expatriates. Any expatriate remuneration package needs to be designed to achieve the following major objectives:

- Attract employees who are qualified and interested in international assignments;
- Facilitate the movement of expatriates from one subsidiary to another, from home to subsidiaries, and from subsidiaries back home;
- Provide a consistent and reasonable relationship between the pay levels of employees at headquarters, domestic affiliates, and foreign subsidiaries; and
- Be cost-effective by reducing unnecessary expenses.

While designing an international remuneration package following problems are faced:

(i) Discrepancies in pay between parent, host, and third-country nationals.
(ii) The need to vary expatriate compensation, depending on the 'life cycle' of the expatriate's family (e.g., young children, children in college, etc.).
(iii) Remuneration issues related to re-entry into the parent country organization.
(iv) Using remuneration programmes that had not changed sufficiently over time to deal adequately with the new international business environment.

Several internal and external factors or determinants influence international compensation.

Internal Factors

Among the internal factors is the

(i) **Goal orientation of the MNC**. Broadly, the goal may be pursuit of economic or non-economic benefits. A non-governmental organization, which seeks to realize cultural goals, will obviously have less attractive compensation package than a firm which produces and sells goods and services for profit.

An MNC's capacity to pay affects both the levels and types of international compensation. Compensation packages should be cost-effective for the international business.

(i) **The competitive strategy** of the MNC will most likely influence the nature of international compensation.
(ii) Attitudes, values, and beliefs about the relative value of employee contributions and international compensation elements such as cash compensation, benefits, perquisites, and employee ownership plans across the MNC are inherent in the organizational culture. The latter also influences the degree to which employees are compensated on the basis of seniority, in contrast to personal connections or performance.
(iii) Workforce characteristics such as age, education level, qualifications, and experience, along tastes and preferences of employees and employee relations will result in different international remuneration approaches. Finally, the strategic role of each subsidiary will have considerable influence on international compensation strategy.

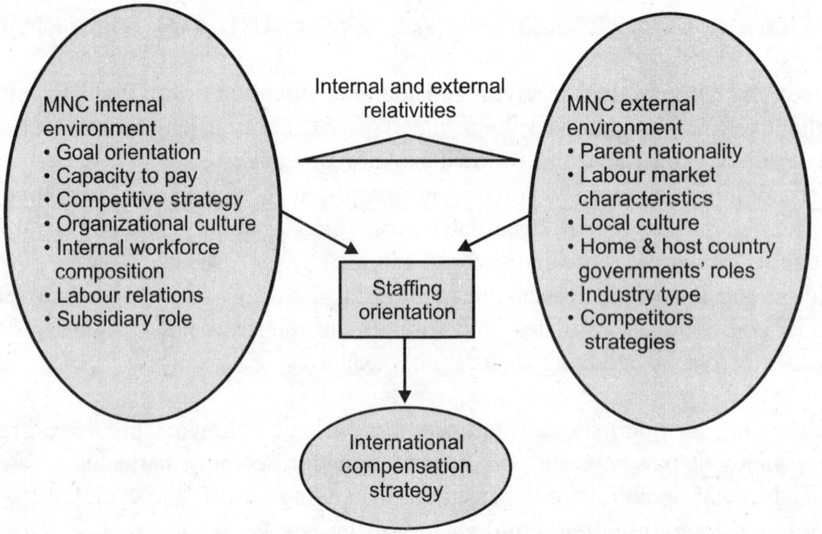

Fig. 16.6. Internal and External Variables Influencing International Compensation Strategy
Source: Anne-Wil Harzing, *et al.*, International Human Resource Management, p. 311.

External Factors

In addition to internal variables, certain factors which are external to the MNC also influence internal compensation.

(i) Nationality of the parent company is one such external factor.
(ii) Local culture influences international compensation strategy through the dominant societal values, norms, attitudes, and attitudes towards salary differences.
(iii) Other influences include labour market characteristics of supply and demand, and skill levels, ages and experience of those in the labour market.
(iv) The roles of home and host country governments in labour relations will also affect the level of government regulation of the labour market and the employment relationship, including remuneration of the workforce.
(v) Industry type and competitor's strategy are also important external determinants.

Any expatriate remuneration package should seek to equalize the cost of living at home and living abroad. The remuneration package generally comprises the following benefits:

The components of international compensation comprise base salary, benefits, incentives, taxes, allowances, and long-term benefits.

- **Base Salary:** The term base salary acquires a somewhat different meaning when employees go abroad. In a domestic setting, base salary denotes the amount of cash compensation that serves as a benchmark for other components (e.g., bonuses and benefits). For expatriates, it is the primary component of a package of allowances, many of which are directly related to base salary (e.g., foreign service premium, cost-of-living allowance, housing allowance) as well as the basis for in-service benefits and pension contributions. It may be paid in home or host-country currency. The base salary is the foundation block for international remuneration whether the employee is a parent-country or third-country national.

- **Benefits**: Benefits constitute a major element of the remuneration of a regular employee. These benefits comprise a similar, or even larger, portion of expat remuneration. However, several thorny issues surround remuneration for expatriates. These include:
    - Whether MNCs should maintain expatriates in home-country benefit programmes, particularly if these programmes are not tax-deductible; and
    - Whether MNCs have the option of enrolling expatriates in host-country benefit programmes and/or making up any difference in coverage.
- **Incentives:** In recent years some international businesses have been designing special incentive programmes for keeping expats motivated. In the process, a growing number of firms have dropped the ongoing premium for overseas assignments and replaced it with a one-time lump sum premium. For example, in the early 1990s over 60 per cent of MNCs gave ongoing premiums to their expats. Today, the figure has come down to 50 per cent and the declining trend continues. The lump sum payment has at least three advantages. First, expats realize that they are paid this only once and that too when they accept an overseas assignment. So the payment tends to retain its motivational value. Secondly, costs to the company are losses because there is only one payment and no future financial commitment. Thirdly, because incentive is a separate payment, distinguishable from regular pay, it is more readily available for saving or spending.
- **Taxes:** The final component of the expatriate's remuneration relates to taxes. Multinationals generally select one of the following approaches to handle international taxation.
    - Tax equalization: The firms withhold an amount equal to the home-country tax obligation of the expatriate, and pay all taxes in the host country.
    - Tax protection: The employee pays upto the amount of taxes he or she would pay on remuneration in the home country. In such a situation, the employee is entitled to any windfall received if the total taxes are less in the foreign country than in the home country.
- **Allowances:** Allowances are an inevitable feature of international compensation. One common allowance relates to the cost-of-living allowance—a compensation for differences between the home country and foreign assignment. This allowance is designed to provide the expatriate with the same standard of living that he or she enjoyed in the home country, and it may cover a variety of expenses, including relocation, housing, education, and hardship. Spouse assistance, housing allowance, home leave allowance, relocation allowance and educational allowance are the other allowances provided for in the expatriate compensation.
- **Long-term Benefits:** The most common long-term benefits offered to employees of MNCs are employee stock option schemes. Traditionally stock option plans were used as a means for companies to reward top management or key people of the organization. However, it is increasingly gaining popularity amongst wholly owned technology companies to retain and reward employees across the organizations. This is stemming from the fact that all employees can create an impact on the organization's performance and will directly impact its profitability. Hence, the primary objectives for providing stock options are to reward and improve employee performance and/or attract/retain critical talent across the organization.

INTERNATIONAL LABOUR RELATIONS

The HRM function of an international business is typically responsible for international labour relations. From a strategic perspective, the key issue in international labour relations is the degree to which organized labour can limit the choices of an international business. A firm's ability to integrate and consolidate its global operations to realize experience curve and location economies can be limited by organized labour, constraining the pursuit of a transnational or global standardization strategy. Prahalad and Doz cite the example of General Motors, which gained peace with labour unions by agreeing not to integrate and consolidate operations in the most efficient manner. General Motors made substantial investments in Germany—matching its new investments in Austria and Spain. This is at the demand of the German metal workers' unions.

One task of the HRM function is to foster harmony and minimize conflict between the firm and the organized labour. In this section, three aspects concerning international labour relations are discussed as under:

1. The Concerns of Organized Labour

Labour unions generally try to get better pay, greater job security, and better working conditions for their members through collective bargaining with the management. Unions' bargaining power is derived largely from their ability to threaten to disrupt production, either by a strike or some other form of work protest. This threat is credible, however, only insofar as the management has no alternative but to employ union labour.

The first principal concern of domestic unions about multinational firms is that the company can counter its bargaining power with the power to move production to another country. Ford, for example, very clearly threatened British unions with a plan to move manufacturing to Continental Europe unless British workers abandoned work rules that limited productivity, showed restraint in negotiating for wage increases, and curtailed strikes and other work disruptions.

The second concern of organized labour is that an international business will keep highly skilled tasks in its home country and farm out only low-skilled tasks to foreign plants. Such a practice makes it relatively easy for an international business to switch production from one location to another as economic conditions warrant. Consequently, the bargaining power of organized labour is once more reduced.

The third concern arises when an international business attempts to import employment practices and contractual agreements from its home country. When these practices are alien to the host country, organized labour fears the change will reduce its influence and power. This concern has surfaced in response to Japanese multinationals that have been trying to export their style of labour relations to other countries. For example, much to the annoyance of the United Auto Workers (UAW), many Japanese auto plants in the United States are not unionized. As a result, union influence in the auto industry is declining.

2. The Strategy of Organized Labour

Organized labour has responded to the increased bargaining power of multinational corporations by taking three actions:

- trying to establish international labour organizations;
- lobbying for national legislation to restrict multinationals; and
- trying to achieve international regulations on multinationals through such organizations as the United Nations.

These efforts have not been very successful. In the 1960s, organized labour began to establish international trade secretariats (ITSs) to provide worldwide links for national unions in particular industries. The long-term goal was to be able to bargain transnational with multinational firms. Organized labour believed that by coordinating union action across countries through an ITS, it could counter the power of a multinational corporation by threatening to disrupt production on an international scale. However, the ITSs have had virtually no real success.

A further impediment to cooperation has been the wide variation in union structure. Organized labour has also met with only limited success in its efforts to get national and international bodies to regulate multinationals. Such international organizations as the International Labour Organization (ILO) and the Organization for Economic Cooperation and Development (OECD) have adopted codes of conduct for multinational firms to follow in labour relations. However, these guidelines are not as far reaching as many unions would like. They also do not provide any enforcement mechanisms. Many researchers report that such guidelines are of only limited effectiveness.

3. Approaches to Labour Relations

International businesses differ markedly in their approaches to international labour relations. The main difference is the degree to which labour relations activities are centralized or decentralized. Historically most international businesses have decentralized international labour relations activities to their foreign subsidiaries because labour laws, union power, and the nature of collective bargaining varied so much from country to country. It made sense to decentralize the labour relations function to local managers. The belief was that there was no way the central management could effectively handle the complexity of simultaneously managing labour relations in a number of different environments.

Although this logic still holds, there is now a trend towards greater centralized control. This trend reflects international firms' attempts to rationalize their global operations. The general rise in competitive pressure in industry after industry has made it more important for firms to control their costs. Because labour costs account for such a large percentage of total costs, many firms are now using the threat to move production to another country in their negotiations with unions to change work rules and limit wage increases. Because such a move would involve major new investments and plant closures, this bargaining tactic requires the input of headquarters management. Thus, the level of centralized input into labour relations is increasing.

In addition, the realization is growing that the way work is organized within a plant can be a major source of competitive advantage. Much of the competitive advantage of Japanese automakers, for example, has been attributed to the use of self-managing teams, job rotation, cross-training, and the like in their Japanese plants. To replicate their domestic performance in foreign plants, the Japanese firms have tried to replicate their work practices there. This often brings them into direct conflict with traditional work practices in those countries, as sanctioned by the local labour unions, so the Japanese firms have often made their foreign investments contingent on the local union's accepting a radical change in work practices. To achieve this, the headquarters of many Japanese firms bargains directly with local unions to get union agreement to changes in work rules before committing to an investment. For example, before Nissan decided to invest in northern England, it got a commitment from British unions to agree to a change in traditional work practices.

IHRM COMPETENCIES–AN EXERCISE

The competencies for IHRM are highlighted in the following steps:

Step One: Define international human resource management and describe IHRM's three main activities which are as under:

- Acquisition
- Employment
- Human resource development

Step Two: Identify factors affecting employee acquisition, discuss steps to reduce the effects of skilled labour shortages, and describe different factors that affect recruitment. It includes:

- Seasonality
- Job dissatisfaction
- High labour turnover
- Demographic and lifestyle changes
- Shortage of training facilities, trainers
- Rapid hotel development
- Low birth rates

Step three: Explain the purpose of different types of new employee orientation programmes in different countries.

- Imported labour/immigration
- Job perceptions
- Family or educational status
- Hotel class
- Joint venture hiring

Step four: Discuss the importance of training and the requirements for a successful training program abroad.

- Analyze the situation
- Consider the training options
- Prepare trainers
- Prepare the trainees

Step five: Identify several kinds of cultural based motivations, describe various decision-making styles, and identify factors that contribute to communication in a multicultural environment including strategies for managing language differences.

- Motivation and productivity
- Decision-making
- Communication

Step Six: List the basic elements of compensation and benefit packages and explain variances between countries.

- Hourly rate
- Overtime
- Service charge contributions
- Tips
- Non-wage benefits
- Paid holidays
- Home leaves
- Meals
- Subsidies
- Pension plans

Step Seven: Describe the state of international relations concerns and strategy of organized labour.

Step Eight: Describe the global performance management and appraisal.

REVIEW QUESTIONS

1. What is international human resource management? Discuss its main characteristics and nature.
2. What are the factors affecting international human resource management? Discuss the strategic functions of IHRM.
3. Discuss the different approaches to international staffing policy. What are the important determinants of international staffing policy?
4. Explain HRM functions at global level.
5. Discuss the different approaches to international staffing policy. What are the staffing policy determinants?
6. What are the basic issues involved in recruiting and selecting managers for foreign assignments?
7. Why do expatriate managers fail in global assignments? Suggest measures to reduce expatriate failure rates.
8. Discuss management development and strategy adopted in global human resource management.
9. What factors affect the performance of HR personnel in foreign assignment?
10. Discuss international compensation strategy. What are the factors that influence international compensation strategy?
11. What are the competencies for international HRM? Give a brief discussion of the steps involved in it.

12. Write notes on the following:
    (a) components of international compensation
    (b) issues of international labour relations

CASE STUDY

16.1 McDonald's International HR

One of the best known companies worldwide is McDonald's Corporation. The fast-food chain, with its symbol of the golden arches, has spread from the United States into 91 countries. With over 18,000 restaurants worldwide, McDonald's serves 33 million people each day. International sales are an important part of McDonald's business, and over 50 per cent of the company's operating income results from sales outside the United States. To generate these sales, McDonald's employs over one million people, and by 2000, McDonald's had grown to over two million employees.

Operating in so many different countries means, that McDonald's has had to adapt its products, services, and HR practices to legal, political, economic, and cultural factors in each one of those countries. A few examples illustrate how adaptations have been made. In some countries, such as India, beef is not acceptable as a food to a major part of the population, so McDonald's uses lamb or mutton. To appeal to Japanese customers, McDonald's has developed teriyaki burgers. Separate dining rooms for men and women have been constructed in McDonald's restaurants in some Middle East countries.

HR practices also have had to be adapted. Before beginning operations in a different country, HR professionals at McDonald's research centre determine how HR activities must be adjusted. One method of obtaining information is to contact HR professionals from other US firms operating in the country and ask those questions about laws, political factors, and cultural issues. In addition, the firm conducts an analysis using a detailed outline to ensure that all relevant information has been gathered. Data gathered might include what employment restrictions exist on ages of employees and hours of work, what benefits must be offered to full-time and part-time employees (if part-time work is allowed), and other operational requirements. For instance, in some of the former communist countries in Eastern Europe, employers provide locker rooms and showers for their employees. These facilities are necessary because shower facilities, and even consistent water supplies, are unavailable in many homes, particularly in rural areas around major cities. Also, public transportation must be evaluated to ensure that employees have adequate means to travel to work.

Once a decision has been made to begin operations in a new country, the employment process must begin. Often, McDonald's is seen as a desirable employer, particularly, when its first restaurant is being opened in a country. For instance, in Russia, 27,000 people initially applied to work at the first Moscow McDonald's, which currently has over 1,500 employees. Because customer service is so important to McDonald's, recruiting and selection activities focus on obtaining employees with customer service skills. For worker positions such as counter representative and cashier, the focus is to identify individuals who will be friendly, customer service-oriented employees. A "trial" process whereby some applicants work for a few days on a conditional basis may be used to ensure that these individuals will represent McDonald's appropriately and will work well with other employees.

For store managers, the company uses a selection profile emphasizing leadership skills, high work expectations, and management abilities appropriate to a fast-paced restaurant environment. Once applicant screening and interviews have been completed, individuals are asked to work for upto a week in a restaurant. During that time both the applicants and the company representatives evaluate one another to see if the job "fit" is appropriate. After the first group of store managers and assistant managers are selected, future managers and assistant managers are chosen using international promotions based on job performance.

Once the restaurants are staffed, training becomes crucial to acquaint new employees with their jobs and the McDonald's philosophy of customer service and quality. McDonald's has taken its Hamburger University curriculum from the United States and translated it into 22 different languages to use in training centres throughout the world. Once training has been done for trainers and managers, they then conduct training for all employees selected to work at McDonald's locations in the foreign countries.

Source: Robert L. Mathis and John H. Jackson, Human Resource Management, South Western, 2000, pp. 135-136.

Questions

1. Identify cultural factors that might be important in a training programme for food handlers at McDonald's in Saudi Arabia.
2. Rather than focusing on the differences, what similarities do you expect exist among McDonald's customers and employees in both the United States and abroad?

16.2: MOLEX Makes Global HR

Molex, a 70-year-old manufacturer of electronic components based in Chicago, is the world's second largest manufacturer of electronic components. The company established an international division to coordinate exporting in 1967, opened its first overseas plant in Japan in 1970 and a second in Ireland in 1971. From that base, Molex has evolved into a global business that generated about 61 per cent of its \$·1.84 billion in revenues outside of the United States. The company operates some 50 manufacturing plants in 21 countries and employs more than 16,000 people worldwide, only one-third of who are located in the United States. Molex's competitive advantage is based on a strategy that emphasizes a combination of low costs, excellent customer service, and mass production of standardized products that are sold globally. Manufacturing sites are located in countries where cost conditions are favourable and major customers are close. Since the 1970s, a key goal of Molex has been to build a truly global company that is at home wherever in the world it operates and that proactively shares valuable knowledge across operations in different countries. The human resources function of Molex have always played a central role in meeting this goal.

As Molex grew rapidly overseas, the human resource management (HRM) function made sure that every new unit did the same basic things. Each new entity had to have an employee manual with policies and practices in writing, new employee orientation programmes, salary administration with a consistent grading system, written job descriptions, written promotion and grievance procedures, standard performance appraisal systems that were written, and so on.

Beyond these things, however, Molex views HRM as the most localized of functions. Different legal systems, particularly with regard to employment law, different compensation norms, different cultural attitudes to work, different norms regarding vacation, and so on—all imply that policies and programmes must be customized to the conditions prevailing in a country. To make sure this occurs, Molex's policy is to hire experienced HRM professionals from other companies in the same country in which it has operations. The idea is to hire people who know the language, have credibility, know the law, and know how to recruit in that country.

Molex's strategy for building a global company starts with its staffing policy for managers and engineers. The company frequently hires foreign nationals who are living in the United States, have just completed MBAs, and are willing to relocate if required. These individuals will typically work in the United States for a while, becoming familiar with the company's culture. Some of them will then be sent to their home country to work there. Molex also carefully screens its American applicants, favouring those who are fluent in at least one other language. Molex is unusual for a US company in this regard. However, with more than 15 languages spoken at its headquarters by native speakers, Molex is committed to multilingual competency. There is also significant hiring of managers and engineers at the local level.

Here, too, a willingness to relocate internationally and foreign language competency are important, although this time English is the preferred foreign language. In a sign of how multinational Molex's management has become, it is not unusual to see foreign nationals holding senior positions at company headquarters. In addition to Americans, individuals of Greek, German, Austrian, Japanese, and British origin have all sat on the company's executive committee, its top decision-making body.

To help build a global company, Molex moves people around the world to give them experience in other countries and to help them learn from each other. It has five categories of expatriates: (1) regular expatriates who live in a country other than their home country for three-to-five-year assignments (there are approximately 50 of these at anyone time), (2) "inpats" who come to the company's US headquarters from other countries, (3) third-country nationals who move from one Molex entity to another (for example, Singapore to Taiwan), (4) short-term transfers who go to another Molex entity for 6 to 9 months to work on a specific project, and (5) medium terms who go to another entity for 12 to 24 months, again to work on a specific project.

A high level of intracompany movement is costly. For an employee making $75,000 in base salary, the total cost of an expatriate assignment can run as high as $2,50,000 when additional employee benefits are added, such as the provision of schooling and housing, adjustments for higher costs of living, adjustments for higher tax rates, and so on. Molex also insists on treating all expatriates the same, whatever their country of origin, so a Singapore expatriate living in Taiwan is likely to be living in the same apartment building and sending his child to the same school as an American expatriate in Taiwan. This boosts the overall costs, but Molex believes that its extensive use of expatriates pays back dividends. It allows individuals to understand the challenges of doing business in different countries, it facilitates the sharing of useful knowledge across different business entities, and it helps to lay the foundation for a common company culture that is global in its outlook.

Molex also makes sure that expatriates know why they are being sent to a foreign country, both in terms of their own career development and Molex's corporate goals. To prevent expatriates from becoming disconnected from their home office, the HRM department touches base with them on a regular basis through telephone, email, and direct visits. The company also encourages expatriates to make home office visits so that they do not become totally disconnected from their base and feel like a stranger when they return. Upon return, they are debriefed and their knowledge gained abroad is put to use by, for example, placing the expatriates on special task forces.

A final component of Molex's strategy for building a cadre of global minded managers is the company's in-house management development programmes. These are open to a wide range of managers who have worked at Molex for three years or more. Molex uses these programmes not just to educate its managers in finance, operations, strategy, and the like, but also to bring together managers from different countries to build a network of individuals who know each other and can work together in a cooperative fashion to solve business problems that transcend borders.

Sources: J. Laabs, "Molex Makes Global HR Look Easy," Workforce, March 1999, pp. 42-46; and M. Solomon, "Foreign Relations," Workforce, November 2000, pp. 50-56.

Questions

1. What multinational strategy is Molex pursuing—localization, international, global standardization or transnational?
2. How would you characterize the approach to staffing used at Molex? Is this appropriate given its strategy?
3. Molex is very successful in its use of expatriate managers. Why do you think this is the case? What can be learnt from Molex's approach?
4. How does the human resource function at Molex contribute to the attainment of its multinational strategy?

REFERENCES

1. Daniels John, and Radebaugh Lee H. (2002). "International Business", Pearson Education Asia, Delhi, pp. 664-670.
2. Luis R. Gomez-Mejia, *et al.*, (2003). "Managing Human Resources", Prentice-Hall of India, p. 555.
3. Cynthia D. Fisher, *et al.*, (1997). "Human Resource Management", Houghton Miffin Company, p. 765.
4. Peter J. Dowling, *et al.*, (1999). "International Human Resource Management", South Western College Publishing Co., p. 3.
5. Anne-Wil Harzing and Joris Van Ruysseveldt (Eds.). (2004). "International Human Resource Management", Sage Publication, p. 66.
6. Robert L. Mathis and John H. Jackson, (2000). "Human Resource Management", South Western, pp. 135-136.

Index